PUBLIC ATTITUDE

austrian embassy bangkok
2013–17

An embassy building, representative of one nation in another cultural area, therefore acts as an important social, cultural, and technological link; respecting the characteristics of both countries results in a symbiotic space. In this particular structure, Austrian achievements in research, energy, and technology mesh with the culture-specific Thai way of living and related building traditions.

Respect for social features of Thai life and analysis of traditional Thai building typologies, were the points of departure for the design process. The main challenge was integrating Thai ways into the requirements of a high-security office building based on European standards, alongside special energy solutions to meet climatic factors like high temperature, high humidity, and heavy rainfall. A common space is included in the form of a main courtyard with existing trees and shady areas for social interactions, used by employees and visitors during exhibitions, and it also serves as a protected area in emergencies.

The building's main traditional resources are detachment, natural airflow, cantilevered roofs, and shady trees. Direct sun has been prevented from affecting the inner construction layers in several ways. A detached steel roof with photovoltaic modules prevents direct sun from heating up the concrete roof, and a detached laterite layer with ventilating airflow keeps it away from the inner prefabricated concrete walls. Existing old trees, which have a high value in Thai society, are integrated into the holistic and sustainable design and used both as landscape elements and for their shading qualities to protect the glass facades from extended solar impact. All glass elements enable high light transmission, low solar energy transportation, and high heat insulation. The correct combination of these three values prevents artificial light during the daytime, thus preventing the inside from getting hot and permitting the building to cool down at night.

For energy production, the photovoltaic roofs work as a solar energy factory; and for reduced energy consumption, the fresh air is cooled down by the main air-handling unit and sent to single-fan coils. No batteries are needed, as the energy is consumed during the day when it is produced. Used air flows from the rooms into the courtyard through overflow louvers and is partly guided back to the fan coil in the suspended ceiling of the corridors. For watering plants in the dry season, a cistern has been implemented under the flat roofed area.

The structural concept of the buildings also follows the idea of sustainability. The structures are designed as concrete skeletons, filled in with local materials. The three materials—laterite (conglomerate stone), teak (from a state-run plantation), and glass/aluminum—are perfect for meeting the concept of a functional envelope. On the outside, laterite and perforated teak create a secure but transparent surface. Glass enables office spaces to extend into the courtyard, creating a pleasant atmosphere for employees and visitors, with a feeling of closeness to nature. Laterite, once used for temples, has an interesting appearance and a wonderful natural red color. Perforated teak is used as an air ventilation element around the courtyard and serves as a protection filter toward the street. Besides its political and cultural importance, the building ensemble serves as an indicator of mutual respect, traditional knowledge, future orientation, energy production, and environmental care.

WDR crossmedia house
2015–16

The *Filmhaus* belonging to Germany's broadcasting company Westdeutscher Rundfunk (WDR) was founded in 1974 and is part of a larger television and radio complex in the historic city center of Cologne, close to the famous cathedral. The existing functional division by media of radio, television, and Internet merges spatially into a *crossmedia house*, and so the old building needed restructuring, redefinition of its structural fabric, and re-presenting to the public realm with an inviting appearance. The introduction of multistory vertical atria has let natural light flood the great depths of the formerly gloomy interior, creating an open atmosphere. The invention of the side-changing vertical atrium, which shifts from the east side of the building to the west over the course of its nine floors, integrates the surroundings in a different way.

A new spatial layout for the different floors, including flexible and distinct working areas, specific communication boxes, and relaxation spaces, forms the functional structure of the building and preserves options for changes without moving walls. Common areas on the ground level face the square and include a public café as a vibrant meeting point along with a waiting area featuring views into the studio next to the public lobby. These common areas are positioned in such a way as to extend the interior space and open it up to its surroundings, thanks to the structure's high ceilings, glazed facade, and communicative character.

The design responds spatially and functionally to the ever-changing flow of the media sector, proving its adaptability to future need, while using the existing structural framework. On the restructured levels, there are 600 working areas with visual access to the light-flooded atria. Plants including large trees are integrated into the layout and support a good microclimate, while inner open staircases connect floors for fast communication when needed.

Sustainability is a particularly important part of the *WDR crossmedia house*, with renewable-energy geothermal probes used as a source for the heating and cooling system. Warm air is refreshed by plants, then moves up the vertical atrium and leaves through roof openings, with cooler air subsequently following through the use of air dynamics. Photovoltaic panels on the atrium-roof produce energy for daytime electricity demand without the use of batteries.

The existing building has acquired new programmatical and spatial qualities for all occupants by means of reprogramming, redefining, and resetting within its structural fabric and decisive outlines.

cluster school

2020

The proposed building is in an up-and-coming area of the 22nd district of Vienna and includes an elementary school, a new middle school, and a day-care facility. Opening onto a public square on the west side, it connects to residential buildings and incorporates shaded seating areas for children, families, and senior citizens. Existing railway tracks on the east provide an opportunity to organize noisy sport facilities without bothering residents. Overall, the outdoor space is generously zoned, with clusters of trees and green or paved areas, resulting in different exercise spots or quieter zones for reading and relaxation.

The spatial layout of the complex follows its intended purpose as a cluster school. Four classrooms adjoin a common area, supported by natural light, and are directly attachted to an outdoor space. Educational team rooms, wardrobes, and cloakrooms are next to them between the clusters and close to the main staircases.

The main entrance to the complex guides pupils and visitors directly into the auditorium, which includes a communal multifunctional space, a canteen, a library, and the administration area, as well as main staircases. They connect all floors above and below ground at a short distance using a simple orientation structure. Indoor sport facilities get natural light from the east and are directly accessible from the wardrobes beside the stairs, as well as from the outside on the south and north for external sport associations. All necessary technical spaces and further services are located underground.

Inside the school, sound-absorbing materials have been applied to walls and ceilings. Thus, the multifunctional and educational areas provide a pleasant, quieter atmosphere. In terms of energy efficiency, the building follows low-tech principles, using concrete elements to regulate heating and cooling and groundwater as a primary source of renewable energy.

campus school

2018–22

The elementary school inside a residential block between Anton-Langer-Gasse and Speisinger Straße in the 13th district of Vienna was in need of an extension. It was important that a kindergarten with four spaces, ten new classrooms, sports facilities, and all necessary auxiliary rooms be located next to the existing buildings, leaving enough outdoor areas for all pupils between the ages of three and ten years. The new three-story building connects to the two existing structures on both floors. Its layout is embedded in the surrounding area, orientating its position to the neighboring residential blocks and the school, adjoining a local park and playground, and expanding upon it with a spacious public area in front of the main entrance.

The kindergarten connects directly to the access from the west through a passage of the residential building, while the main entrance to both institutions is accessible from the east via the park inside the block. Determined by the connection between two existing buildings, the new courtyard structure is elevated about 1.5 meters above the ground and barrier-free. On the west boundary, 919 square meters are dedicated to the youngest children, with group spaces taking advantage of direct outdoor access from the inside. Eliminating differences in height, the interior expands onto the green, dividing into quiet and more active play zones that adapt to the children's needs, with several zones dedicated to experiencing nature.

Bounding the east side of the plot, the remaining 2,340 square meters of the property accommodate an extension to the elementary school. The separate entrances for the kindergarten and the school allow for a functional structuring of the interior spaces, creating ten additional educational rooms and two generous multifunctional group spaces. An inner courtyard—a protected break-out area accessible via the basement—ensures that daylight enters all spaces across each floor, guaranteeing easy orientation within the indoor spaces and emphasizing its open, circular character. New workshop rooms and creative studio areas, as well as a fully equipped sports hall, can be found in the daylight-flooded basement.

connected with max
2001

The concept for *connected with max* seeks to reintegrate an economically weak area next to the old harbor into Valencia's generally well-functioning urban network. Once very active, this part of the city now lacks cultural, educational, leisure, and social interaction zones for young and elderly residents. The scheme therefore addresses a wide range of programmatic issues, including edutainment, welfare (communication platform), inspiration (studios and galleries), and pleasure space. In response to the long, rectangular site, *connected with max* establishes a diagonal pedestrian network throughout the site that interlinks with existing footways and introduces vectors that catch light and attention. Individual areas within the plot are shaped by pathway intersections, vectors of light, functional positioning, and the volumes of surrounding buildings. Valencia's city fabric thus actively nourishes the decision processes, creating a site with individual units that dedicate its spaces to specific uses.

Taking into account the low-income area and creating direct opportunities for interaction and exchange, the proposal introduces three dimensional overlays as tools of programmatic and spatial construction. Thus it includes various essential welfare facilities, as well as a care center, a spiritual site, a youth center, and a hostel; and, to enhance educational facilities, it introduces a kindergarten, a school, a mobile library, and a computer center. Furthermore, to cover the need for leisure, and commercial services, the proposal offers a bar and restaurant, a supermarket, and some other shops to serve the needs of everyday life.

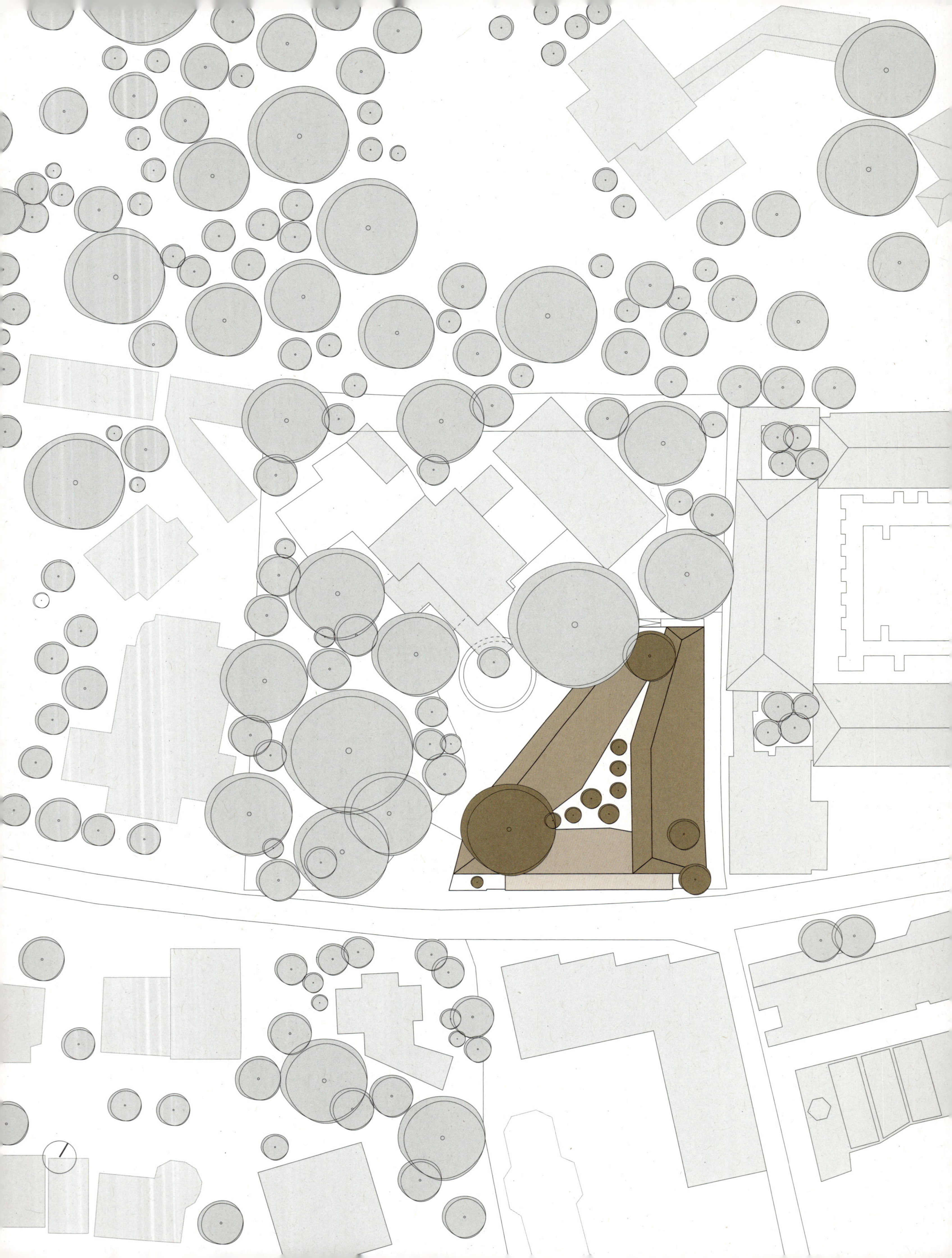

austrian embassy bangkok
10120 Bangkok, TH

See pp. 8–20

PROGRAM
Embassy and consulate, outdoor facilities, innovative and local materiality

DIMENSIONS
Plot area 1,740 m^2, GFA 1,271 m^2, covered area 961 m^2, PV roof 590 m^2, courtyard area 610 m^2

CLIENT
BMEIA Federal Ministry Republic of Austria, European and International Affairs, Vienna

PROJECT TEAM
Marlies Breuss, Michael Ogertschnig, Suchon Mallikamarl, Johannes Müller, Alexsander Garber, Peter Hundt, Chloe Priou, Elitsa Tsankova

CONSULTANTS
ghp gmeiner | haferl & partner zt gmbh (structural engineer), Four Aces bangkok (consultants), Russ Ingenieure GmbH, PGG Blueberg Engineering, PSMC Bangkok (building systems), IPJ Ingenieurbüro (building physics and building simulation), Power Line Engineering (PLE) Bangkok (building contractor), Aero Bangkok (photo voltaic)

PHOTOGRAPHY
Ketsiree Wongwan, Pichak Thananchaibut

AWARDS
STAATSPREIS ARCHITEKTUR AUSTRIA 2021, nomination; ENERGY GLOBE AWARD THAILAND 2020; EUROPEAN ARCHITECTURE AWARDS 2020; ICONIC Award – Best of Best for Innovative Architecture 2019; Austrian Green Planet Building Award 2018; Green GOOD DESIGN AWARD 2018; Architizer A+ Awards 2019, finalist; LEAF Leading European Architects Forum Award 2019, shortlisted; Mies van der Rohe Award 2019, nomination; The Plan Award 2019, honorable mention; first prize, EU-wide two-stage general planning tender competition

PUBLICATIONS (SELECTION)
BEST OF AUSTRIA 2018, Zurich, Edition Park Books, October 2019 (ISBN 978-3-03860-217-0).
Mathias Boeckl, "Zeitgenösische Architektur in Österreich – HOLODECK," in *Architektur.aktuell*, Vienna, 2020.

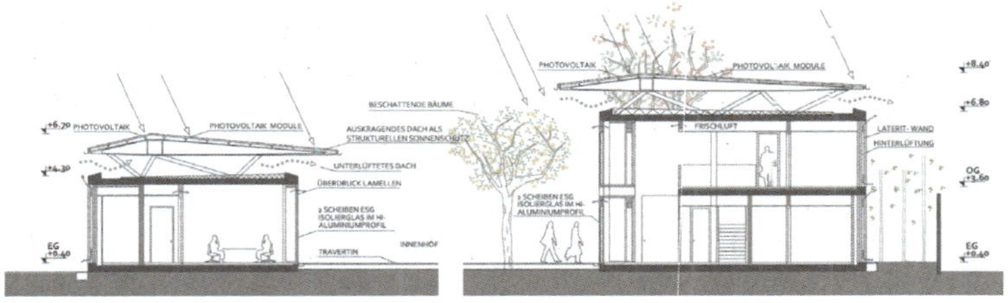

"The sensitive handling within context, resources, and environmental influences, combined with the achievement of maximum energy efficiency, makes the building an ambassador for forward-looking, holistic building."

—*working environments. spaces of productivity.*, Münster, Deutscher Architektur Verlag, 2021, p. 213 (trans. by the ed.)

Site plan
1:750

5 15 30 50 m

1 Public area
2 Entrance to embassy, events
3 Entrance to visa section
4 Semipublic courtyard
5 Security guard
6 Main courtyard
7 Embassy
8 Visa section
9 Multifunctional area

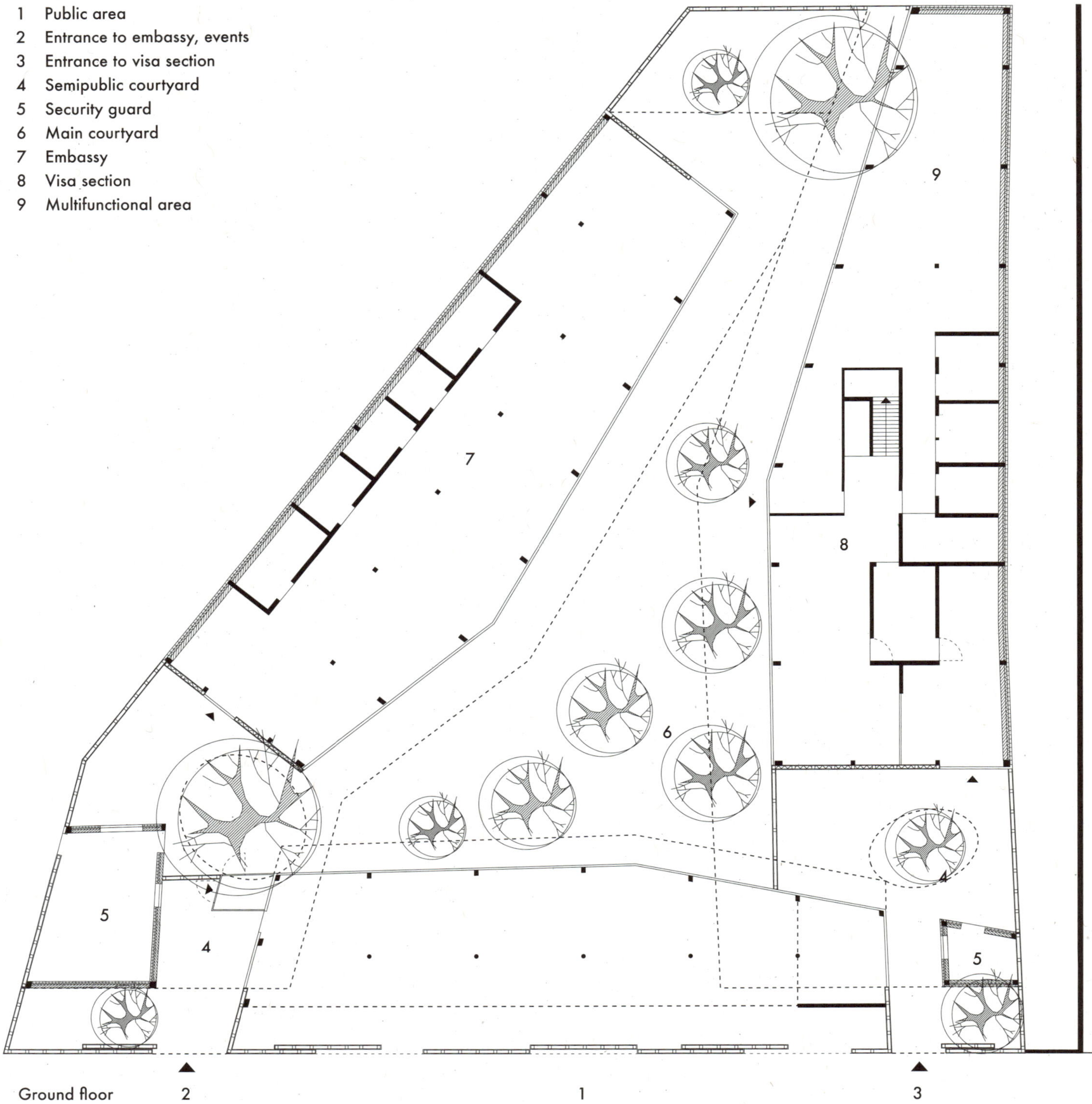

Ground floor

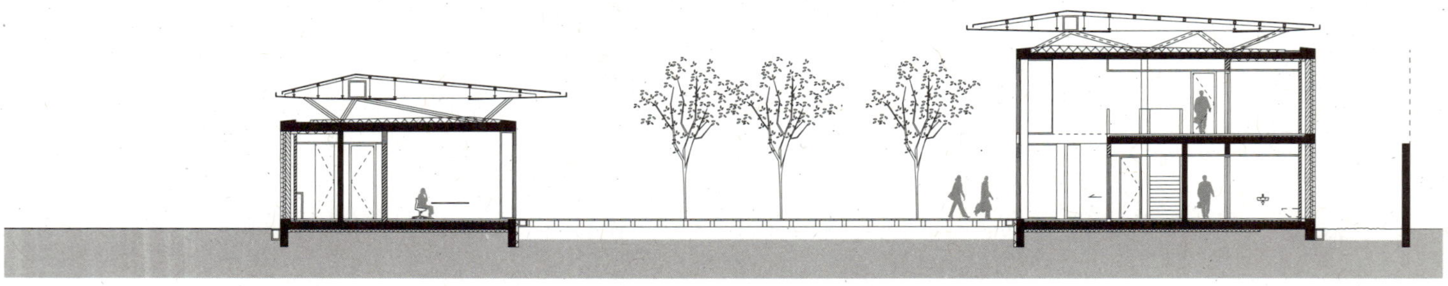

Sections
1:250

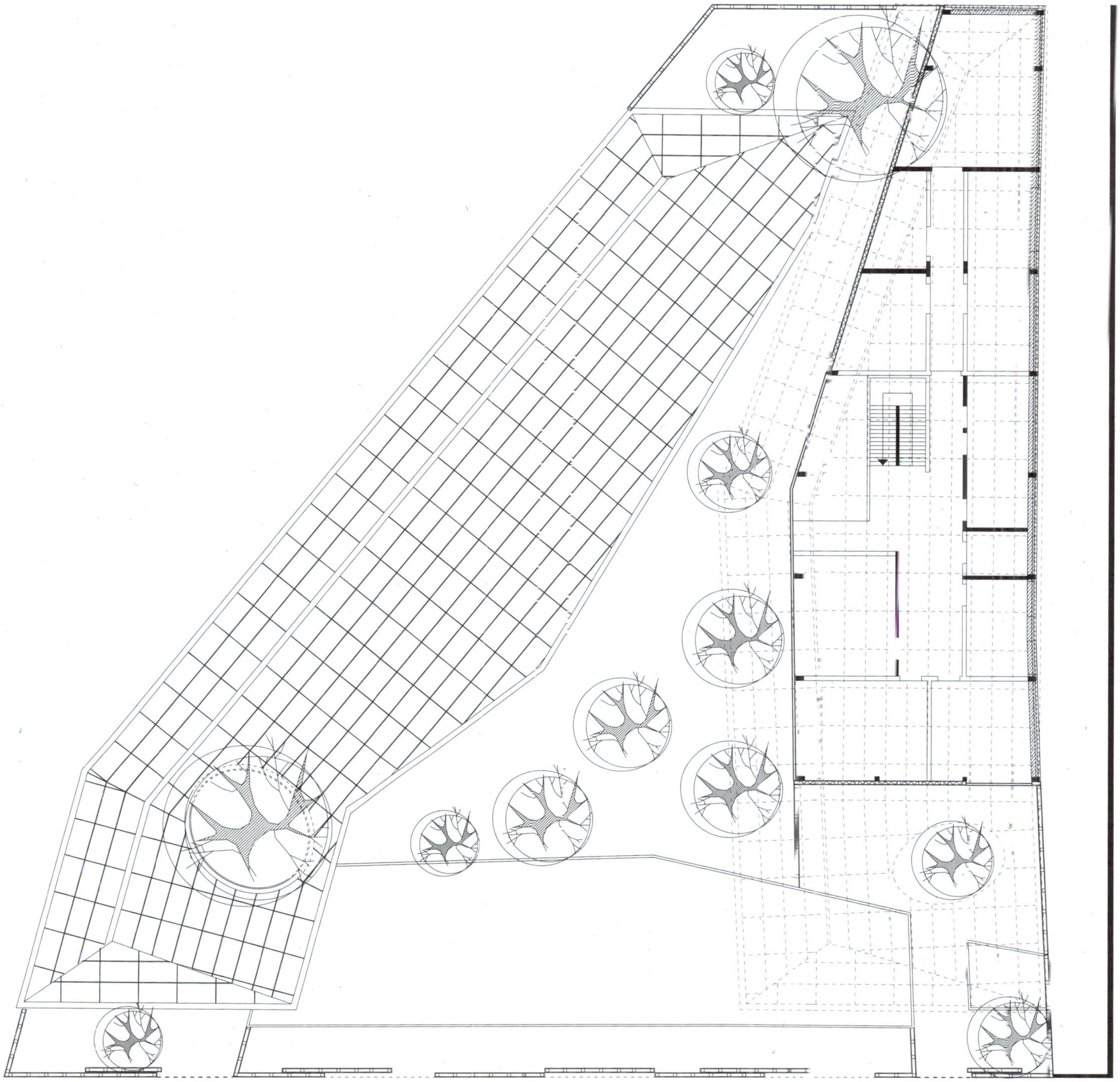

First floor

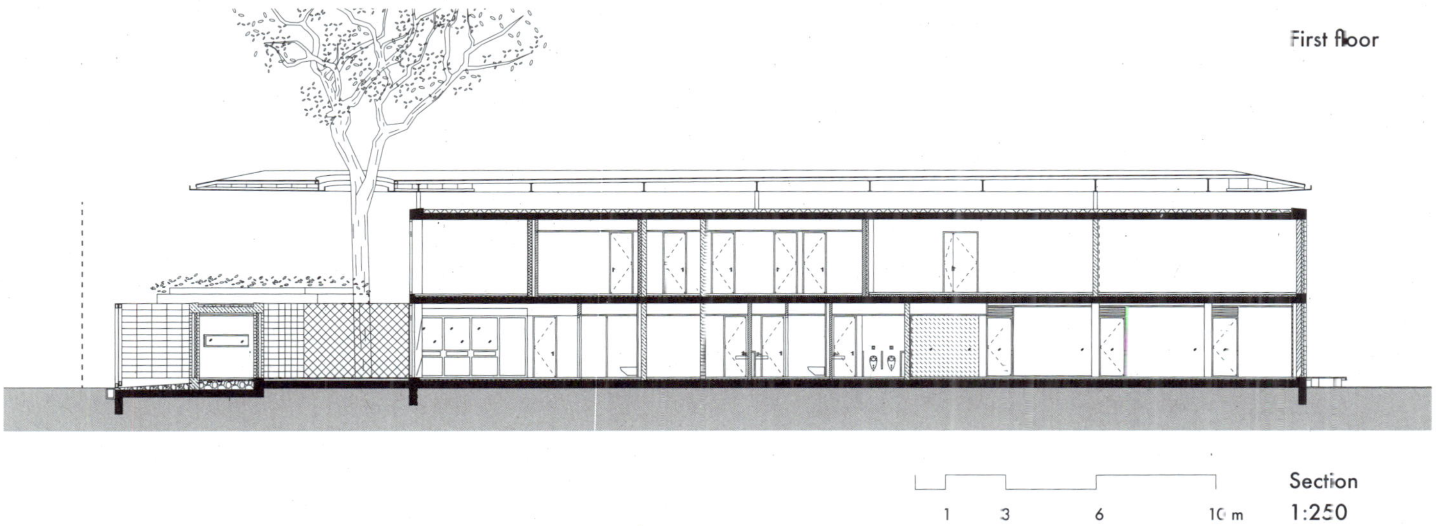

Section
1:250

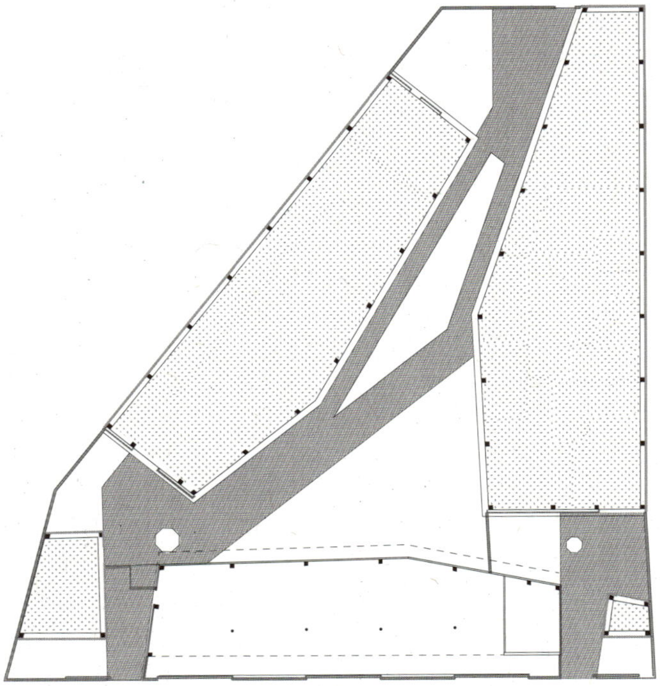

Materials ground floor

Travertine
- Inner travertine
- Outer travertine

Perforated teak panel

Laterite bricks

590 m² solar cell roof
207 m² green roof
610 m² courtyard area
879 m² functional area

- 8 existing trees
- 1 rainwater cistern
- 2 biological waste water treatment plants

1 Teak

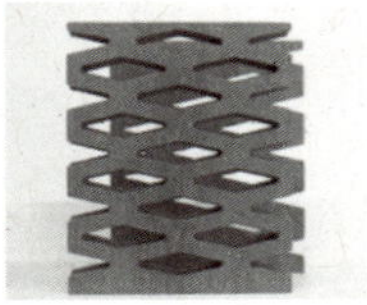

2 Laterite

3 Travertine

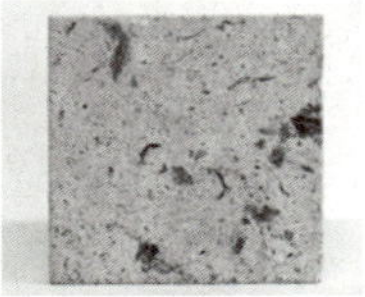

4 Photovoltaic element

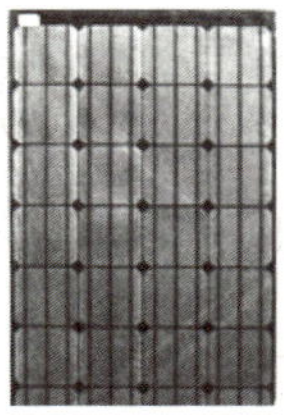

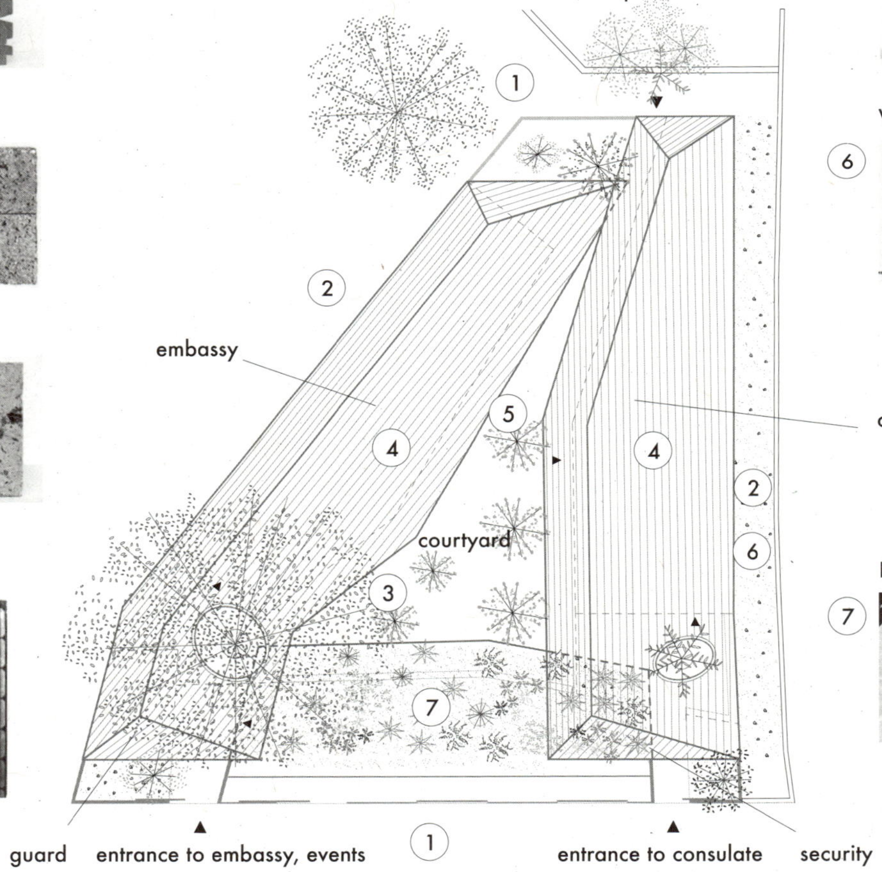

5 Sun-protecting glass

6 Waste water treatment

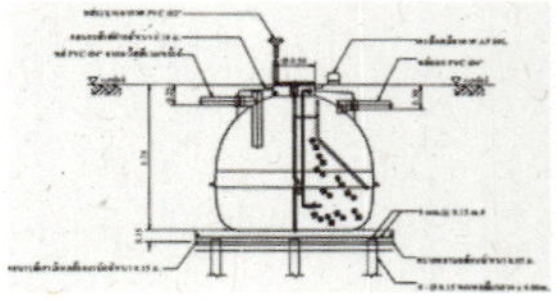

7 Rain water cistern

Materials and trees
1:500

5 10 20 40 m

1 Wate-proofing mounted on a clamping profile
2 Clamping profile RAL 7016
3 Permanent elastic joint
4 Water glass surface
5 Mount waterproofing on Sika waterbar or similar
6 Gap 10 mm
7 Insect screen
8 Waterproofing and vapor-proof barrier at joints and connections to Taxca wall, conc-ete ceiling and slab
9 Ventilation
10 Drip tray
11 Laminated safety glass
2 × 6 mm clear glass
+ 14 Ar
+ 6 mm clear glass
T = 65 % – g = 0.37 – u = 1.1 W/m²K
12 Aluminum frame
13 Waterproofing and vapor-proof barrier mounted on window profiles and substructures
14 Waterproofing and vapor-proof barrier at joints and connections to rising walls to a hight of min. 300 mm
15 Separation layer (e.g. waterproofing)
16 Insect screen
17 Gap 10 mm
18 Water glass surface, offered product similar to EverCrete Vetrofluid
19 Gutter cover, steel 3 × 10 mm
20 Grass
21 Support layer
22 Slope
23 Gutter 30/50 prefab concrete element
24 Drainage hose e = 3,000 mm
25 Wall junction, aluminum channel 10 × 10 mm
26 Window frame enlargement
27 Plaster slat and sealant
28 Edge strip, including sealant
29 Water proof admixture
30 Brick wall, lost formwork

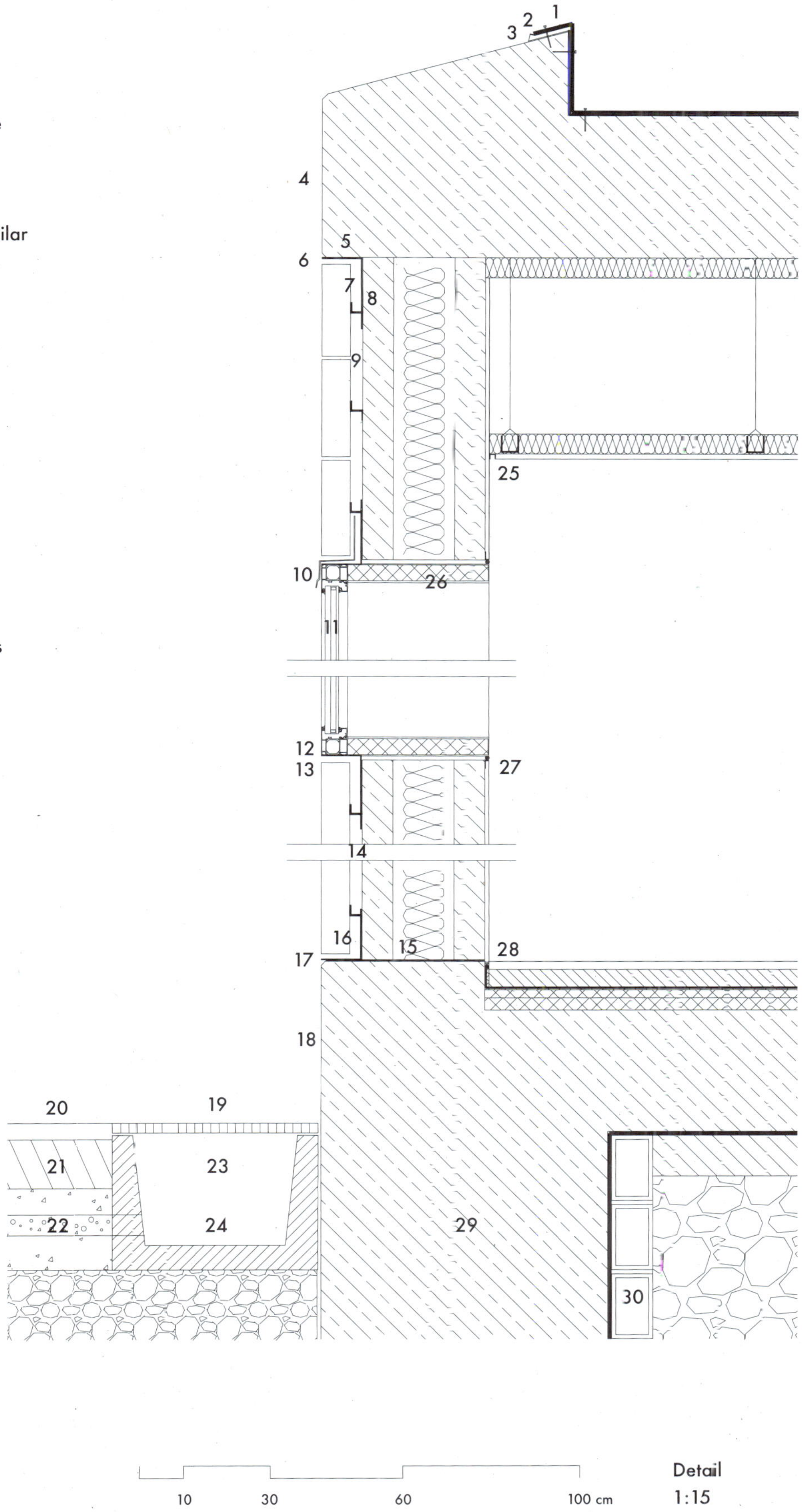

Detail
1:15

Overview
steel substructure
HEA 100

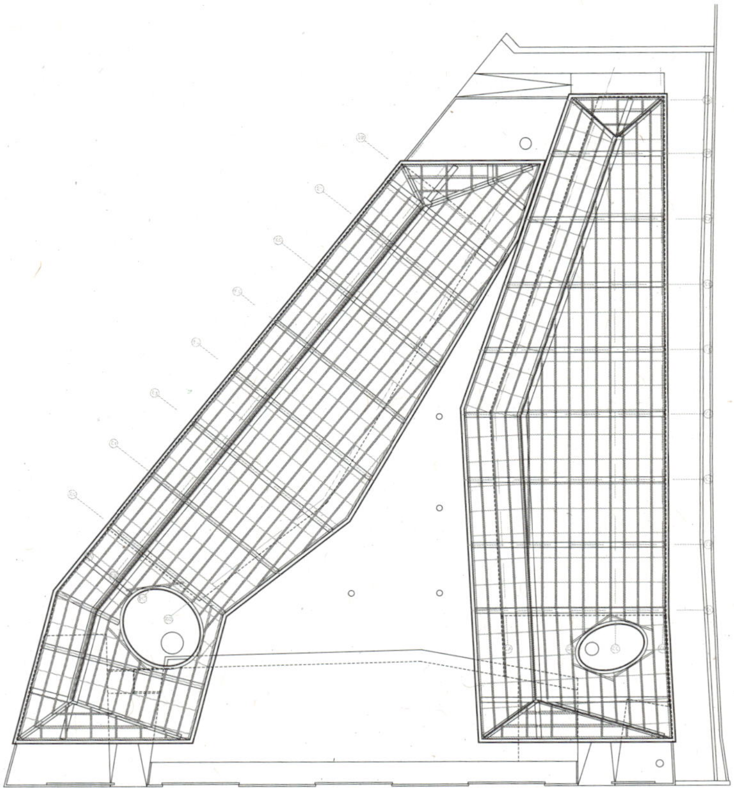

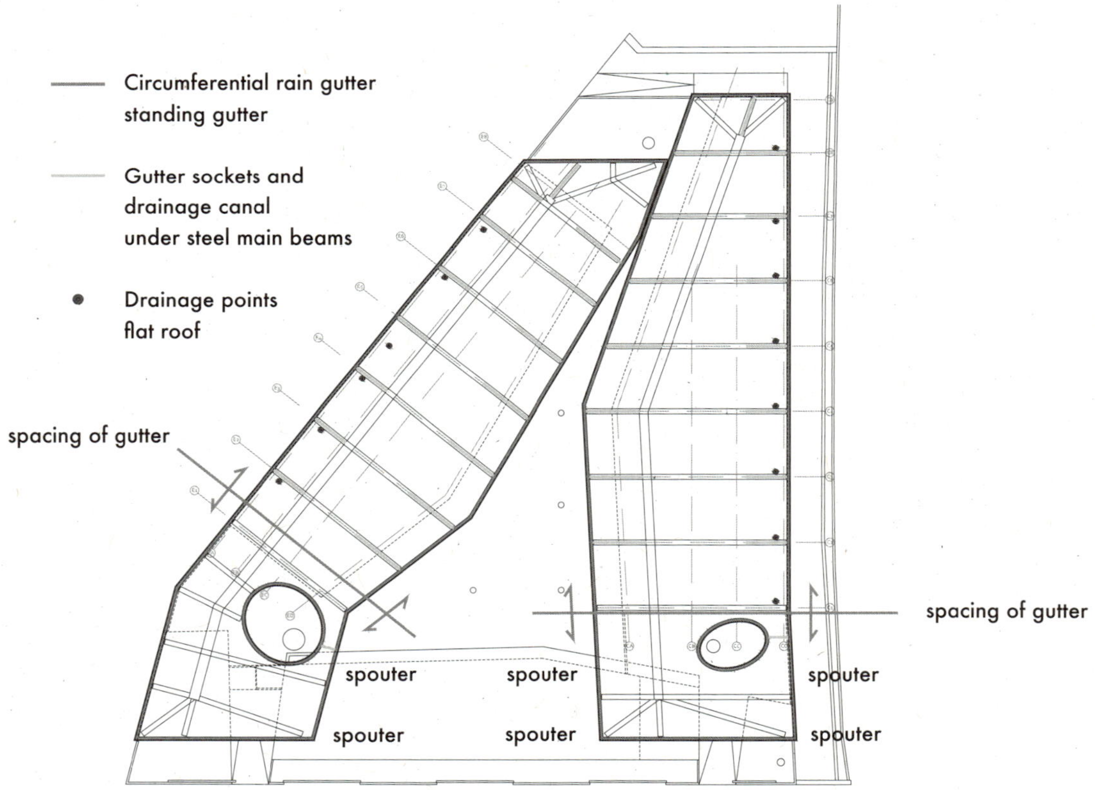

Photovoltaic roof

Overview drainage
over gutter, socket
and drainage canal

1:500

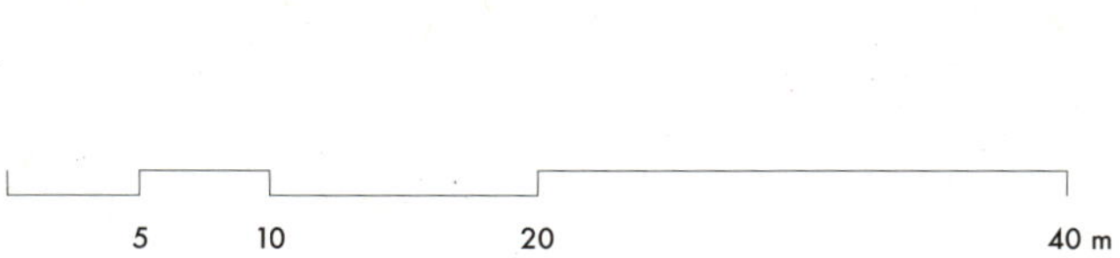

1 Eaves board, aluminum black, 76 mm high
2 Flashing, aluminum sheet 2 mm, painted black
3 Rain gutter, steel galvanized, painted black
4 Head cladding, composite, black high gloss
5 Bracket for head cladding, adjustable
6 Rain collector 50 × 350 mm, steel galvanized, painted black
7 Gutter hook, every 500 mm, steel galvanized, painted black
8 HEA 100 by main contractor
9 Lower end bracket, aluminum, black anodized
10 Photovoltaic element
11 Photovoltaic frame
12 Solar rail, aluminum, black anodized
Cut areas painted black

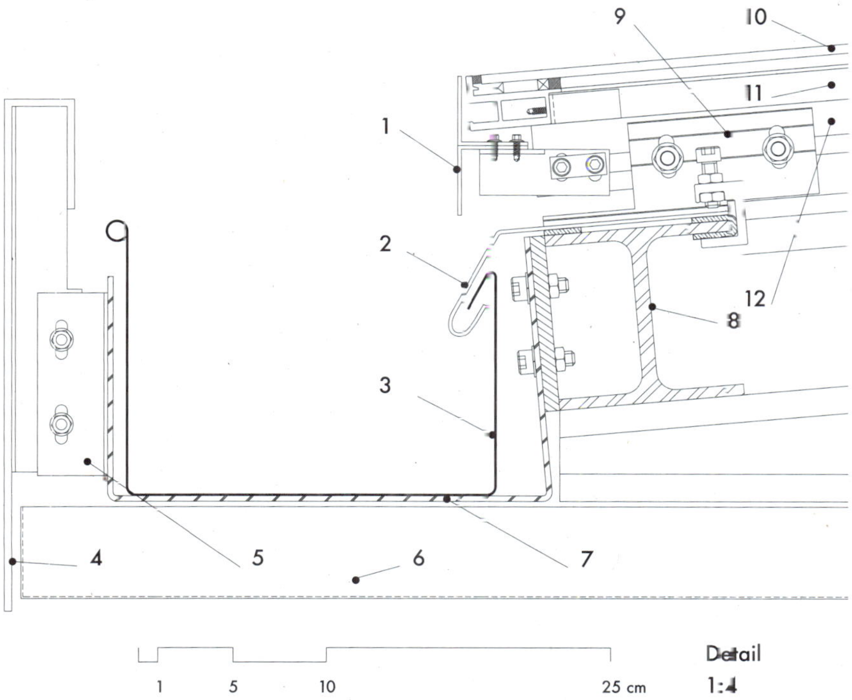

Detail
1:4

1 End profile, T-profile steel 600/400 according to static requirement, surface black high gloss
2 Z-profile steel coated, selectively according to static requirements
3 Inlet plate, coated aluminum
4 PV module, point bearing on Z-profiles
5 HEA 100 on site with 8 mm head plate (100 × 100 mm) every 500 mm with 2 holes ∅ 10.5
6 Main beam welded, coated
7 Gutter as required, gutter spigot in channel
8 Rainwater channel below main girder, sheet steel edged 50 × 350 mm, coated
9 L-profile aluminum 600/300 according to static requirement, surface black
10 4 mm Alucobond black high gloss
11 Bottom edge for Alucobond
12 Gutter hook
13 Circumferential fastening profile Ertex Intevo or equivalent
14 Hammer head plate, black surface
15 Z-profile steel coated, selectively according to static requirement, surface black
16 Height adjustability as required and elastic support
17 HEA 100 on site

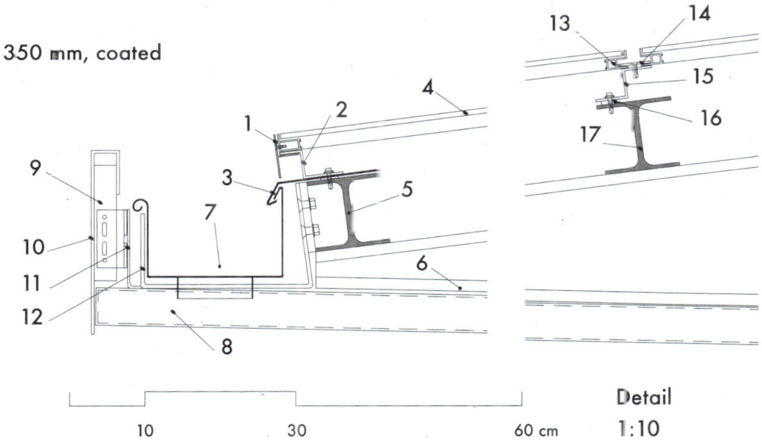

Detail
1:10

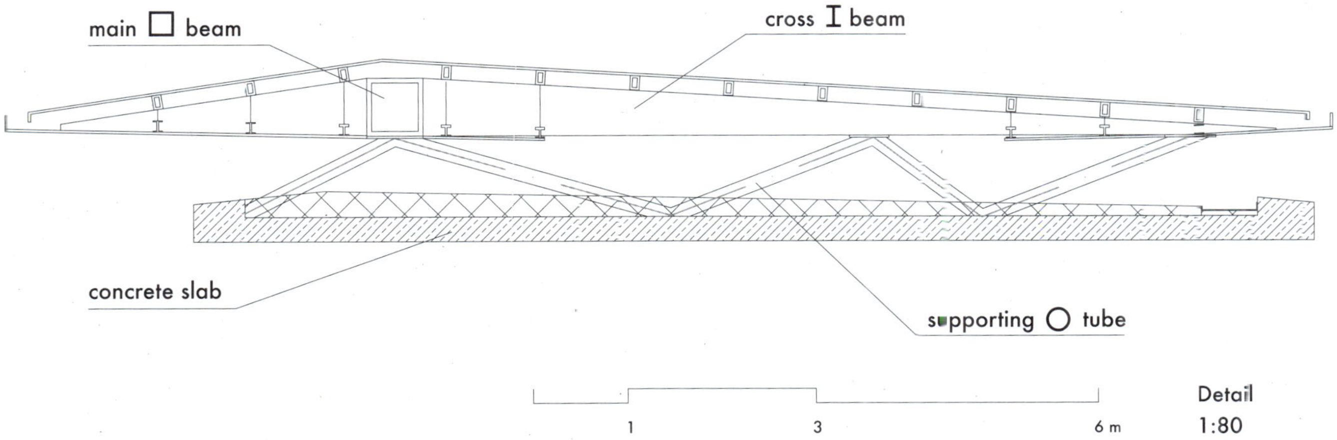

Detail
1:80

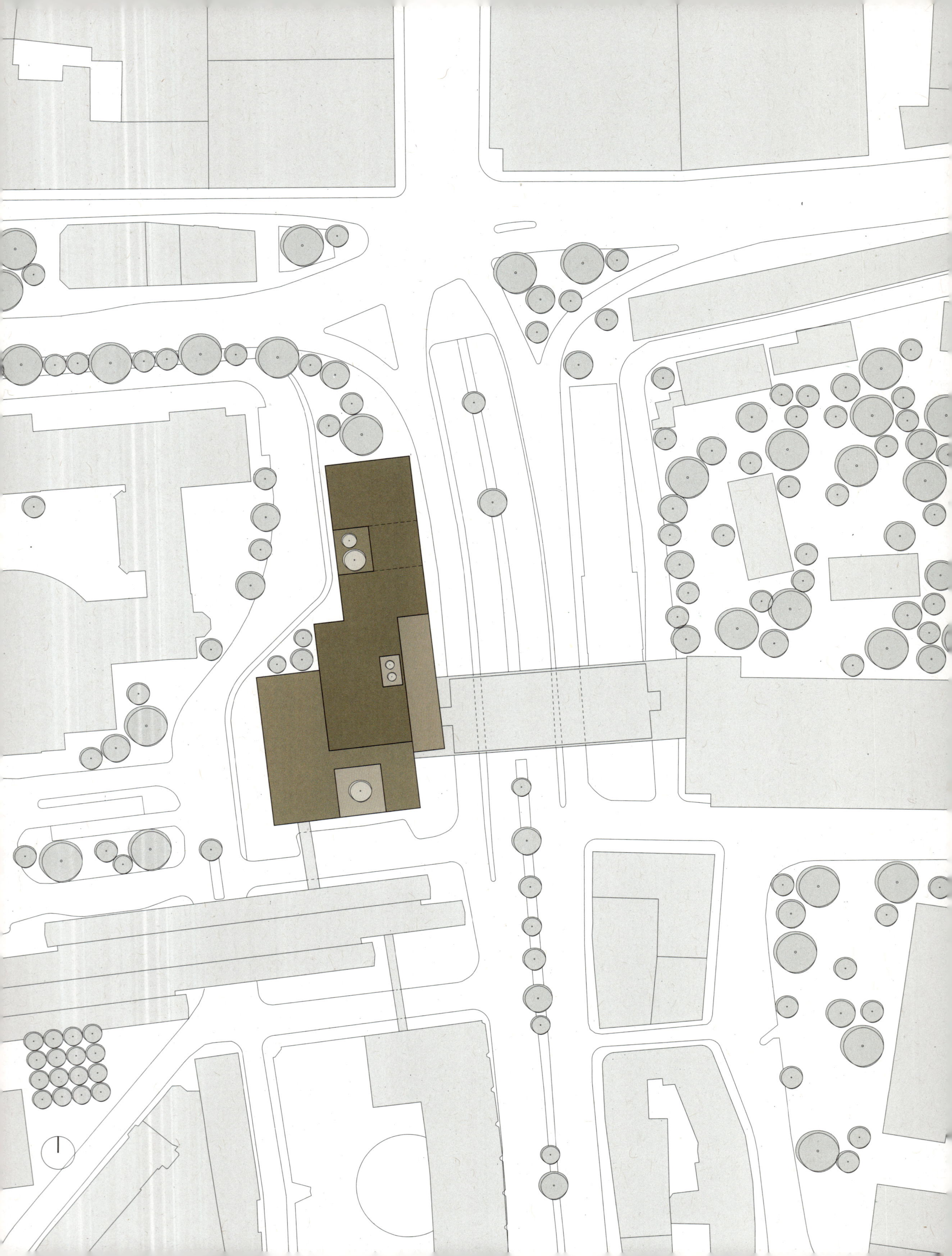

WDR crossmedia house
50667 Cologne, DE

PROGRAM
Cross media house, vertical atria, office building, television studio, event hall, hospitality, restructure, conversion

DIMENSIONS
Gross floor area 21,567 m², gross net area 18,390 m², floor space 12,980 m²

CLIENT
Westdeutscher Rundfunk WDR, Cologne, Germany

PROJECT TEAM
Marlies Breuss, Michael Ogertschnig, Hannes Zergoi, Isabel Gares Sala, Adam Myczkowski, Marcel Schwab, Peter Szilagyi

CONSULTANTS
kwi and IPROconsult (building systems), IPJ Ingenieurbüro P. Jung (building physics), KPPK (structural engineer), ISRW Dr.-Ing. Klapdor (acoustics), Diete + Siepmann Ingenieur (building management)

MODEL-MAKING
archimodell, Vienna

AWARDS
Winning group, EU-wide two-stage general planning tender competition

PUBLICATIONS (SELECTION)
"Kölnische Rundschau online," WDR online, Cologne, May 1, 2015.
Competition online, online portal (https://www.e-architect.com/germany/wdr-crossmedia-house-in-cologne), 2016.

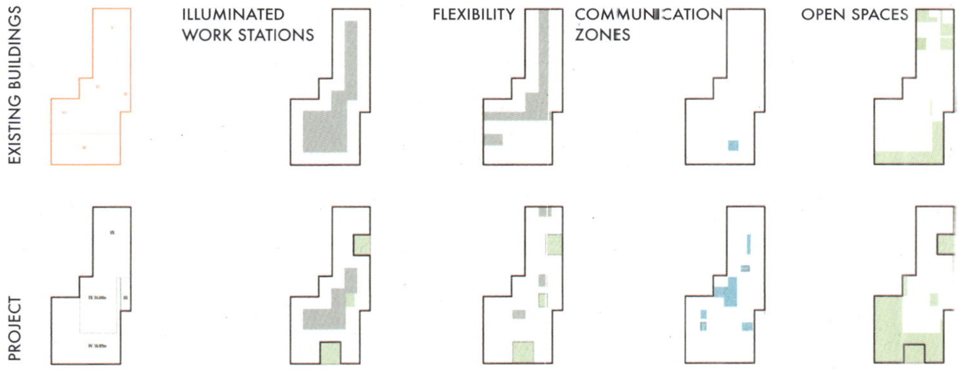

"The architecture is contemporary and, in particular, the greened atriums succeed in creating a high quality of interior space that does not restrict flexibility, representing spaces of retreat and providing orientation."

—Excerpt from the jury protocol, 2015 (trans. by the ed.)

Site plan
1:1,000

10 25 50 m

page 209

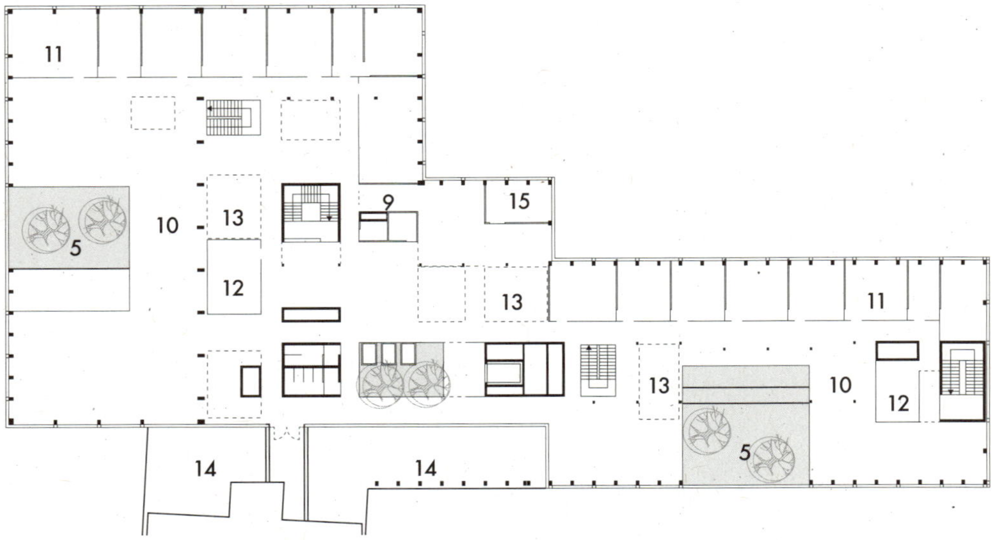

Third floor

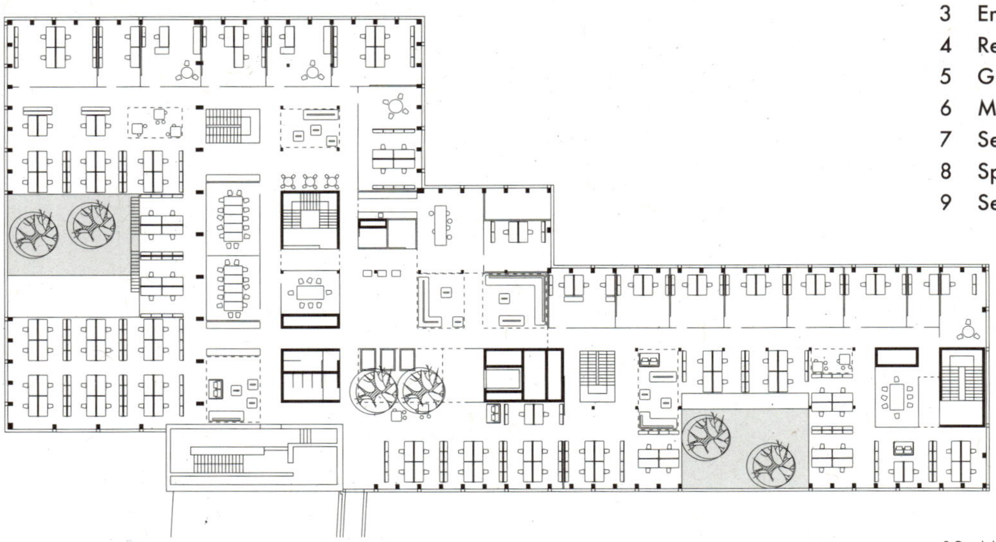

Second floor

1 Common public area
2 Entrance for pedestrians
3 Entrance for cyclists
4 Restaurant
5 Green atrium
6 Multifunctional space
7 Secure area
8 Sports zone
9 Service area

10 Multifunctional area
11 Office spaces
12 Meeting boxes
13 Communication area
14 Terraces for relaxation
15 Balconies for relaxation

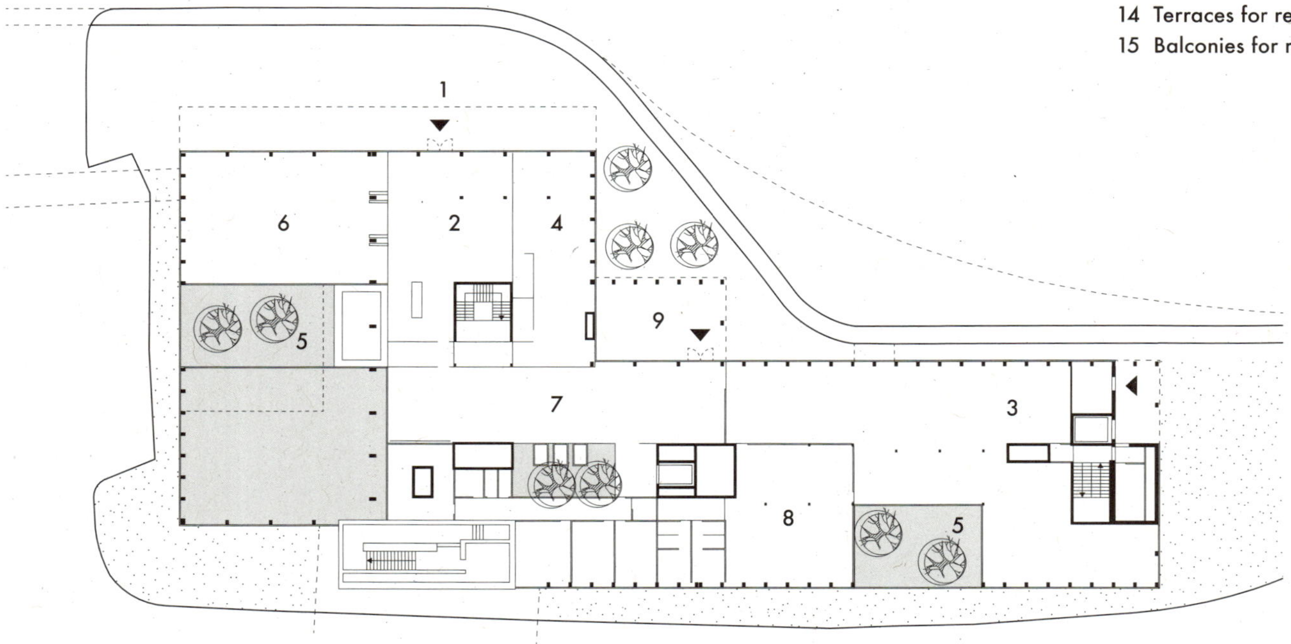

Ground floor
1:650

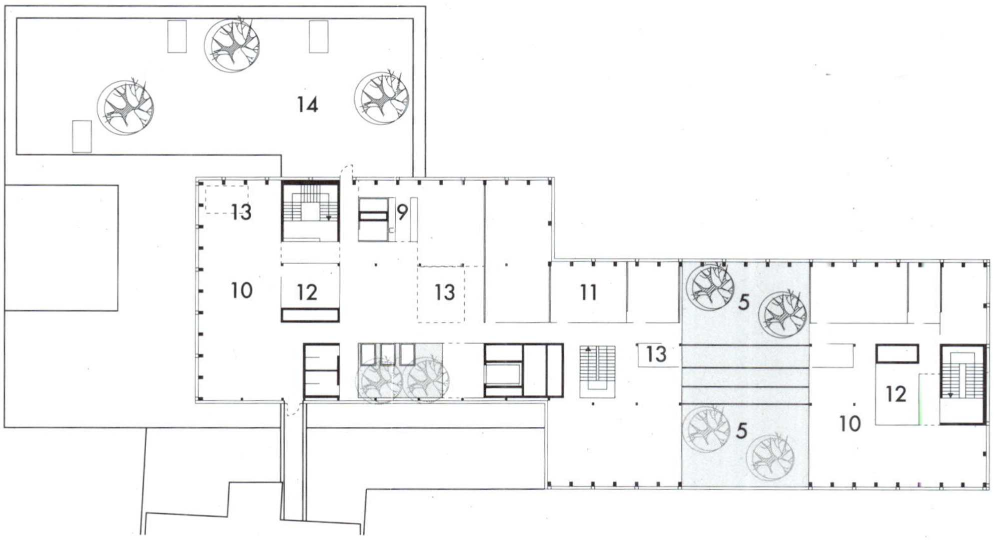

Fourth floor

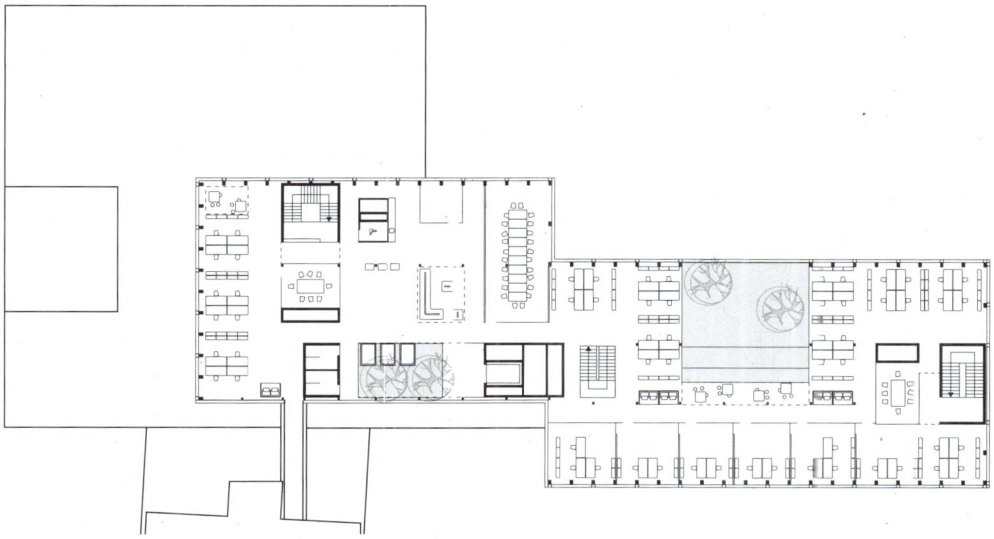

Eighth floor

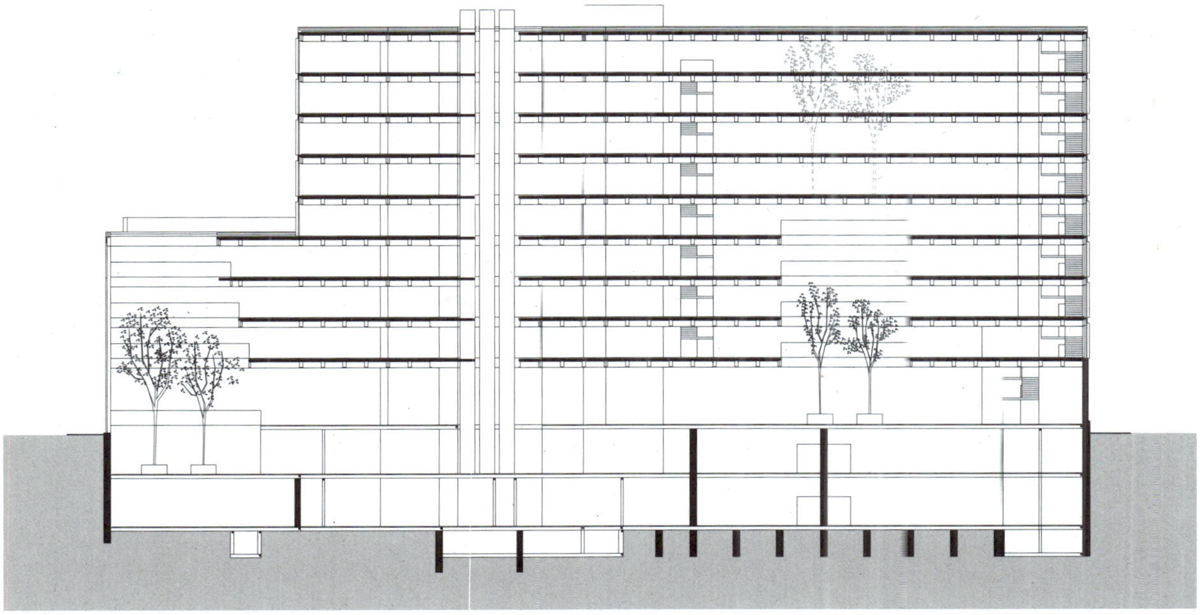

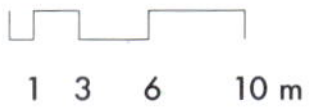

Longitudinal section
1:650

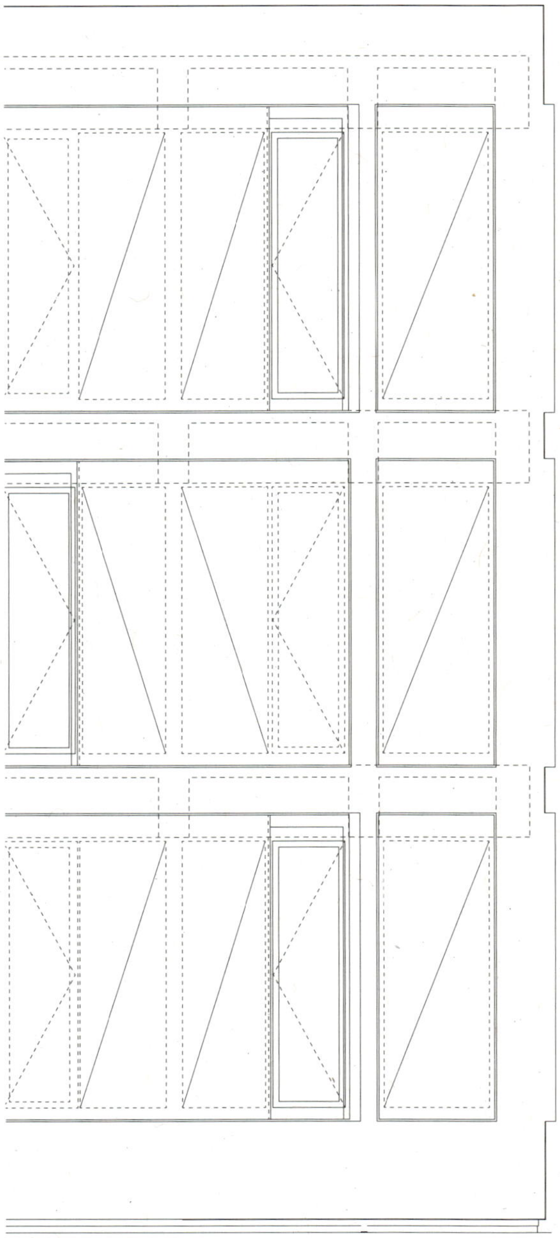

Sections of
facade
1:75

10 60 100 cm

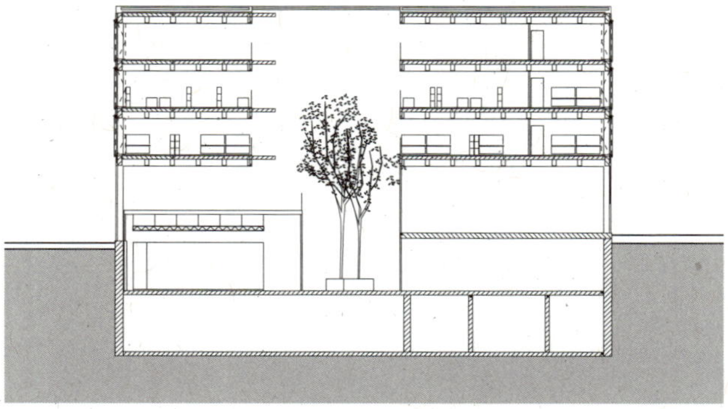

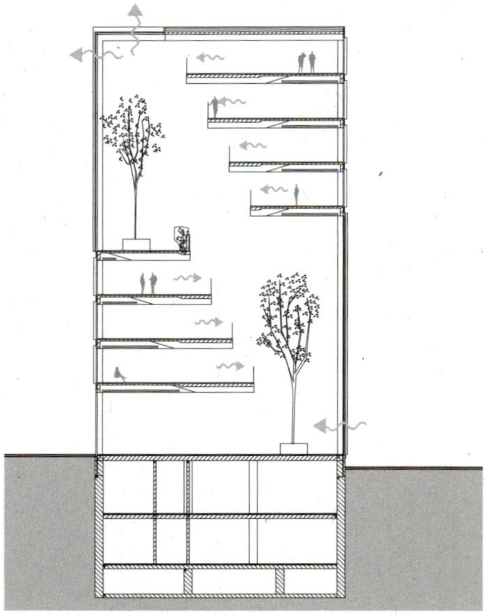

Sections
1:650

1 3 6 10 m

Section

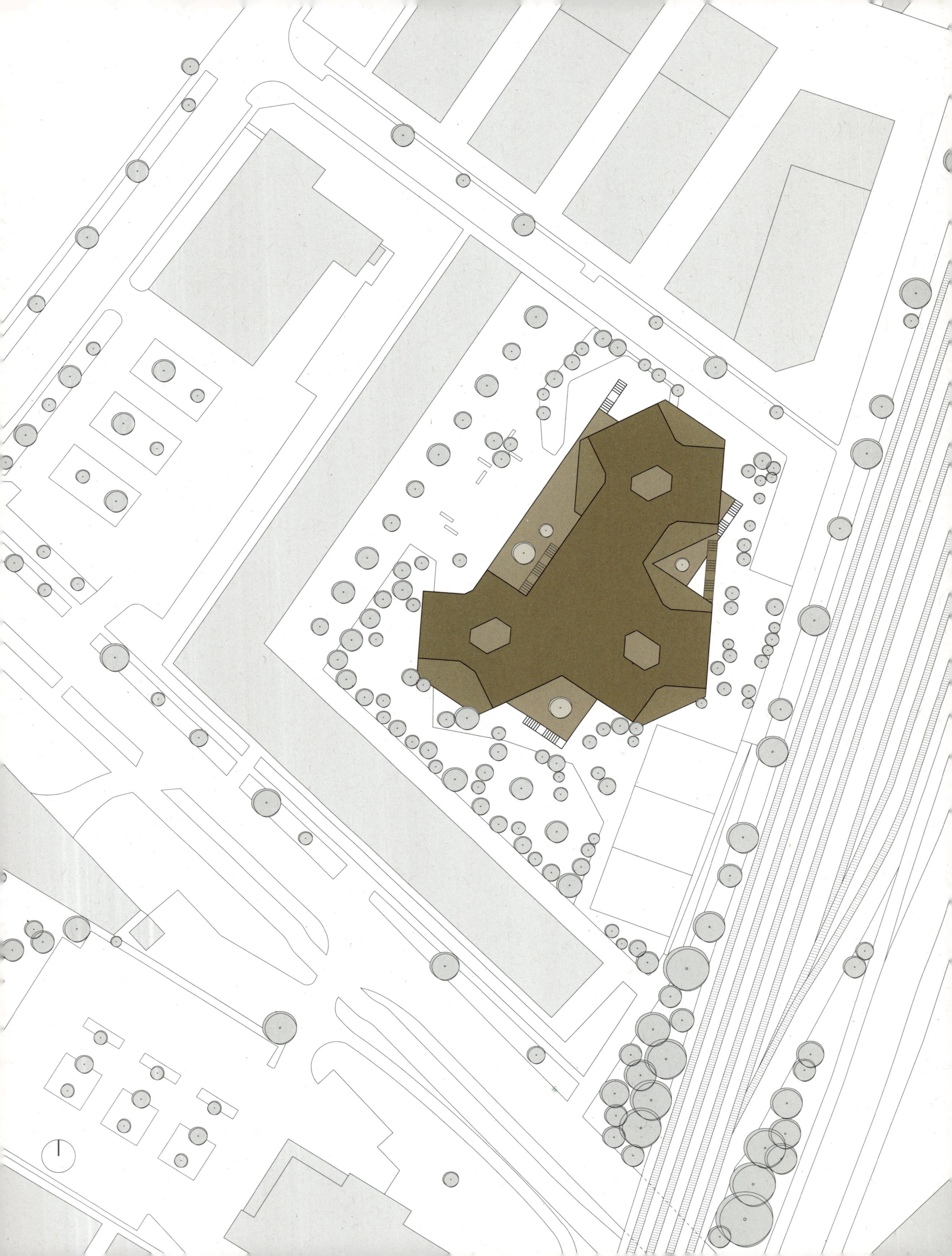

cluster school
1220 Vienna, AT

PROGRAM
School and day-care, educational zones, library, auditorium, cafeteria, gym, communal outdoor areas

DIMENSIONS
Gross floor area 9,070 m², gross net area 8,187 m², floor space of classrooms 5,955 m²

CLIENT
City of Vienna, MA19 – Architektur und Stadtgestaltung

PROJECT TEAM
Marlies Breuss, Michael Ogertschnig, Alessandro Zerbi, Kira Röblitz, Anika Lindwedel, Philipp Schulten

CONSULTANTS
ghp gmeiner | haferl & partner zt gmbh (structural engineer), kwi (building systems),
Dipl-Ing. Erich Röhrer and Dipl.-Ing. Ianko Ivanov (fire protection)

MODEL-MAKING
archimodell, Vienna

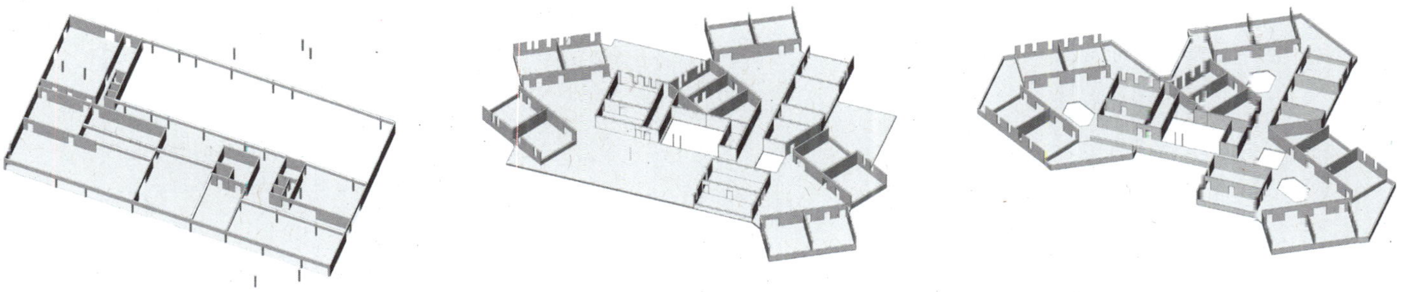

"The structure makes its function as a cluster school clearly recognizable through its form and appearance."

—HOLODECK architects, project description for the competition, 2020 (trans. by the ed.)

Site plan
1:1,000
10 25 50 m

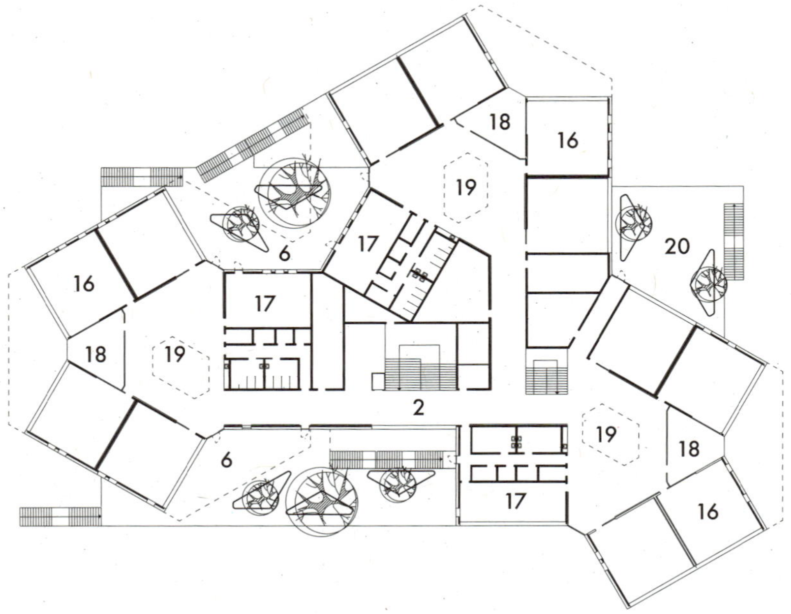

First floor

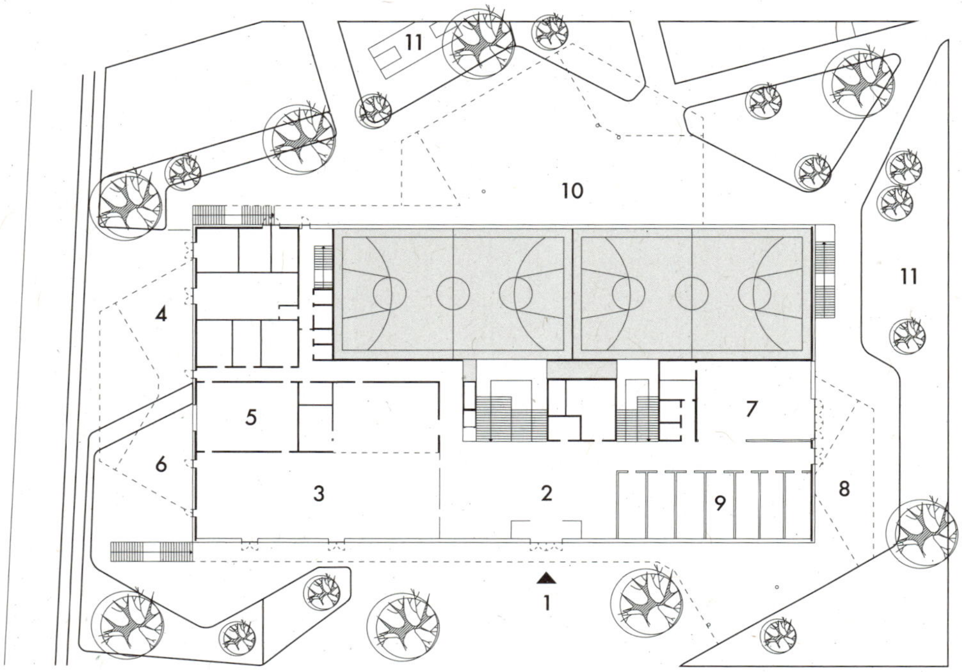

Ground floor

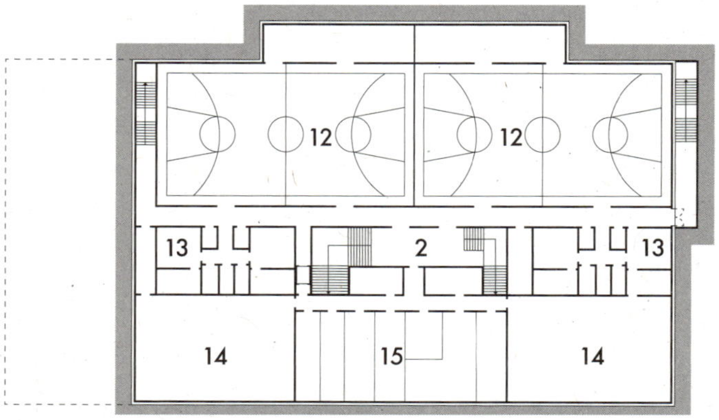

Basement floor
1:850

1 5 10 25 m

Second floor

Third floor

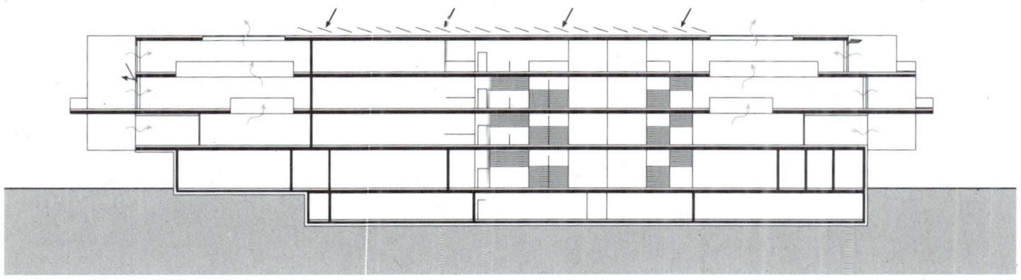

1	Common public square	7	Library	14	Building systems
2	Main circulation	8	Outdoor terrace	15	Storage area
3	Multifunctional space, cafeteria	9	School administration	16	Classroom for pupils
4	Delivery area	10	Outdoor covered area	17	Educational team
5	Kitchen	11	Green islands	18	Indoor loggia
6	Terraces for relaxation	12	Sports hall	19	Multifunctional area
		13	Service room	20	Teaching balconies

Section
1:850

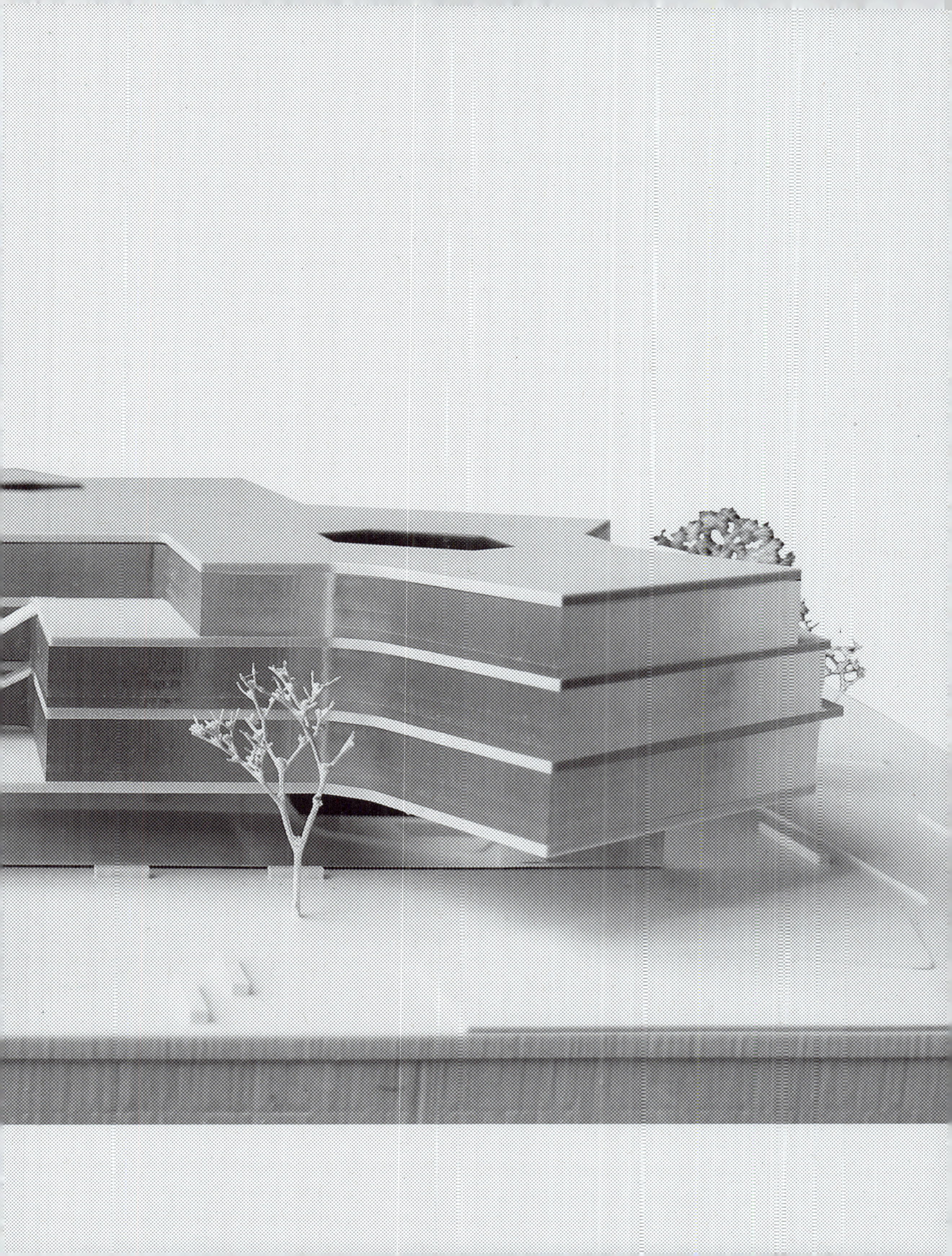

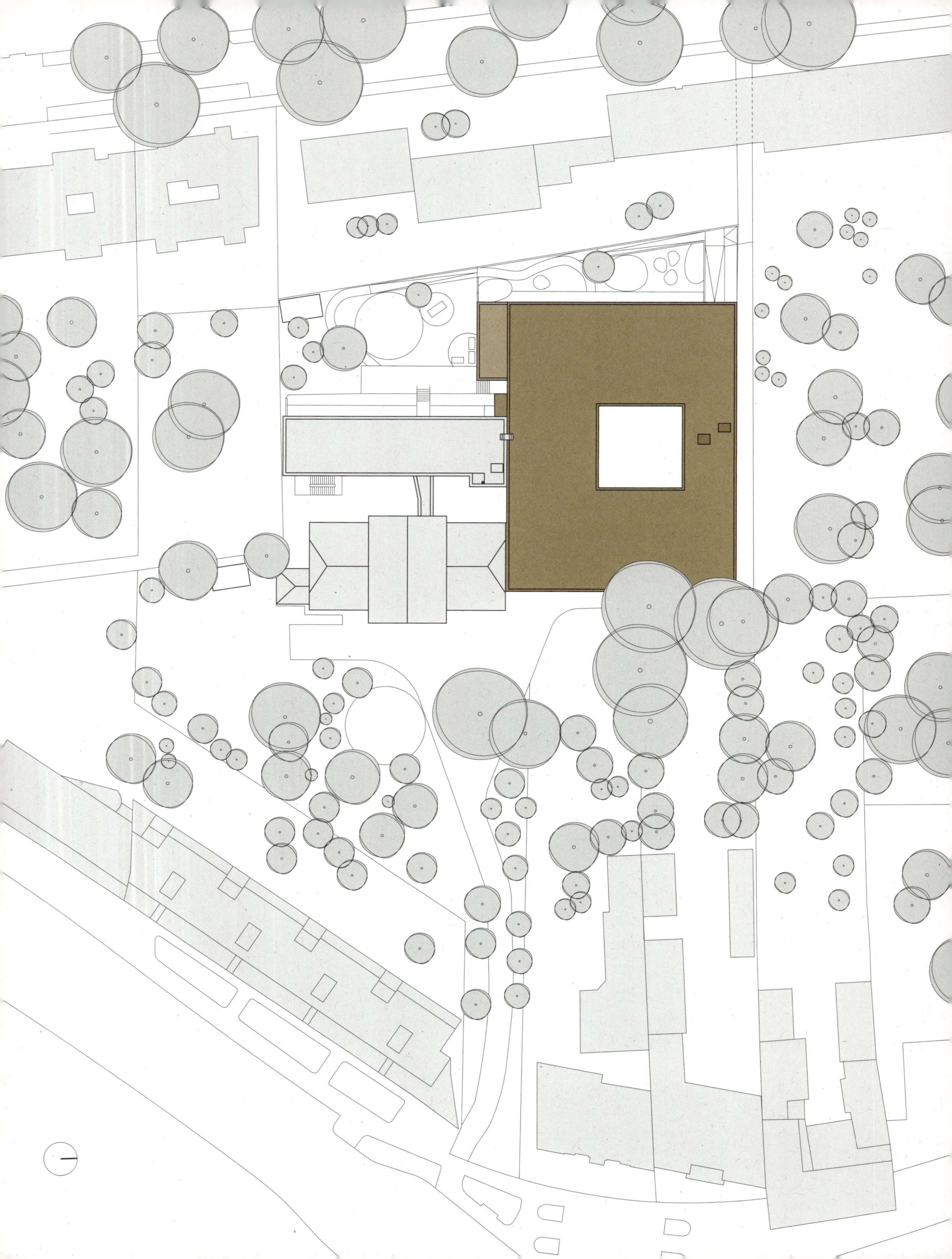

campus school
1130 Vienna, AT

See pp. 22–27

PROGRAM
School campus, group- and classrooms, multifunctional spaces, gym, workshop and service space, urban courtyard, extension

DIMENSIONS
Gross floor area 5,355 m², gross net area 4,672 m²

CLIENT
City of Vienna, MA19 – Architektur und Stadtgestaltung
Bauunternehmung Granit GmbH

PROJECT TEAM
Marlies Breuss, Michael Ogertschnig, Vedran Zonic, Alessandro Zerbi, Bernhard Hofinger, Kira Röblitz

PROJECT COOPERATION
Veit Aschenbrenner Architekten

CONSULTANTS
ghp gmeiner | haferl & partner zt gmbh (structural engineer), Kräftner Landschaftsarchitektur (landscape design), Röhrer Ziviltechniker and Vasko+Partner Ingenieure ZT GmbH (building physics and fire protection), Russ Ingenieure and Franye Gebäudetechnik (building systems), Elektro MMS GmbH (electrical engineering), DI Johann Wöss (cultural technology)

PHOTOGRAPHY
Kurt Hörbst, Susanne Veit Aschenbrenner

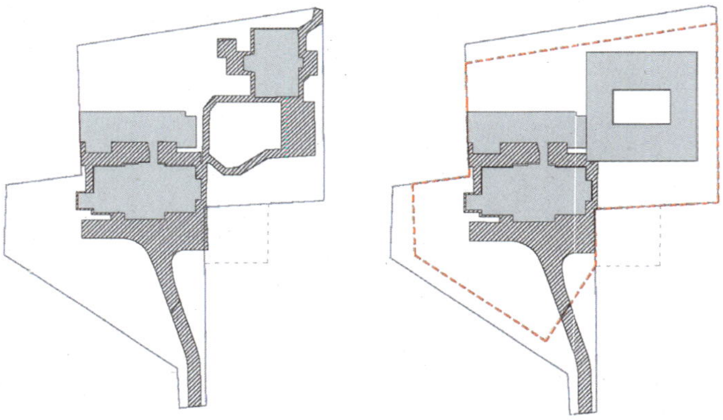

> “The existing, already extended school building will be supplemented with a courtyard structure, using minimal surface and fitted into the surrounding park landscape.”

—HOLODECK architects, project description, 2017 (trans. by the ed.)

Site plan
1:725

10 25 50 m

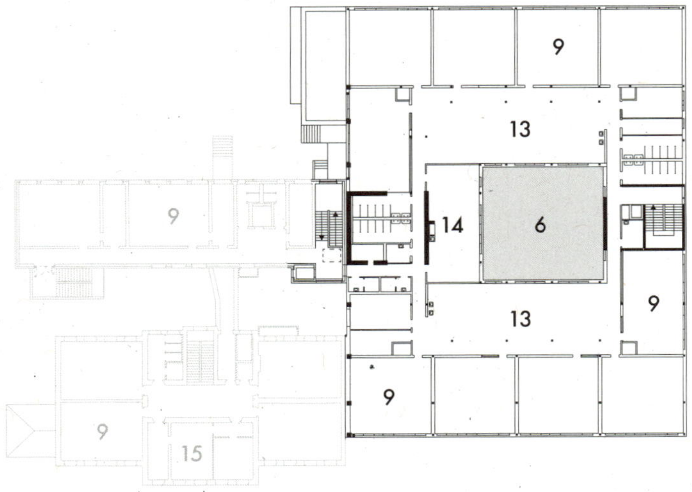

First floor

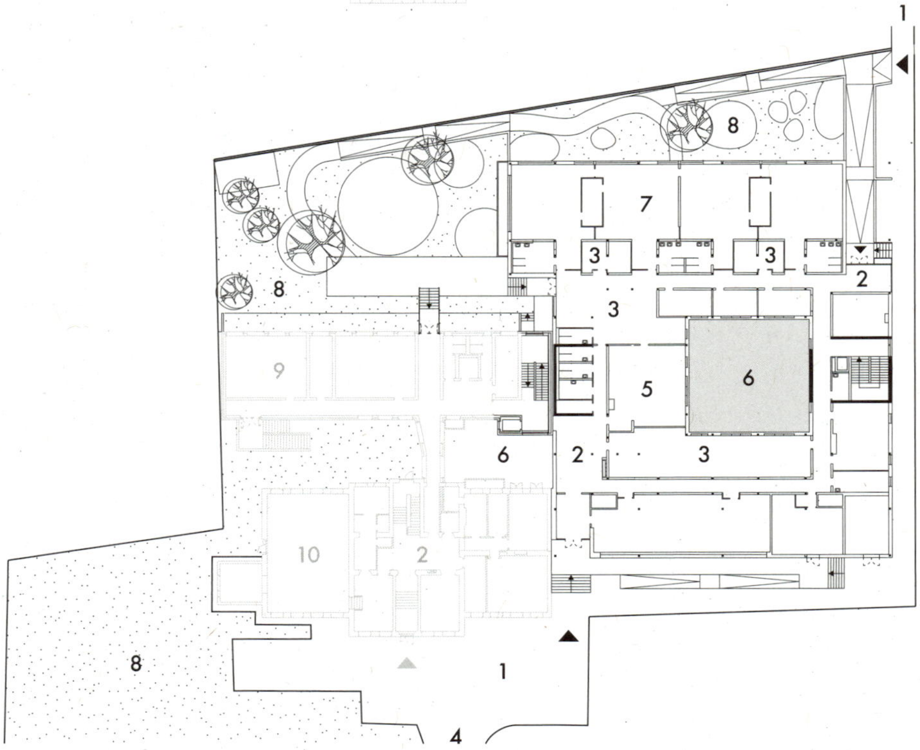

Ground floor

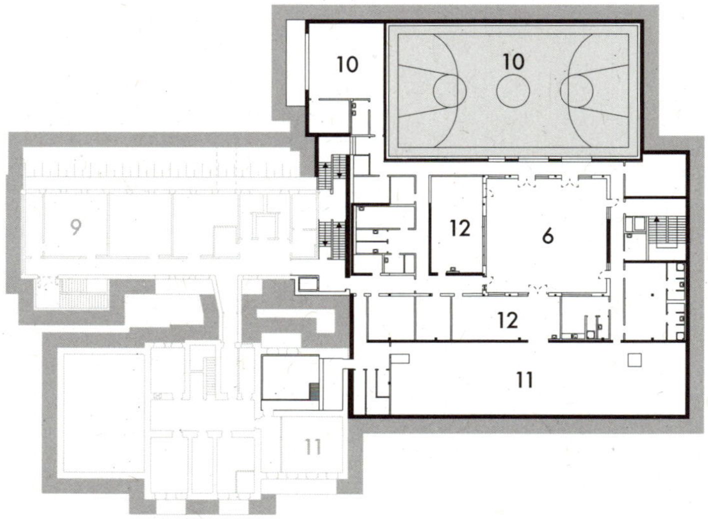

Basement floor
1:850

1 Common public area
2 Main circulation
3 Multifunctional space, cafeteria
4 Delievery area
5 Kitchen
6 Common courtyard
7 Classroom, kindergarten
8 Outdoor playground
9 Classroom for pupils
10 Sports hall
11 Building systems
12 Workshop spaces
13 Multifunctional area
14 Educational team
15 Administration

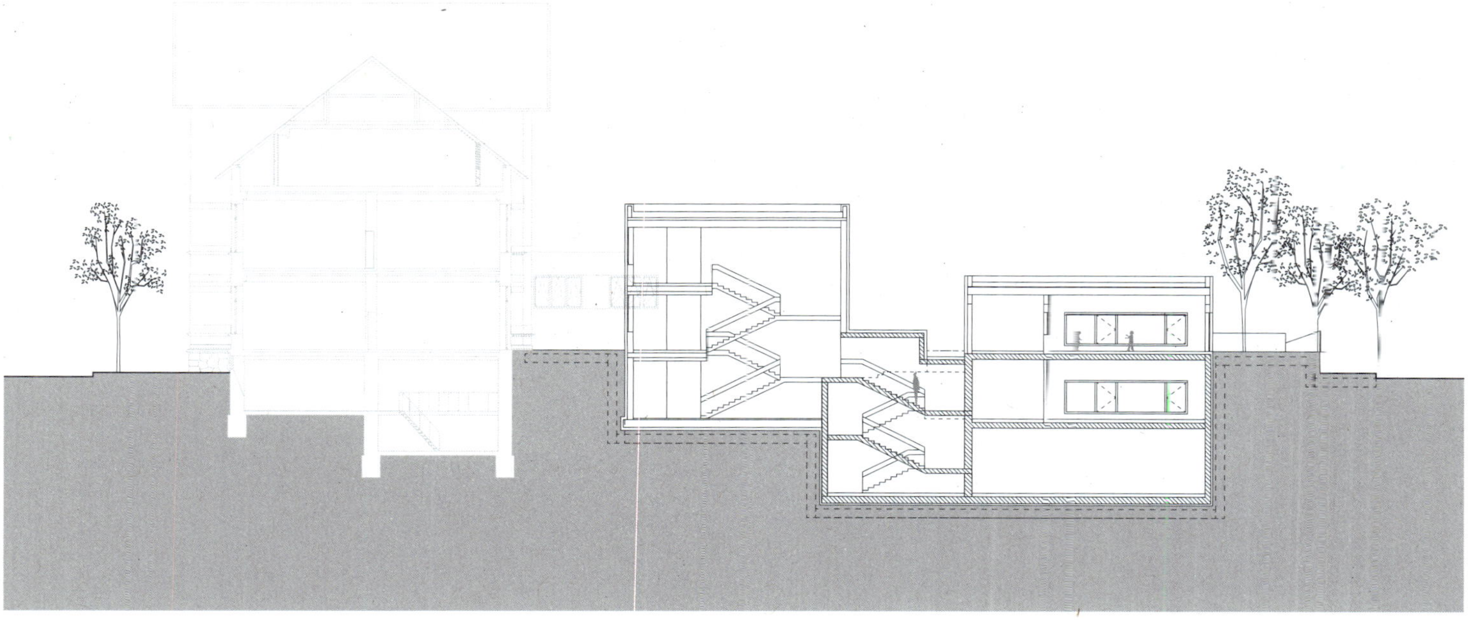

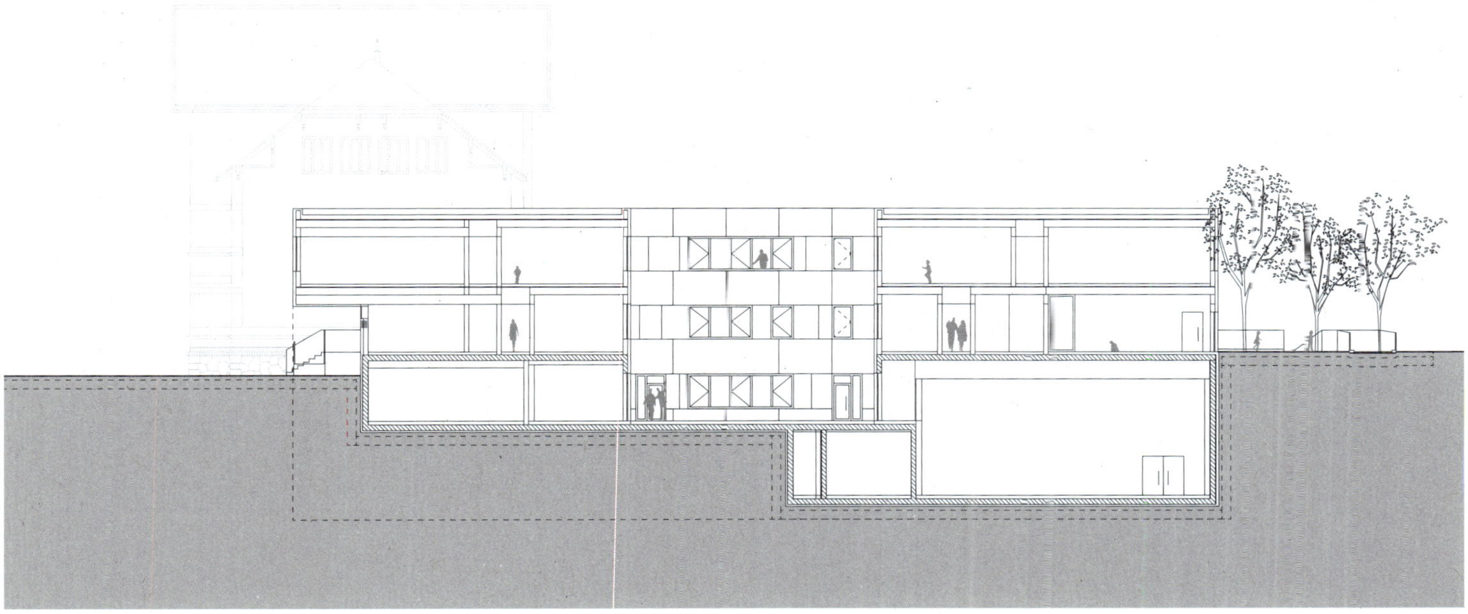

1 5 10 25 m

Longitudinal sections
1:400

2001
PUBLIC ATTITUDE

connected with max
46024 Valencia, ES

PROGRAM
Urban development, restructuring of a city quarter

DIMENSIONS
Plot area 14,800 m², gross floor area 12,880 m²

CLIENT
City of Valencia, Spain

PROJECT TEAM
Marlies Breuss, Michael Ogertschnig, Peter Hofstetter, Christine Schmauszer, Florian Waldmayer

INTERNATIONAL CONSULTANTS
Joann Blackburne (London), Manuel Garcia Barbero (Barcelona), Marc Spinner (Berlin)

PUBLICATIONS (SELECTION)
Laboratorio di progettazione architettonica 4, Milan, 2014.
Nick Dunn, *Architectural Modelmaking*, London, Laurence King Publishing, 2014/2020 (ISBN 10:9781780671710)

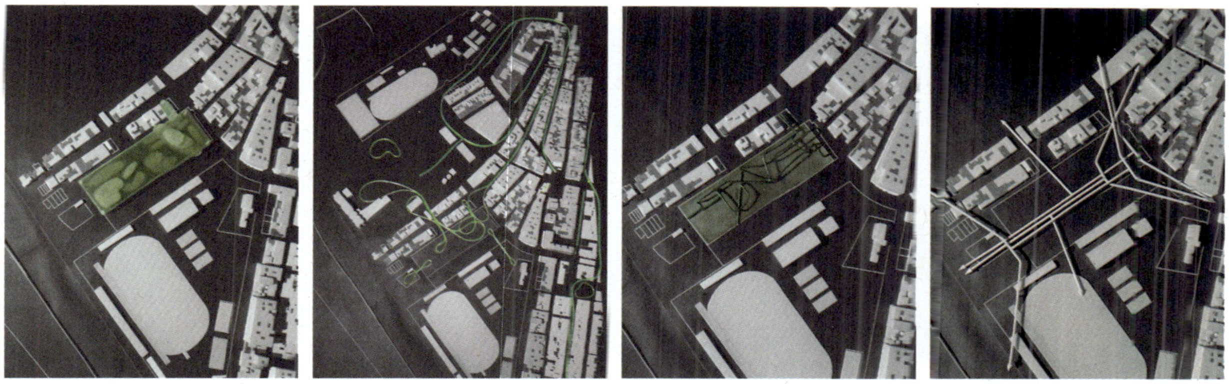

“The strategy to urbanize this area of Valencia is based on the method of overlay, interaction, infiltration, and creation of new program structures.”

—HOLODECK architects, project description for the competition, 2001 (trans. by the ed.)

Site plan
1:1,500

10 30 60 100 m

page 229

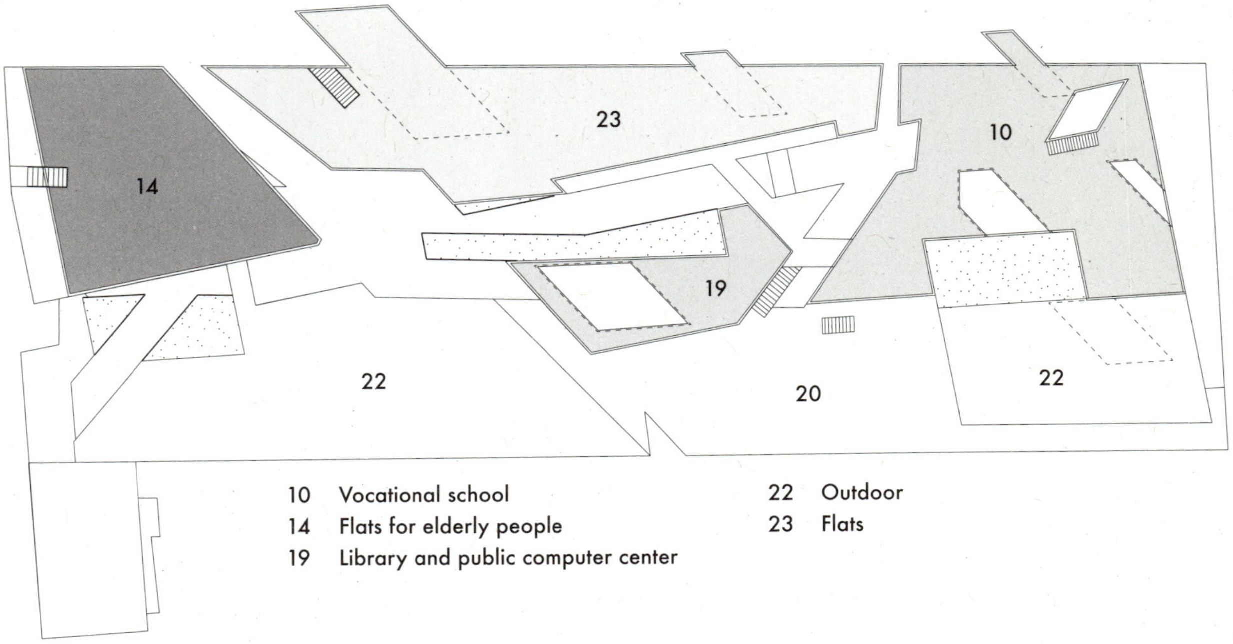

10 Vocational school
14 Flats for elderly people
19 Library and public computer center
22 Outdoor
23 Flats

Second floor

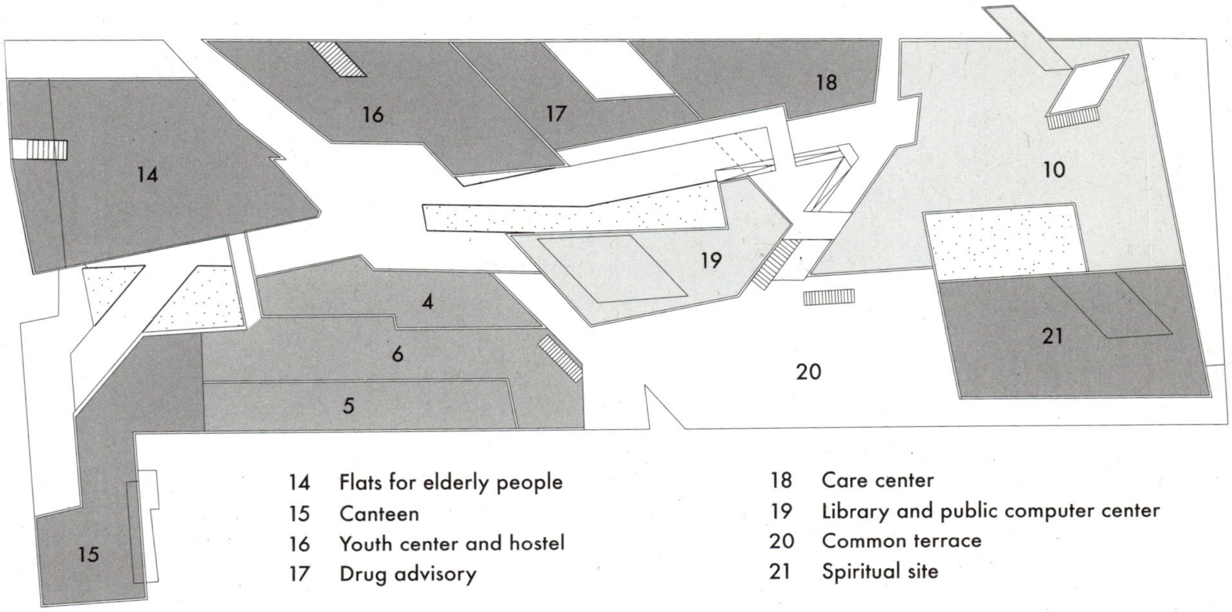

14 Flats for elderly people
15 Canteen
16 Youth center and hostel
17 Drug advisory
18 Care center
19 Library and public computer center
20 Common terrace
21 Spiritual site

First floor

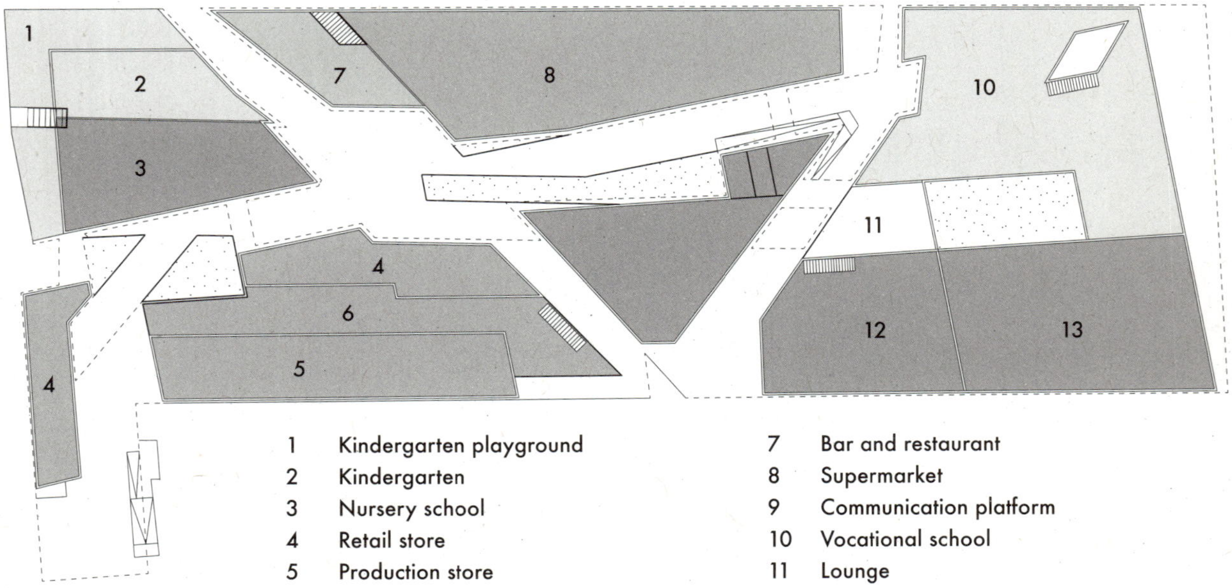

1 Kindergarten playground
2 Kindergarten
3 Nursery school
4 Retail store
5 Production store
6 Interior market place
7 Bar and restaurant
8 Supermarket
9 Communication platform
10 Vocational school
11 Lounge
12 Medical center
13 Convalescent home

Ground floor
1:1,100

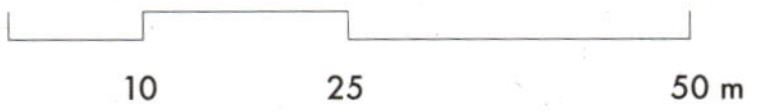

PROGRAMATIC STRUCTURE

PLEASURE SPACE
MONEY NET
WELFARE
INSPIRION
EDUTAINMENT
FLATS
OPEN AREA

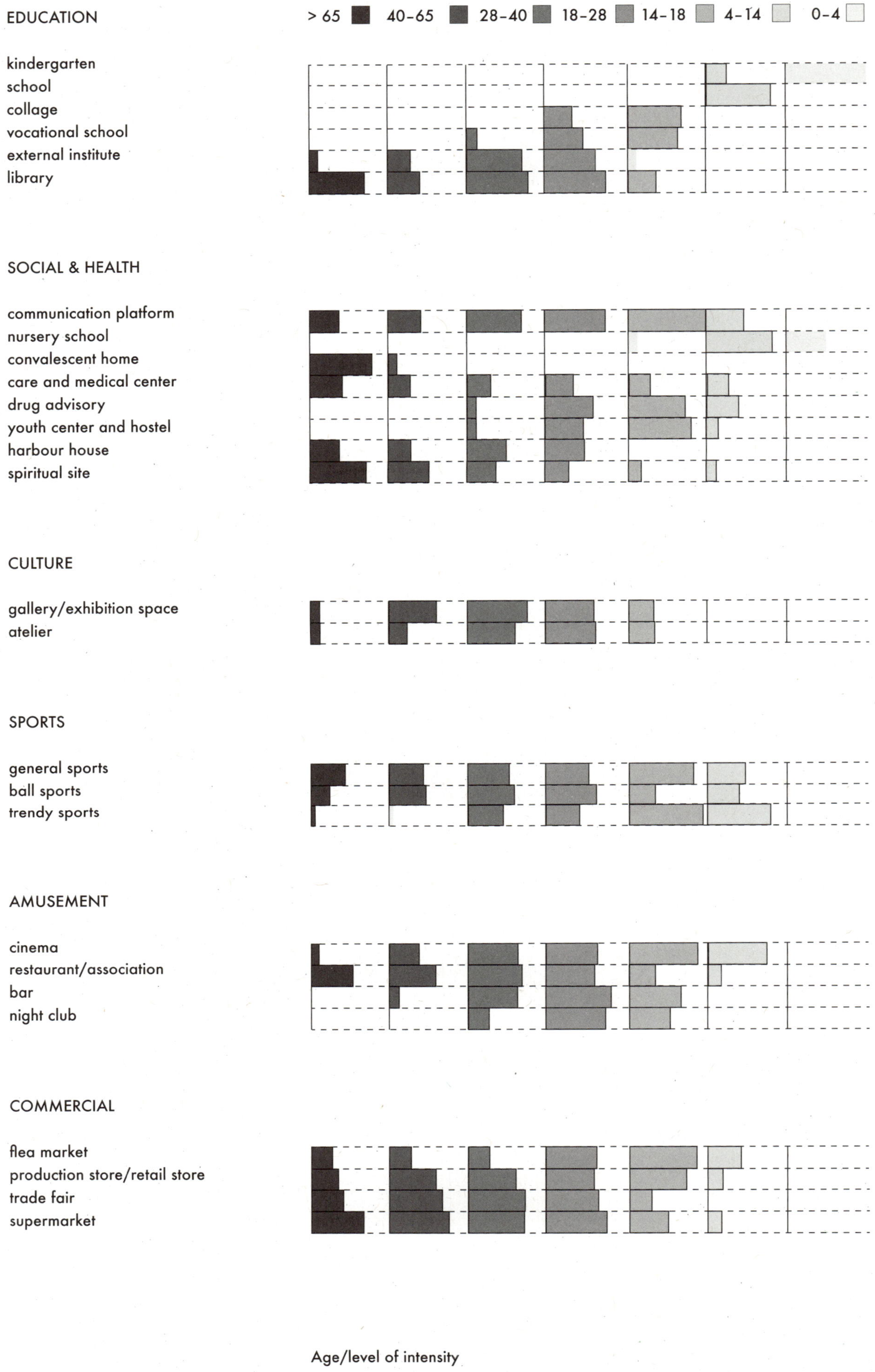
EDUCATION
> 65
40–65
28–40
18–28
14–18
4–14
0–4
kindergarten
school
collage
vocational school
external institute
library
SOCIAL & HEALTH
communication platform
nursery school
convalescent home
care and medical center
drug advisory
youth center and hostel
harbour house
spiritual site
CULTURE
gallery/exhibition space
atelier
SPORTS
general sports
ball sports
trendy sports
AMUSEMENT
cinema
restaurant/association
bar
night club
COMMERCIAL
flea market
production store/retail store
trade fair
supermarket
Age/level of intensity

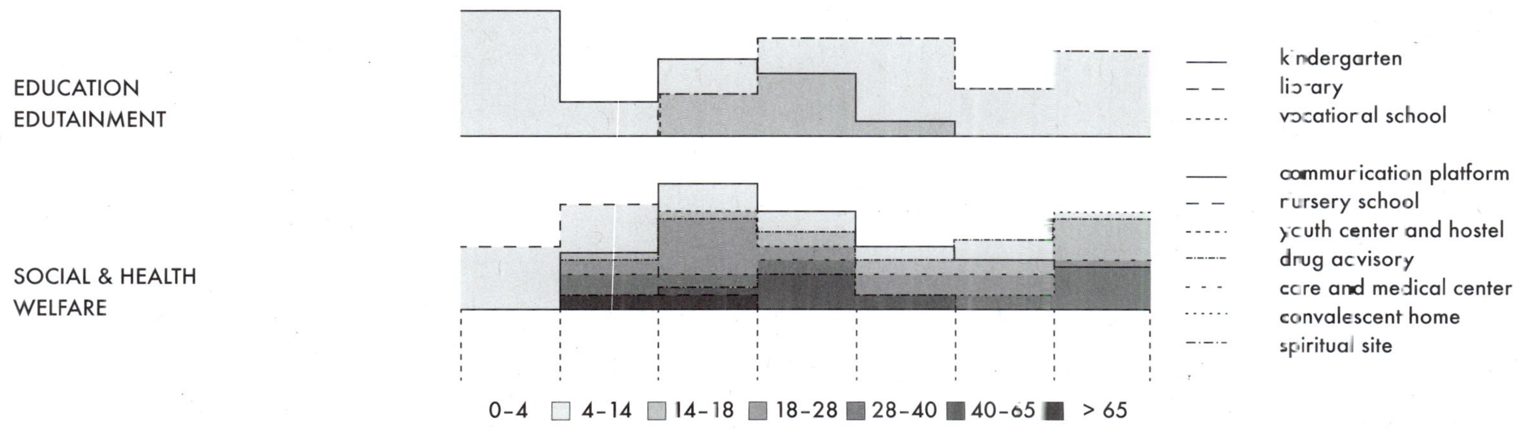

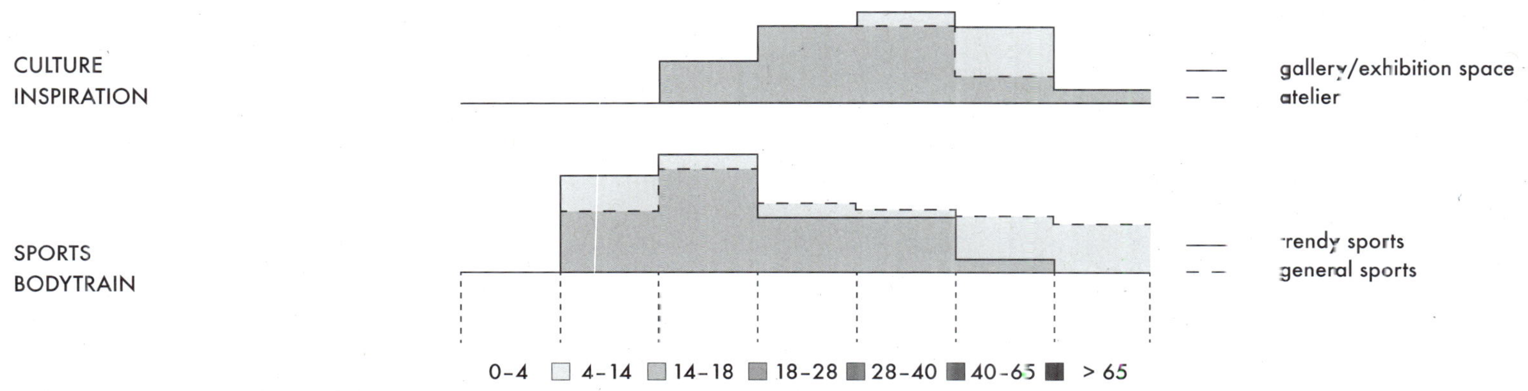

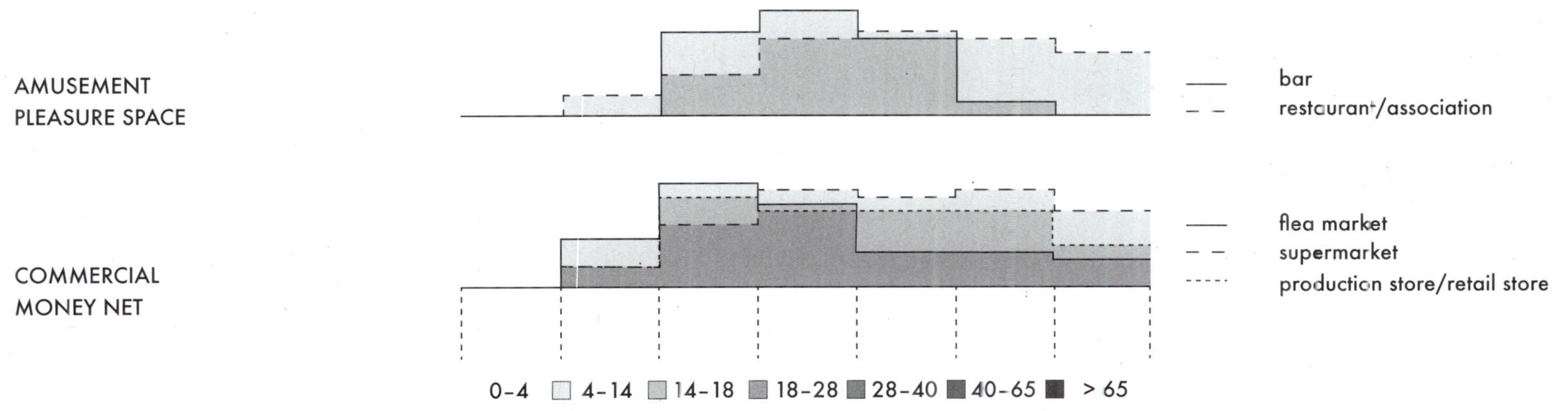

Age/level of intensity

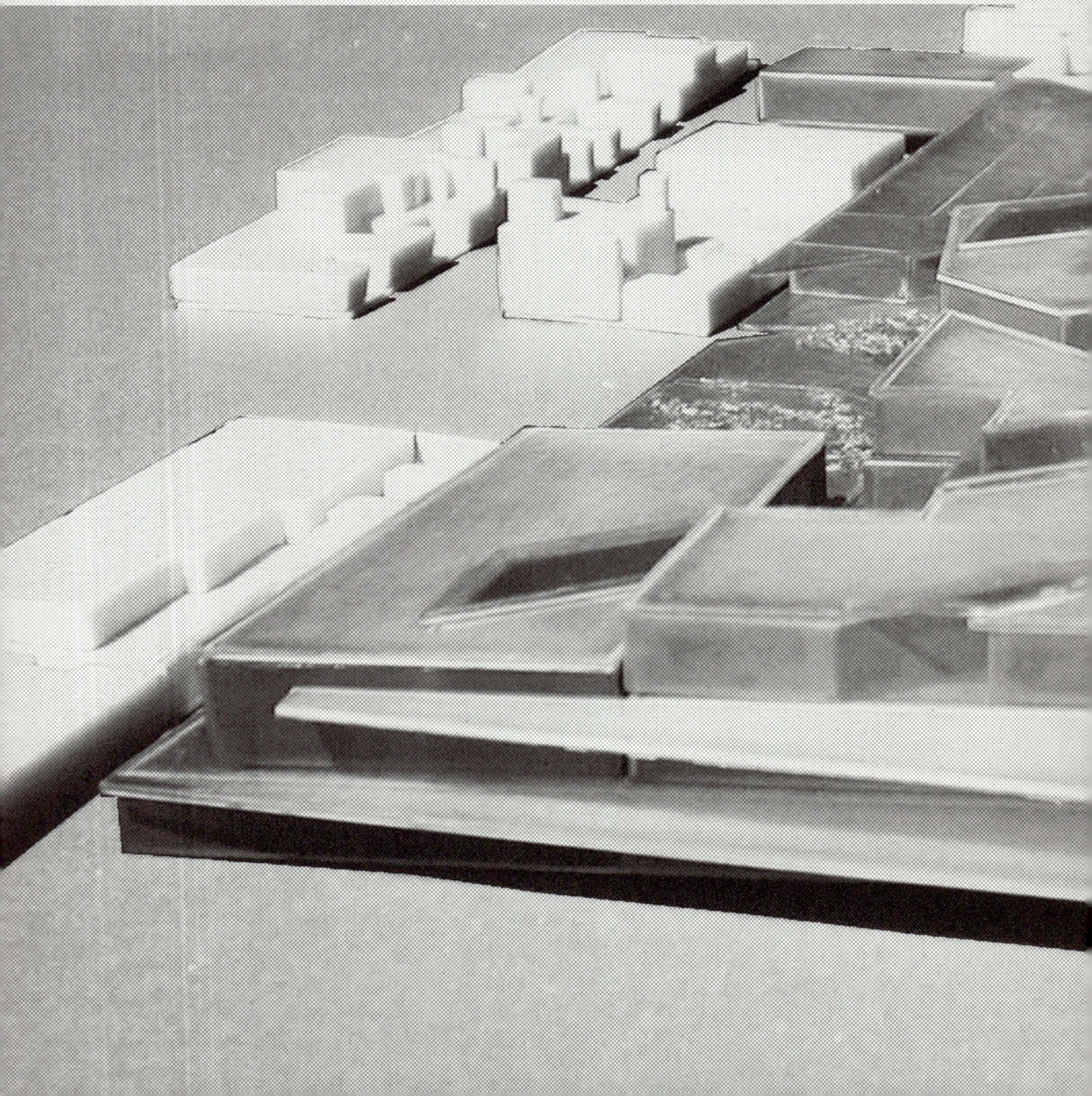

FLEXIBLE REUSE

wirtschaftspark breitensee and breitensee studios
2009–15

The main objective of this project is transforming a nineteenth-century production site into a welcoming mixed-use location in the twenty-first century. Inspired by existing infrastructure the concept focuses on the local need and desire for a creative hub next to the Sargfabrik, a very specific housing project in Vienna designed by BKK2. Now equipped to cover a wide range of offers, the ensemble provides everything necessary to accommodate so-called creative industries, manufacturing companies, office space for artificial intelligence and technology firms, media representatives, and more. A specific ambience that represents creative production is generated using existing and innovative components.

The reinterpretation of this industrial estate results in *wirtschaftspark breitensee* taking up some 25,000 square meters of the restructured area. Analyzing the "functional loop of a truck" to deliver goods defined the site layout conceptually and physically, and articulated the new building within the block. Surrounding facades of different periods were analyzed and transformed into a new configuration and pattern of transparent, translucent, and opaque parts. Linking the existing and the new construction, a bridge connects the outer block with the inner island, where a glass-roofed patio serves as a venue for festivities and interaction between different companies. Outdoor spaces, such as balconies and terraces, support communication, and their appearance creates a visible connection between old and new architecture.

To provide maximum flexibility, the new structure based on prefabricated components with supporting heights of 3.2 meters on main levels, up to 5.8 meters, permitting natural light from both sides. This open floor plan—a new loft interpretation with inner service zones—offers different options for uses such as office or production space, or even sport facilities. The whole structure follows a low-tech approach using specific materials, such as specially invented translucent glass elements to minimize solar radiance, insulated aluminum panels to prevent an outside view in, and more. No suspended ceilings or raised floors are used, so as to permit adaptability when working requirements change and to minimize maintenance costs. The roof extension for breitensee studios, on top of the commercial building, facing Goldschlagstrasse, presents these interventions to the public and invites people to visit the inside yard of the *wirtschaftspark breitensee*. The attic offers two-level studios for creatives, such as graphic and web designers or software programmers, and, with its moving form and outdoor spaces, shows the new vividness inside the building block.

EnBW co-working spaces
2018

The *EnBW co-working spaces* with its 6,950 square meters of ground area, is owned by the Baden-Württemberg energy company EnBW, whose main headquarters are right alongside. Good public transport links and direct connection to a nearby highway influenced the city of Karlsruhe to turn this former industrial area into a new vibrant quarter featuring cultural areas, housing projects, and multifunctional spaces alongside existing atmospheric buildings. A boulevard with trees, the Durlacher Allee, leads from the Adenauerring around the city core, with its castle and all main cultural institutions, to the restructured neighborhood in an up-and-coming area that includes this plot.

Connecting to this promenade, big, open, partly covered outdoor spaces were created, with a restaurant on the ground level and generous staggered terraces facing south on the upper levels. These serve as areas for relaxation and meeting for all employees and guests from spring to autumn. Inside the spacious building, in the atrium, two large islands with plants, water, and trees at ground level provide the basis for a good indoor climate. These gardens are visible and accessible from every level via staircases and bridges, creating an agreeably relaxing atmosphere.

The four upper levels with open galleries support up to 27,000 square meters of multifunctional office spaces with four main service zones, which act as supporting cores for the suspended construction, keeping all levels free of columns. Inside the facade, made of three main glass elements, are diagonal steel beams between the thermal activated concrete ceilings, suspended inside with steel cables from the framework roof. Meeting rooms, shops, hospitality units, and event areas are located on the public ground floor. Flexible areas, including office and recreational spaces, are divisible into areas with a minimum size of 12 square meters and take up all the upper floors, extending into the south-facing terraces. Geothermal energy, gained from piling below the building, and cooled air, obtained from ground water, are part of the sustainable strategy, as are photovoltaic panels on the roof made of folded elements. Together with its inner microclimate, the whole building works as a future-orientated co-working space.

hall 01

1999–2000

The hardware store Eisenwaren Geiger on the edge of Sankt Veit an der Glan, in Carinthia, lacked an area to display its products to clients, such as newly opened big houseware dealers in the area had. The owner, aged sixty-two, decided to build a new structure on the site to enable him to compete with the larger companies.

Our design maintains the existing delicate steel structure of the former storage hall (which could not be built in the same way, due to new security and fire protection regulations) while expanding and renewing the surrounding structural components. The vast space is not divided but supplemented with a parallel steel structure, a gallery, and two small spaces in front of and alongside the hall, so as to create more exhibition area and to attract customers.

All materials are of low-budget specification, and most come from the client's stock, which includes various industrial prefabricated systems. Homogeneity is created through resourceful application and detailing, using prefabricated elements in unexpected combinations. The old pitched roof, formerly consisting of single plates, is covered with prefabricated, insulated aluminum panels that merge into the west facade and continue down to ground. Adjacent to the facade in the east, there is an additional structure made of industrial, translucent glass components and recessed under the overhanging section of the roof. In the north, a tailor-made wired glass forms a ventilated facade opening onto the inside for daylight.

The entrée pavilion welcomes all clients and consists of unframed insulated glass panels, mounted on a bar made of fair-faced concrete. The restructuring of the building itself has therefore created a marketing instrument for Eisenwaren Geiger without any additional advertising costs.

gewerbehof missindorf

2007–10

This restructuring of spaces originating from the turn of the nineteenth century represents the start of a process of change in the industrial hub *gewerbehof missindorf*. A new face has been created to present to the public realm, a suspended, light-filled café that welcomes everyone from inside and outside. Next to this public meeting point for all employees and guests, there is an innovative TV studio called *okto* that works as a private and self-organized hub for all kinds of creatives who want to show their films, music, stories, and so forth, to the public. Visual connections between the café and the studio provide an insight into TV production, which normally takes place behind walls or black curtains.

On the upper levels, one existing floor, organized with small rooms along a corridor, is given a new spatial layout for creative workers in the twenty-first century. Shared office zones are situated next to large windows on both sides of the now loft-like office area, supplemented with bookable meeting rooms and storage areas on the side of the hallway. A flexible system offers the possibility of creating connecting spaces and utilization of areas on demand while dividing costs for shared functions. Outdoor facilities, like balconies and small terraces, are also introduced for micro-breaks and communication.

The structural system of a skeleton follows the idea of flexibility, with only acoustic panels for sound absorption suspended from the old load-bearing ceilings. Piping, ducting, and supporting technical installations are mounted visibly in the corridor, and can so be removed or added to without heavy maintenance costs. Profilit glass, an industrial product from the 1960s, separates the outer working areas from the inner zones and allows natural light to flow into the corridor.

experience center

2018

Formerly a turbine-testing facility located on an airfield, the existing building with its specific sound emission features will now serve as an exhibition area, the first-ever experience center for the Mercedes G class all-terrain vehicle. Preserving the character and structure of the old industrial hall with its huge entrance doors, the restructuring as an *experience center* uses simple architectural interventions. The vast sliding doors continue to flank the main entrance but are now immobilized, to preserve the indoor-outdoor energy balance, and a glass partition inserted, the lower part of which can be opened and closed.

Inside, the vast space is kept as it was, adapted by the insertion of window embrasures in the 2.5-meter-thick metal walls and completed by additional spaces. A lounge stands inside like a display case, connected to the ground floor by just two supports, a staircase and an elevator that have been incorporated. Reception, workshop, and sales areas are located in between the metal panels of the outer walls. The western and eastern wings contain sanitary areas, the kitchen, and secondary rooms. A platform strip beside the entrance hovers above the main space, connecting the two wings and additional spaces.

The building's thermal envelope is developed to be flexible. A coating protects the outer shell from solar radiation and prevents the inner spaces from overheating in summer. All glass elements are equipped with an anti-reflective filter to separate external from internal conditions.

headquarters post
2013

Austria's postal service decided to locate its main Vienna administration at an old site next to the Rochusmarkt subway station and Grete-Jost-Park in the 3rd District. The scheme was to include an existing building, formerly housing a 1920s switching center and post and telegraph office. The multifunctional program on the lower floors, with retail shops, restaurants, a grocery store, and a post office, serves as link to the market and residential areas around and as an indoor connection to the park facilities at the back.

Typologically, the new development follows a block structure with inner courtyards but respects neighboring residential houses by reducing the roof height on the sides facing them. The courtyards allow natural light to reach all office spaces on the inner facades down to the ground floor, using generously sized skylights. Four cores with vertical infrastructure—elevators, staircases, and sanitary rooms—give access to the whole building, from the underground parking up to the roof terraces, for the 1,200 employees and various guests. A small urban plaza next to the Rochusmarkt and at the beginning of Erdbergerstrasse offers an outdoor waiting and relaxing area beside the narrow subway station. From there, two main entrances guide vistors either into the lobby with a security point on the first floor or to the retail area on the ground floor and leading to the main entrance on Landstrasser Hauptstrasse and the U3 subway.

In addition to the ground-floor plaza, a private roof terrace with a garden on the sixth floor provides space for relaxation and outdoor meetings. The overall building with its module-based facade follows the principles of a low-tech structure, prioritizing human needs for openable windows, a pleasant atmosphere, and flexible working areas with screens, as well as the common outdoor garden. Structurally, the principle of a skeleton enhances future adaptations to accommodate changes in working procedures.

remise amstetten
2021–24

The perfect location of the old *Remise Amstetten*—five minutes from the main railway line (a main east–west rail link)—lends meaning to this new development. Technological innovations around the end of the nineteenth and the start of the twentieth century, plus the need to service and maintain more than fourteen diesel locomotives at the same time, necessitated this circular railway shed with a diameter of more than 120 meters and a turntable in the middle. During over 100 years of use, especially during wartime, renovations and adaptions were made for larger and stronger engines, but the main layout was retained. After periods of abandonment, it became an event and identity location for residents of the surrounding neighborhood who formed a citizens' initiative to keep the atmosphere of the Remise intact.

The existing brick wall toward the old water tower and the huge wooden doors facing the hub are part of the new design, as well as two overhanging office floors above the 4.8-meter-high ground floor and the 4.2-meter-high first floor that visually works as a transparent joint between old and new. Three indented courtyards on the outside and corresponding light wells on the inside provide natural light to the inner areas and lend structure to the building. The main entrance from the railway station into the new area at the east side of the Remise leads through the fully glazed passage with a bistro, common lounge, and co-working spaces on the two sides. Three functional cores with elevators, stairs, sanitary rooms, and vertical infrastructure shafts organize the floors and support all their functional requirements. Tea kitchen areas as communication zones, server and storage rooms, and rentable meeting spaces complete the flexibly arranged floors, which offer units of 60 to 1,200 square meters.

As a flexible skeleton structure, the low-tech building includes thermal activation of the concrete core to aid heating and cooling, with primary energy tapped from renewable energy sources below the building and photovoltaic panels on the roof for local energy demands. Fresh air comes via openable windows and tubes suspended from the ceiling. Outside textile sun shades reduce the effects of solar radiance while providing views at all seasons.

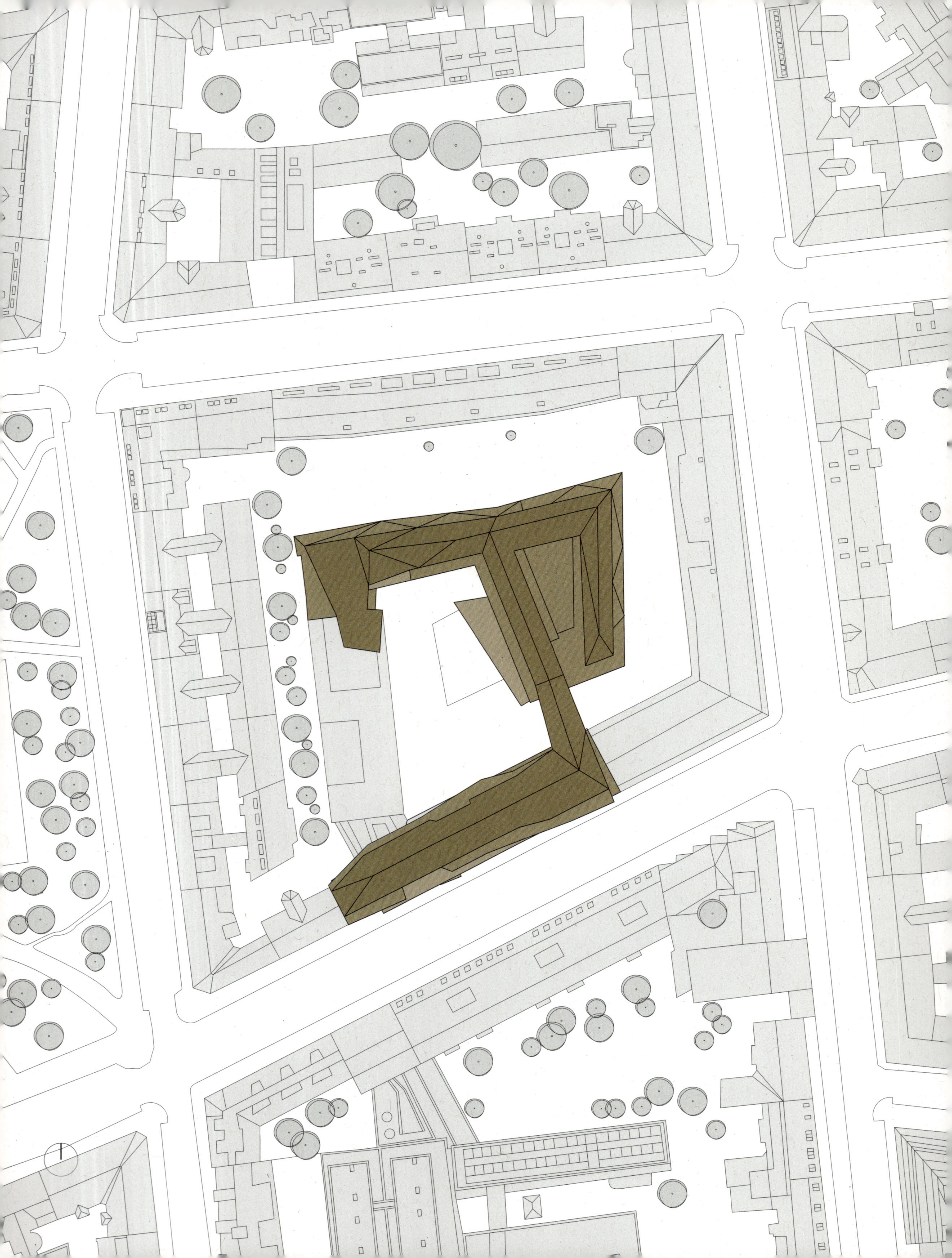

wirtschaftspark breitensee and breitensee studios
1140 Vienna, AT

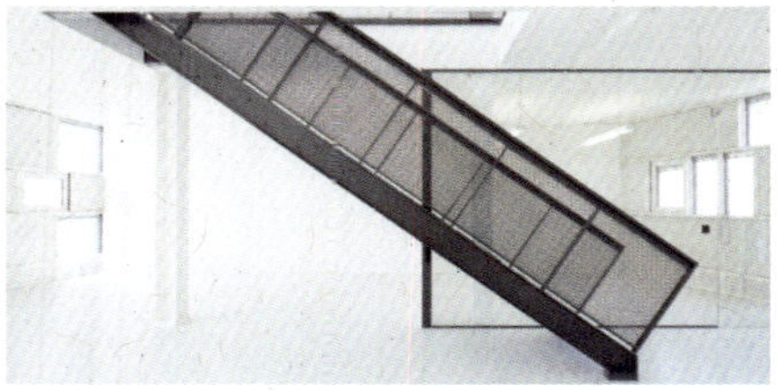

See pp. 28–38

PROGRAM
Urban development, business park, offices, studios, extension

DIMENSIONS
Plot area 9,494 m², GFA business park 10,300 m², GFA Breitensee studios 2,400 m²

CLIENT
Wien Holding, Vienna, Austria

PROJECT TEAM
Marlies Breuss, Michael Ogertschnig, Hannes Zergoi, Johannes Müller, Stefanie Gänger, Kieu Giang Hoang, Jiri Huske, Sven Klöcker, Niels Merschbrock, Helena Miller, Christian Mörtl, Carolin Saile

CONSULTANTS
Vasko+Partner Ingenieure ZT GmbH (building physics), CD-Consult Ziviltechniker (structural engineer)

MODEL-MAKING
Stefanie Gänger, Kanade Inaba

PHOTOGRAPHY
Wolfgang Thaler

AWARDS
First prize, invited competition
GEBAUT 2013 – Stadtgestaltung Wien
Ernst A. Plischke Award 2014, nomination

PUBLICATIONS (SELECTION)
Wojciech Czaja, "Einer macht den Lärm, und alle profitieren," *Der Standard*, Vienna, January 27, 2010.
Angela Djuric, "Neues Zentrum für junge, innovative Unternehmen," in *Der Aufbau – PERSPEKTIVEN*, 2012 (ISSN 0004-7805).

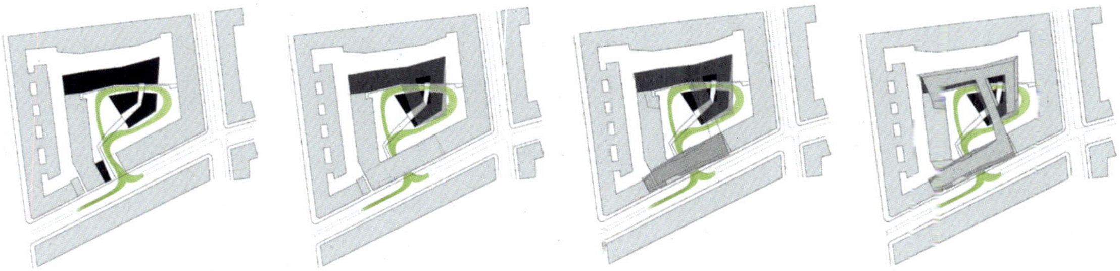

"With a grand gesture, their design connects the existing building with additions and extensions to form a multilayered new whole."

—Isabella Marboe, "Gewerbehof wird Wirtschaftspark," *Architektur.aktuell* 12 (2014), Vienna, p. 2 (trans. by the ed.)

Site plan
1:1,000

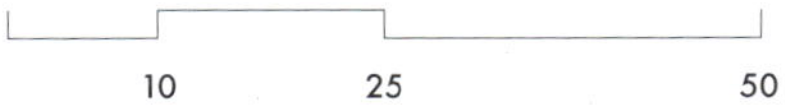

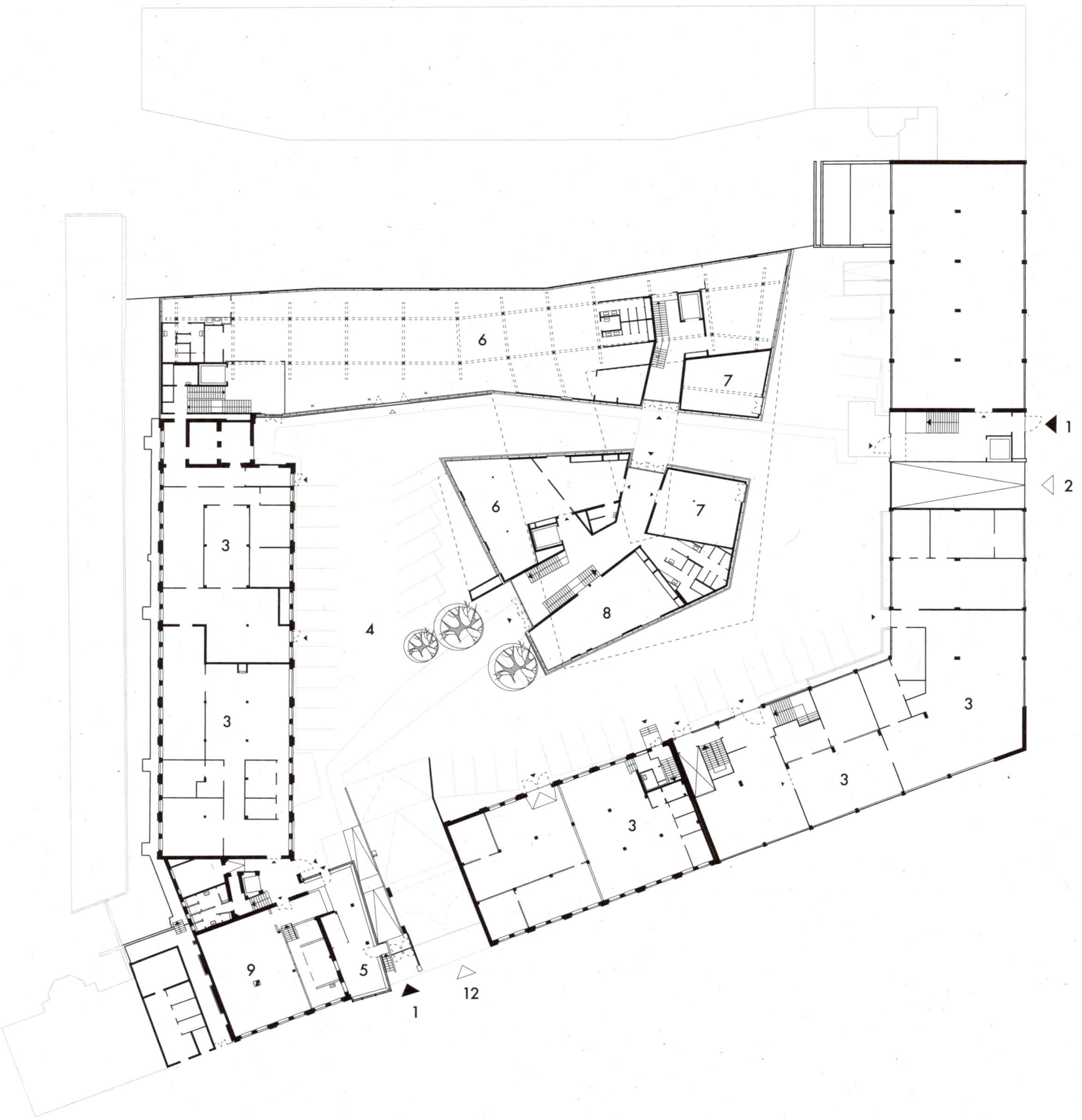

1 Entrance
2 Entrance to garage
3 Existing production companies
4 Common service courtyard
5 Restaurant
6 Multifunctional space
7 Waste disposal area
8 Seminar spaces
9 Television studio
10 Terraces
11 Interior atrium
12 Entrance to courtyard
13 Meeting space

Ground floor
1:650

1 3 6 10 m

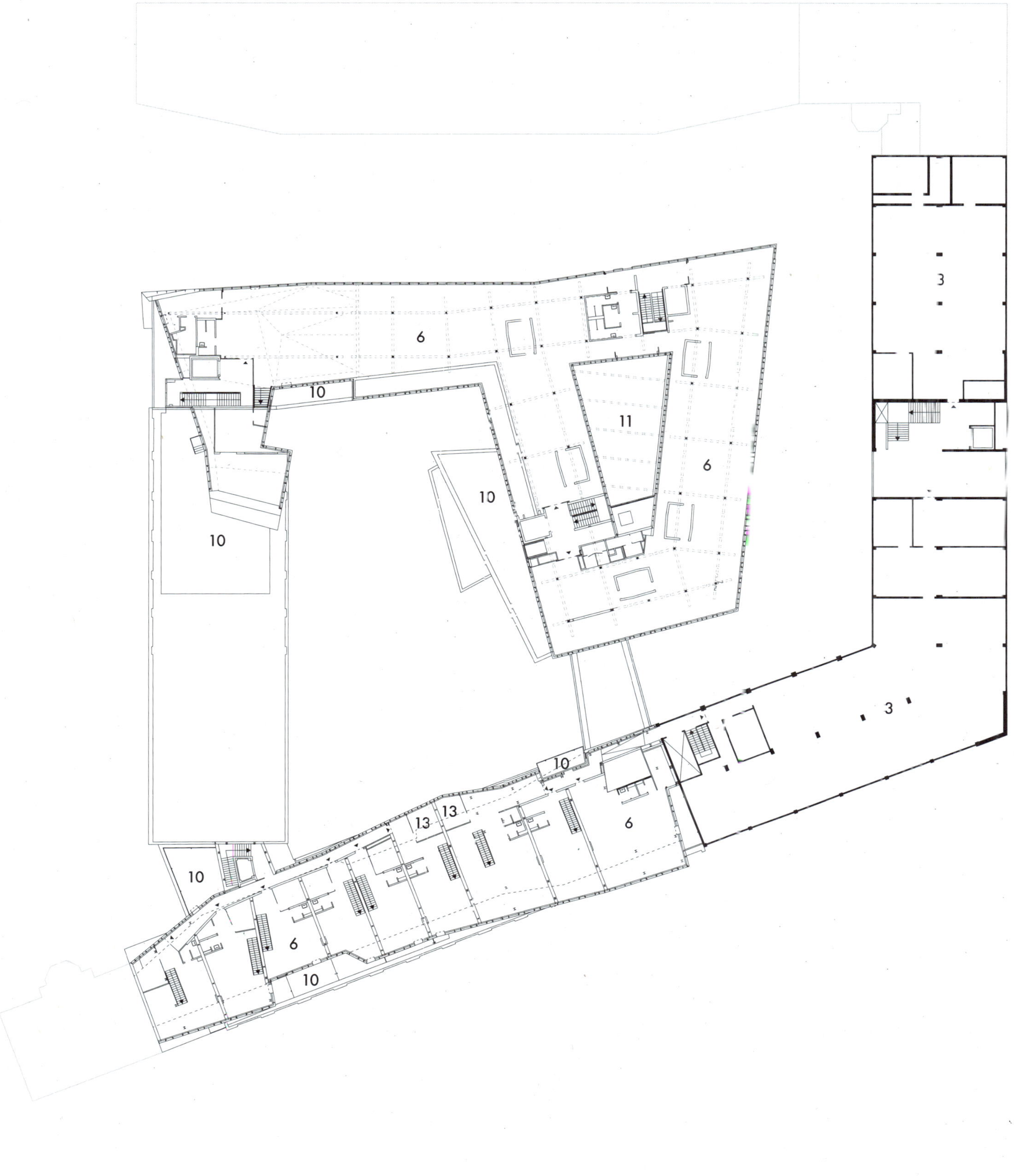

Third floor
1:650

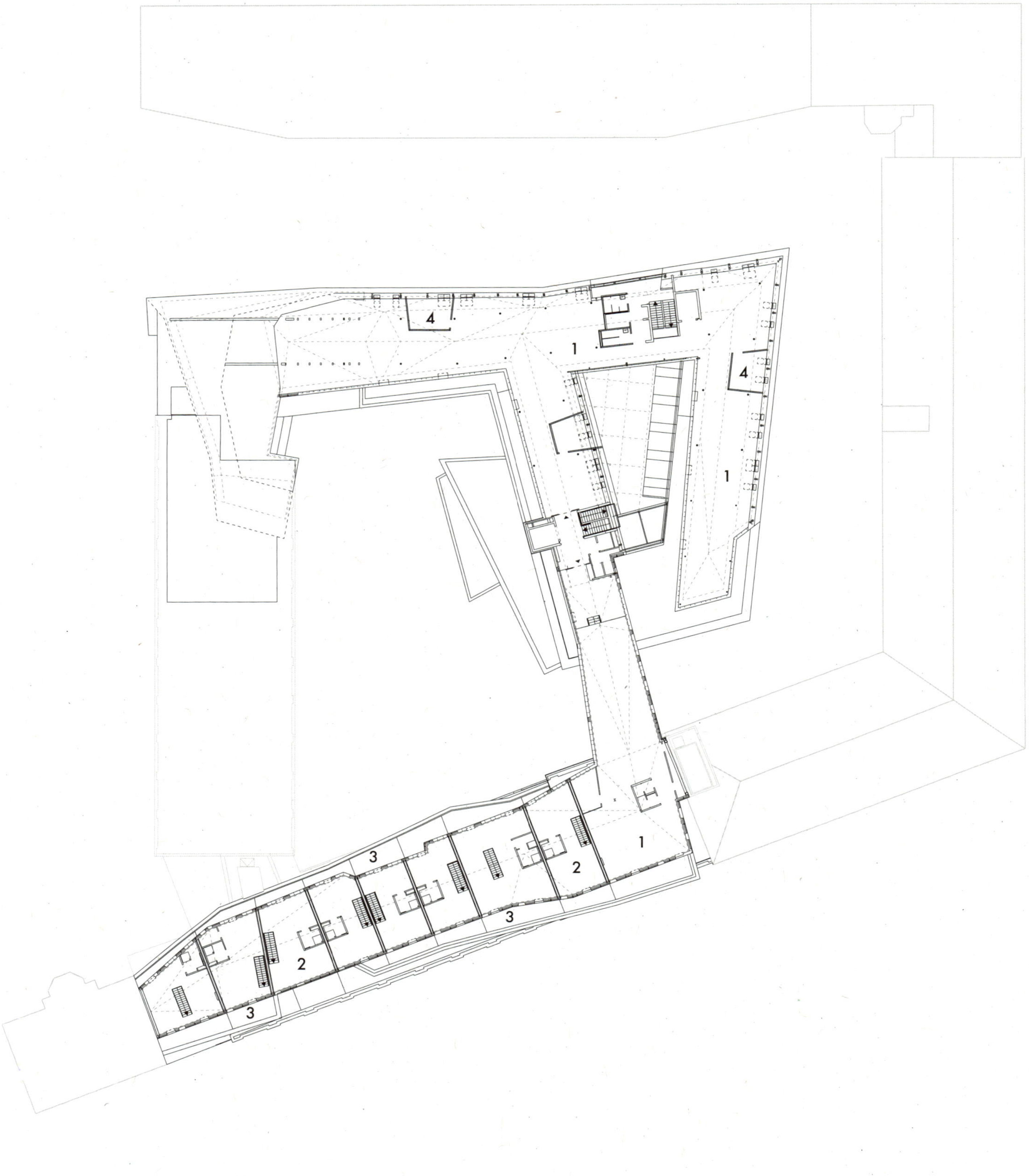

Top view
1:650

1 3 6 10 m

1 Multifunctional space
2 Creative studios
3 Terraces
4 Service boxes

Facade

1 Opaque element
- high isolated two-part aluminum insert unit
- surface inside with acoustic perforation
- outside RAL Design 1002005
- inside RAL 9010 matt

2 Translucent element
- fix-framed glazing with sunshade coating neutral 25% and mounted aluminum woven fabric
- 50% open, RAL Design 1002005
- in L-steel frame
- openable for cleaning access

3 Transparent element
- fix-framed glazing or tilt and turn windows
- sunshade coating neutral 25%
- triple-insulation glas
- 0.5 W/m²K

4 Basic system steel facade
- high isolated post and beam facade
- width 50 mm, cover profile 12 mm
- RAL Design 1002005

5 Steel subconstruction
- T-profile 120 × 8 mm
- partly welded
- RAL 9010

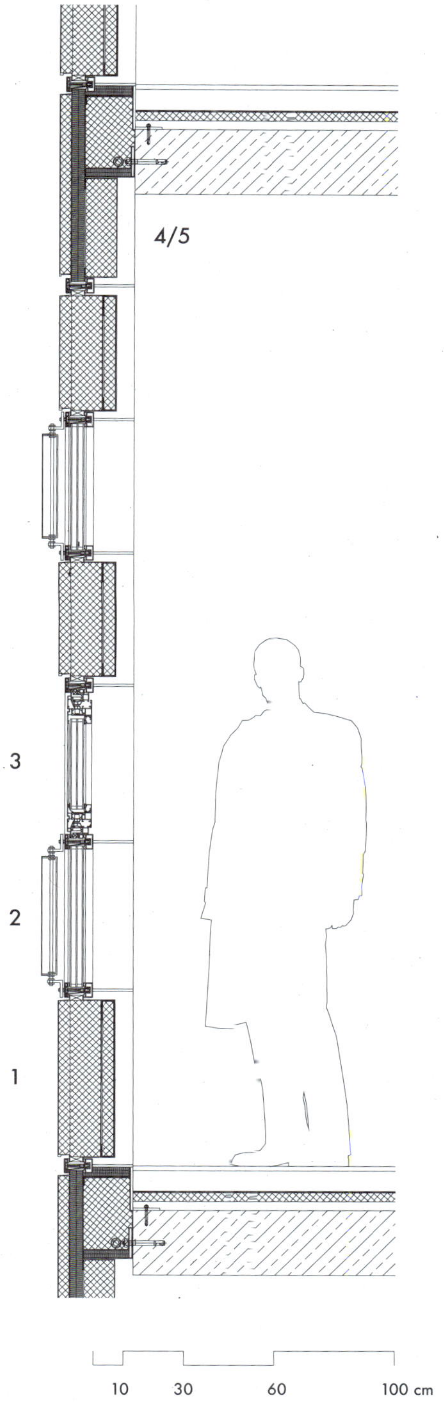

Detail
1:25

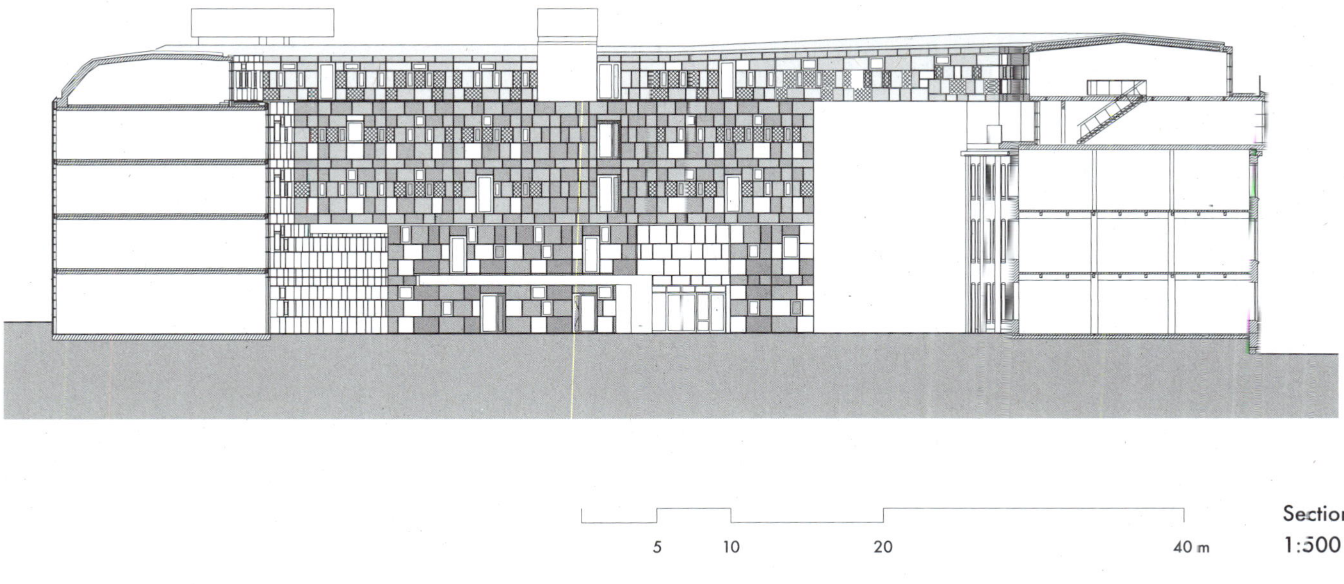

Section
1:500

2018
FLEXIBLE REUSE

EnBW co-working spaces
76131 Karlsruhe, DE

PROGRAM
Offices, co-working spaces, open floor plan, interior atrium, recreation areas, auditorium, restaurants

DIMENSIONS
GFA 34,712 m², floor space of offices 27,099 m², green islands 1,574 m²

CLIENT
EnBW Energie Baden-Württemberg

PROJECT TEAM
Marlies Breuss, Michael Ogertschnig, Jennifer Wei Zhang, Alessandro Zerbi, Dilara Ceren Oylum, Yoanna Dimitrova

CONSULTANTS
Bollinger & Grohman Ingenieure (structural engineer), IPJ Ingenieurbüro (building physics)

MODEL-MAKING
archimodell, Vienna

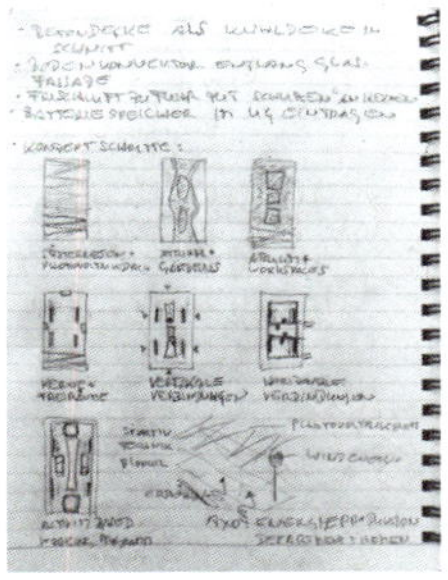
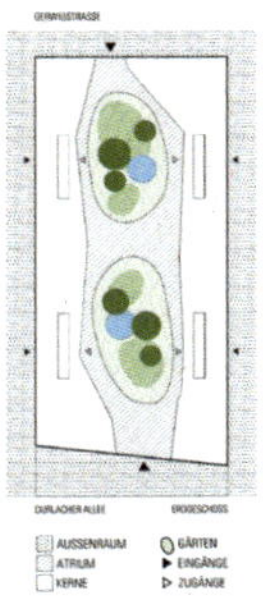
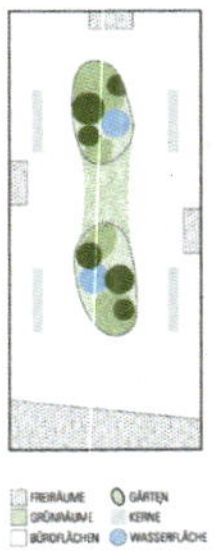
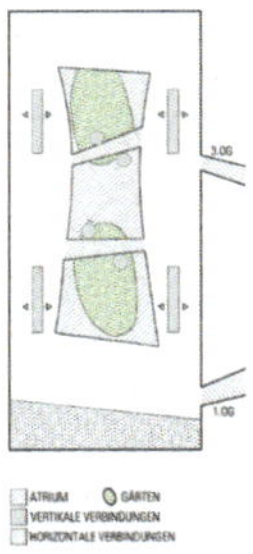
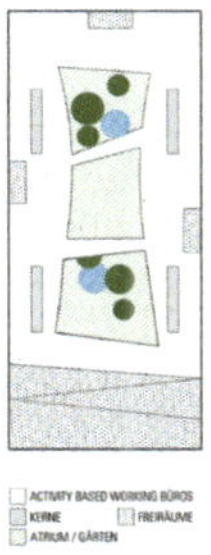
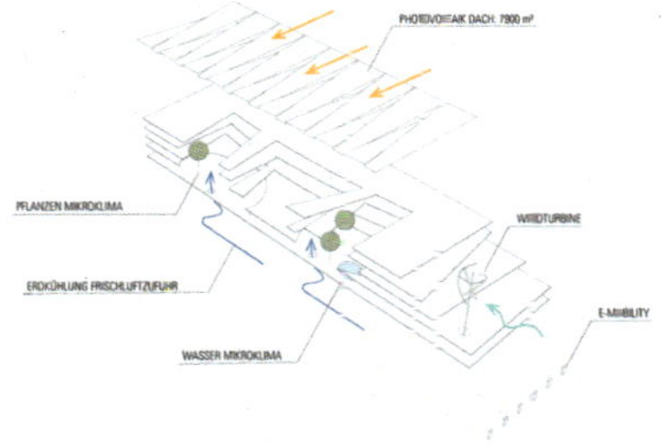

> “The concept appears light and elegant with its generous terraces facing Durlacher Allee and the Schlachthofareal, with the white ceiling bands of the facade and the widely projecting canopy.”

—Excerpt from the jury protocol, 2018 (trans. by the ed.)

Site plan
1:1,500

10 30 60 100 m

page 251

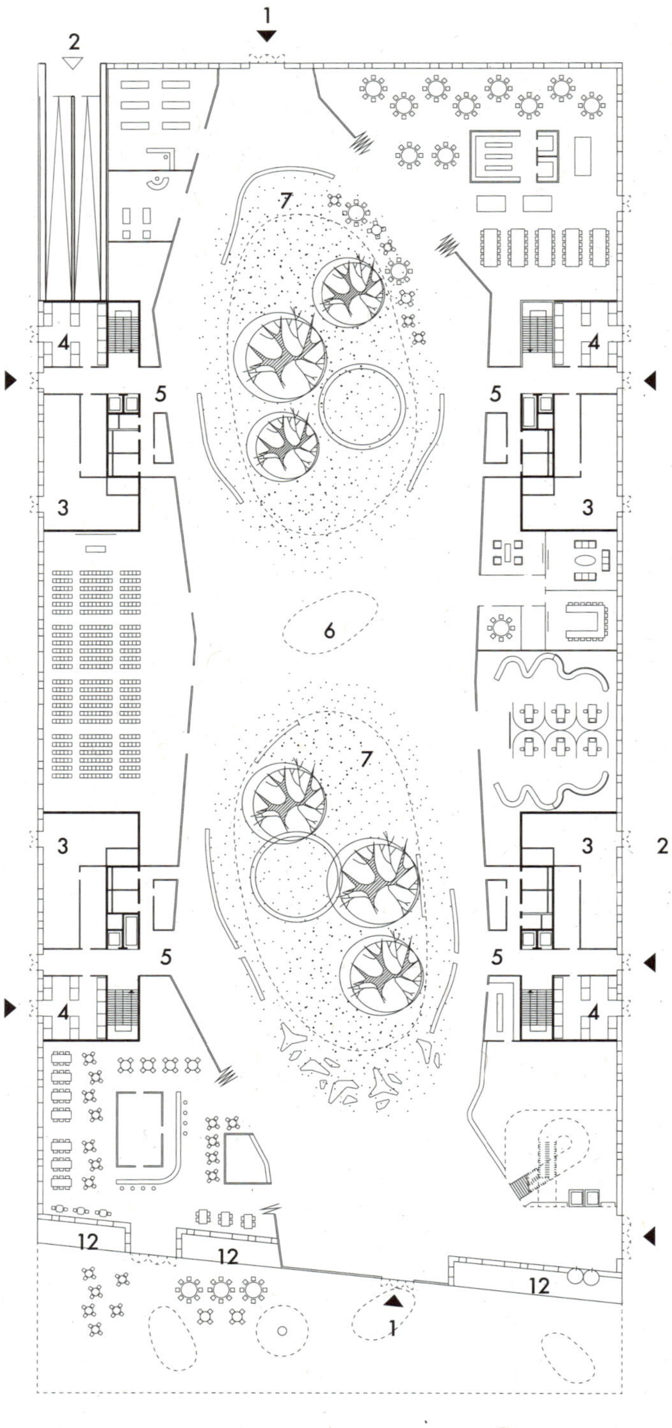

Ground floor

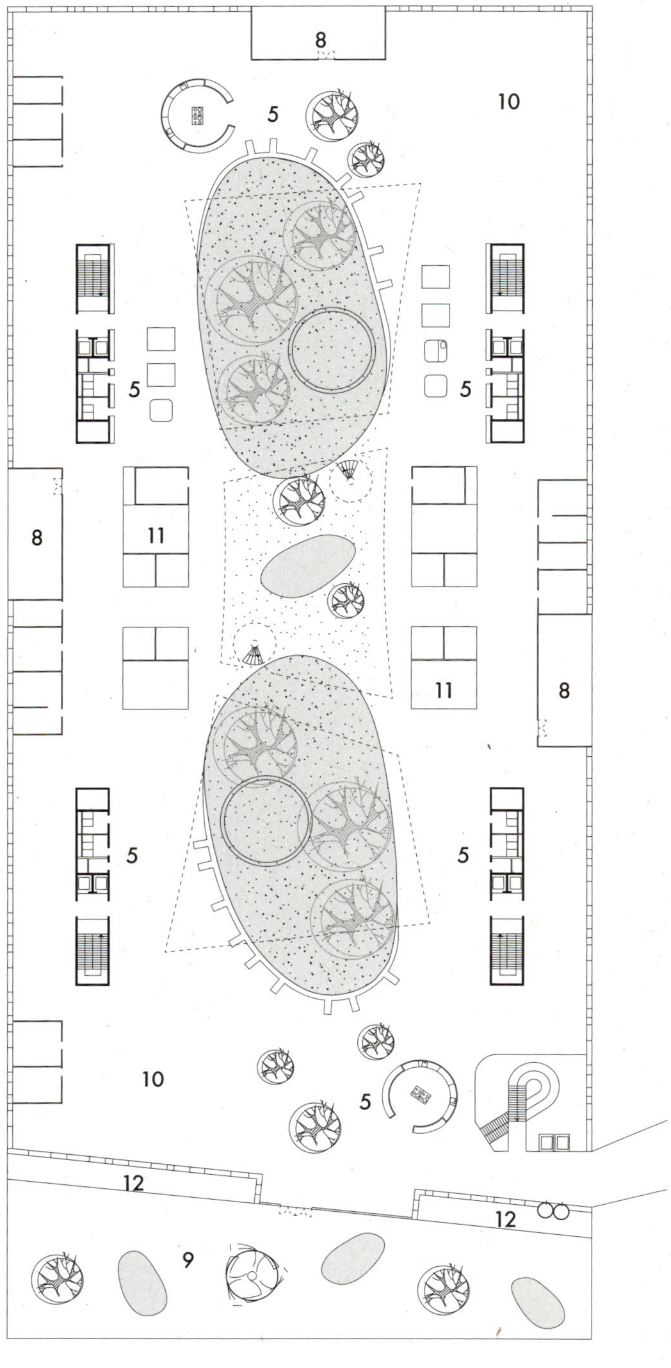

First floor

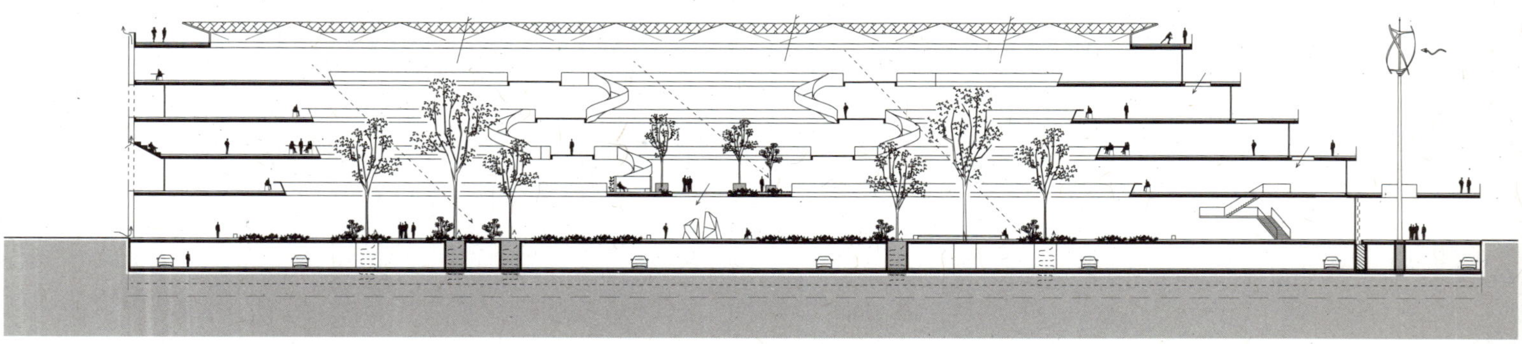

Longitudinal section
1:850

1 5 10 25 m

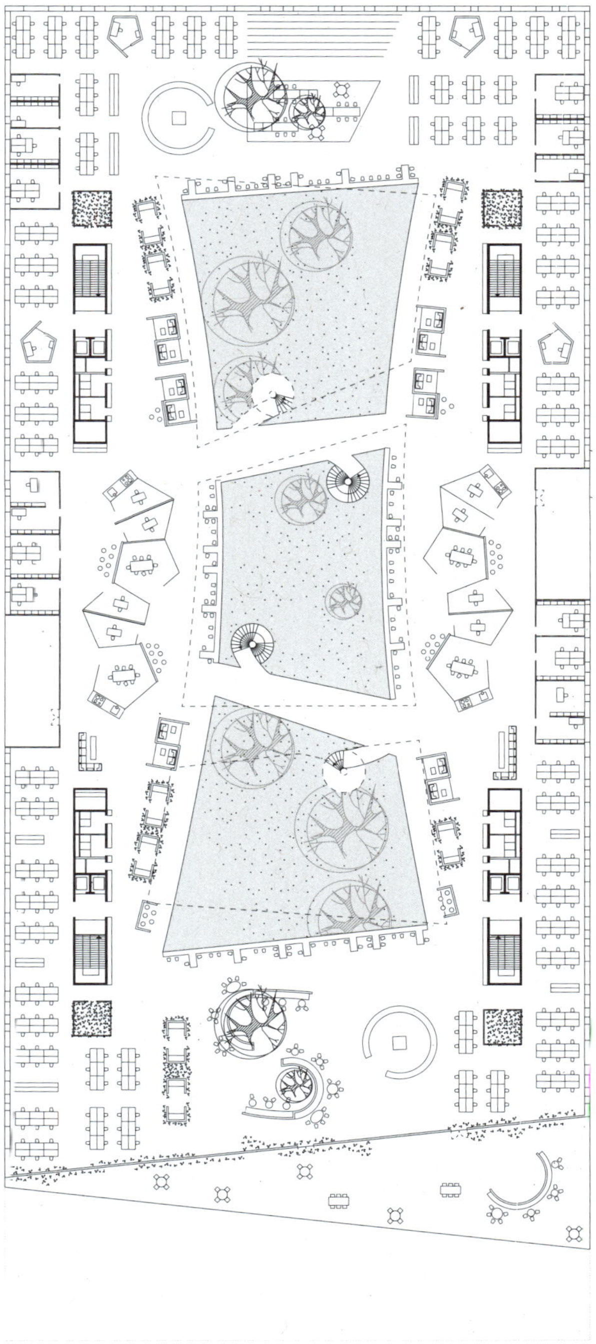

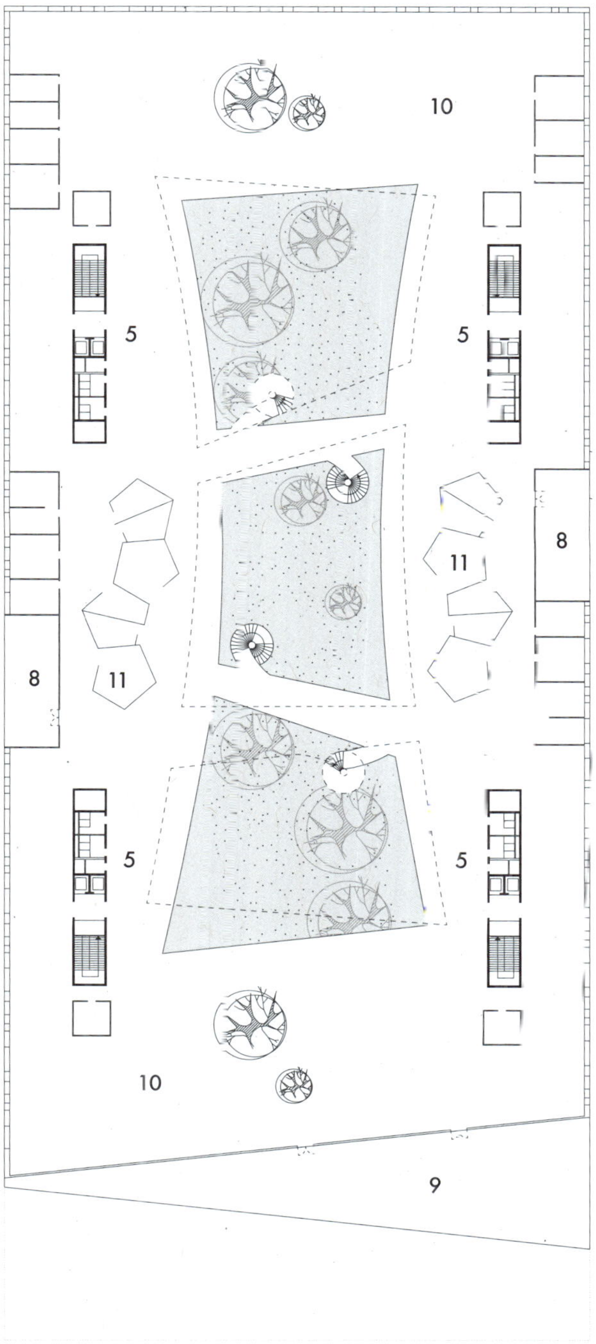

Second floor

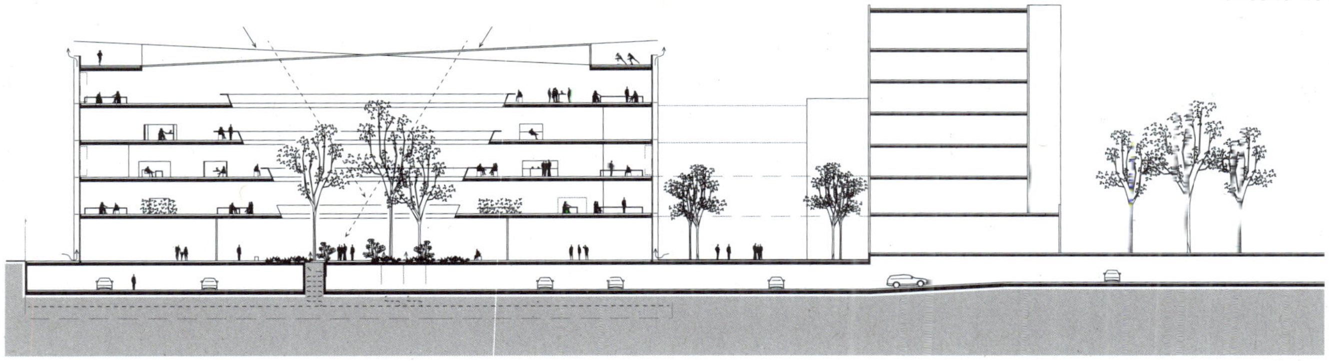

1 Main entrance
2 Entrance to garage
3 Bicycle parking
4 Waste disposal area
5 Service areas
6 Common inner courtyard
7 Green islands
8 Balconies for relaxation
9 Terraces for relaxation
10 Multifunctional office areas
11 Meeting rooms
12 Winter garden

Cross section
1:850

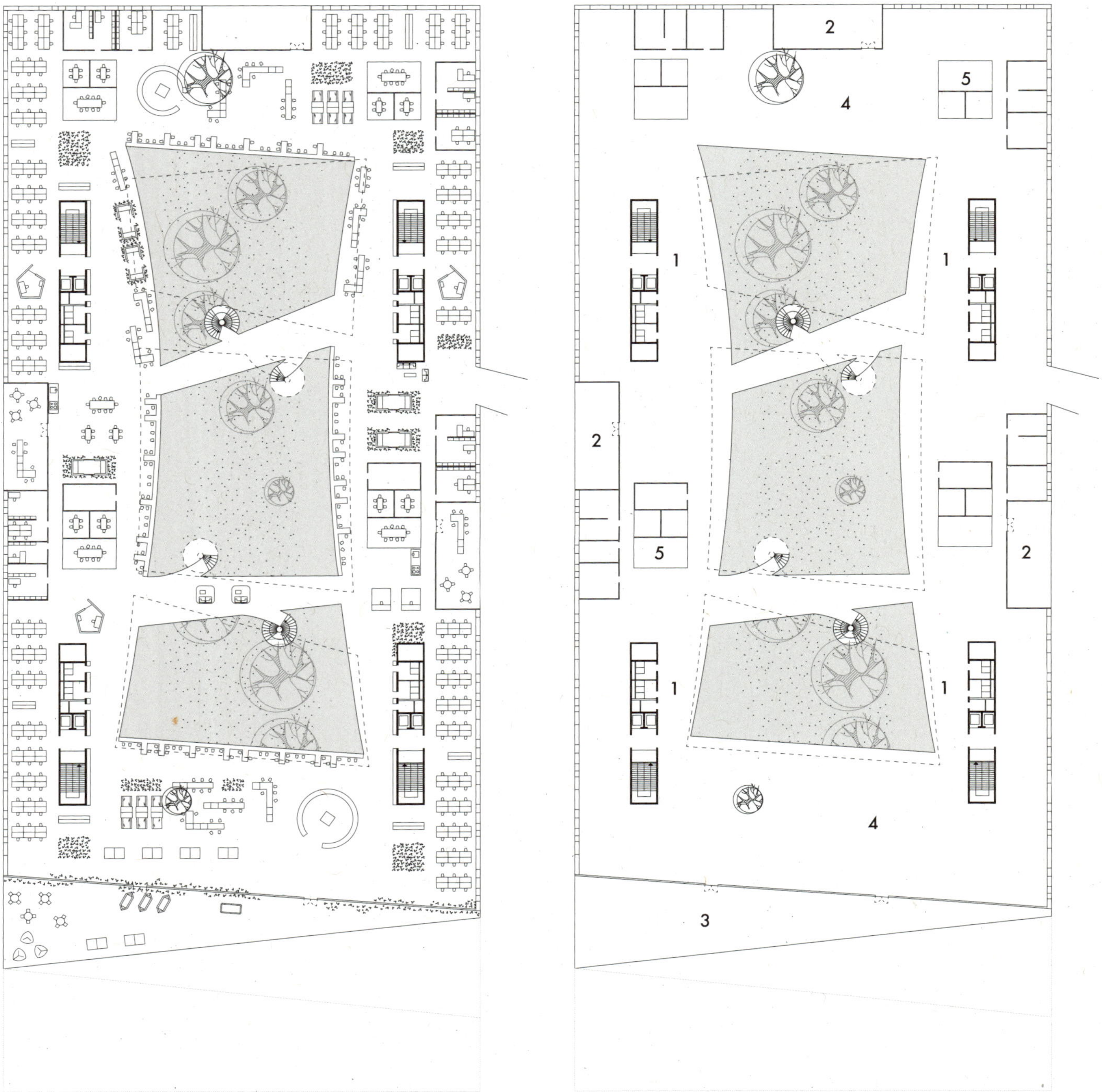

Third floor

1 Service areas
2 Balconies for relaxation
3 Terraces for relaxation
4 Multifunctional office areas
5 Meeting rooms

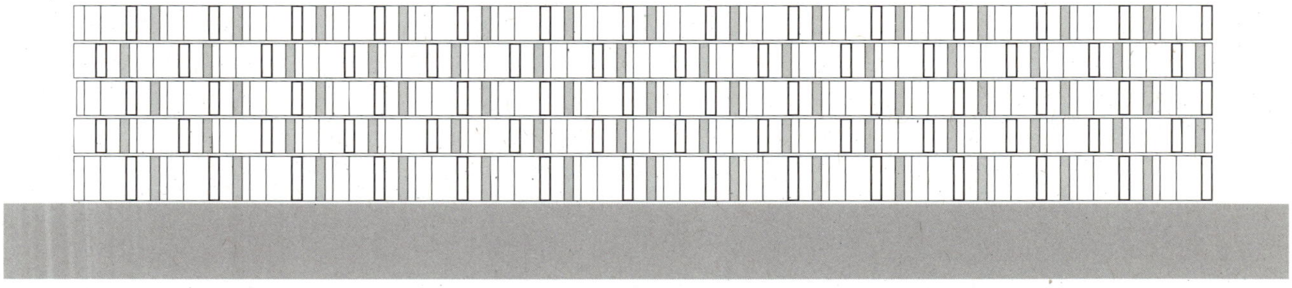

Facade
1:850

1 5 10 25 m

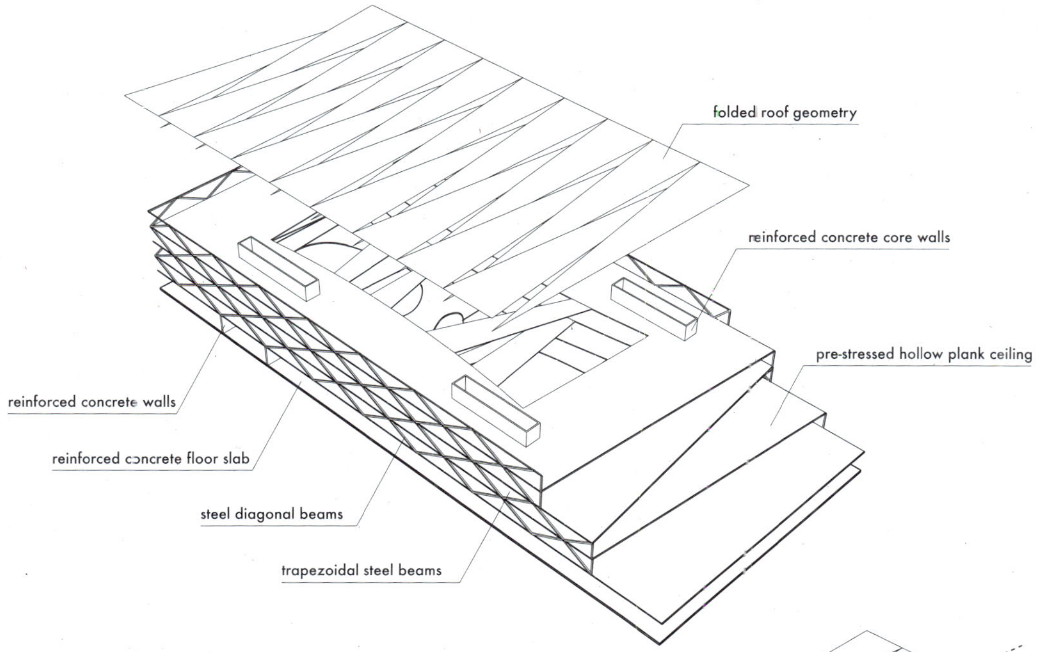

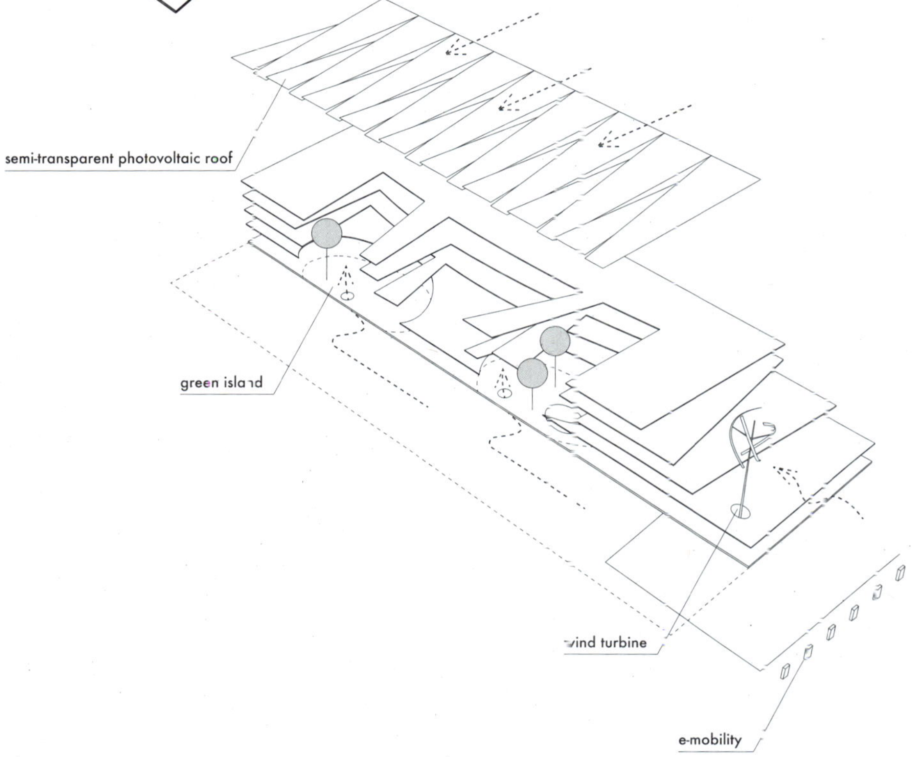

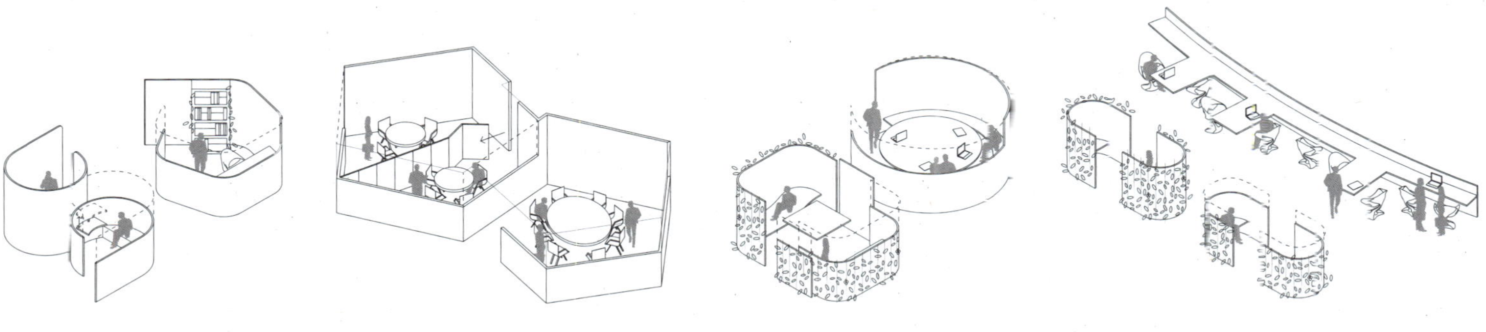

Structure and furniture

hall 01
9300 St. Veit an der Glan, AT

See pp. 39–43

PROGRAM
Industrial building and trade showroom, retail building with storage, restructure, extension

DIMENSIONS
Plot area 1,500 m², GFA 900 m², floor space 600 m²

CLIENT
Geiger Franz & Söhne, St. Veit an der Glan, Austria

PROJECT TEAM
Marlies Breuss, Michael Ogertschnig, Susanne Schmall

CONSULTANTS
Kastner & Moser Zivilingenieur (structural engineer), Puppitz (facade)

PHOTOGRAPHY
AT Neubau

PUBLICATIONS (SELECTION)
"hall 01" in *Scl-Arc 1*, newsletter, Los Angeles, March 2001.
"Kis osztrák épitészet, hall 01," *OCTOGON 4*, Budapest, April 2002.

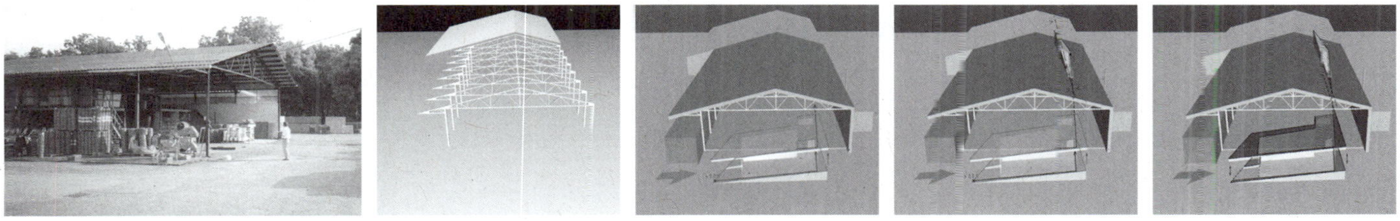

"Here HOLODECK.at combines an absolute low-cost strategy with an ambitious design concept. Keeping both in balance so that no single component nor the surroundings as a whole are overstrained."

—Otto Kapfinger, "Urbane Häutung," *Architektur.aktuell* 9 (2001), Vienna and New York, Springer, p. 145 (trans. by the ed.)

Site plan
1:650   1 3 6 10 25 m

page 259

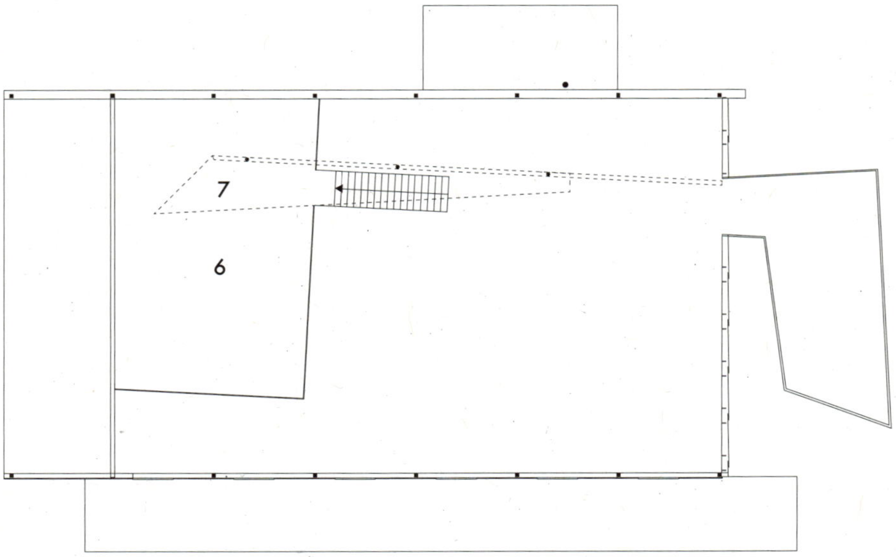

First floor

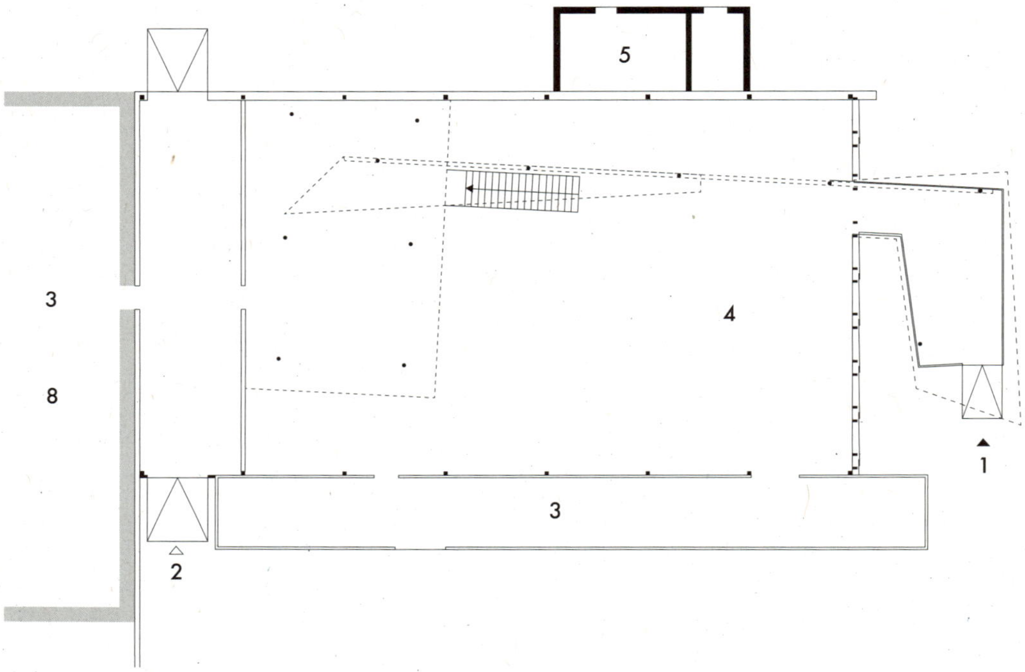

Ground floor

1 Entrance
2 Delivery entrance
3 Exhibition space
4 Retail space
5 Building systems
6 Gallery level
7 Skyligtht vector
8 Storage space

1:300

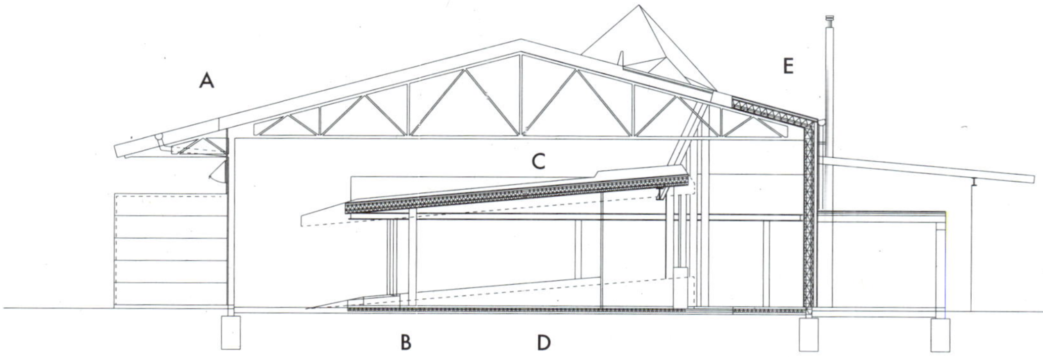

Section with details

Detail A / roof

Trapezoidal sheet
Roof battens 25/50 mm
Counter battens 50/50 mm
Bitumen sheet 350 g
Solid wood formwork 24 mm
Rear ventilation 40 mm
Mineral wool 200 mm
Mineral wool 100 mm
Vapor barrier
Air layer 35 mm
Aluminum sheet

Detail B / floor

Mastic asphalt
Unreinforced concrete
150 mm
Waterproofing
Extruded polystyrene 80 mm
Sealing
Blinding layer
Separating layer
Anti-capillary layer

Detail C / entrance roof

Trapezoidal sheet
Roof battens 25 mm
Counter battens 50/50 mm
Sarking Membrane
Fleece
Formwork 24 mm
Insulation 160 mm
Insulation 80 mm
Battens 30/50 mm
Vapor barrier
Plaster fireboard 15 mm
Plaster fireboard 15 mm
Plaster

Detail D / floor

Oil coating
Cement screed
Vapor barrier
Impact-sound insulation
TDP 50/45 mm
Protective concrete
Separating layer
Damp-proofing
Blinding layer
Separating layer
Anti-capillary layer

Detail E / roof / facade (unheated)

Aluminum sheet
Rear ventilation
Insulation 80 mm
Insulation 80 mm
Wooden bricks 250 mm
Aluminum sheet

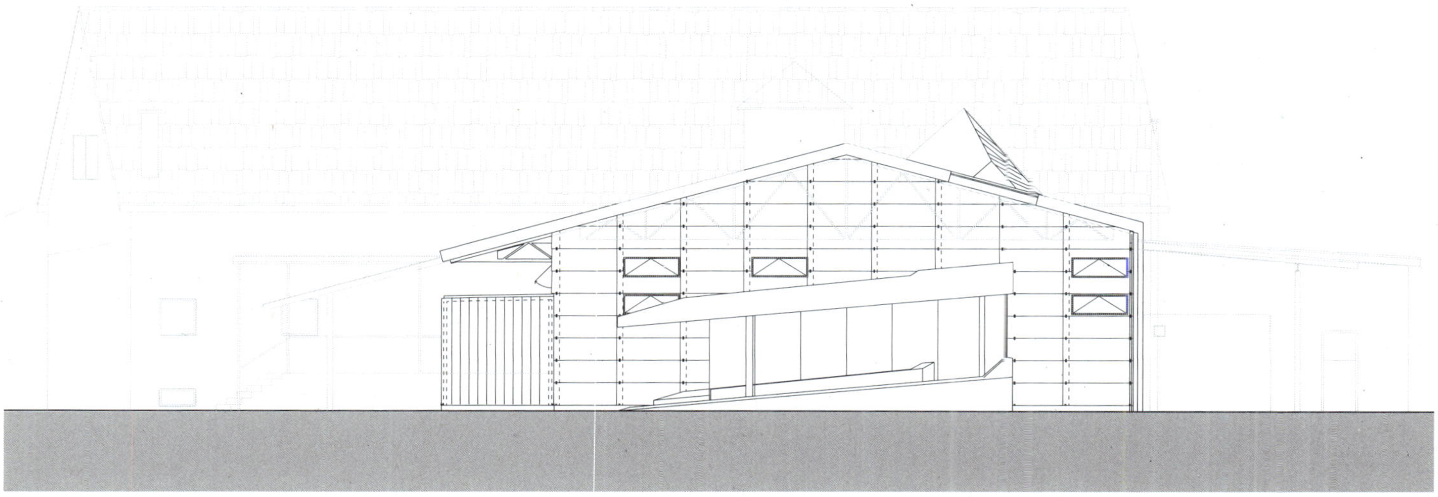

Northern elevation
1:200

fachmarkt
sanitär
geiger
metall

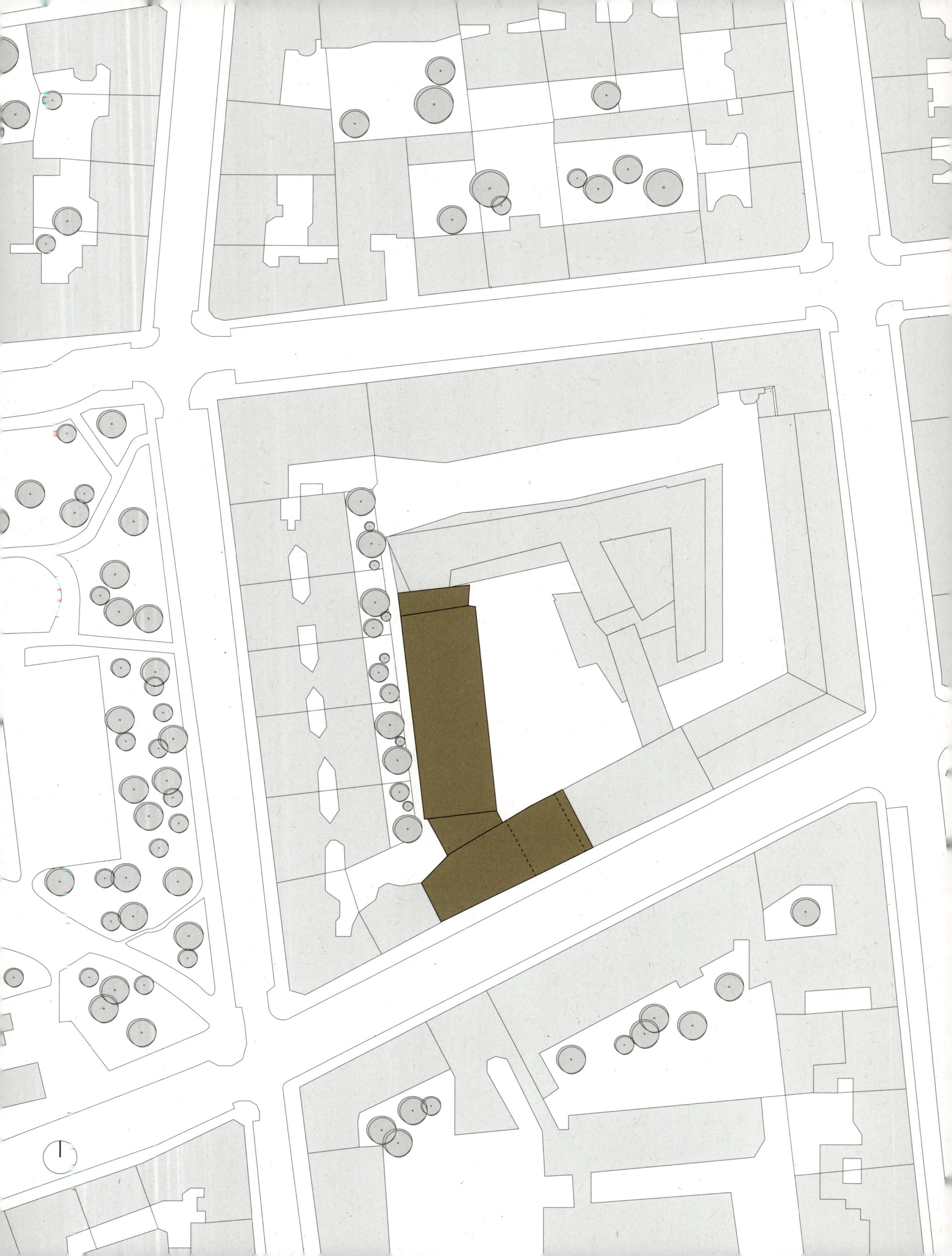

gewerbehof missindorf

1140 Vienna, AT

See pp. 44–49

PROGRAM
Industrial hub, café, television studios, offices, restructure, conversion, extension

DIMENSIONS
GFA 1,400 m^2

CLIENT
Wien Holding, Vienna, Austria

PROJECT TEAM
Marlies Breuss, Michael Ogertschnig, Robert Pippan

CONSULTANTS
Vasko+Partner Ingenieure ZT GmbH (building physics), CD-Consult Ziviltechniker (structural engineer)

PHOTOGRAPHY
Wolfgang Thaler

AWARDS
First prize, invited competition
GEBAUT 2009 – Stadtgestaltung Wien
Bauherrenpreis 2010, nomination

PUBLICATIONS (SELECTION)
"Gewerbehof," *Wettbewerbe – Architekturjournal* 263/264, WERBA Werbe- und Verlags-Gesellschaft, September 2007 (ISSN 1015-4477).
"Wohnen: Arbeiten – Flexible Verhältnisse," *Architekturtage 2012*, guided tour, Vienna, June 2, 2012.

"A casual, modern café with a transparent steel and glass facade protrudes like a box onto the sidewalk and thus takes possession of public space: it emphasizes the incision and passage and conveys the feeling of being right where the action is."

—Isabella Marboe, "Gewerbehof wird Wirtschaftspark," *Architektur.aktuell* 12 (2014), Vienna, p. 6 (trans. by the ed.)

Site plan
1:1,000

10 25 50 m

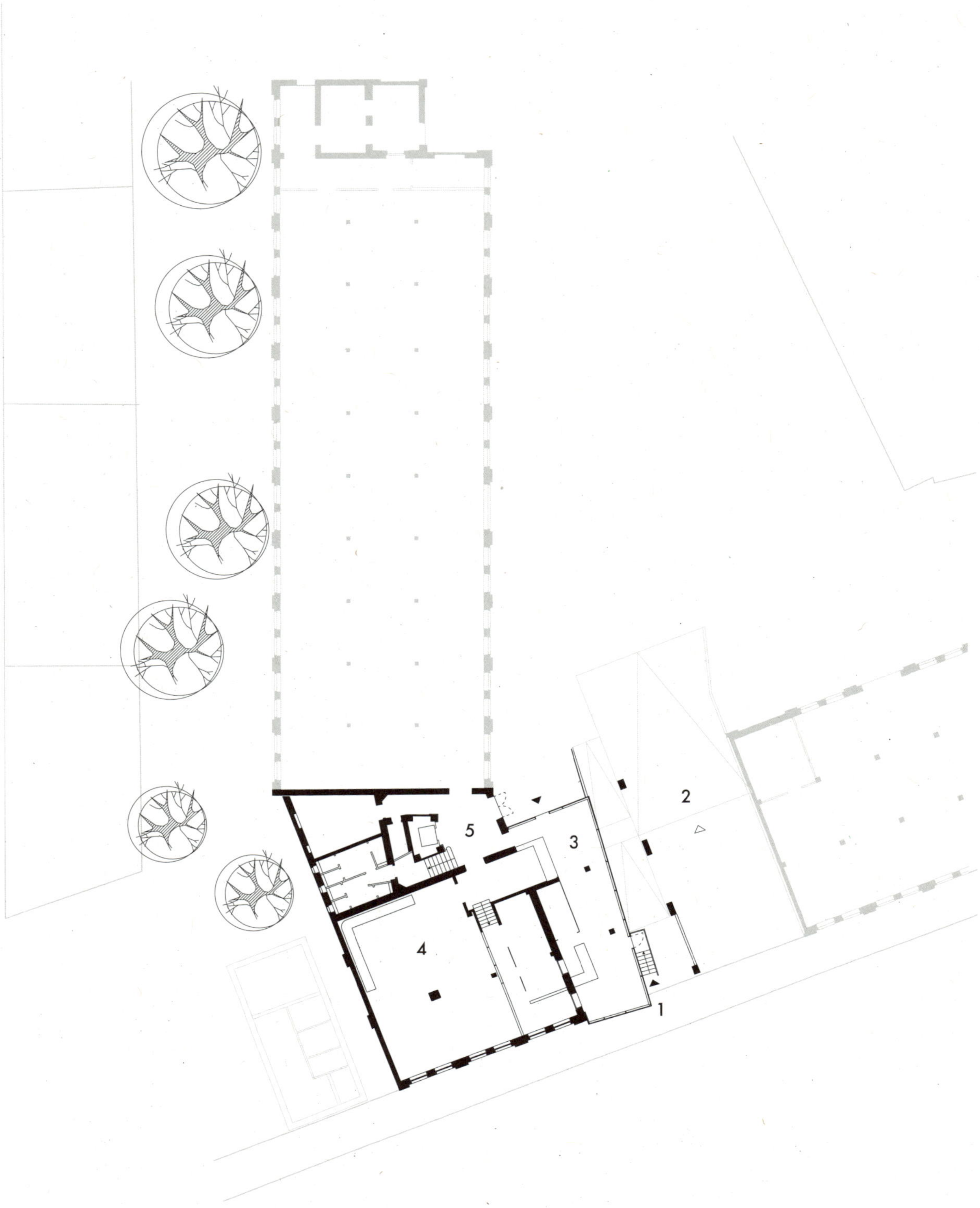

Ground floor

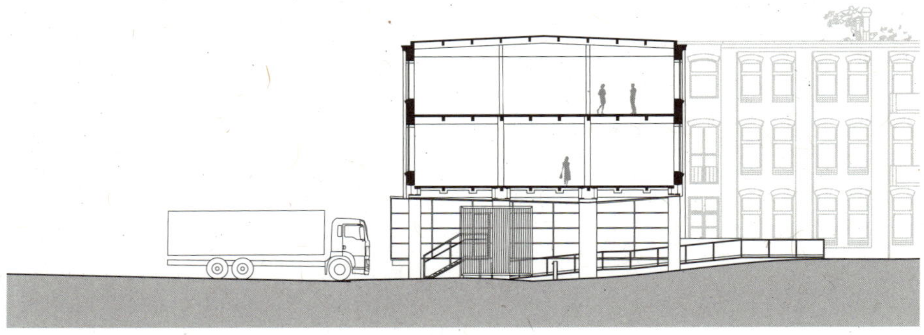

Section
1:450

1 3 6 10 m

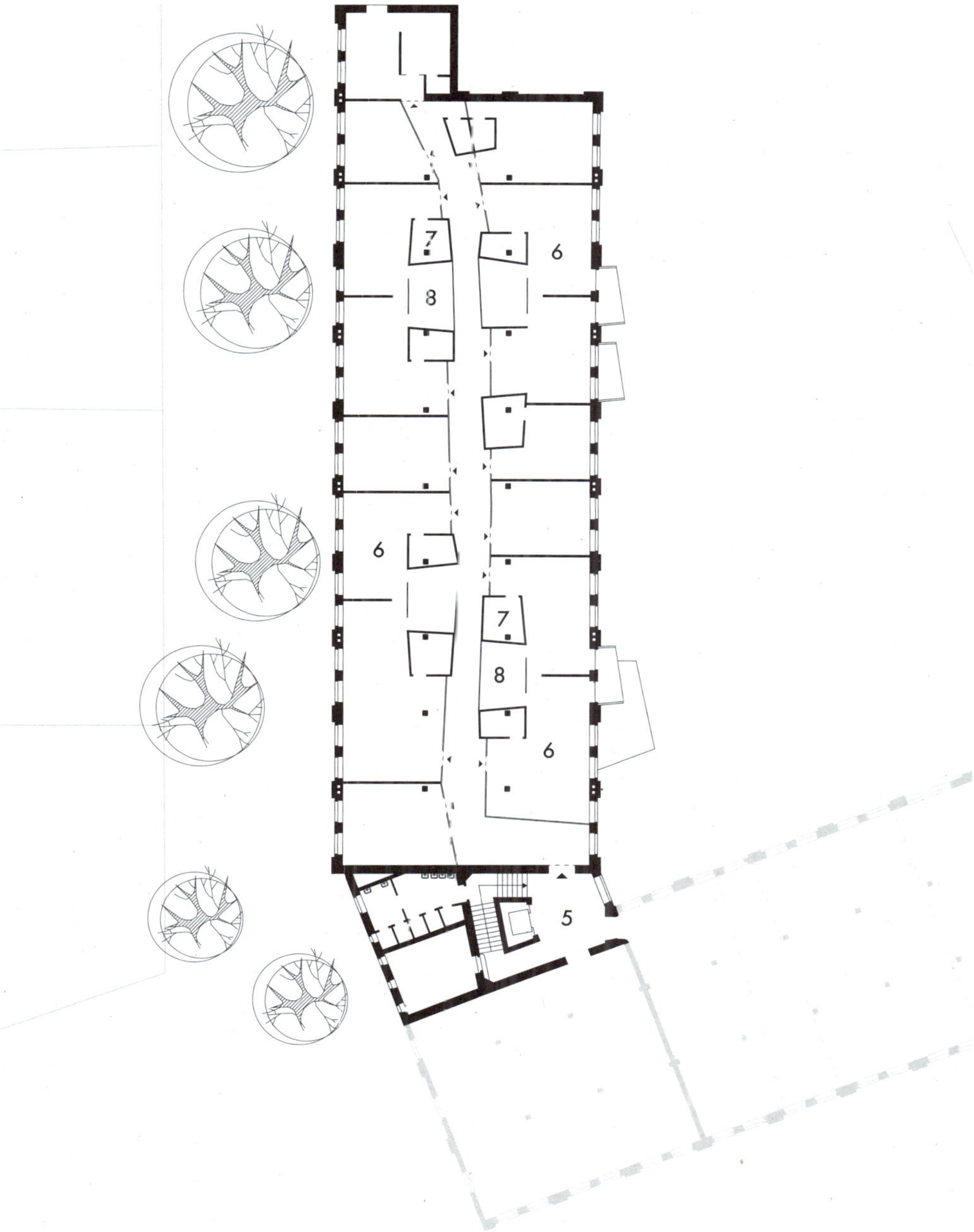

Second floor

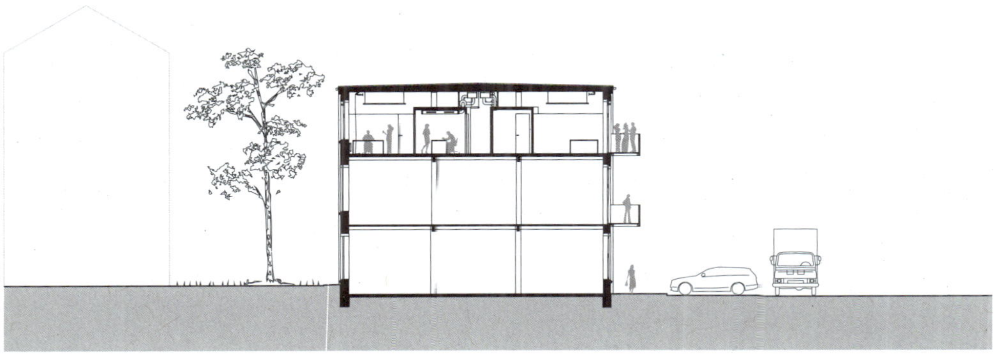

1 Entrance to café
2 Entrance to courtyard
3 Restaurant/café
4 Film studio
5 Staircase
6 Shared office spaces
7 Storage spaces
8 Meeting space

Cross section
1:450

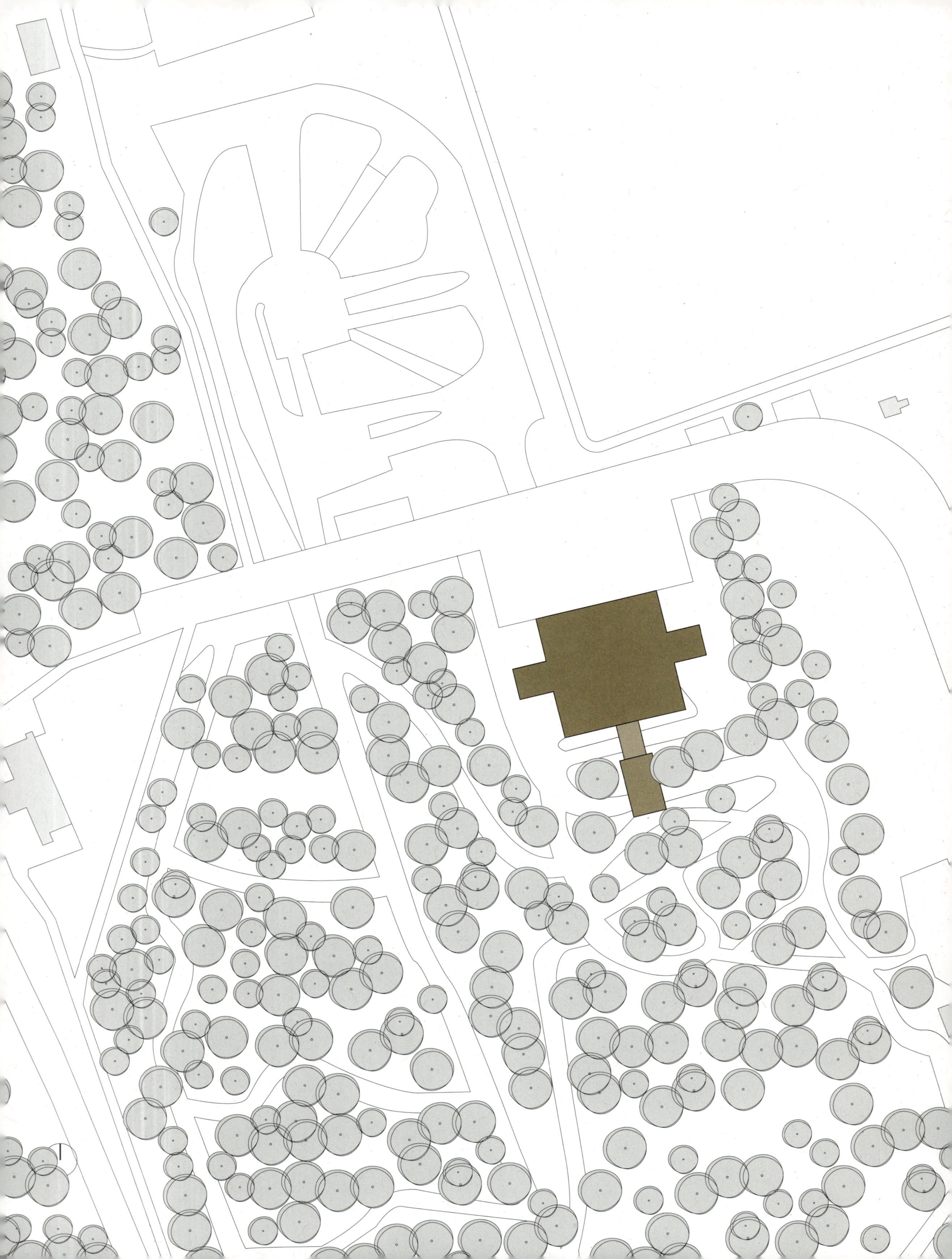

2018
FLEXIBLE REUSE

experience center
8401 Kalsdorf near Graz, AT

PROGRAM
Event center, workshops, training, conference, exhibition, driving experience course, restructure, conversion

DIMENSIONS
GFA 1,619 m², plot area 1,098 m²

CLIENT
Mercedes G-Class GmbH and Daimler AG

PROJECT TEAM
Marlies Breuss, Michael Ogertschnig, Lars Oberländer, Marc Werner

AWARDS
First prize, invited competition

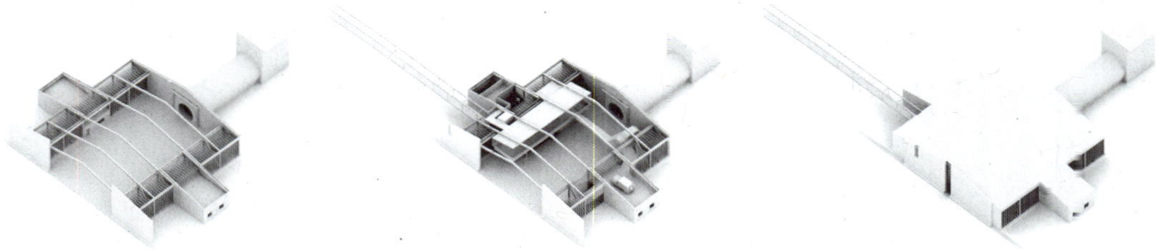

“The existing building with its industrial character is preserved in its shape and structure and transformed into a multifunctional spatial network through interventions.”

—HOLODECK architects, project description for the competition, 2018 (trans. by the ed.)

Site plan
1:1,000

10 25 50 m

page 271

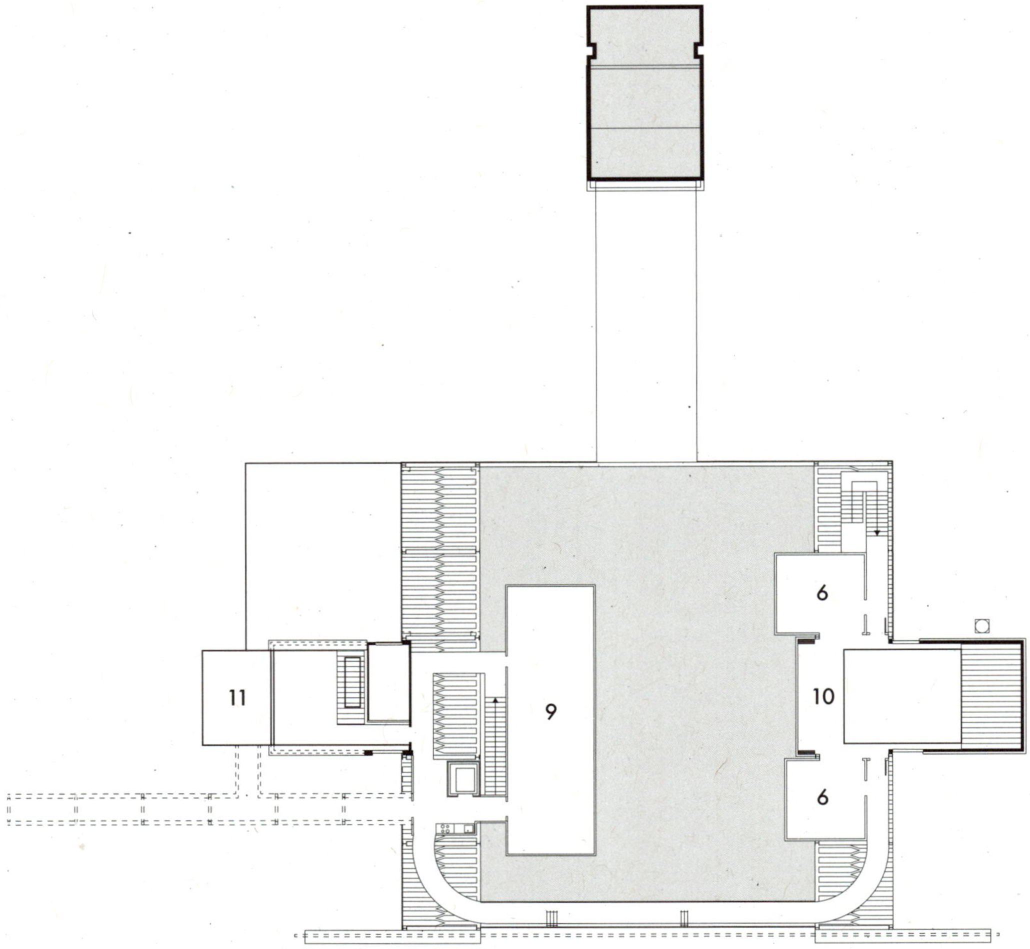

First floor

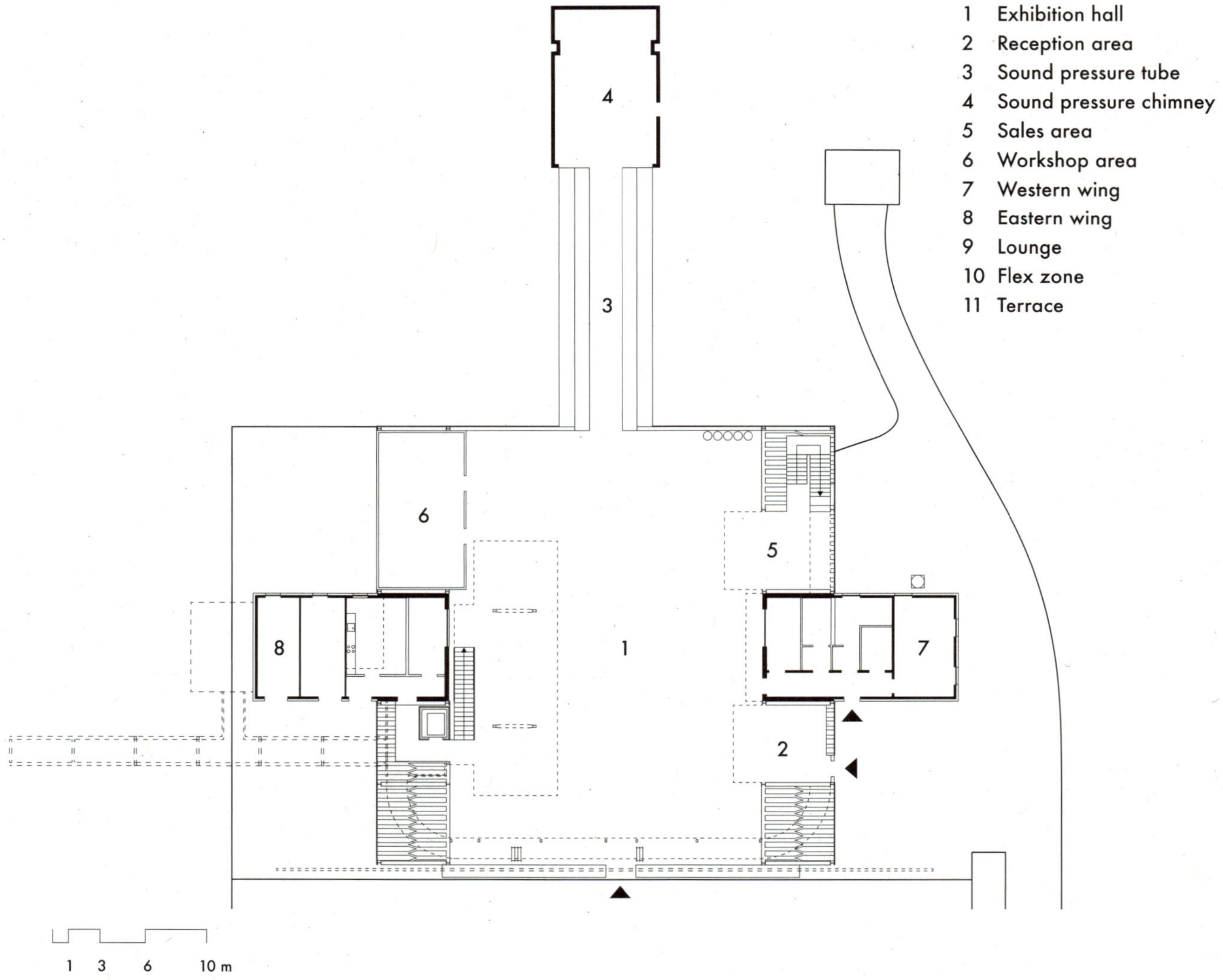

Ground floor
1:450

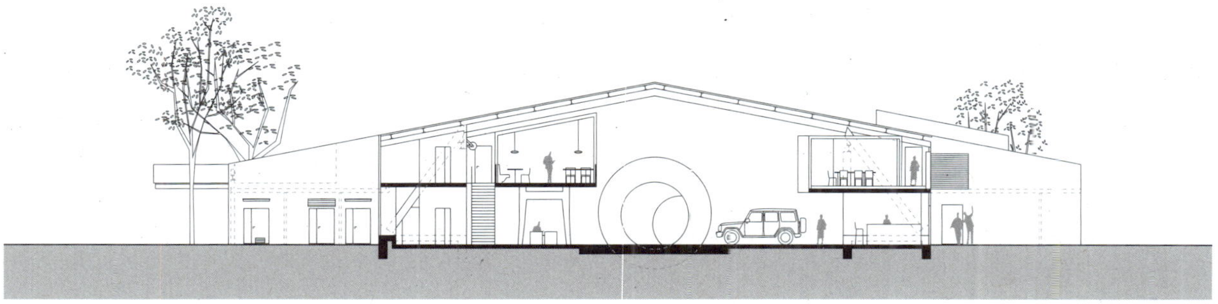

Longitudinal section

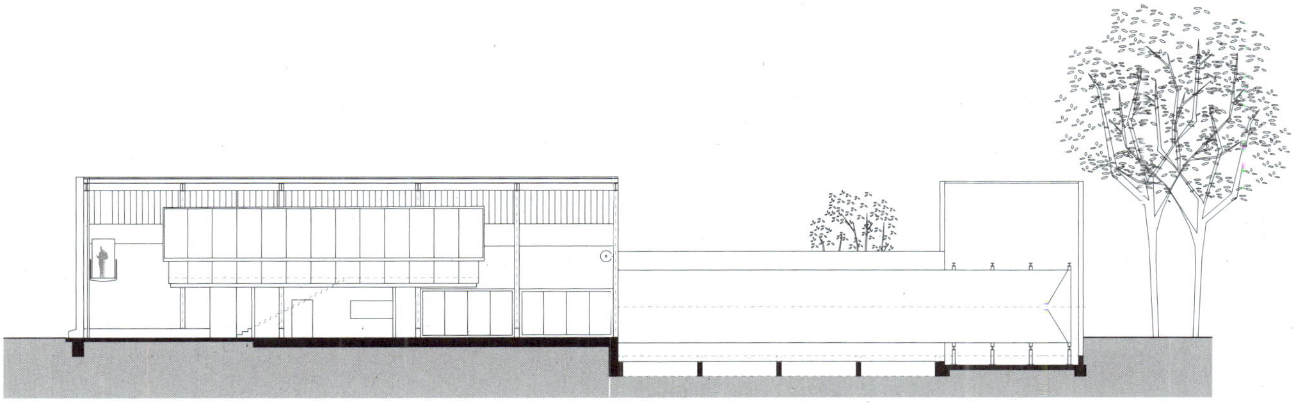

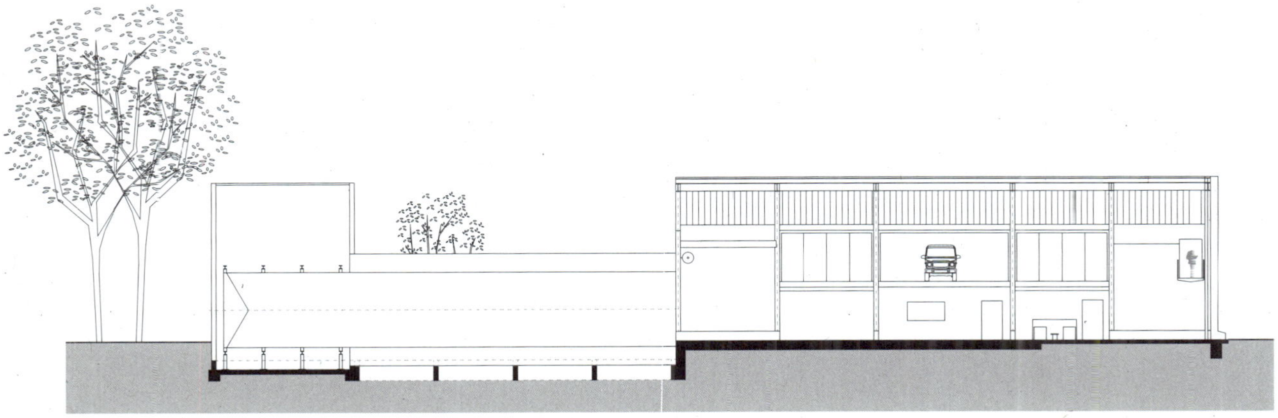

1 5 10 25 m

Sections
1:400

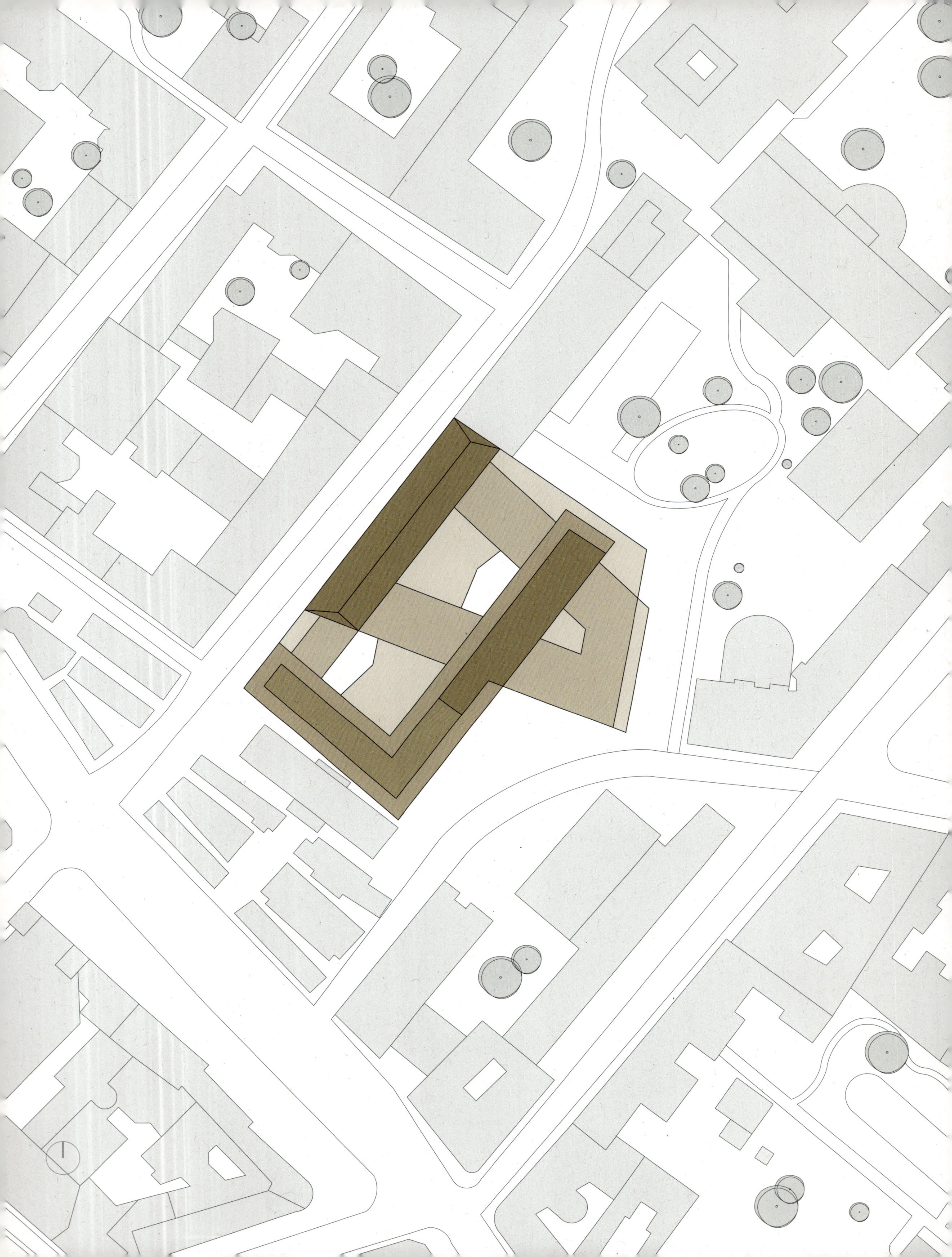

2013
FLEXIBLE REUSE

headquarters post
1030 Vienna, AT

PROGRAM
Urban design, office spaces, retail and retreat, underground parking, restructure, extension

DIMENSIONS
Plot area 5,178 m², GFA 47,315 m², gross net area 41,637 m²

CLIENT
Post AG, Austria

PROJECT TEAM
Marlies Breuss, Michael Ogertschnig, Hannes Zergoi, Michal Bugan, Peter Hunct, Chloe Priou, Karolina Wolny

CONSULTANTS
KPPK (structural engineer), kwi (building systems), merl (sustainability)

MODEL-MAKING
archimodell, Vienna

RENDERINGS
isochrom, Vienna

AWARDS
Second Prize, EU-wide open two-stage general planning tender competition, 2013

PUBLICATIONS (SELECTION)
Architekturjournal – Wettbewerbe, Bohmann Druck und Verlag, September/October 2013.

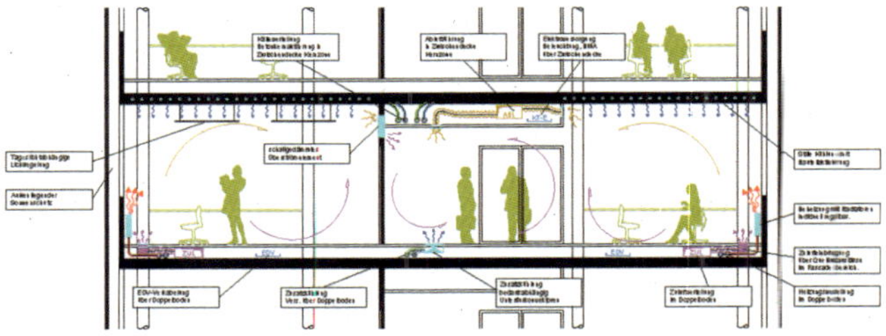

Building services standard floor office

“The calm overall attitude of the facade with its coordinated modulation is appreciated, as is the appropriately scaled design of the single-story base zone.”

—Excerpt from the jury protocol, 2013 (trans. by the ed.)

Site plan
1:1,000

10 25 50 m

page 277

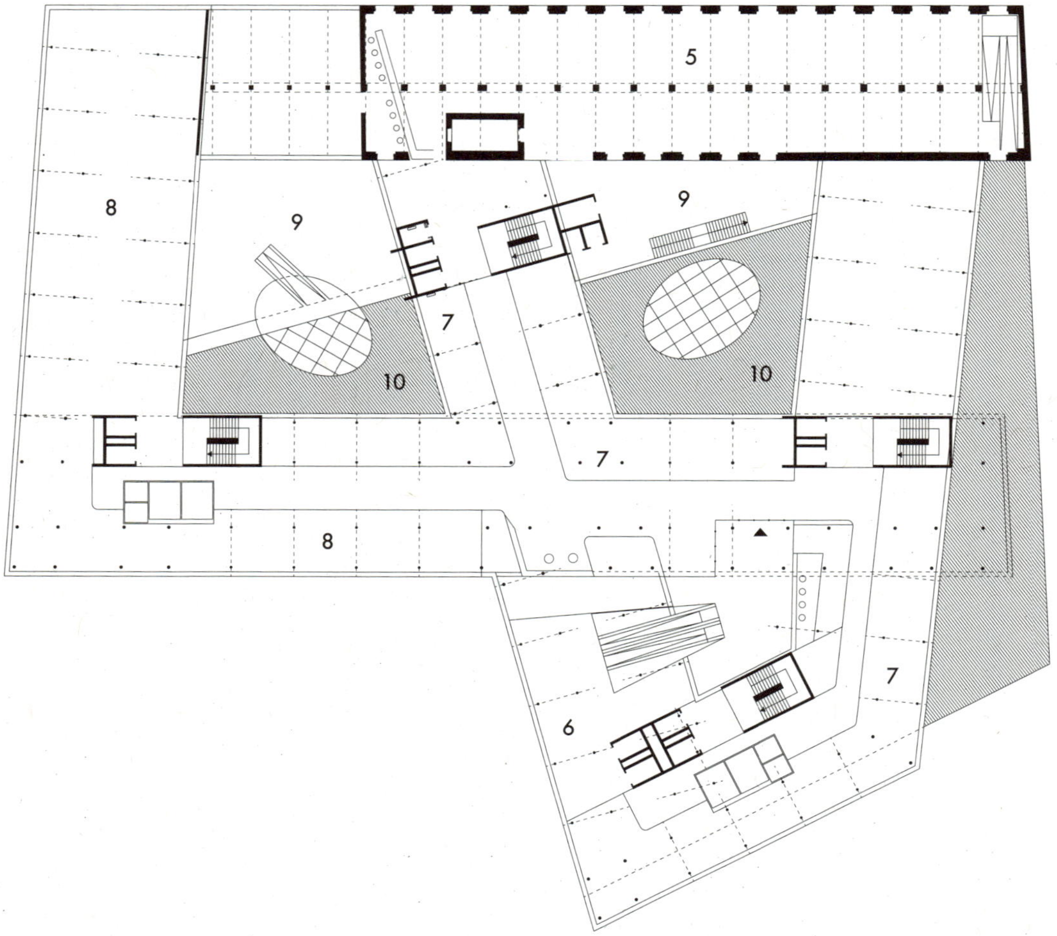

First floor

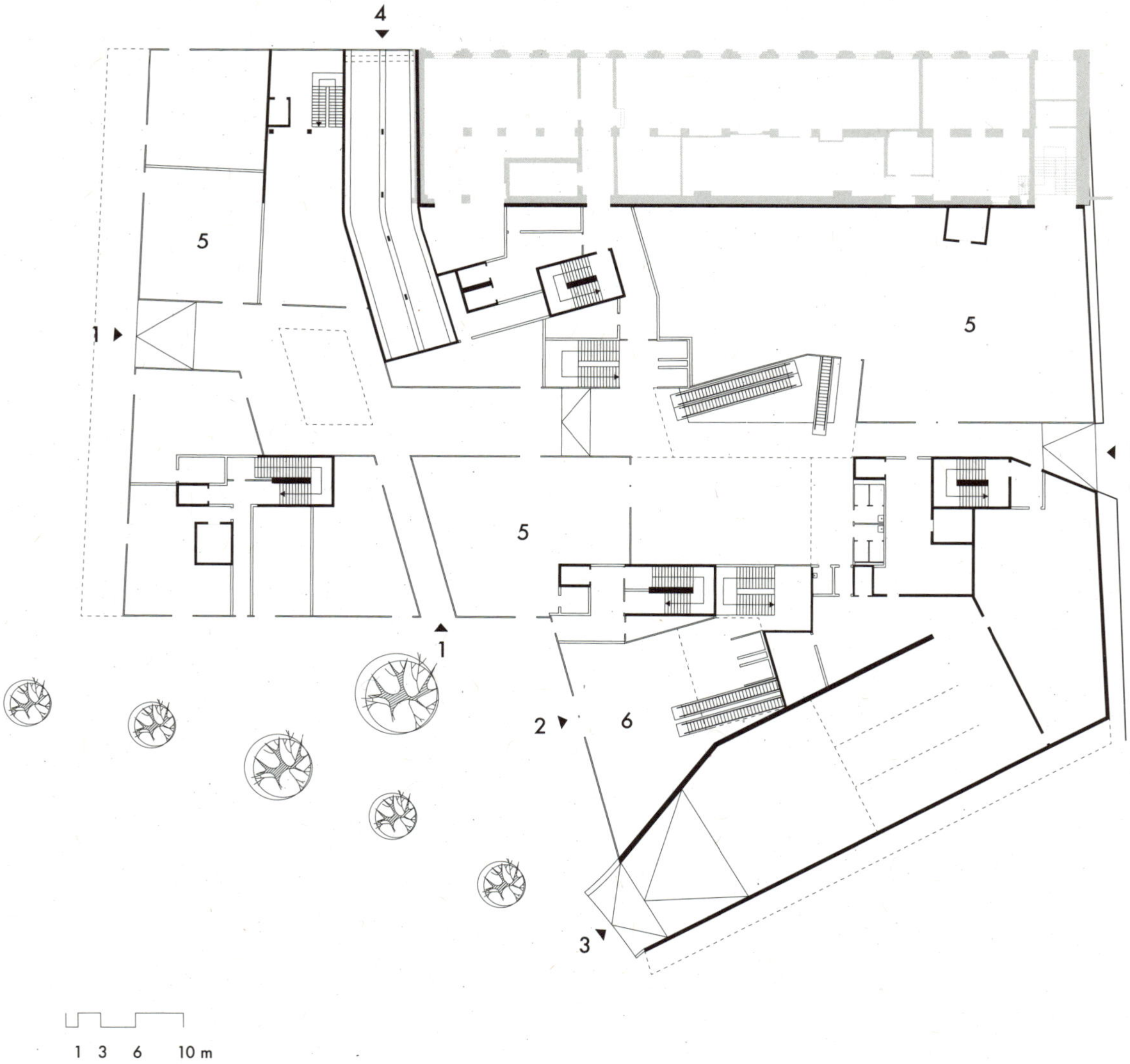

Ground floor
1:650

1 Entrance to mall
2 Entrance to headquarters
3 Deliveries underground
4 Entrance to garage
5 Shops/restaurant
6 Lobby
7 Meeting rooms
8 Office spaces
9 Indoor atrium
10 Outdoor atrium

Typical floor plan

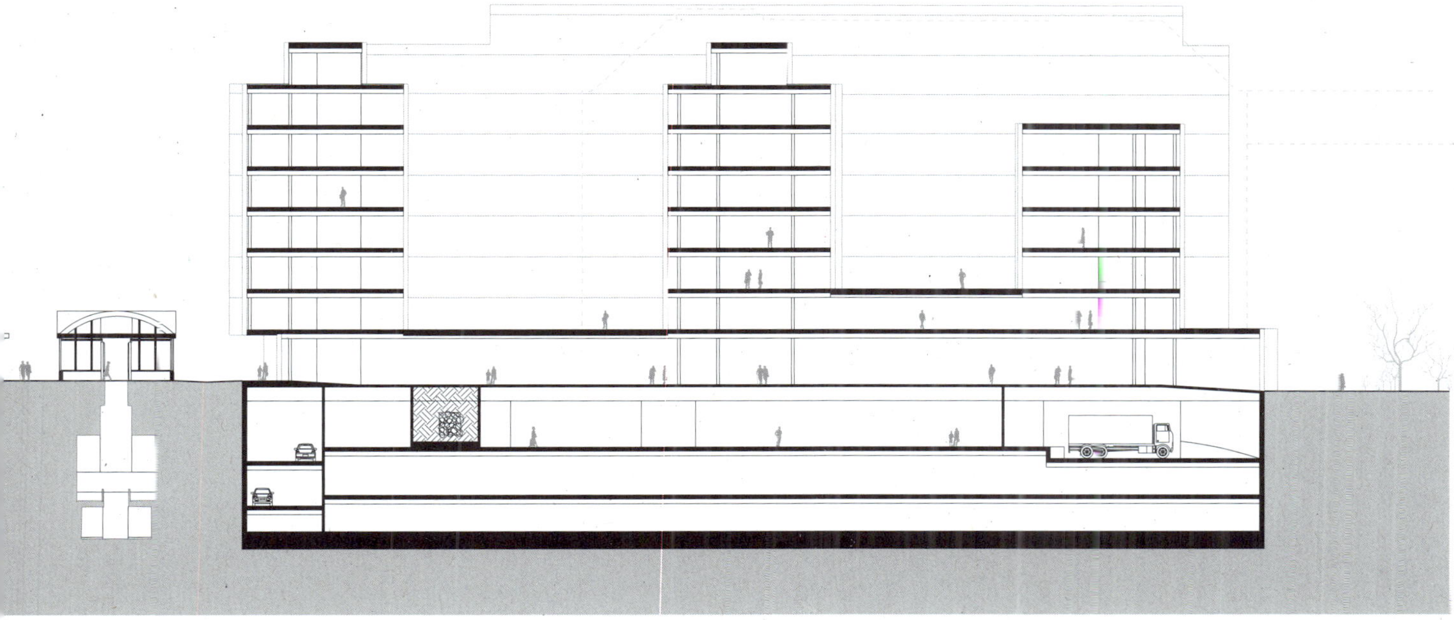

Longitudinal section
1:650

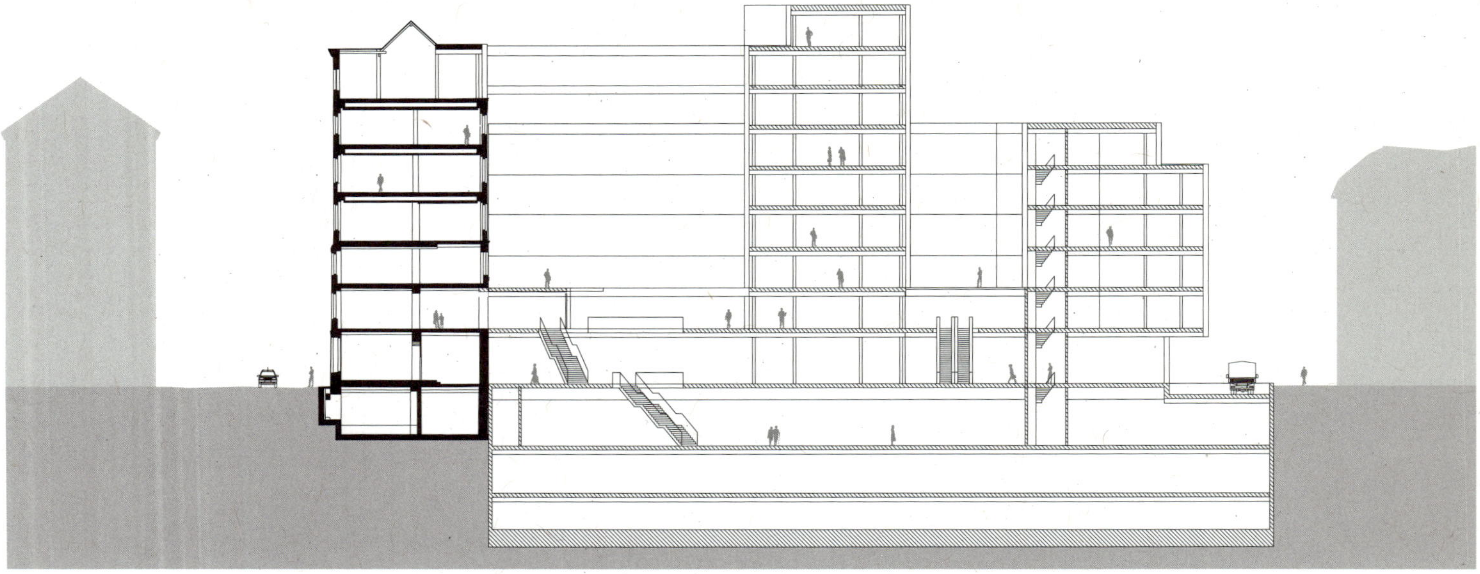

Sections
1:650

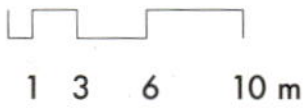

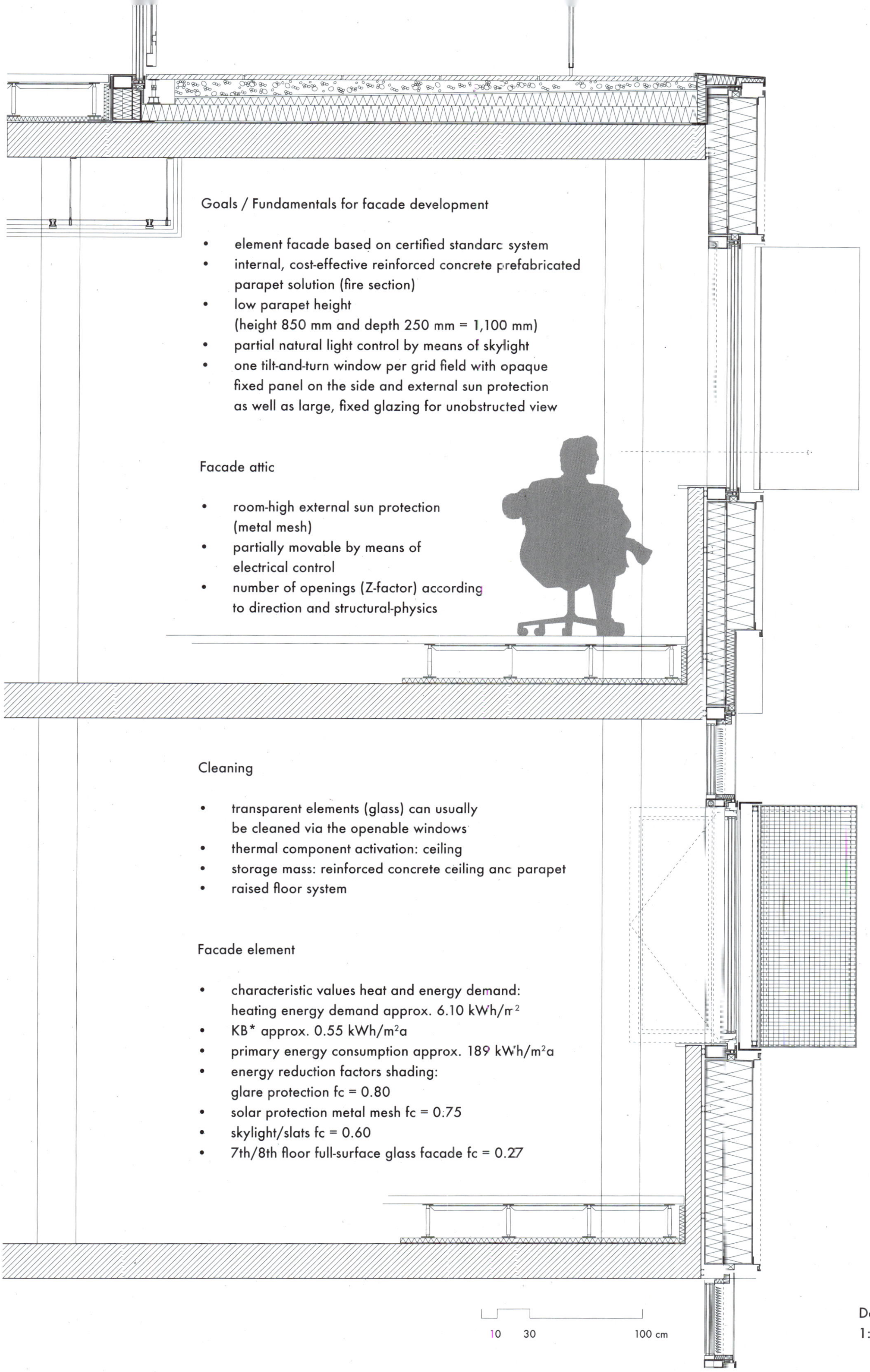

Goals / Fundamentals for facade development

- element facade based on certified standard system
- internal, cost-effective reinforced concrete prefabricated parapet solution (fire section)
- low parapet height (height 850 mm and depth 250 mm = 1,100 mm)
- partial natural light control by means of skylight
- one tilt-and-turn window per grid field with opaque fixed panel on the side and external sun protection as well as large, fixed glazing for unobstructed view

Facade attic

- room-high external sun protection (metal mesh)
- partially movable by means of electrical control
- number of openings (Z-factor) according to direction and structural-physics

Cleaning

- transparent elements (glass) can usually be cleaned via the openable windows
- thermal component activation: ceiling
- storage mass: reinforced concrete ceiling and parapet
- raised floor system

Facade element

- characteristic values heat and energy demand: heating energy demand approx. 6.10 kWh/m^2
- KB* approx. 0.55 kWh/m^2a
- primary energy consumption approx. 189 kWh/m^2a
- energy reduction factors shading: glare protection fc = 0.80
- solar protection metal mesh fc = 0.75
- skylight/slats fc = 0.60
- 7th/8th floor full-surface glass facade fc = 0.27

2021–24
FLEXIBLE REUSE

remise amstetten
3300 Amstetten, AT

PROGRAM
Multifunctional, innovative low-tech building, restaurant, co-working, offices for creative industries, new typology of a school, roof garden, restructure, extension

DIMENSIONS
GFA 13,500 m^2, plot area 8,954 m^2

CLIENT
ecoplus NÖ Wirtschaftsagentur GmbH

PROJECT TEAM
Marlies Breuss, Michael Ogerschnig, Marc Werner, Iva Olujic, Arber Koni, Sarah Gold, Elisa Cesarini, Angelika Krayer, Pavao Markulin Grgic, Elena Perez y Schneider

CONSULTANTS
ghp gmeiner | haferl & partner zt gmbh and ferro & partner (structural engineers), Welatech (building systems), DI Karin Graf (landscape design), IPJ Ingenieurbüro P. Jung (energy and building physics), Dipl-Ing. Erich Röhrer (fire protection), ÖSTAP Engineering & Consulting GmbH (percolation), Ingenieurbüro Fritsch (kitchen planning), umdasch Store Makers (gastronomy planning), IBO (certification)

MODEL-MAKING
archimodell, Vienna

AWARDS
First prize, EU-wide two-stage tender competition 2021

"The overall look is one of impressive simplicity, clarity and understated elegance, and shows a coherent evolution of the master plan."

—Excerpt from the jury protocol, 2021 (trans. by the ed.)

Site plan
1:1,500

10 30 60 100 m

Ground floor
1:500

5 10 20 40 m

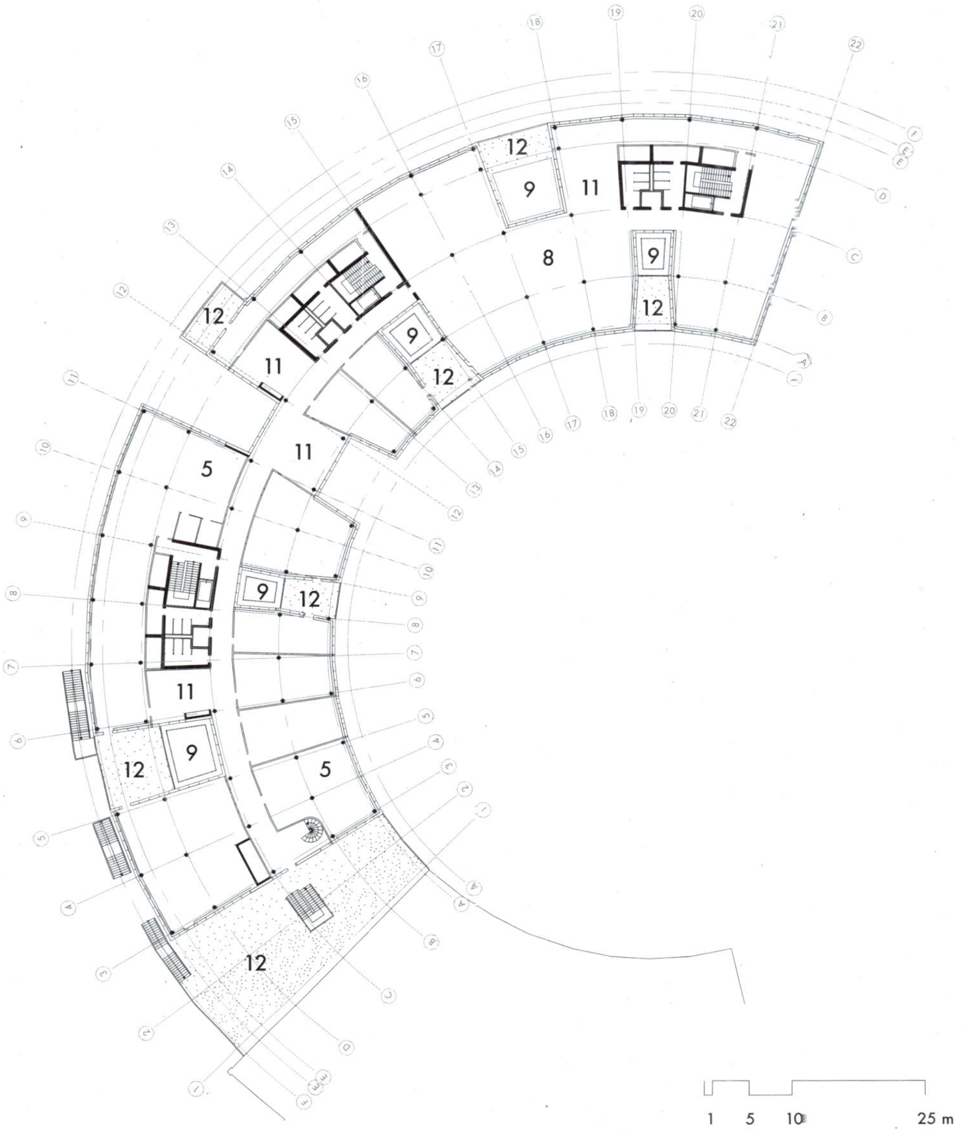

1 Entrance to lobby
2 Entrance to staircase
3 Delivery
4 Multifunctional area
5 School 42
6 Restaurant
7 Kitchen
8 Office spaces
9 Courtyard
10 Skylight
11 Common zone
12 Terrace

First floor
1 850

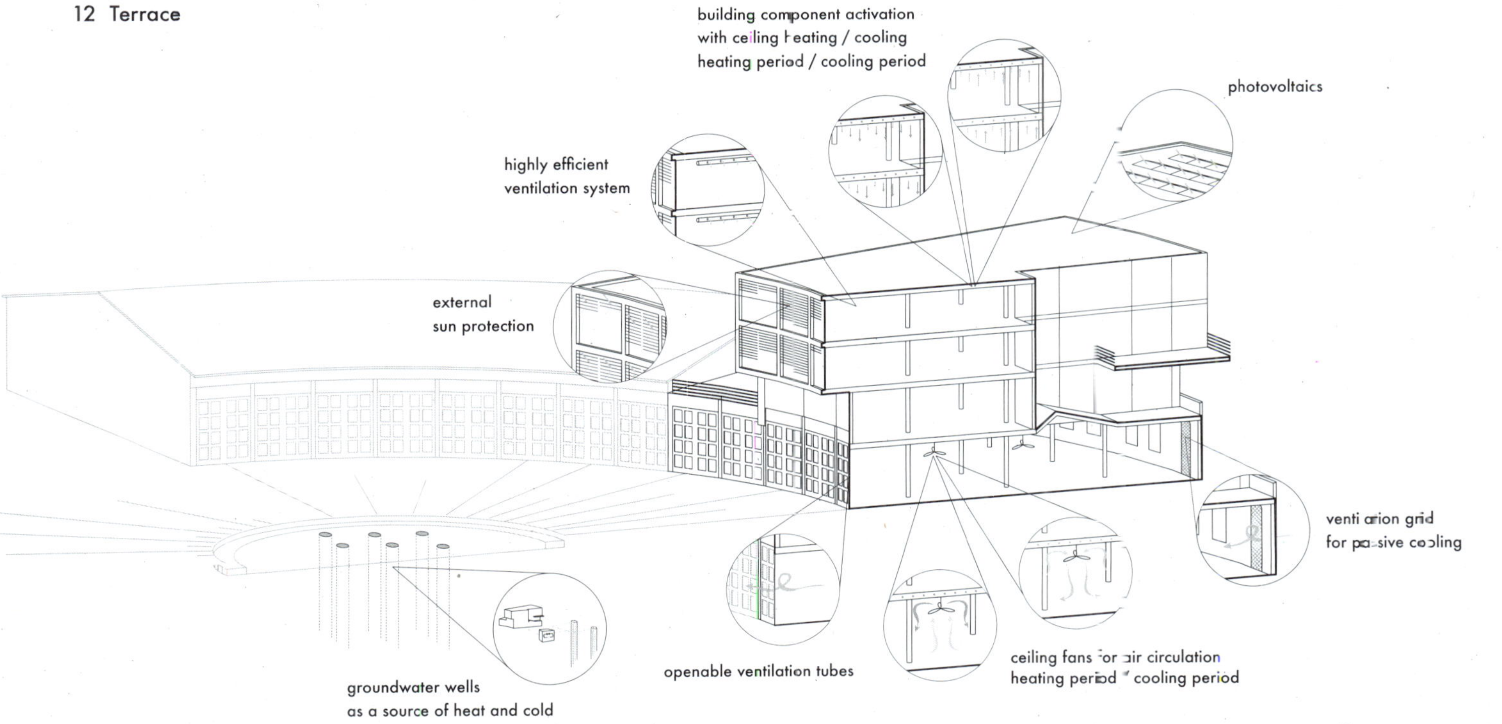

Energy concept

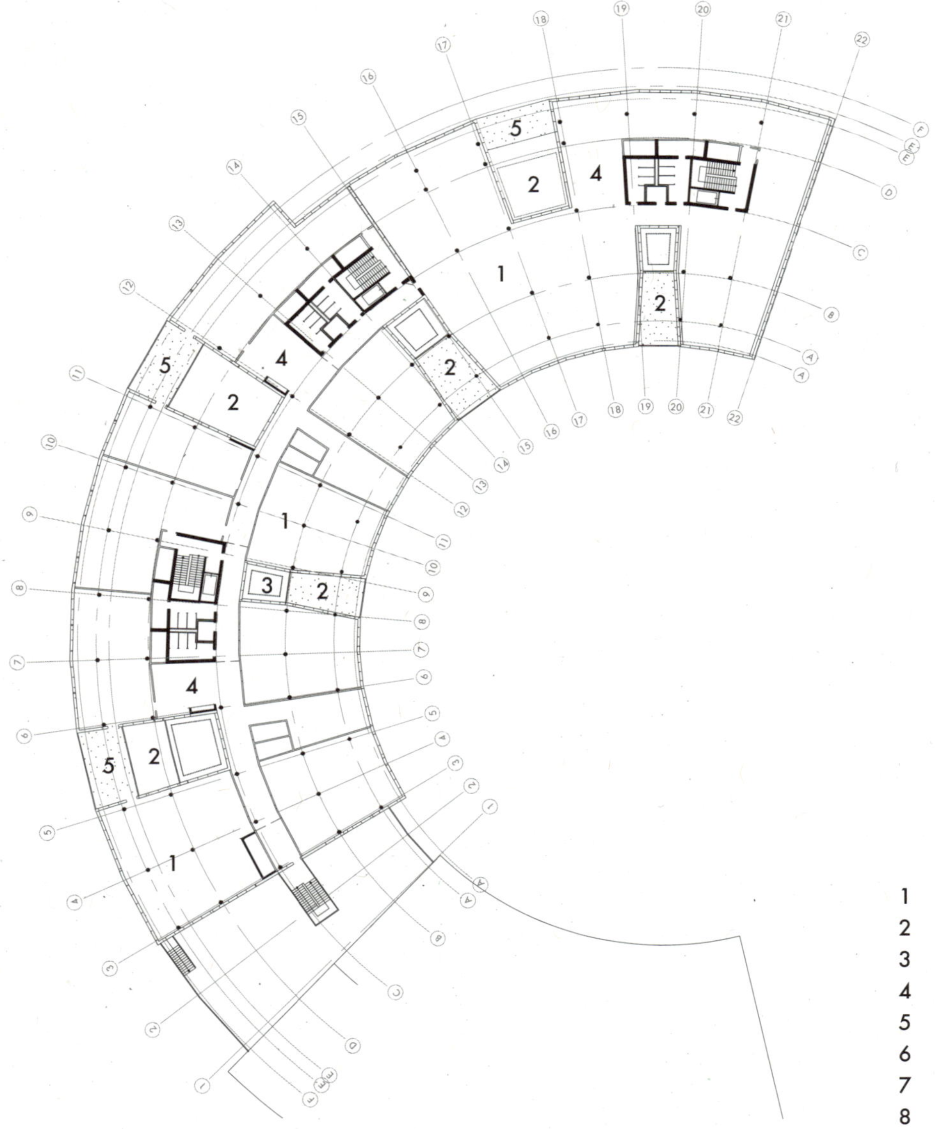

1 Office spaces
2 Courtyard
3 Skylight
4 Common zone
5 Terrace
6 Roof terrace
7 Green roof
8 Photovoltaic panels

Second floor
1:850

1 5 10 25 m

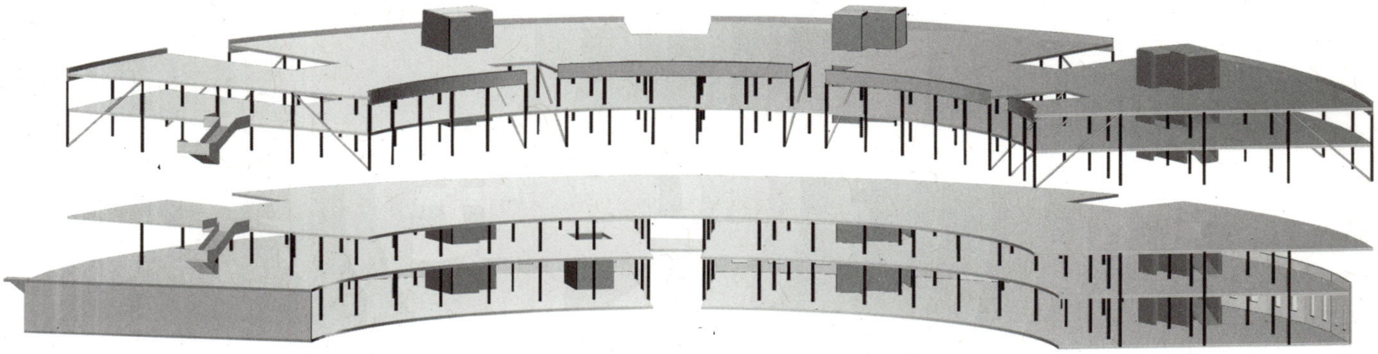

Structural concept

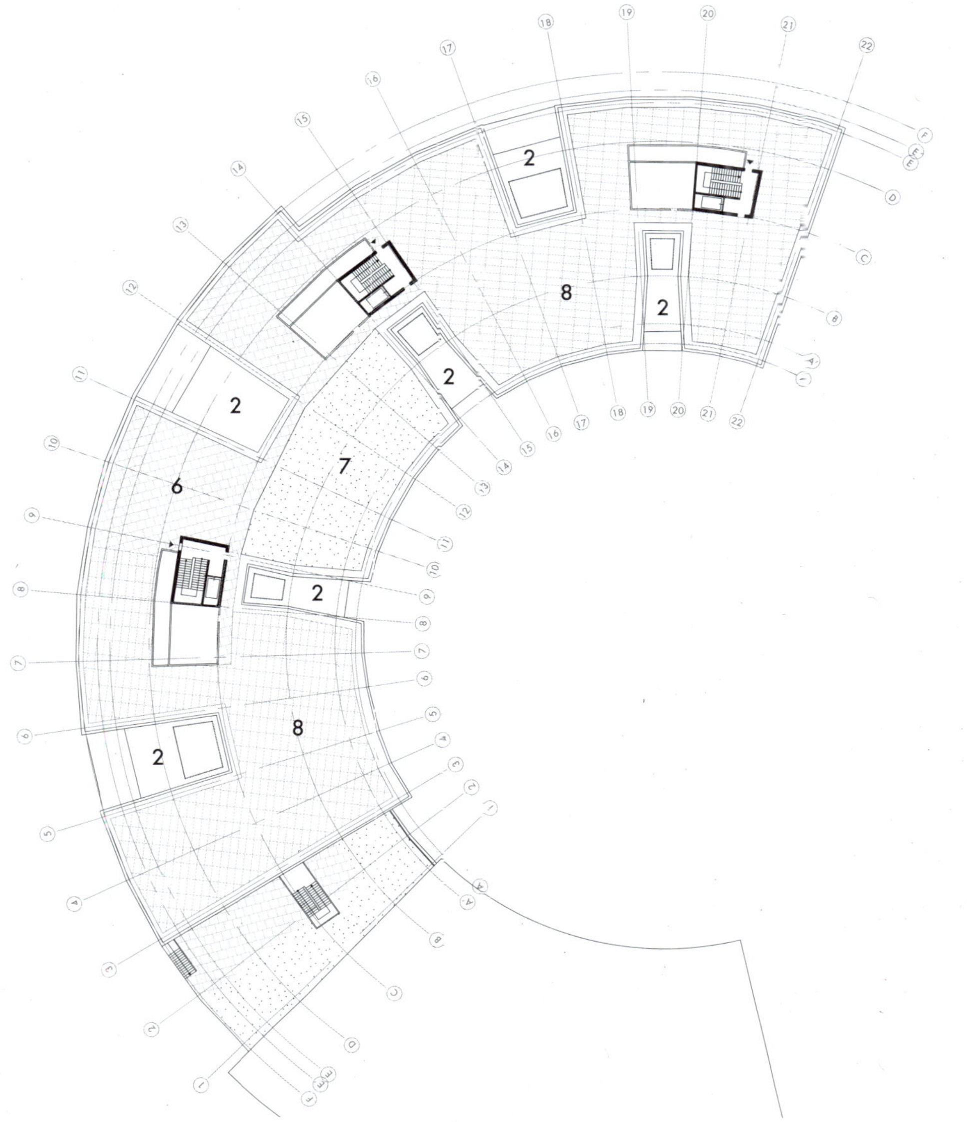

Top view

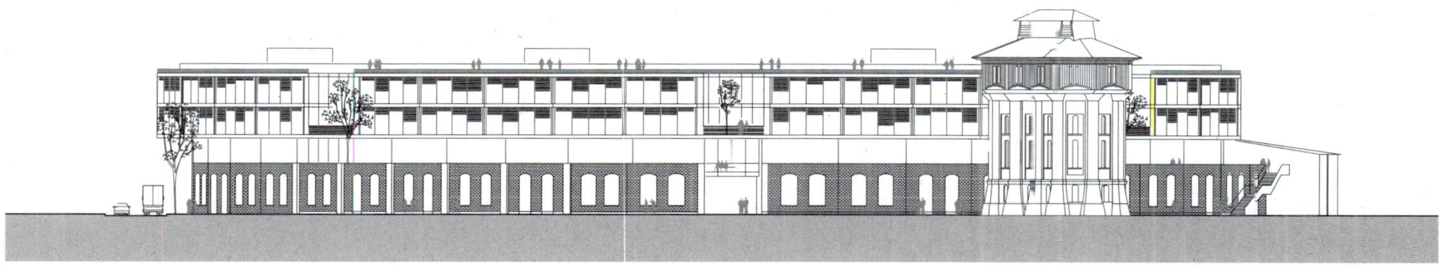

1 5 10 25 m

Elevation
1:850

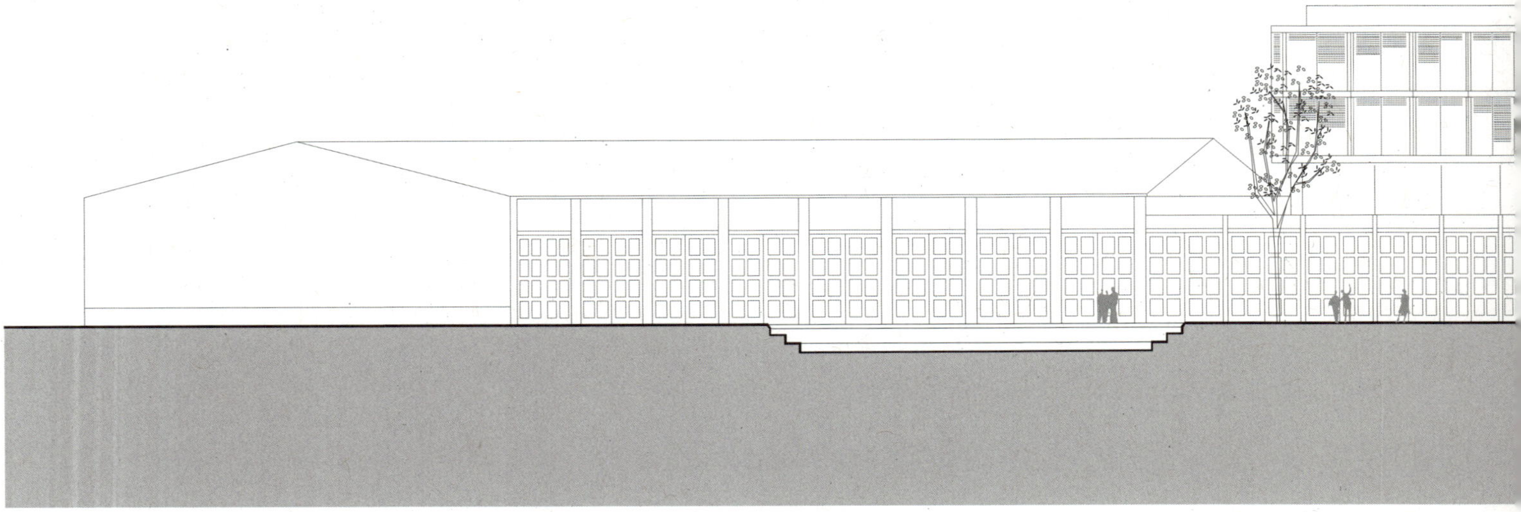

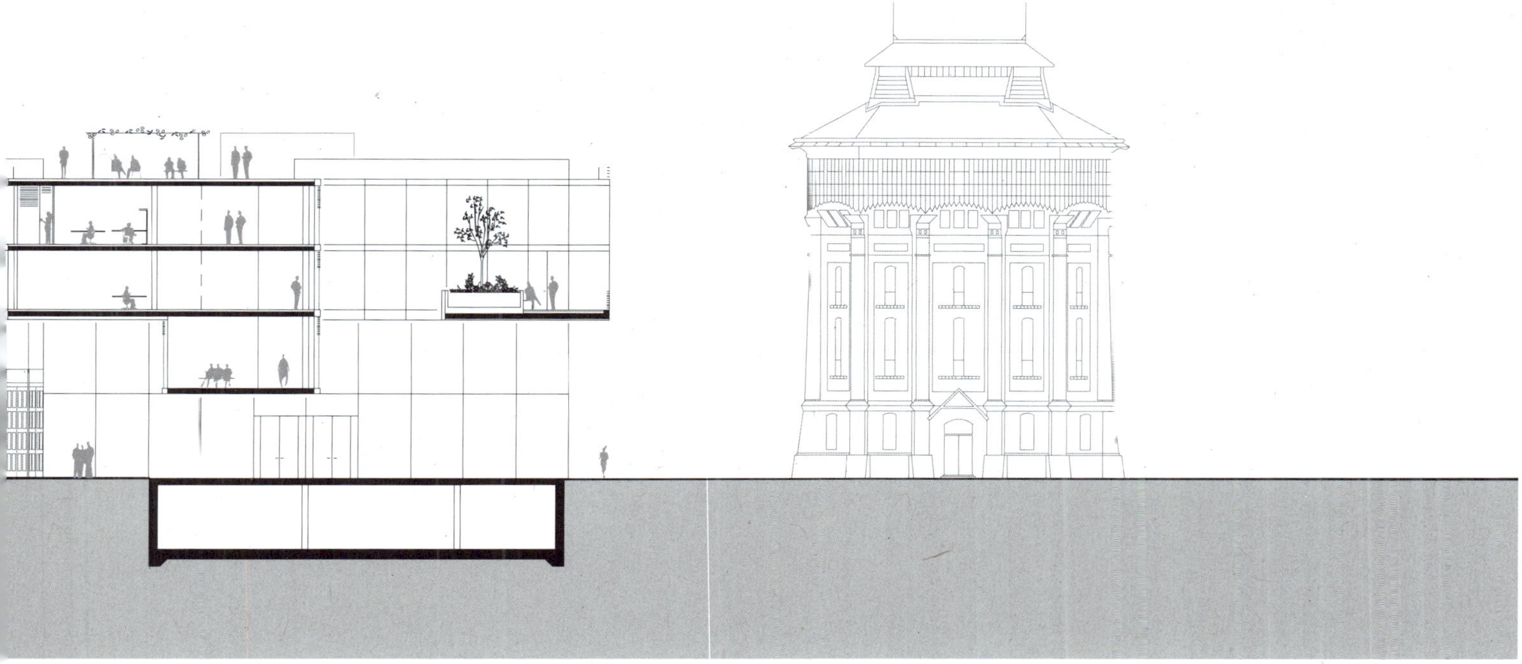

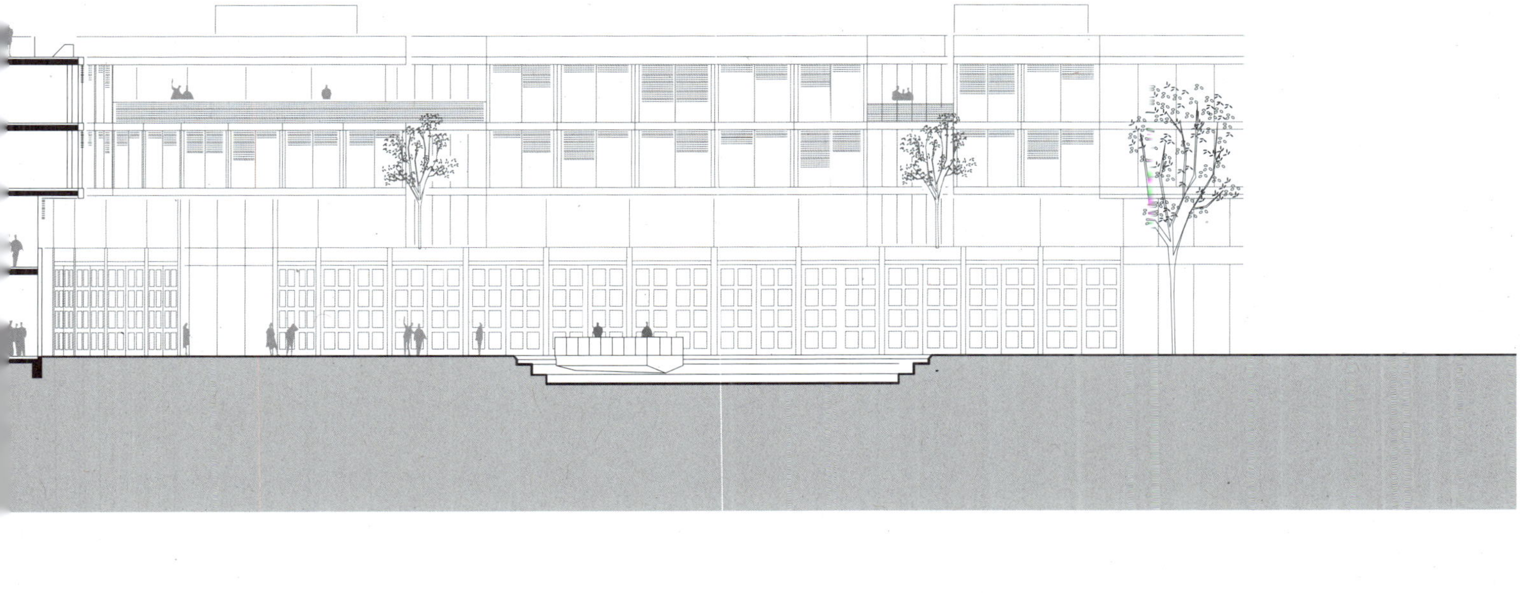

Sections
1:400

HUMAN
HABITAT

urban topos

2009–11

In the multicultural neighborhood in the Fifteenth District of Vienna, most of the dwellings were built in the last 150 years. The main urban housing typologies are low-rise residential blocks, buildings from the *Gründerzeit* period, so-called *Gemeindebauten* and detached units.

One of these unfinished housing blocks, with a detached building at one end, introduces the shape of *urban topos*, making it the transitional element between the two different types of dwelling, a blockhouse and a stand-alone building. The Z-shaped site, offering both wide and enclosed views, is on a road that rises toward a hill and a park across the street. This location inspires the concept of a building based on topography complete with "endless" terraces and balconies stretching across its whole length.

All elevations are treated in the same way, no matter which direction they are facing: the urban street or the green, semipublic courtyard. Two features that define the facades reference the rhythm of the adjacent buildings and harmonize with the surroundings. The first is the extended aluminum plates that run around the building, surrounding its outdoor areas—the balconies and terraces of various sizes. Their gently reflective finish allows the sun to penetrate and brighten the enclosed outdoor areas, while blocking views from ground level into the private and semiprivate spaces. A further feature of the facades is the lava-colored panels behind the aluminum bands and the sun-protecting elements in the same color. Varying in opacity, these elements react to different surroundings and optimize the private indoor and outdoor spaces. The overall effect is to create a feeling of openness and community with private areas for retreat.

The ground floor includes a foyer that connects all zones of the building, allowing for direct views into the inside and the yard at the back. A concrete bench in front of the building has the feeling of a retreat zone, inviting passers-by to sit and rest. Similarly, all apartments face in two directions and expand spatially until hitting the aluminum railing. This results in an indoor area that almost doubles in size. Floor-to-ceiling glazing enables direct access to the outdoor spaces, and the living areas extend beyond their physical thresholds into semiprivate spaces on the balconies and terraces, and thus further into the urban realm. The interior spaces remain flexible, with light-structure, internal walls that are removeable to create one vast open area. The proposal accommodates twenty flats across six residential floors, and an underground parking lot. There are four types of open-floor apartments, with predominately two- and three-bed variations. The building proves itself sustainable, with long-lasting and low-tech structural and material elements, including cross ventilation and district heating.

stratified townscape

2005–08

The residential building is located in the Fifth District of Vienna in between two mid-nineteenth-century *Gründerzeit* buildings, on a site with a maximum building depth of 15 meters and a plot size of 15 by 30 meters. Four principles—through views from the street into the courtyard, gardens for every floor, two-sided apartments, and a glass facade facing the yard—are the main parameters of the design. The street facade fits into the sequence of perforated facades and is created by a perspective view, as clear room heights differ from neighboring houses due to building costs and maximum usable floors.

Views into to the semipublic green courtyard from the street create a different sort of urban living in comparison to the enclosing walls of old buildings without transparency and connections. The garden remains open to the public eye, offering wide-reaching views, but it still contains a variety of private zones within. A bright plastered surface with horizontal planting areas adjacent to each floor transforms into a climbing lawn, an extension of the backyard, growing on the back elevation of the building. This creates garden galleries outside of every window; living spaces turn into winter gardens using large glass facades and the "greenfilter concept." This newly developed structure in front of the west facade gives the user the chance to arrange plants, creating a kind of concervatory of more than 20 square meters rather than a balcony of 8 square meters that also overshadows the neighbors living below. The garden galleries are made of zinc metal sheets, with different depths and dimensions. All fourteen units open onto it. Although their structure does not allow the tenants to step onto them, this is outweighed by the fact that the galleries' position right by the living room brings a private lawn directly into the large spaces instead of creating individual small balconies. In the apartments, natural light has less impact beyond 6 meters inside, therefore sanitary rooms or kitchens are placed in the center. All flats face both ways and offer open floor plans if desired and use natural cooling by cross ventilation and district heating.

tions below the outer walls, just some adjustments to the masonry in between, and a new elevator beside the existing stairs, connecting storage rooms in the cellar with the rooftop.

from the street, because it integrates perfectly into the surroundings.

roof transformations

2009-11

Close to the new main railway station in Vienna, in the Fourth District, towers a *Gründerzeit* building that was damaged in the Second World War and rebuilt during the 1950s. Positioned at the junction of two streets where the terrain falls toward the Wien, the little river that gives its name to the city, these two street axes are conceptually turned into a visual axis and become one main design parameter. Other influential factors are rotation, natural light, green areas, functional elements, and views.

The layout of the floor plan is turned by 13 degrees, to reduce interference for residents across streets, and all four apartments are organized as maisonettes in such a way as to give privacy for outdoor spaces on both levels. Two skylights bring natural light into the wide, two-story volumes, whereas green areas—called "greenfilter"—protect sleeping spaces from being visible and create a feeling of life in nature combined with the benefits of urban living. Inside the four apartments, the main functional elements, like kitchen and sanitary areas, zone spaces but do not limit them. An airy setting for all four flats with maximum glass areas in all directions—some openable for cross ventilation, some connected to green areas and private terraces—results in a new typology of rooftop.

This is a lightweight structure made of steel and wood, so its weight requires no strengthening of founda-

urban reflections

2007-12

In the historic First District of Vienna—where most of the national government buildings are, as well as St. Stephen's Cathedral, Hofburg Palace, Otto Wagner's Postsparkasse building, Looshaus, et cetera—a lot of multifunctional buildings nowadays serve as speculative assets for investors. It remains the only one of Vienna's twenty-three districts that has a decreasing number of residents in 2020; since 2005 almost 7 percent of residents have left the inner city. *urban reflections* is a rooftop extension on a building inside the medieval Schottenviertel quarter situated between Sterngasse and Salvatorgasse; it belongs to a local family and is intended to offer additional living spaces. Of major importance is its integration into the urban fabric, where since the fourteenth century cupolas, dormers, and flat roofs have defined this dense area's surrounding roofscape that is mostly subject to heritage protection.

The design revolves around the manifold geometric forms of adjacent roofs, the transition from common to private spaces, and the implementation of greenery and astonishing views. The resulting "roof-folding" creates an architectonic mediator between dormers and cupolas, privacy and community, as well as greenery for protection and relaxation. Even with 900 square meters of floor area organized on two and three stories, the vast volume is hardly seen

cliffhouse

2001-02

The existing family house in Tel Aviv is based on the modern, open floor plan, which provides individual zones set within continuous spaces. In this specific case, it creates an undifferentiated flow between three levels of house and gardens. In the absence of spatial complexity and dynamics, the client has asked for an interior that creates atmosphere and places for assigned functions.

Analyzing the existing conditions, the design proposal keeps the openness but uses a conceptual *stripe of continuity, reflection*, and *layering of materials* that moves within the three levels. Wherever an intervention is appropriate, the *stripe creates a functional element*, while still referring to the interconnecting concept, using the same set of defined materials. A programmatic matrix of significant sensual characteristics—like haptics, optics, and scent—is determined for interventions like boards, tables, wardrobes, vitrines, shelving, and so on, which carefully subdivide spaces while containing the open floor plan. Fully enclosed spaces are kept to a minimum, yet plenty of privacy is provided. Bespoke elements and their positioning allow visual connections to be established between these spaces and interrupt unwanted sightlines, where retreat zones are required.

2005–06

Next to the popular Yppenplatz in Vienna's Sixteenth District, this former pantyhose factory at the rear of a building complex remained unused until a small developer sold some spaces as empty lofts. The nineteenth-century building now accommodates mostly artists and some elderly residents. Inside the ground level there are still some ceilings like Wiener Platzldecke (Kappendecke) that give a specific atmosphere. The decision to maintain the 180-square-meter loft unpartitioned demanded a specific approach, eschewing walls but embracing possibilities for generating spaces. Le Corbusier's open floor plan with only pilotis combined with floating, moveable curtains to create functional units seemed suitable for keeping the spatial generosity.

Three temporary units are defined as *Körperkultur* (mind and body training), *Wellnessort* (daily care), and *Pflanzenoase* (plant oasis), and using them creates a secondary space for other functional demands, like zoning for guests. The surrounding walls are partly turned into *Speicherwände* (walls for storage), offering space enough for all kinds of devices, clothes, appliances, and dishes. Only the cooking apparatus and wardrobes are fixtures. To light the interior space (maximum length 23 meters, and width 8 meters into the depth of the building), four existing skylights, underfloor lighting, and a large terrace space are installed for the comfort of residents during the day and at night. Luminescent floor joints, intermittently appearing and following the walls, reinforce the effect of fluid space, connect different spatial zones, and carry the light into the interior.

urban topos
1050 Vienna, AT

See pp. 50–56

PROGRAM
Residential building, 20 apartments, surrounding terraces and balconies, underground parking, bicycle parking

DIMENSIONS
Plot area 626 m², covered area 341 m², GFA 3,241 m², floor space 2,615 m²,
useable living area 1,325 m², balconies and terraces 471 m²

CLIENT
CER Immobilienentwicklung GmbH, Vienna, Austria

PROJECT TEAM
Marlies Breuss, Michael Ogertschnig, Carolin Saile, Christian Rottensteiner, Nana Schilling, Stefan Staehle

CONSULTANTS
Riebenbauer (building services), Röhrer Ziviltechniker (building physics), Ruzicka Ziviltechniker (structural engineer),
Reichel Architekten (site supervision)

PHOTOGRAPHY
Hertha Hurnaus

AWARDS
Best architects 14 – Multiple Storey Buildings, winner
GEBAUT 2011 – Stadtgestaltung Wien 2012, distinction

PUBLICATIONS (SELECTION)
GEBAUT 2011, exhibition catalogue, exhibition of MA19, Vienna, 2011.
Bauvisite 155, Turnergasse, Österreichische Gesellschaft für Architektur, ÖGFA, Vienna, May 13, 2011.
Isabella Marboe, "Immer Neues erfinden," *H.O.M.E.*, November 2013.

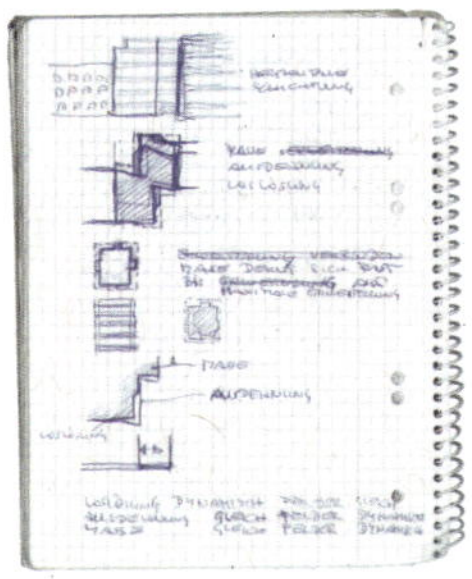

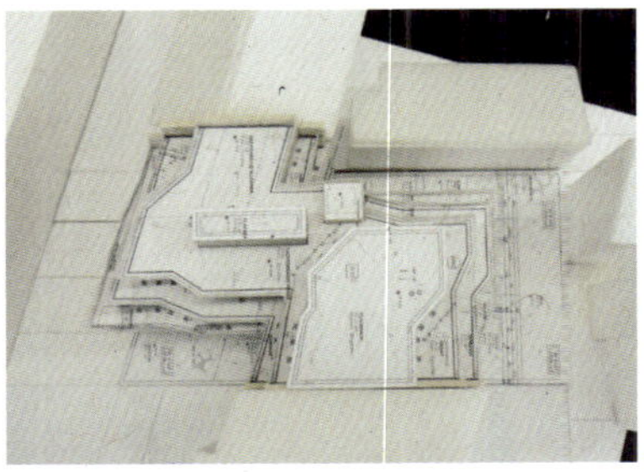

"Urban Topos is a piece of landscape in the city: memorable, walkable, sunlit, and a little different at every corner."

— Isabella Marboe, "Ein Stadthaus als Landschaft – Ein Haus mit Charakter," *Architektur.aktuell* 6 (2012), Vienna and New York, Springer, p. 84 (trans. by the ed.)

Site plan
1:500

5 10 20 40 m

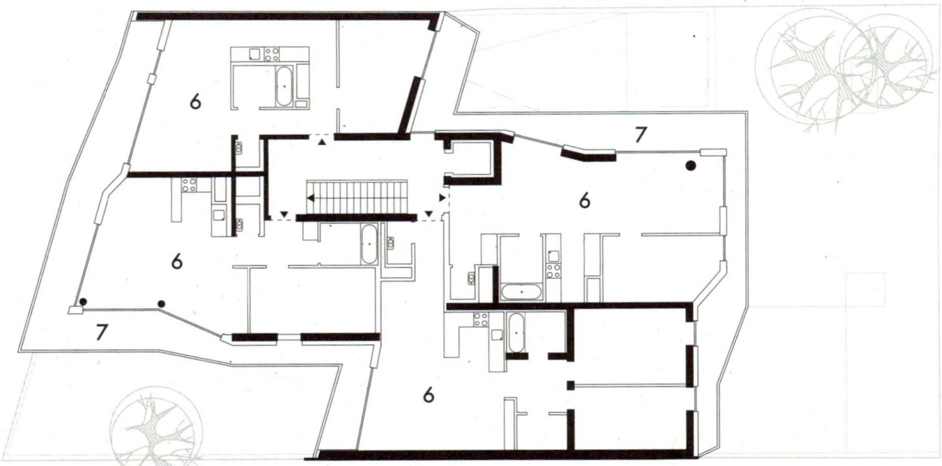

First floor

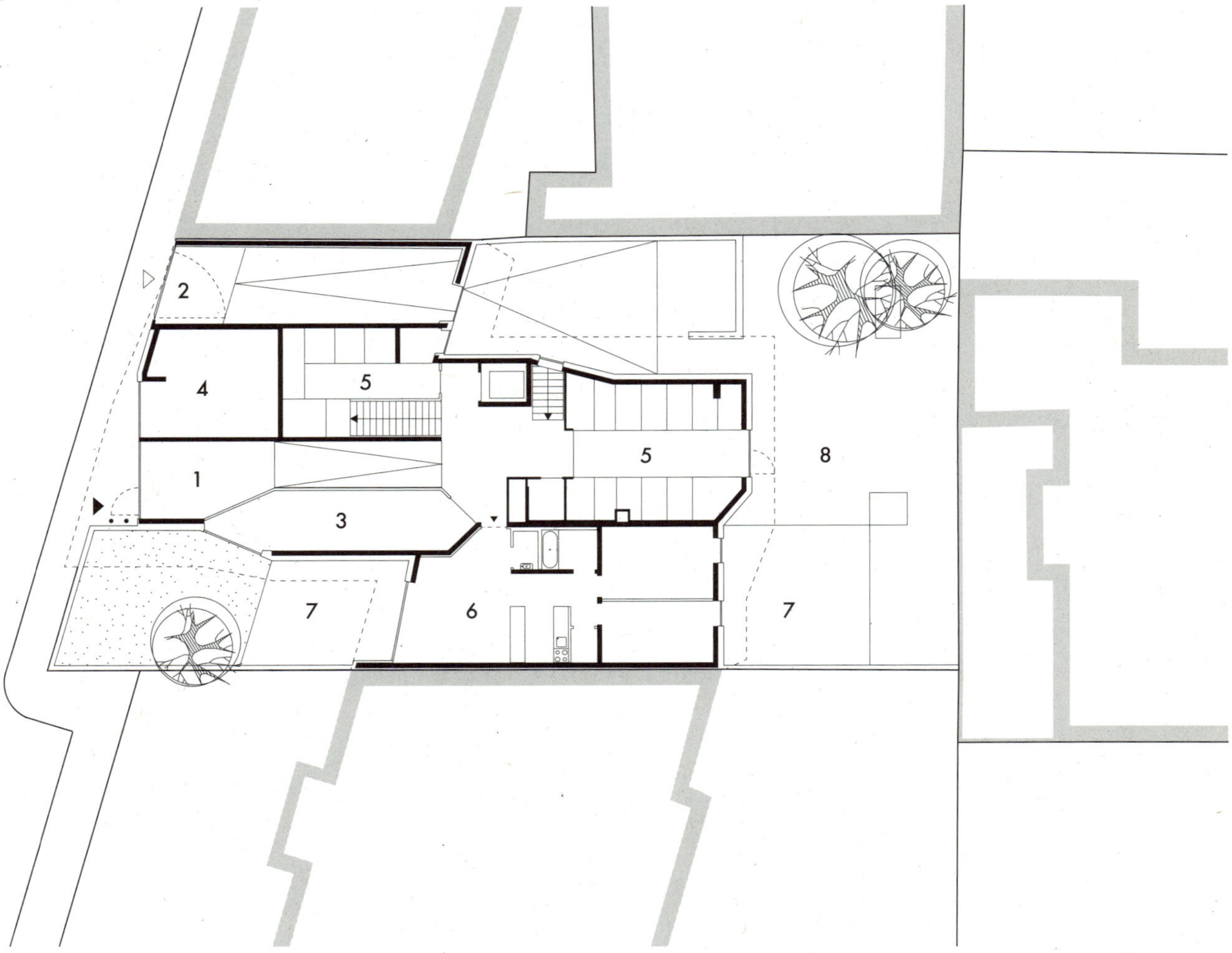

1 Entrance
2 Entrance to garage
3 Bicycle parking
4 Waste disposal area
5 Storage spaces
6 Housing unit
7 Terraces for relaxation
8 Semipublic area

Ground floor
1:300

1 3 6 10 15 m

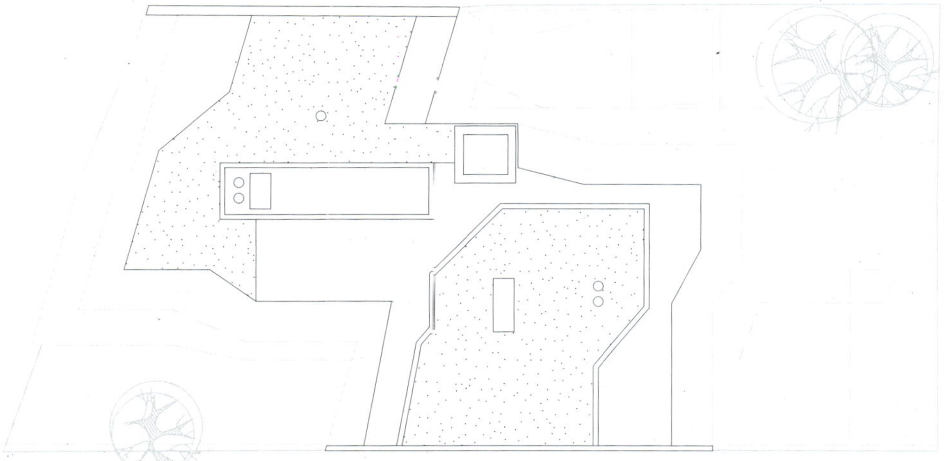

Second top floor

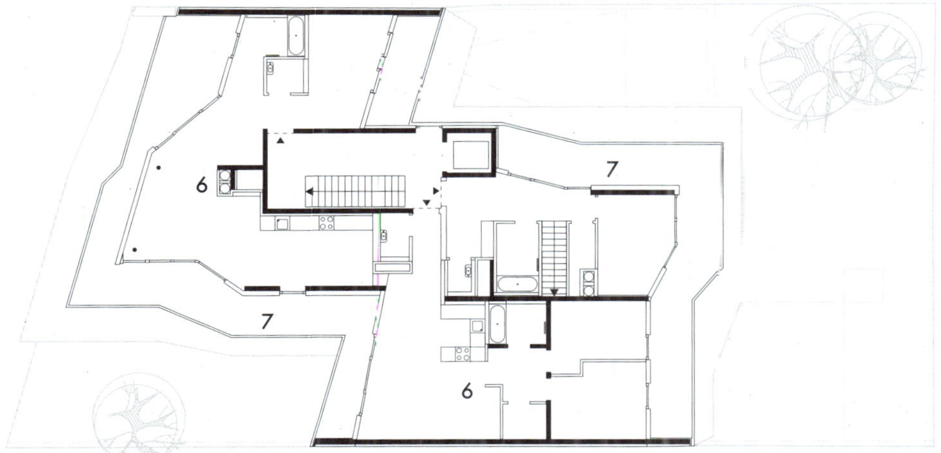

First top floor

Section

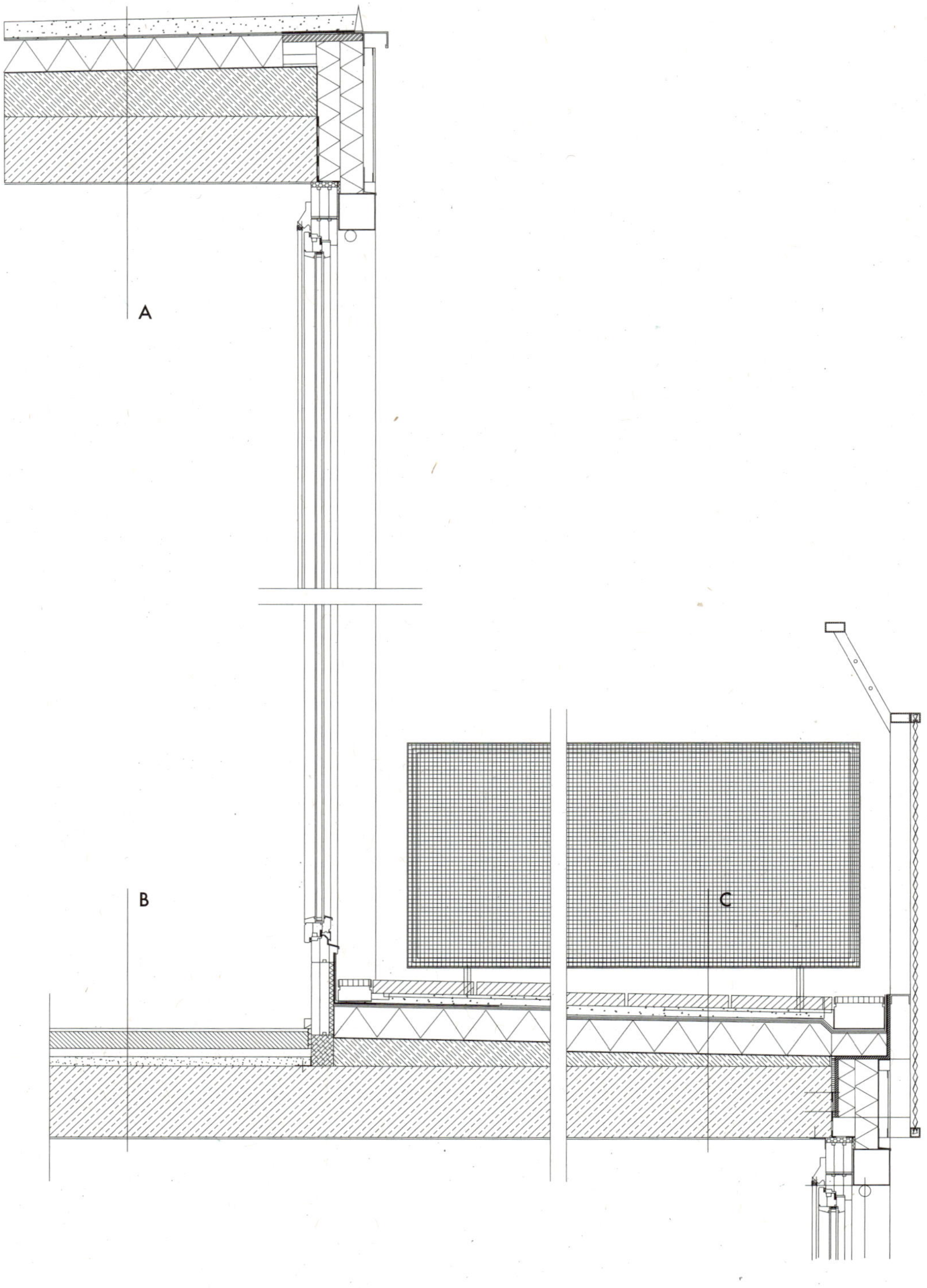

Detail A / extensive green roof

Plant substrate 100 mm
Filter fleece 2 mm
Drainage 40 mm
Root-barrier membrane 3 mm
Foil sealing 2 mm
EPS insulation 160 mm
Vapor pressure equalization layer
Bituminous primer
Concrete (gradient) 20–140 mm
Reinforced concrete ceiling 300 mm
Plaster

Detail B / floor

Solid parquet 10 mm
Screed 60 mm
PAE-foil
Mineral wool sound impact insulation 40 mm
Polystyrene concrete 40 mm
Reinforced concrete ceiling 250 mm
Thin plaster

Detail C / terrace

Screed plates 40 mm
Gravel 8/16 >30 mm
Filter fleece
Rubber mat 5 mm
Bituminous roof sealing 10 mm
Vapor pressure equalization layer
Polyurethane insulation 100 mm
Vapor barrier
Concrete (gradient) 30–85 mm
Reinforced concrete ceiling 250 mm
Plaster 5 mm

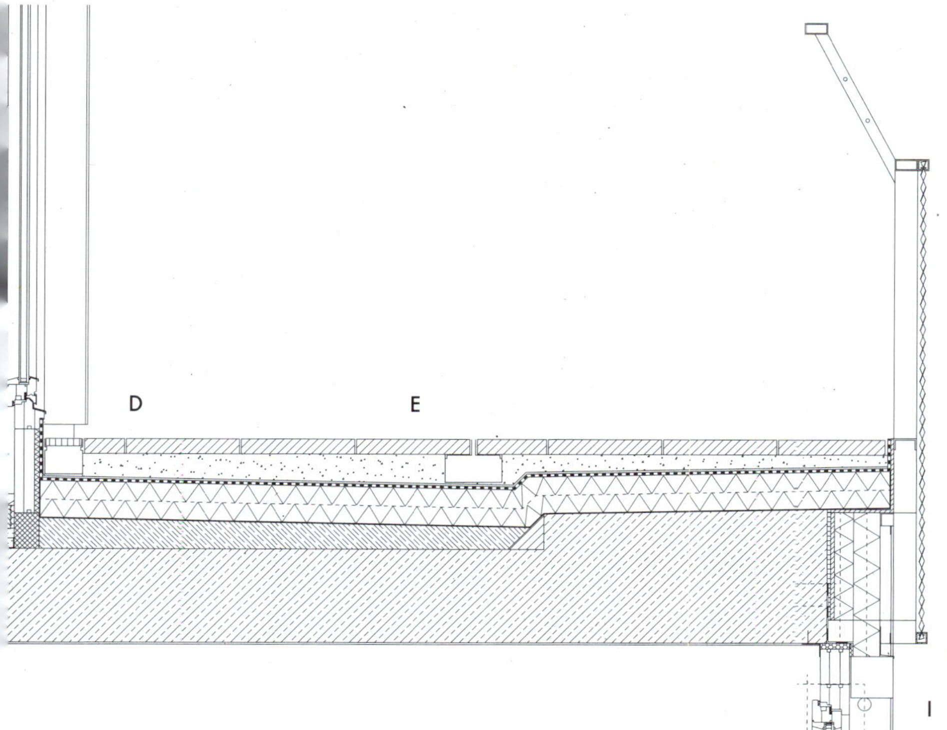

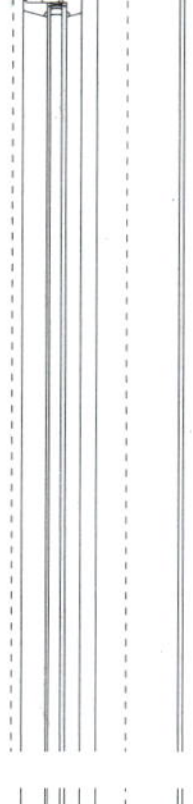

Detail D / facade

Frontedge lateral facade connection
Top edge gutter/concrete (gradient)
Sealing in accordinance norm
Cover sheet, aluminum
Facade drainage channel, perforated

Detail E / terrace

Screed plates 40 mm
Gravel 8/16 >30 mm
Filter fleece
Rubber mat 5 mm
Bituminous roof sealing 10 mm
Vapor pressure equalization layer
Polyurethane insulation 100 mm
Vapor barrier
Concrete (gradient) 30–85 mm
Reinforced concrete ceiling 250 mm
Plaster 5 mm

Detail F / facade

Mounting window inside with
an aluminum angle
Crank
Structural attachement joints

Detail G / railing

RHS handrail, galvanized steel
Anodized aluminum profiled edging 30/30 mm
RHS post, galvanized steel
Infill expanded aluminum metal
Steel angle, galvanized
Point-fixing of posts, axial dimension 1,200 mm
Chamfered silicon edge
Drip edge with 100 mm distance, parallel to outer edge

Detail H / facade

Cover strip
Edge insulation strips
Point-fixing according to window

Detail I / facade

Fixation inside aluminum angle
Cavity filled with foam
Cover sheet
Insect screen
Fixation outside thermally separated

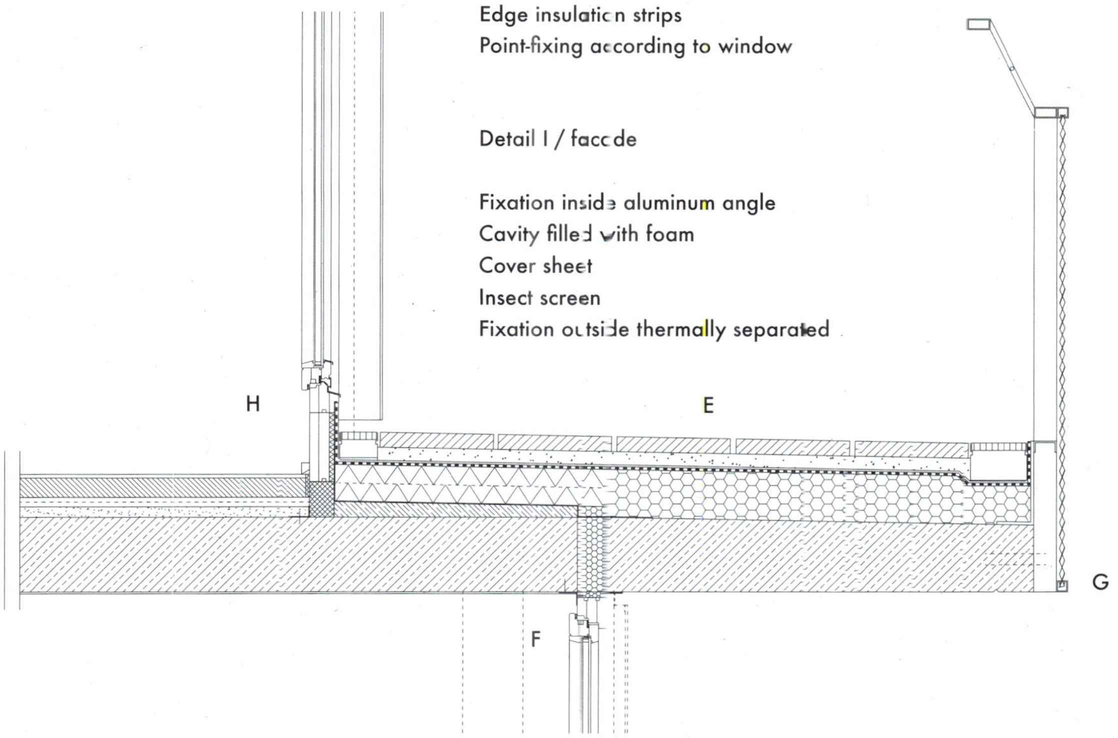

10 30 60 100 cm

Details
1:20

stratified townscape
1050 Vienna, AT

See pp. 57–61

PROGRAM
Residential building, 12 apartments, underground parking, bicycle parking

DIMENSIONS
Plot area 510 m², covered area 221 m², GFA 1,884 m², useable living area 1,191 m², gross net area 1,263 m²

CLIENT
Kallco, Vienna, Austria

PROJECT TEAM
Marlies Breuss, Michael Ogertschnig, Ulrich Hagen, Stephan Goos, Jan Chladil, Grischa Fischer, Alexej Kolyschkow, Jan Conradi

CONSULTANTS
3:0 Landschaftsarchitektur (landscape architecture), Manfred Bruck ZT (building physics), KPPK (structural engineer), KREINER architektur (site supervision), Riebenbauer (building systems)

PHOTOGRAPHY
Hertha Hurnaus

AWARDS
First prize, national competition

PUBLICATIONS (SELECTION)
"Wohnen im verdichteten Gebiet," *Der Standard*, Vienna, December 13, 2008.
TURN On Architekturfestival with "Wohnbau Gießaufgasse und Wolfsberg." Radiokulturhaus Wien, Vienna, March 7, 2009.

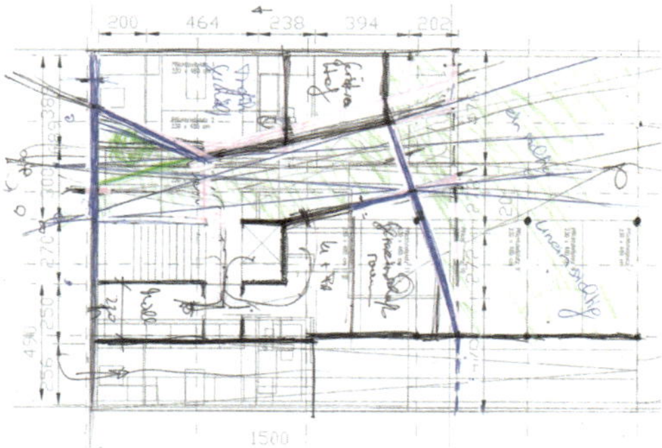

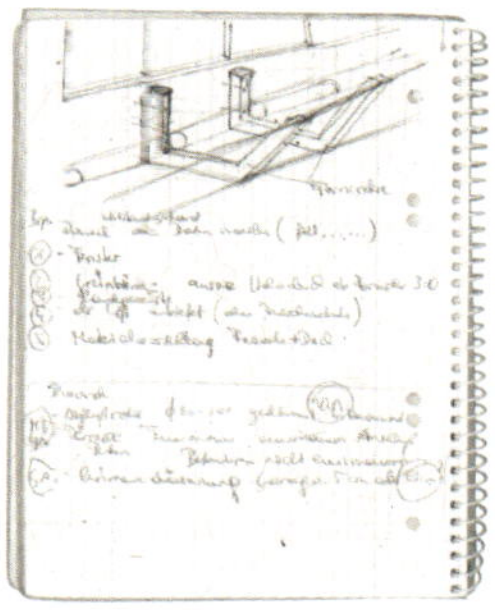

"The housing complex unfolds its irresistible qualities as a folded green landscape, a big step towards reading a building as a topography …."

—Elke Krasny, *oris – magazine for architecture and culture*, 58 (2009), Zagreb, p. 62.

Site plan
1:500

5 10 20 40 m

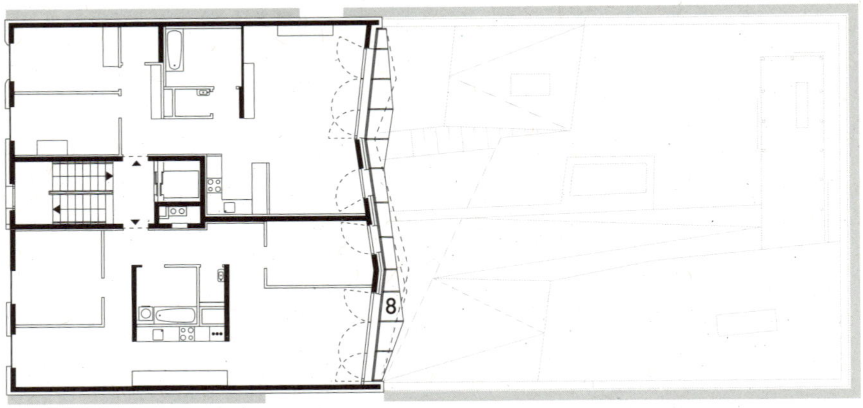

Fourth floor

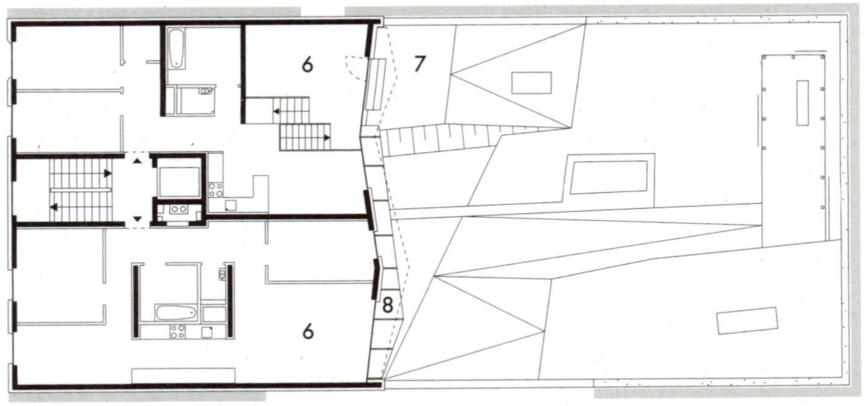

First floor

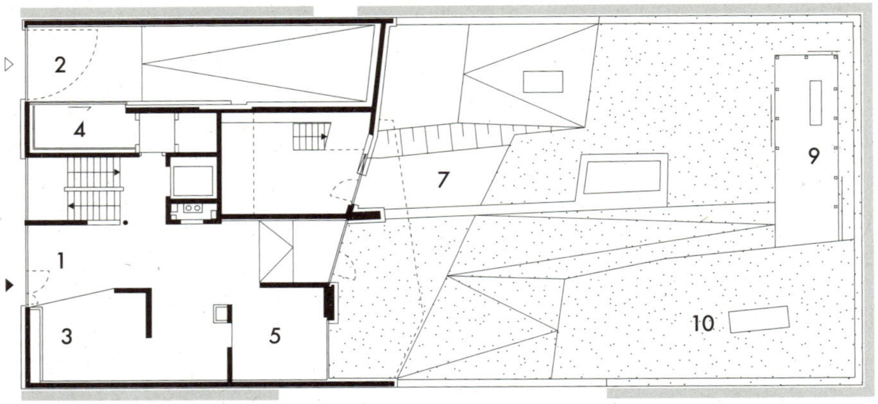

Ground floor
1:300

1 3 6 10 15 m

1 Entrance
2 Entrance to garage
3 Bicycle parking
4 Waste disposal area
5 Storage spaces
6 Housing unit
7 Terraces for relaxation
8 Green filter
9 Semipublic arbor
10 Courtyard

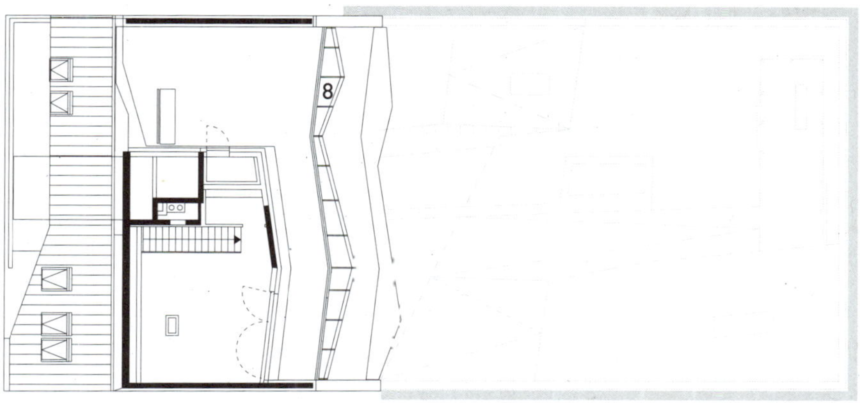

Second top floor

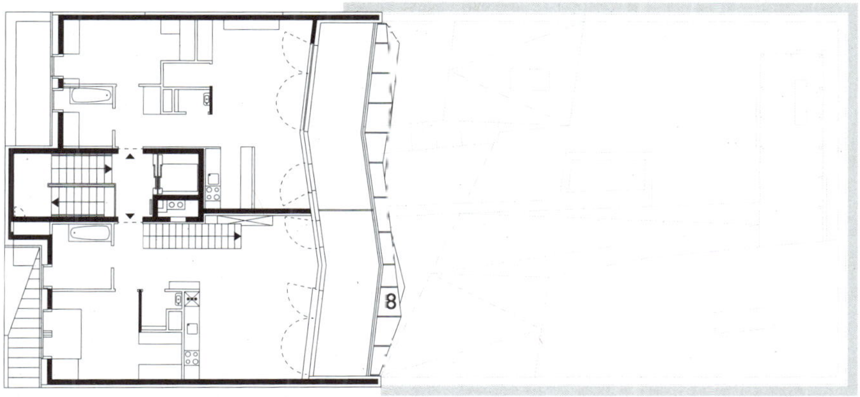

First top floor

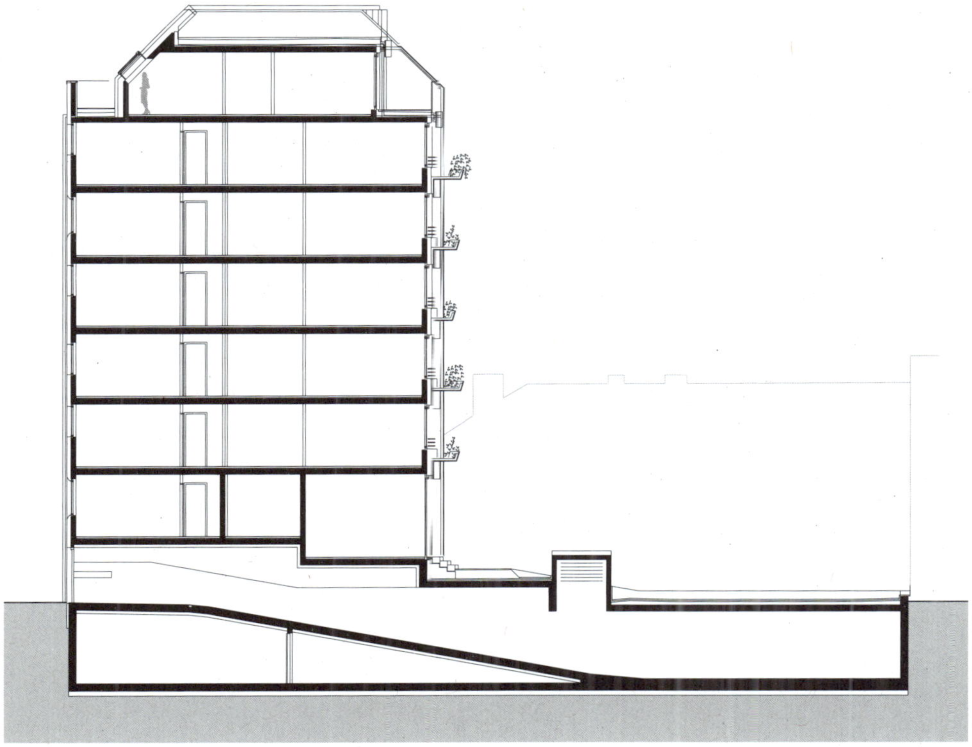

Section

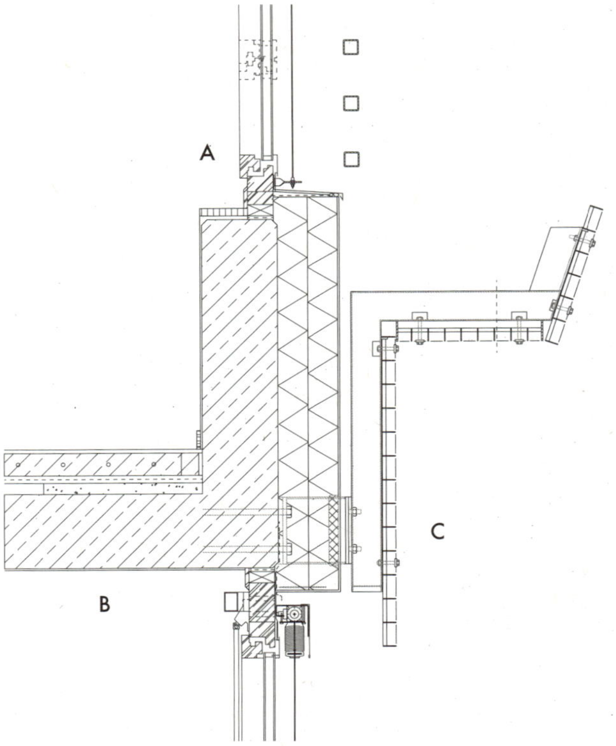

Detail A / window ledge

Hand railing SHS 40 mm outside
Galvanized fixation on concrete wall
Window ledge, sharp edged inside
Plaster
Reinforced concrete wall 200 mm
Baseboard

Detail B / floor

Floor covering
Screed 75 mm
PAE-foil
Mineral wool impact sound
insulation board 25/20 mm
Polystyrene concrete
Reinforced concrete ceiling 200 mm
Thin plaster

Detail C / balcony element

Galvanized u-steel 80/80 mm
Grating 64/128/35 mm, galvanized
Stainless steel edging
Grating 40/88/2/35 mm, galvanized
Stainless steel edging
Grating 64/128/35 mm, galvanized
Stainless steel edging
Galvanized SHS 80 mm
Dowel
Elastomic bearing
Galvanized SHS 80 mm, filled with foam
Sealing tape
Insect screen and weather hood
External blinds

Detail
1:20

10 30 60 100 cm

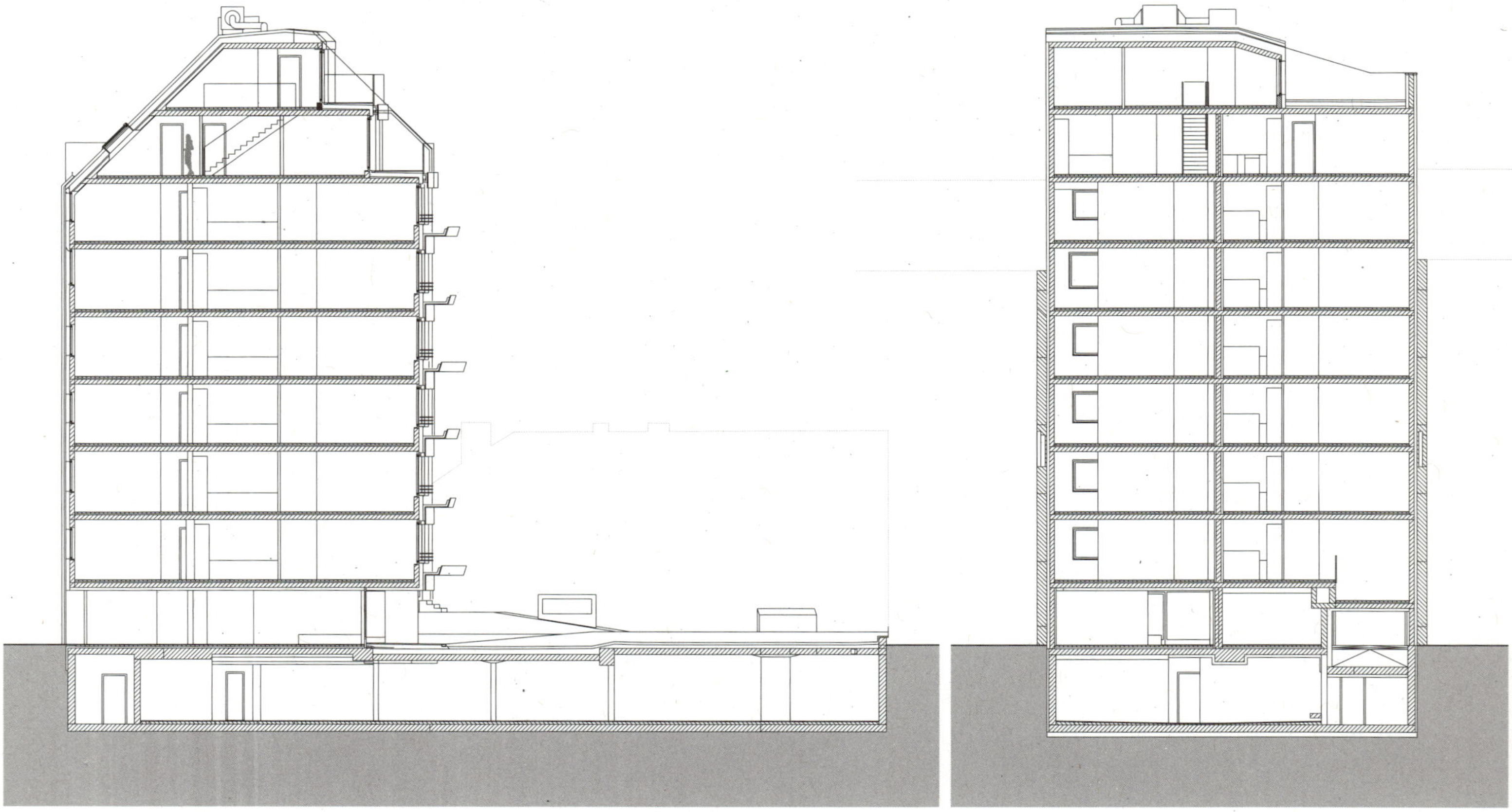

Sections
1:300

1 3 6 10 15 m

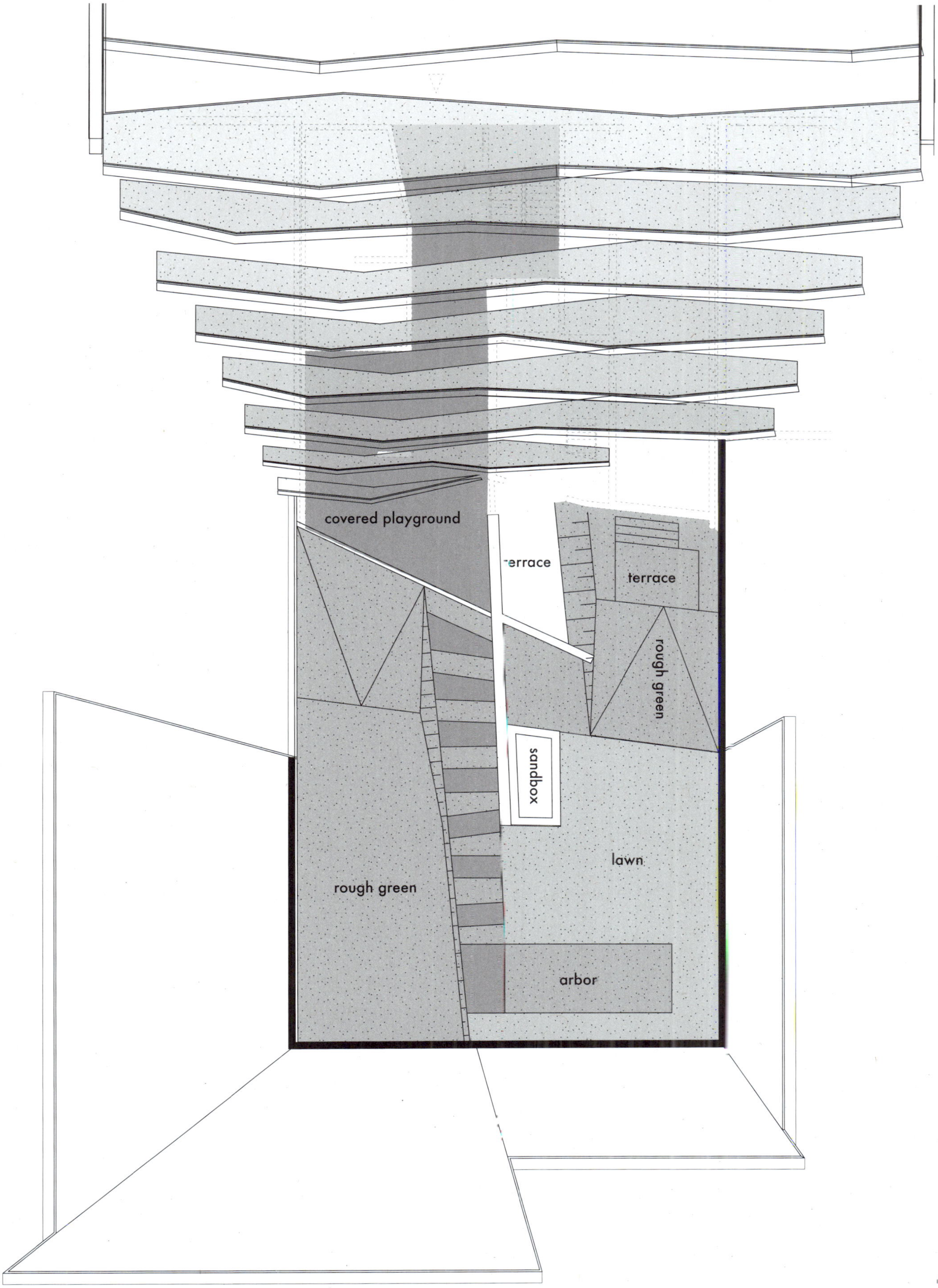

Axonometric projection

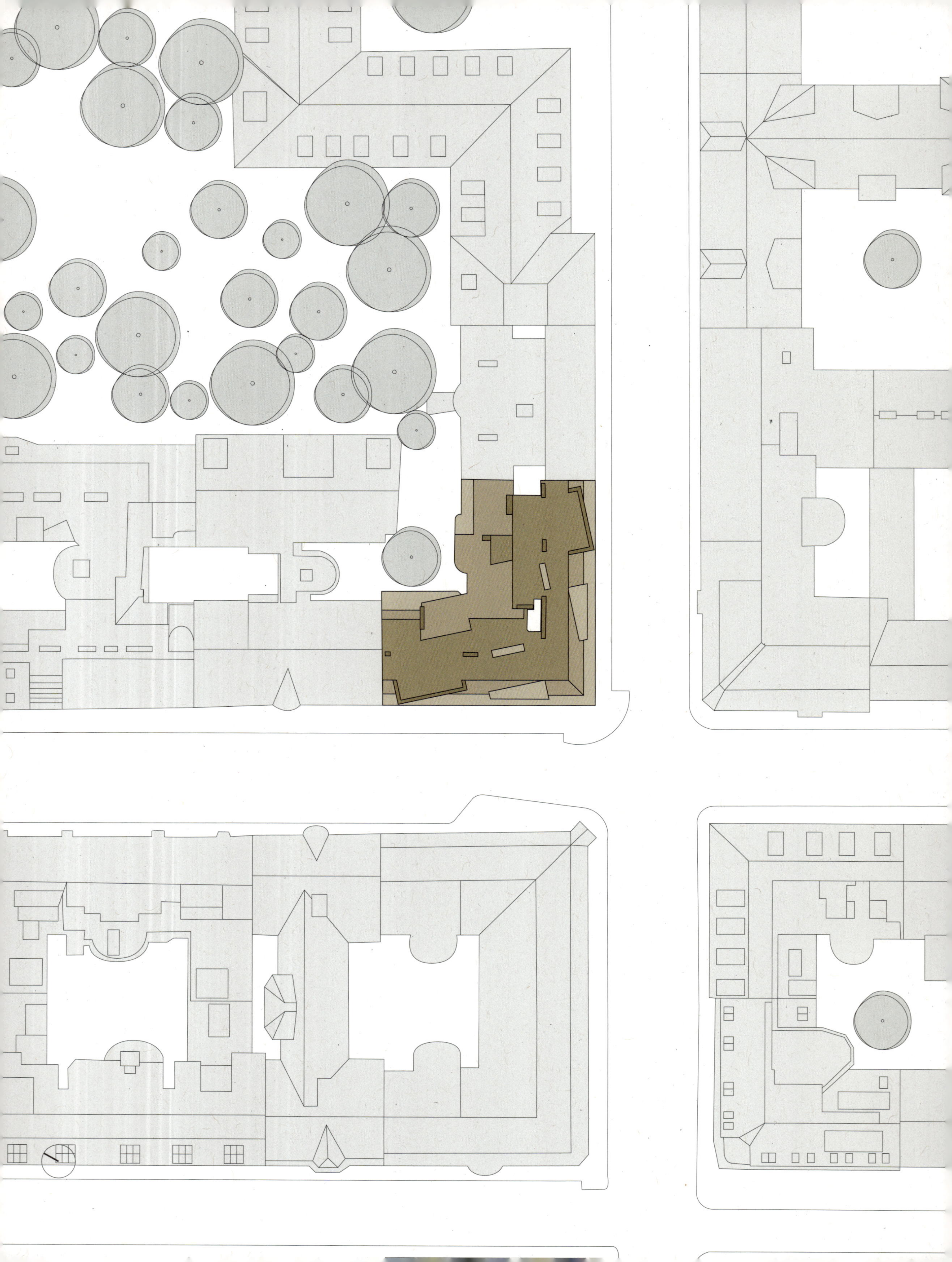

roof transformations
1040 Vienna, AT

See pp. 62–67

PROGRAM
Rooftop, attic conversion, four apartments, elevator, green filters, terraces

DIMENSIONS
Plot area 653 m², covered area 548 m², floor space 540 m², useable living area 518 m², terraces 118 m²

CLIENT
IMMOWERT Immobilieninvest GmbH, Vienna, Austria

PROJECT TEAM
Marlies Breuss, Michael Ogertschnig, Marc Wohlschak, Laura Reinartz, Christian Rottensteiner

CONSULTANTS
KPPK (structural engineer, building physics), Riebenbauer (building systems)

PHOTOGRAPHY
Wolfgang Thaler

AWARDS
First prize, invited competition
28. Stadterneuerungspreis (urban renewal prize), honorable mention

PUBLICATIONS (SELECTION)
"Roof transformations," *Architektur Fachmagazin: Dach & Wand*, Perchtoldsdorf, September–October 2013 (ISBN 1606-4550).
Isabella Marboe, "Immer Neues erfinden," *H.O.M.E.*, November 2013.
Aufstocken mit Holz: Verdichten, Sanieren, Dämmen, Basel, Birkhäuser, April 2014 (ISBN 978-3-03821-506-6).

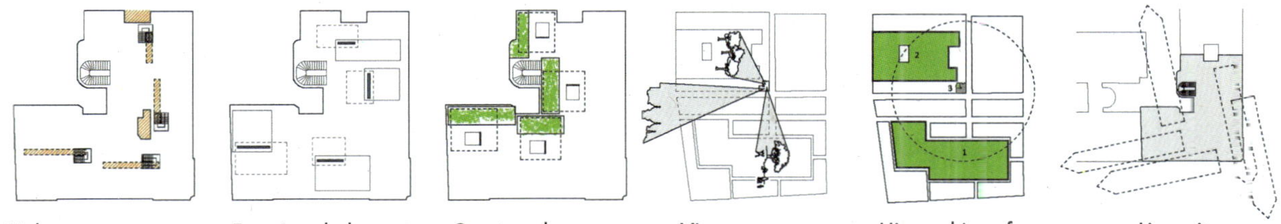

Halos › Light spaces | Functional elements | Courtyard › Greenfilter | Views › Molding | Hierarchies of green spaces | Linearity › Twist

"The light-flooded rooms with their generously dimensioned private open spaces create a comforting ambiance. This has created perfect oases of tranquillity above the rooftops of the pulsating metropolis."

—Markus Mooser, Marc Forestier, Mélanie Pittet-Baschung, and Charles von Büren, "Ruheoase über den Dächern Wiens," in *Aufstocken mit Holz*, Basel, Birkhäuser Verlag, 2014, p. 151 (trans. by the ed.)

Site plan
1:500

5 10 20 40 m

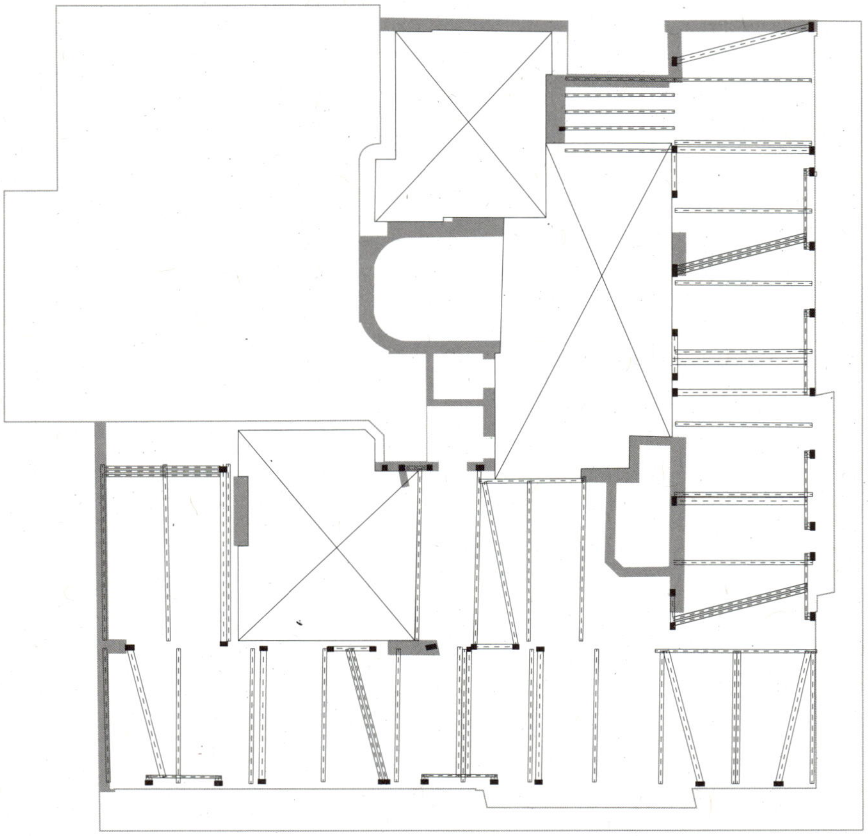

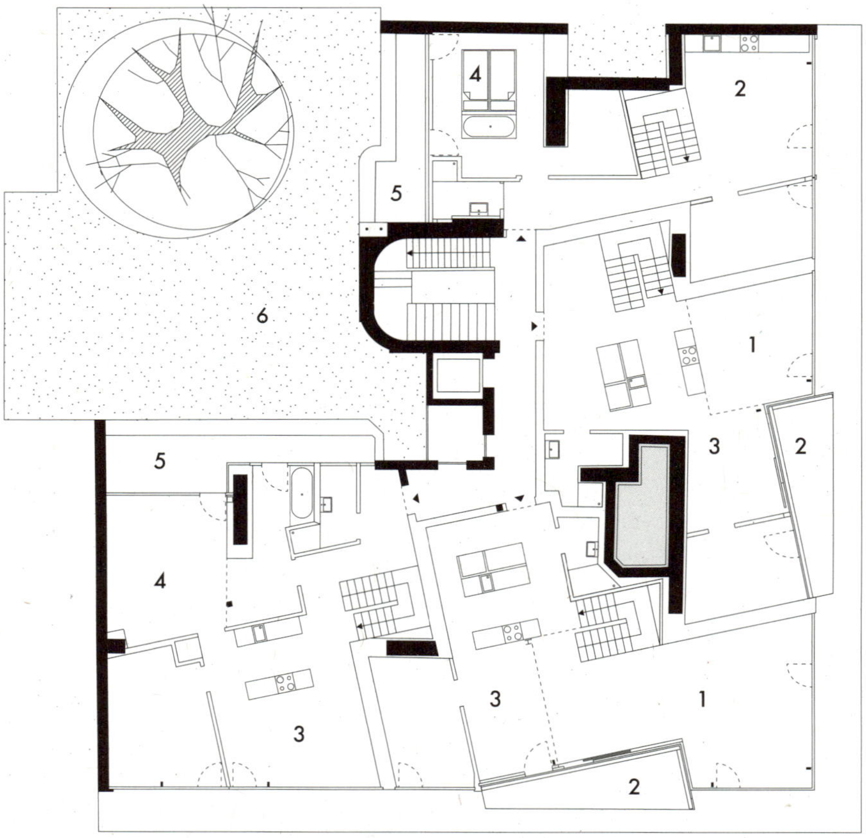

First top floor

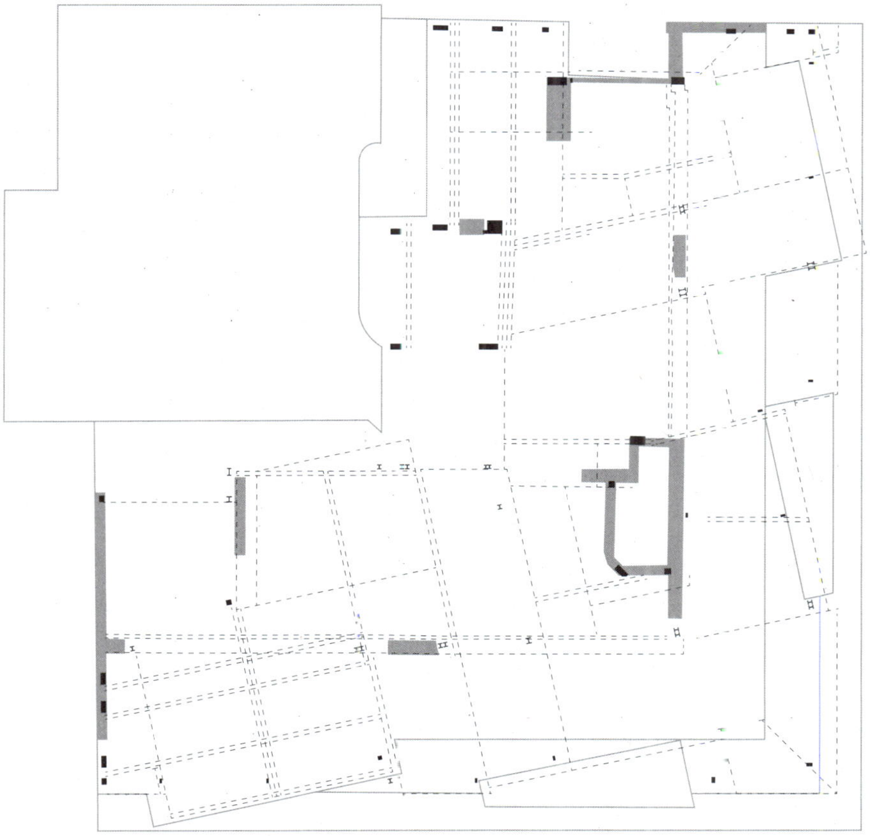

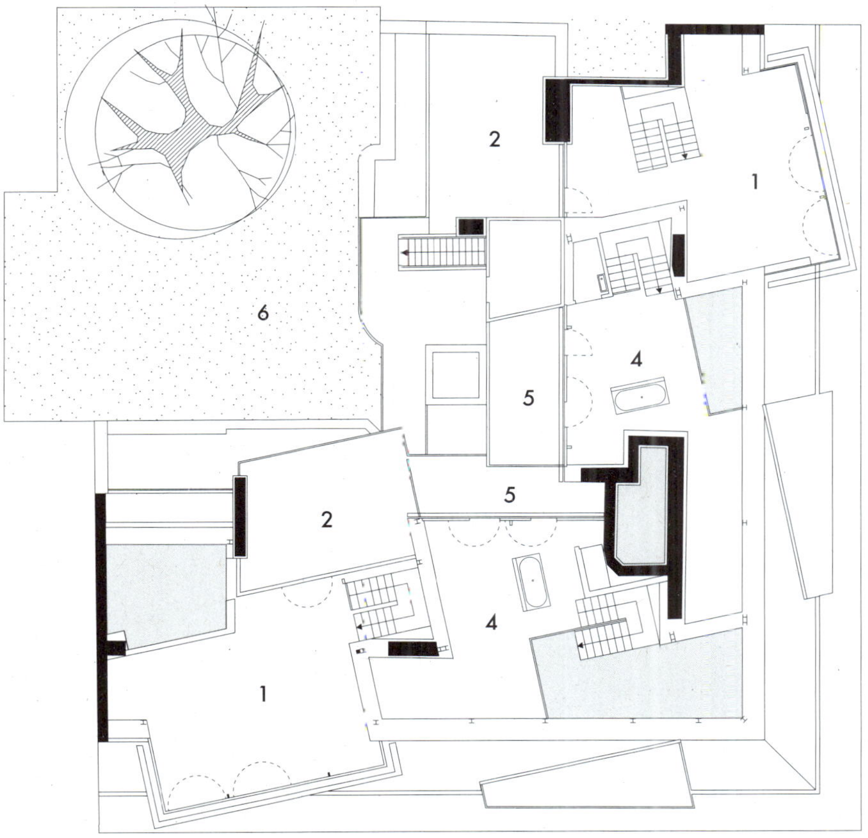

Second top floor

1 Common private space
2 Terraces for relaxation
3 Eating/cooking area
4 Individual space
5 Green filter
6 Semipublic area

1 3 6 10 m

1:250

Detail A / roof

Aluminum composite panel 4 mm
Substructure 90 mm, on 50 mm trapezoidal strip
Double layered bituminous sealing 10 mm
(alternatively: one layer foil)
OSB board 22 mm
Mineral wool 340 mm between rafters 100/340 mm
Plasterboard 15 mm
Plasterboard 15 mm
Vapor barrier 1,500/1,800 mm
Open formwork 27 mm between spring bows

Detail B / floor

Wood flooring 15 mm
Underfloor heating 20 mm
Dry screed fireboard REI60 25 mm
Mineral wool sound impact
insulation insulation 20 mm
Laminated timber ceiling 140 mm
Cap profile 16 mm
Plasterboard 15 mm
Plasterboard 15 mm

Detail C / terrace door

RHS according to statics
Lift- and slide door wood, aluminum
PRO 1,400/800/125 mm with fire-proof coating
Lift- and slide door wood, aluminum
Circumferential sealing tape inside and outside
Wooden threshold

Detail D / terrace floor

Duckboards 40 mm
Gravel 50 mm
Rubber mat 10 mm
Bituminous roof sealing, two layers with vapor
pressure equalization layer 10 mm
Plaster on grating 20 mm
Polyurethane insulation to falls 140 mm
EPS insulation 75 mm (+equalizing layer of
polystyrene concrete max. 20 mm
Vapor barrier
Top concrete layer 65 mm

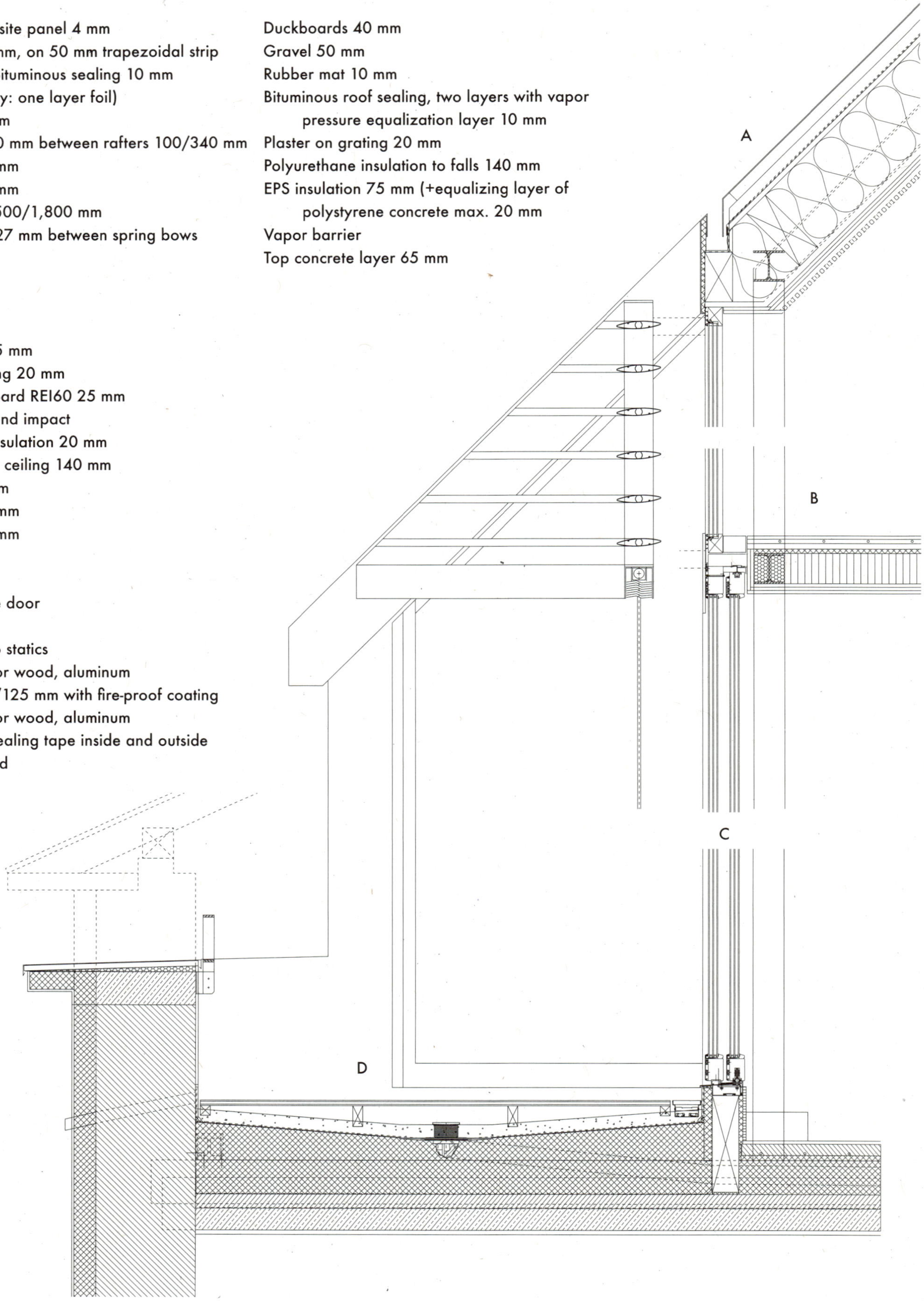

Details
1:25

10 30 60 100 cm

Detail A / roof

Gravel/concrete plates 50 mm
Vapor-permeable membrane
OSB board 22 mm
Mineral wool between timber beams 100/200 mm
Vapor barrier
Open formwork 27 mm between spring bows
Plaster fireboard 15 mm
Plaster fireboard 15 mm
Covering REI60

Detail B / facade

Wooden beam 80/220 mm
Window with circumferential sealing tape
Wood, aluminum tilt-and-turn window
RHS with fire-proof coating 1,400/800/125 mm
External solar shading louvres fixed

Detail C / facade

RHS with fire-proof coating 1,400/800/125 mm
External solar shading louvres fixed
Wood, aluminum tilt-and-turn window
Rock wool insulation strip
Window with circumferential sealing tape
Insulation-filled cladding
Aluminum composite panel A2

Detail D / floor

Wood flooring 15 mm
Underfloor heating 20 mm
Dry screed fireboard REI60 25 mm
Mineral wool sound impact
insulation 20 mm
Laminated timber ceiling 140 mm
Cap profile 16 mm
Plaster fireboard 98/15 +
1x plaster fireboard 15 mm
2x plaster fireboard 15 mm
Expansion joint
Background lighting behind plasterboard
Insulation
Window with circumferential sealing tape
RHS with fire-proof coating 1,400/800/125 mm

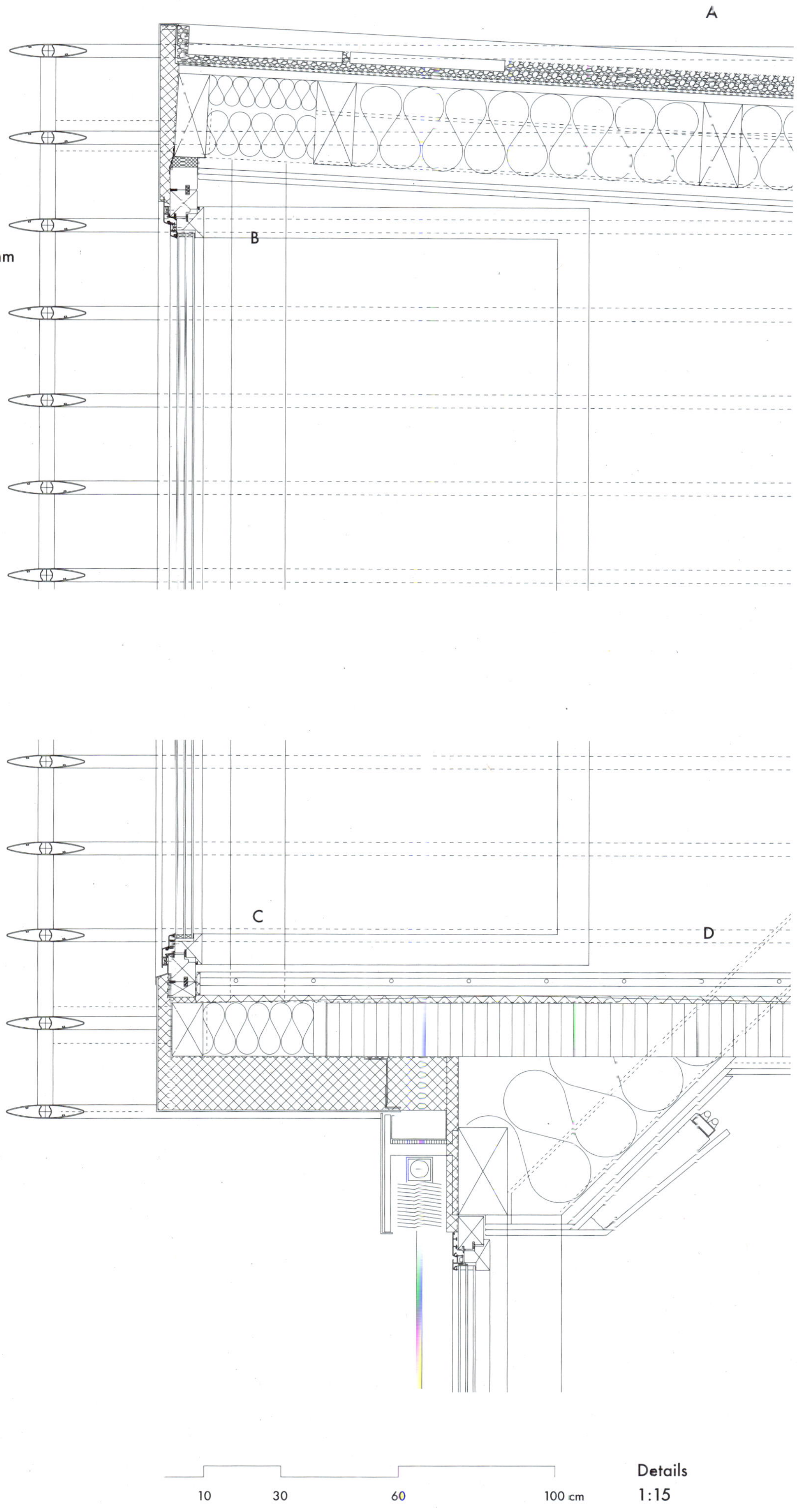

Details
1:15

urban reflections
1010 Vienna, AT

See pp. 68–71

PROGRAM
Rooftop, attic conversion, eight duplex apartments, garage with elevator, green filters, terraces

DIMENSIONS
Covered area 354 m², floor space 1,420 m², useable living area 1,185 m², terraces and green filter 233 m²

CLIENT
A. Muzicant Stiftung, Vienna, Austria

PROJECT TEAM
Marlies Breuss, Michael Ogertschnig, Jan Chladil, Stefan Förg, Stephan Goos, Sven Klöcker, Alexej Kolyschkow, Christian Mörtl, Christian Rottensteiner, Sebastian Uhl

PROJECT COOPERATION
Architekt Weinmann (building renovation and site supervision)

CONSULTANTS
KPPK (structural engineer), Riebenbauer (building systems), Röhrer Bauphysik (building physics), Pasteiner (roof)

PHOTOGRAPHY
Josef Herfert, HOLODECK architects archive

AWARDS
First prize, invited competition
IFA Award – international prize for facade design
Best Building of the Year 2017 – archdaily housing projects worldwide, nomination

PUBLICATIONS (SELECTION)
Axel Sowa, "Combles viennois, Vienne, Austriche," *l'architecture d'aujoud'hui*, Paris, May–June 2006 (ISBN 2-858938571).
Christine Müller, "Meister der Spurensuche," *SKIN – Das Fachmagazin für intelligente Gebäudehülle 1*, Vienna, May 2012.

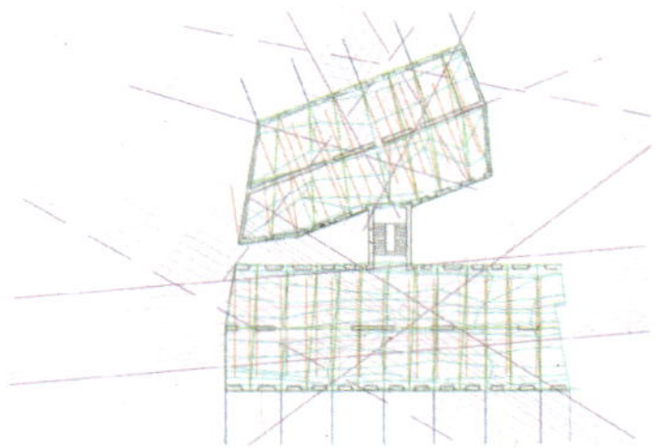

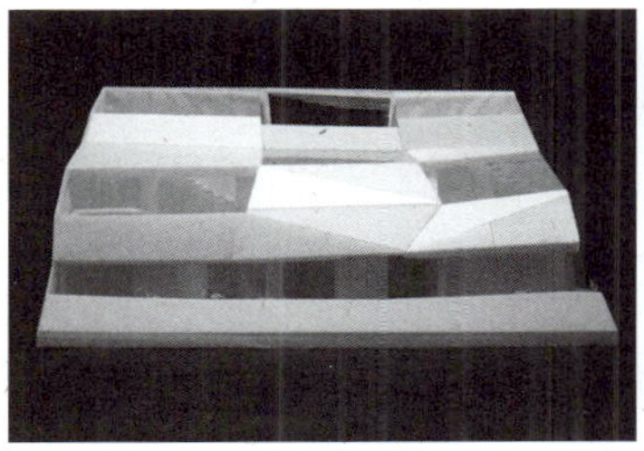

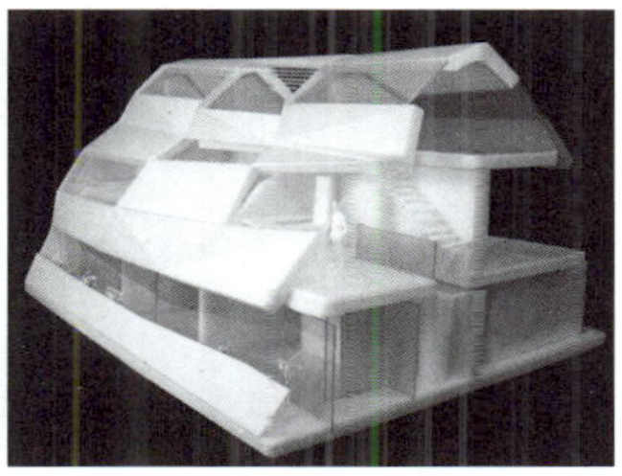

"This work has deeply marked the imagination of dwellings under the attic space."

— Axel Sowa, "Combles viennois," in *l'architecture d'aujourd'hui* 364, 2006, p. 59.

Site plan
1:500

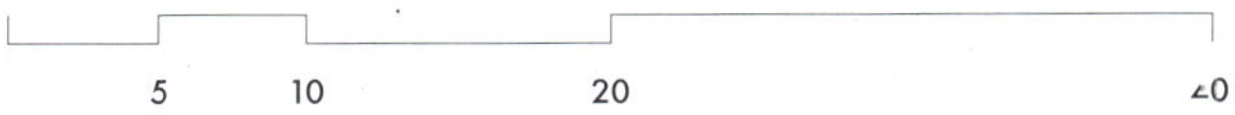

page 325

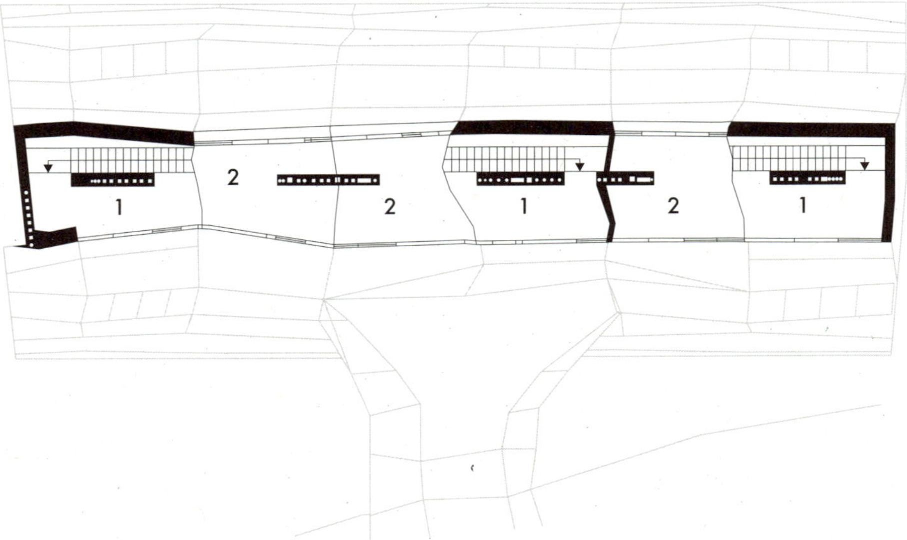

Third top floor

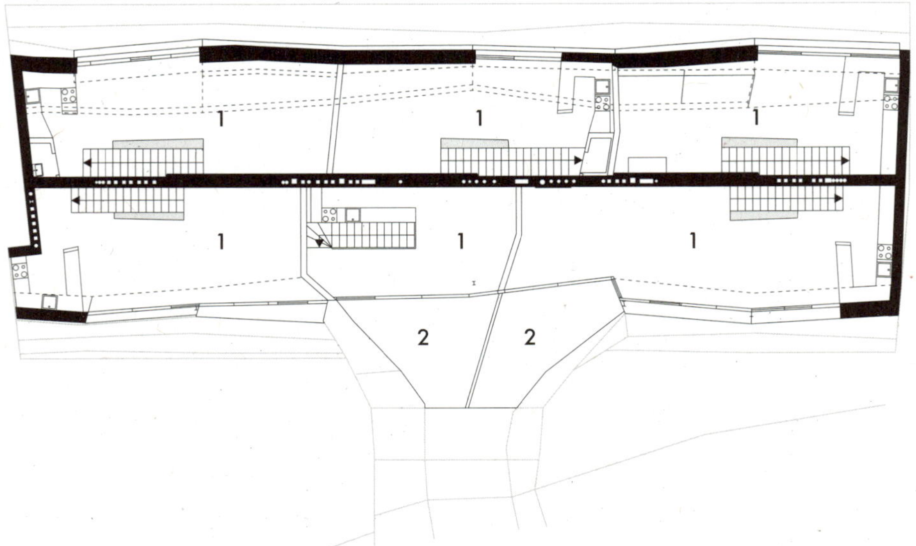

Second top floor

1 Common private space
2 Terraces for relaxation
3 Individual space
4 Green filter
5 Semipublic area

First top floor
1:300

1 3 6 10 15 m

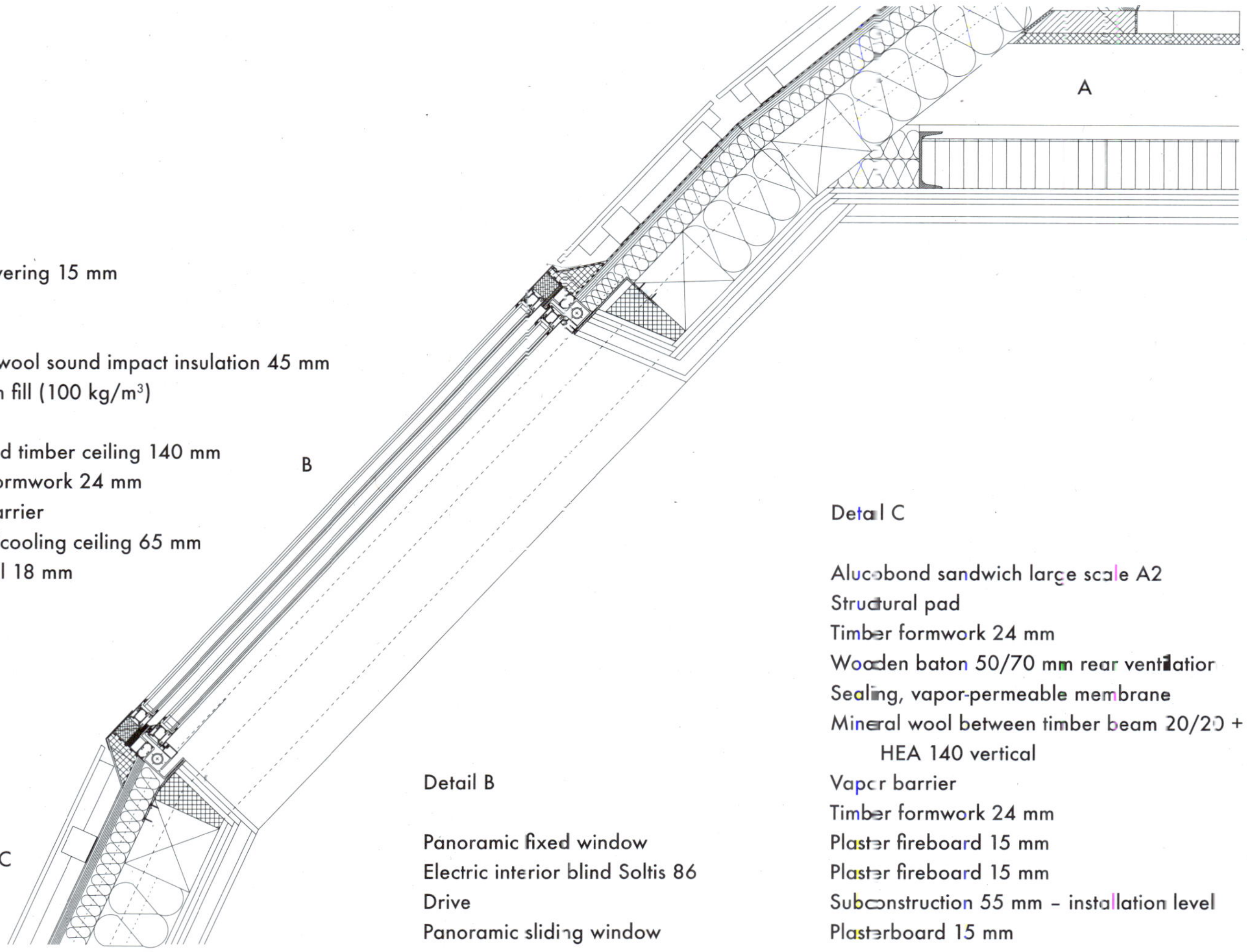

Detail A

Floor covering 15 mm
Dcreed
PE-foil
Mineral wool sound impact insulation 45 mm
Insulat on fill (100 kg/m^3)
PE-foil
Laminated timber ceiling 140 mm
Timber formwork 24 mm
Vapor barrier
Heating/cooling ceiling 65 mm
Fermacell 18 mm

Detail B

Panoramic fixed window
Electric interior blind Soltis 86
Drive
Panoramic sliding window

Detail C

Alucobond sandwich large scale A2
Structural pad
Timber formwork 24 mm
Wooden baton 50/70 mm rear ventilation
Sealing, vapor-permeable membrane
Mineral wool between timber beam 20/20 +
HEA 140 vertical
Vapor barrier
Timber formwork 24 mm
Plaster fireboard 15 mm
Plaster fireboard 15 mm
Subconstruction 55 mm – installation level
Plasterboard 15 mm

10 30 60 100 cm

Details
1:20

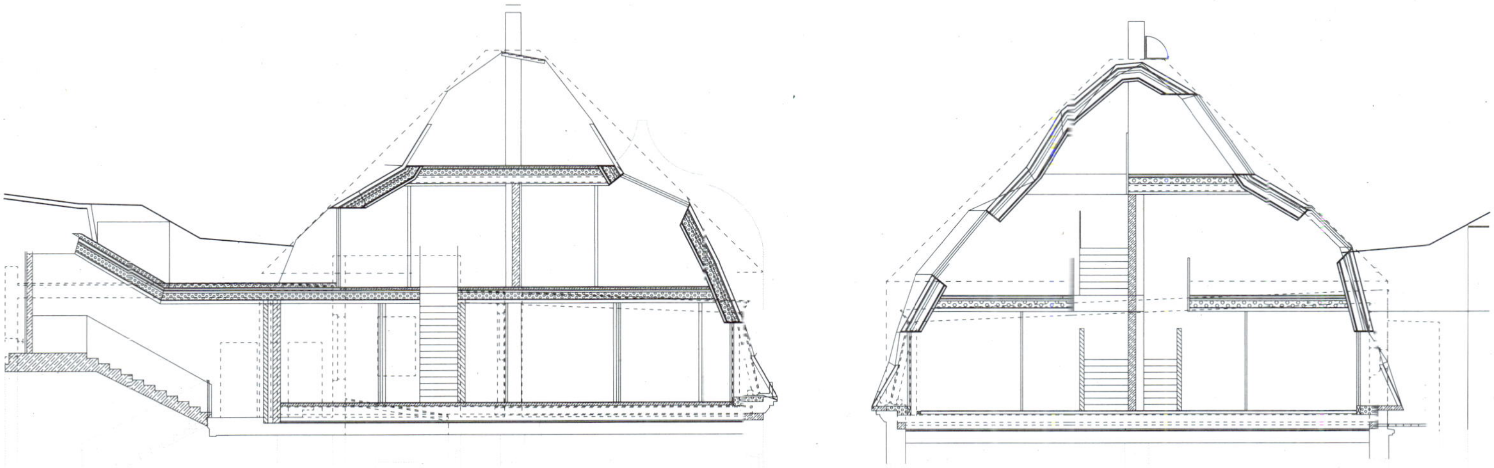

1 3 6 10 15 m

Sections
1:3C0

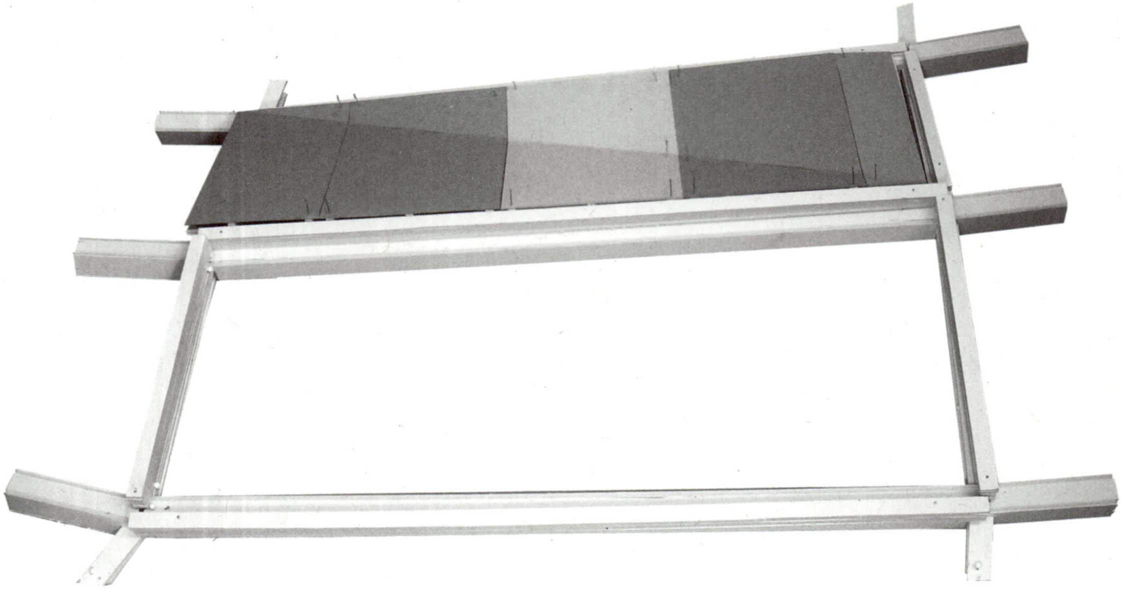

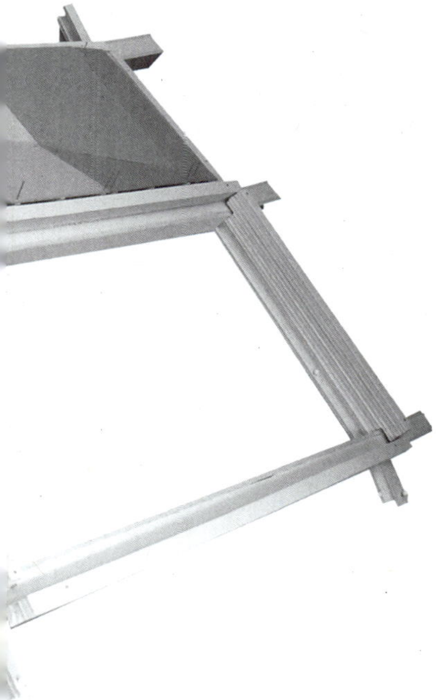

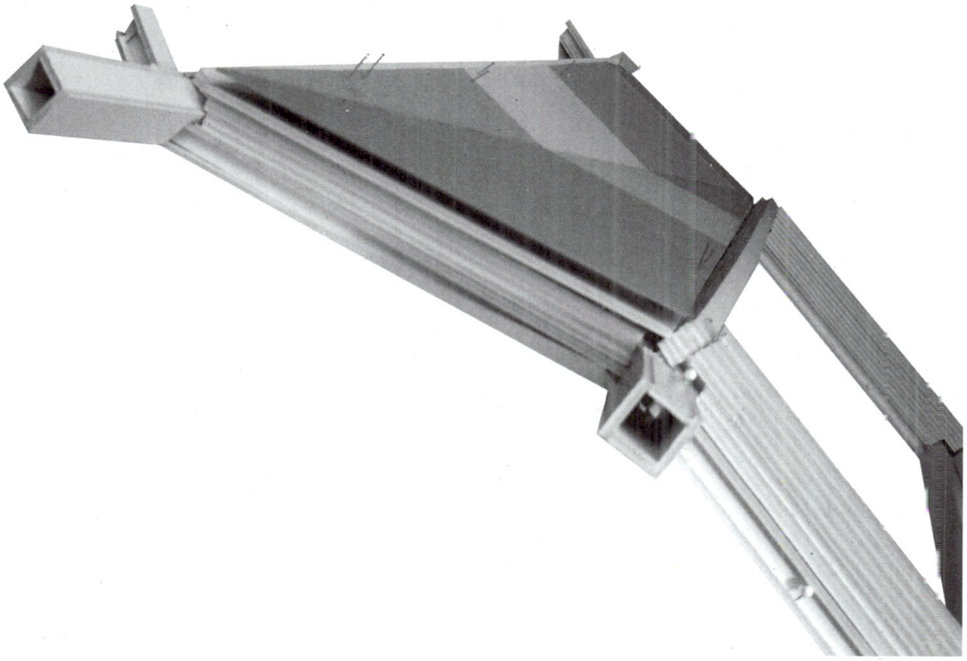

2001–02
HUMAN HABITAT

cliffhouse
4664915 Tel Aviv, IL

PROGRAM
Interior architecture, spatial organization

DIMENSIONS
GFA 1,100 m², plot area 2,200 m²

CLIENT
Private

PROJECT TEAM
Marlies Breuss, Michael Ogertschnig, Christine Schmauszer, Gerold Strehle

PUBLICATIONS (SELECTION)
Annett Zinsmeister and Tobias Wallisser, "Wie gehen wir warum wohin," in *JOUR FIXE Zeitgenössische Positionen in Architektur, Design, Kunst*, Berlin, DOM Publishers, 2010 (ISBN 978-3-86922-034-5).
Nick Dunn, *Architectural Modelmaking*, London, Laurence King Publishing, 2014/2020 (ISBN 88-86701-90-X).

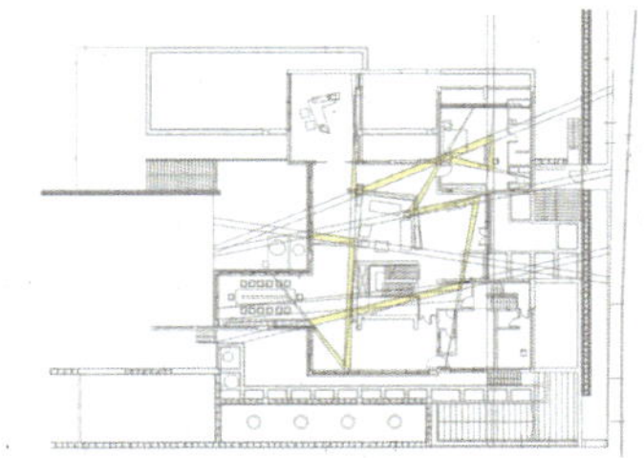
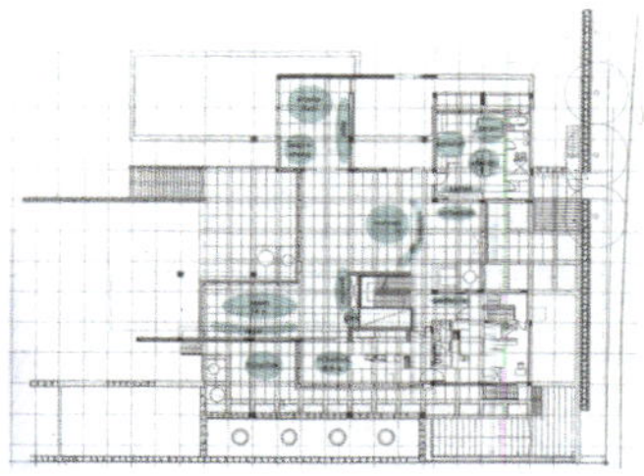
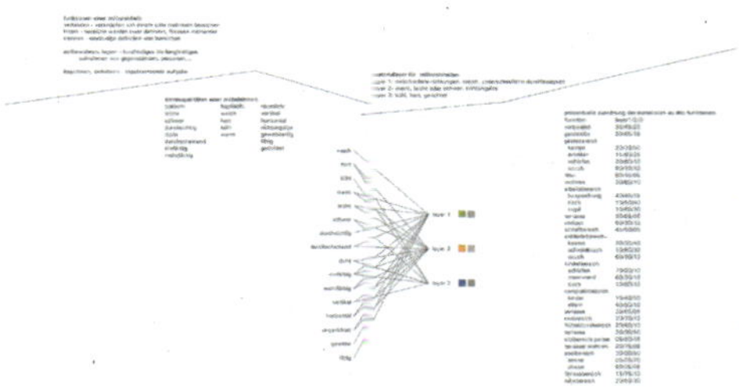
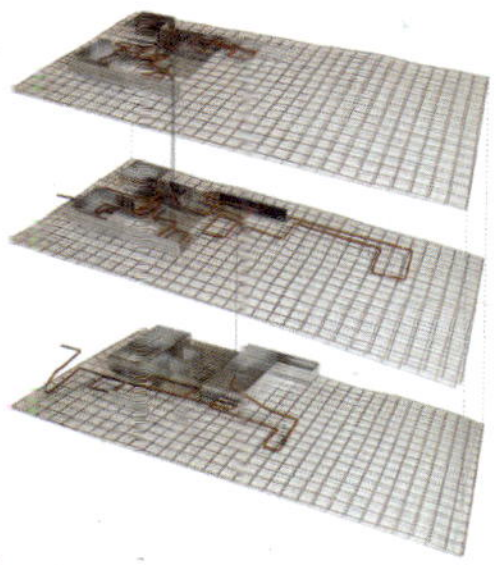

"The concept follows the idea of continuity, reflection, and material overlay. We define a connecting band of space with materials, determined by haptic and spatial textures."

—HOLODECK architects, project description, 2001 (trans. by the ed.)

Site plan
1:1,500

10 30 60 100 m

page 333

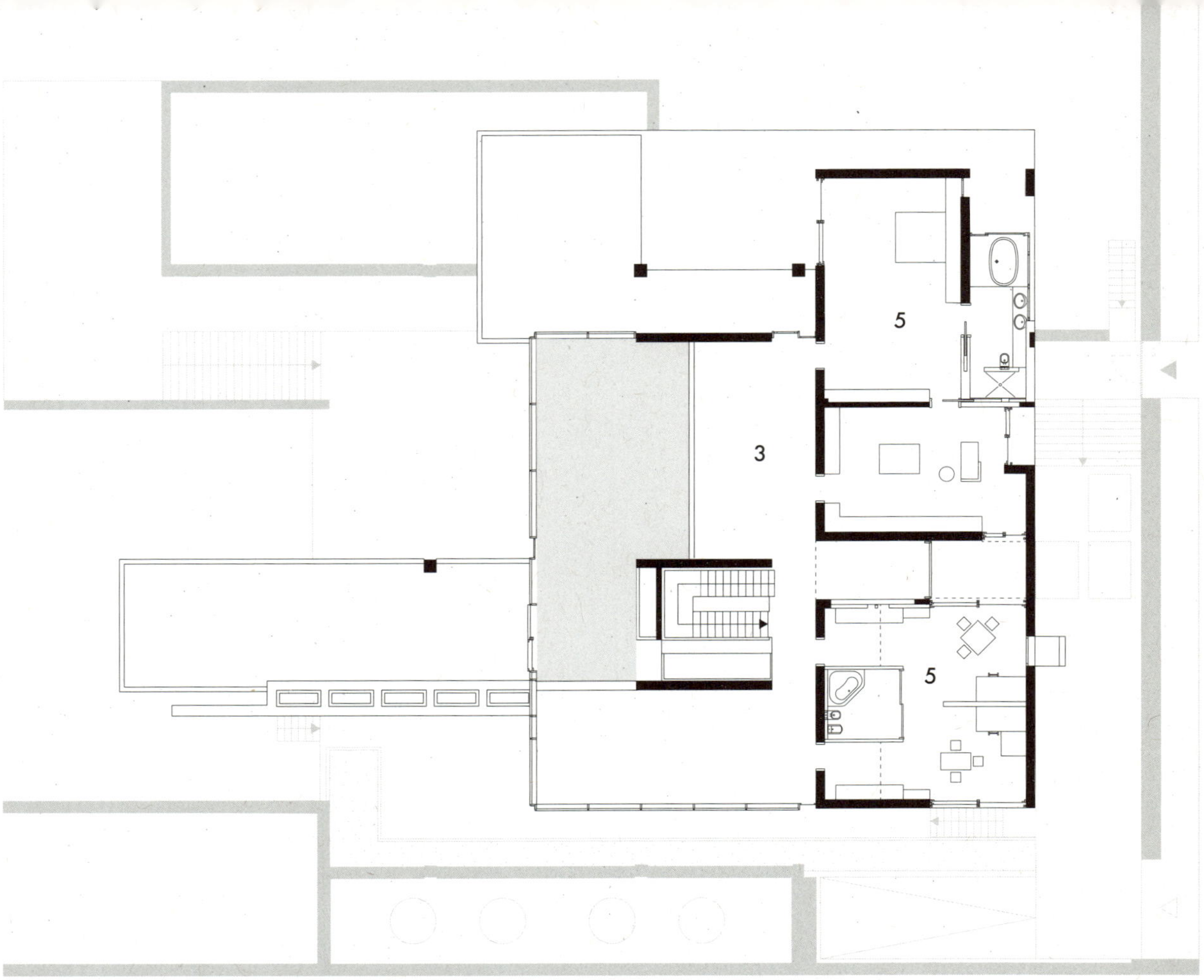

First floor

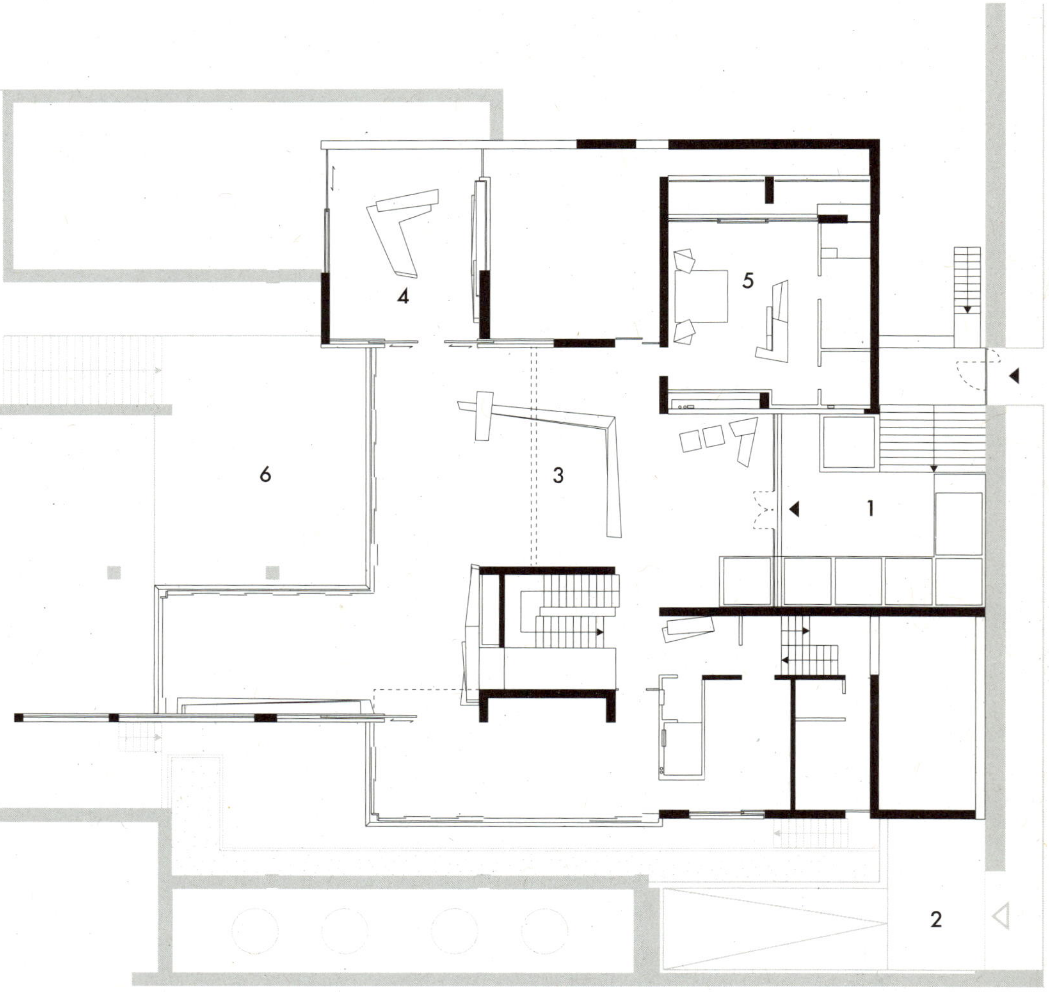

1 Entrance
2 Entrance to garage
3 Common private space
4 Working area
5 Individual private spaces
6 Terraces for relaxation

Ground floor
1:300

1 3 6 10 15 m

Ground floor – filter

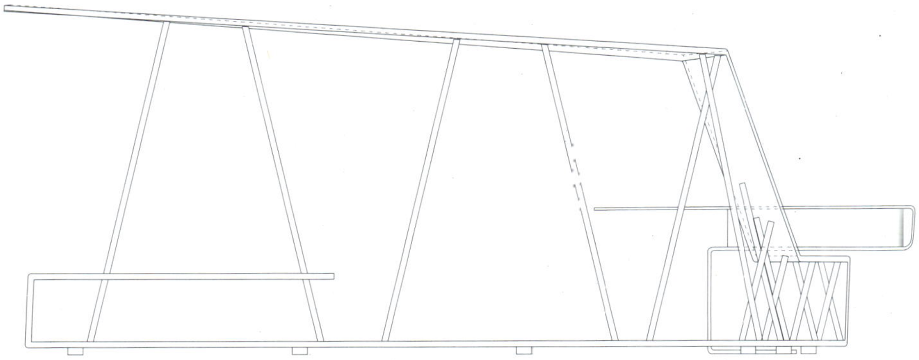

Longitudinal elevation – filter

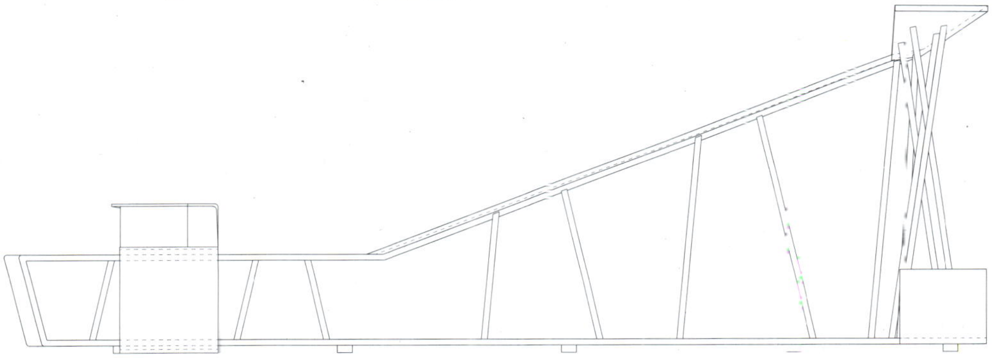

Lateral elevation – filter

10 30 60 100 cm 1:50

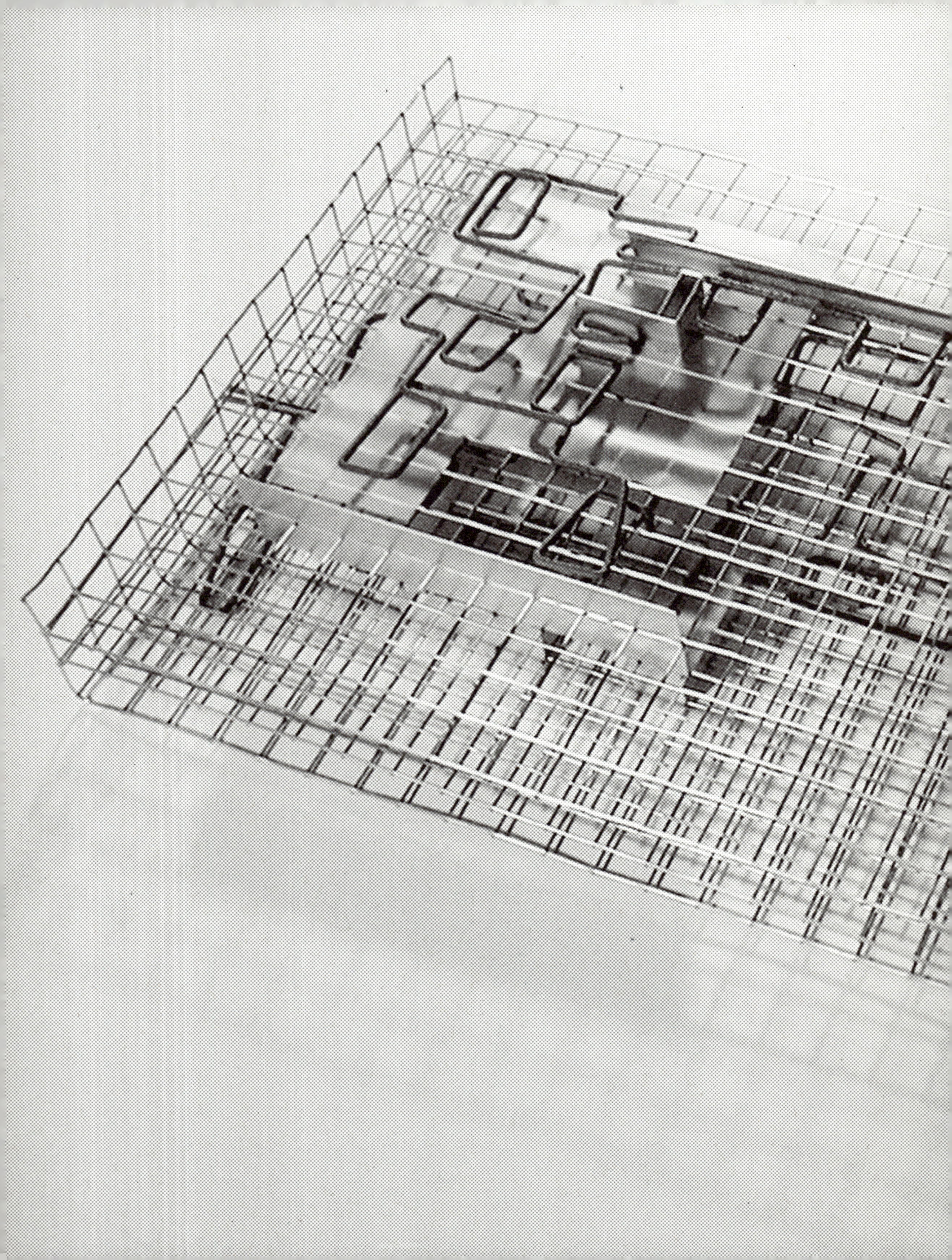

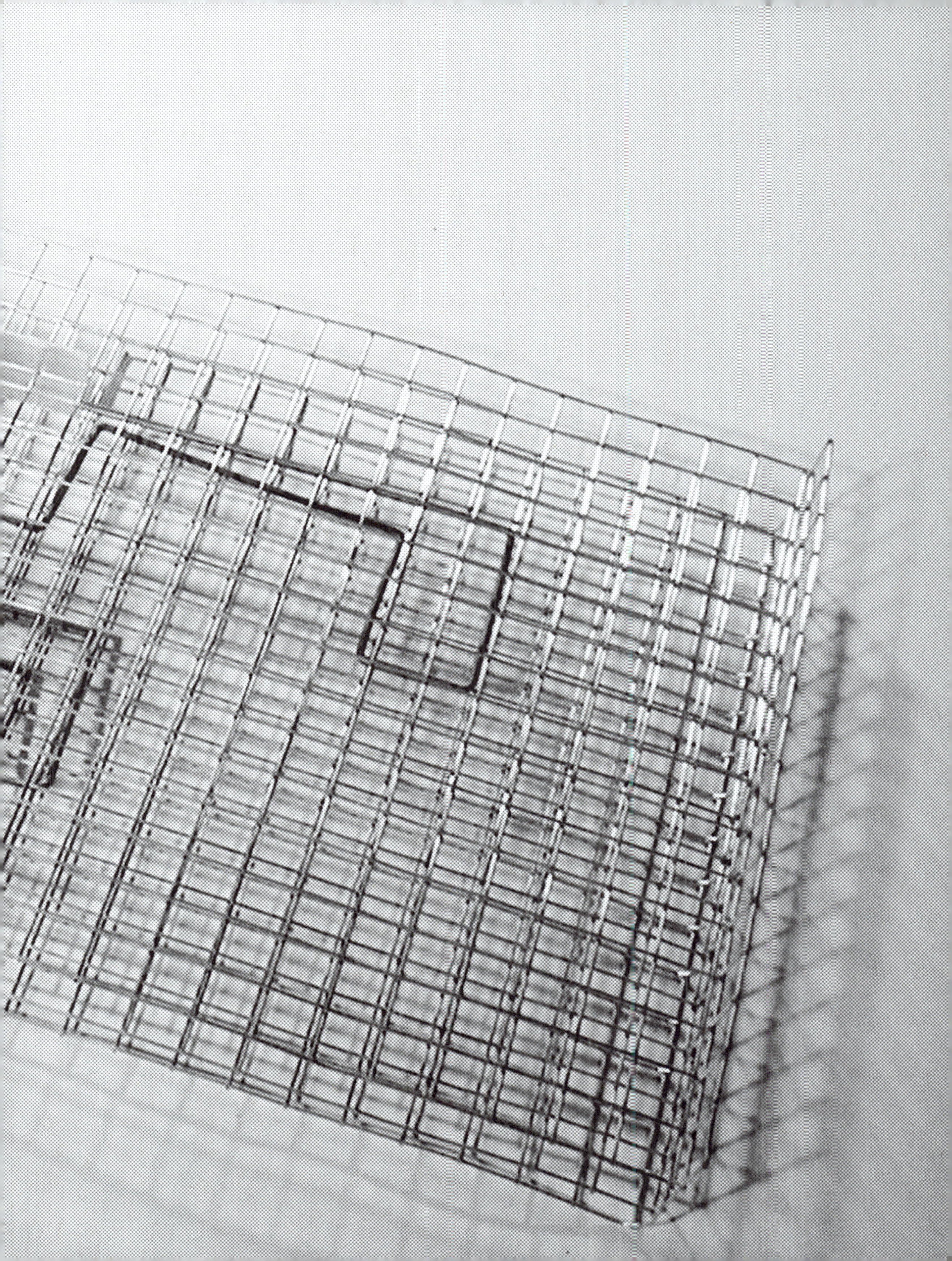

spatial appropriation
1170 Vienna, AT

See pp. 72–76

PROGRAM
Residential building, former textile production space, restructure, conversion

DIMENSIONS
Useable living area 175 m^2 and terraces 34 m^2

CLIENT
Private

PROJECT TEAM
Marlies Breuss, Michael Ogertschnig, Stephan Goos

CONSULTANTS
KPPK (structural engineer), Röhrer Ziviltechniker (building physics)

PHOTOGRAPHY
Grazia Ike Branco

PUBLICATIONS (SELECTION)
Isabella Marboe, “Inseln im Raumfluss,” *Der Standard*, Vienna, September 19, 2007.
“Architektur von Innen,” *Architekturtage 2006*, Vienna, May 17, 2006.
“Architekturtage Österreich,” *ZIB 1*, ORF 1, Vienna, Austria, June 11, 2006.

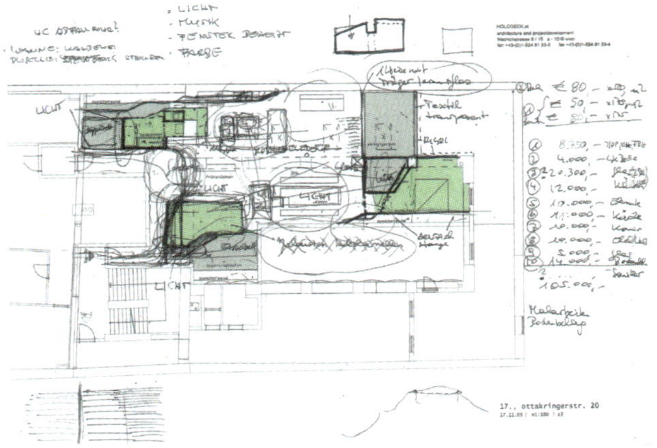

“Organically shaped runners suspended from the ceiling define different islands of space where you can indulge in mental and physical well-being.”

—Isabell Marboe, “Inseln im Raumfluss,” *Der Standard*, September 15, 2007, p. 12 (trans. by the ed.)

Site plan
1:830

10 25 50 m

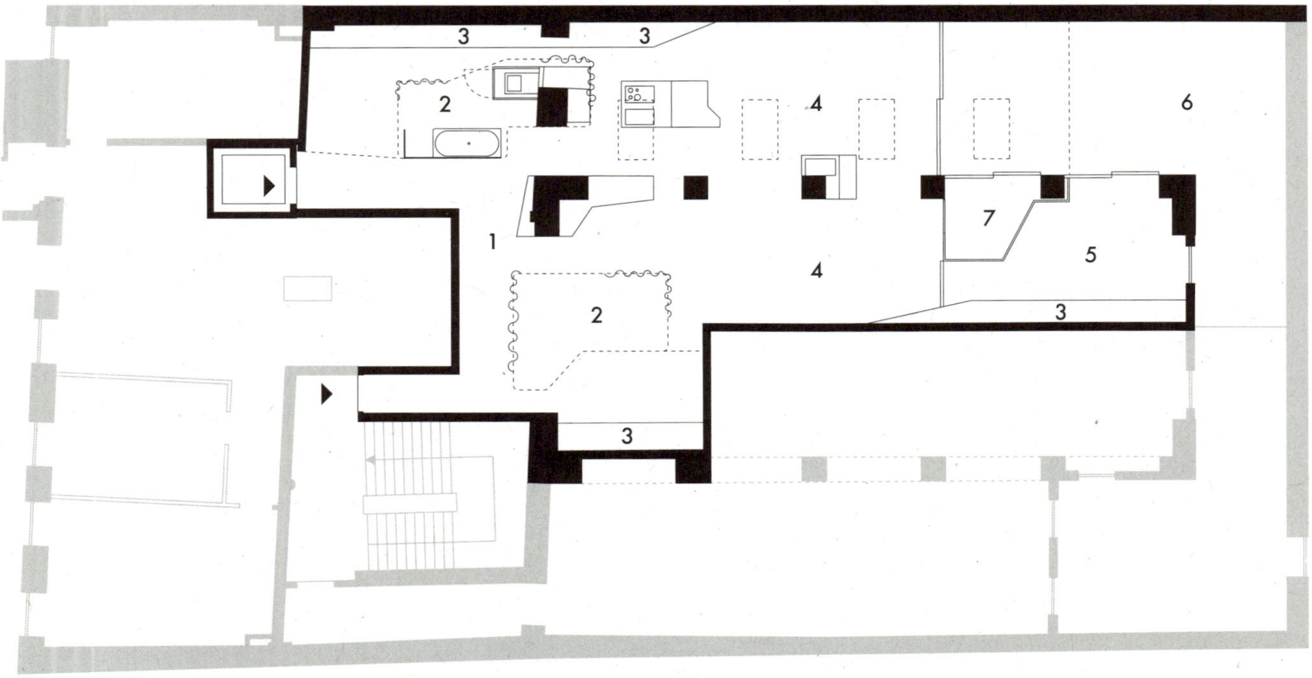

Ground floor

1 Entrance
2 Temporary spaces
3 Storage spaces
4 Common private space
5 Individual space
6 Terraces for relaxation
7 Winter garden

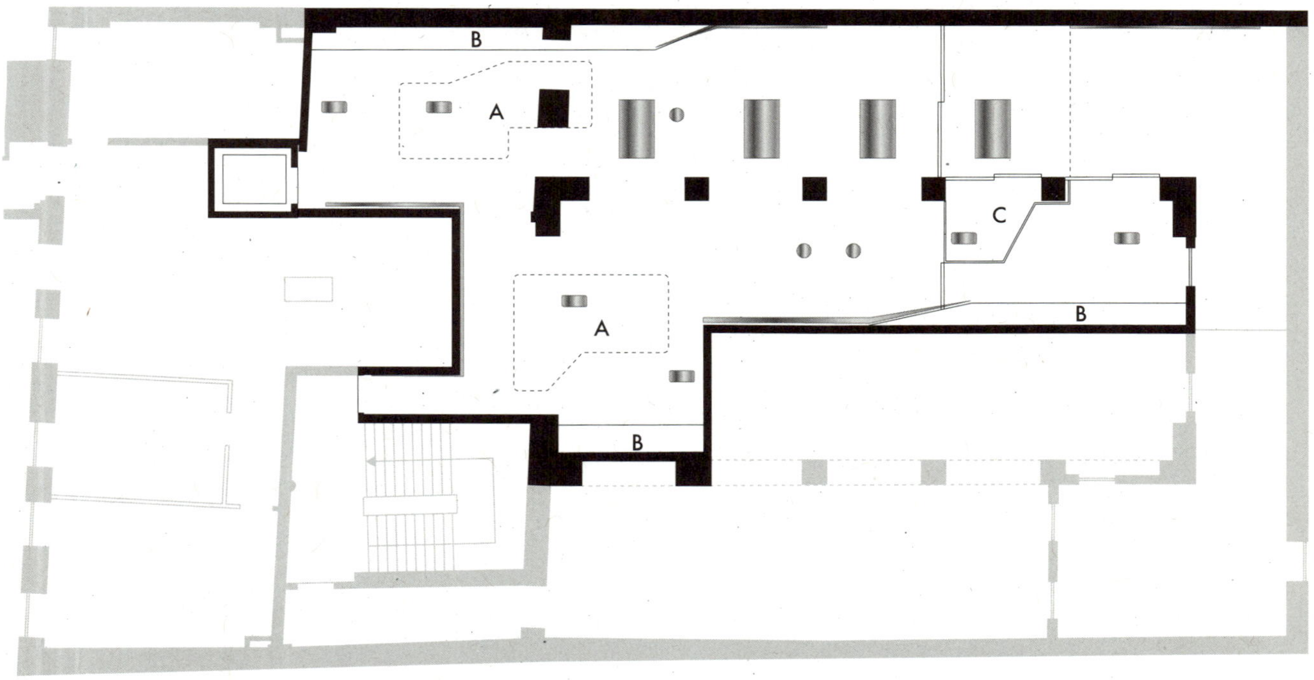

A Temporary spaces
B Storage spaces
C Plant area
Light spaces

1:200

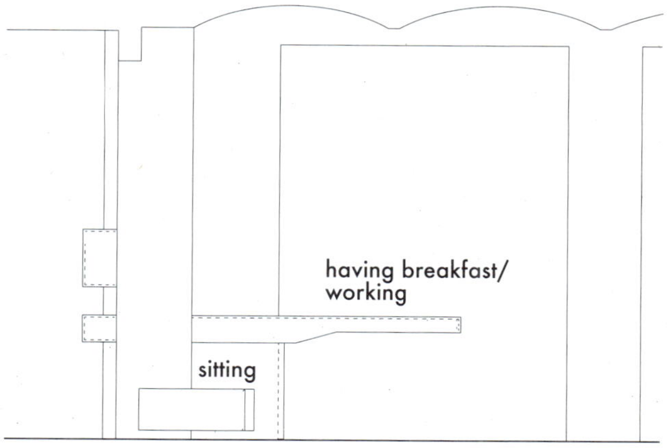

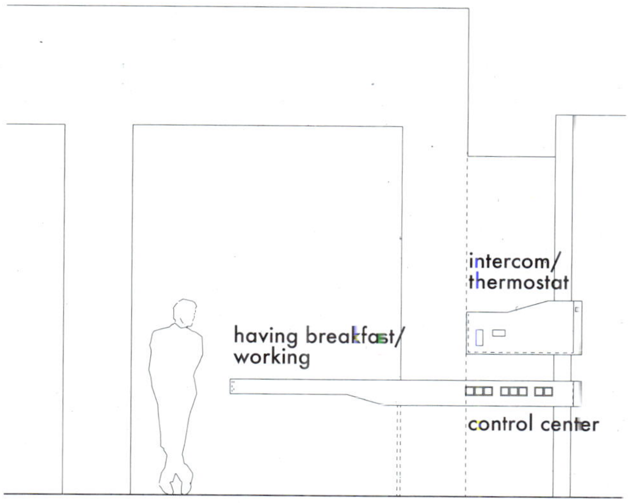

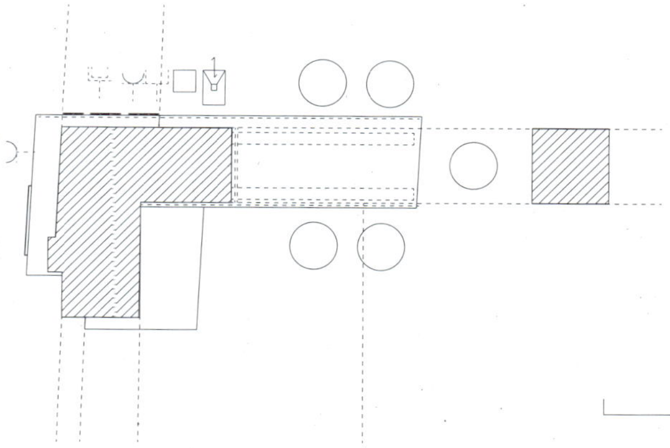

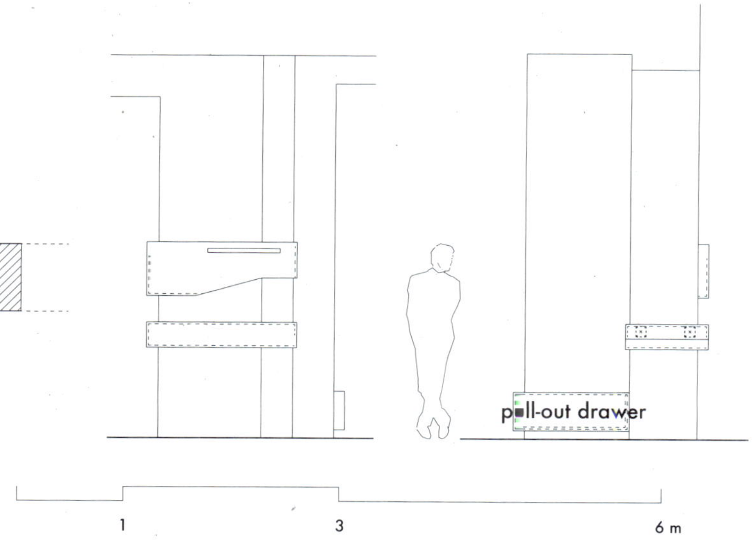

Details
1:70

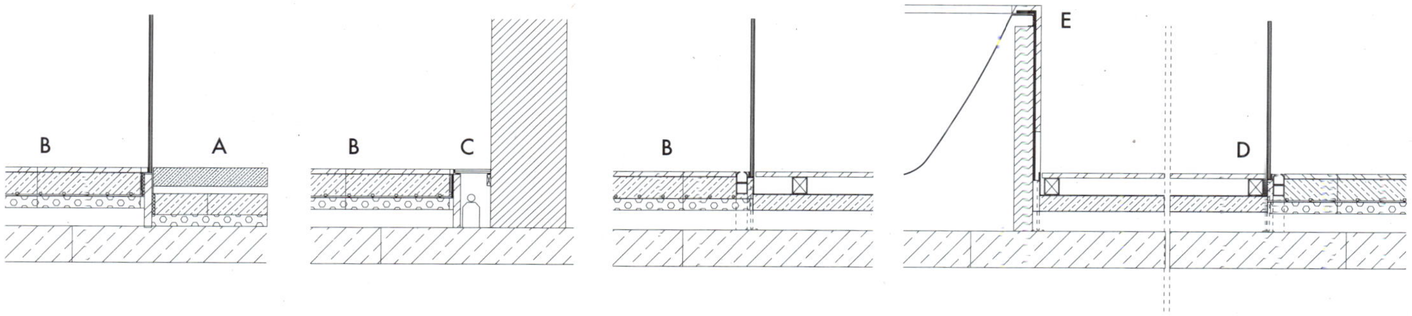

Detail A / floor construction

Screed tiles 60/60 mm
Mortar bed 20 mm
Anhydrite screed 50 mm
Foil
Impact sound insulation board 32 mm

Detail B / floor construction

Parquet Wenge 14 mm
Anhydrite heating screed 64 mm
Foil
Impact sound insulation board 32 mm
Equalizing layer EPS W/20 50 mm

Detail D / glass partition wall

Toughened glass 10 mm
Runner 30 × 30 mm flush to the floor (U/S)
Metal bracket for glass
h: 14 mm, w: 12 mm
Base, height adjustable for shower tray
Wooden grating on subconstruction

View bathtub

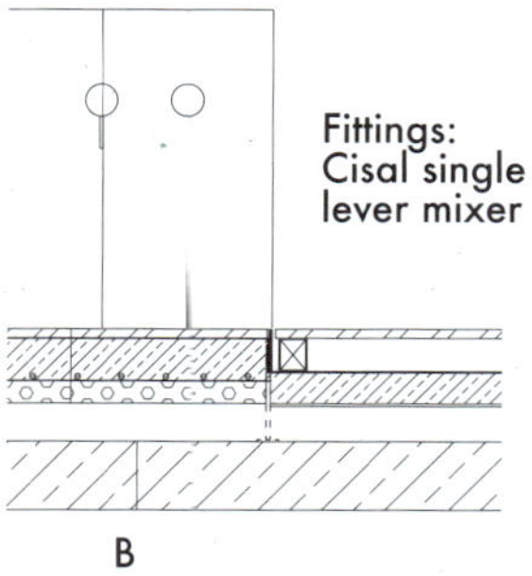

Detail C / floor wall joint

Laminated sheet glass (LSG) 10 mm
Mounting strip 15 mm
Form board 20 mm

Detail E / bath

Bathtub 1,800 × 800 mm
Bath cladding
Wenge on mounting plate

10 30 60 100 cm

Details
1:20

ALLOVER LANDSCAPE

22 tops

2002–08

The public developer Gemeinnützige Wohnungsgesellschaft der KELAG acquired a property on the edge of the town of Wolfsberg next to agricultural land and a constellation of single-family homes. In the 1970s, the company put up a three-story building that aroused discontent among locals because of its large scale and the impact on their homes. *22 tops* settles into its surrounding context, preserving scale and the views of the immediate next-door single-family homes and the adjacent larger-scale building; during the approval process, the continuation of the project was supported by all neighbors. The development takes on the narrow site's east–west positioning, including an embankment, which had been described as too complicated for an affordable social housing complex supported by public funds. The design is based on the continuing landscape of adjacent fields folding into user spaces, creating apartments with private terraces, balconies, and loggias next to semipublic outdoor areas on the ground level. Thus, the elongated body of the scheme gradually tapers its mass down from four stories, embedding itself in the ground and creating a two-story development with units on the other side, leaving open views for neighboring houses.

That architectural folding is supported by structural elements using insulated concrete masses and white plaster, while all other walls are filled with dark, air-ventilated and corrugated plexiglass mounted in lightweight modules. A glass foyer relieves any sense of the mass of the apartment block, allowing for direct views onto the entrance area that leads to the vertical circulation, elevator, and stairs. In the parking lot below the building complex, parking places are embodied into the land to allow cross ventilation via natural air supply, and bicycle storage and waste cans are sited outside, easily accessible from the street. The continuity from landscape to architectonic folding creates an architectural structure that adapts to the surrounding nature and the wishes of all residents.

roof landscape

2010–11

This project offers an expansion atop an existing residential building in the densely urbanized eighth district of Vienna, limited by varying zoning regulations. It spreads over a narrow area, 76 meters long but only 8 meters wide, in between other residential properties and abuts a major street at the front end, offering an expansive view across garden treetops at the back. Responding in shape to the changing heights of neighboring buildings, as well as being guided by the Viennese zoning laws that fundamentally direct its development. The roof proposal offers possibilities for various semipublic break-out spaces for all residents, as well as for the new one- and two-story apartments directly beneath.

Within this narrow site, *roof landscape* provides differently usable terraces and gardens available to children, families, and the elderly who have limited access to green areas, especially in this dense district, with its lack of parks. Areas for urban gardening, sports and games, communication, and relaxation are located on top of the building. The lower levels are connected by three staircase cores that give residents the chance to escape the confines of existing small apartments of around 30 square meters.

looped house

1999–2001

The design of *looped house* evolved from the natural continuation of the surrounding landscape into the main building layout. The house sits on a gentle slope in Grossweikersdorf, part of the hill above the village where the central church designed by Joseph Emanuel Fischer von Erlach stands. By using the slope to provide direct access to an upper and lower level, the building merges with the surrounding contours, and a natural split level can be created. For example, an approaching bicycle or car moves down and vanishes below the terrace platform adjacent to the living area, and enters the home from downstairs. Self-propelled guests and residents, on the other hand, walk up a slight inclination and share the main entrance with a small view onto that terrace platform.

Internally, the overall layout of the house is based on a rise of four levels. After one enters, a ramp next to the entrance leads across a half-landing directly into the living space, thus giving access to the southwest-facing terrace above the open-air parking. A second pathway at ground level leads guests via a multifunctional and top-open sanitary area to the dining and cooking space, which has a northeast facing breakfast terrace attached. Beside the long half-story ramp, a staircase directly connects all four levels. The family's private rooms are on the west side of the building and incorporate direct access into the large west-orientated garden. Ceiling-to-floor windows are carefully positioned in large format, and residents will experience a variety of different viewpoints as they move across the house's various levels.

In view of the land footprint of single-family plots *looped house* was designed from the outset as a part of a *Teppichsiedlung* (carpet settlement), allowing potential new buildings to connect along all sides of the plot, without any intrusion or disruption to the family's well-being.

embedded house
2005–08

On the edge of Heiligengeist, a small village between Gailtal and Drautal, there is a hillside with extensive green land next to some homes, with an astounding view toward the city of Villach. Here sits the *embedded house*. Using the typology of the barn and the descending slope, this family home is embedded in the natural topography. From the road the building looks like no more than a roof covering a parking space for vehicles. The residence itself is interwoven with the landscape, creating outside spaces for relaxation and communication. Structurally, the house is made of exposed concrete on the inside and, on the outside, an earth-toned plaster facade that echoes the natural colors of its immediate vicinity.

On the upper floor, one large, fluid space serves family life, including a shaded outdoor area, and it also includes the parents' rooms. On the lower level there are two children's rooms with an adjacent outside play area connected to the landscape. On all sides facing east, south, and west, the large double-glazed wooden window frames extend from floor to the ceiling except some spatial creations for seats and protection. A small gravel path follows the glass line to protect the floor from being watered by condensation along the inner glass.

To integrate the elongated building into its surroundings, the roof is covered with 30 centimeters of soil and plants.

floating house
2003–05

This project reflects the longing of urban families for a house in the countryside, away from a stressful life and embedded in a joyful landscape. *floating house* embodies characteristics of a refuge, so that the family can leave behind all traces of rushed and pressured working life. For this reason, the small working space is adjacent to the main house, only accessible by separate entrance, making this area into a transitional zone between city and countryside. Family members can therefore physically leave the urban context behind, the moment they step through the front door and enter the landscape-like house.

The layout of the house itself is driven by the user program, specified by the family members using our diagram strategy, as well as by the concept of moving away from the earth into the air. *floating house* creates a continuity between outside and inside, between being anchored on the ground and floating in the air, between realistic and conceptual, between the built environment and nature. Arranged following a pattern of continuous movement, the interior spaces start at the level of adjacent landscape and move upward until they are hovering above the ground, where they become an extensive projection of the surroundings. Each change of direction marks a change of function. The wardrobe and the living areas are on the split-level ground-floor, followed by the dining and cooking space with its view onto the upper inner courtyard and, on the other side, the village. The parents' master sleeping and private retreat zones are around the first corner, followed by the children's spaces with a direct entry to the upper courtyard. The upper level, which is 25 meters long, draws the surrounding farmland and woods into the inner spaces through a huge glass window, while underneath it the whole-family rooms on the ground level extend into the landscape.

earthquake memorial
2004

The proposal for the *earthquake memorial* starts with thorough research about earthquakes in Taiwan, as the island is often hit by tremors of different intensities. In 2003, the city of Nantou suffered a major quake and the government of Taiwan decided to donate a memorial to the victims. Close to Nantou, in Taichung City's Wufeng District, the memorial is located on a green area. The approach espouses the idea of an active memorial and does not only serve the culture of memory. It introduces an interactive setting that gives visitors information on historic earthquakes, creates spaces for contemplation and remembrance, but also introduces large-scale structures that react to earth movements and operate as warning signs to the population. A changing topography, with differentiating terrain levels in the center of the memorial garden, hosts the library with books about earthquakes and a café, as well as public services. The park-like landscape, filled with and distant from the residential buildings, allows the memorial to offer different spaces for mourning and for remembrance.

Due to a very active terrain and constant tectonic movements, all large structures reaching into the sky are dedicated to registering the Earth's real-time activities. Transforming accelerograph data readings into frequencies that affect the skin of the four visitors' viewing structures (earthquake responding drums) instantaneously translates Earth movements by changing the color and light intensities of the structures' facades.

22 tops
9400 Wolfsberg, AT

See pp. 88–96

PROGRAM
Residential building, 22 apartments, parking deck, gardens, terraces

DIMENSIONS
Useable living area 1,077 m², balconies and terraces 991 m², covered area 1,930 m²

CLIENT
Gemeinnützige Wohnungsgesellschaft der KELAG, Klagenfurt, Austria

PROJECT TEAM
Marlies Breuss, Michael Ogertschnig, Manuel Garcia Barbero, Gernot Köfer,
Peter Pschill, Christine Schmauszer

PHOTOGRAPHY
Paul Ott

CONSULTANTS
Bau&Plan (construction coordination), energie:bewußt Kärnten (energy),
KFW/Vorstädtische Kleinsiedlung (site supervision), OBERRESSL & KANTZ ZT (structural engineer),
Röhrer Bauphysik (building physics)

AWARDS
Landesbaupreis Kärnten (national construction prize Carinthia), honorable mention
Ugo Rivolta European Award, nomination

PUBLICATIONS (SELECTION)
Nicole Büchl, "Wohnen mit der Landschaft," *architektur fachmagazin*, Laser Verlag, April 2003.
"Wohnen mit der Landschaft," *architektur*, magazine, Laser, Vienna, May 2009.
Otto Kapfinger, in Neue *Architektur in Kärnten*, Salzburg, Pustet, March 2006 (ISBN 3-7025-0515-6).

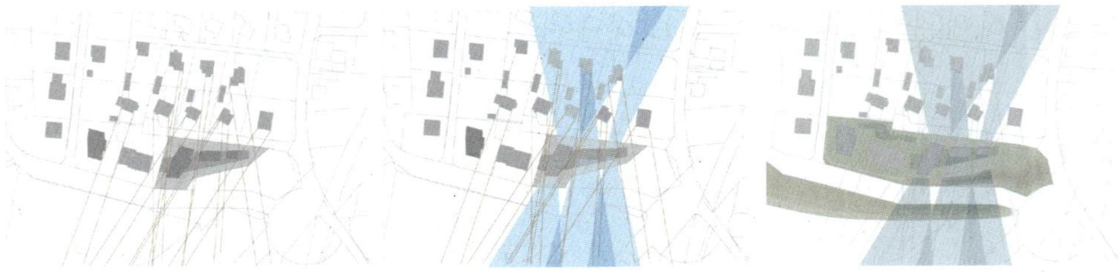

"Like a folded landscape, the building develops out of the landscape and embeds itself, confidently yet discreetly, in the existing surroundings."

—Brigitte Amort, "Bauen im Kontext," in *SKIN*, June 2009, p. 20 (trans. by the ed.)

Site plan
1:750

5 15 30 50 m

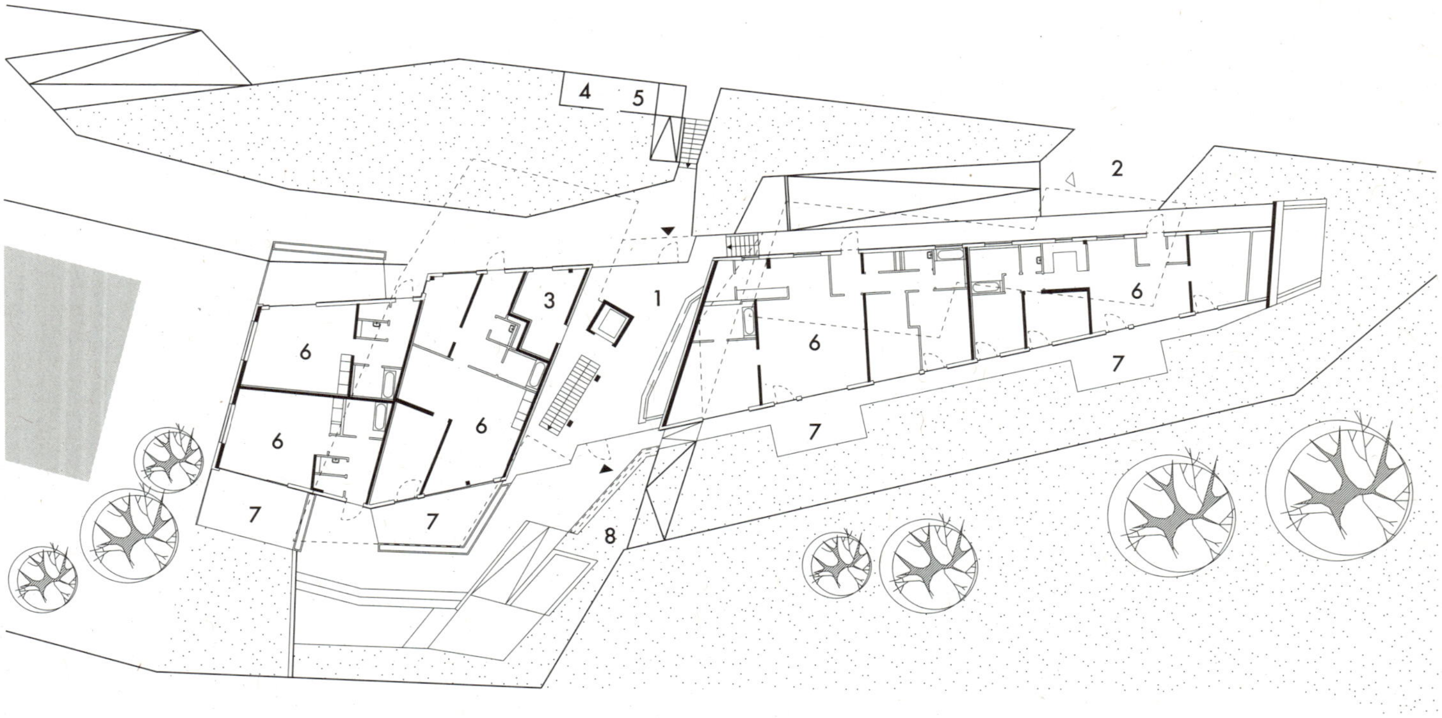

Ground floor

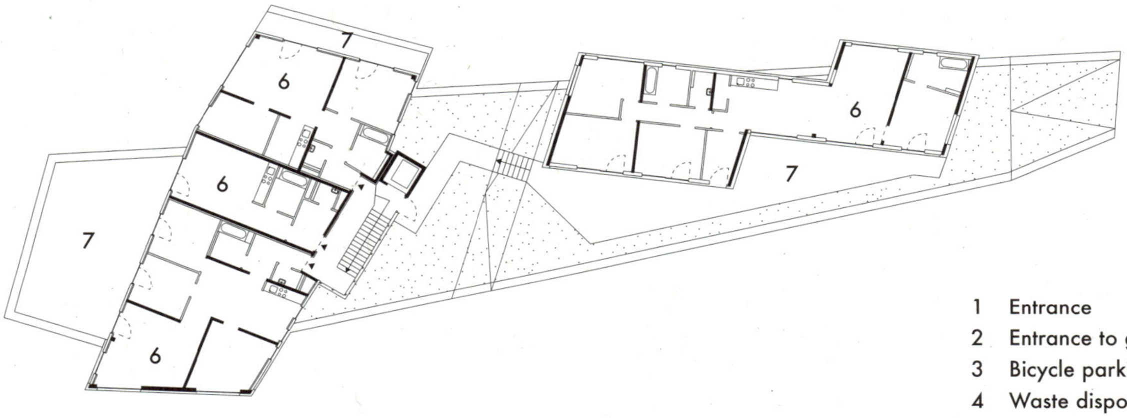

First floor

1 Entrance
2 Entrance to garage
3 Bicycle parking
4 Waste disposal area
5 Storage space
6 Housing unit
7 Terraces for relaxation
8 Semipublic area

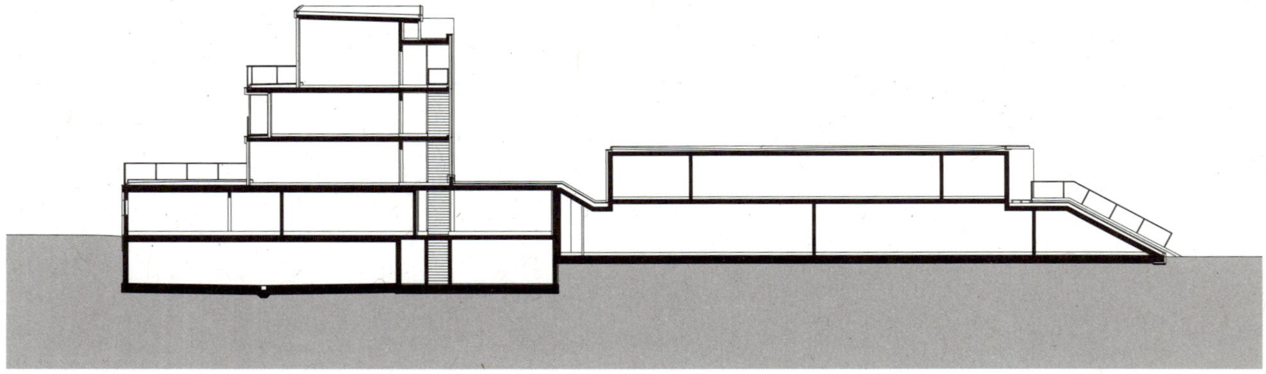

Longitudinal section

1:450

1 3 6 10 m

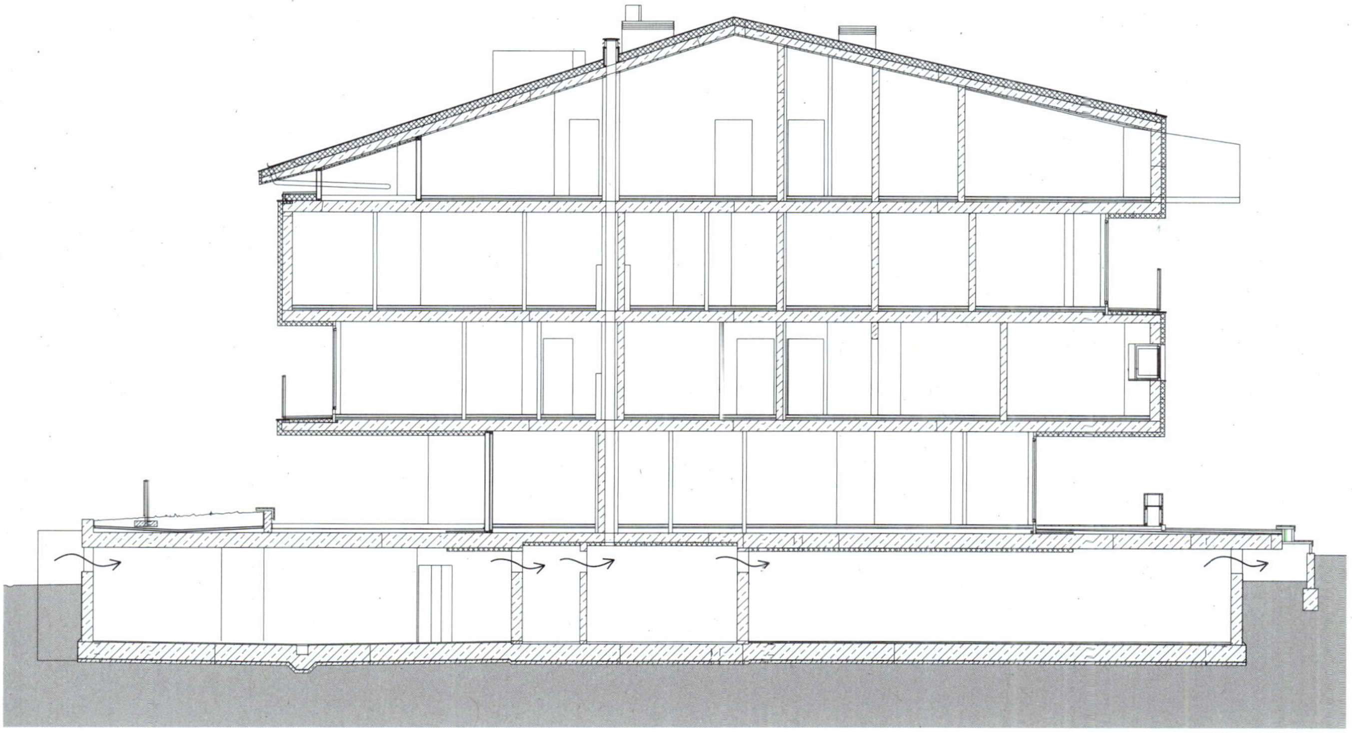

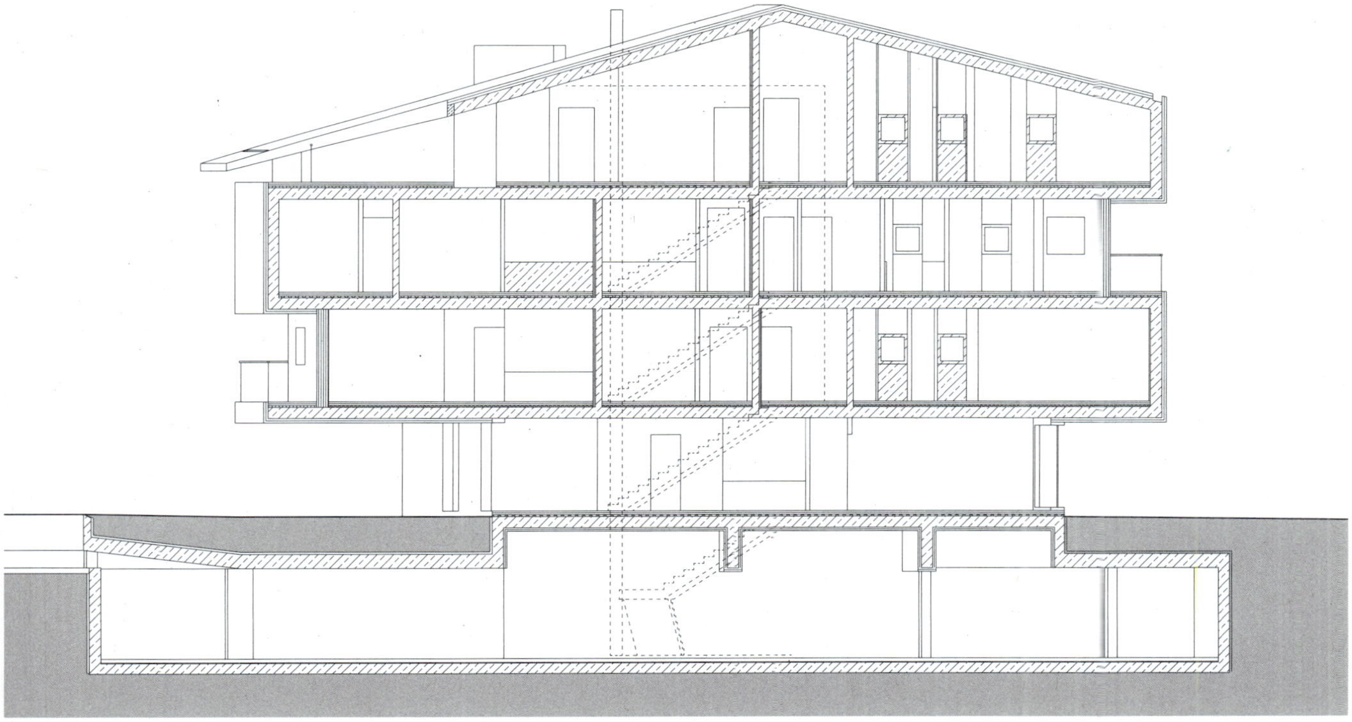

Cross sections
1:200

Detail A / roof

Bituminous sealing with slate granules
Capping sheet 4 mm
Underlay 3 mm
EPS insulation 200 mm
Vapor barrier
Bituminous primer
Reinforced concrete ceiling 260 mm
Plaster-based filler

Detail B / floor

Solid parquet 10 mm
Screed 60 mm
PAE-foil
Mineral wool sound impact insulation 30 mm
Polystyrene light concrete 40 mm
Reinforced concrete ceiling 300 mm
Plaster-based filler

Detail C / facade

Plasterboard 15 mm
Mineral wool/installation level 50 mm
Vapor barrier
OSB board 16 mm
Mineral wool between wooden poles 120 mm
OSB board 16 mm
Vapor-permeable sarking membrane UV-resistant
Perspex wave 21 mm

Detail D

Wood mounting strip

Detail E

Sarking membrane adhesively bonded to concrete

Detail F

EPS insulation 120 mm
Plaster 3 mm

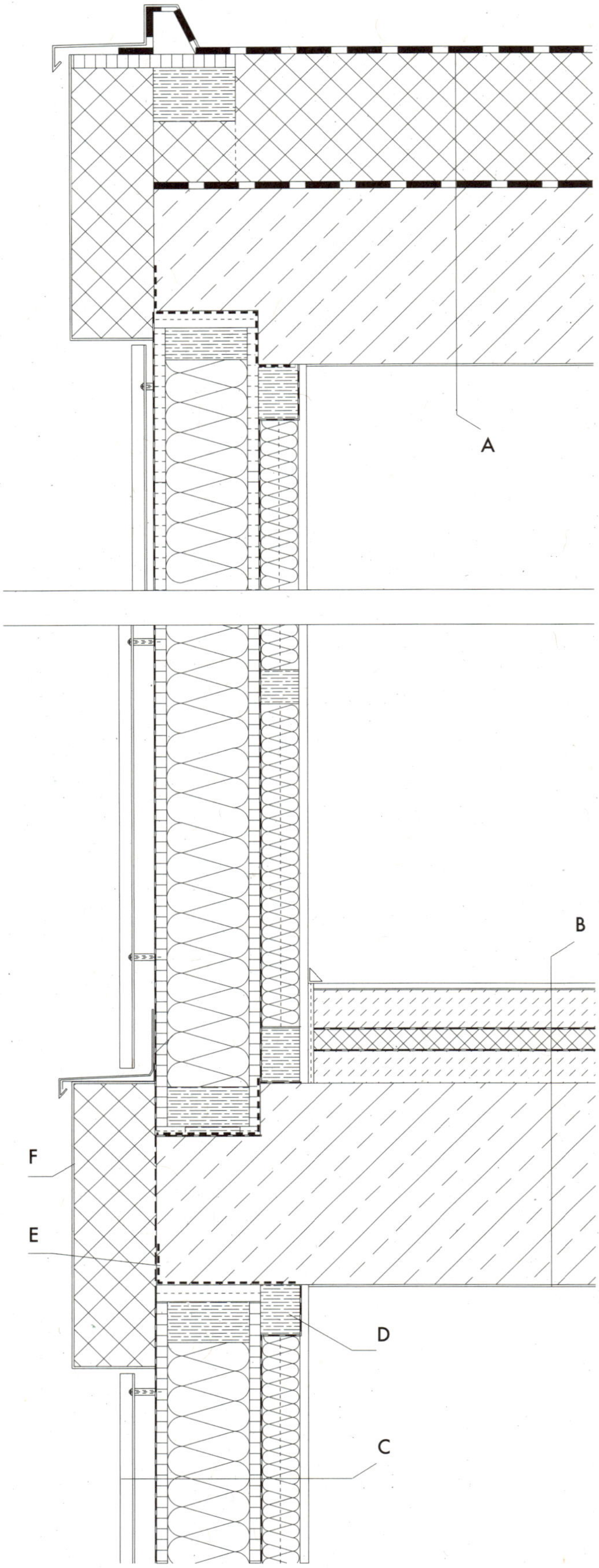

Details
1:10

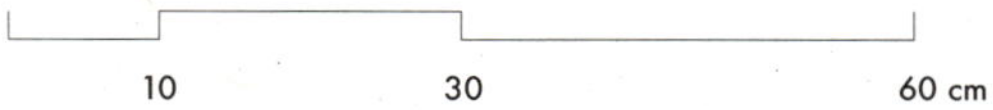

Detail A / extensive green roof

Plant substrate 100 mm
Filter fleece 2 mm
Drainage layer 40 mm
Root-barrier membrane 3 mm
Foil sealing 2 mm
EPS insulation W30 160 mm
Vapor pressure equalization layer
Bituminous primer
Concrete (gradient) reinforced concrete ceiling 300 mm
Plaster

Detail B / ventilated facade

Plasterboard 15 mm
Mineral wool/installation level 50 mm
Vapor barrier
OSB board 16 mm
Mineral wool between wooden poles 120 mm
OSB board 16 mm
Vapor-permeable sarking membrane UV-resistant
Perspex wave 21 mm

Detail C / floor in contact with the ground

Solid parquet 10 mm
Screed 60 mm
PAE-foil
Mineral wool sound impact insulation 40 mm
PAE-foil overlapping and heat-sealed
EPS insulation 140 mm
Polystyrene light concrete 40 mm
Reinforced concrete foundation base plate 300 mm
Foil sealing 5 mm
EPS insulation 60 mm

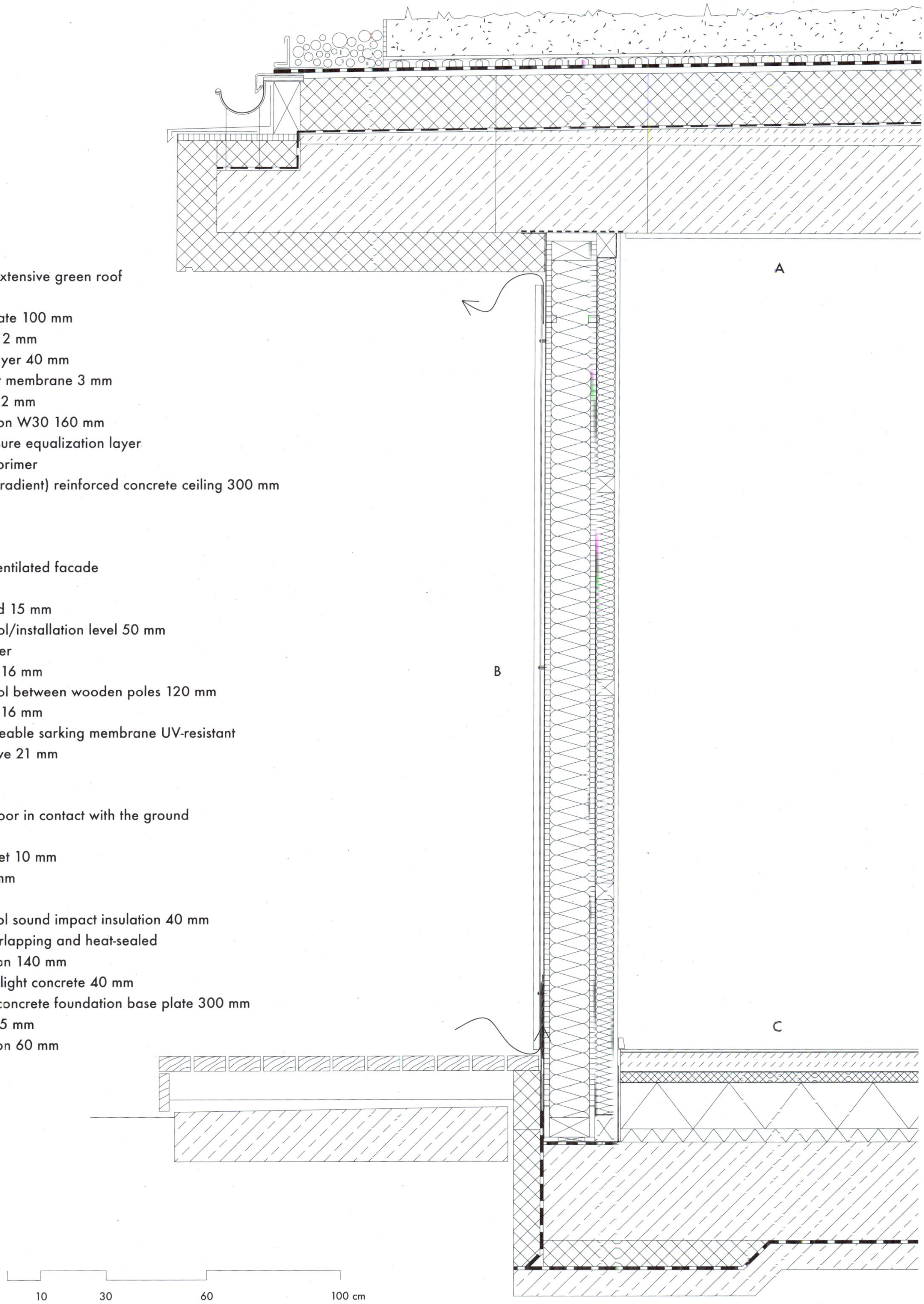

Details
1:15

roof landscape
1070 Vienna, AT

PROGRAM
Residential building, rooftop conversion, green terraces, roof gardens

DIMENSIONS
Useable living area 1,368 m², terraces and green areas 322 m²

CLIENT
IMMOWERT, Vienna, Austria

PROJECT TEAM
Marlies Breuss, Michael Ogertschnig, Christian Rottensteiner, Maria Ferragud Saez, Oguz Örgün, Metape Can

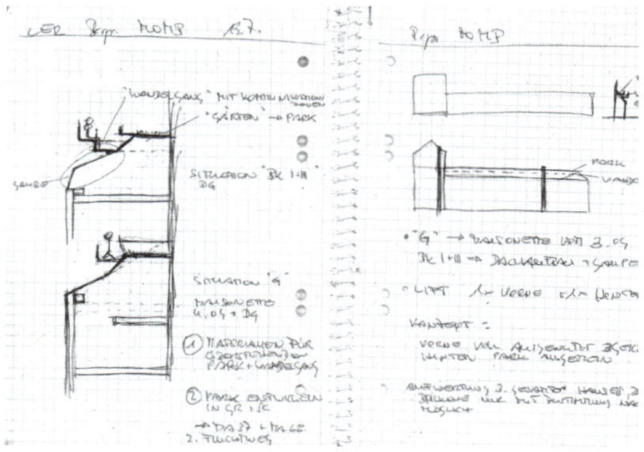

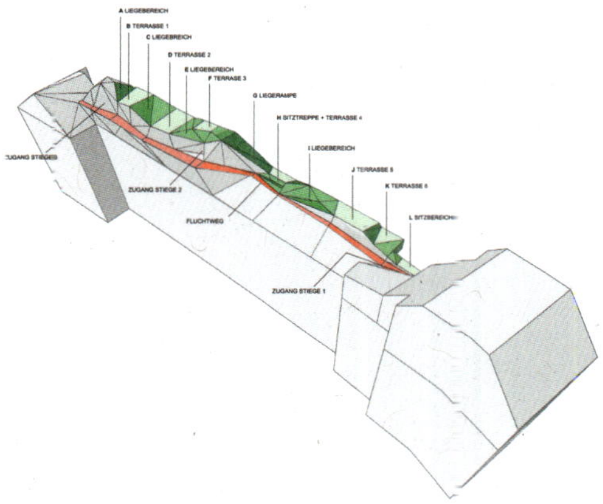

“The complex roof landscape serves as a green relaxation area for all residents and is intended as a park landscape in the dense Josefstadt area.”

—HOLODECK architects, project description, 2010 (trans. by the ed.)

Site plan
1:500

5 10 20 40 m

page 359

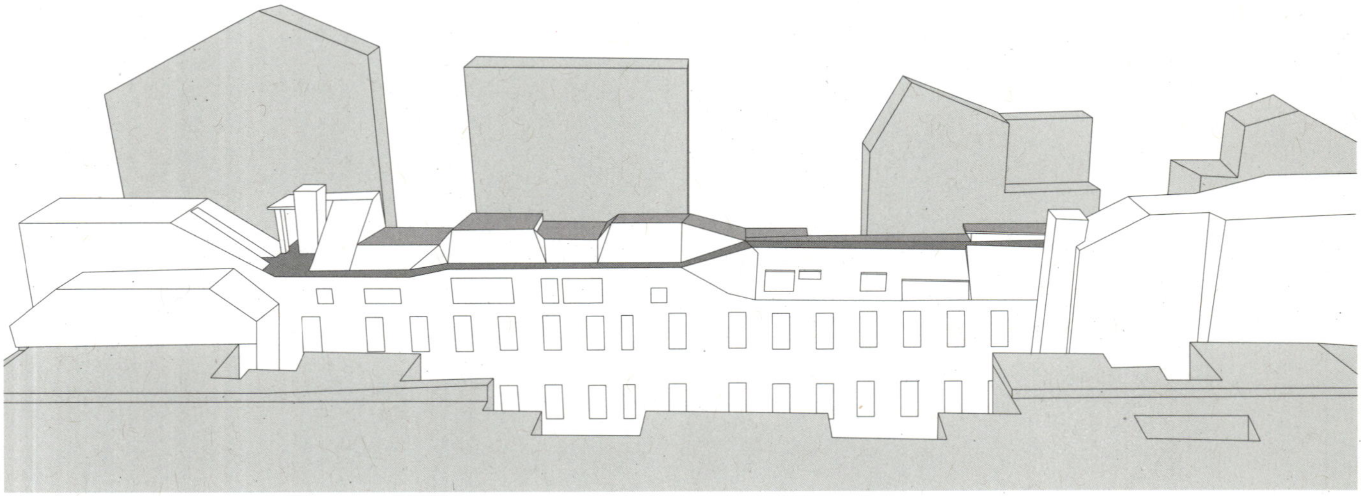

Axonometric
projection

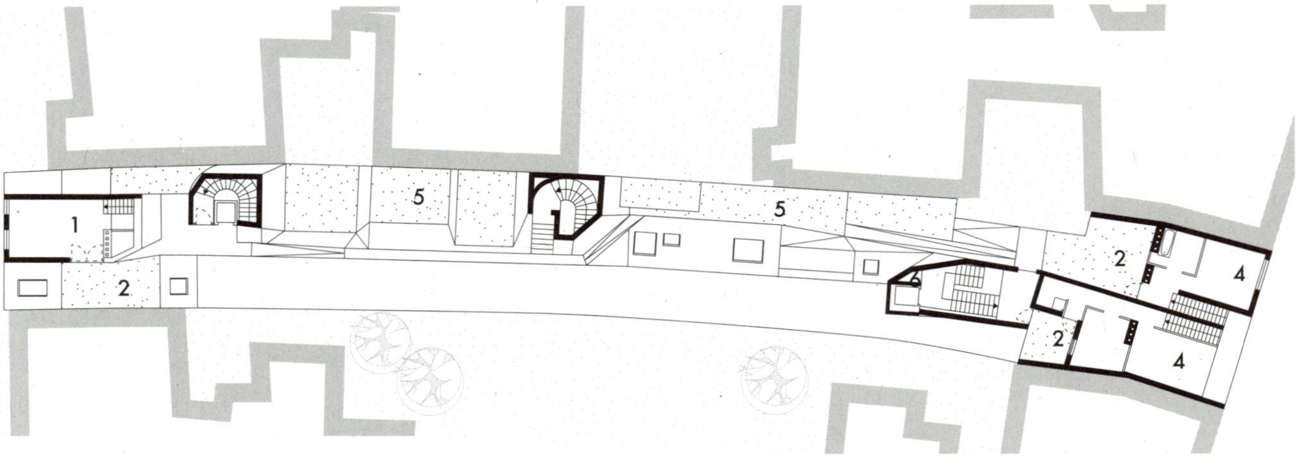

Top view

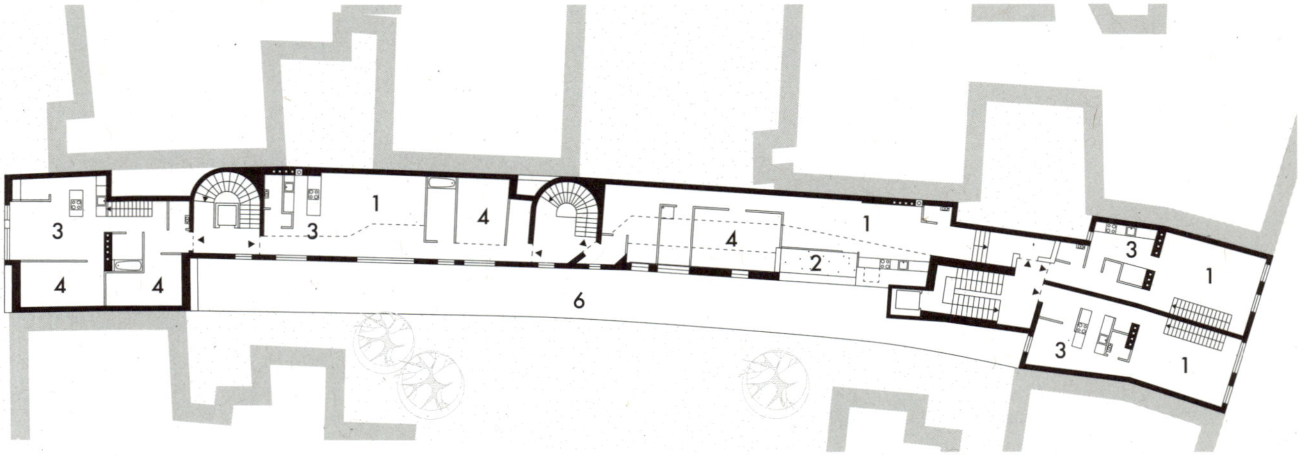

Top floor
1:450

1 3 6 10 m

1 Common private spaces
2 Terraces for relaxation
3 Eating, cooking area
4 Individual spaces
5 Green semipublic terraces
6 Semipublic courtyard

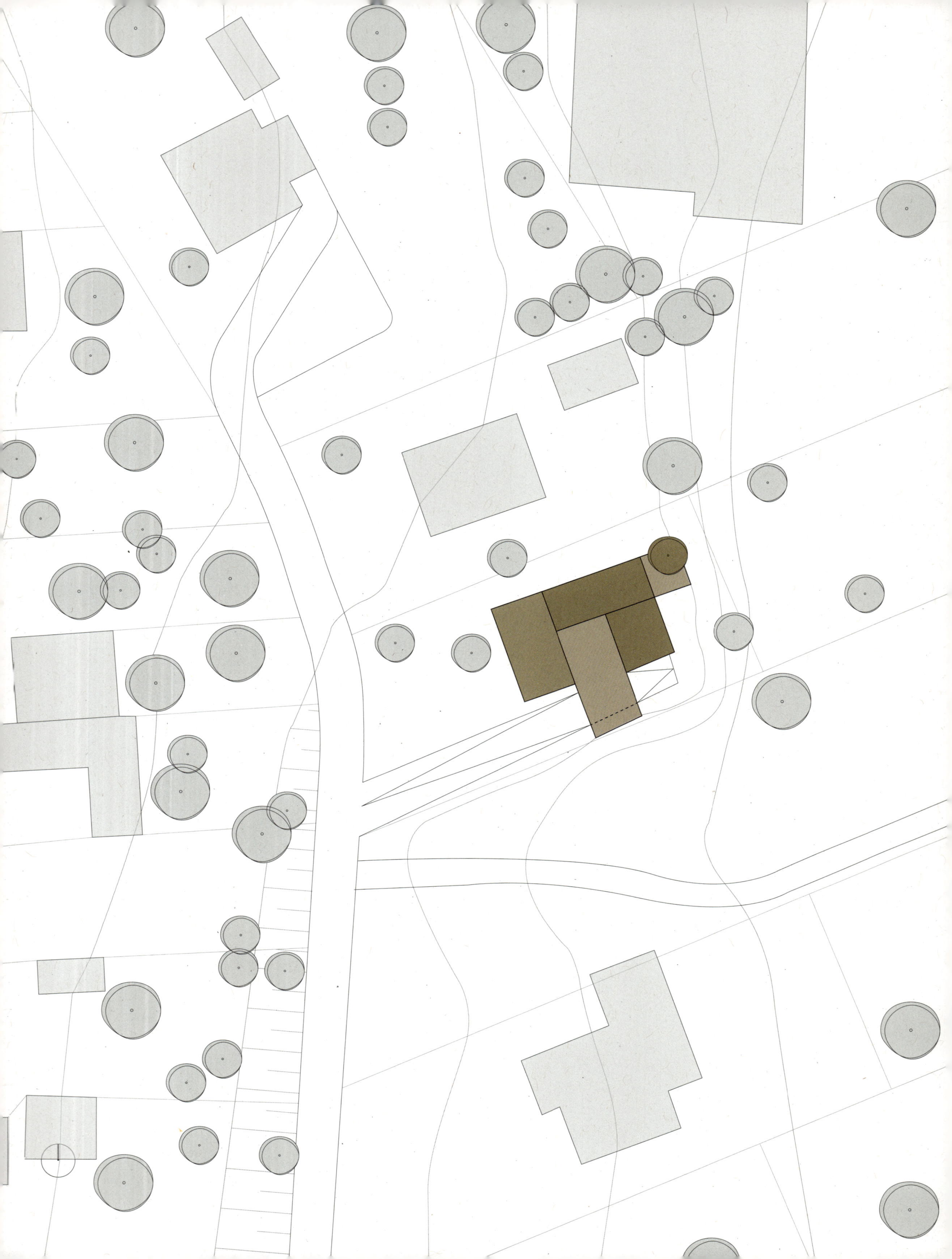

looped house
3701 Großweikersdorf, AT

See pp. 97–103

PROGRAM
Residential building, family with children

DIMENSIONS
Plot area 234 m², floor space 1,100 m²

CLIENT
Private

PROJECT TEAM
Marlies Breuss, Michael Ogertschnig, Susanne Schmall, Christine Schmauszer

CONSULTANTS
KPPK (structural engineer), Röhrer Ziviltechniker (building physics)

PHOTOGRAPHY
Veronika Hofinger

PUBLICATIONS (SELECTION)
Brigitte Simma, "Looped House 2001, Architekturpreis 2003," *Beton + Zement*, April 2003 (ISSN 0514-2946).
Barbara Jahn, "Looping im Haus," *WOHNEN*, February–March 2003 (ISBN 9 004575 001661).

"The space flows—insights and views are made possible from every point in the house."

—Barbara Jahn, "Looped House," *Wohnen*, February–March 2003, p. 73 (trans. by the ed.)

Site plan
1:500

5 10 20 40 m

page 365

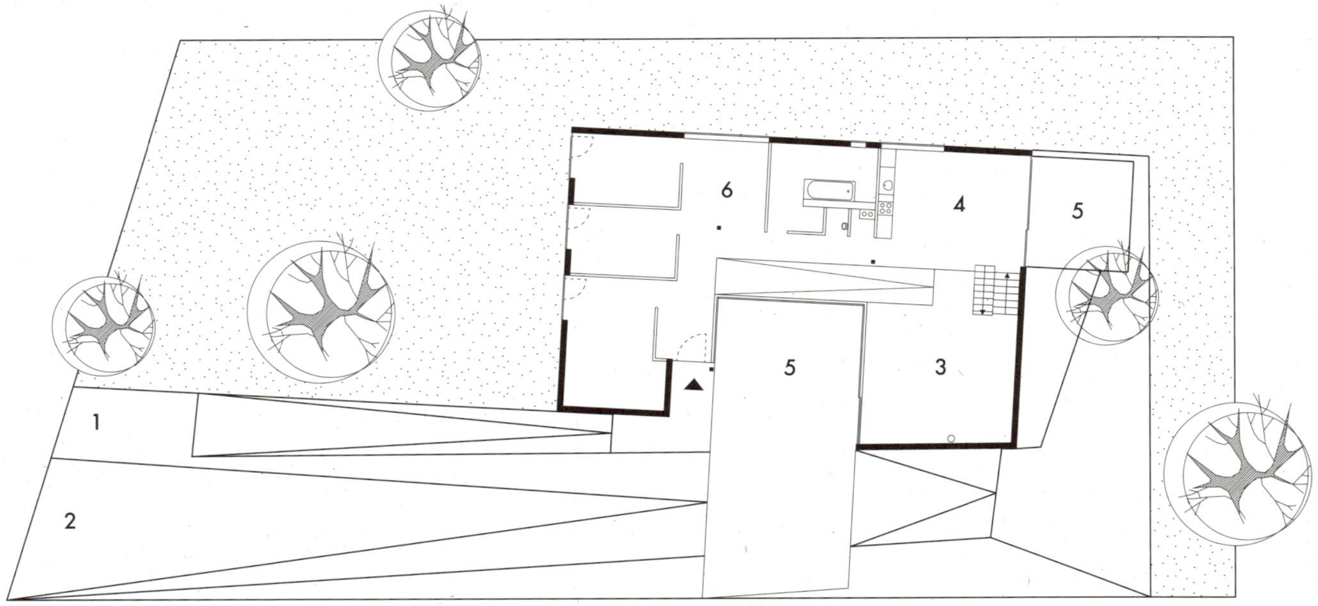

Ground floor

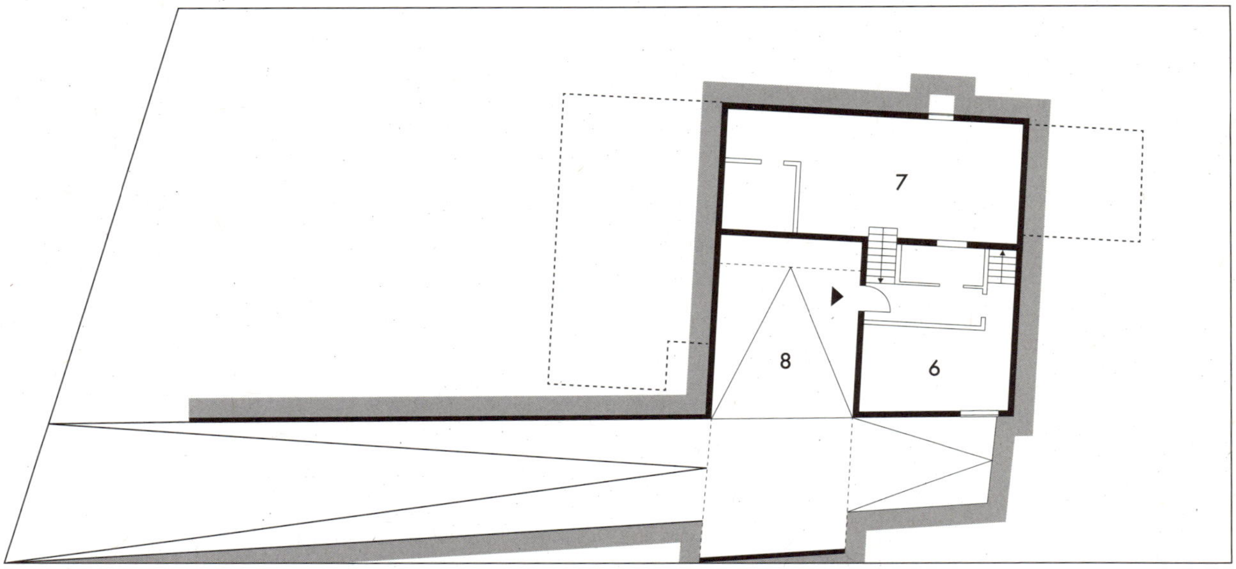

Basement floor

1 Entrance
2 Entrance to parking area
3 Common private spaces
4 Eating, cooking area
5 Terraces for relaxation
6 Working area
7 Building systems
8 Car parking

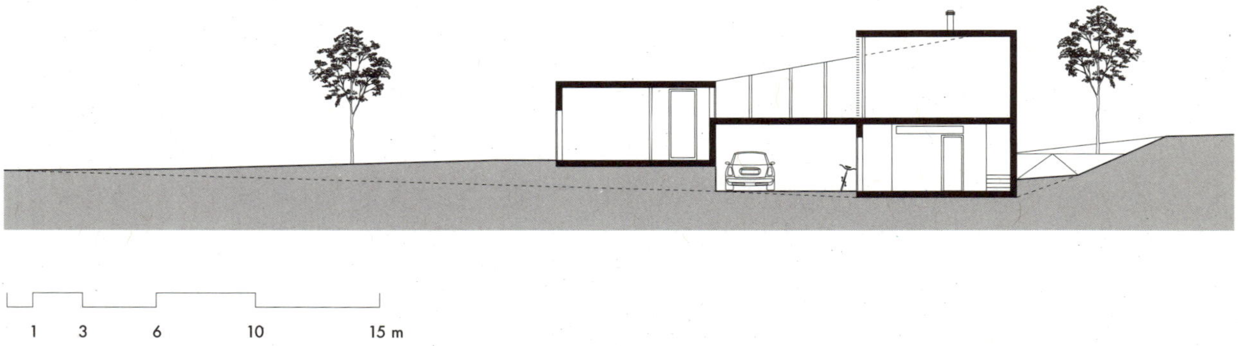

Section
1:300

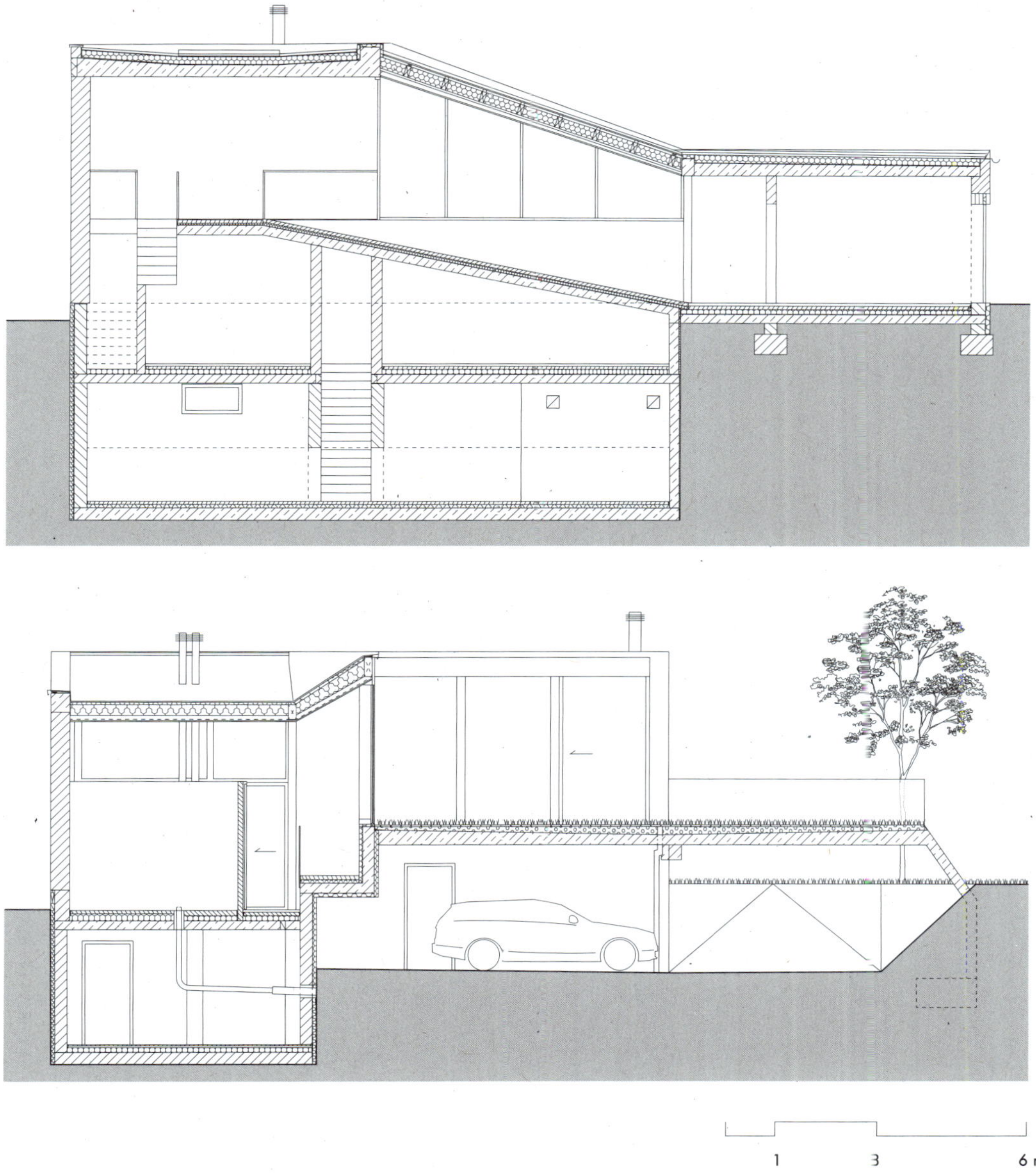

Sections
1:150

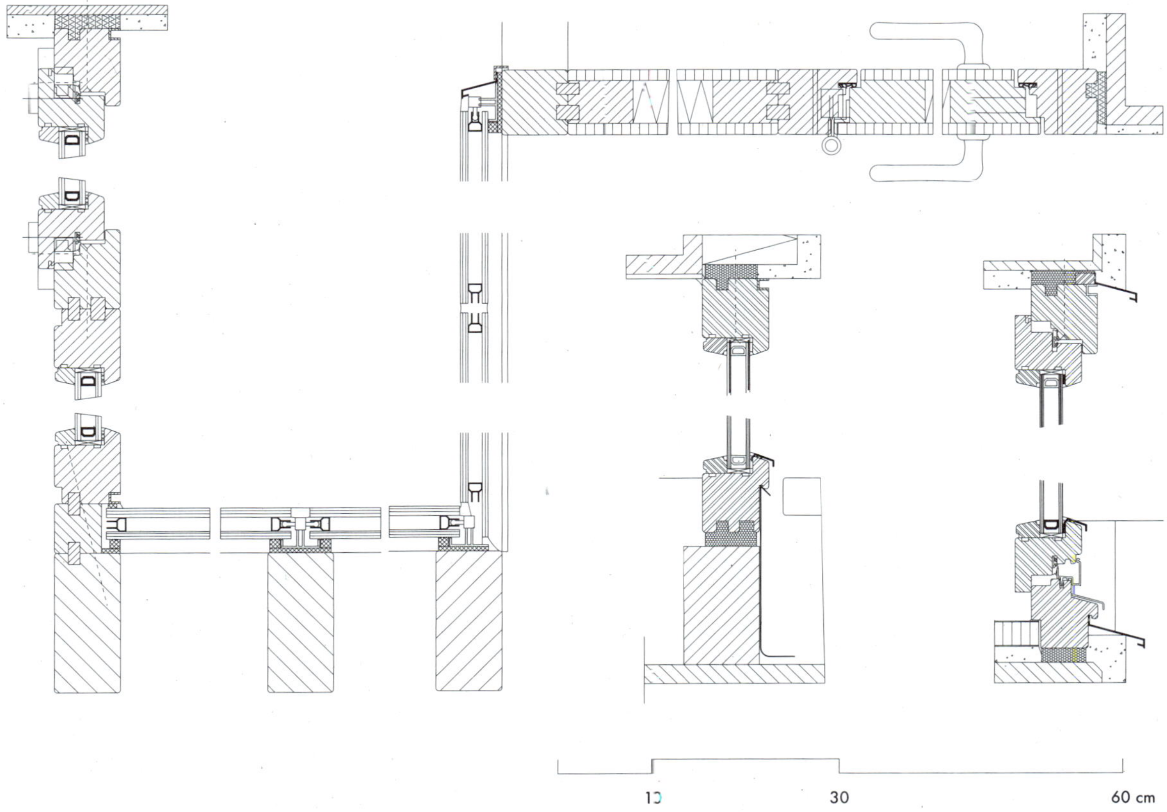

Details of wooden
windows and doors
1:8

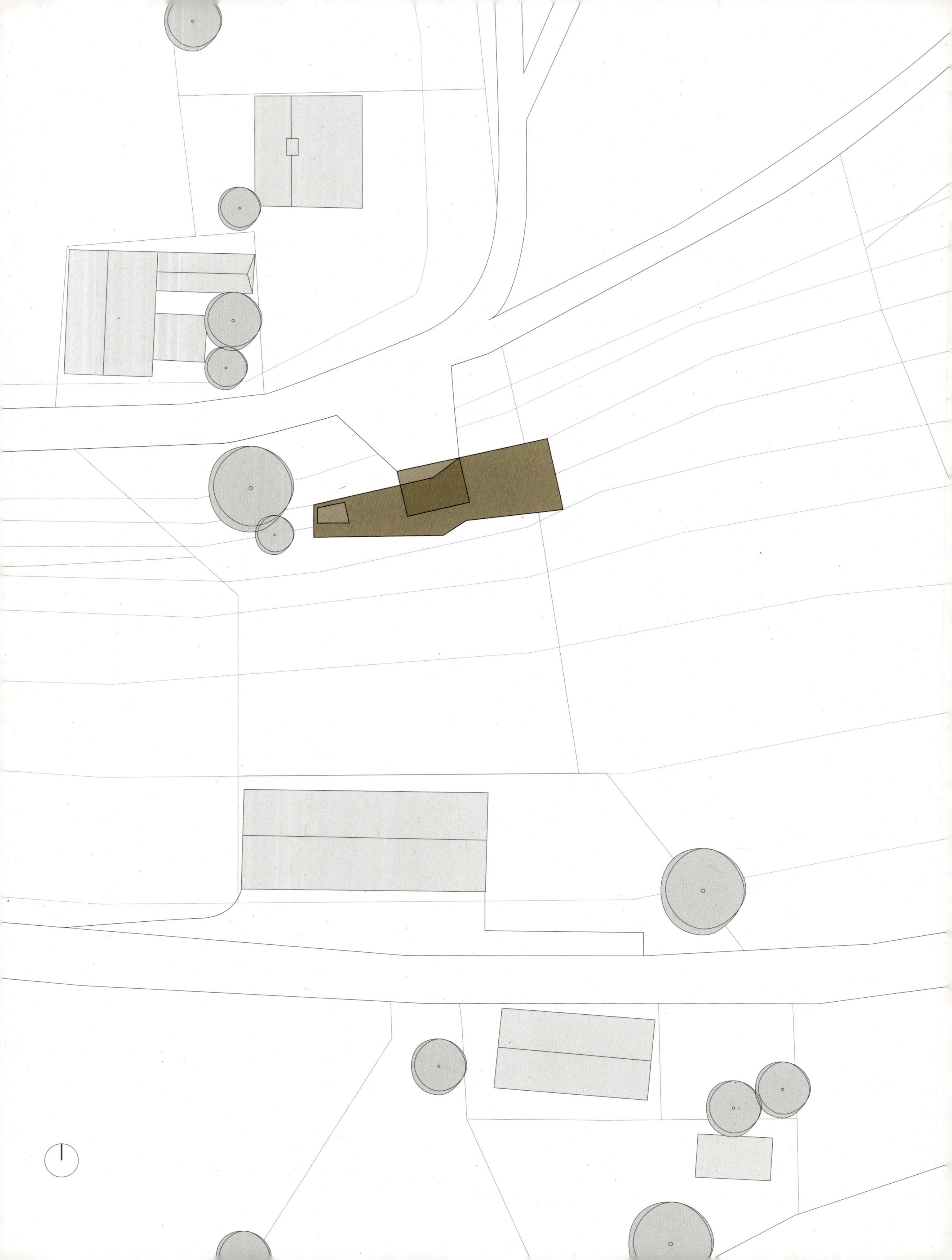

2005–08
ALLOVER LANDSCAPE

embedded house
9500 Heiligengeist, AT

See pp. 104–11

PROGRAM
Residential building, family with children

DIMENSIONS
Plot area 5,250 m², GFA 294 m², covered area 168 m², floor space 229 m², terraces 50 m²

CLIENT
Private

PROJECT TEAM
Marlies Breuss, Michael Ogertschnig, Gernot Köfer, Sebastian Uhl

CONSULTANTS
BUILD.iNG Baumanagement (construction management)

PROJECT MANAGER
BM Rest, Villach

PHOTOGRAPHY
Günter Stöger, Rita Laslberger

AWARDS
Landesbaupreis Kärnten (national construction prize Carinthia), honorable mention
Das beste Haus (best house), AzW (Architekturzentrum Wien), nomination

PUBLICATIONS (SELECTION)
"Fünf Mal Baupreis," *Die Brücke*, Klagenfurt, March 2011.
Susanne Mitterbauer, "Das Auto steht am Dach," *Besser Wohnen*, August 2014 (ISBN 9-022500-001005-08).
Michelle Galindo, "Masterpieces," in *Country House, architecture + design*, Berlin, Braun Publishing, June 2011 (ISBN 978-3-03-768-072-8).

"This room, however, is not a Mies van der Rohe glass box, but rather looks like a habitable polypore in which glazing has been inserted, a pleasant atmosphere in which one is connected to nature without being exposed to it."

—Excerpt from the jury protocol of the Landesbaupreis, 2010, p. 18 (trans. by the ed.)

Site plan
1:500

5 10 20 40 m

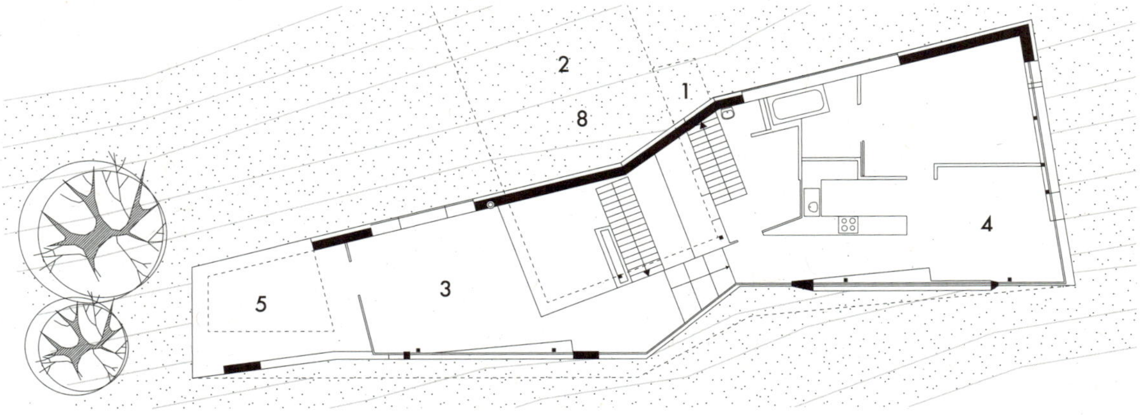

Ground floor

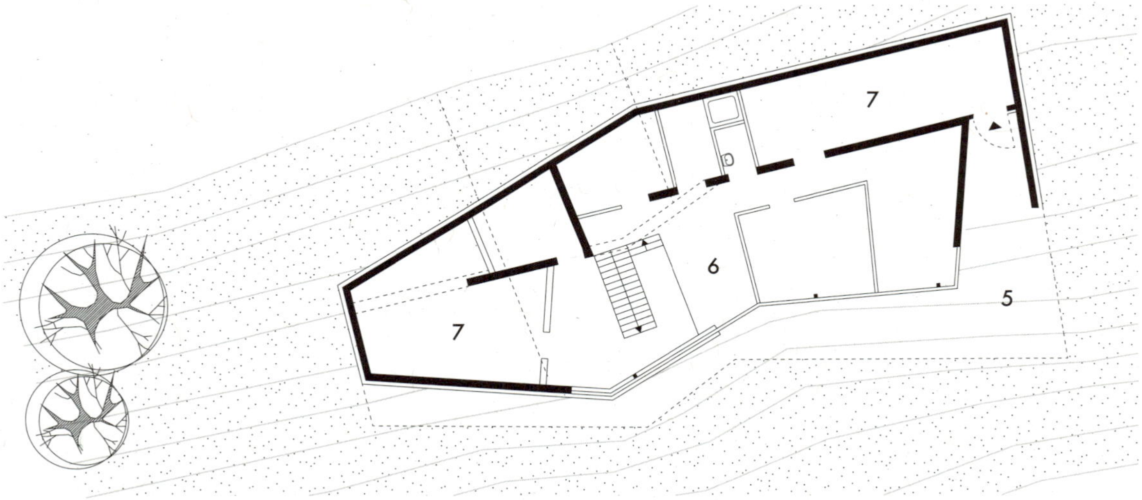

Basement floor

1 Entrance
2 Entrance to parking area
3 Common private space
4 Eating, cooking area
5 Terraces for relaxation
6 Working area
7 Building systems
8 Car parking

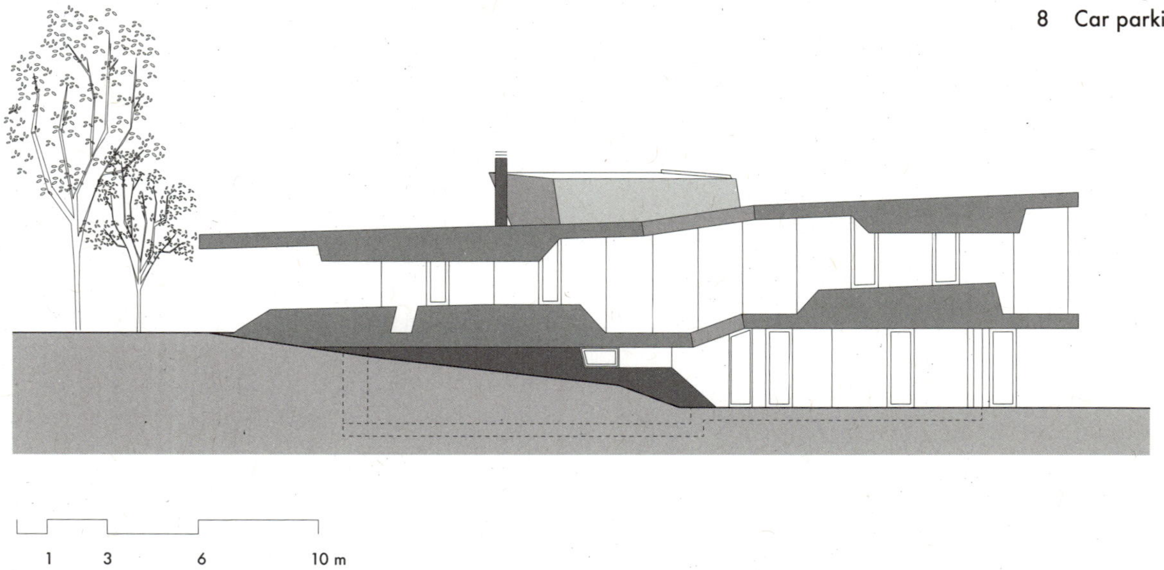

South view
1:250

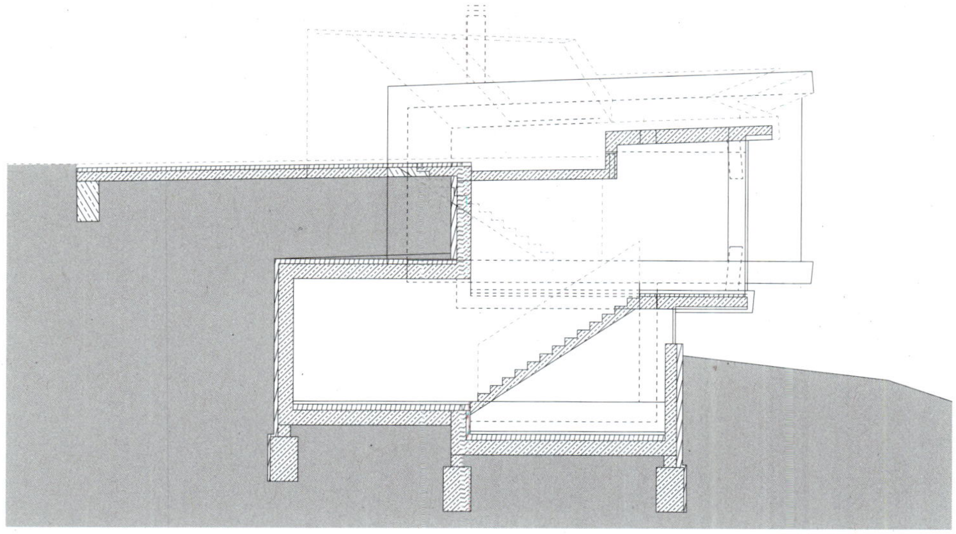

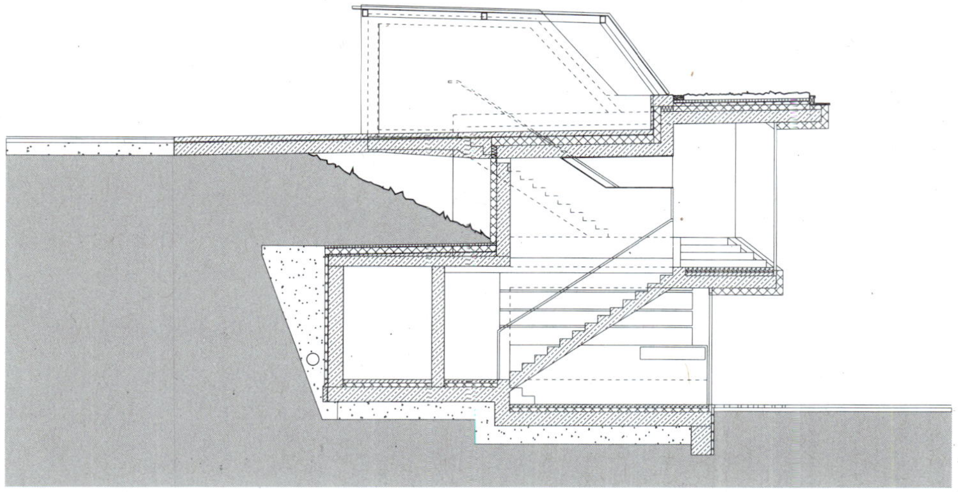

Sections

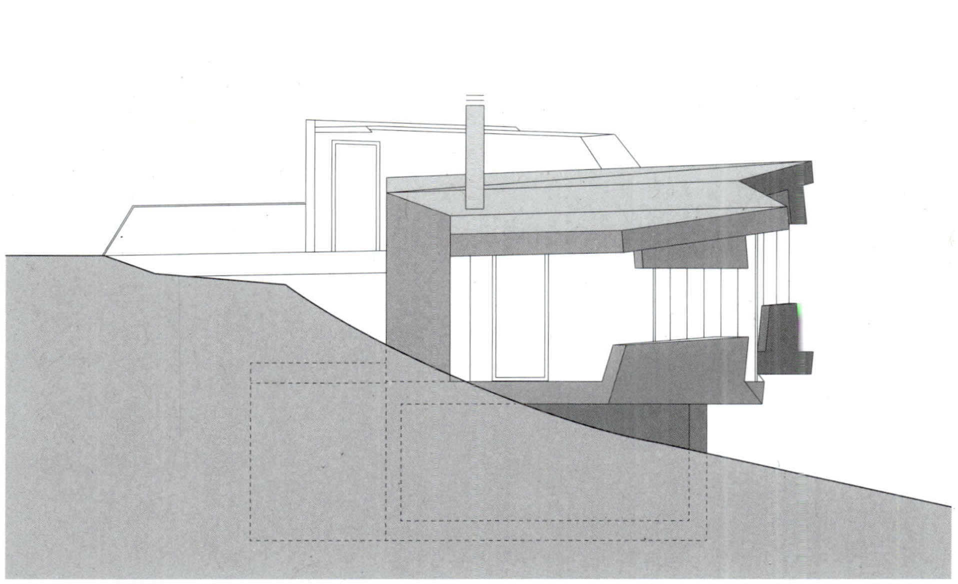

1 3 6 m

West view
1:150

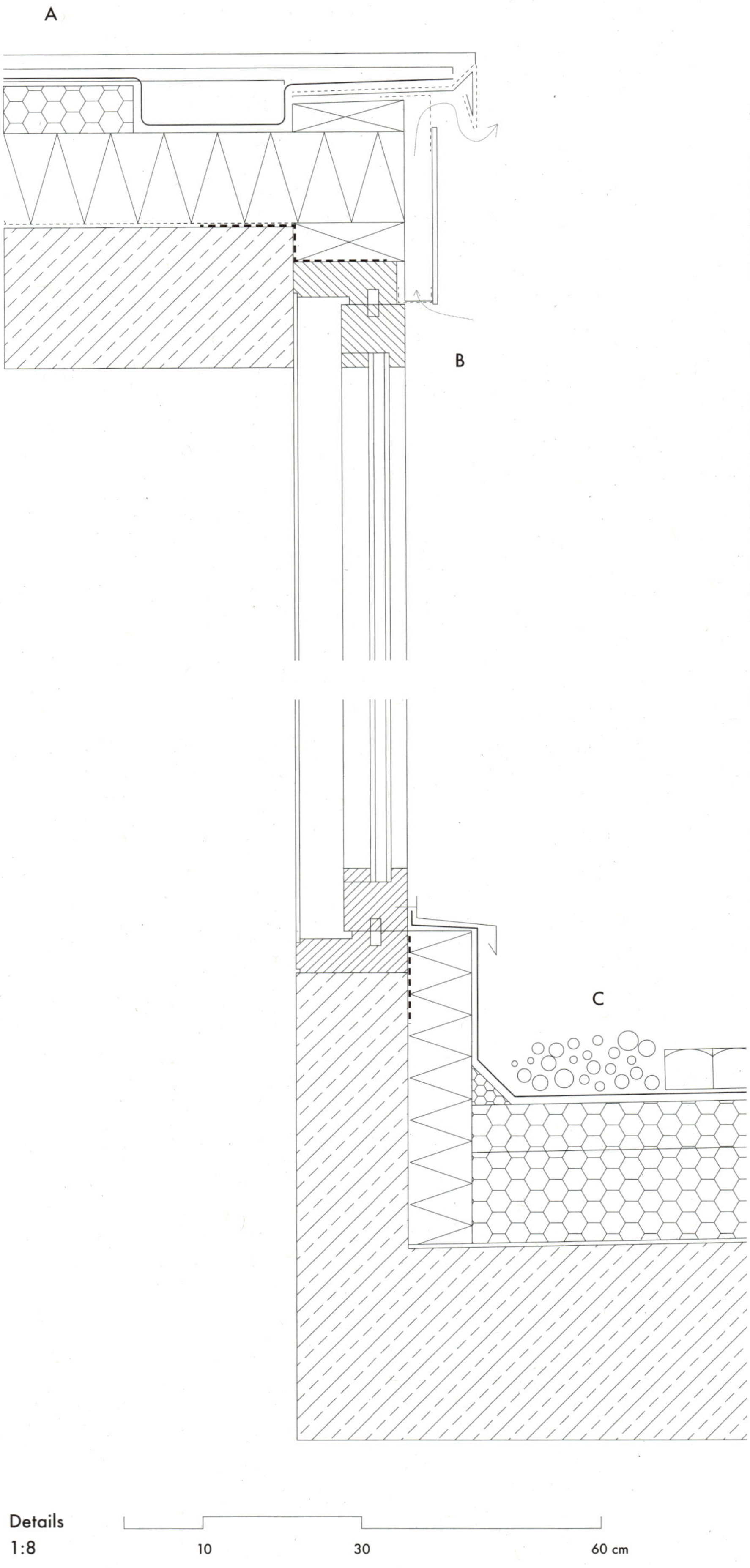

Detail A / roof

Roof sealing 2 mm
EPS W25 insulation 60 mm
EPS W25 insulation 120 mm
Primer and bituminous vapor barrier 3 mm
Reinforced concrete ceiling 180 mm

Detail B / facade

Foils sheet metal
Insect screen
Fibre cement plates 6 mm on wooden substructure
Reveal element/cladding with shadow groove 140 × 55 mm
Frame fixed glazing 800 × 80 mm
Underside frame = underside ceiling
Insect screen
Sealings high point min. 150 mm
Gravel border

Detail C / floor

Plant substrate 200 mm
Filter fleece 2 mm
Drainage layer 40 mm
Root-barrier membrane 3 mm
Roof sealing 2 mm
EPS W25 insulation 60 mm
EPS W25 insulation 120 mm
Primer and bituminous vapor barrier 3 mm
Reinforced concrete ceiling 250 mm

Detail A / roof

Roof sealing 2 mm
EPS W25 insulation 60 mm
EPS W25 insulation 120 mm
Primer and bituminous vapor barrier 3 mm
Reinforced concrete ceiling 180 mm

Detail B / floor

Isokorb according to statics
Infiltration ditch 60 mm
Covering: cast iron grating
Infiltration ditch connection on DN50
Galvanized steel sheet, laid into formwork

Detail C / floor

Screed 80 mm
Separating layer
Impact-sound insulation 32 mm (TP 35/32)
Heat sealed separating layer
Perlite fill (expanding) 70 mm
Reinforced concrete ceiling 250 mm
EPS-F 14 insulation 140 mm
Counter-battens/rear ventilation 35 mm
Fibre cement board 6 mm

Detail D / facade

Reveal element with shadow groove 140 × 55 mm
Frame fixed glazing 80 × 80 mm
Underside frame = underside slab
Steel angle 170 × 170 mm primed and coated
Frame fixed glazing 80 × 80 mm
Frame top edge = floor slab level
Glavanized steel sheet/aluminum
Insect screen

Detail E / facade

Foils sheet metal
Insect screen
Treated wood plank 140 × 35–40 mm
Wood mounting strip
Mounting frame
Reveal covering with shadow groove 70 × 15 mm
Insect screen
Fibre-cement plate 6 mm on wooden substructure
Pine/mahogany 60 × 40 mm,
in between XPS 50 mm
Solid leaf door outside, veneered inner surface
Pine/mahogany, cementer
Sill on wood mounting strip
Galvanized steel sheet coated

Detail F / floor

Asphalt concrete AB8 35 mm
Load distributing slab according
to statics 120 mm
PAE-foil
PAE-foil
DIV pe sealing layer 5 mm
DIV pe sealing layer 5 mm
Reinforced concrete ceiling (gradient)
250–410 mm

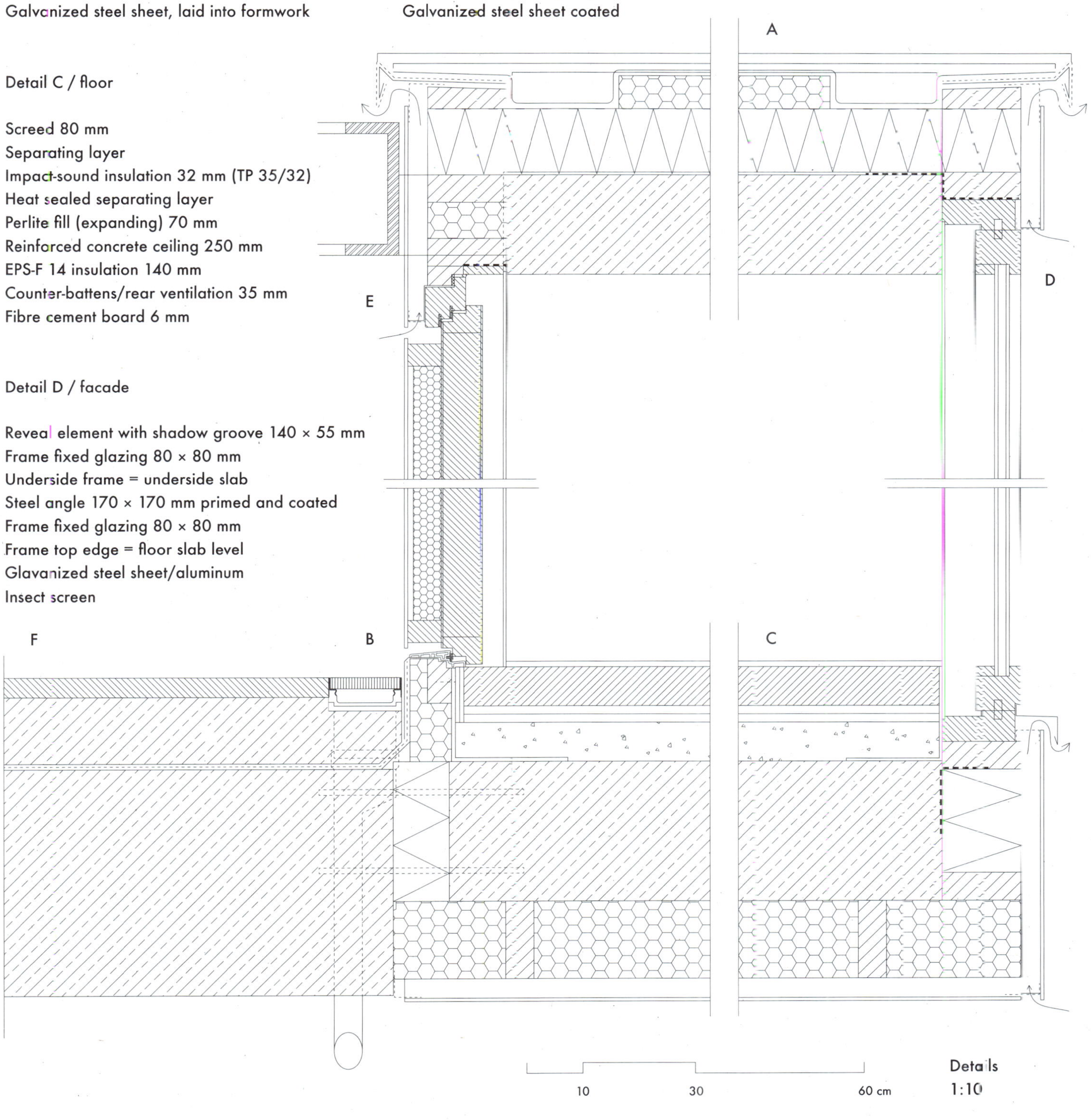

Details
1:10

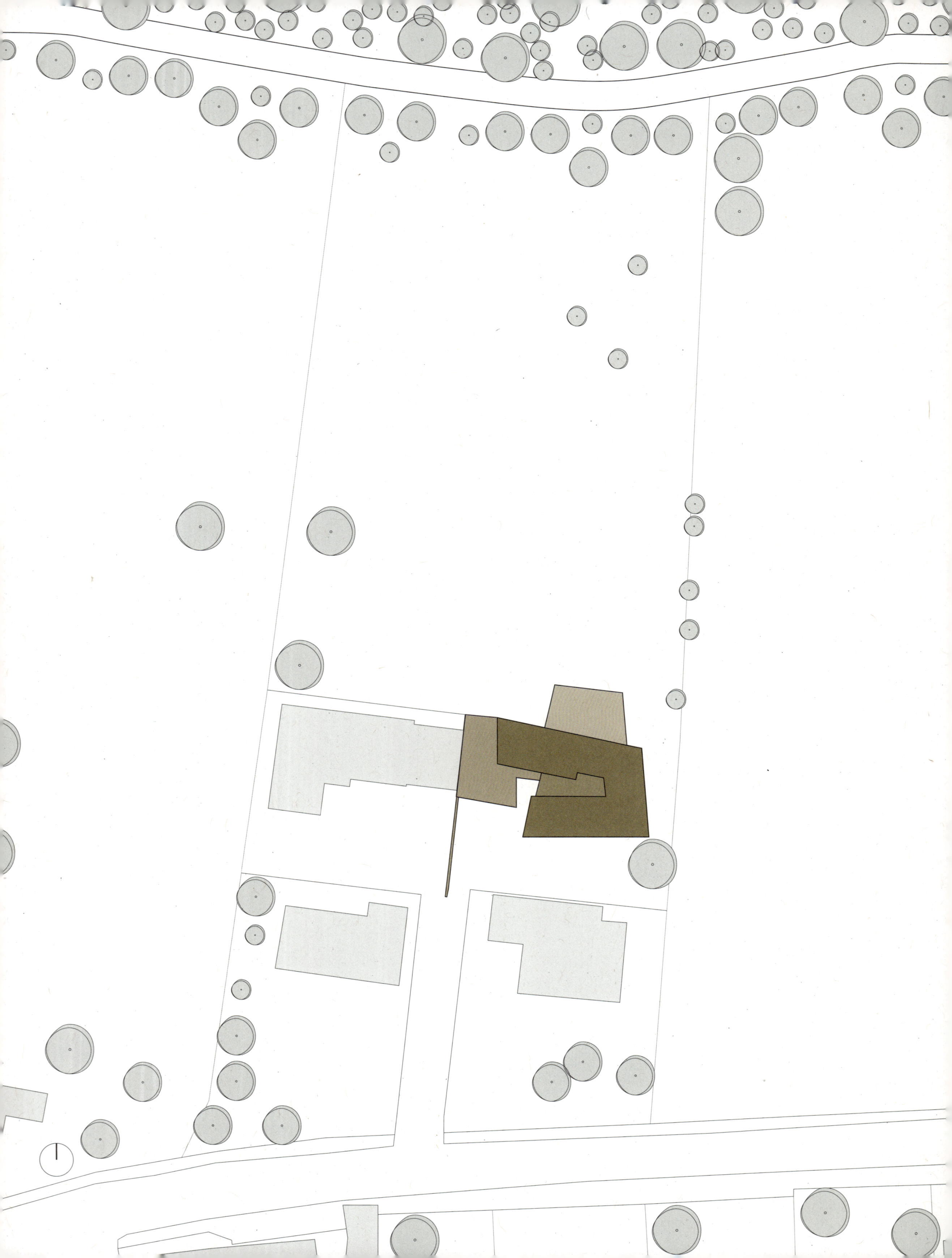

floating house
2500 Siegenfeld, AT

See pp. 112–19

PROGRAM
Residential building, family with children

DIMENSIONS
Plot area 696 m², covered area 250 m², GFA 439 m²

CLIENT
Private

PROJECT TEAM
Marlies Breuss, Michael Ogertschnig, Manuel Garcia Barbero, Ana Curto, Franz Moser, Sebastian Uhl

CONSULTANTS
KPPK (structural engineer), Röhrer Bauphysik (building physics)

PHOTOGRAPHY
Hertha Hurnaus, Grazia Ike Branco

AWARDS
Ecola Award 2008, nomination

PUBLICATIONS (SELECTION)
Isabella Marboe, "Hauslandschaft in den Siegenfeldern," *Der Standard*, Vienna, June 4, 2005.
Elke Krasny, "Floating House in Siegenfeld," *Architektur.aktuell – Integration*, Vienna and New York, Springer, October 2005.
"floating house, Niederösterreich – Wohnhaus mit Steuerberaterkanzlei," *Beton Zement – 2005 Architekturpreis der österreichischen Beton- und Zementindustrie*, June 2005 (ISSN 0514-2946).

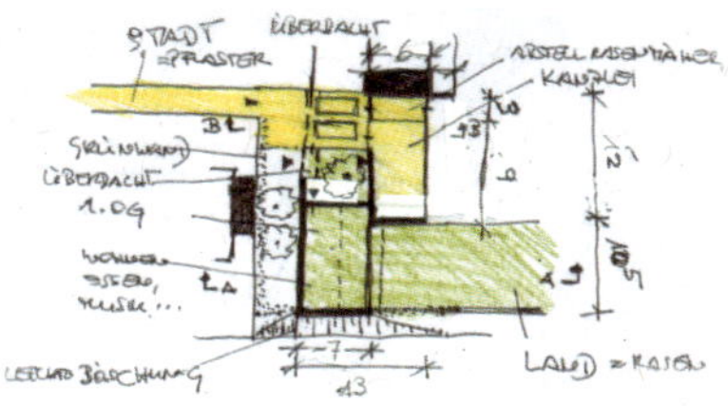

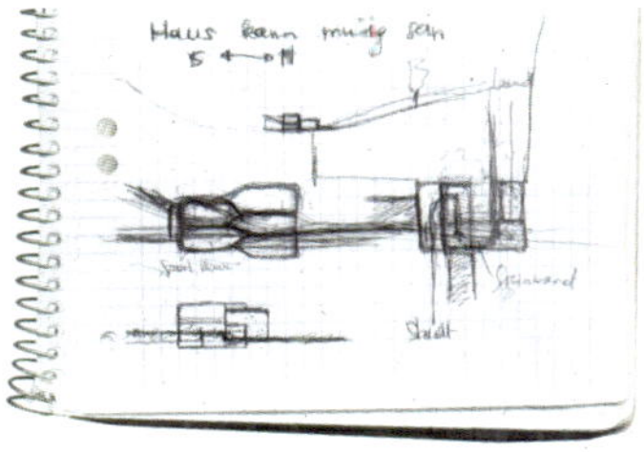

"The house is designed in response to the context and landscape. The result is a complex, multilayered, continuous space that floats above the fields."

—Álex Sánchez Vidiella, *Minimal: Le grand livre du minimalisme*, Barcelona, Maomao Publications, 2007, p. 222.

Site plan
1:500

5 10 20 40 m

page 379

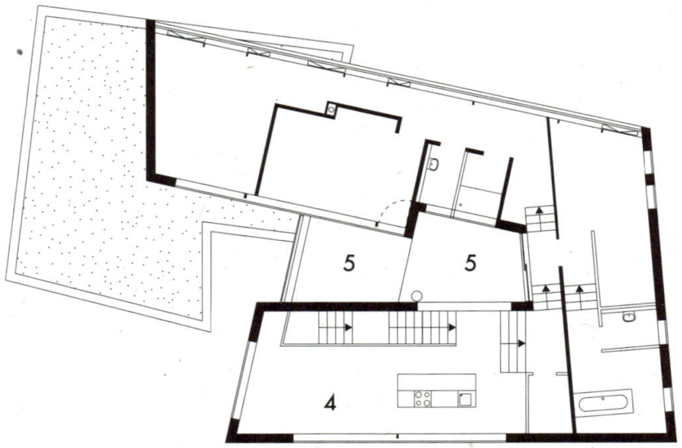

First floor

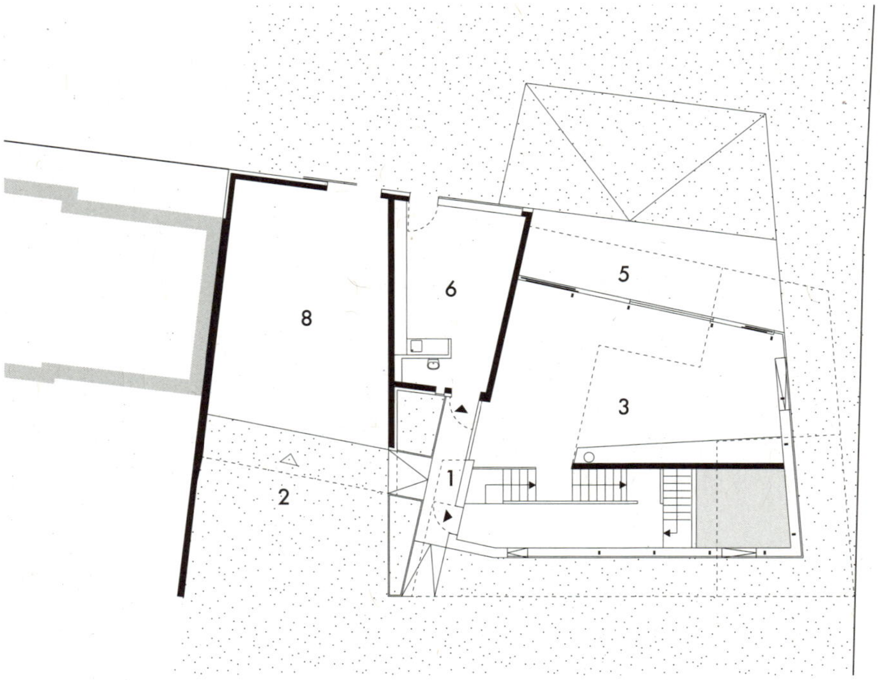

Ground floor

1 Entrance
2 Entrance to parking area
3 Common private space
4 Eating, cooking area
5 Terraces for relaxation
6 Working area
7 Building systems
8 Car parking

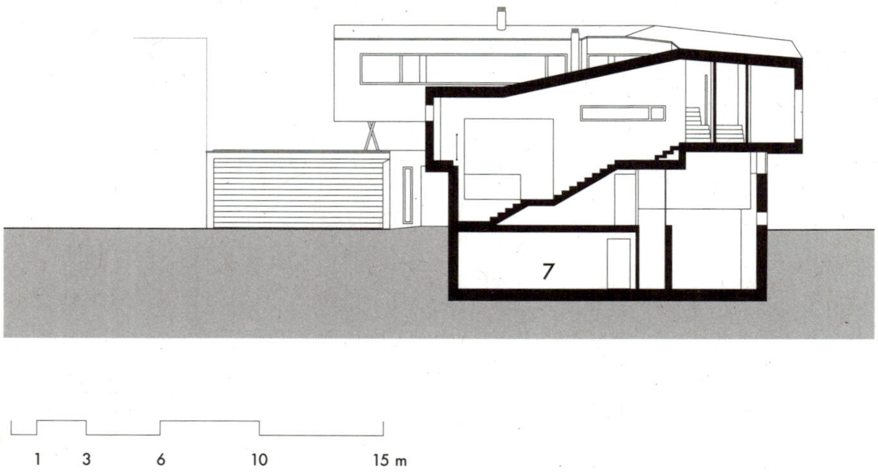

Section
1:300

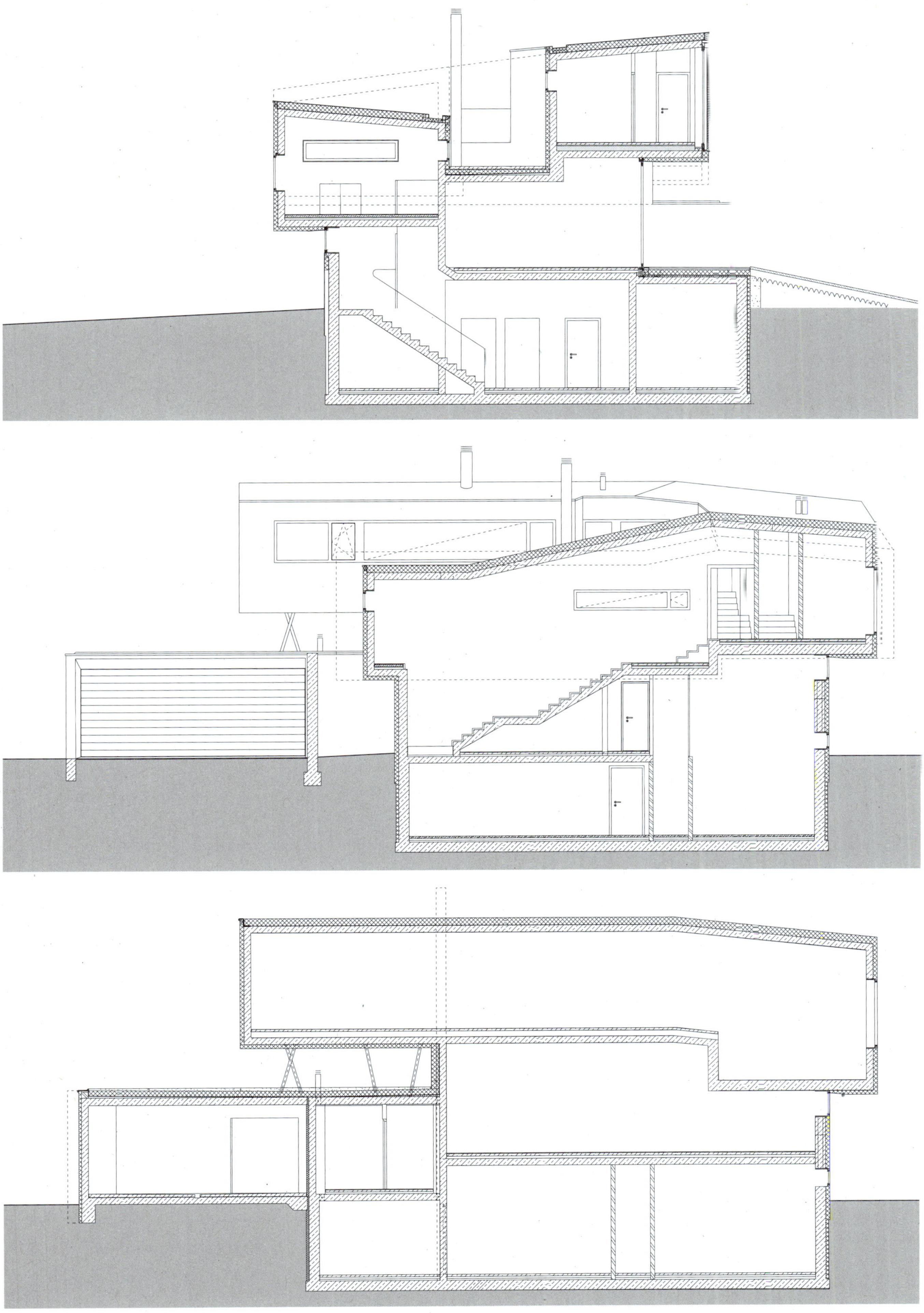

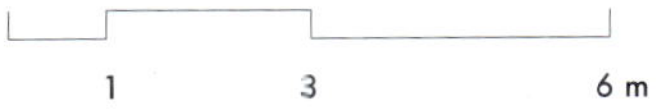

Sections
1:150

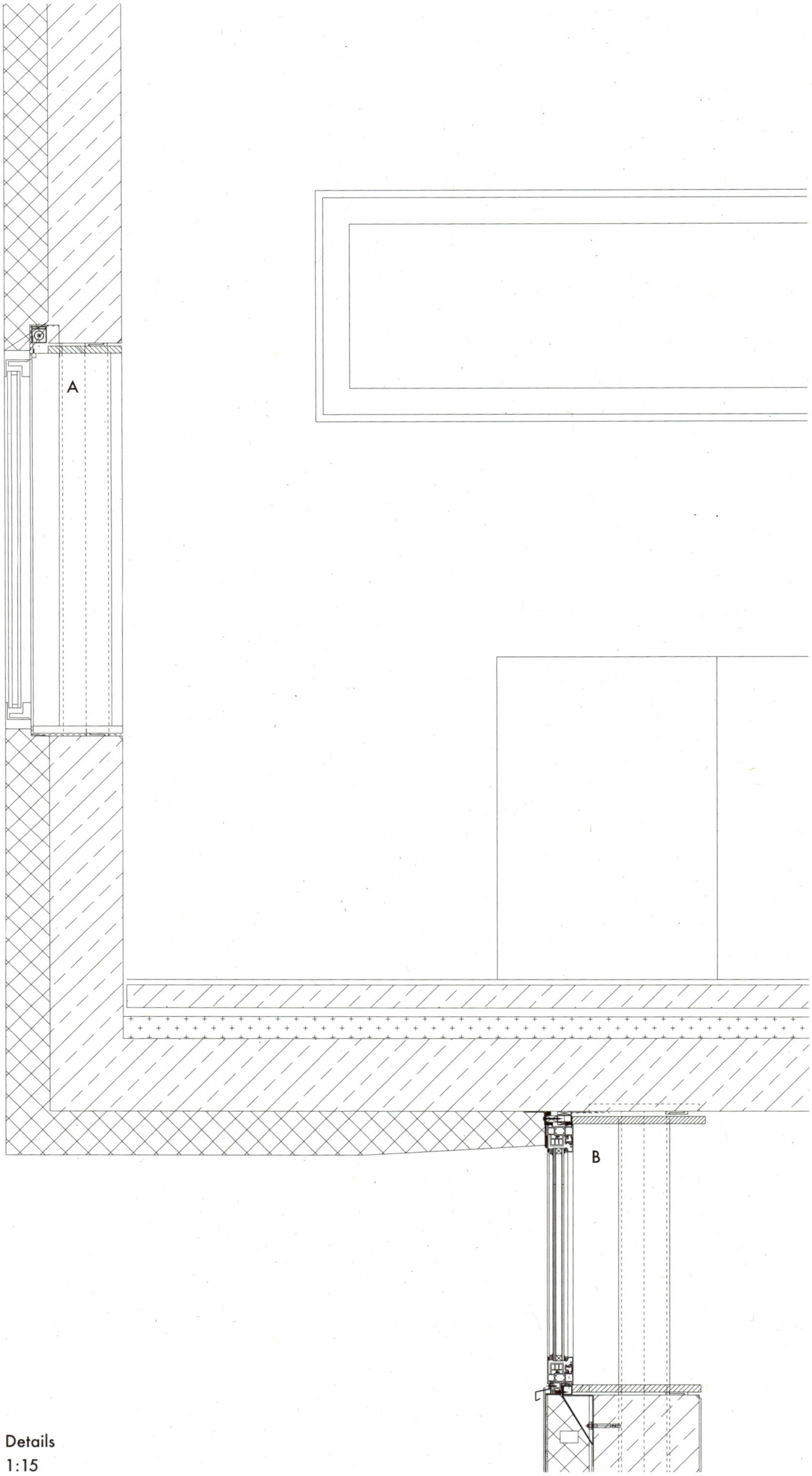

Detail A / window

Vapor barrier completely bonded
Sun protection roller blind, inside,
h: 460 mm, w: 410 mm
Wooden reveal covering
Column RHS 1,400/800/63 mm ST37/2
Vapor barrier completely bonded

Detail B / window and facade

Purenit
Compriband pre-compressed
Steel RHS DIN 2395 40/20/2
R2BL 300/300/20
Vapor barrier
Foil sealing aluminum profile
Joint tape
Insulation
Column RHS 1,400/800/63 mm ST37/2
Wooden reveal covering

Details
1:15

Detail A / roof

Foil sealing 1.5 mm
EPS insulation 2 levels overlapping
Vapor barrier, PE-foil
Reinforced concrete ceiling 200 mm
Thin Plaster

Detail B / facade

Foil sheet metal
Mounting wood baton 20/8 mm
Insulation
Substructure
Reinforcement every 350 mm
Sealing membrane
Anchor bolt M8x/75/10/23
Adhesive anchor every 3,500 mm
Mounting frame
Aluminum 2 mm
Column RHS 1,400/800/63 mm ST37/2
Plaster dark
Aluminum sheet 1.5 mm RAL 7016
Compriband pre-compressed
Pipe construction-reinforcement

Detail C / facade

Stainless steel angle RAL 7021
Hinge
Aluminum 2 mm RAL 7021
Electric heating element
Reinforcement mat in levelling compound
Pipe construction reinforcement
Steel substructure
Insulation

Detail D / facade

Purenit
Compriband pre-compressed
Foil
Aluminum 2 mm
Foil
Vapor barrier
Joint tape
Steel substructure
Insulation

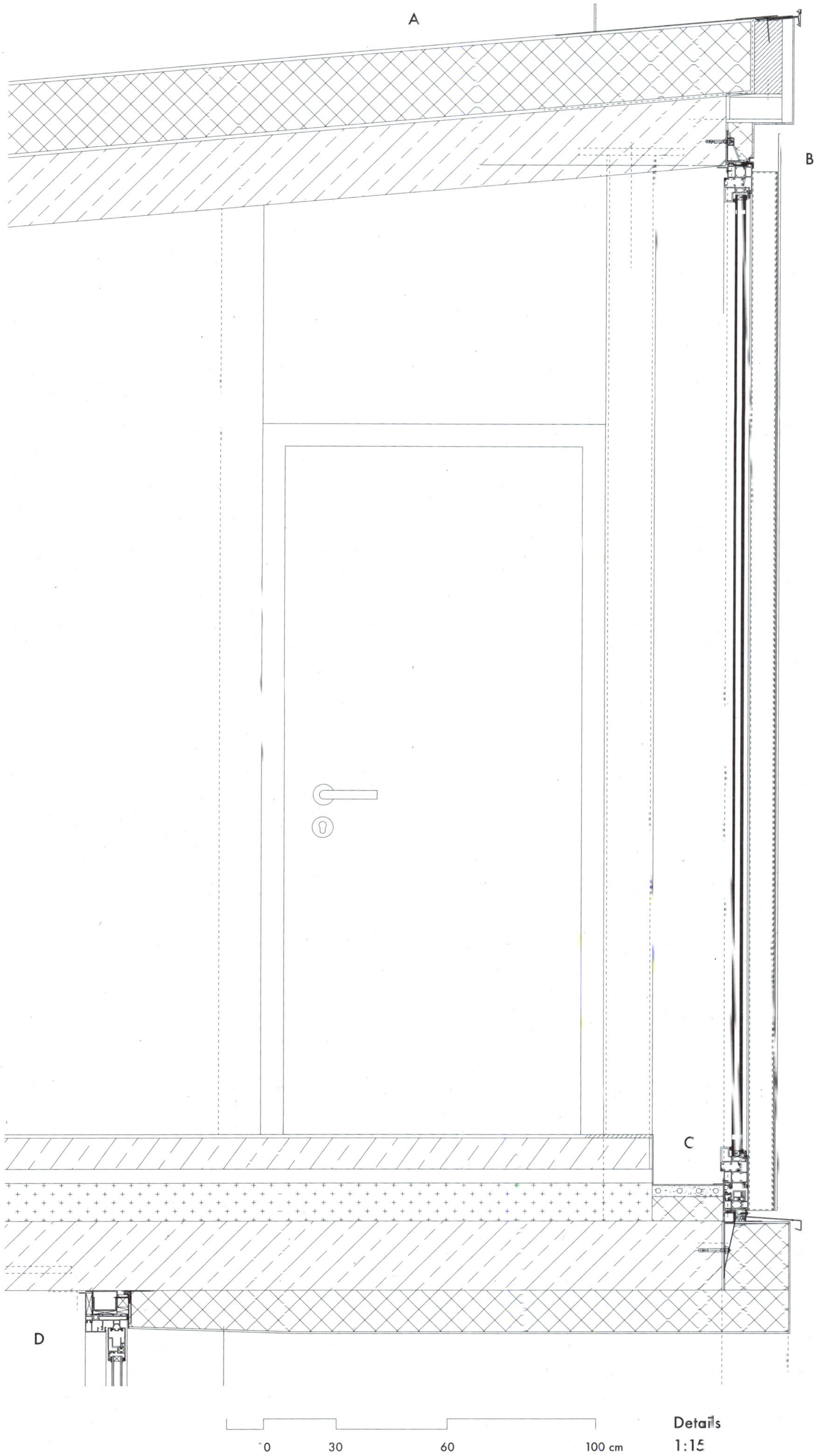

Details
1:15

earthquake memorial
413 Wufeng, Nantou, TW

PROGRAM
Cultural building, landscape design, earthquake memorial, restructuring of landscape

DIMENSION
Plot area 20,000 m²

CLIENT
PDRC (Post-Disaster Recovery Commission) and AIROC (Architecture Institute of China), Nantou, Taiwan

PROJECT TEAM
Marlies Breuss, Michael Ogertschnig, Henry van Hoeve, Misa Shibukawa

AWARD
International open competition, honorable mention

PUBLICATION
921 chichi earthquake memorial, AIROC & PDRC, Taiwan, April 2004 (ISBN 957-01-6963-X).

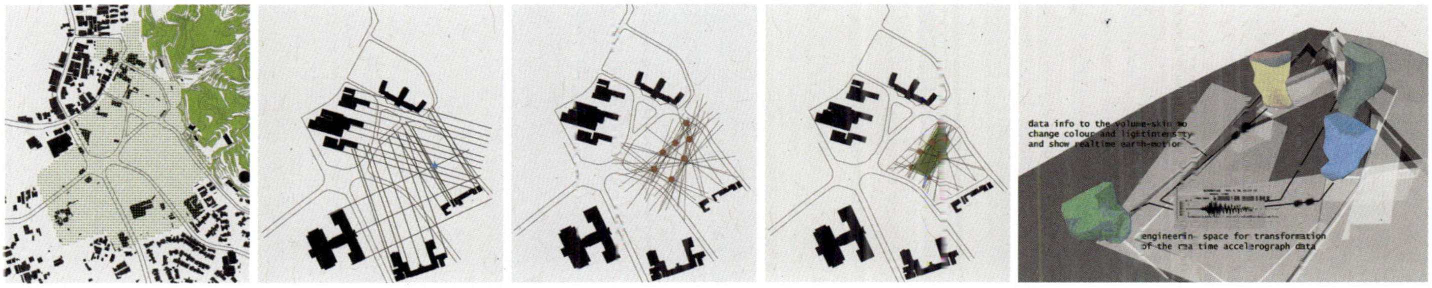

“I believe the true completion of architecture is not in the physical completion of a building. Instead, it is at the stage of recording and ruminating on the significance and value of architecture, sharing these aspects with the wider world.”

—Lee Jeong Hoon, “The Moment When Architecture is Truly Complete,” in *Pergola of The Clue at NINE BRIDGES: Architecture and Technology Resembling the Nature*, Seoul, Space Books, 2018, p. 7.

Site plan
1:1,500
10 30 60 100 m

page 387

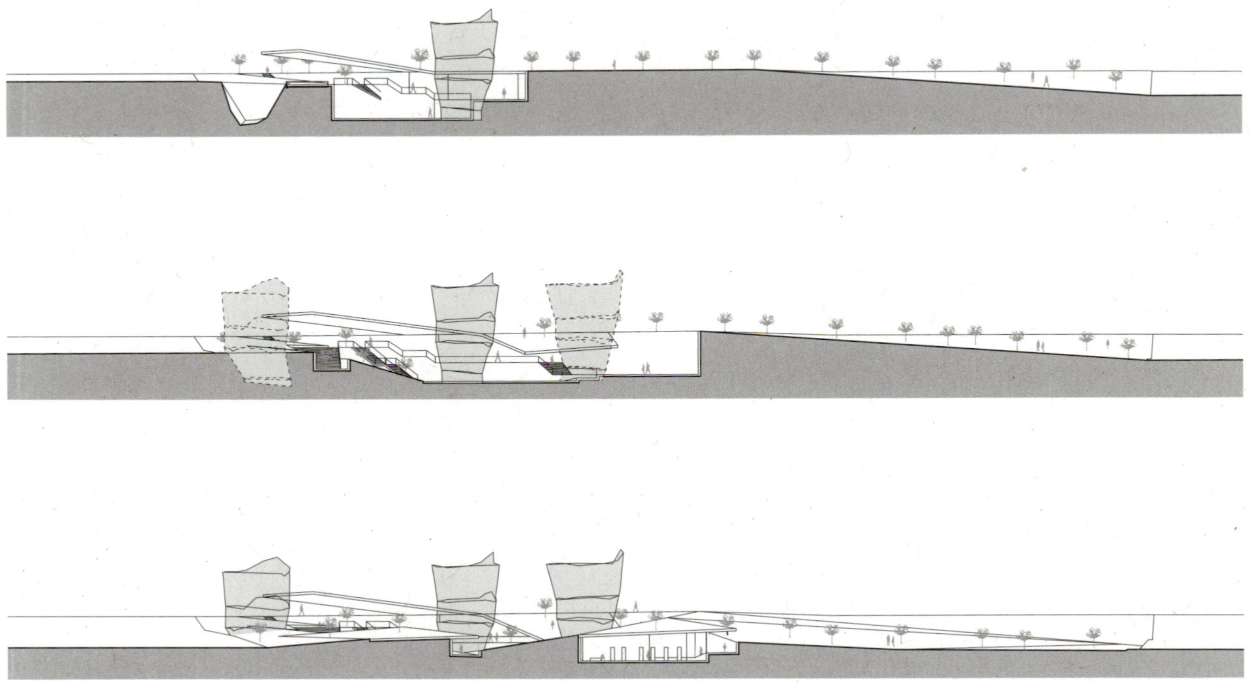

Sections

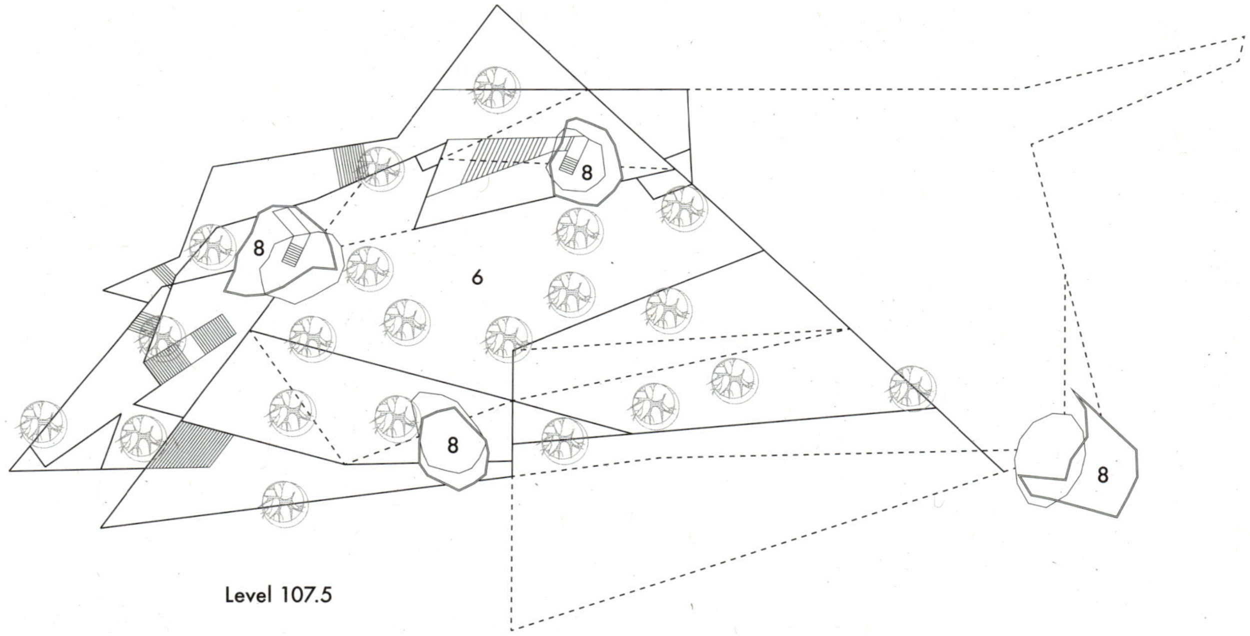

Ground floor

Level 107.5

1:850

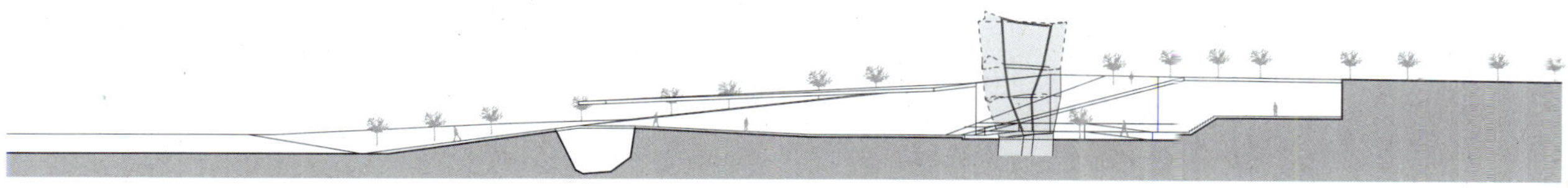

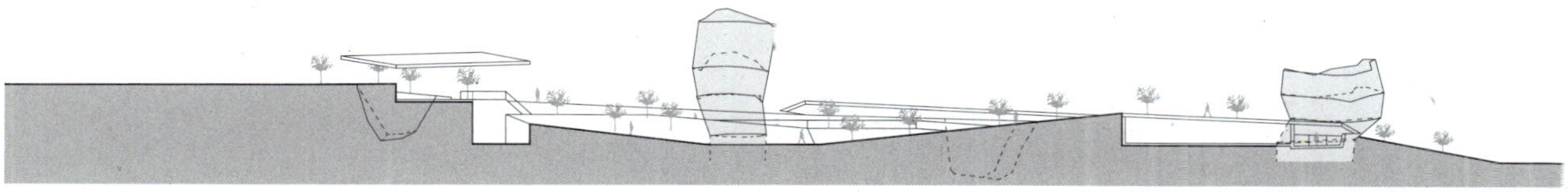

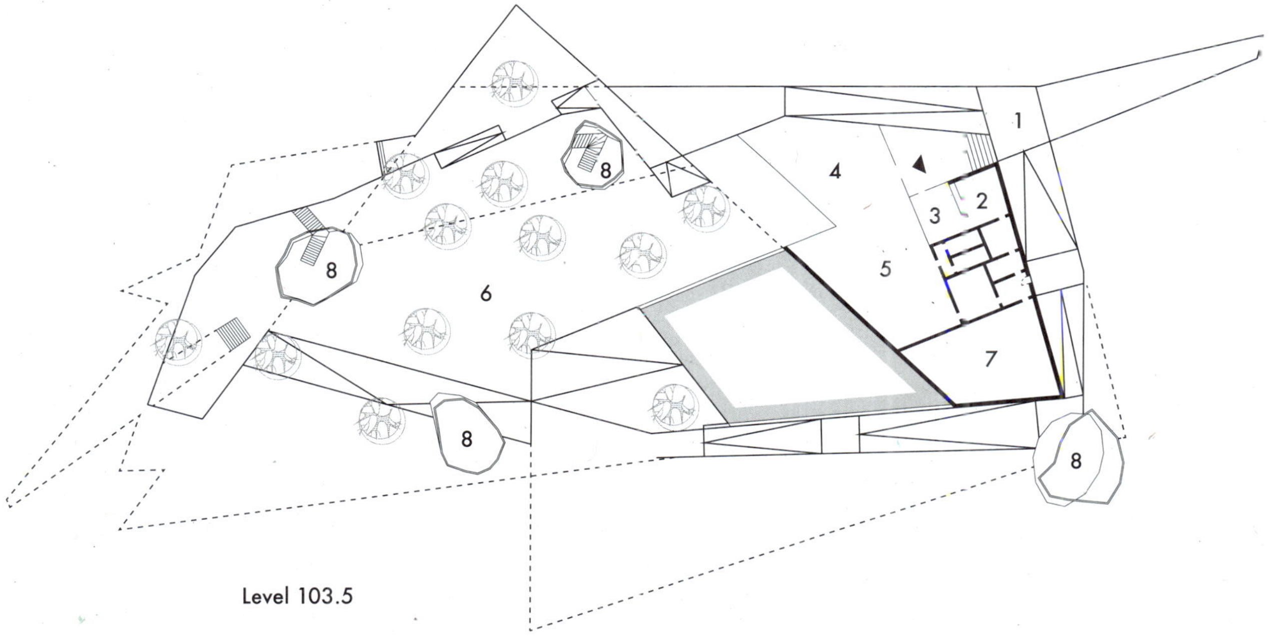

Level 103.5

1 Main entrance
2 Information
3 Service space
4 Cafe
5 Library area
6 Public courtyard contemplation area
7 Technical room
8 Earthquake responding drums

SOCIAL CULTURE

kulturzentrum mattersburg /
zentrum für kultur
und forschung
2016–22

The kulturzentrum mattersburg/ zentrum für kultur und forschung (Center for Culture and Research) complex in Mattersburg by the architect Herwig Graf—a restructuring and extension of the 1976 cultural center—houses important public amenities and organizations, such as a literature house, an adult education center, and a large performance hall, with an interlinking multipurpose foyer, and a *Gasthaus*, a typical Austrian venue for socializing and dining. Originally created to support the region's culture (as the first of five Center for Culture) by Burgenland's Cultural Councillor Gerald Mader with support of State Councilor Fred Sinowatz, it now also houses the state library and state archive of Burgenland, at the instigation of the present Governor Hans Peter Doskozil.

Sensitively repositioned in the park-like landscape, the overall scheme sits between the sloping Wulkalände and a steep railway embankment, forming a generous public square to integrate the derelict but protected area between the former cultural center and the still operational school and sports complex. The expressive and sculptural volumes of the existing brutalist, exposed-concrete building, as well as the structuralist northern part of the complex, all from the same period, are preserved, since they represent Burgenland's political history and cultural identity.

The proposed spatial layout pursues the idea of a vivid and active space where people of all ages are welcome and will love to meet. Two existing and newly built concrete masses—with a glass and steel foyer, 6.05 meters high, in between—reflect the inner organization pertaining to all the different functions. On the ground floor there is an event hall, accommodating about 410 visitors, the exhibition and lecture spaces hosting seventy people, and the dining rooms with an adjacent outside area embedded in the west lawn. On the first floor, office spaces, a library, and archive rooms find their place and are connected by a bridge that guides users to the different destinations via the multipurpose foyer. On this level, the outdoor area with the existing brutalist fountain invites visitors to read outside and enjoy the sunlight from the west. Most spaces adapt to multifunctional usage during the day and evening. The appealing, connective layering inside the existing and new spaces shows the ensemble as a contemporary interpretation of spatial sequences, inviting guests and users to experience culture and science in specific historic and contemporary surroundings.

archiv der avantgarden
2017

The *archiv der avantgarden* (Archive of the Avant-Gardes) stands on the Königsufer beside the Elbe River, between Dresden's historic Innere Altstadt and the more recent Innere Neustadt, the newer urban settlement across the river. Opening up in both directions, the site becomes a space for democracy, research, and encounter. The building was designed in the eighteenth century by Zacharias Longuelune as the Neustadt Watchtower, to protect the old inner city across the Augustus Bridge, and was later enlarged during the Baroque period into the existing *Blockhaus*. Its function changed several times until it became an administrative building, most recently housing the Sächsische Akademie der Wissenschaften (Saxon Academy of Sciences and Humanities). In 2013, however, it was flooded and not restored. In 2016, the City of Dresden decided to make the Blockhaus available as a research space and event center for the comprehensive avant-garde archive donated to the public by Egidio Marzona. This collection holds important and unique works from this influential period of the twentieth century—including original letters, sketches, drawings, paintings, prototypes, and objects.

The almost symmetrical building is accessed from the Innere Neustadt only, which is the reason for creating a new temporary structure on the side facing the river—above the Baroque garden and directly connected to the Augustus Bridge. This terrace, called the "democracy platform," doubles the volume from the inside to the outside and welcomes researchers and visitors from around the world attending outdoor workshops, festivals, and cultural events. There is a strong focus on public access to the archival spaces—integrating all security demands—and to the adjacent reading zones and exhibition areas distributed over five levels. Fitted into the protected space of the historic Baroque Blockhaus, the vertical design connects all stories via air spaces and sight lines. A created matrix—which includes philosophers like Ludwig Wittgenstein, musicians like John Cage, artists like Marcel Duchamp or Joseph Beuys, and architects like Ludwig Mies van der Rohe—defines both spatial and content-oriented arrangements. In addition to public interaction (workshops, exhibitions, discussions), quiet zones for studying books, films, and digital media serve researchers from all over the world—creating a source of inspiration, serving as a catalyst for visitors' streams of thought, and encouraging relationships with research platforms.

culture park pecs

2007

culture park pecs includes a series of indoor and outdoor contemporary exhibition spaces for the new Modern Hungarian Art Gallery in Pécs, Hungary. Influenced by sight lines and the neighboring buildings (including a masonry wall that wraps around the site), the observer focuses conceptually on individual museum structures that emerge out of the landscape. Their positioning initiates new open spaces in between, which, rather than becoming transitional areas for visitors, grow into a landscape for culture and exchange. An outdoor podium evolves, making use of a slight incline in the ground and introducing a stage for open-air performances and art lectures.

Like the tip of an iceberg, the structure's visible surface bespeaks the complexity of its invisible interior: the further spaces at the underground levels. Approaching *culture park pecs*, seamlessly embedded in the surrounding landscape, visitors are invited into an entrance building next to the pedestrian pathway, and then directed further into the gallery's interior spaces. The exhibition areas are divided into four main galleries. The one directly underneath the outdoor podium is the vast space that visitors encounter first, as they penetrate the depths of the museum. Starting at the underground level, they move, space by space, through the gallery, passing through exhibitions that include conceptual places of content, and then upward, step by step, until they reach the last and highest exhibition area, some 10 meters above the ground, looking back over the surrounding area and the wider landscape.

walk into rhythm

2000

walk into rhythm was proposed as an initial urban investment after the devastating war in Sarajevo, leaving local residents optimistic about their future. Taking its cue from the urban context, the concept uses a historical axis as a visual axis to locate a public square next to the Miljacka River and the parliament destroyed in 1992. It then turns the visual axis into a walkway that slowly but steadily guides visitors upward, an uptilted pedestrian space connecting all the floors, concert halls, and the panorama platform on top. The programmatic shape of the concert halls and the passage in between lends form to the building *walk into rhythm* and creates an envelope that does not hide its functions.

Passage and concert halls are set in a surrounding landscape conceptually designed as a composition. Walking slowly along the inclined promenade one is lead to the entrance areas of each concert hall, different in size and orientation. Finally, at the top, a public space offers guests views of the back gardens, and a restaurant serves as a relaxation area during concert intermissions. All serving rooms are located along the walkway and can be used by the guests. The building and its volume are determined by the interior organization of music halls and waiting areas, and the promenade—and lighted interior spaces—display all visitor activities to Sarajevo's inhabitants.

kinderkunstlabor

2020

The city of Sankt Pölten has extended its cultural institutions to include a space for children, where they can encounter contemporary art. A park-like area has been selected for this, next to the Festspielhaus, Landesmuseum, Klangturm, and Landesbibliothek and close to the State government Landhaus, yet adjacent to a busy street. Taking the existing infrastructure and local changes as vital parameters, the project reflects the area's up-and-coming status as an extension of the surrounding culture and landscape. It proposes a space for children to make contact with artists working in painting, sculpture, photography, music, and literature, as well as multimedia and various other interdisciplinary forms of art production. The idea is to create a building for creativity that motivates children to experience various art techniques, experiment with media, and create their own works of art.

Three levels are organized horizontally along the street, to protect the outdoor areas inside Altona Park from traffic noise. Ramps guide children through the building, passing different kinds of trees that are incorporated into the spatial arrangement. Children are continually connected to nature as they stroll from one exhibition area to the next, until they reach the first floor and the experimental laboratories for their own art productions. One of these spaces extends beyond the footprint of the structure and, enclosing a nearby Metasequoia redwood tree, hovers above ground. The office rooms, on the second floor, can be quickly accessed via a central staircase and elevator close to the entrance area and café.

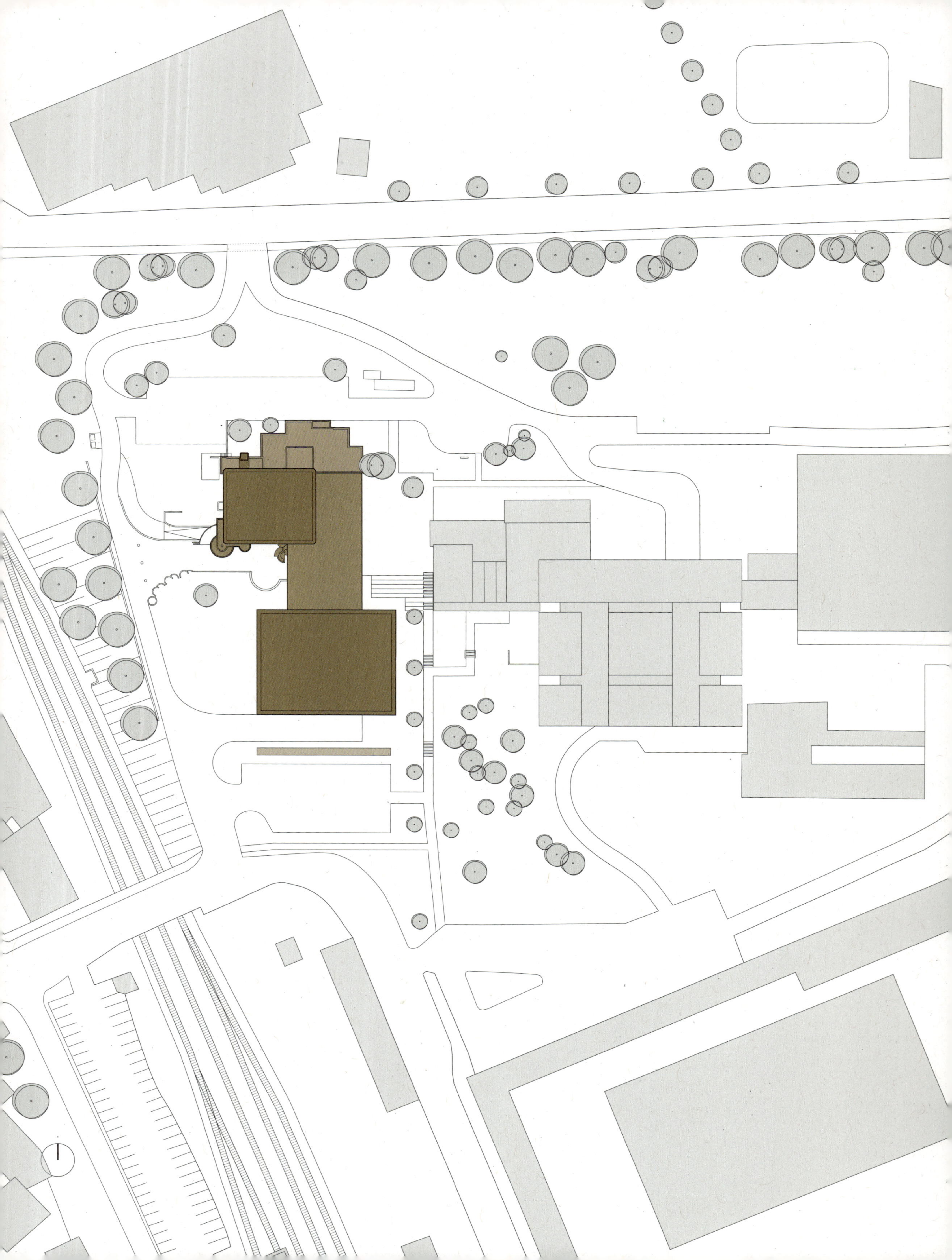

kulturzentrum mattersburg / zentrum für kultur und forschung

7210 Mattersburg, AT

See pp. 138–51

PROGRAM
Cultural center, state library, state archive, literature house, vocational school, event hall, youth meeting area, inn (restaurant), renovation, restructure, extension

DIMENSIONS
GFA 5,769 m^2, gross net area 4,745 m^2

CLIENT
LIB – Landes Immobilien Burgenland GmbH

PROJECT TEAM
Marlies Breuss, Michael Ogertschnig, Marc Busquets, Lars Oberländer, Marc Werner, Iva Olujic, Alexander Garber, Mija Mikuz, Johannes Müller, Simon Pranter, Richard Szilvassy

CONSULTANTS
KPPK (structural engineer and building physics), kwi (building systems), Dr. Pfeiler (acoustics)

ARTIST
Paul Muehlbauer

MODEL-MAKING
archimodell, Vienna

PHOTOGRAPHY
Wolfgang Thaler

AWARDS
First prize, EU-wide two-stage tender competition 2016

PUBLICATIONS (SELECTION)
Claudia Rinne, "Kulturzentrum Mattersburg, Burgenland: ein langer Neubeginn," *Architektur.aktuell*, Vienna, September 2018.
"Kulturzentrum Mattersburg: Sanierung, Um- und Zubau," in *Wien. Niederösterreich. Burgenland* (2018).

"The result is a successful combination of old and new, which interprets the architectural theme of Brutalism in an exciting contemporary way."

—*alt bau neu* 1 (2022), p. 43 (trans. by the ed.)

Site plan
1:1,000

10 25 50 m

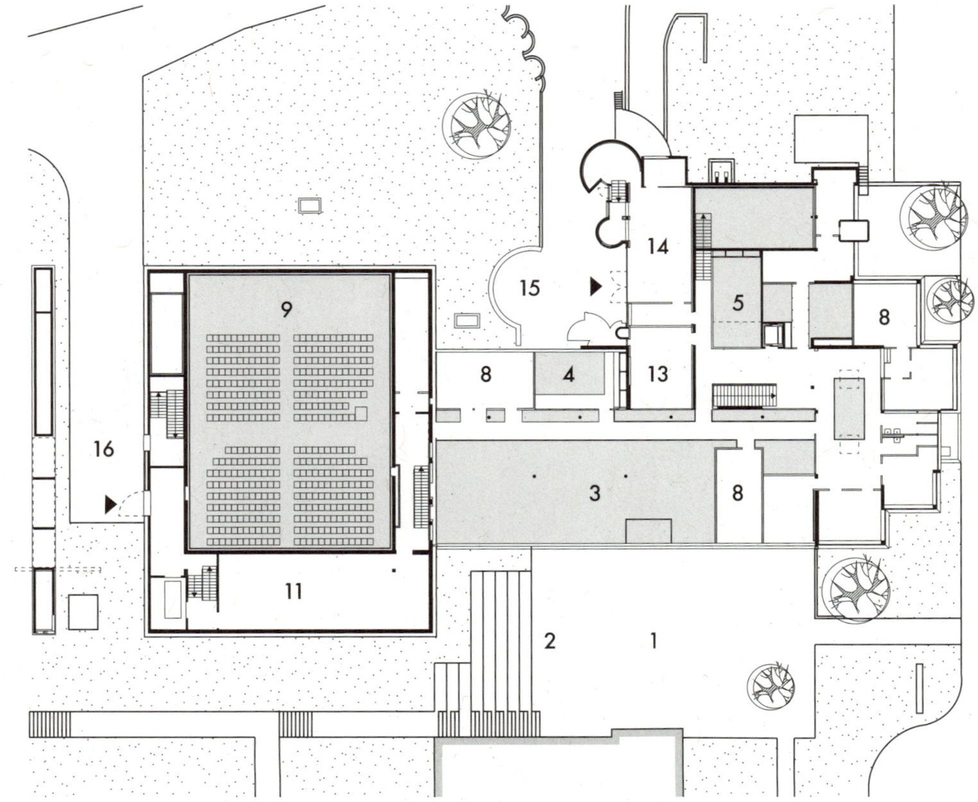

First floor

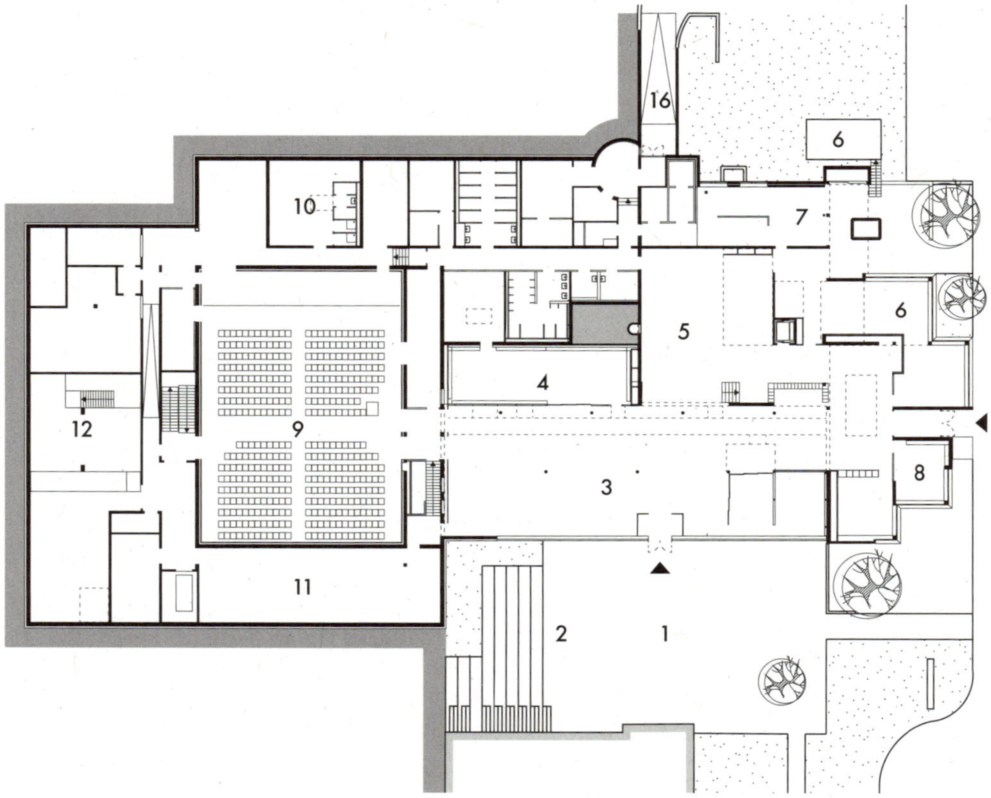

Ground floor
1:650

1 Public square
2 Outdoor podium
3 Multifunctional foyer
4 House of literature
5 Exhibition space
6 Restaurant with terraces
7 Cooking area
8 Office spaces
9 Event hall
10 Artists area
11 National archive
12 Building systems
13 Adult education space
14 Library/reading area
15 Common courtyard
16 Delivery area
17 Multifunctional space

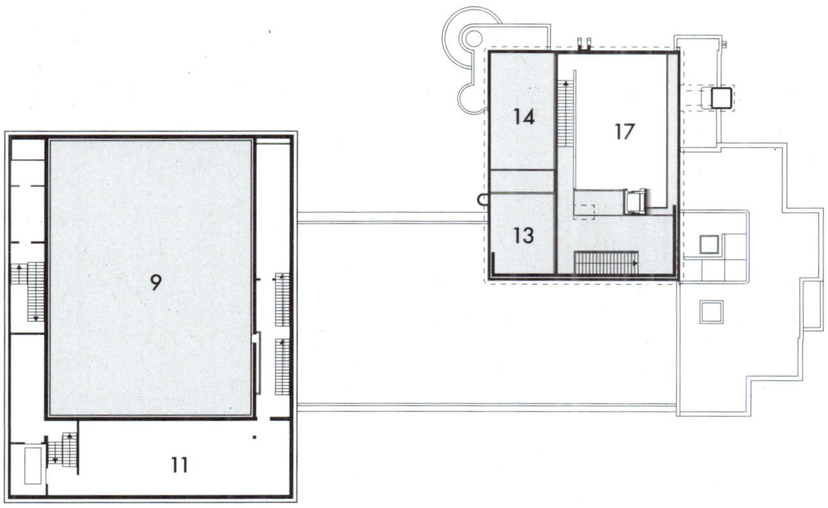

Second floor

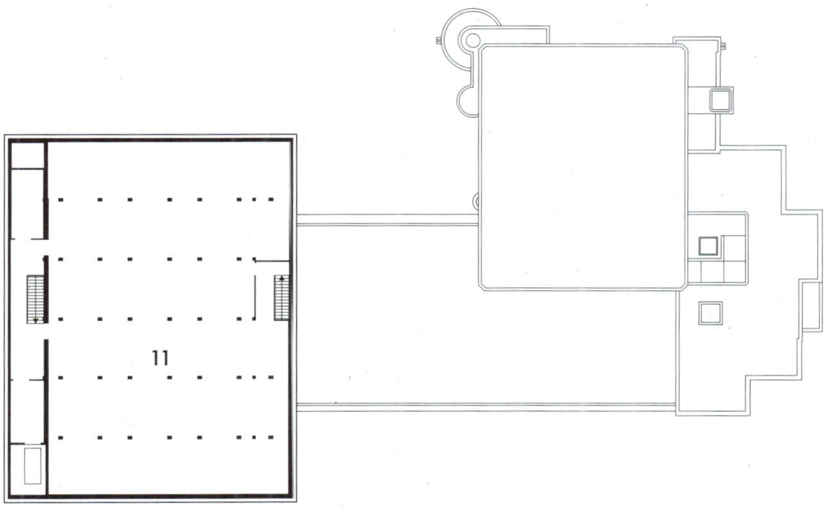

Third floor

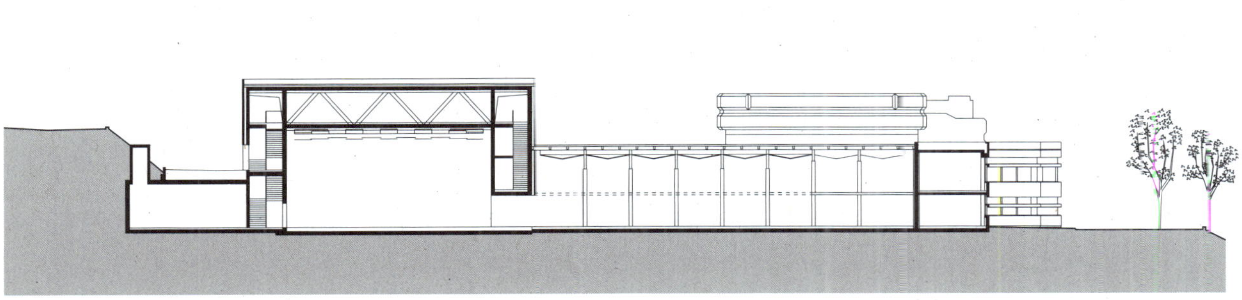

Section

1:650

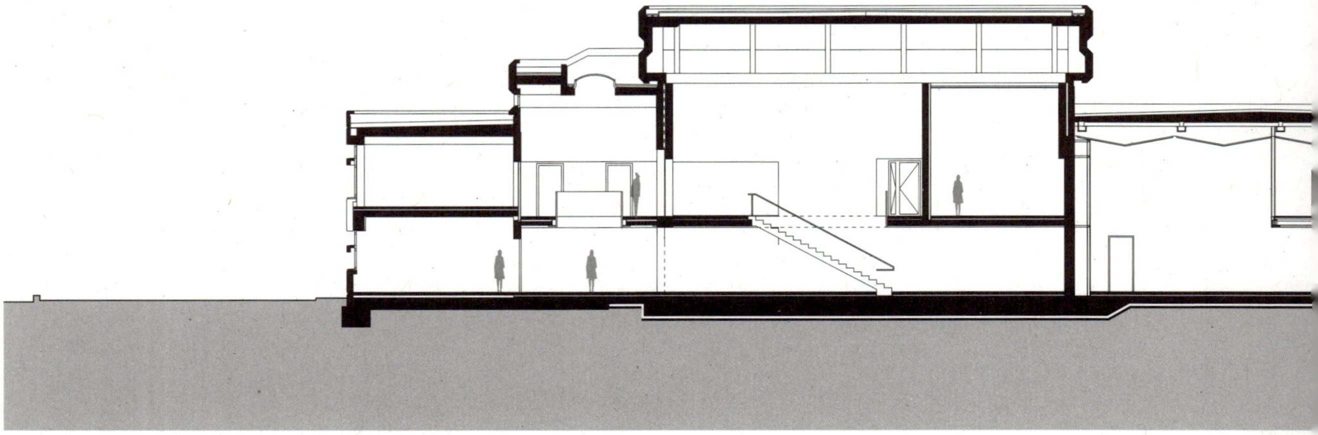

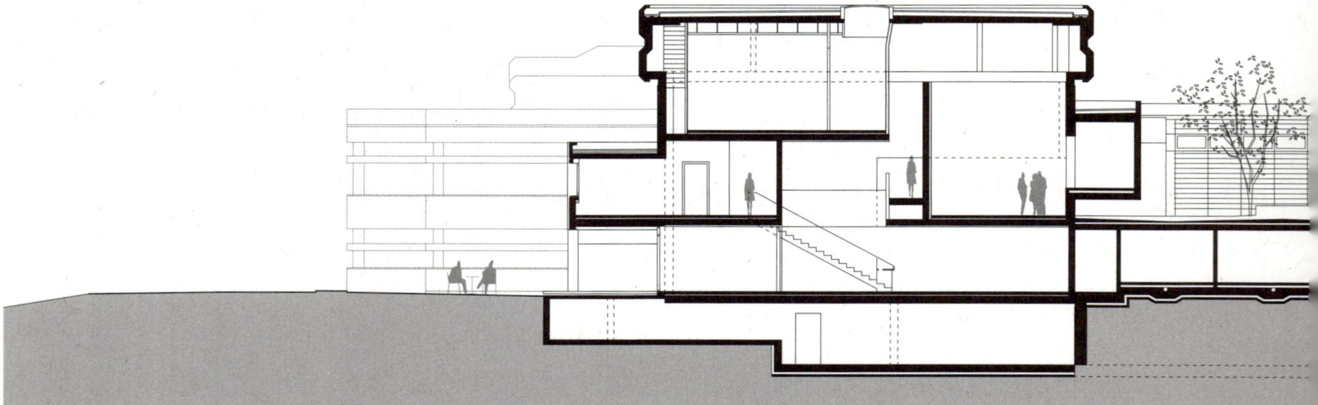

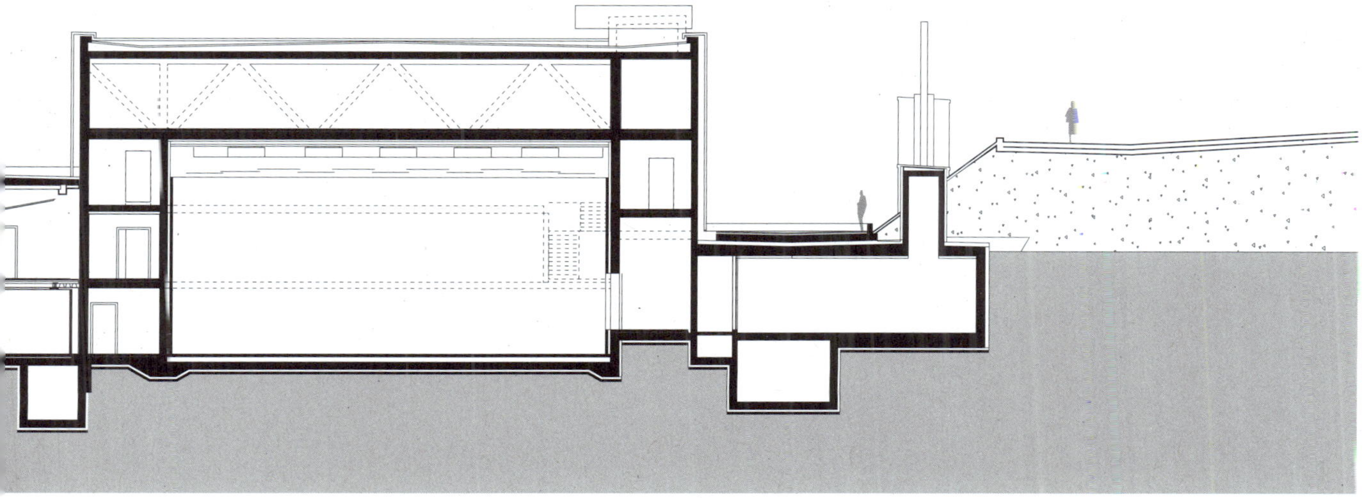

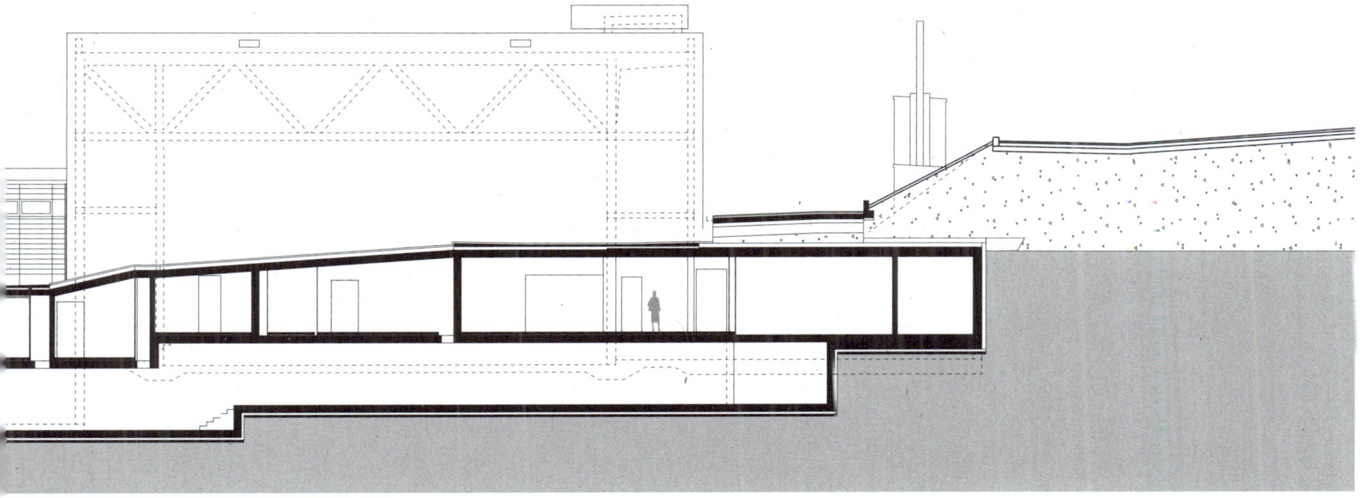

Sections
1:300

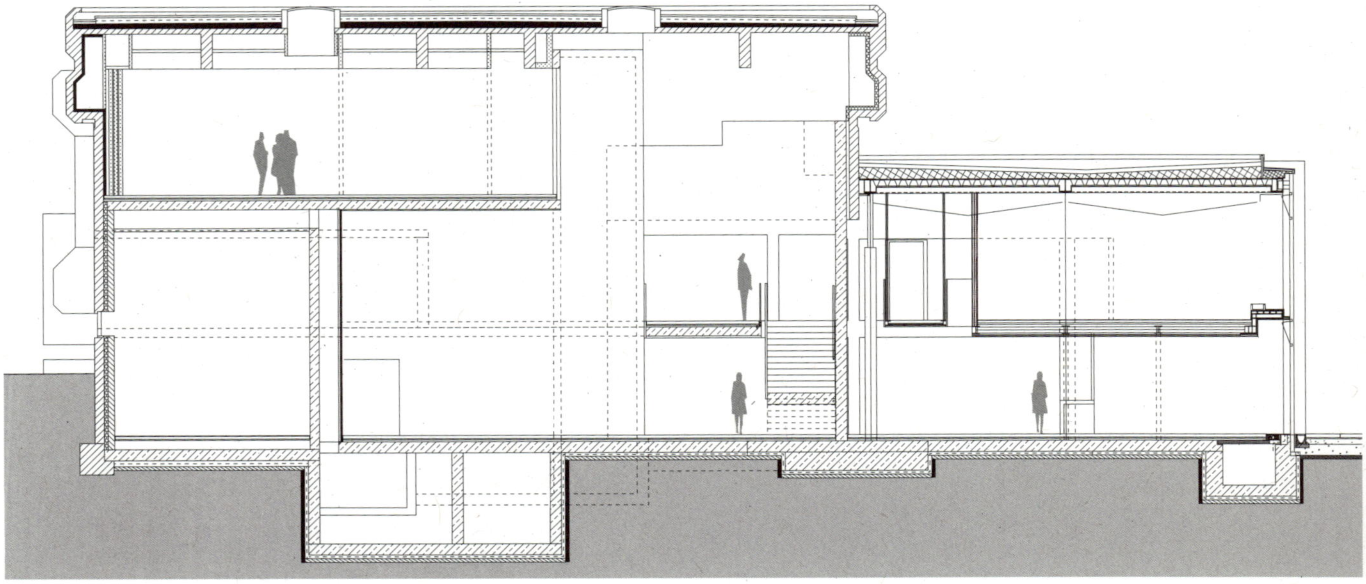

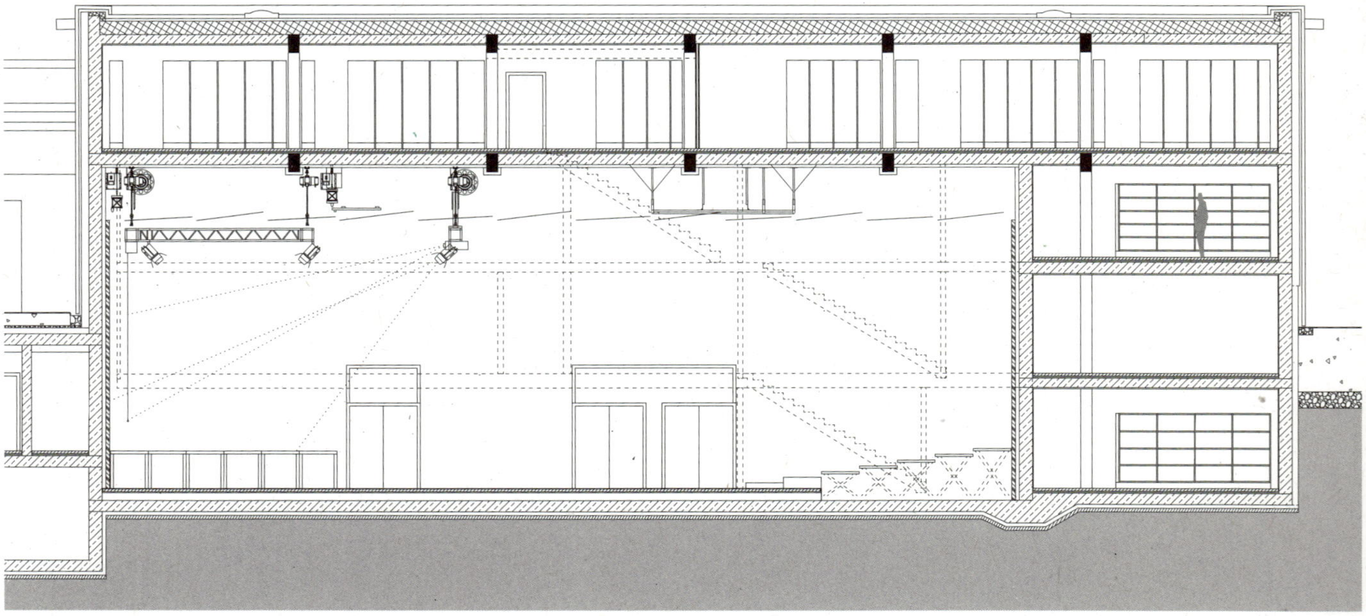

Sections
1:200

1 3 6 10 m

Detail A / roof

Substrate for extensive green roofing 80 mm
Drainage and filter layer 20 mm
Double layered polymer bitumen sealing
Lower layer: cold-bonded elastomeric membrane,
root resistant and fleece reinforced
Upper layer: film laminated elastomeric membrane with
root barrier, copper band insert, glass mat insert
EPS insulation (gradient) falls 190–300 mm
Elastomeric bitumen vapor barrier
Load distributing galvanized sheet metal 1 mm
Trapezoidal sheet metal 8 mm
Plaster fireboard 15 mm
Insulation 50 mm
Acoustic panel 15 mm

Detail B / facade

Mullion/transom facade wide 50 mm
Sun protection insulation glazing (neutral)
1,0 W/m²K g = 0,23
Inside sunscreen textile fc value 0,56 (offices)

Detail C / floor

Blinding layer 100 mm
XPS insulation 100 mm
Polyethylene film, double layered, fleece reinforced
Concrete slab 300 mm
Sealant 5 mm
Bonded fill 46 mm
Polyethylene film
Impact-sound insulation 30 mm
Polyethylene film
Anhydride screed 75 mm
Tiles in thin-bed 14 mm

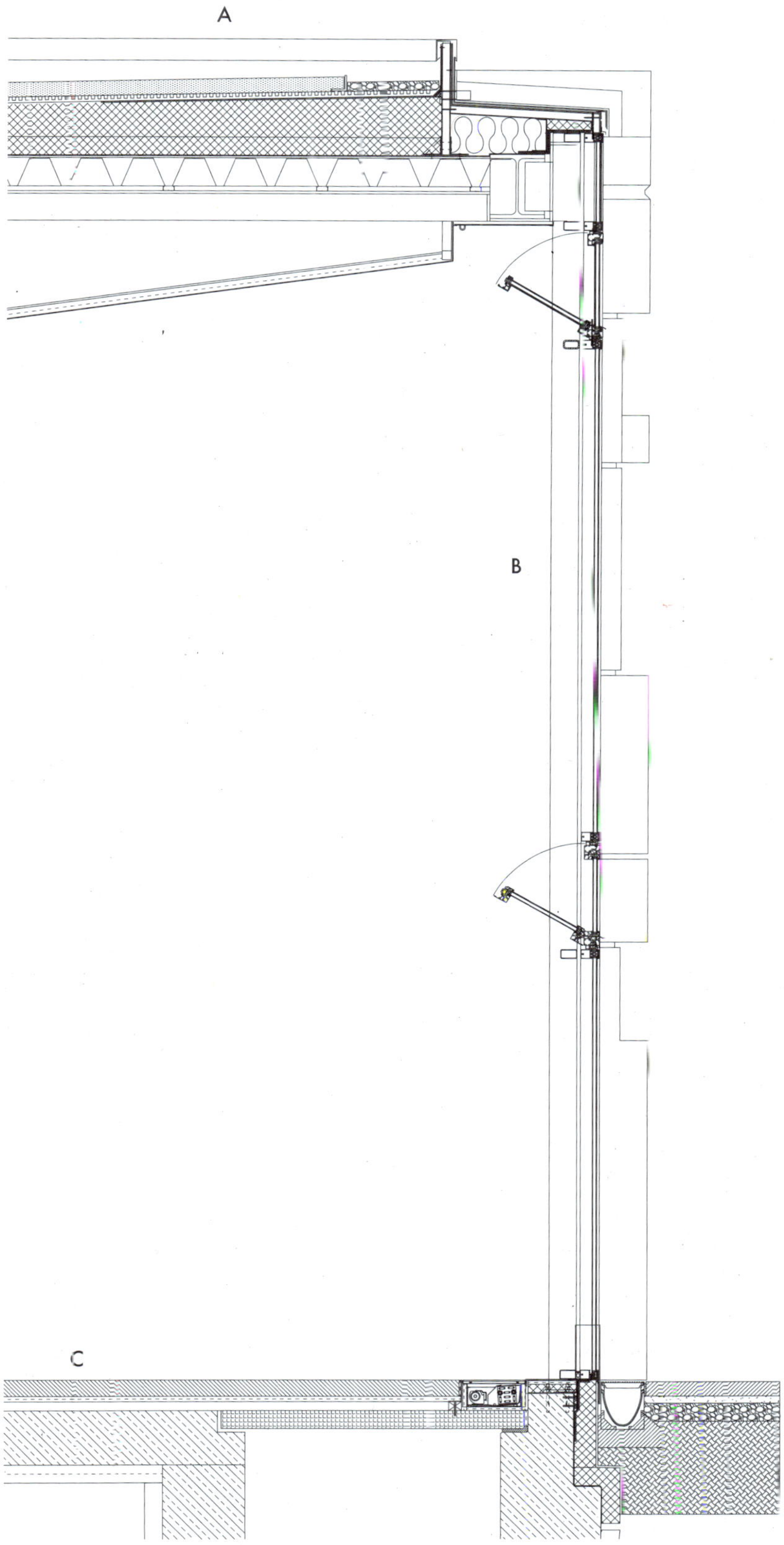

Details
1:40

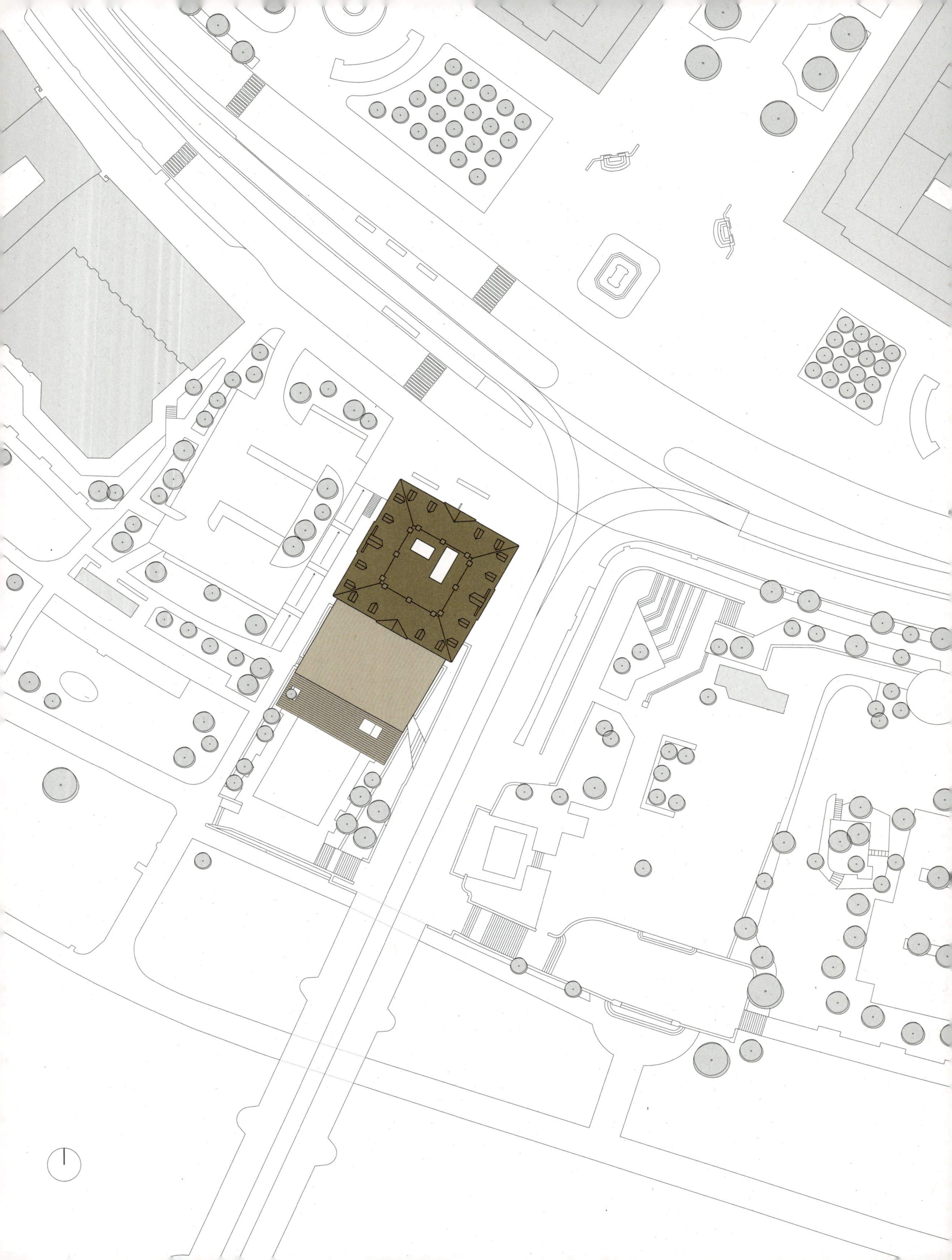

archiv der avantgarden
01097 Dresden, DE

PROGRAM
Museum and exhibition spaces, conversion, redevelopment, restructure

DIMENSIONS
GFA 4,762 m², gross net area 3,457 m²

CLIENT
Staatliche Kunstsammlung Dresden

PROJECT TEAM
Marlies Breuss, Michael Ogertschnig, Lars Oberländer, Lisa Götz, Amanda Riedel, Alessandro Zerbi

CONSULTANTS
ghp gmeiner | haferl & partner zt gmbh (structural engineer), IPJ Ingenieurbüro
P. Jung (energy and building physics), kwi and IPRO (building systems)

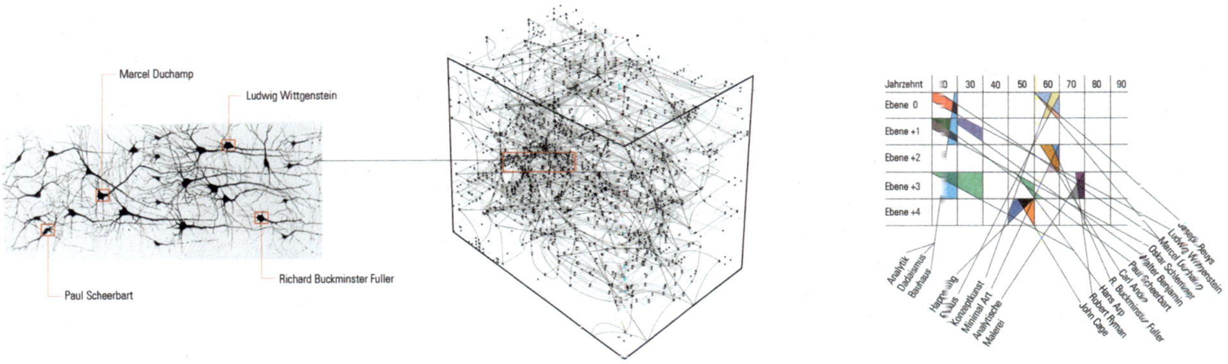

> “Democracy is a spatial practice that takes over specific spaces, often spaces of the everyday and even spaces that were not intended for the purpose, the physical stuff—cities, space bodies—they matter.”

—Yasmin Vobis, experts discuss “Architecture of Democracy,” in *Lecture*, hosted by Harvard and MIT.

Site plan
1:1,000

10 25 50 m

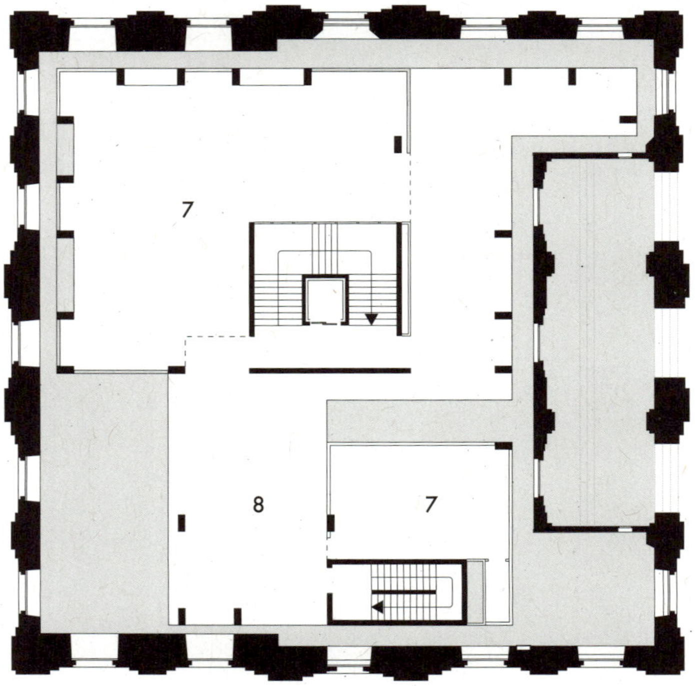

First floor
1:350

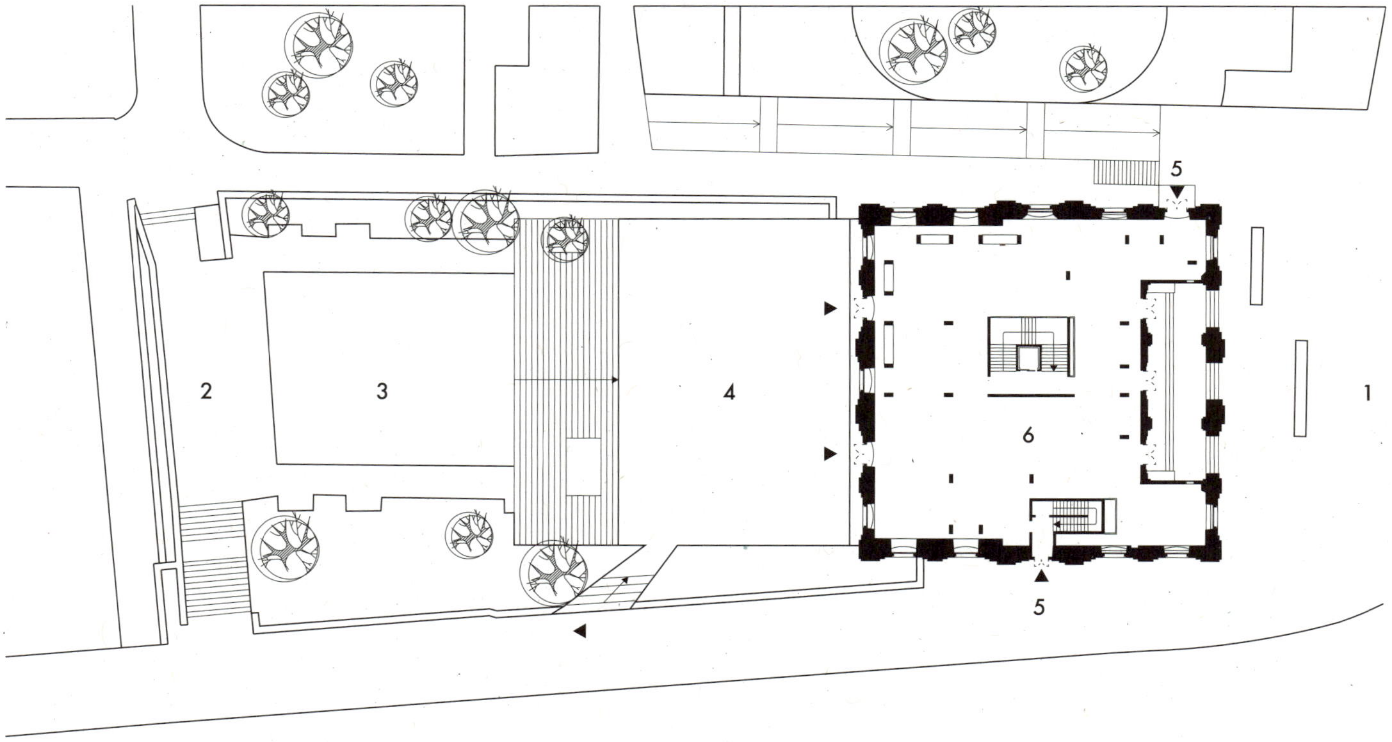

Ground floor
1:650

1 3 6 10 m

1 Common public area
2 Public river walkway
3 Baroque garden
4 Democratic plateau, river terrace
5 Delivery area
6 Multifunctional space
7 AdA archive
8 Exhibition space
9 Reading area
10 Public discussion space
11 Office area
12 Common courtyard

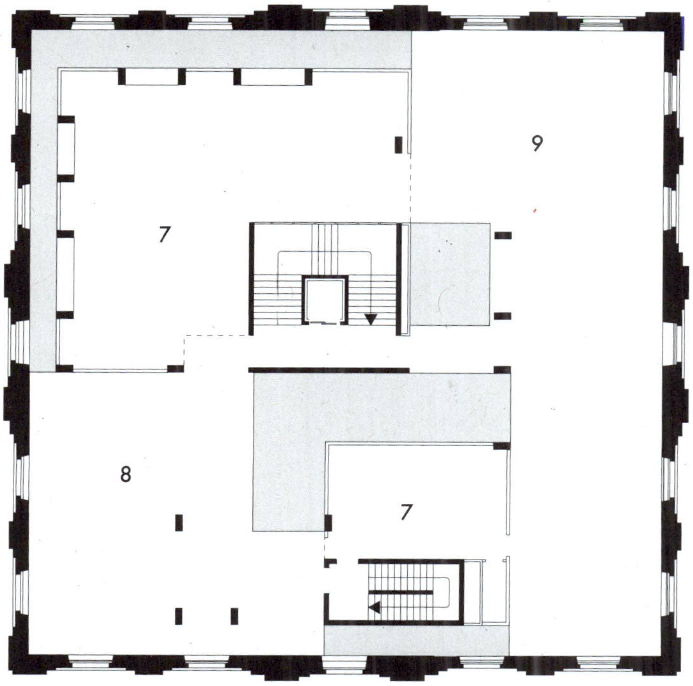

Second floor

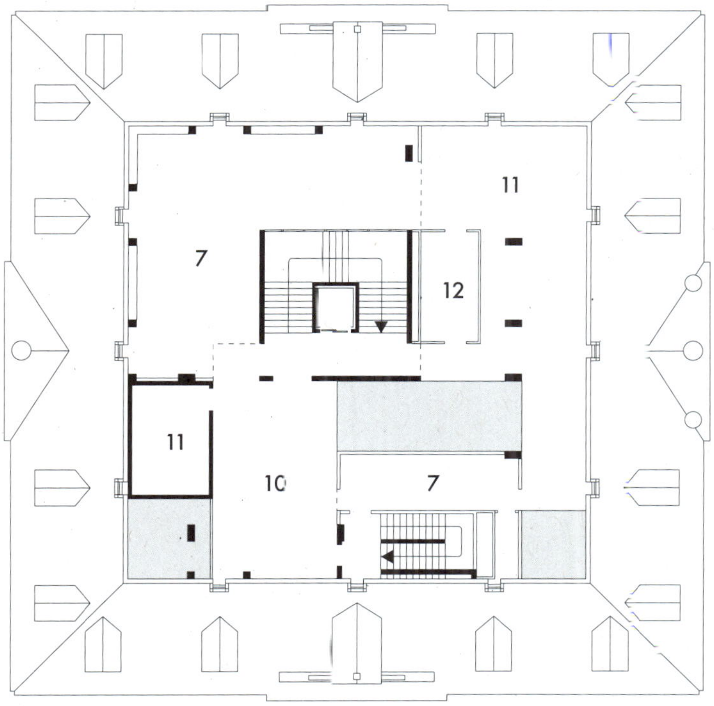

1 3 6 10 m

Fourth floor
1:350

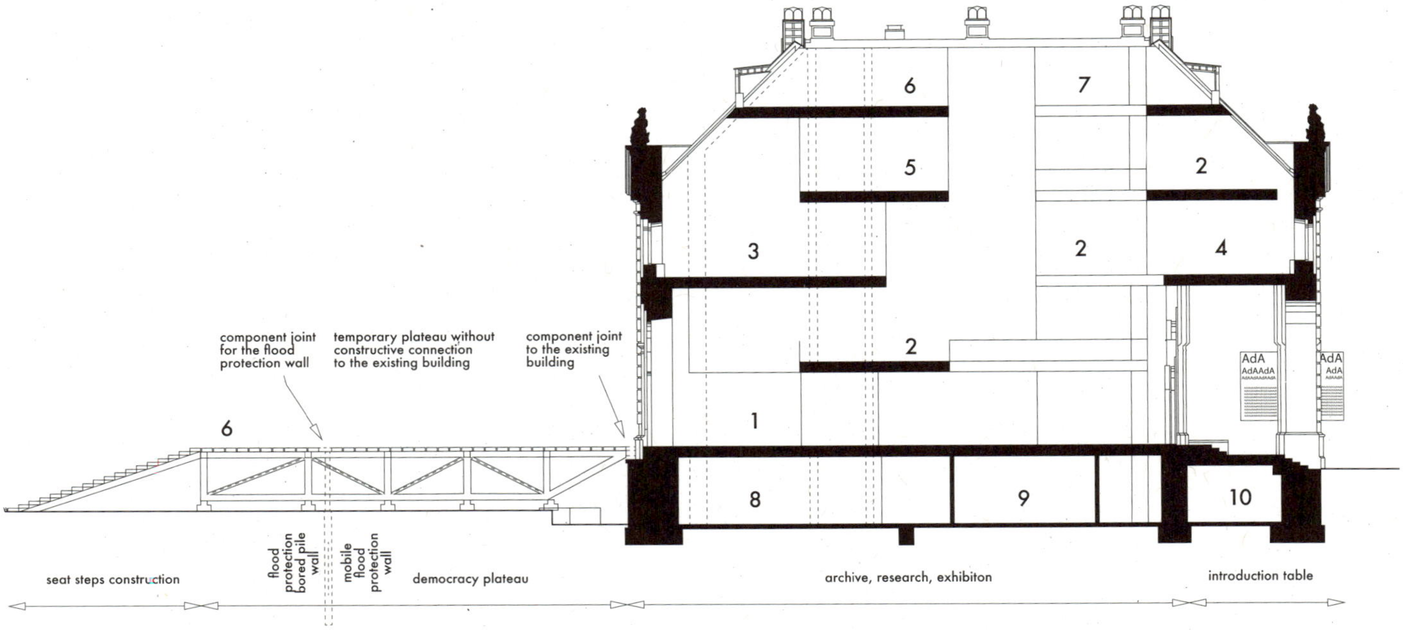

1 Foyer
2 Exhibition
3 Research
4 Open access library
5 Photography/digital
6 Democratic plateau, river terrace
7 Staff area
8 Technical area
9 Bathroom facilities
10 Storage area

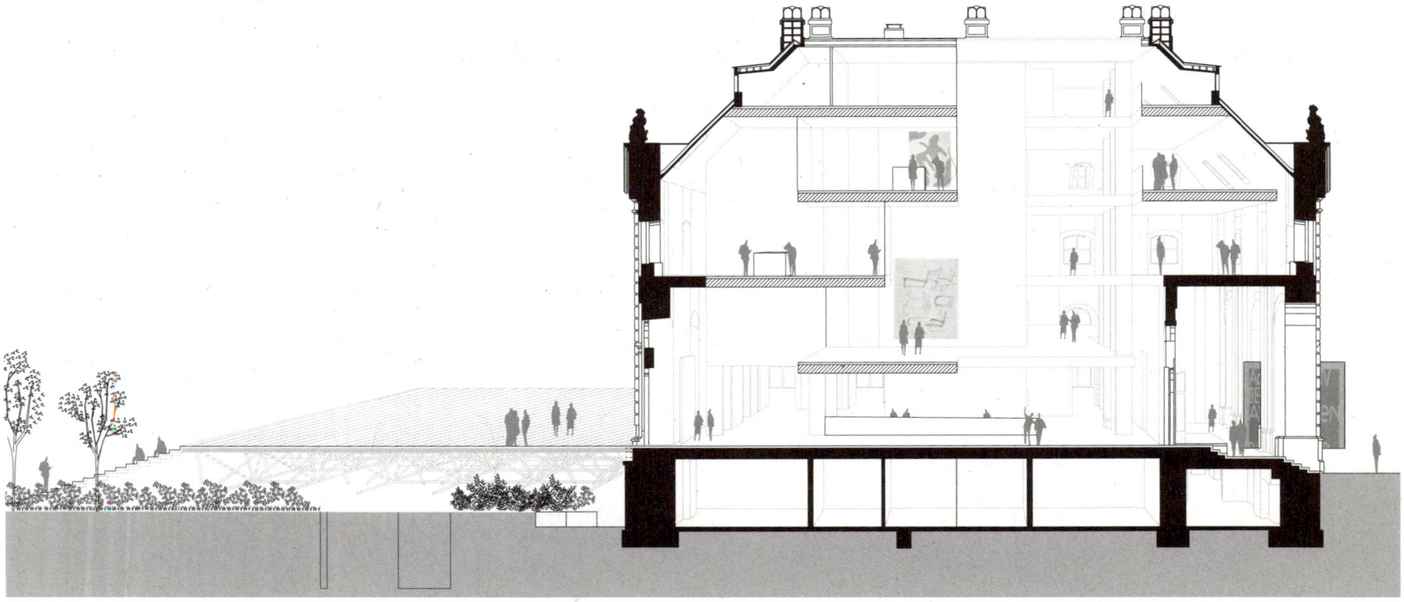

Cross section
1:350

1 3 6 10 m

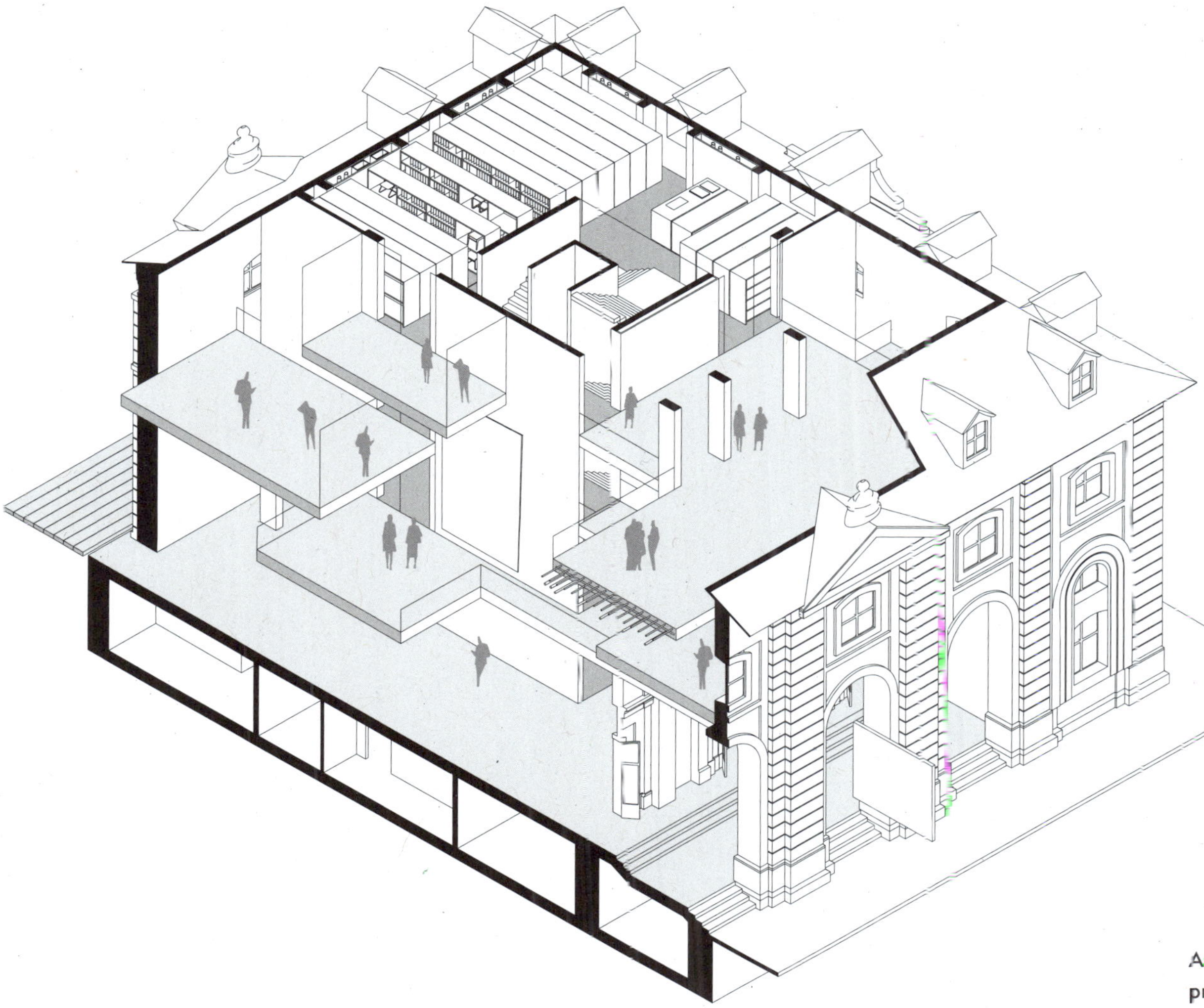

Axonometric
projection

1 Augustus Bridge
2 Foyer/bar area
3 Cash desk
4 Archives
5 Research
6 Storage
7 Packing room
8 Distributing depot
9 Exhibition level
10 Common courtyard

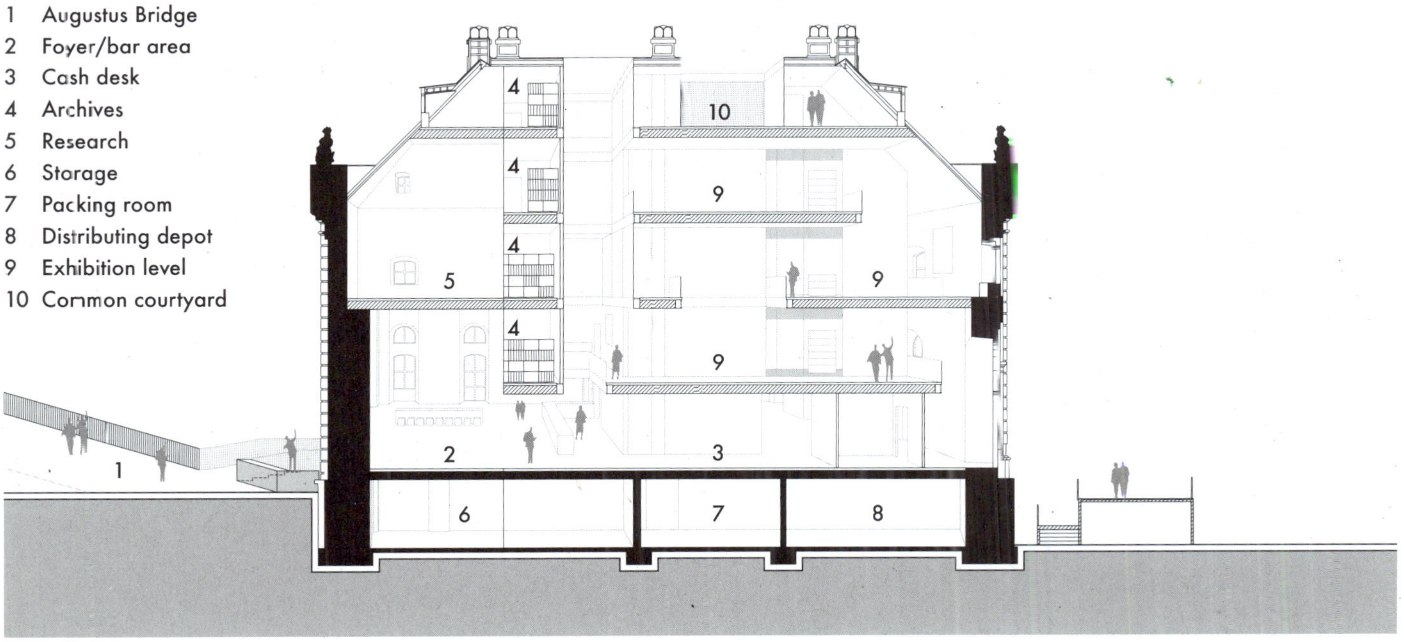

Longitudinal section
1:350

culture park pecs
7621 Pécs, HU

PROGRAM
Museum area with four galleries, cultural building, extension

DIMENSIONS
Plot area 2,834 m², GFA 7,806 m²

CLIENT
City of Pécs – European Cultural City of the Year 2010

PROJECT TEAM
Marlies Breuss, Michael Ogertschnig, Elisa Gersdorf, Ulrich Hagen, Sven Klöcker

AWARDS
International open competition – Pécs 2010, European Capital of Culture, special mention

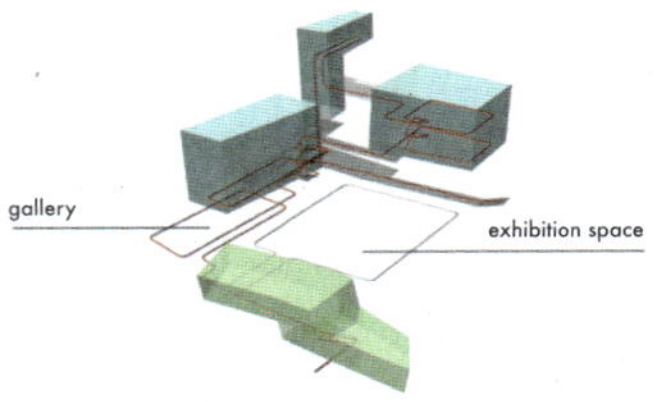

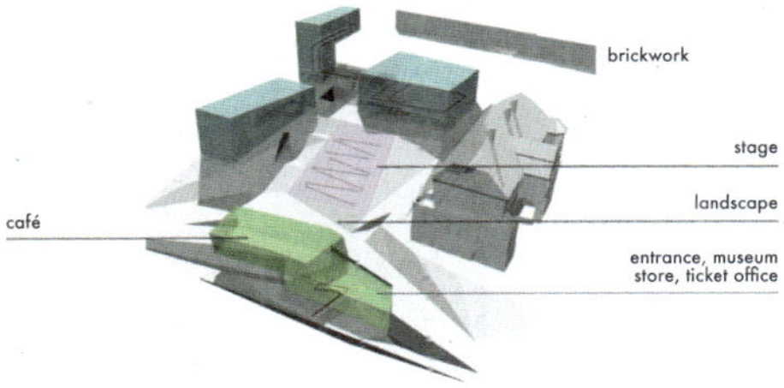

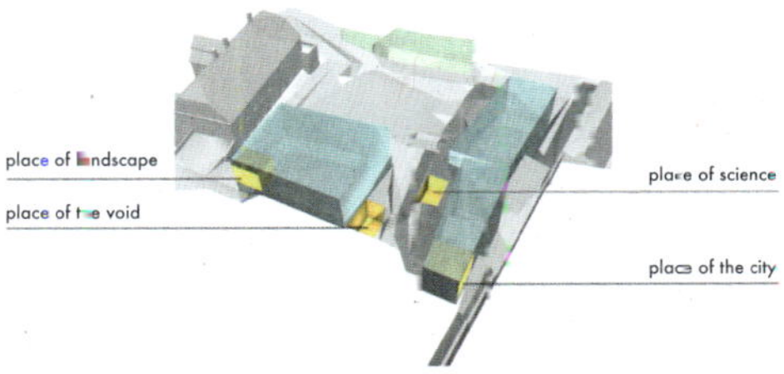

“The impulse behind the creation of an earthbound form ... is often to reveal the hidden and turn it into architecture.”

—Aaron Betsky, *Landscrapers: Building With the Land*, Thames and Hudson, 2002, p. 18.

Site plan
1:1,000

10 25 50 m

page 415

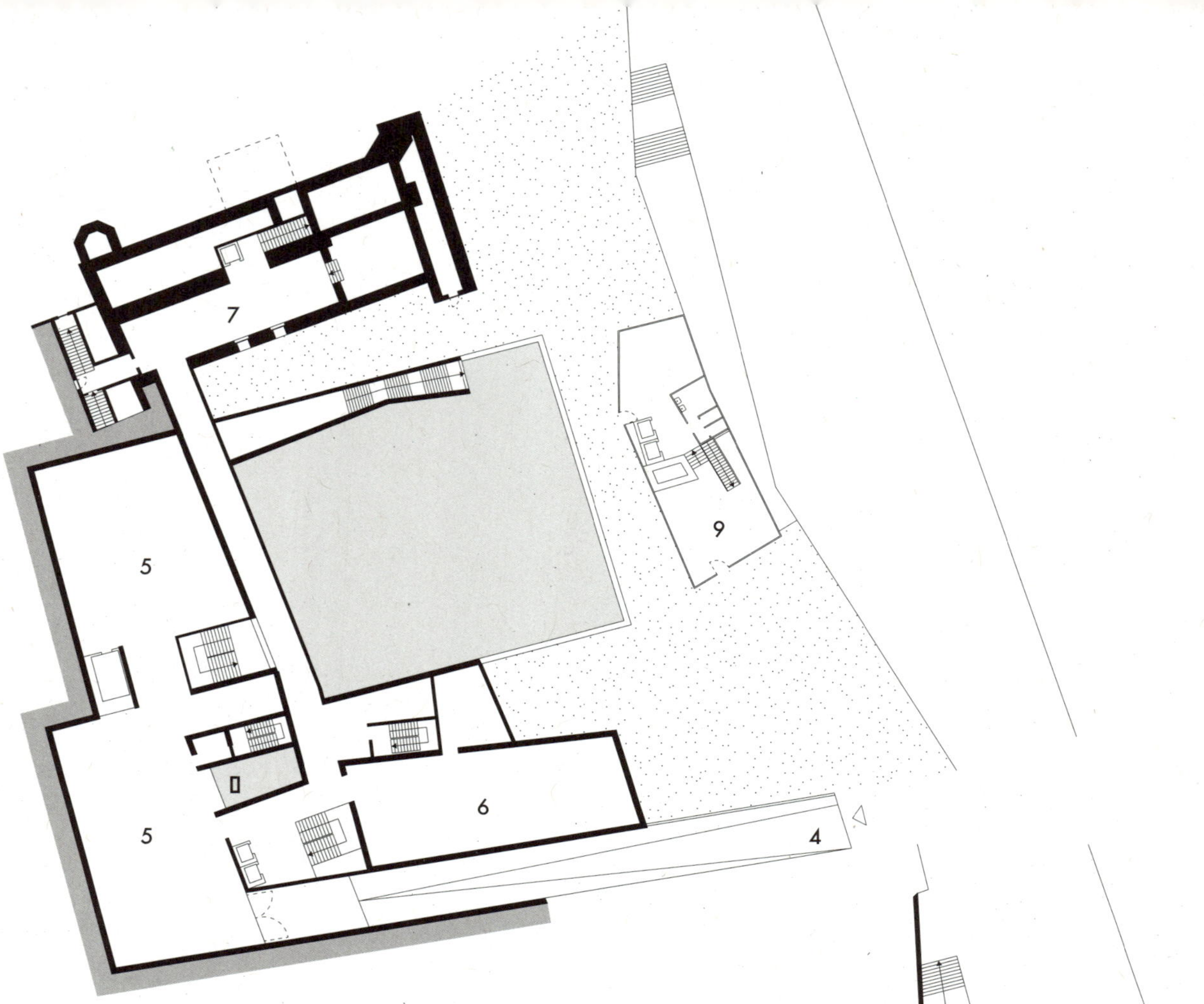

First floor

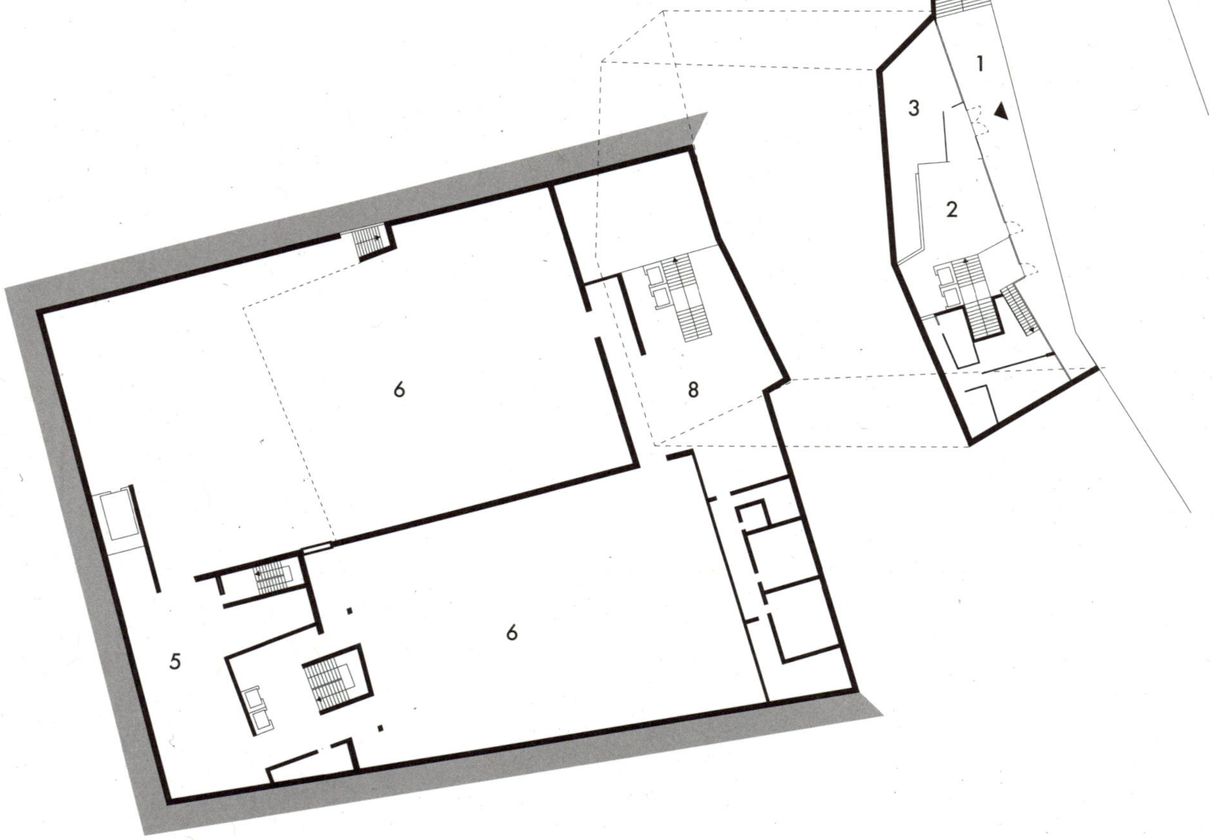

Ground floor
1:650

1 3 6 10 m

1 Public entrance area
2 Multifunctional foyer
3 Shop space
4 Delivery area
5 Storage area
6 Exhibition space
7 Existing museum
8 Service area
9 Restaurant
10 Library
11 Administration
12 Outdoor podium

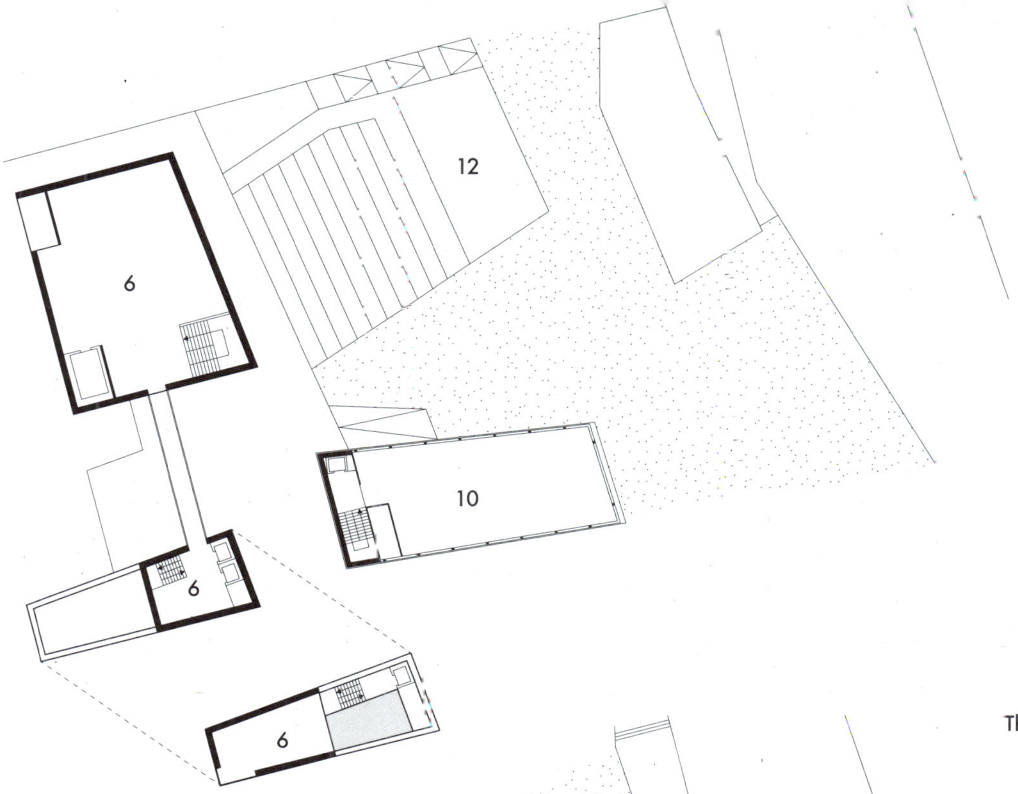

Third floor

Second floor

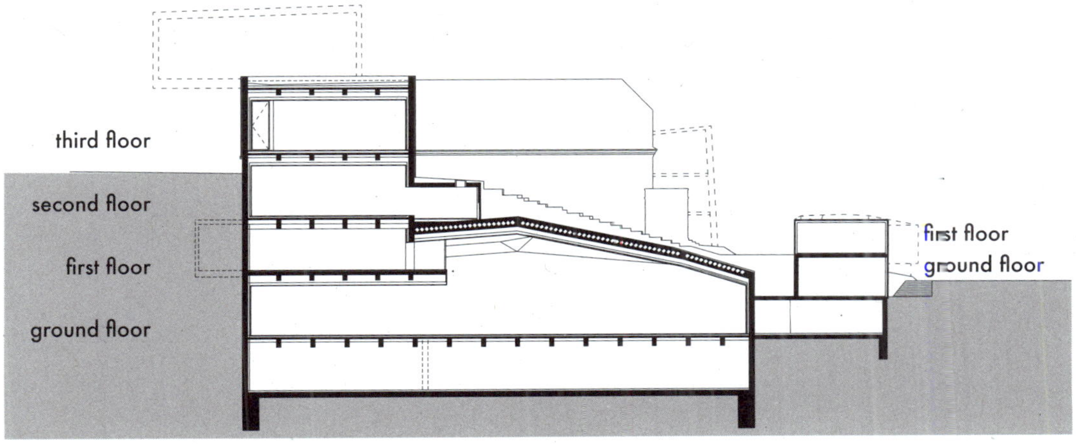

Section
1:650

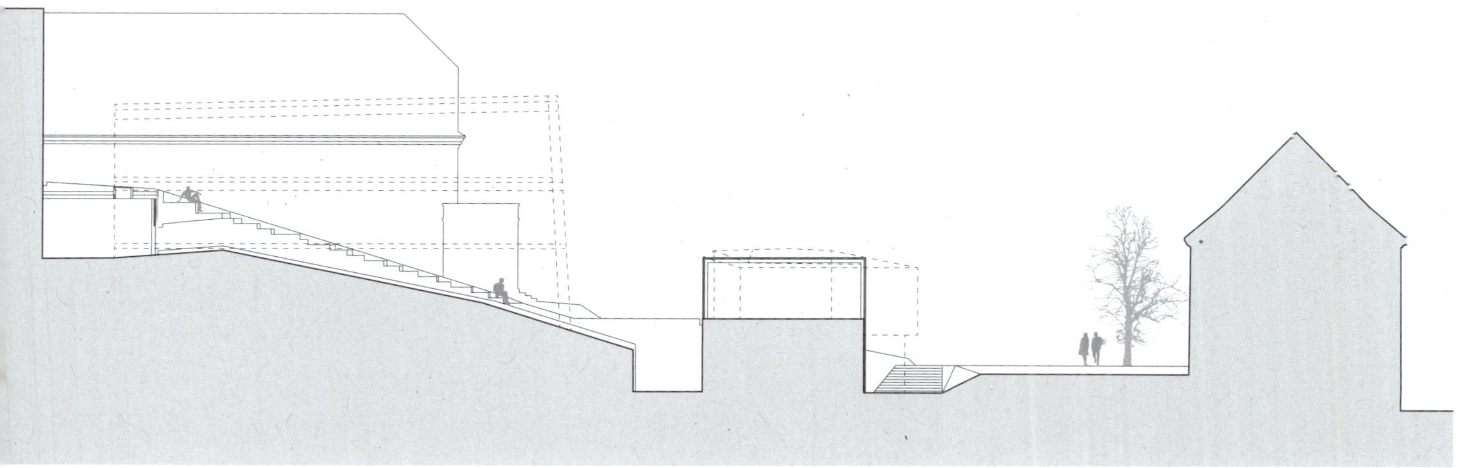

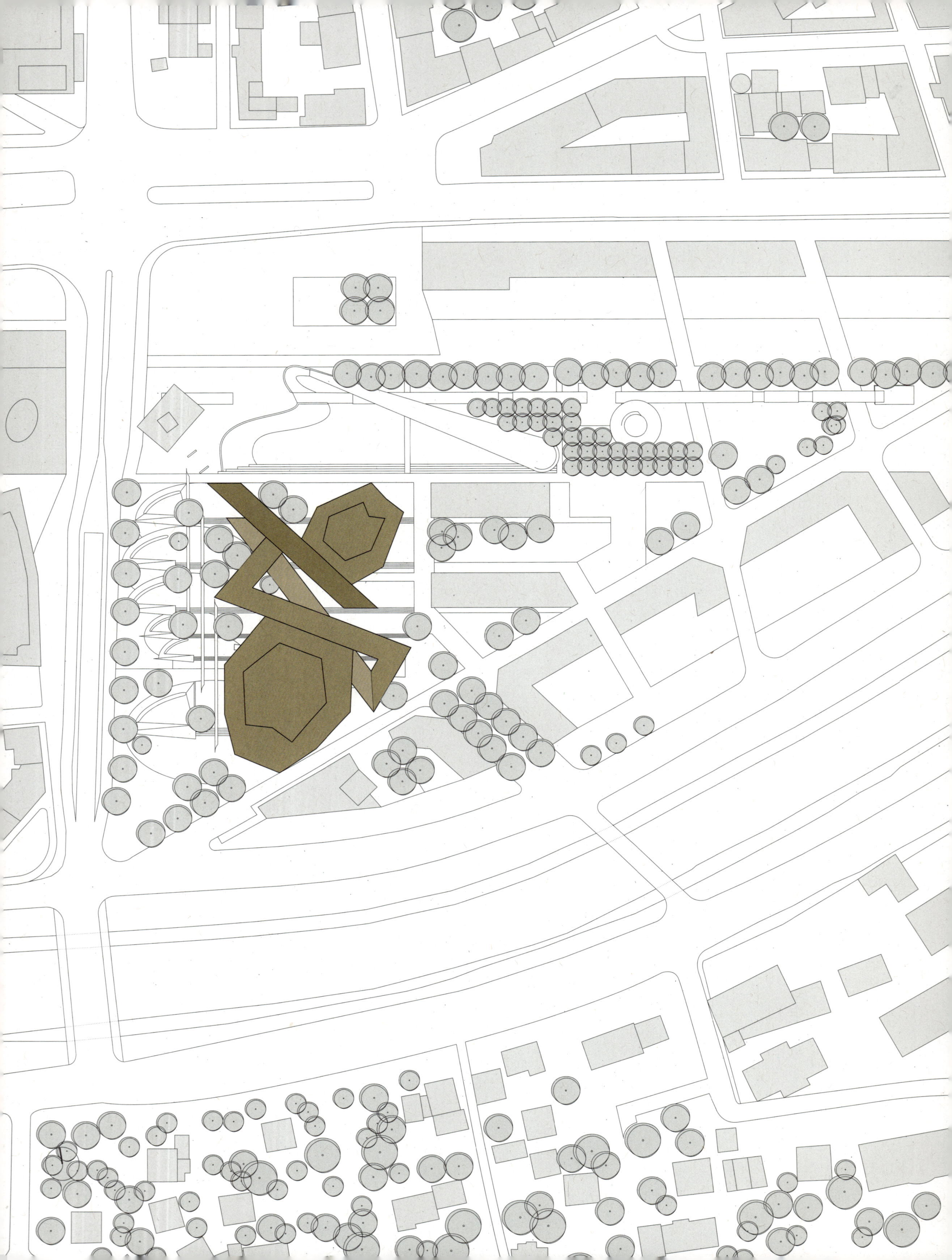

2000
SOCIAL CULTURE

walk into rhythm
71000 Sarajevo, BA

PROGRAM
Cultural building, concert halls with lounge, urban walkway, public gardens

DIMENSIONS
GFA 7,125 m^2

CLIENT
Sarajevo Canton & AS.A.S (Association Architects of Sarajevo)

PROJECT TEAM
Marlies Breuss, Michael Ogertschnig, Heidelinde Holzinger, Stefan Schodenböck, Susanne Schmall, Christine Schmauszer

AWARDS
International open competition, honorable mention

PUBLICATIONS (SELECTION)
IX Biennial of Young Artists From Europe And The Mediterranean, exhibition, Mattatoio Testaccio, Rome, June 1999.
Young European Architects, CLEAN edizioni, Naples, 2000 (ISBN 88-86701-90-X).
Sarajevo Concert Hall, competition catalogue, Rome, February 2000.
Francesco Ghio and Donata Tchou, *Sarajevo Concert Hall*, 2000 (ISBN 88-8125-406-9).

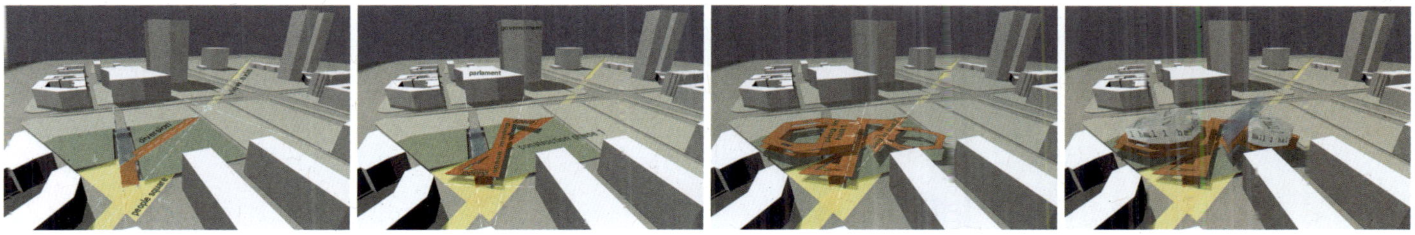

"The inclusion of the historic axis within the design for the redeveloped area calls attention to its importance and its new interpretation."

—HOLODECK architects, project description for the competition, 2000 (trans. by the ed.)

Site plan
1:1,500

10 30 60 100 m

page 423

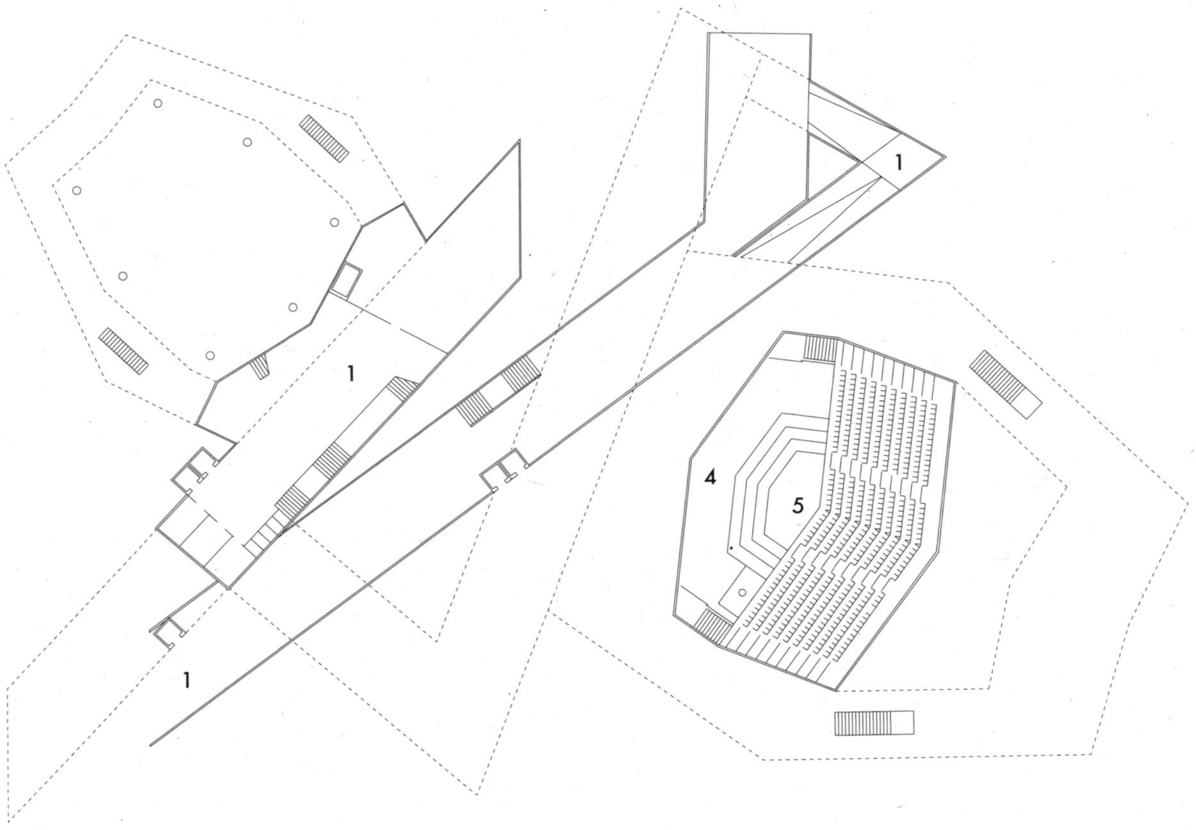

Level +2.70 m

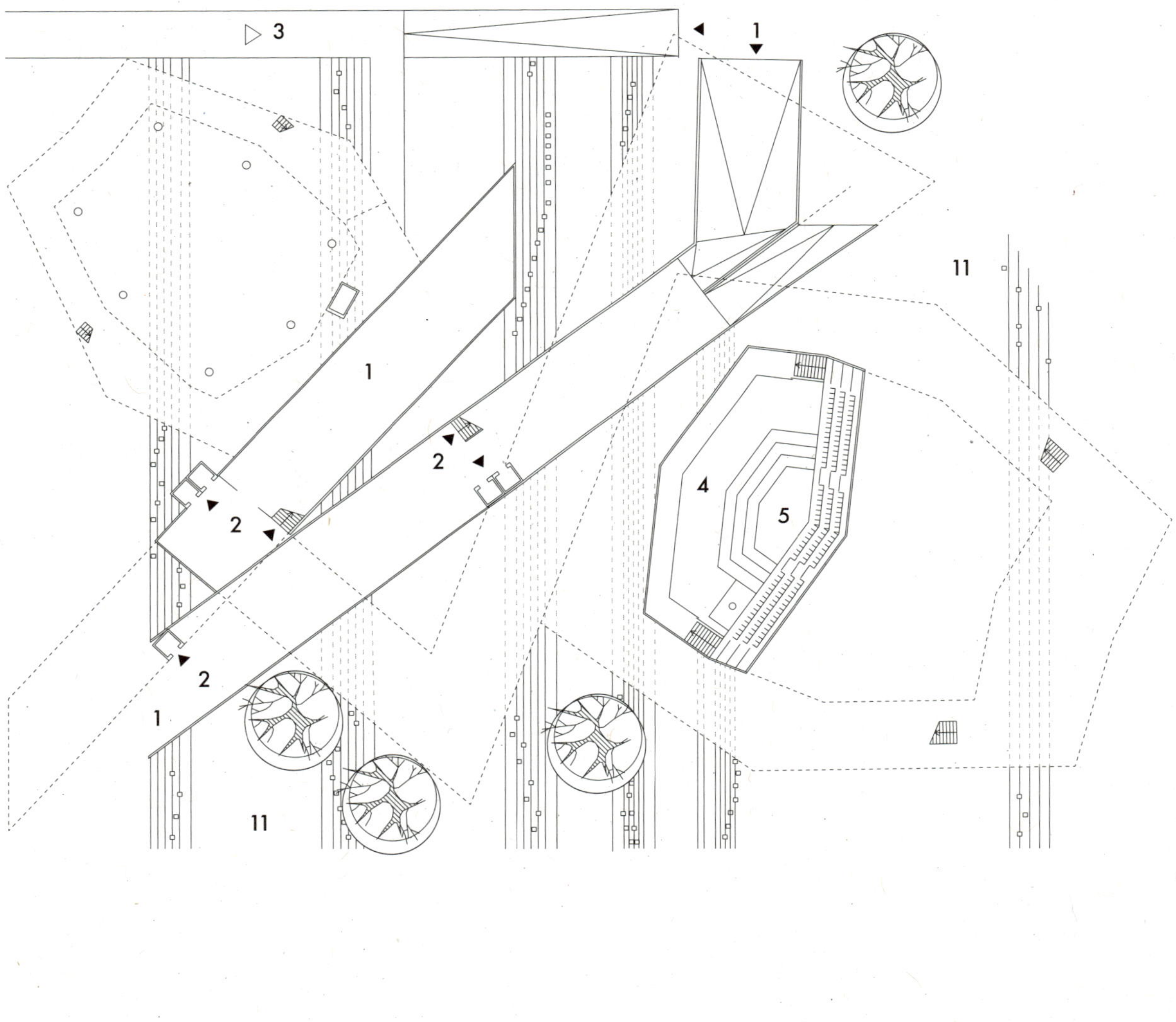

Level +1.50 m
1:650

1 3 6 10 m

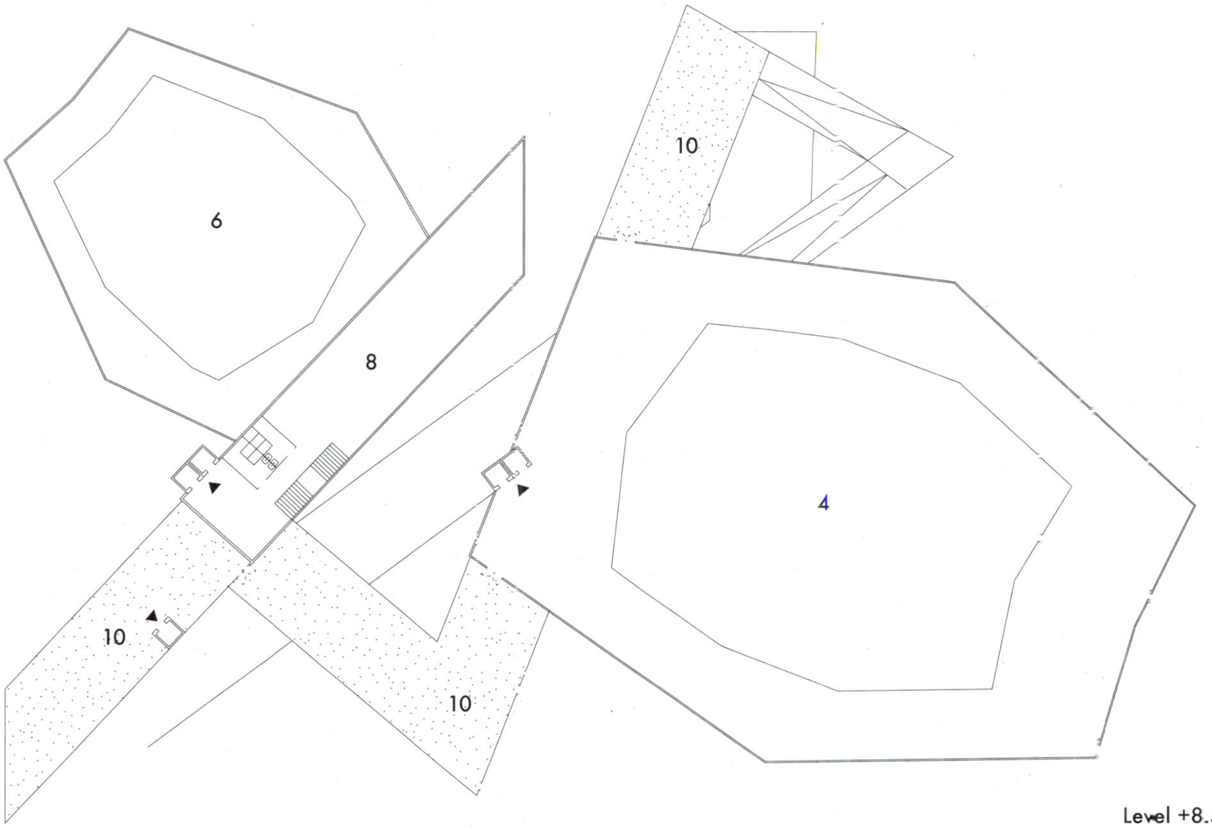

Level +8.50 m

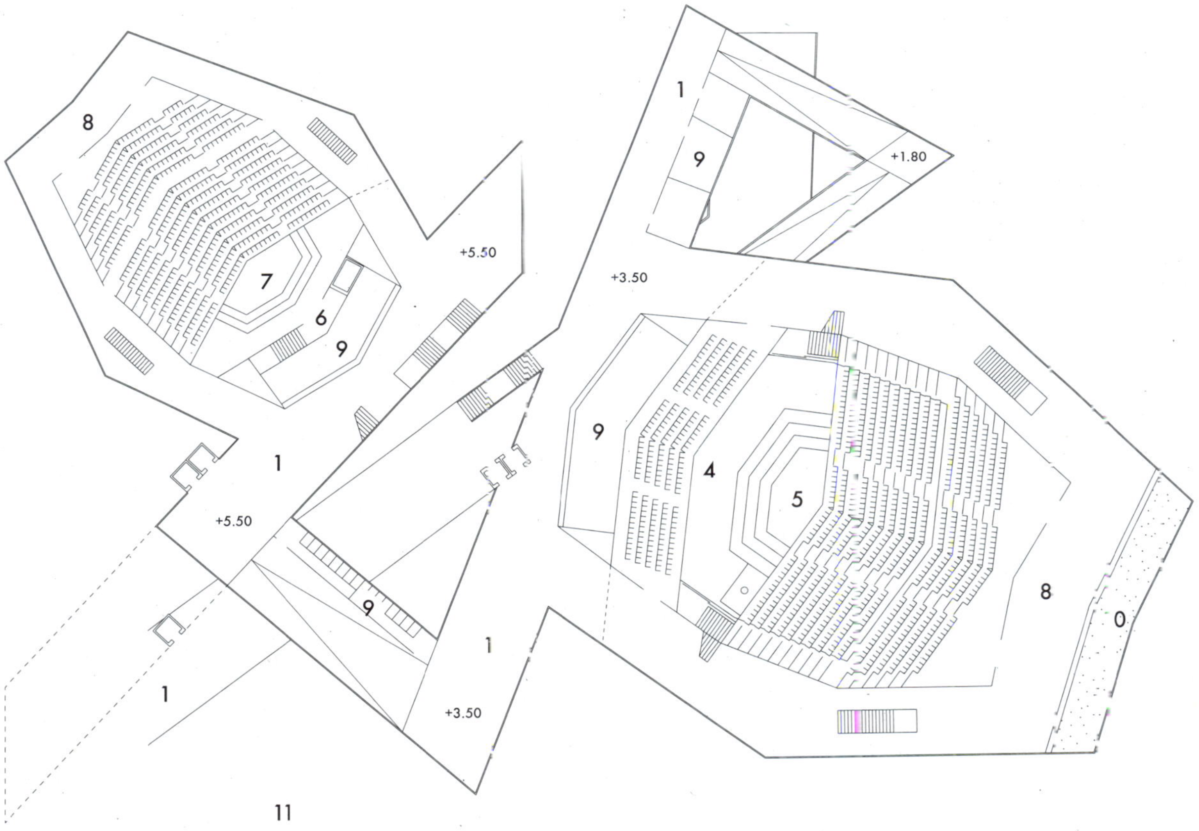

1 Public walkway
2 Entrance for pedestrians
3 Entrance to garage
4 Grand concert hall
5 Orchestra
6 Small concert hall
7 Orchestra
8 Reception area
9 Service spaces
10 Terraces for relaxation
11 Public garden

Leve +5.50 m
1:650

1 hall 1

hall hall 2 hal

kinderkunstlabor
3100 St. Pölten, AT

PROGRAM
Exhibition spaces, café, labs, library, meandering ramp, integrated trees

DIMENSIONS
Floor space 2,377 m², GFA 2,800 m², park playing area 1,024 m²

CLIENT
City of St. Pölten

PROJECT TEAM
Marlies Breuss, Michael Ogertschnig, Alessandro Zerbi, Zois Alexandros Chionidis, Marc Werner, Julia Binder

CONSULTANTS
DI Karin Graf (landscape design), ghp gmeiner | haferl & partner zt gmbh (structural engineer), IPJ Ingenieurbüro P.Jung (energy and building physics)

MODEL-MAKING
archimodell, Vienna

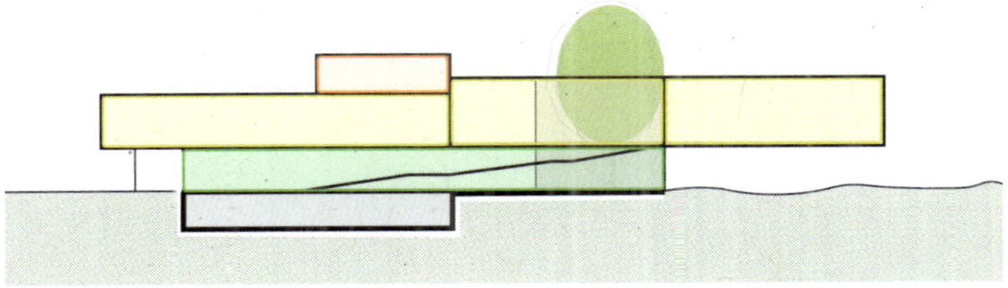

"The architecture is inspired by the interaction of open space and existing trees with the building, responding to the genius loci and local changes."

—HOLODECK architects, project description for the competition 2020 (trans. by the ed.)

Site plan
1:1,000
10 25 50 m

page 429

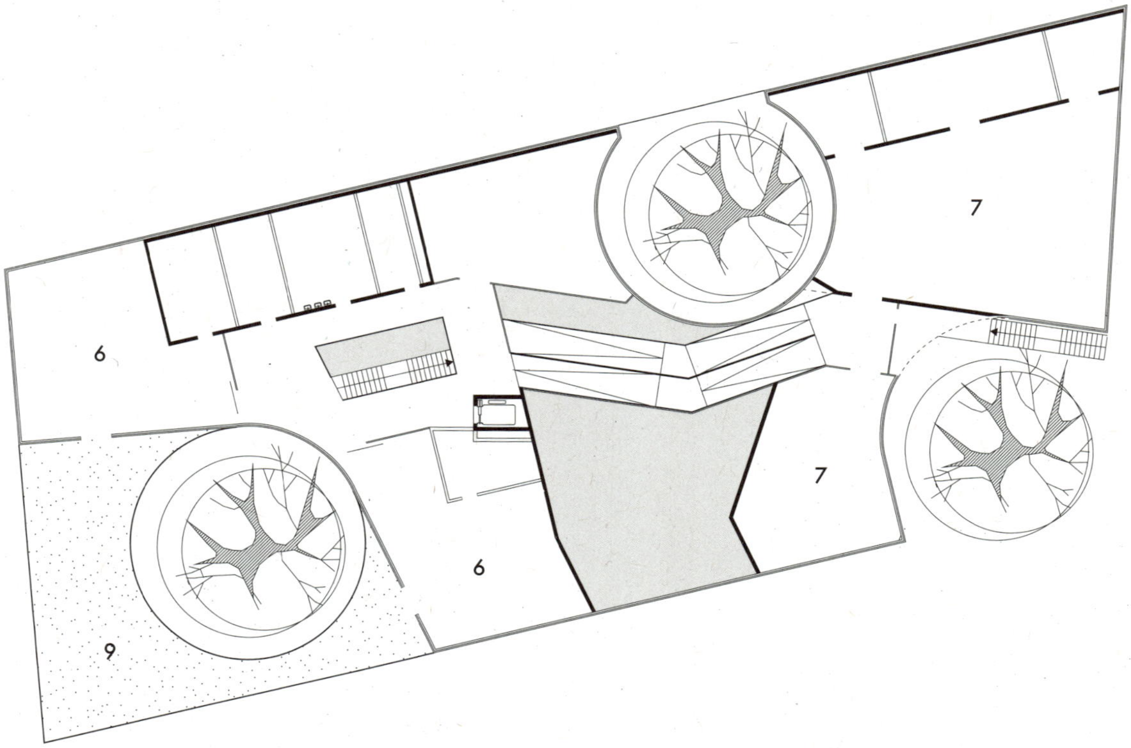

First floor

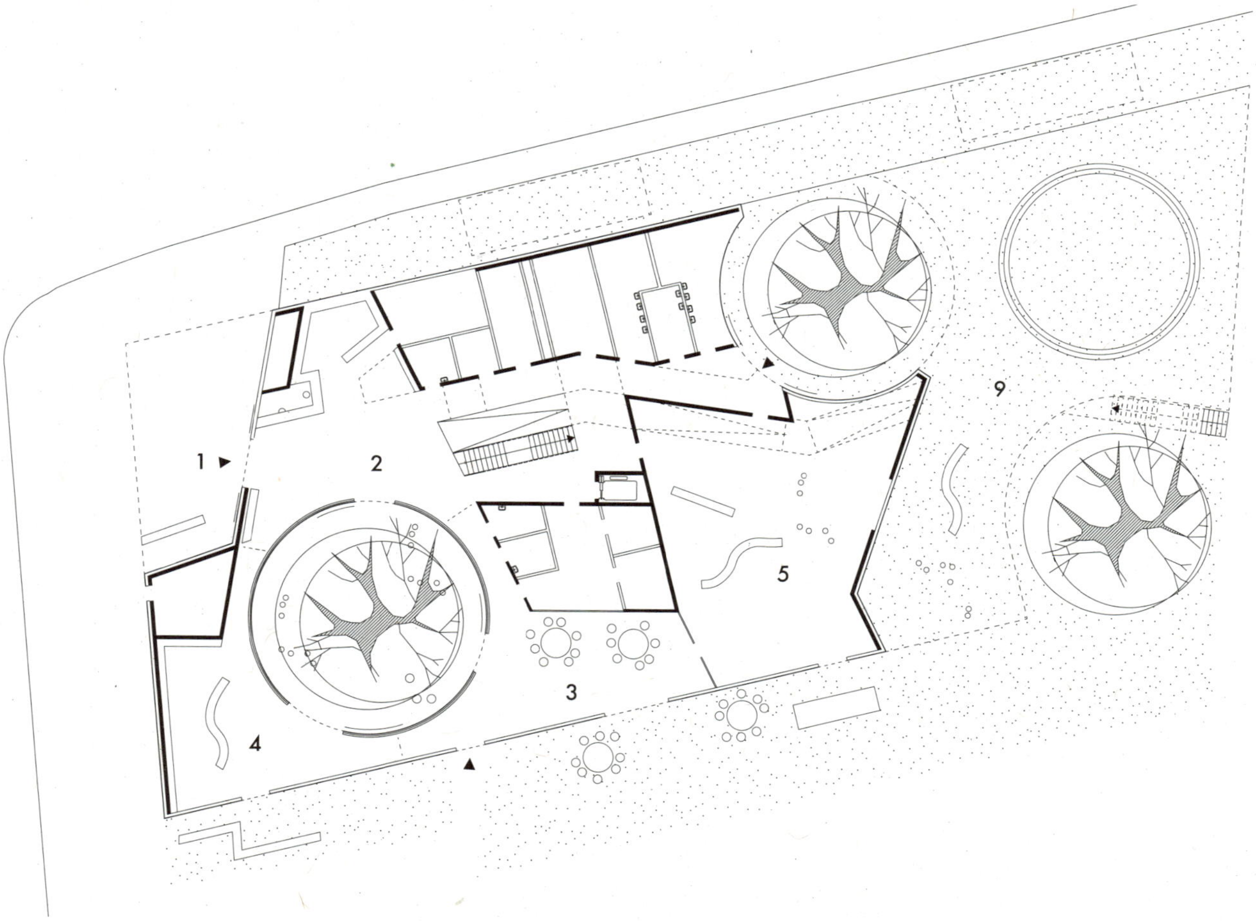

Ground floor
1:450

1 3 6 10 m

1 Entrance
2 Main hall
3 Café
4 Library
5 Children's play area
6 Workshop spaces
7 Exhibition
8 Administration
9 Outdoor areas

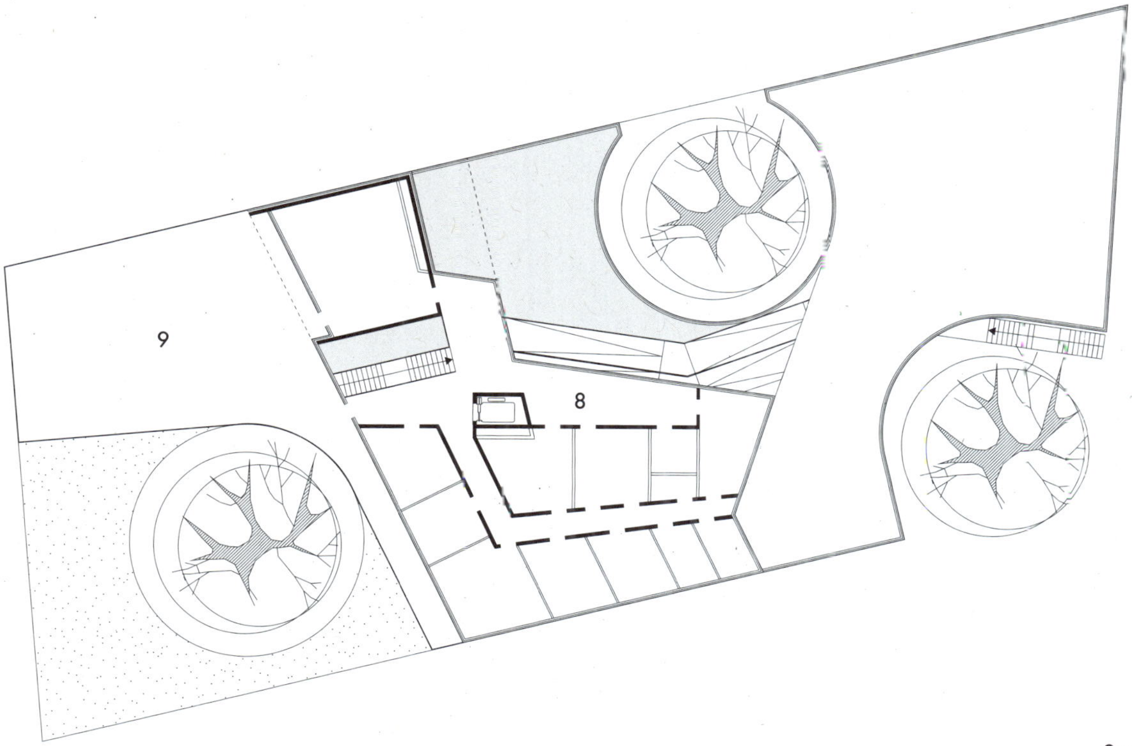

Second floor

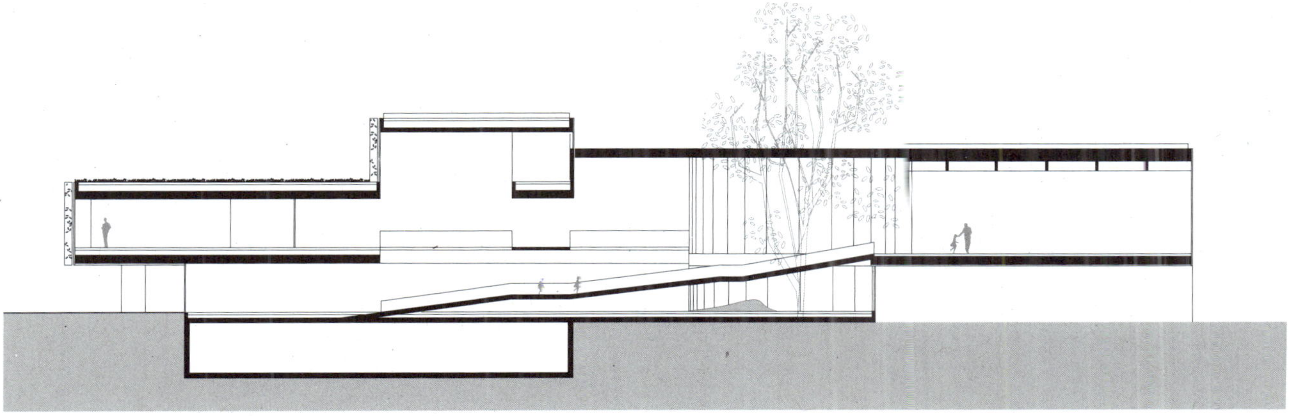

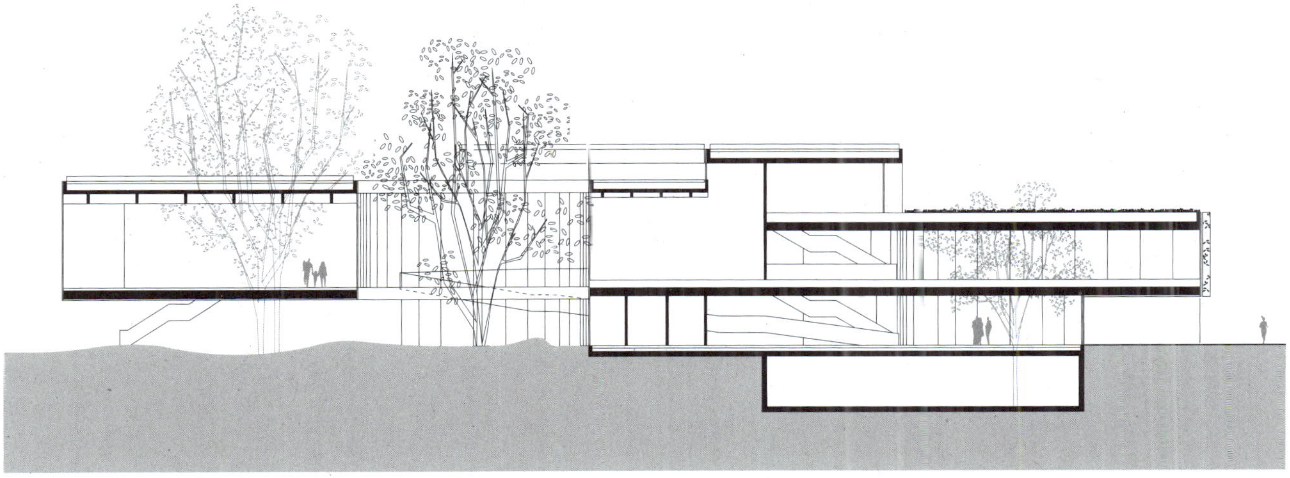

Sections
1:450

ART
POSITIONS

aktionsraum 1

2011

The design for the *aktionsraum 1* exhibition at the MUMOK in the MuseumsQuartier began with a question: How can *Viennese Actionism* be shown in an exhibition setting so long after it happened? Based on the comprehensive archive owned by Egidio Marzona, including accurate documentation on the avant-garde collective displaying in Munich, the exhibition establishes an appropriate space to represent the work produced in an intensive one-year period in the early 1970s. A chronological timeline of the group's actions—*Aktionen*, presented on a floating table in the contemporary space at the MUMOK—sets out the narrative of this avant-garde art movement. Documentary materials—writings, letters, sketches, official notifications, omission declarations, protocols, and more—were collected by Alfred Gulden and have now been carefully selected by Sophie Haaser and Rainer Fuchs for each *Aktion*, to show the impact of this period on society and the arts. All the happenings or performances have been placed in chronological order, each in a recycled glass case within the now timeless floating exhibition display, and the information is amplified by films and prints projected onto the surrounding walls.

First, approaching the exhibition space, visitors encounter a dark room, showing an original extract from the film *Aktionsraum-1 oder 57 Blindenhunde* to introduce the theme. Then, moving past a black heavy curtain, they enter the main exhibition space with the floating chronology band, to be welcomed by the original artwork *Waterbed* by Klaus Rinke, and start their passage through the exhibition and through the chronologies. Simply suspended from the ceiling the 84-meter-long table carries forty-eight glass boxes, representing the contents of all the avant-garde performances or installations of this one-year period of *Aktionen* in Munich. The visitors are guided chronologically through each of the groups' happenings or temporary installations, outlining their act of resistance and defiance.

marzona book collection

2003–04

The main concept for *Wie Bauen? Das Buch der Moderne* (How to Build? The Modernist Book), an exhibition at the Architekturzentrum Wien (AzW), is based on an idea of a cityscape. The curator Elisabetta Bresciani carefully selected 520 books from Egidio Marzona's vast book collection, now open to researchers in the Archiv der Avantgarden (Archive of the Avant-Gardes) in Dresden, classifying them into eight subject areas—housing; theory and practice; countries; materials and construction; isms; monographs; didactics; and urban planning. The selection not only includes work by various artists, architects, and critics, but it also highlights the methodologies of breaking boundaries and creating spatial relationships. The order of the performing/presented books follows the so-called "ism" strategy for displaying and exhibiting art books. Are we seeking a certain style of architectural representation, a formal guide for constructing spaces? Or is it about freeing our approach from certain methods? In a literal sense, the design of the exhibition takes the contents, reads into them, and creates a moving landscape of bookshelves representing various views.

Supported by thirty-two iron frames, the moving wooden shelves reveal the world of books, and thus a world of personalities. The landscape responds to the diversity of people and their writings, providing visitors to the AzW's temporary exhibition hall with an experimental spatial experience. The literature is displayed so as to provide an adequate and nonhierarchical overview of the selected fields. Rhythmically positioned, the shelves move slightly, shifting horizontally or vertically, and create a vivid atmosphere. By means of overlays, the design provides a dynamic reading process as one walks through chronologically or crossways, interweaving with the exhibition setup. Some of the publications, protected by an acrylic-glass cover, allow a view of their contents; others remain closed. In the dedicated reading zone, and using protective white gloves, visitors can take a particular book out of the safe librarian world and study its contents.

double vision dürer kentridge

2015–16

In the Sonderausstellungshalle at the Kulturforum in Berlin, a spatial laboratory for experimenting with exhibition displays has been installed by the curators Elke Werner and Andreas Schalhorn. Creating a dynamic dialogue between the works of Albrecht Dürer and William Kentridge, seven curatorial themes reference the two significant artists. Their work is arranged in precise spatial sequences including different ways of observing and perceiving art. As part of a research project at the Freie Universität Berlin, *double vision* expands on the various methods of printing that originated in the sixteenth and twentieth centuries.

Nine existing height-adjustable square light elements, designed by the architects Heinz Hilmer, Christoph Sattler, and Thomas Albrecht, are the keynote of the conceptual design. Minimal spatial interventions, with low-partition walls and some specifically designed elements, further the ideas of experimenting with the display of printing technologies. Various positions of height and light intensity follow the curators' themes and support the discourses constructed by the display. Specific elements, such as a softcover platform or a large table with seats for reading, aim to actively introduce visitors into an experimental dialogue with the carefully selected original prints. They invite viewers to lie or sit down, so as to familiarize themselves with the themes of the artwork, and thus to become active participants.

One part of the exhibition presents the works of Albrecht Dürer, which can be surveyed closely with a movable magnifying glass installed on tracks. In another part, one of Kentridge's prints—an artwork showing his steps of creative production—has been enlarged on a transparent membrane and projected onto the exhibition floor for the visitors to physically follow, and let themselves be part of his creative process. All the sensory elements incorporated in the conceptual design result in this being perceived as an experimental space for displaying art.

codicil

2002

codicil is a temporary cultural structure—an art space—that weaves into a large arterial road in Athens. The proposal for this exhibition area recognizes the lack of cultural institutions in this economically highly evolved neighborhood and adds a footnote to an infrastructure that focuses mainly on consumption. Hence, the art structure is imagined as obstructing the course of traffic and is positioned as a sort of tangible yet almost floating gallery in the middle of a six-lane road—an intervention counteracting the relentless flow of commercial traffic and the lack of public art in the area.

Approaching the busy street, pedestrians encounter a light structure on a traffic island with a shell that takes on the characteristics of the fast-paced surroundings. Its materiality—an envelope of fiberglass and thermoplastic pepcore—allows the art to be contained safely within, while giving the occupants of the vehicles whizzing by on either side of the structure a view. All elements are prefabricated and can be quickly installed without closing the affected road. A pedestrian crossing connects the separated neighborhoods bordering the very busy arterial road and lets the public encounter art installations on already established plots.

mobile 01

2002

In 2001, the Landesjugendreferat (Provincial Youth Department) in Burgenland commissioned us to create an exhibition booth to attract the attention and support of young people. *mobile 01* was our interpretation of a fair stand for teens. It can be moved from one place to another and addresses the needs of an adaptable youth center. It includes a lounge to relax in, a DJ table for playing music, storage space for laptops and brochures, a refrigerator and a counter for serving drinks and selling tickets. Taking the form of a trailer, the two-ton vehicle can easily be attached to a towing vehicle and moved across the country. Its shape and exterior shell are determined by the pragmatic positioning of the user spaces inside. Grouped together, the clusters claim the necessary space and ensemble to form *mobile 01*.

The programmatic loop enables the maximally reduced spaces to contain all functional services, and even to accommodate up to five people. The layout has been based on different functional modules. An Internet access point—a must-have for young people, even in 2002—is incorporated into the structure and can be accessed from the outside, and there are boxes on the front and the rear to broadcast the music to the surroundings.

Made by Peter Fattinger in cooperation with Susanne Schmall, *mobile 01* was handcrafted over just three months in an old Viennese warehouse. Its body, a lightweight timber structure, was concealed by a weather-resistant polyester resin coating, which at that time was perfect for creating a permanent skin in a sky-blue hue. When completed, *mobile 01* was approved by the structural authorities and licensed by the Austrian automobile authority as a trailer for use on public streets.

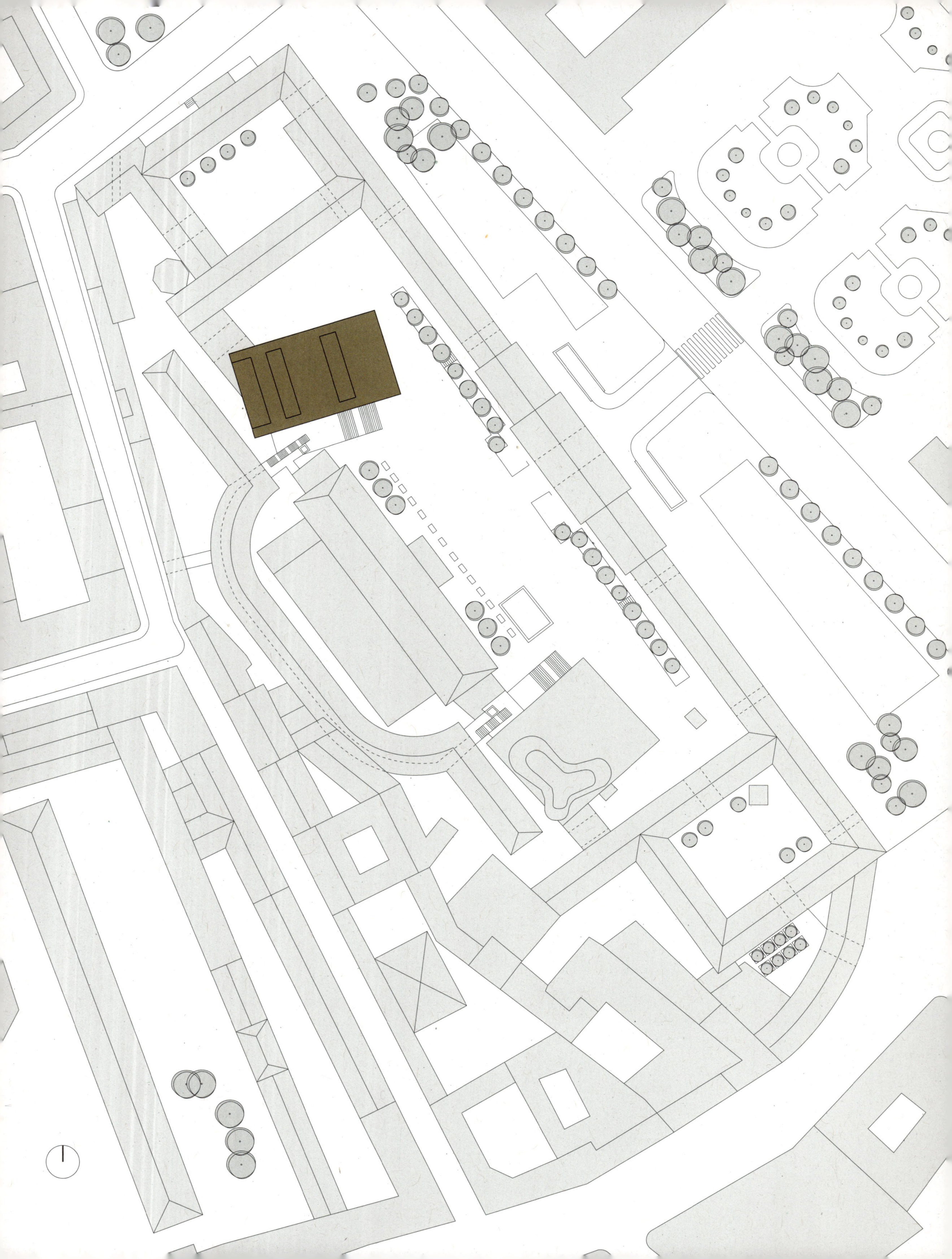

aktionsraum 1
1070 Vienna, AT

See pp. 152–54

PROGRAM
Exhibition concept and architecture

DIMENSIONS
Floor space 831 m² (large space 636 m², small space 195 m²)

CLIENT
MUMOK, Museum of Modern Art Foundation Ludwig Vienna

PROJECT TEAM
Marlies Breuss, Michael Ogertschnig, Christian Rottensteiner

CURATORS
Rainer Fuchs and Sophie Haaser

PHOTOGRAPHY
Barbara Mair

PUBLICATIONS (SELECTION)
Aktionsraum 1, catalogue for the exhibition at the MUMOK, published by Sophie Haaser, Rainer Fuchs, Museum Moderner Kunst Stiftung Ludwig Vienna, 2011 (ISBN 978-3-902490-78-0).
Anne Katrin Feßler, "Publikumsstörung," *Der Standard*, Vienna, March 3, 2011.
Matthias Dusini, "Auferstanden aus dem Vitrinengrab," *Falter* 13/11, Vienna, March 30, 2011.

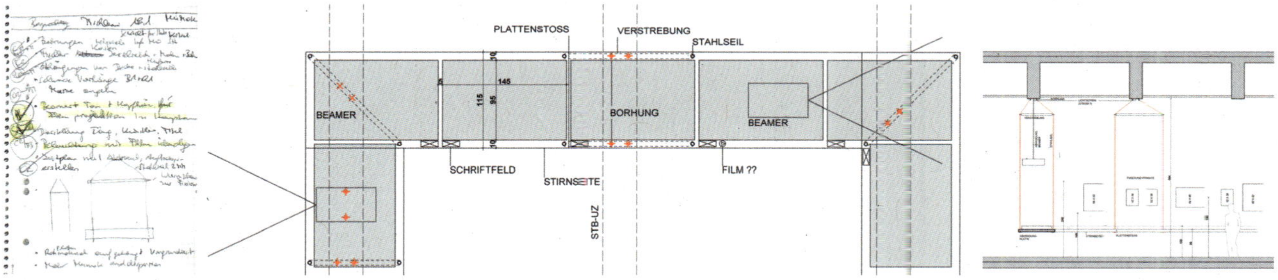

"The showcases, meanwhile, hang from the ceiling, appearing free of spatial gravity. This floating in space allows the entire display of archival material to appear as linear 'text,' folded on itself, which can be seen and also read by the visitor."

—Sophie Haaser and Rainer Fuchs, "Social Critisism with Perspectives," *Aktionsraum 1*, Vienna, MUMOK, 2011, p. 17.

Site plan
1:1,500

10 30 60 100 m

page 439

FABRO
BEKLEIDUNG
ZERREISSPROBE
ANIMA SOUND
ABREAKTIONSSPIEL
EXPANSION
ENTWIRREN
EINER SCHNUR
DENKLEIT
BALKEN
AUSSCHNITT
AKTIONSRAUM
BROT
GRUSS ATTERSEE

1 Announcer 1
2 Information booklets
3 Announcer 2
4 Wall text
5 Information area

Floor plan
1:150

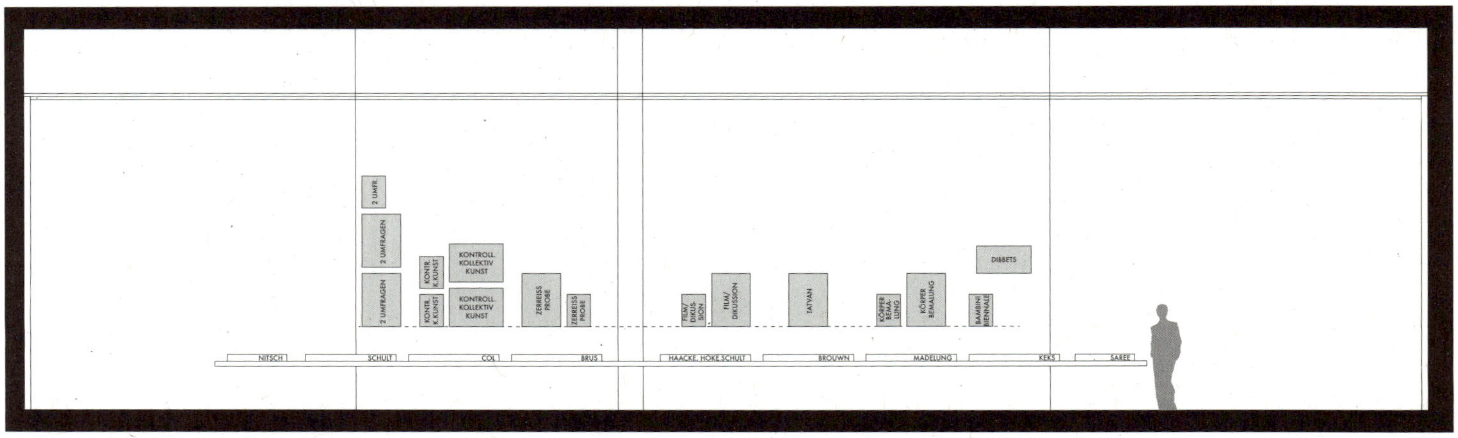

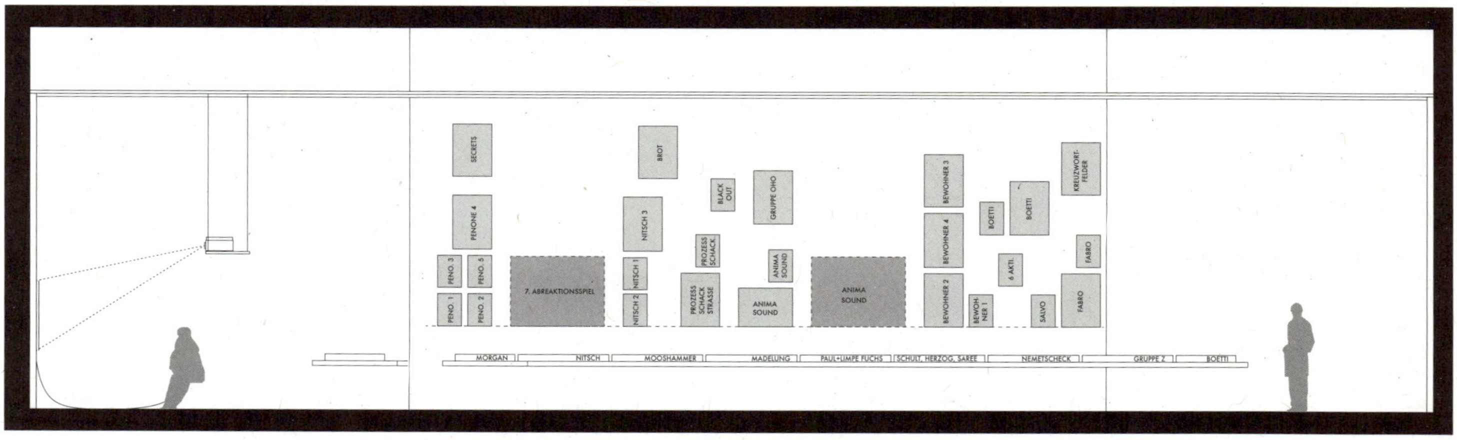

Sections
1:120

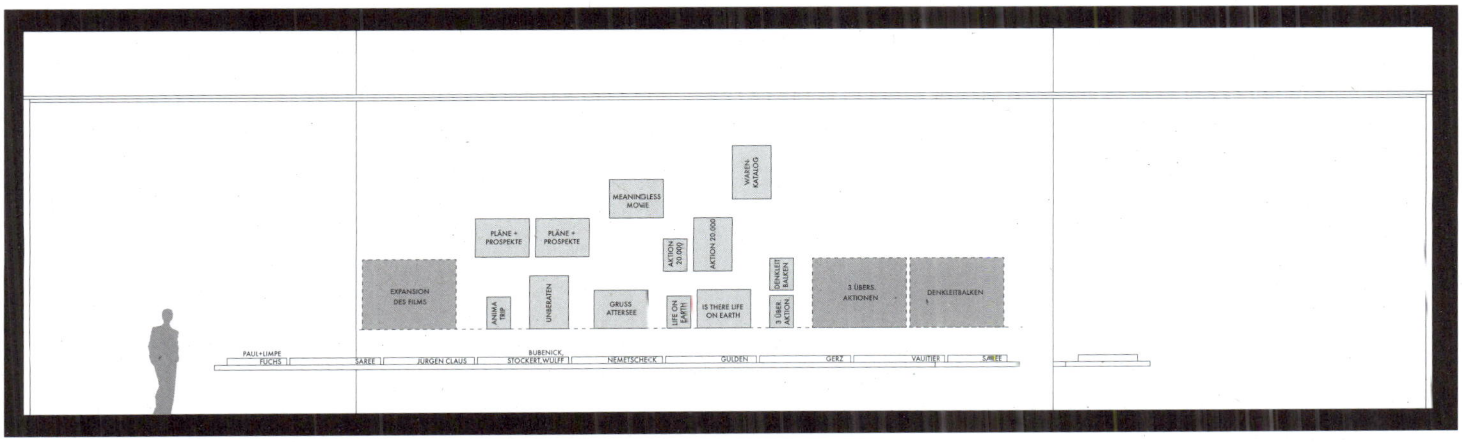
WAREN-KATALOG
MEANINGLESS MOVIE
PLÄNE + PROSPEKTE
PLÄNE + PROSPEKTE
AKTION 20.000
AKTION 20.000
EXPANSION DES FILMS
ANIMA TRIP
UNBERATEN
GRUSS ATTERSEE
LIFE ON EARTH
IS THERE LIFE ON EARTH
DENKLEIT BALKEN
3 ÜBER. AKTION
3 ÜBERS. AKTIONEN
DENKLEITBALKEN
PAUL+LIMPE FUCHS
SAREE
JURGEN CLAUS
BUBENICK, STOCKERT, WULFF
GULDEN
GERZ
VAUTIER

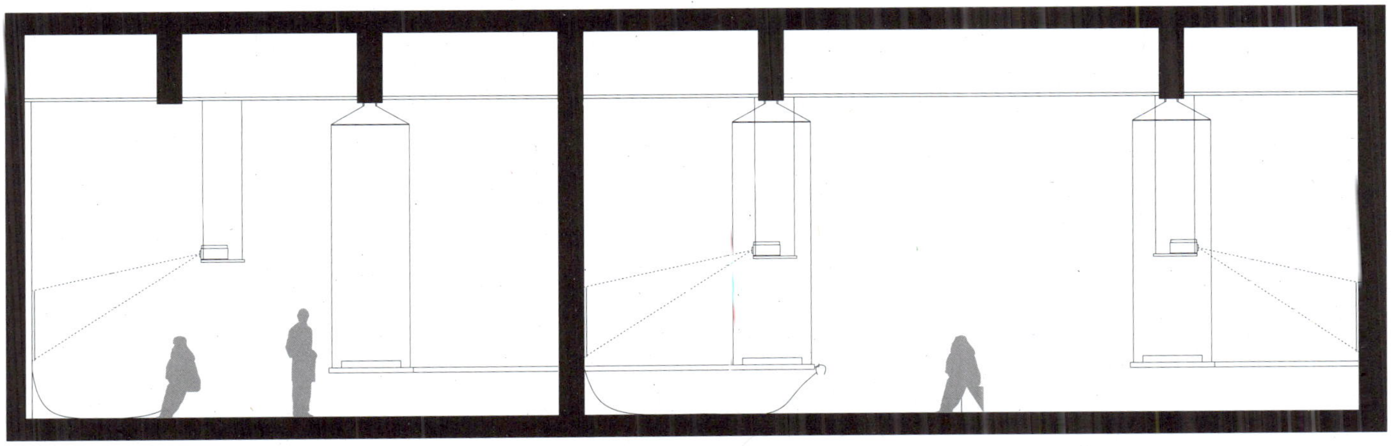

	MÄRZ 1969	APRIL	MAI	JUNI	JULI	AUG	SEPT	OKT	NOV	DEZ	JAN 1970	FEBR	MÄRZ	APRIL	MAI	
1											NEMET-SCHEK	Kinderfasch. GULDEN				
2												SAREE Denkleitbal.				
3													Hess. TV "und"		Maurer	
4													MOSHAM-MER			
5				Situation 5.Juni				Kartei				PENONE			Mauer	
6									HA Schult				FUCHS		Zeitspur	
7																
8				Biennale Nürnberg				Info 5 "Vorarbeit"	Bern Eröffnung							
9						Multilith										M
10								Kassel Prospect				Agentzia fällt aus Fasch.Dienstag		SALVO		A
11														BOETTI		C
12																
13							Kassel				CLAUS		PROZESS Schackstr.			
14					Anzeige Mag. Kunst								NEMET-SCHEK			
15				Schackstr.	Italien		Info 1 – 4		HÖKE							
16									HÖKE		MADELUNG Finanzbefr.					
17																
18								LINDOW/BORLAT RINKE MORGAN						FABRO TONELLO		
19				Wember		Pläne ein			PLÄNE + PROJEKTE				GRUPPE Z		ca. Düsseldorf	E
20				Staeck								MORGAN				
21				Sens-action	mieten Halle											
22												NITSCH Lesung	Urlaub		NITSCH Dokument.	
23																T H
24							WC			FUCHS	UNBERATEN					B
25				Frankfurt											Zwischen-bericht	
26				Düsseldorf												
27				Krefeld								NITSCH				
28				Köln								NITSCH		MEIER Tonsäule Kiste	Wien	
29																
30										SAREE mög-lich	GERZ			Zeitzeichen		
31					Bern						VAUTIER					

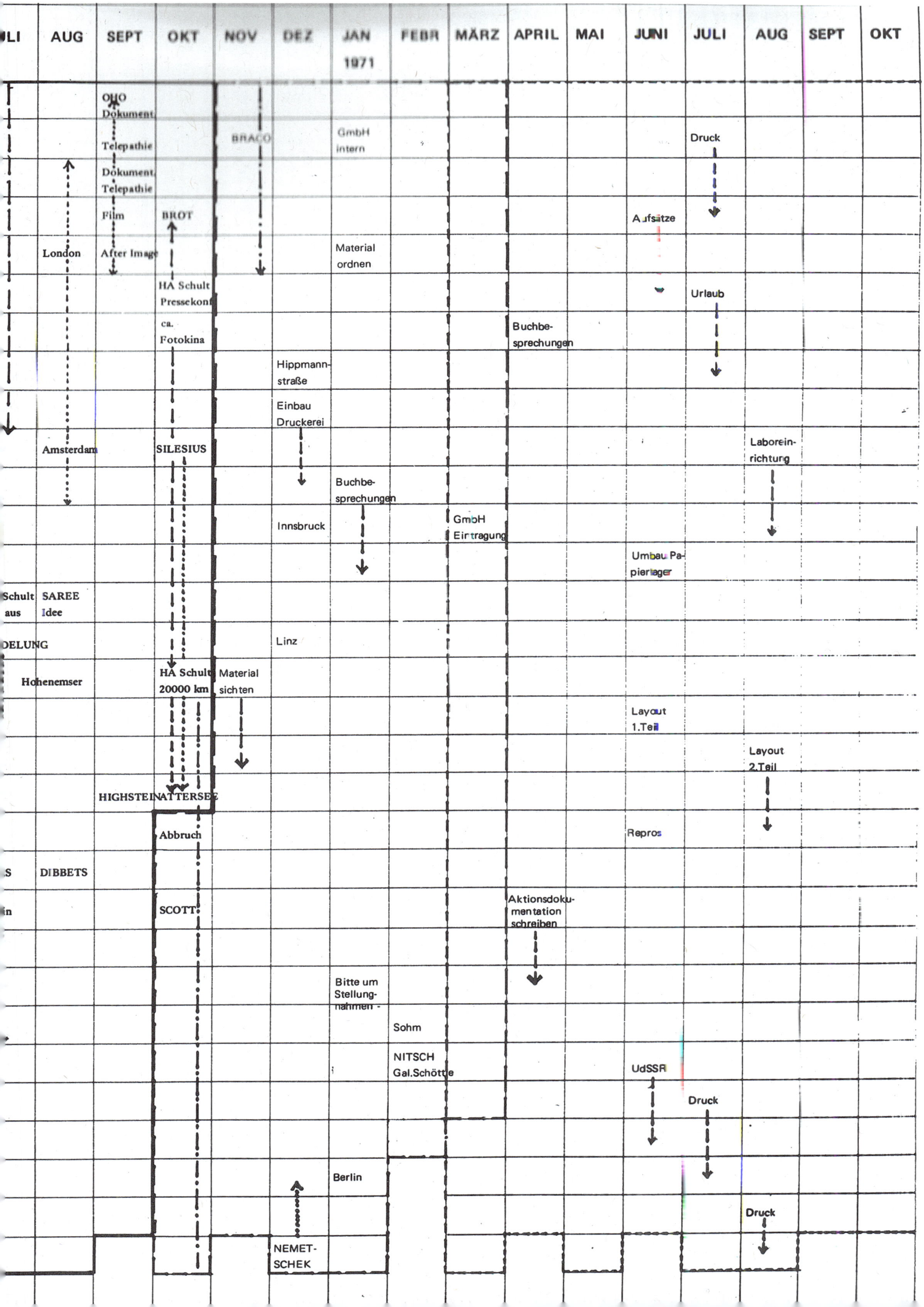

LI
AUG
SEPT
OKT
NOV
DEZ
JAN 1971
FEBR
MÄRZ
APRIL
MAI
JUNI
JULI
AUG
SEPT
OKT
OHO Dokument.
Telepathie
Dokument. Telepathie
Film
After Image
London
Amsterdam
BRACO
GmbH intern
Material ordnen
BROT
HA Schult Pressekonf
ca. Fotokina
SILESIUS
Hippmann-straße
Einbau Druckerei
Buchbe-sprechungen
Innsbruck
GmbH Eintragung
Buchbe-sprechungen
Druck
Aufsätze
Urlaub
Laborein-richtung
Umbau Pa-pierlager
Schult aus
SAREE Idee
DELUNG
Linz
Hohenemser
HA Schult 20000 km
Material sichten
Layout 1.Teil
Layout 2.Teil
HIGHSTEIN
ATTERSEE
Abbruch
Repros
S
DIBBETS
in
SCOTT
Aktionsdoku-mentation schreiben
Bitte um Stellung-nahmen
Sohm
NITSCH Gal.Schöttle
UdSSR
Druck
Berlin
Druck
NEMET-SCHEK

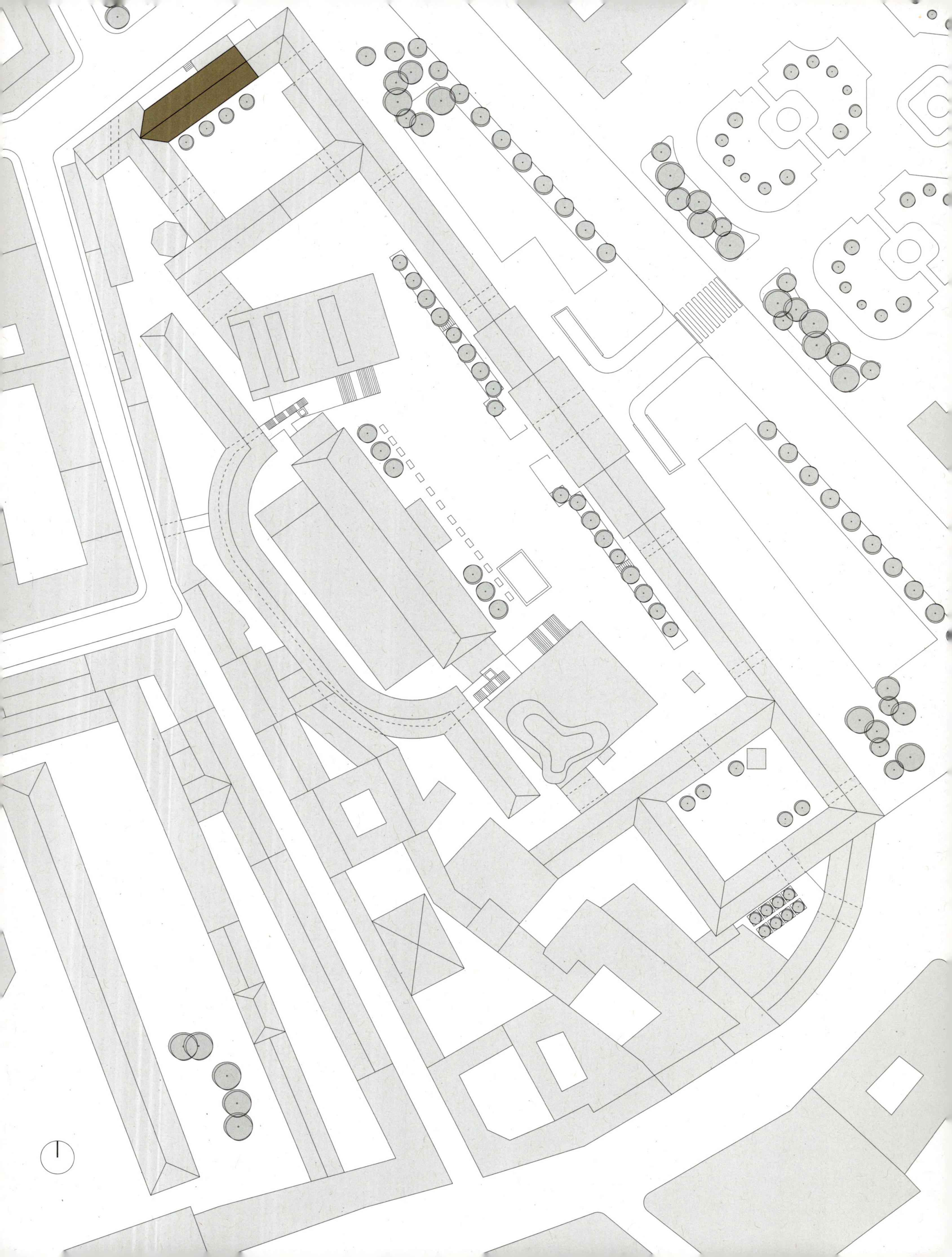

marzona book collection
1070 Vienna, AT

See pp. 155–57

PROGRAM
Exhibition concept and architecture

DIMENSIONS
Floor space 306 m²

CLIENT
Architekturzentrum Wien

PROJECT TEAM
Marlies Breuss, Michael Ogertschnig, Marc Spinner, Jakob Spriestersbach

CONSULTANTS
Kerstin Gust and Monika Platzer, AzW, Elisabetta Bresciani

CURATOR
Elisabetta Bresciani

PHOTOGRAPHY
Veronika Hofinger

PUBLICATIONS (SELECTION)
"Wie bauen? Das Buch der Moderne," *domus* 866, Milan, January 2004.
"How to Build the Modernist Book," *Arredamento Mimarlik*, Istanbul, November 2003.
"Das Buch der Moderne," *StadtBauwelt* 48, Berlin, December 2003.
"Ein Jahrhundert Architekturgeschichte," *Architektur.aktuell*, Vienna and New York, Springer, December 2003.
"Bloß keine Fingerabdrücke," *Frankfurter Allgemeine Zeitung*, December 29, 2003.

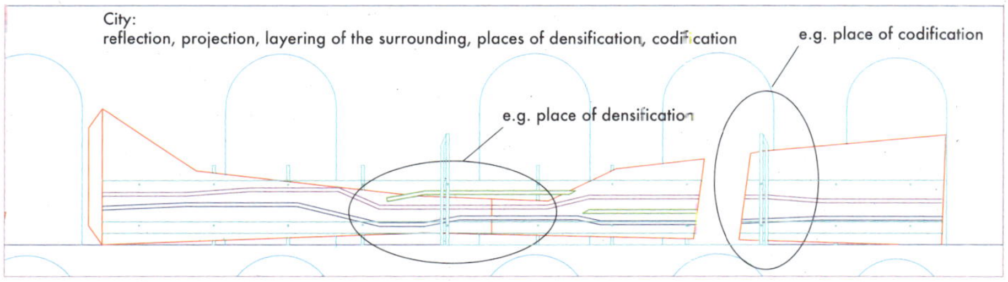

"The exhibition is not only a method of communication but is communication itself. It is a message and a vehicle that can change the message—depending on how the communication is understood."

— Joan Roig, "Objekt und Subjekt in der heutigen Ausstellungsarchitektur," in *Bühnen- und Ausstellungsarchitektur*, Pedro Azara and Carlos Guri Harth (eds.), Munich, dva münchen, 2000, p. 31 (trans. by the ed.)

Site plan
1:1,500

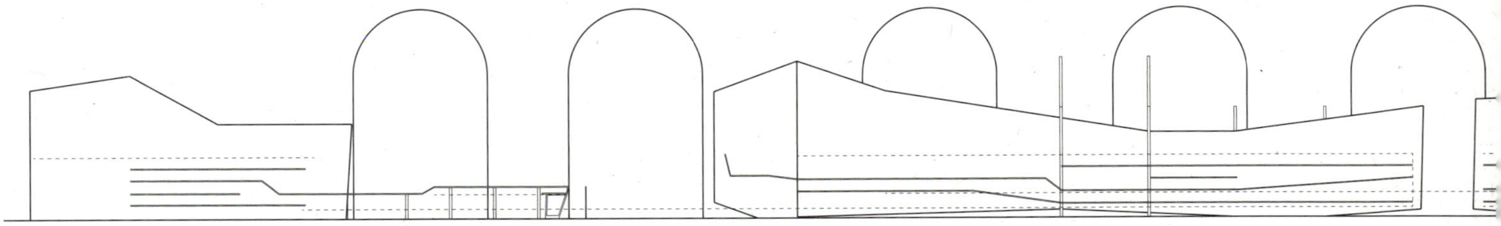
9 Books
10 Reading area
1 Housing
2 Theory and experience

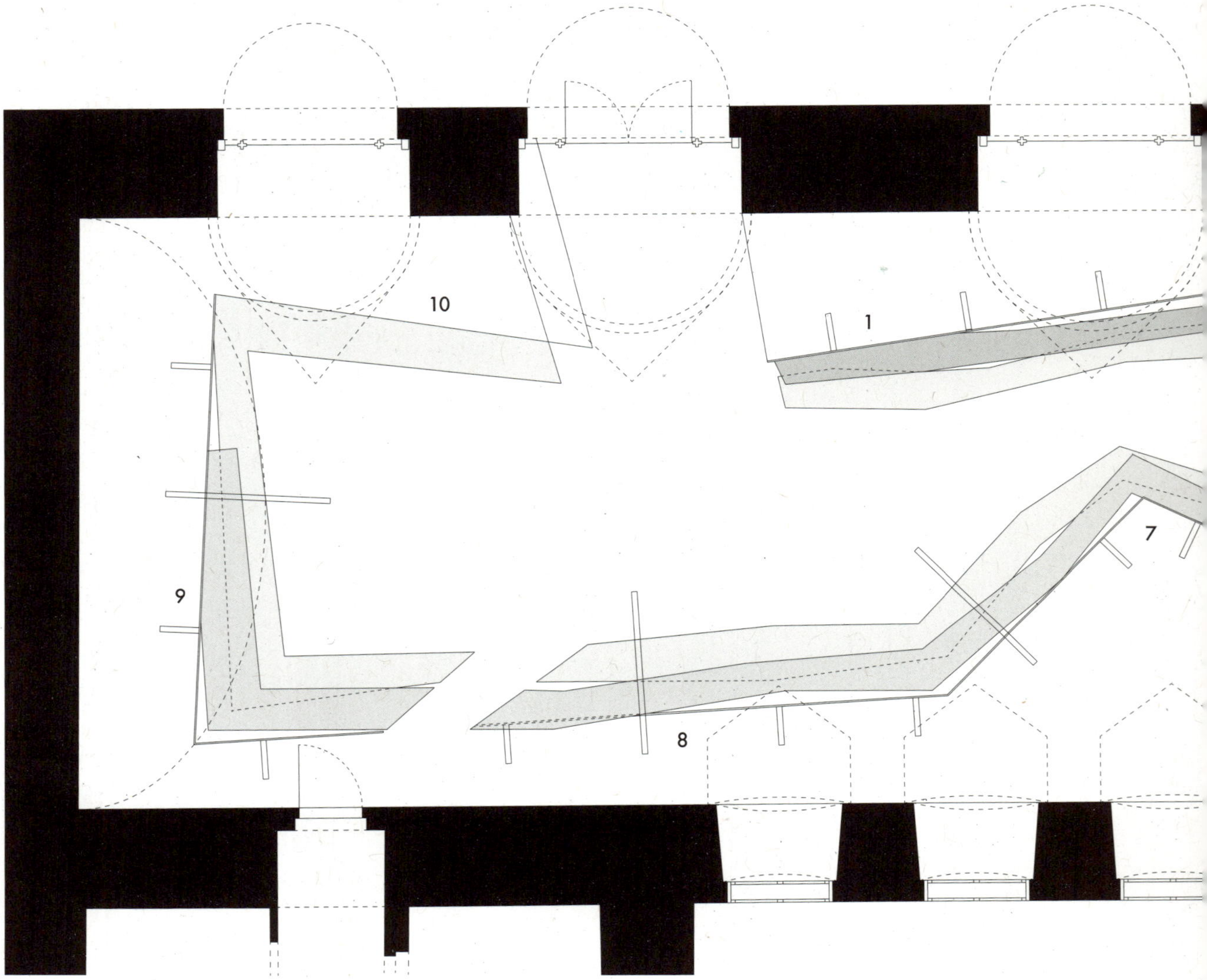
10
1
9
7
8

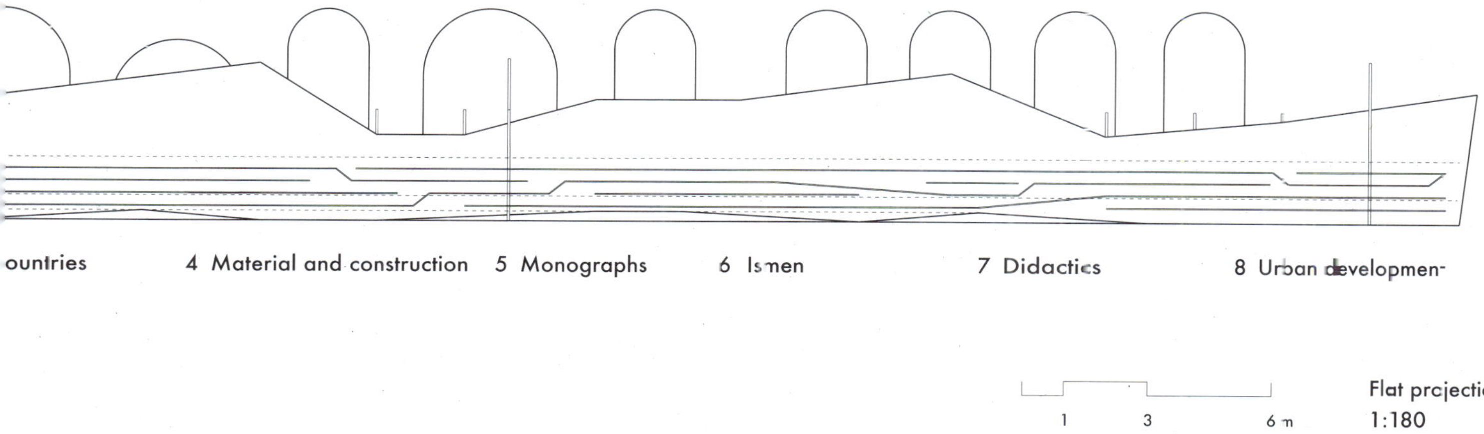

Flat projection
1:180

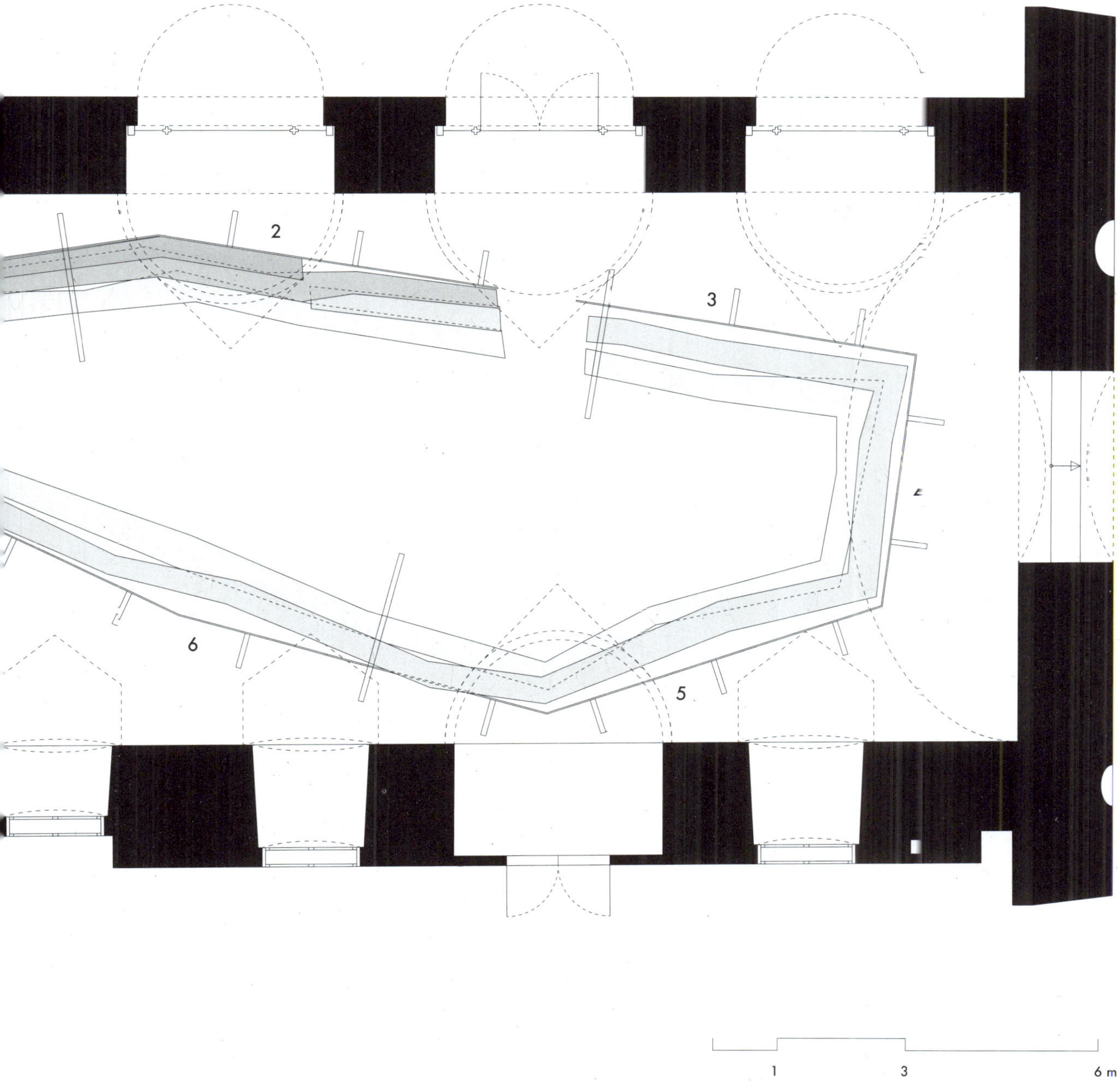

Ground floor
1:100

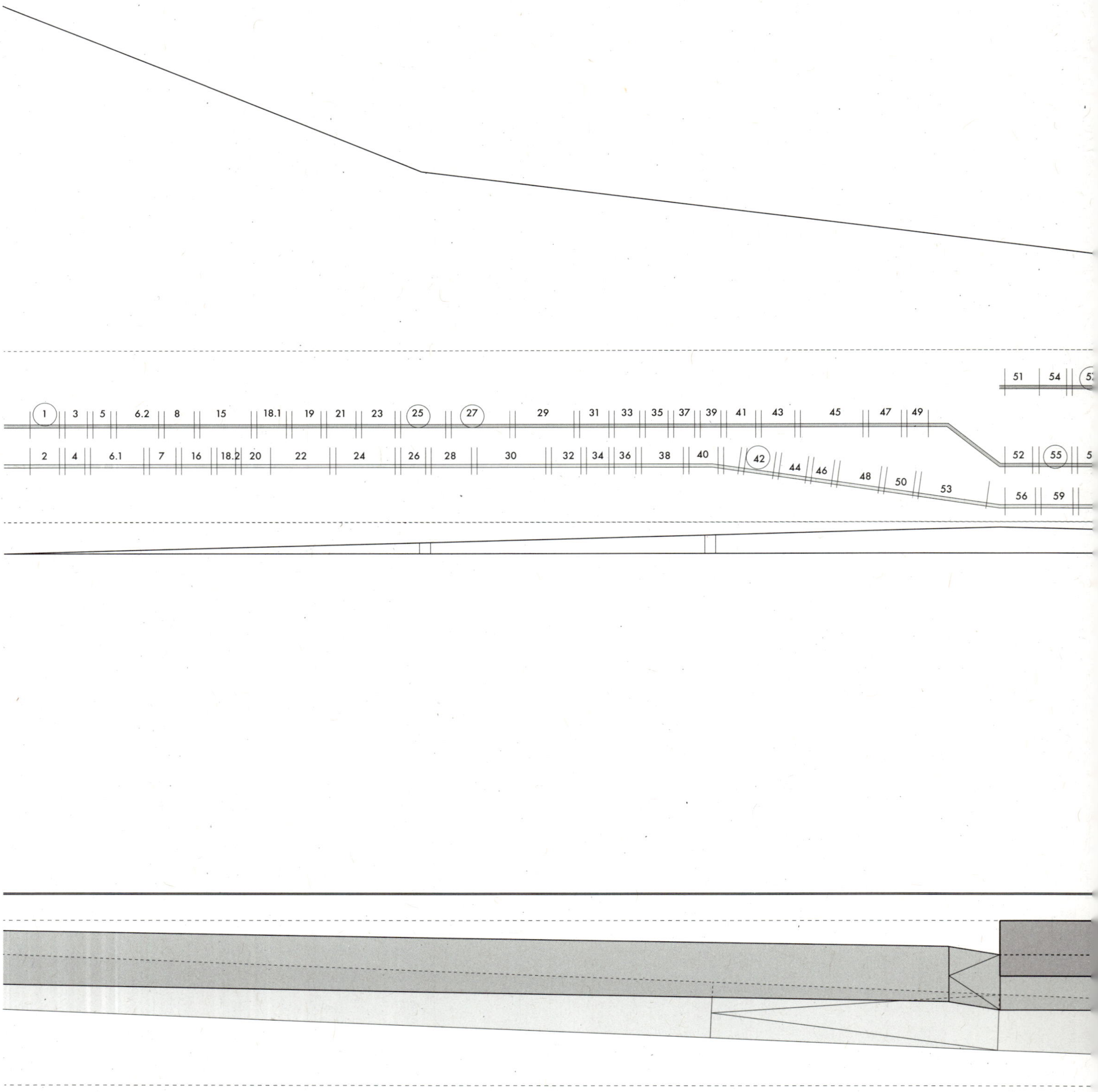
51 54 5
1 3 5 6.2 8 15 18.1 19 21 23 25 27 29 31 33 35 37 39 41 43 45 47 49
2 4 6.1 7 16 18.2 20 22 24 26 28 30 32 34 36 38 40 42 44 46 48 50 53
52 55 5
56 59

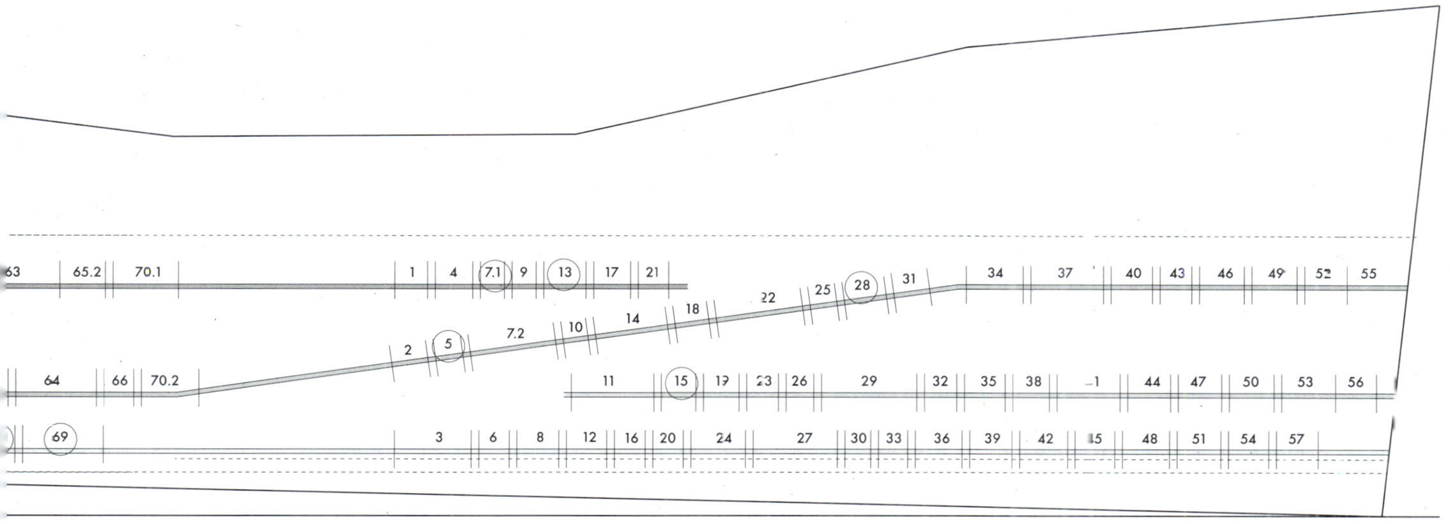

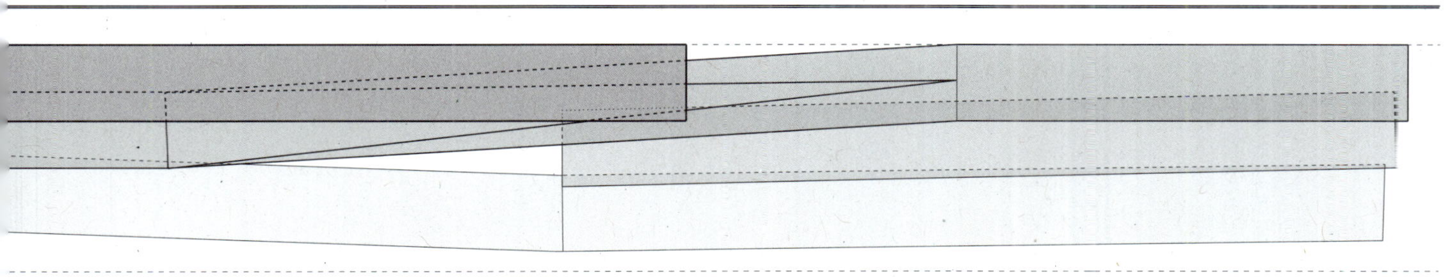

0,5 1 2 m

Details
1:25

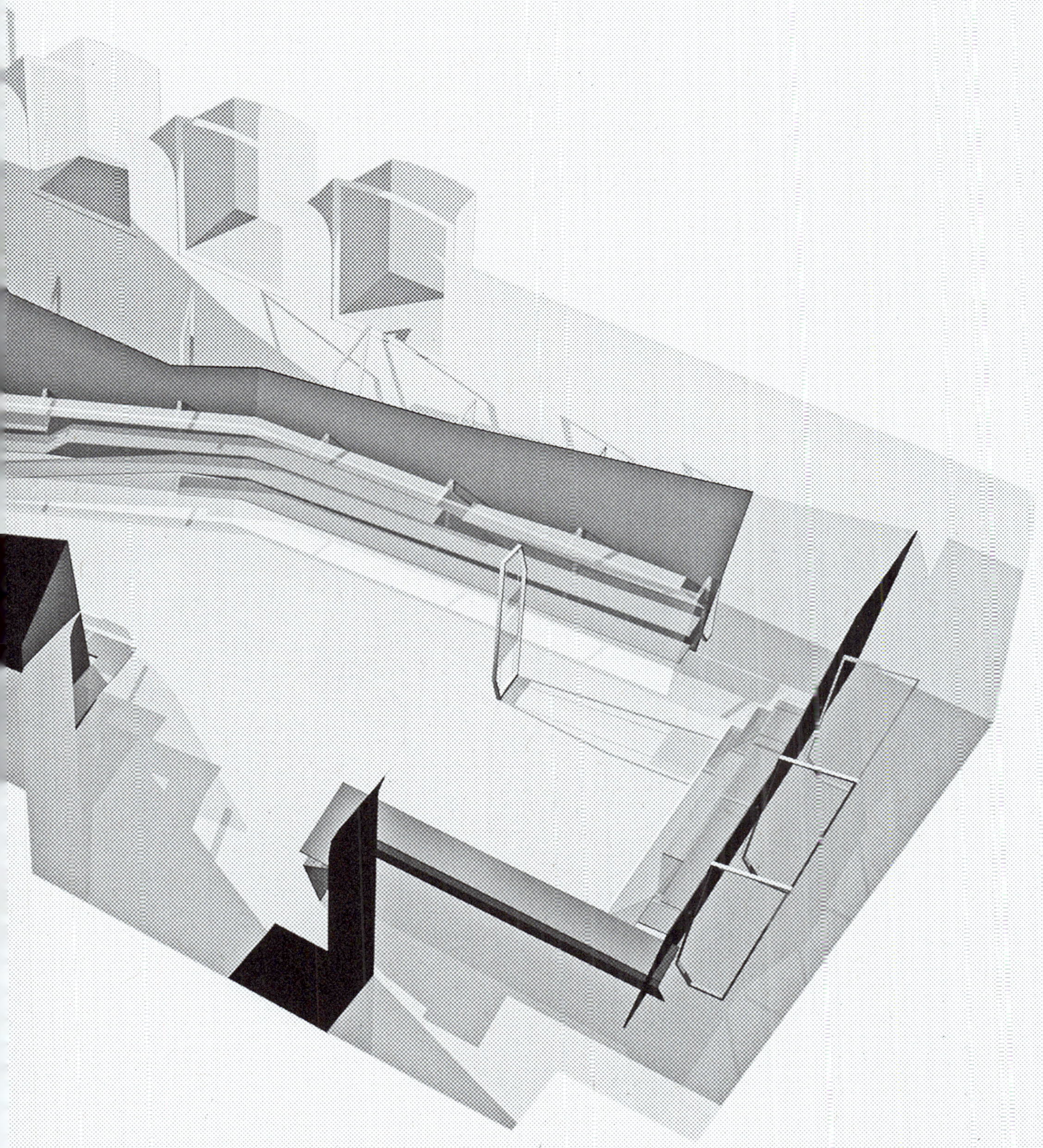

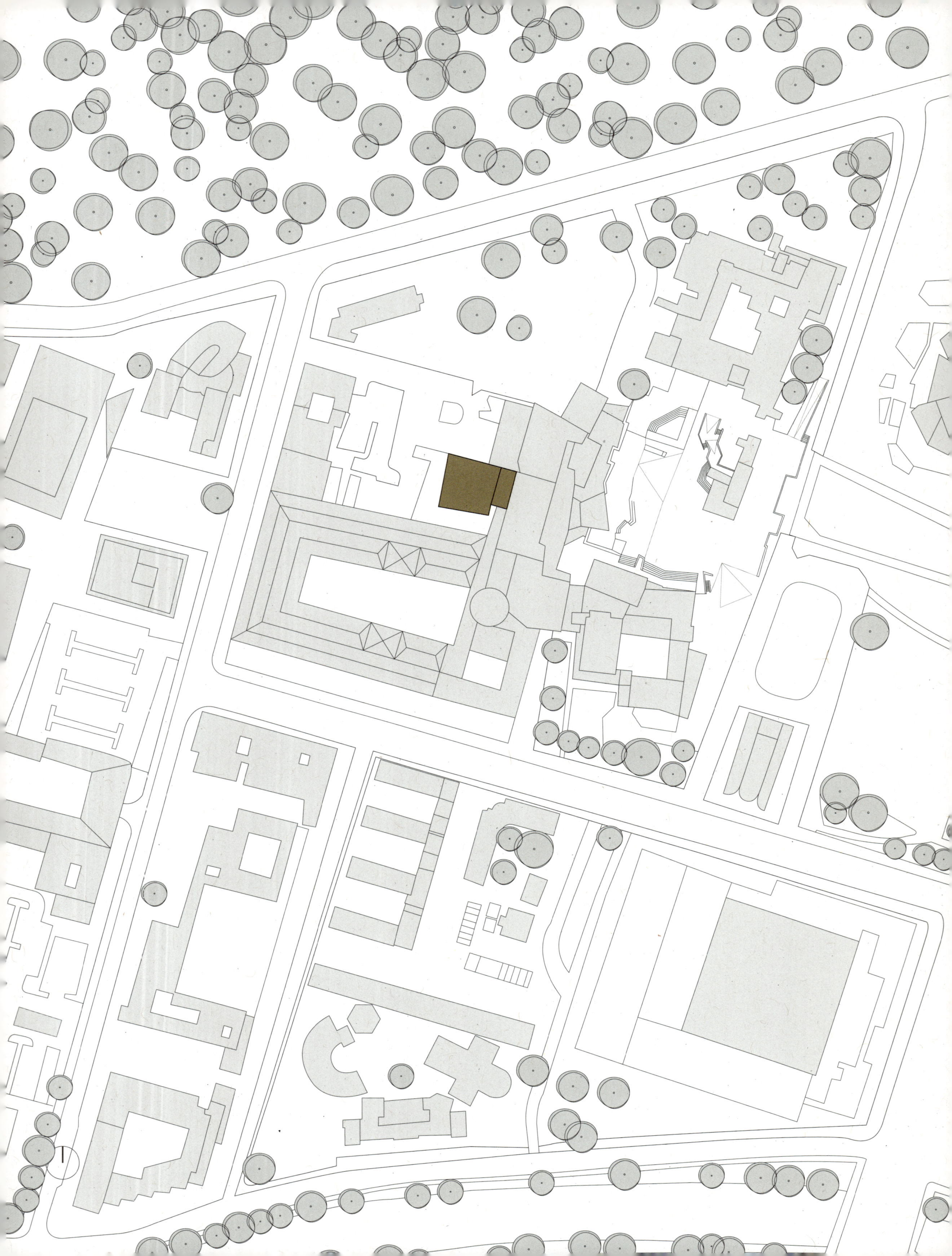

double vision dürer kentridge

10875 Berlin, Kulturforum Berlin, DE

See pp. 158–63

PROGRAM
Exhibition concept and architecture

DIMENSIONS
Floor space 422 m²

CLIENT
Staatliche Museen Kupferstichkabinett (Museum of Prints and Drawings)

PROJECT TEAM
Marlies Breuss, Michael Ogertschnig, Vidosava Petrovic

CURATORS
Elka Anna Werner and Andreas Schalhorn with Nadine Rottau

PHOTOGRAPHY
Christian von Steffelin

PUBLICATIONS (SELECTION)
Marlies Breuss, "On the exhibition architecture," in *DOUBLE VISION: Albrecht Dürer/William Kentridge*, Munich, Sieveking Verlag, 2015 (ISBN 978-3-944874-371).
Irmgard Berner, "Der doppelte Blick," *Berliner Zeitung*, Berlin, December 9, 2015.
"Double Vision, Albrecht Dürer & William Kentridge," *Museums Journal* 4/2015, March 6, 2016.
EVIDENZEN DES EXPOSITORISCHEN, ed. Klaus Krüger, Elke Anna Werner, and Andreas Schalhorn, Bielefeld, transcript Verlag, 2019 (published as e-book ISBN 978-3-8394-4210-4 and print ISBN 978-3-8376-4210-0).
"Die antipodischen Kollegen – Dürer und Kentridge," *Neue Zürcher Zeitung*, Zurich, January 22, 2016.

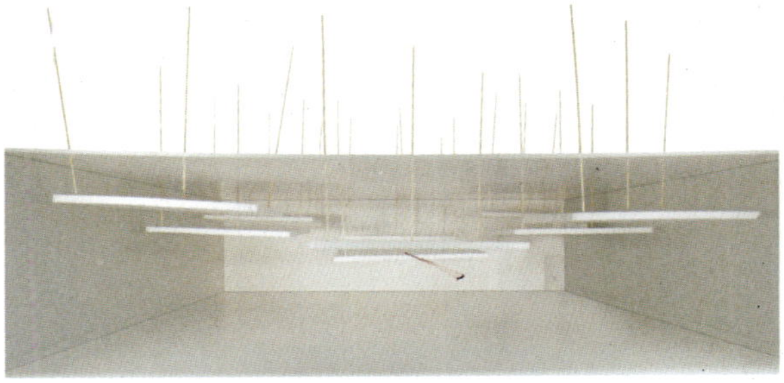

"Giving time and space to seeing … to find other perspectives of perception and analysis."

—Barbara Borek, *Art in Berlin: Dialog in Schwarz-Weiß*, Berlin, November 20, 2015 (trans. by the ed.)

Site plan
1:1,900

10 30 60 100 m

Exhibition system

Ground floor
1:150

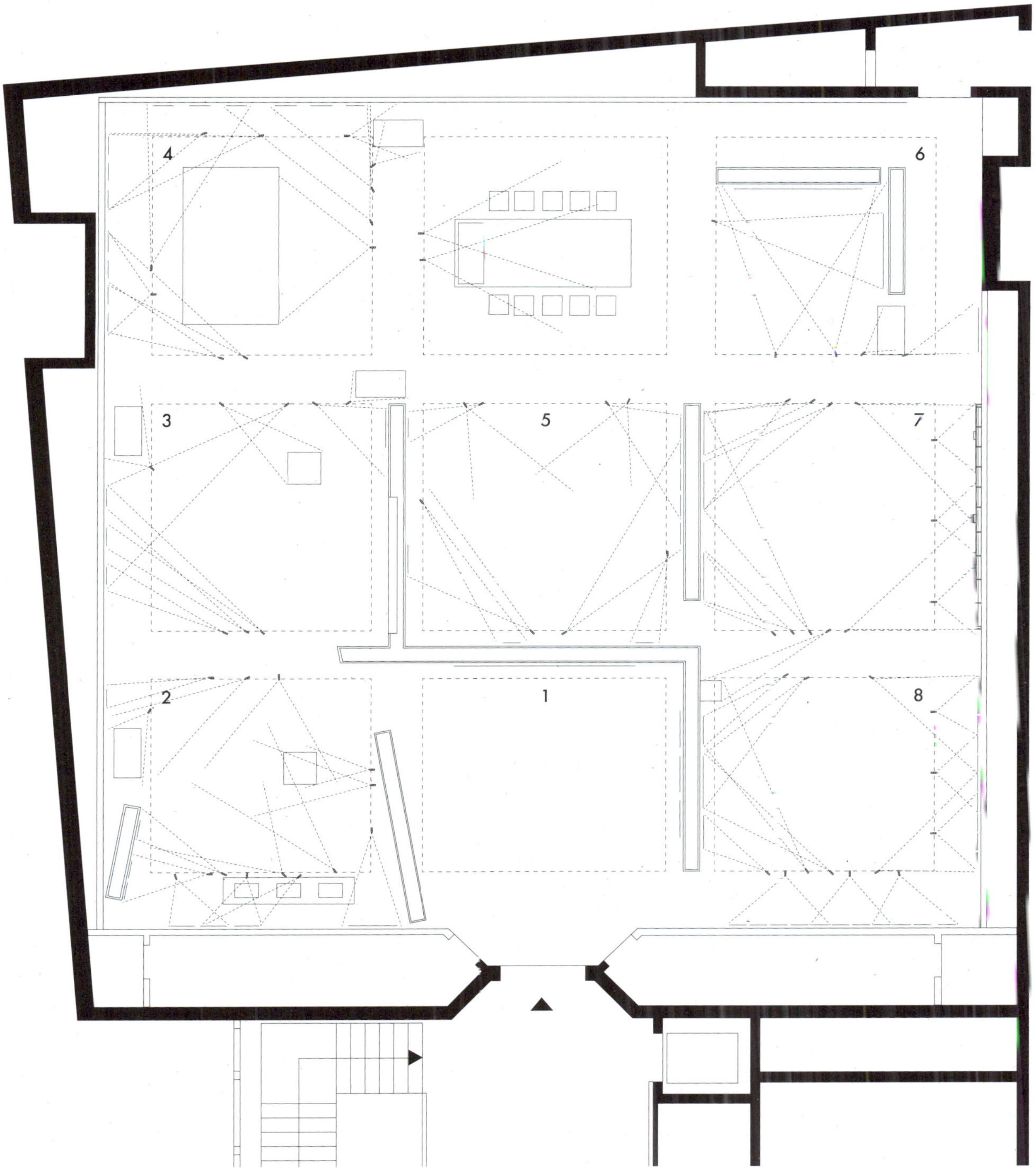

1 Introduction and conclusions
2 Open up perspectives
3 See the unknown
4 Pictures on journeys and in transformation
5 In the thinking space of images
6 Pictures in negotiation and as a prescription
7 Print black, see white
8 Follow images

Lighting system

Ground floor
1:150

1 3 6 m

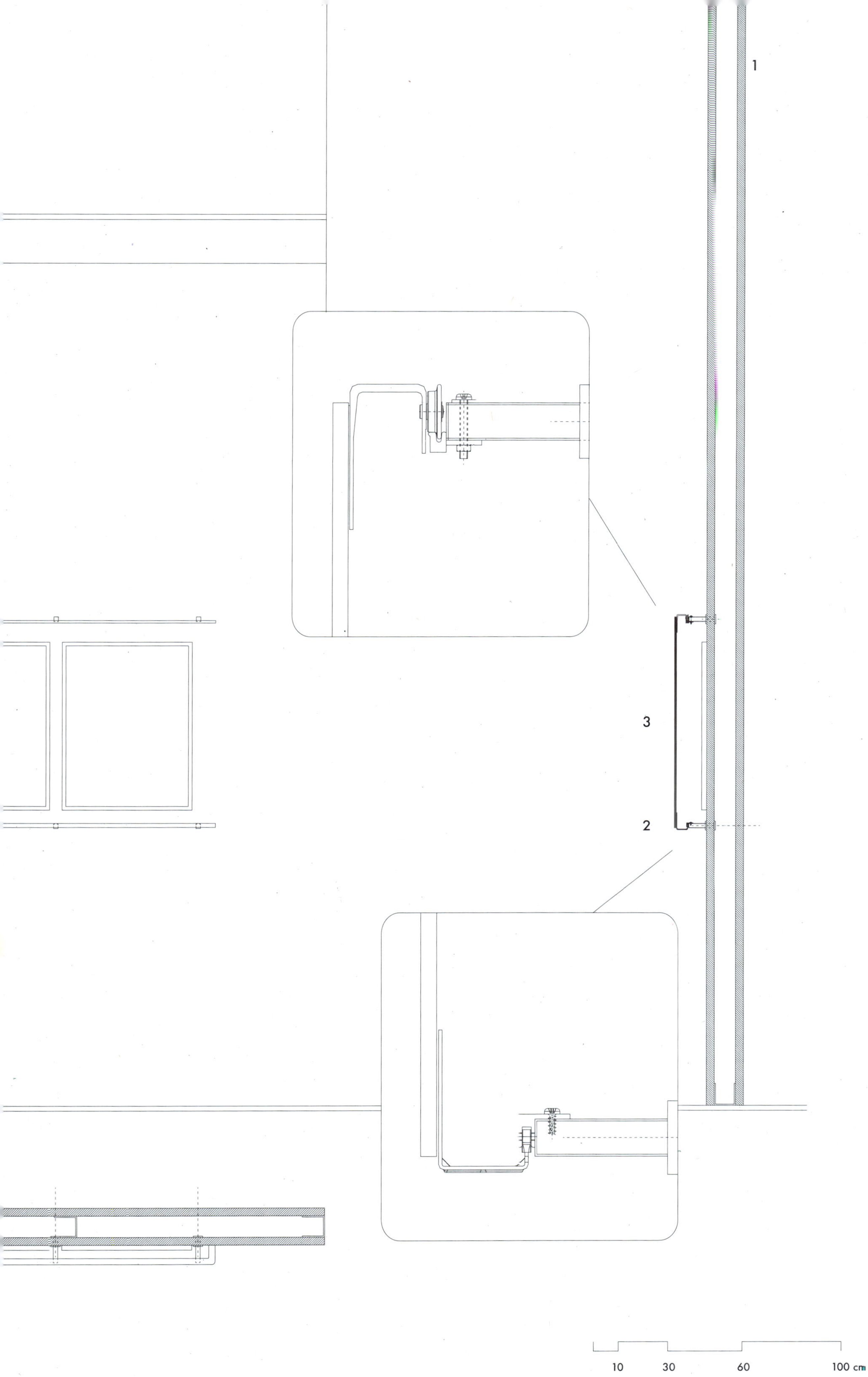

Exhibition elements

1 Existing wall
2 F.e. Hawa 212, toughened glass element 8 mm plus magnifying foil, 120 mm wide
3 Mounted with hollow profiles

Sectional elevation
1:20

Albrecht Dürer

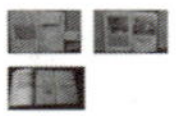

1. Perspektiven eröffnen

Holzschnitt
(cm) 7,5 x 21,5
8,3 x 21,5

Federzeichnung
13,1 x 18,2

Buch, Typendruck Holzschnitt
18.9 x 24,6

Holzschnitt
19,2 x 13,8

2. Ungewisses sehen

Kupferstich
26,1 x 20,2

Kupferstich
18 x 12

Kupferstich
31 x 22

3. Bilder auf Wanderungen und in Verwandlun

Holzschnitt, koloriert (grün, ocker)
23,9 x 29,8

Holzschnitt, Typendruck, mit niederländischem Text, 6. Ausgabe, gedruckt von Hendrik Hondius
23,9 x 29,8

Holzschnitt, Typendruck, mit deutschem Text
23,9 x 29,8

Kupferstich
24,1 x 34,4

Buch, Typendruck Holzschnitt

William Kentridge

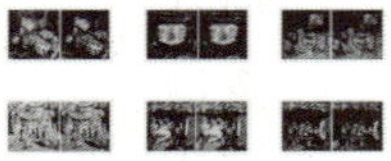

1. Perspektiven eröffnen

brush, ink
(cm) 63 x 70

stereoscopic photogravure
34,3 x 57,15

lithograph printed on Le Nouveau Larousse Illustré Encyclopaedia (1906), chine collé on BFK Rives White paper
78 x 78; 63

2. Ungewisses sehen

steel
45 x 60 x 98

Chine collé with black Canson paper on multiple spreads from Le Nouveau Larousse Illustré Encyclopaedia (c. 1906) on Vélin d'Arches Crème,folded as a Leporello
29 x 25,5 x 200

etching, drypoint, sugarlift
77 x 90

3. Bilder auf Wa

charcoal, red pastel
35.6 x 56 35.5 x

etching, drypoi red pencil on Hahnemühle pa
28,5 x 32,5

5. Bilder in Verhandlungen und als Verordnung

three-coloured lithograph, chine collé on cotton
(cm) 196 x 180

linocut on 30 pages of the Britannica World Language Dictionary, chine collé on Vélin d'Arches
170 x 108

6. Schwarz drucken, Weiß sehen

monotype in black on Fabiano paper
66 x 49,5

linocut on Tableau rice paper and canvas
250,2 x 97,8

etching Vélin d
158 x 1

Im Denkraum der Bilder

upferstich

,8 x 18,5

5. Bilder in Verhandlungen und als Verordnung

Holzschnitt, 195 Druckstöcke
auf 36 Großfoliobogen, Typendruck

357 x 309

6. Schwarz drucken, Weiß sehen

Holzschnitt

32,8 x 28,5

Kupferstich
unfertiger
Zustand

32 x 22,5

Kaltnadelradierung

21 x 18,4

Kaltnadelradierung

21 x 18,4

Kupferstich

32 x 22,5

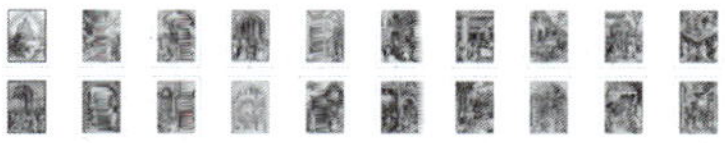

7. Bildern folgen

Holzschnitt

29,7 x 21

und in Verwandlung

ching

x 26

etching,
drypoint

45 x 40

ching, drypoint

5 x 19,5

lithograph, two coloured

45 x 50

4. Im Denkraum der Bilder

collage, ink, pen
red pencil

24,6 x 39,3

photogravure
on handmade
Abaca paper

31,5 x 46

set of 8 stereoscopic
cards, colophon wood
box and stereoscope

9 x 17

silk-screen print on pages of Septem
Linguarum Calepinus (1746),
Journal Northern Transvaal Lands
Co hld (1.1.1927), Historia Natural
Do Brasil (o.J.), Dilftributus (1757)

37,5 x 50,5

aquatinta on
anc 300 g paper

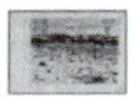

7. Bildern folgen

etching,
drypoint &
aquatinta
on Fabriano
Rosapina
Bianco 220g paper

55,5 x 77,5

charcoal,
red pencil

47 x 66

etching, soft ground,
drypoint, aquatinta,
zinc plate, polycarbon
sheet, on Fabriano
Rosapina Bianco
220g paper

25 x 30

four-colour lithograph,
hand printed on maps from
Bacon's Popular Atlas of the
World (1893) and
The Oxford Atlas (1951),
on Vélin d'Arches Blanc;
cut to a circle and attached
to gramophone record,
metal shaft and handle,
2 vinyl records

80 x 50 x 50

drypoint on vinyl

49,8 x 34,8

etching, drypoint, burnished, some with
engraving on Hahnemühle paper

28,5 x 33

Dear William, liebe Holodeck Architekten

der unaspektuelle Kontextualismus ist gelungen.

Double vision and evidence of scenes, are well worked out and the dimension of your work is great.

See you soon

[illegible]

Genial ♥ ♥

5.1. Thank you so much for the exhibition,

it was academic in a playful way,

I really enjoyed it. I was a fan but now even more so.

Katriina Tuominen, Helsinki, Finland

張瀚文到此一遊

Bia Junqueira

[illegible] - Brazil - GREAT!!!

Interessante Ausstellung!!!

[illegible]

Für Beate

[illegible]

Brilliant juxtaposition

Ashley Harris (South Africa)

Das Tollste dass ich in Monaten gesehen habe!
Total beeindruckend.

(New York)

Sehr schöne Sonderausstellung

IRMA STOLT

Faszinierend und beeindruckend

S. H.

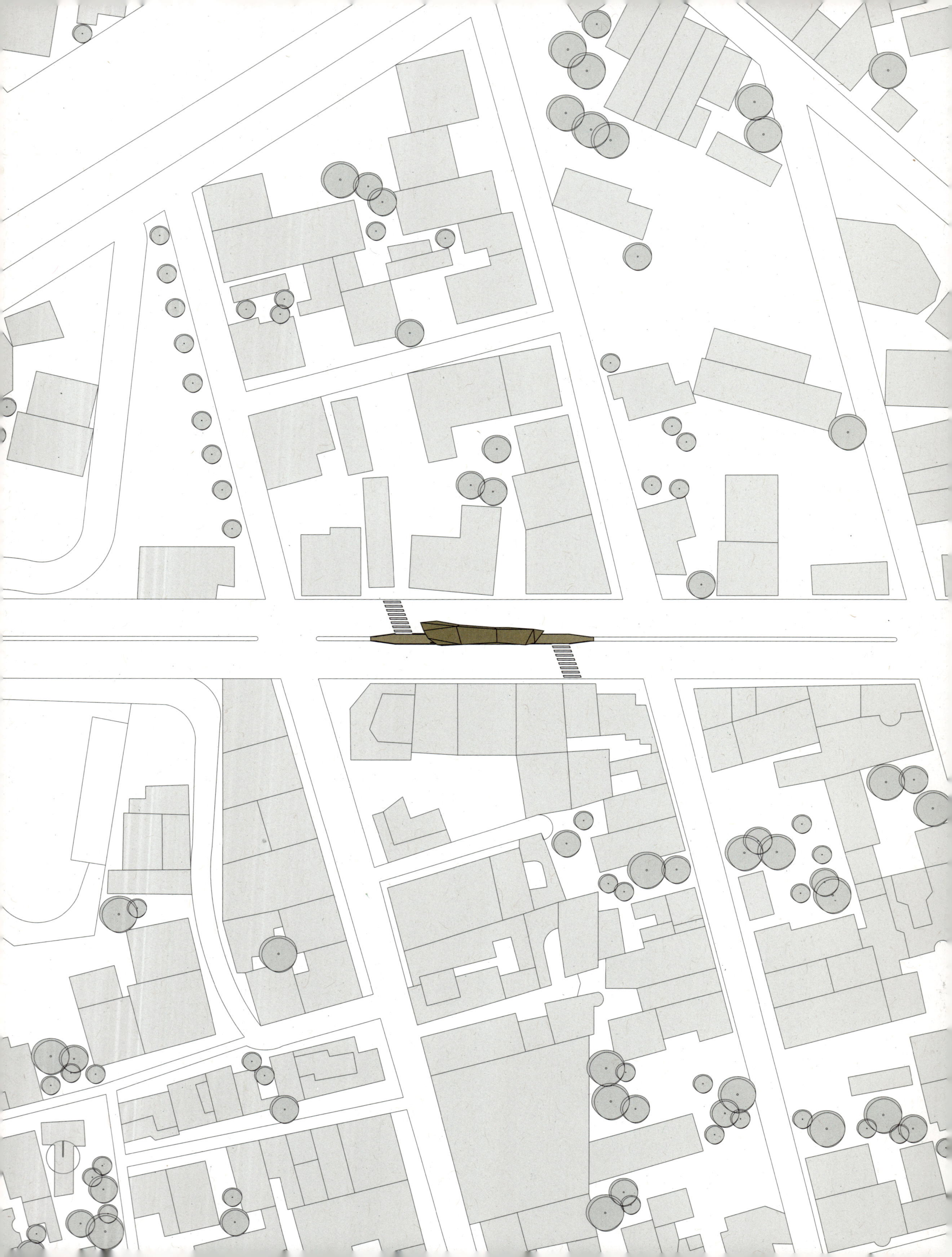

codicil
10682 Athens, GR

PROGRAM
Urban intervention, temporary exhibition space

DIMENSIONS
Floor space 56 m²

CLIENT
City Administration of Athens

PROJECT TEAM
Marlies Breuss, Michael Ogertschnig, Martin Maczutajtis, Susanne Schmall

CONSULTANTS
KPPK, structural engineer

AWARDS
International open competition, honorable mention

PUBLICATIONS (SELECTION)
Nicholas Anastasopoulos, Thanasis Moutsopoulos, Lina Stergiou, and Vaso Trova, “Time-based design,” *Archis* #2, Amsterdam, March 2003 (ISSN 1568-2730).
Ephemeral Structures, exhibition, Heraklion, Crete, May–June 2004.
Peter Lorenz, “*Die Kür:* Perspektiven, Renderings und andere Darstellungsformen,” in *Gebäude Entwerfen: grundlagen, methoden, arbeitshilfen*, Munich, DVA kompakt, May 2010 (ISBN 978-3-421-03667-4).

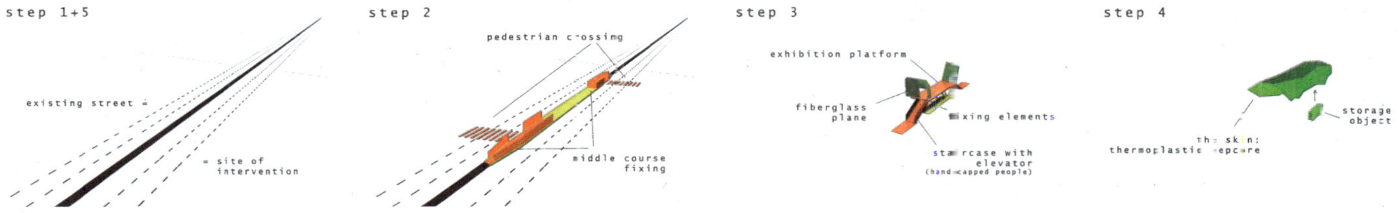

“If we understand time as a malleable substance, then such evanescent structures promise to become our ‘time machines,’ in other words devices that manipulate time and the perception of it.”

—Nicholas Anastasopoulos, “Techniques of time, Ephemeral structures: eternal moments or monumental eternities,” *Archis* #2, 2003, p. 34.

Site plan
1:1,000

10 25 50 m

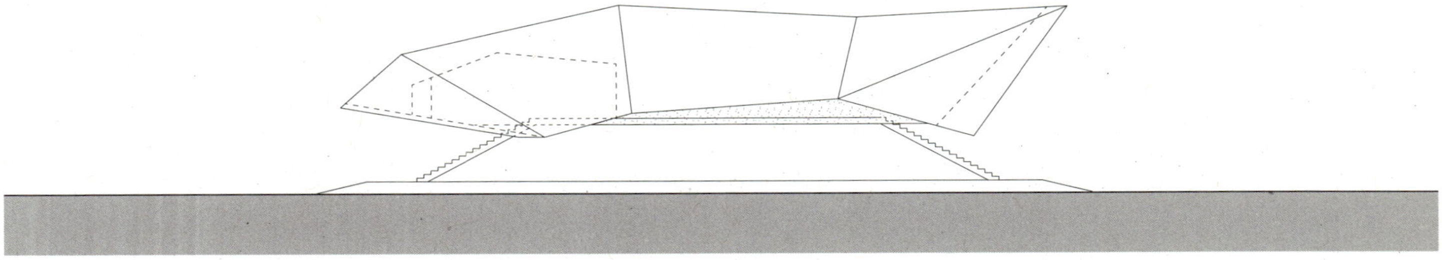

Elevation

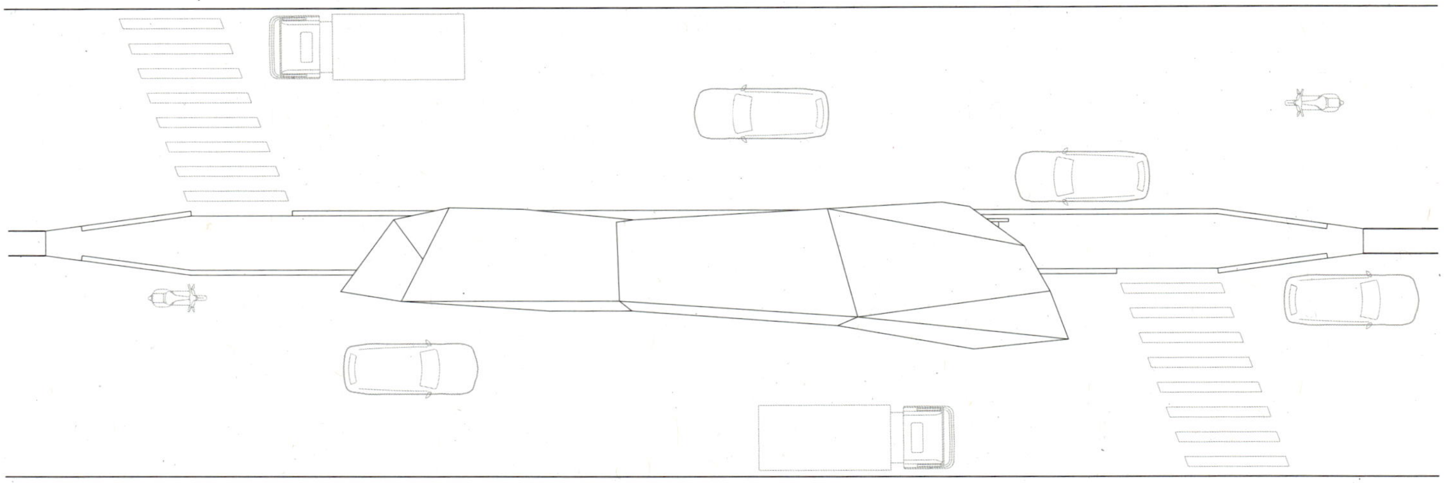

Top view

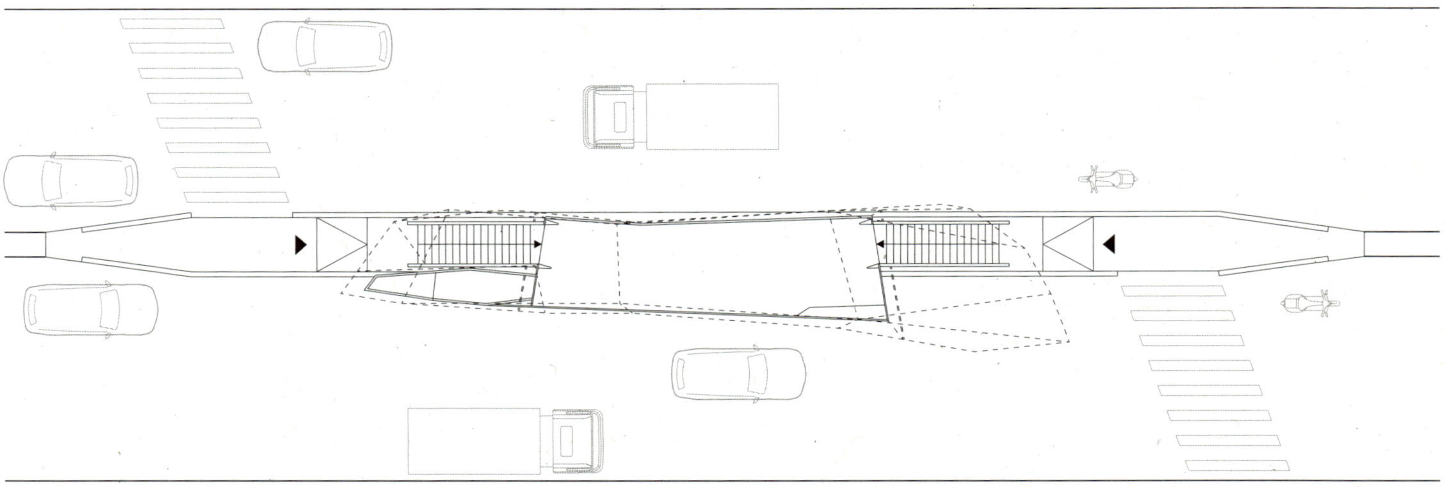

Ground floor
1:300

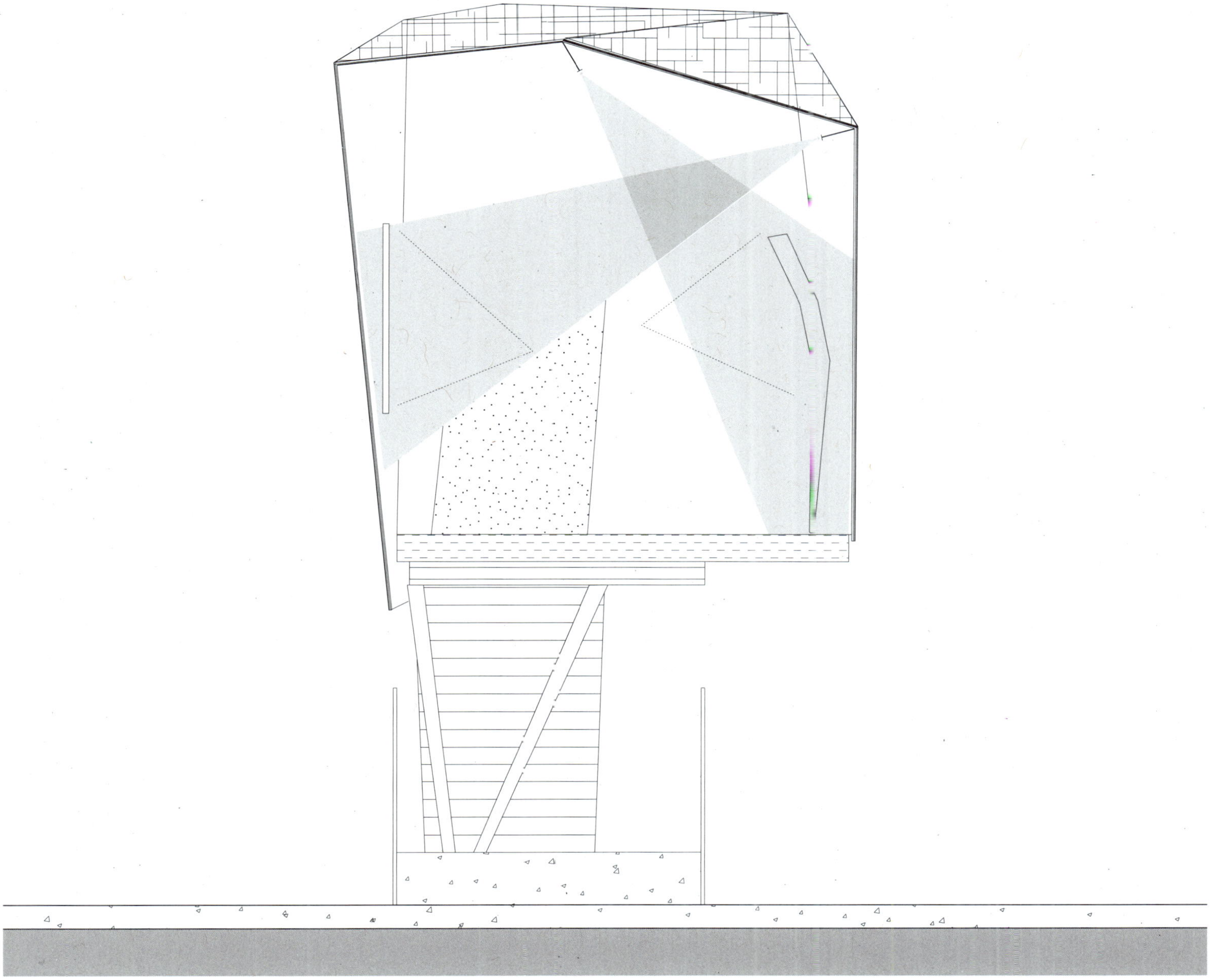

Section
1:50

10 30 60 100 cm

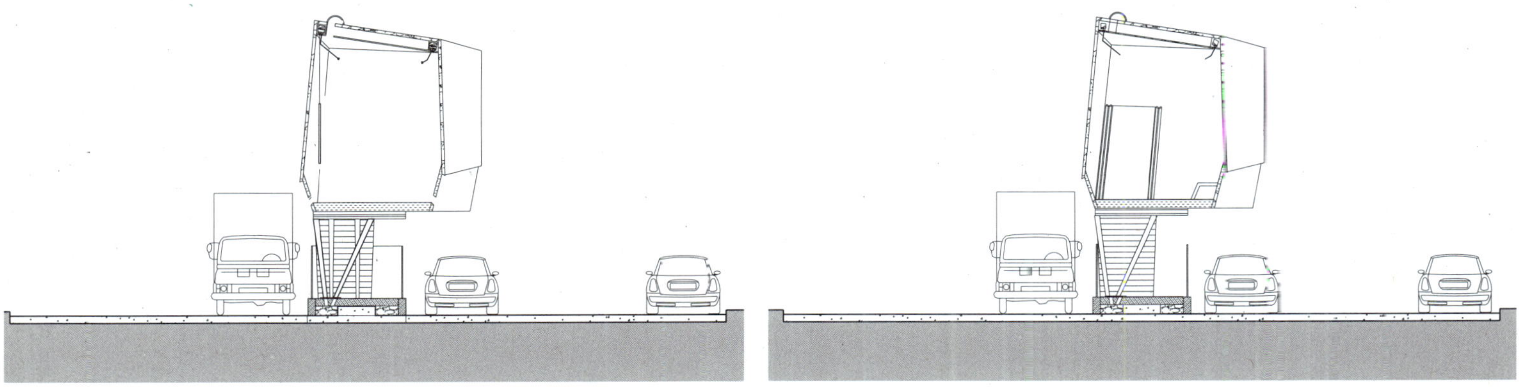

Sections
1:200

1 3 6 10 m

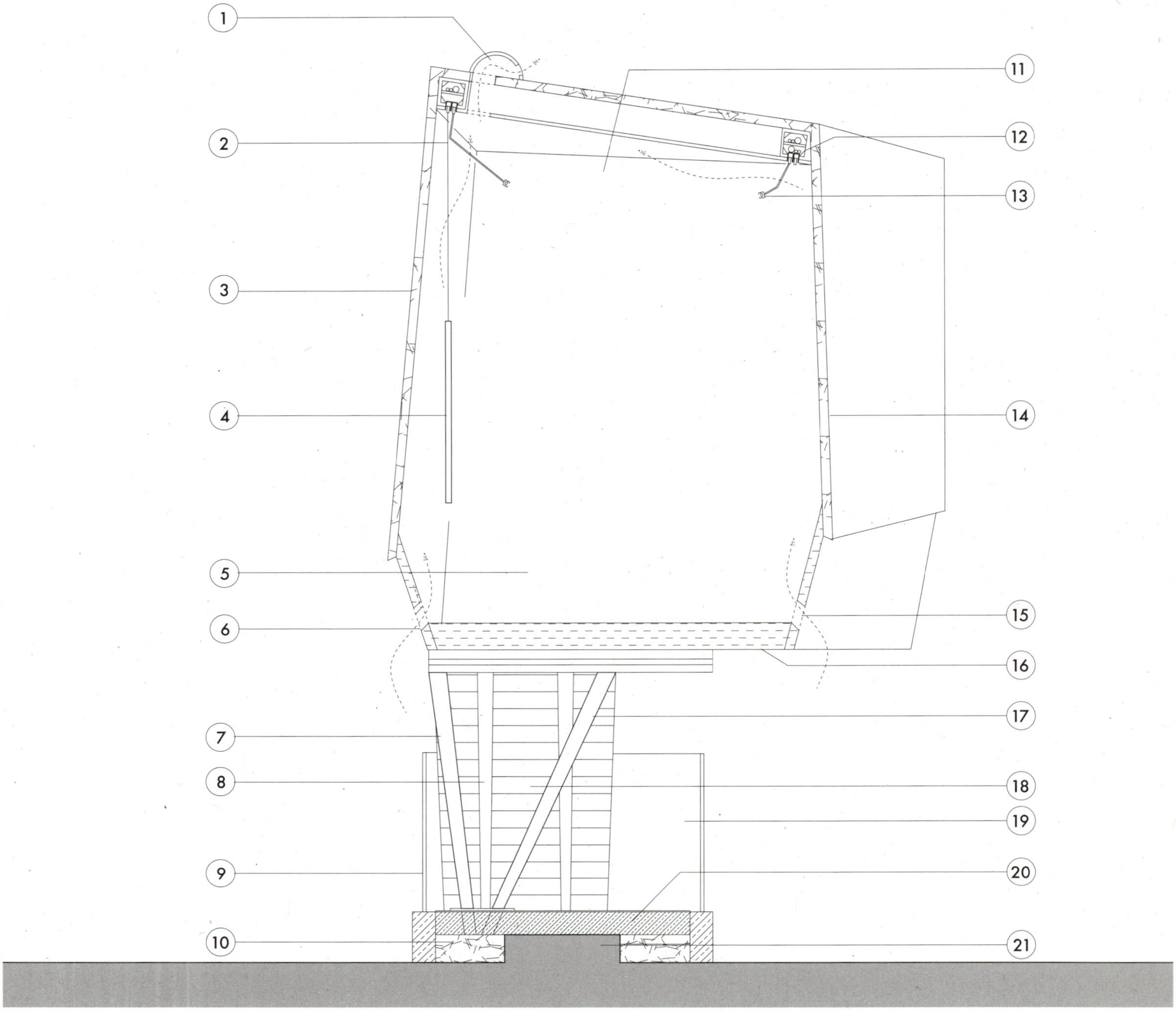

1 Air circulation opening rooftop
2 Presentation hanging system
3 Clear PEP stage, self-supporting composite 8 mm
4 Presentation boards
5 Folding door entrance
6 Air circulation opening ∅ 200 mm
7 Steel structure ∅ 180 mm
8 Staircase construction beam and electric support
9 Concrete bollard 200/400 mm
10 Concrete-filled area
11 Fiberglass panel, opaque 30 mm
12 Tracks
13 Luminaires
14 Fibreglass front panel, transparent
15 Air circulation opening ∅ 200 mm
16 Cross-laminated timber panels 230 mm
17 Steel beams 200 mm
18 Steel staircase with rubber 1,600 mm
19 Fiberglass panels 20 mm
20 Supporting concrete slab with rubber 2,000/3,000/200 mm
21 Existing middle course 1,000/200 mm

Section
1:50

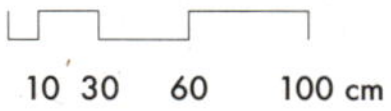

Outlining and supporting system
Mounting phase 1

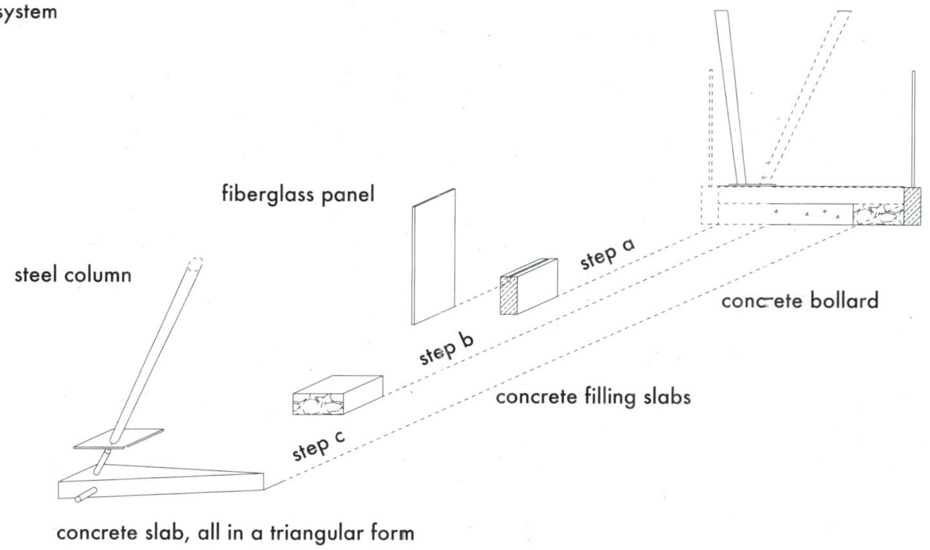

Construction frame and skin
Mounting phase 2

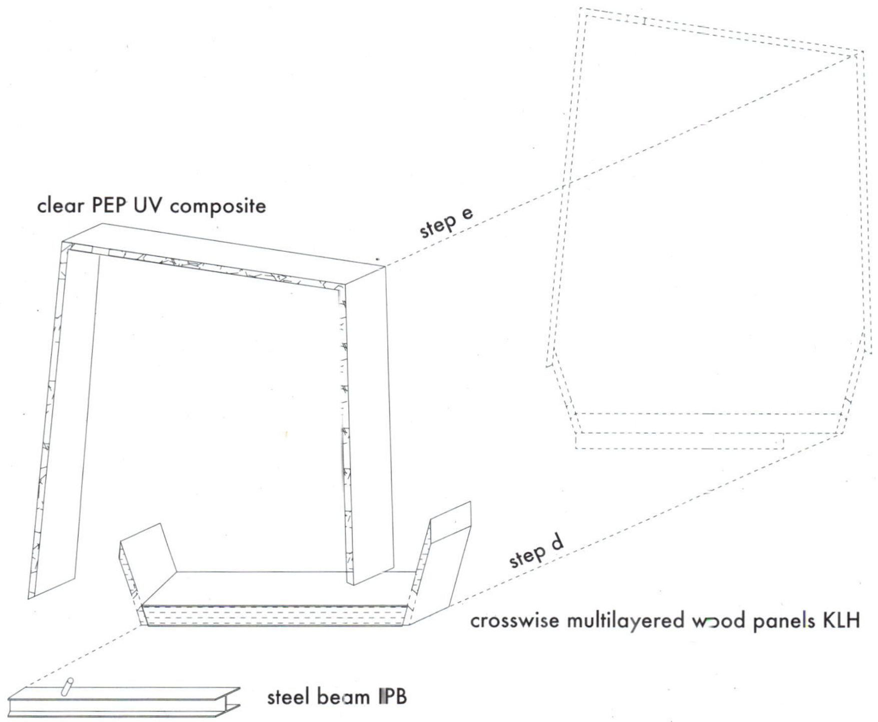

Interior equipment
Mounting phase 3

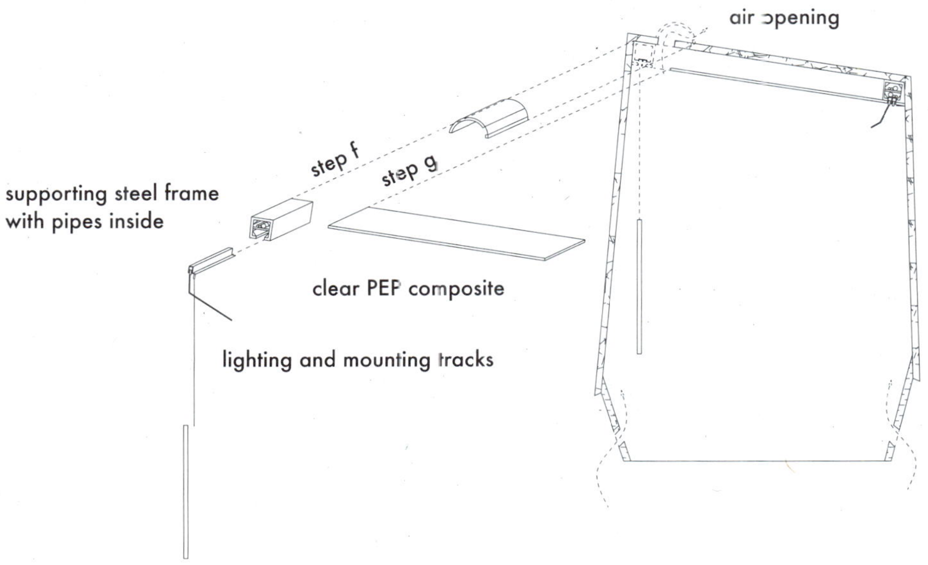

mobile 01
Independent location, variable

See p. 190

PROGRAM
Urban intervention, mobile youth center

DIMENSIONS
Mobile minimal space about 1.4 × 3.5 meter

CLIENT
Jugendreferat Land Burgenland, Eisenstadt, Austria

PROJECT TEAM
Marlies Breuss, Michael Ogertschnig, Martin Maczutajtis, Susanne Schmall

PROJECT COOPERATION
Peter Fattinger

CONSULTANTS
KPPK (structural engineer), Wolf (electrical engineer/technician)

PHOTOGRAPHY
Peter Fattinger

PUBLICATIONS (SELECTION)
"Suburban paradise," *Architektur.aktuell*, Vienna and New York, Springer, June 2003.
"Mobil in der Stadt," *Architektur.aktuell*, Vienna and New York, Springer, March 2004.
Manuela Hötzl and Antje Mayer, "Mobile Immobilie," in *Einfach! Architektur aus Österreich – Die Wahl der Kritiker*, Graz, Verlag Haus der Architektur, 2006 (ISBN 3-901174-61-3).

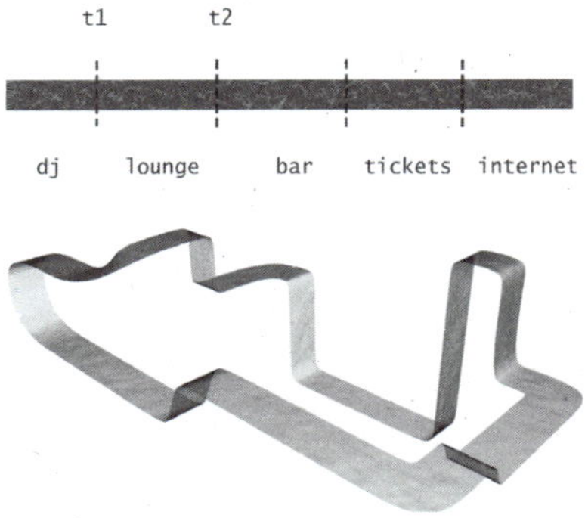

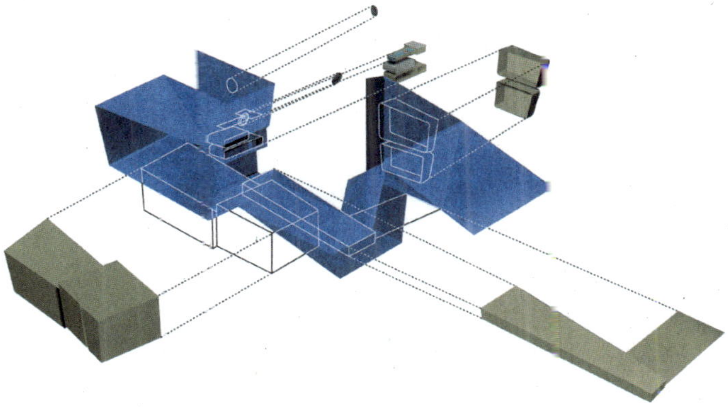

"The temporary stands out from the existing, thus making the city visible anew. The mobile architectures draw their urban energy from their precise setting."

—Elke Krasny, "Mobil in der Stadt," *Architektur.aktuell* 3 (2004), Vienna and New York, Springer, p. 4 (trans. by the ed.)

Phase 1
Programming

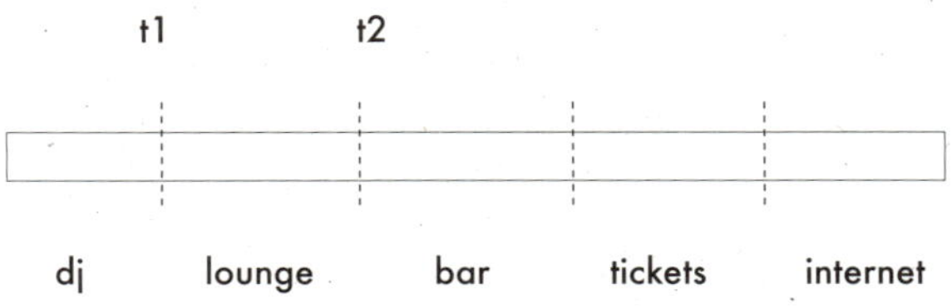

Phase 2
Program loop

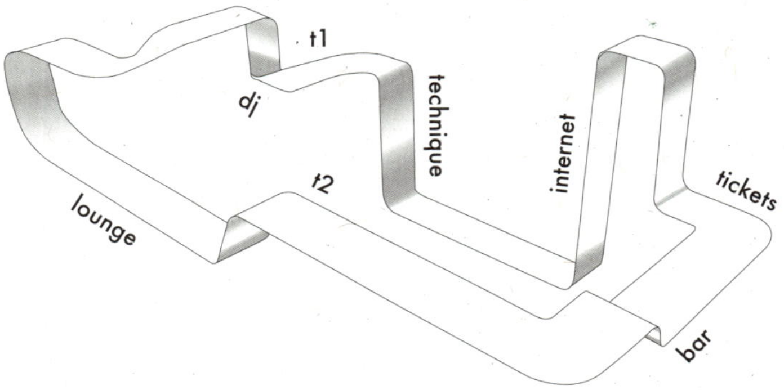

Phase 3
Tools

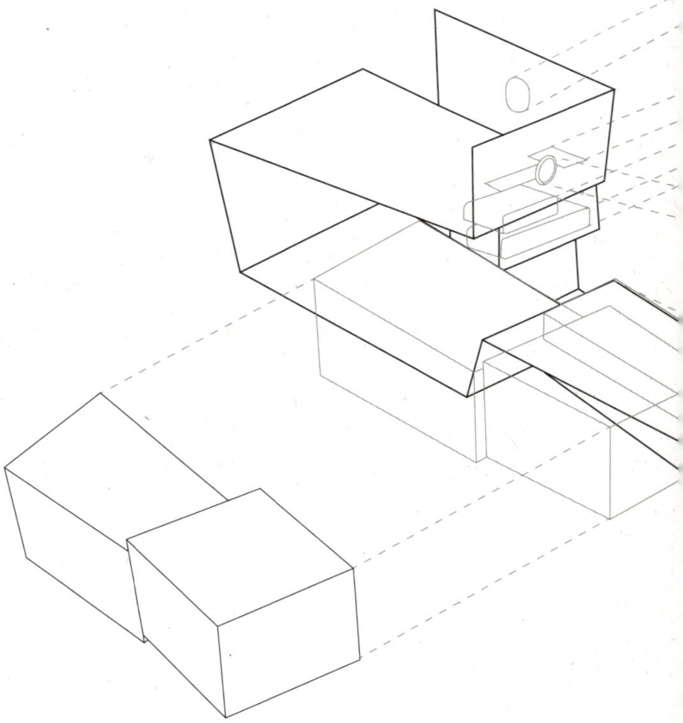

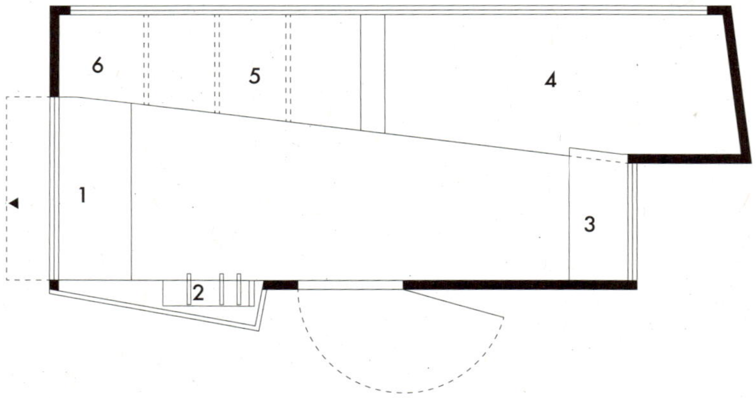

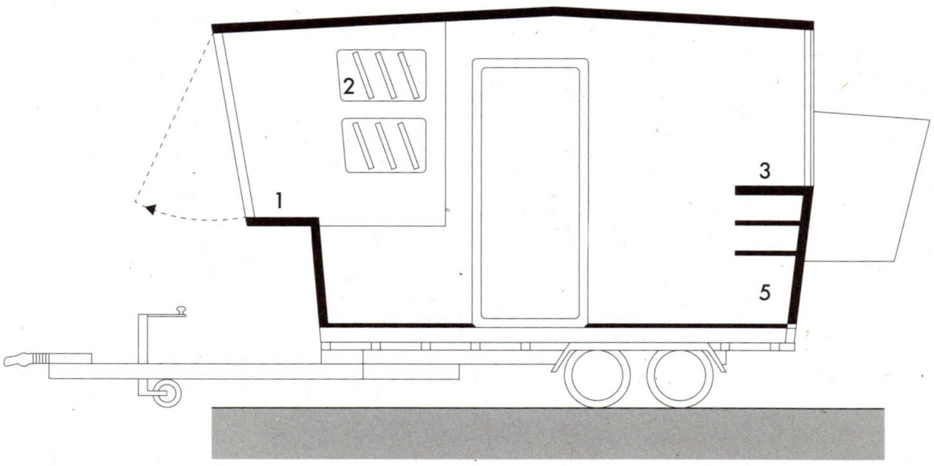

Sections
1:50

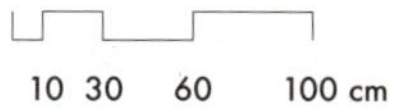

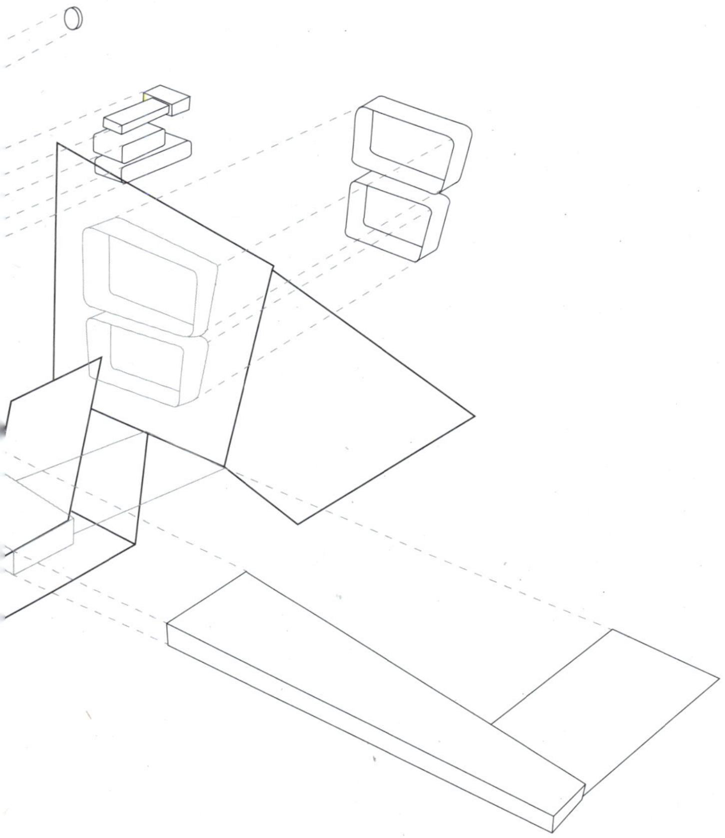

Phase 4
Mobility

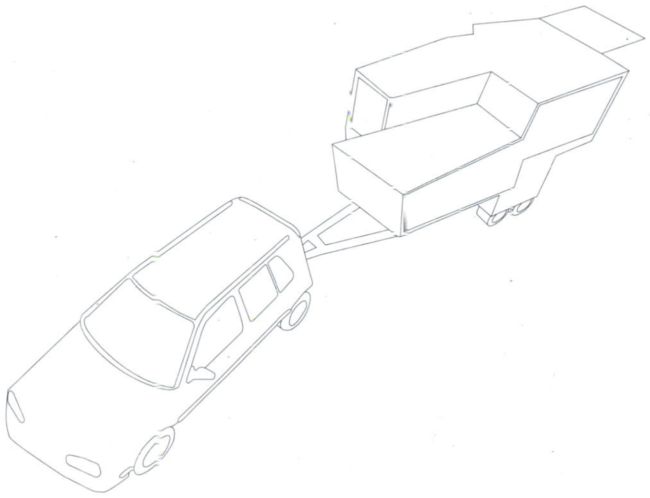

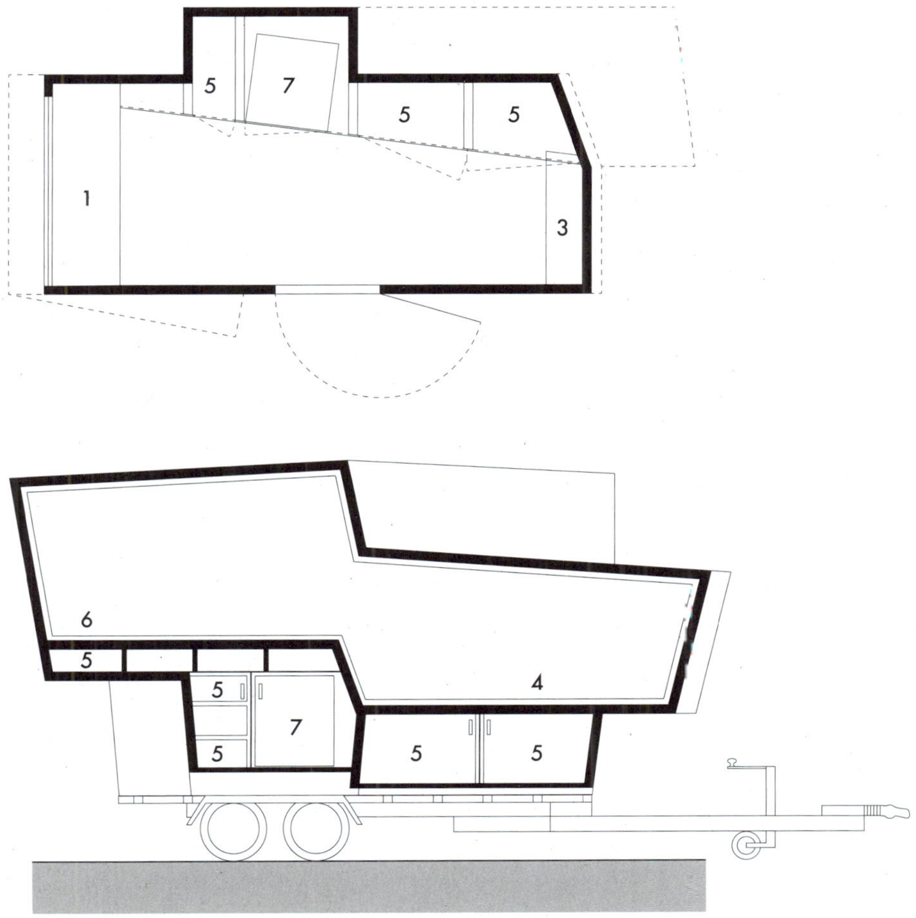

1 Ticket booth
2 Notebooks
3 DJ desk
4 Lounge
5 Storage space
6 Presentation desk
7 Refrigerator

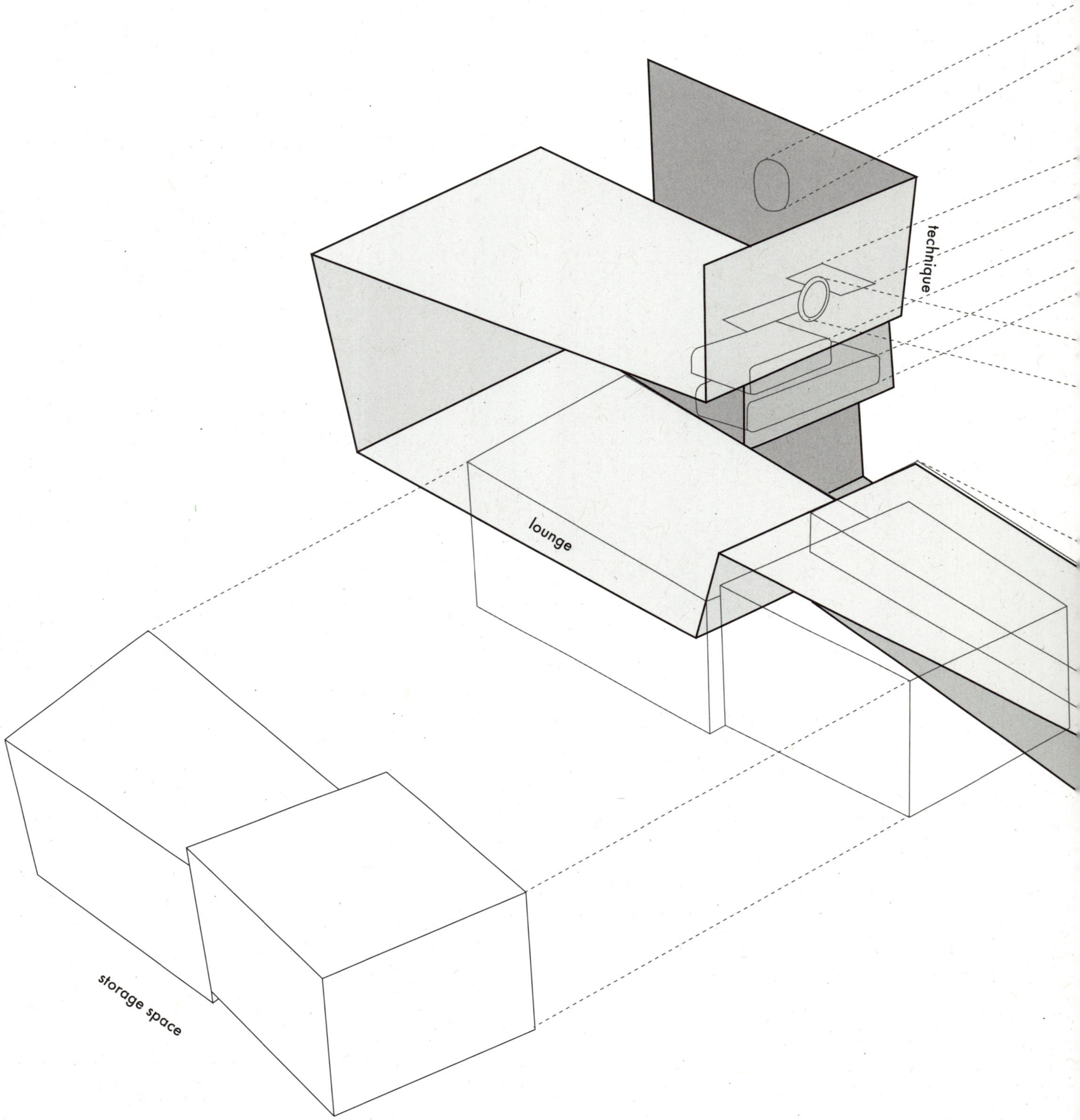
technique
lounge
storage space

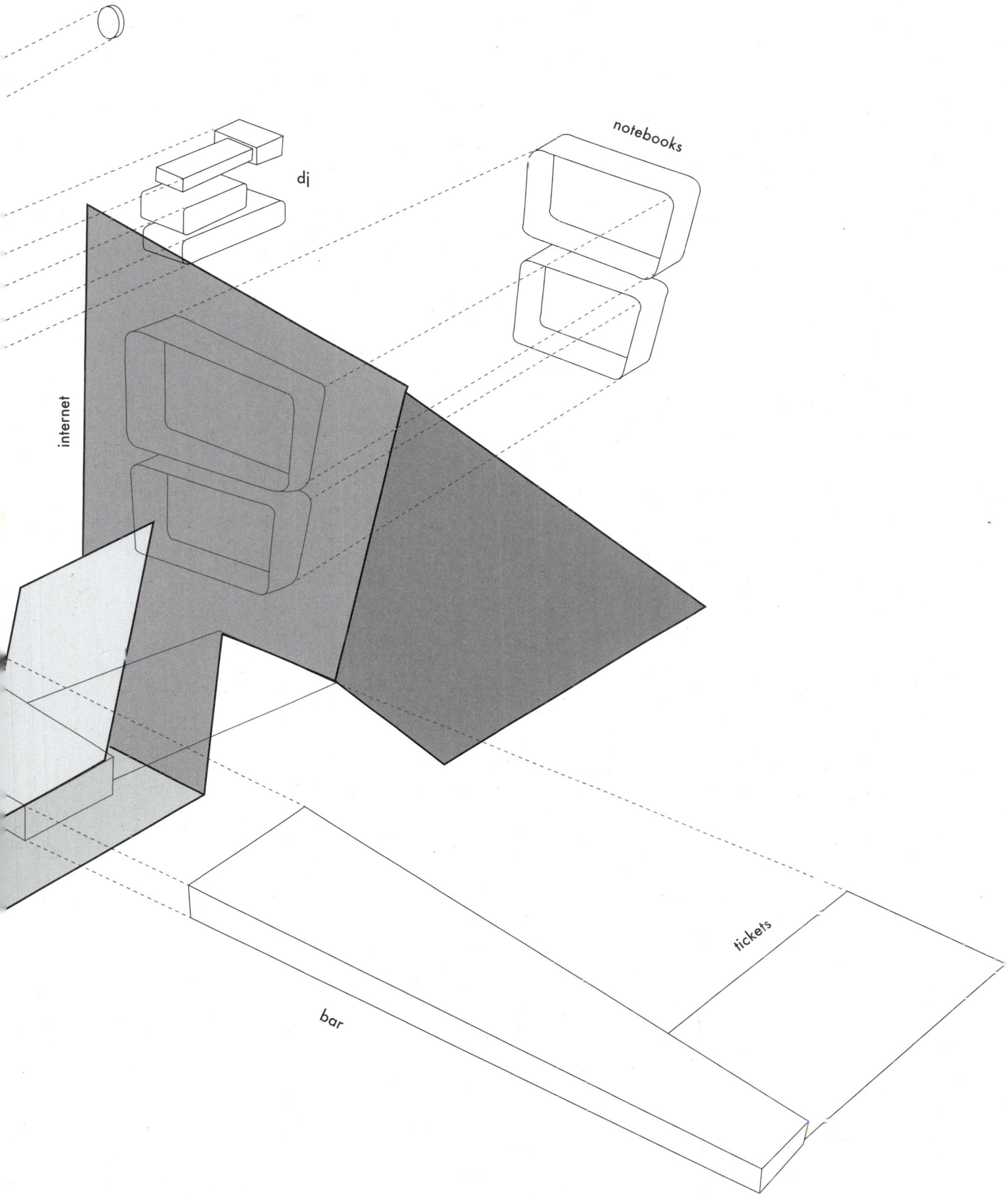
notebooks
dj
internet
tickets
bar

URBAN
STRATEGIES

krieau. viertel zwei plus

2014

The Krieau district of Vienna has a varied history—from a water meadow where courtiers hunted on an islet in the unchanneled arms of the Danube to today's compact, multifunctional urban expansion area including a university quarter. Wedged between the Prater landscape, the urban development axis along the U2 line, the new campus of the Vienna University of Economics and Business, and the historic Trabrennbahn (trotting track), it is an especially significant area. The two sculpture studios (formerly pavilions of art) east of the Trabrennbahn are still preserved from the 1873 Vienna World's Fair. They have a considerable influence, sitting as solitaires symmetrically in relation to the project area and, along with the renovated and updated grandstands, framing the racecourse still in use at the edge of the Prater.

In response to this specific spatial situation, we take the urban concept as based on the landscaped open space, with buildings arranged in between, including an urban square acting as a continuation of the university axis and a connection to neighboring areas. The exact positioning of the buildings is determined by the inclusion of several reference angles to adjacent existing buildings, and the inclusion of links to the U2 station, the Trabrennbahn, and the Prater landscape which hold relevance in terms of city planning. The urban structure emerges out of space-defining distances, proportions, orientation, and numerous intervening spaces that have different amenity values.

Different uses, such as a student hall of residence, various office units, and a residential building, plus a multifunctional ground floor zone in all buildings, make for a lively quarter. Two multistory, green bridges link functionally connected building units at airy heights, provide views, and enhance circulation within the area, which also includes lawns for lying on, and seating and play areas. These areas are augmented by semipublic roof gardens on the milestone building and the studio apartment block. Designed as skeleton structures, all the buildings are flexible and, in the western part, directly connected to the underground car park. All office units are equipped with openable windows and external sun protection, and the apartments are also enclosed by green loggias.

campagne living

2017

At the edge of Innsbruck's extensive residential area of Reichenau, on Radetzkystraße and next to the Langer Weg arterial road and the newly built tram line, the Campagne grounds are a large and important area for development within the city. For the northeastern part, a park is projected, with public open space for recreation, while the southern area has several residential complexes with a multifunctional ground-floor zone; in between, a neighborhood square includes a café as a meeting place. Next to the common areas are parking spaces: those for bicycles are at ground level for quick use, while cars are parked in the underground garage below the southernmost buildings.

The southwestern residential complex, with a semipublic inner courtyard, preserves bicycle or pedestrian routes from Burghard-Breitner-Straße and from the Radetzkystraße intersection in the direction of Langer Weg via the neighborhood square. Its ground-floor zone is also used as a communication area for the residents of Reichenau. Roof gardens situated on buildings in the complex, which are of different heights, serve as semipublic open spaces for the relevant apartments. All occupants have private places of retreat and recreation in their own residential units in the form of a balcony, loggia, or terrace.

Different housing types allow for varying lifestyles, from singles to families with several children, and they are accessed via a porch or central corridor. Each combined structure has a vertical access core connecting all residential floors with the ground-floor zone and the roof gardens. All sanitary areas are positioned at the vertical shafts along the access zone. All this is followed a facade that incorporates loggias, balconies, and generously glazed elements for natural lighting.

low-rise courtyards

2014

At the northeastern edge of the City of Vienna, on the border of Lower Austria (which makes it a rural development), a 26,000-square-meter property on Breitenleer Straße is being considered by the city for a possible Category I/II housing development. In light of an adjacent settlement of single-family homes and allotments, as well as the federal boundary and the continuing demand for affordable housing in Vienna, three different housing types with maximum private open space are considered—terraced housing, multistory housing, and atrium housing—along with the access road, parking spaces, and ancillary areas required under the building code. Terraced housing with an east–west orientation makes for 136 residential units with ground-level open spaces; multi-story housing adds 153 south-oriented units with balconies; and atrium housing yields 181 south-oriented units with directly allocated open spaces on three levels.

The study shows the positive features of the densified low-rise topology of the atrium house or garden courtyard house, especially in regard to privacy and generous open space. Particularly in the 1960s and 1970s, architects such as Roland Rainer (1964 Puchenau Garden City, near Linz, with ground-level L-shaped atrium floor plans) and Fritz Matzinger (1974 residential house in Linz) experimented with this housing form as an alternative to the emerging typology of the high-rise residential building.

public square
2020–21

Situated in Eisenstadt, Austria, on the lower slopes of the southern Leitha Mountains, the project area was mainly agricultural, with meadows and fields, until the Burgenland Landhaus (provincial government building) was erected to the plans of the architect Rudolf Perthen (1926–29). After the Landhaus and the associated housing estate for civil servants were built along Tillstraße, the area served no particular purpose and remained a green space with various wooded areas. In the early 1960s, the terraced parking lot for the employees of the provincial government was built.

Sitting between the Landhaus to the north, the federal secondary school complex to the south, the Eisenstadt district administration to the west, and a residential estate to the east, the inner-city project area will have several urban functions in the future. Supplementing the sloping and green square in front of Esterhazy Palace, at one end of Eisenstadt's pedestrian zone, the new Europaplatz in front of the Landhaus—designed as a terraced area, with horizontal surfaces totaling 130 by 28 meters—offers a site for regional markets and concerts, as well as a place for visitors to linger under the trees and enjoy a cooling fountain in the summer. The avenue of trees in front of the school will be retained as a shady element of the sloping landscape and will be extended as far as Bürgerspitalgasse, so the pupils will still have the same view during their breaks between lessons.

Beneath the public space, a four-story underground parking garage is being built for use by both state employees and the public, with an access road on one side and an exit on the other. Separately, state government vehicles will use the existing ramps beside the Landhaus, exiting directly onto Ingenieur-Hans-Sylvester-Straße.

mirabellplatz s-link station
2021

Salzburg's ambitious S-Link project to provide an underground rapid transit connection from surrounding towns and villages to the city's main station has begun with the first station at Mirabellplatz. Years of traffic jams between surrounding settlements and the Old Town, caused by solo car drivers, should thus come to an end. Mirabellplatz sits among Salzburg's great cultural institutions. Mirabell Palace, Mozarteum University, and Mirabell Gardens flank the square, which opens out eastward to St. Andrä Parish Church. This site has undergone constant spatial changes since the seventeenth century, especially on the northeast side. The S-Link project divides the space through urban structuring and enables redefinition by means of clear zoning.

The west side of the area, adjacent to Mirabell Gardens, is defined as a recreational space with shady trees. Along the arm of the square that is an extension of Dreifaltigkeitsgasse, plenty of covered mobility space is created with several connections to the underground station for regional trains and to wind-sheltered, above-ground bus stops. In the northeast, the town square between the palace and the church, cleared of small-scale fixtures, is opened up for a wide variety of events.

The peculiarity of the site, with the east-facing buildings and the west-facing garden, extends to the wide-span roofscape, which houses all of the lighting elements and anchorages of the overhead wires for the trolleybuses. On the residential buildings, green, prefabricated roof elements provide cooling surfaces, while parallel to the garden a 915-sqaure-meter solar energy system is fitted in so as to meet local electricity consumption.

From above, this floating landscape, made up of roof elements of the same format arranged in different ways, produces a pixelated image that creates a distinctive identity; underneath it is a pleasant, easily adaptable mobility space. Contextually, the roofscape reacts to its surroundings via the different arrangements of the composing elements.

sustainable quarter
2008

The Nordhavnen project area in Denmark, covering 200 hectares beside the sheltered Oresund in the northwest of Copenhagen, will be developed over the next few decades into a multifunctional urban district with 40,000 residents and just as many jobs and bicycles. The shipping piers and some industrial buildings will be preserved, while the remaining areas will be put to various new uses.

An in-depth analysis of preexisting assets and challenges is being carried out via research on the Internet and in libraries, and by gathering information from local people. This will help to define an approach that follows a system of preserving and adapting. Established, distinctive structures such as Fiskerhavnen (fishermen's harbor), but also industrial monuments and docking areas for container ships and cruise ships, will be taken into account in the new district.

Another important consideration is mobility: a fundamental factor in any city. Bicycles are given high priority, with a flexible cycle network including rental shops and maintenance facilities. This is complemented by public transport, such as water taxis, while cars are restricted to specific connecting axes and, ultimately, meet dead ends.

Existing housing typologies in Copenhagen, such as ribbon, terrace, plate, and perimeter-block construction, are being transformed by integration into the bicycle network. Programmatically, there are new housing types, *Living Green* and *Urban Beach*. A structured network of open spaces supplements the bicycle lanes with private, semipublic, and public green spaces (as well as a park left to run wild), including a wind farm on the northern edge of the new urban development area and an urban promenade with a public square in the middle.

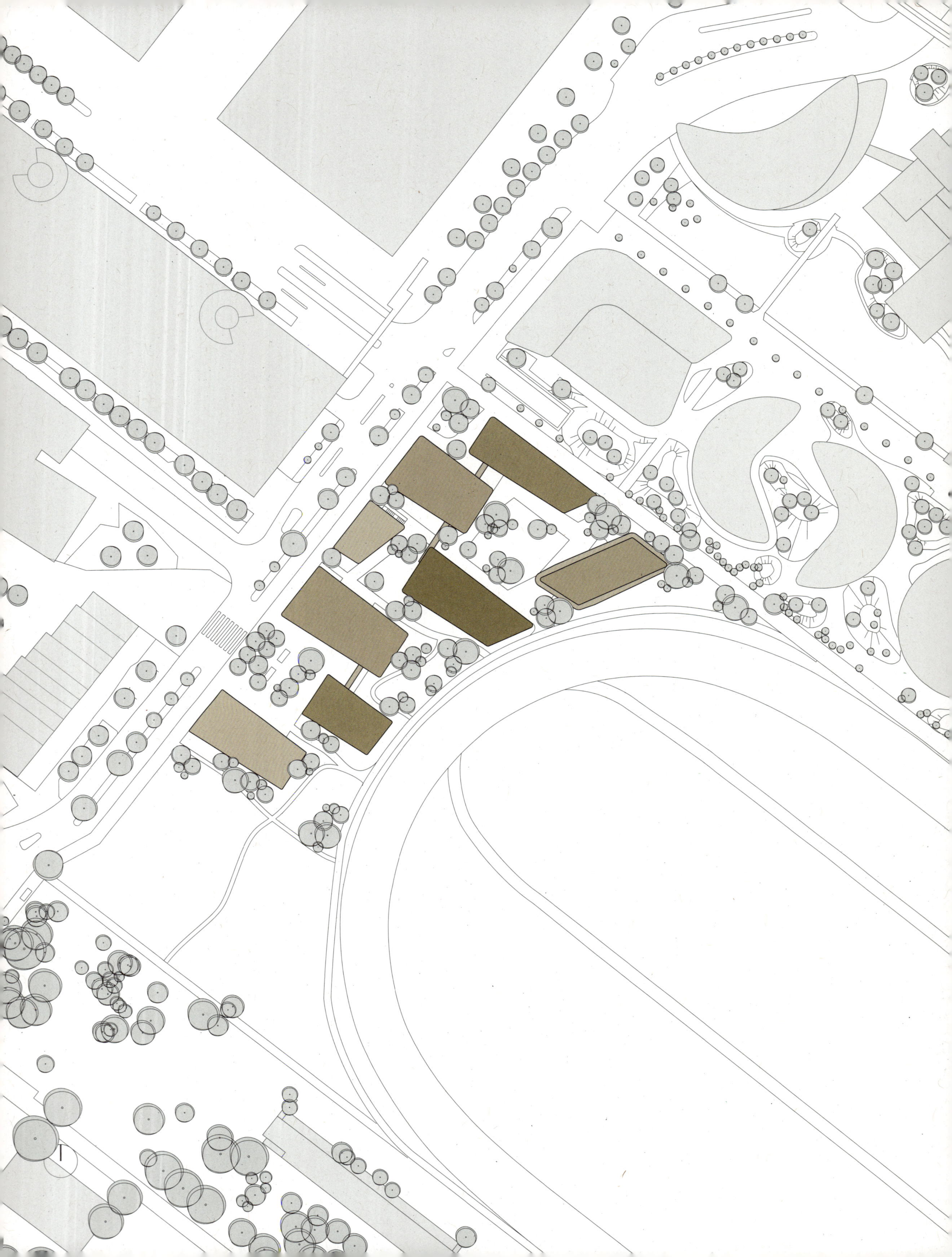

2014
URBAN STRATEGIES

krieau. viertel zwei plus
1020 Vienna, AT

PROGRAM
Urban development, offices, student accommodation, studio apartments, underground parking, public gardens

DIMENSIONS
GFA offices 23,599 m², GFA milestone 12,547 m², GFA studios 6,266 m²

CLIENT
IC Projektentwicklung GmbH, Austria

PROJECT TEAM
Marlies Breuss, Michael Ogertschnig, Hannes Zergoi, Adam Myczkowski, Janine Jakubik,
Laura Llinares, Giacomo Zanin

CONSULTANTS
Röhrer Ziviltechniker (building physics and fire protection), EGKK Landschaftsarchitektur (landscape design),
Dr. Pfeiler ZTGmbH (sustainability assessment)

MODEL-MAKING
archimodell, Vienna

RENDERINGS
on3studio, Hamburg

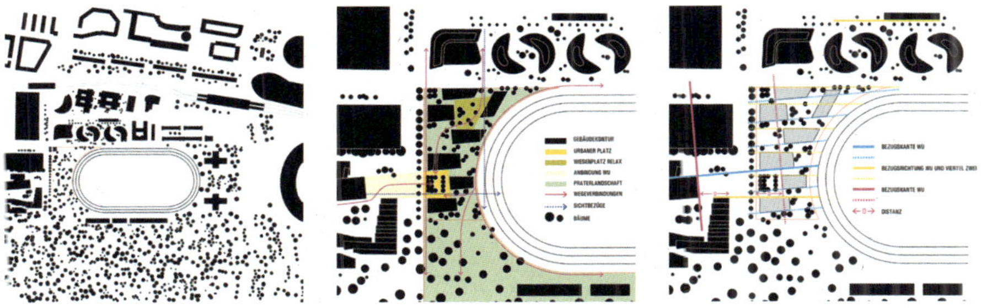

“The sequence of built and unbuilt space derives from the developed rhythm of several parameters, which includes spatial limits, space-determining distances, orientation, and spaces in between.”

—HOLODECK architects, project description for the competition, 2014 (trans. by the ed.)

Site plan
1:1,500

10 30 60 100 m

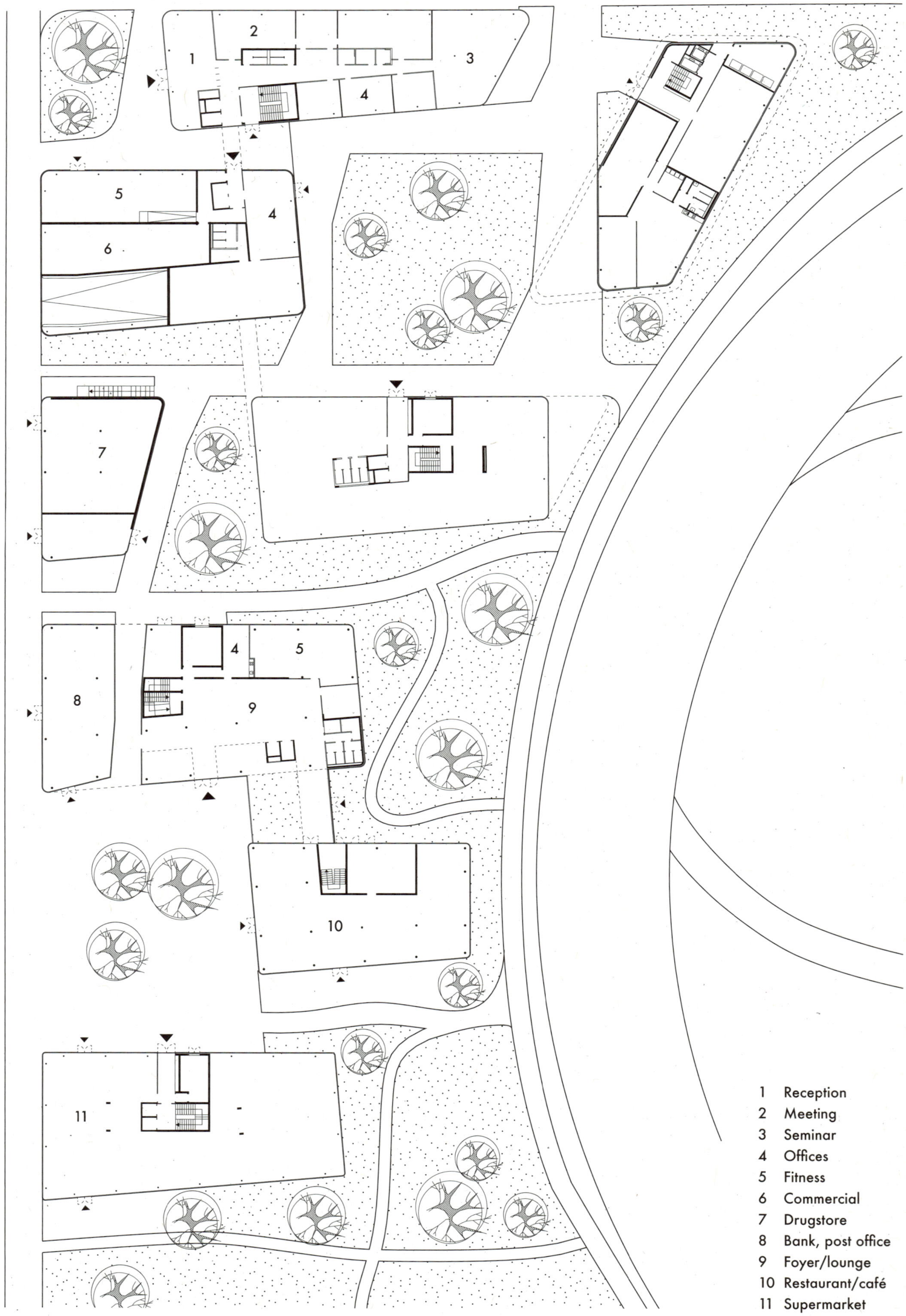

Ground floor
1:650

1 Reception
2 Meeting
3 Seminar
4 Offices
5 Fitness
6 Commercial
7 Drugstore
8 Bank, post office
9 Foyer/lounge
10 Restaurant/café
11 Supermarket

Typical floor plan
1:650

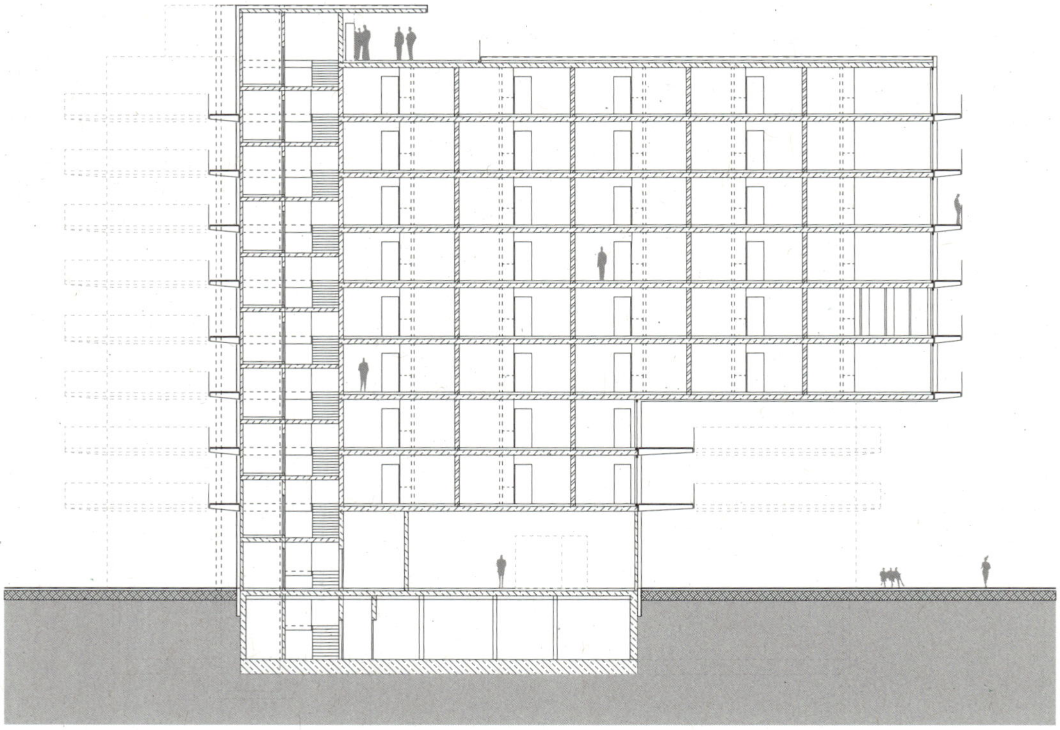

Section studio
1:400

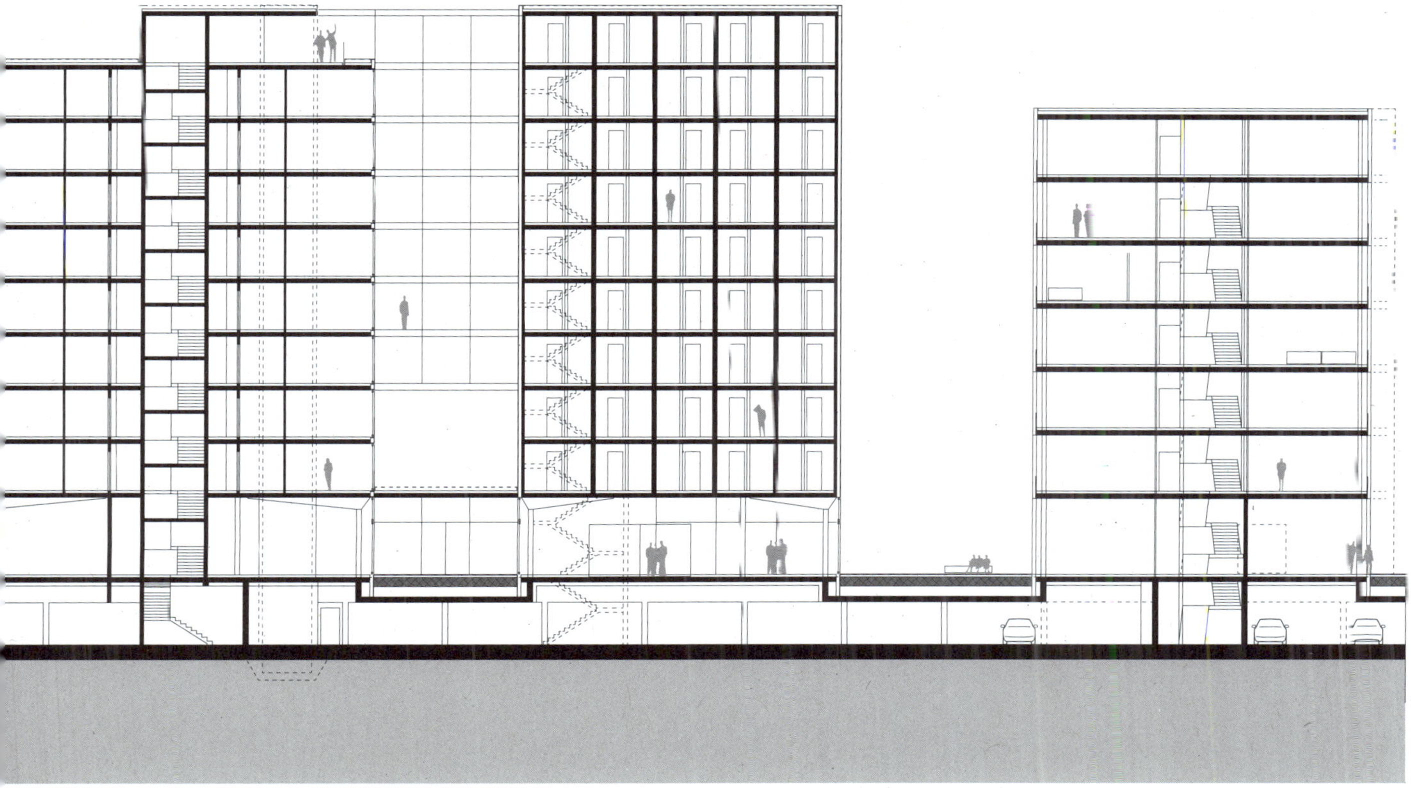

Longitudinal section
1:400

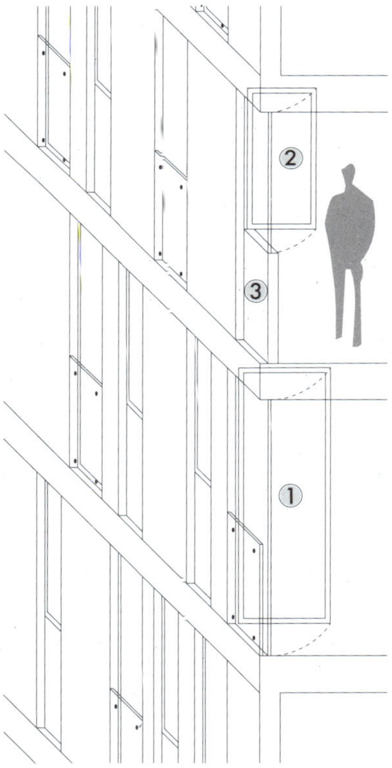

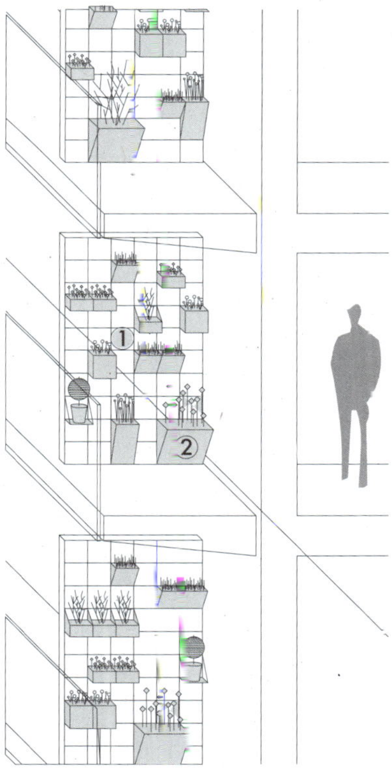

Facade concept

1 French window
2 Tilt-and-turn sash window
3 Opaque panel (partial fire-protection)

Glazed surface/apartment 2.62 m²

1 Opaque panel
2 Parapet
3 Insulating glass/sun protecting film with gradient
4 Tilt-and-turn sash window
5 Mixed slats to direct light
6 Vent window

Loggia partition

1 Vertical garden
2 For sustainable development individual planting and small-scale CO_2 exchange

10 60 100 cm

Details
1:75

campagne living
6020 Innsbruck, AT

PROGRAM
Residential settlement, studio appartments, shared green, underground parking, semipublic roof gardens

DIMENSIONS
GFA 29,496 m², useable living area 18,712 m², terraces and balconies 6,857 m²

CLIENT
Innsbrucker Immobilien GmbH & Co., KG

PROJECT TEAM
Marlies Breuss, Michael Ogertschnig, Marc Busquets, Alexander Garber, Klara Schön, Vedran Zonic

MODEL-MAKING
archimodell, Vienna

AWARDS
Alternate awardee, EU-wide open competition

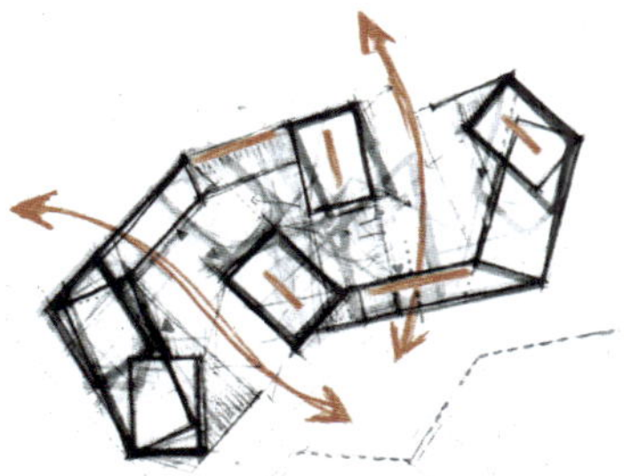

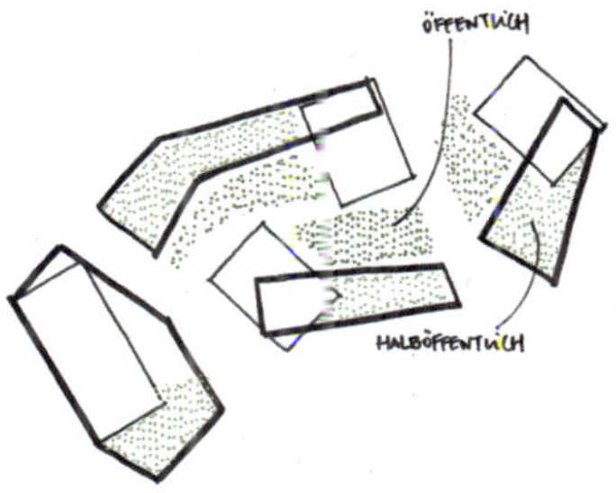

"Between urbanity and landscape, the housing project reacts to both, using qualities of each through overlaying selected parameters."

—HOLODECK architects, project description for the competition, 2017 (trans. by the ed.)

Site plan
1:1,500 — 10 30 60 100 m

page 495

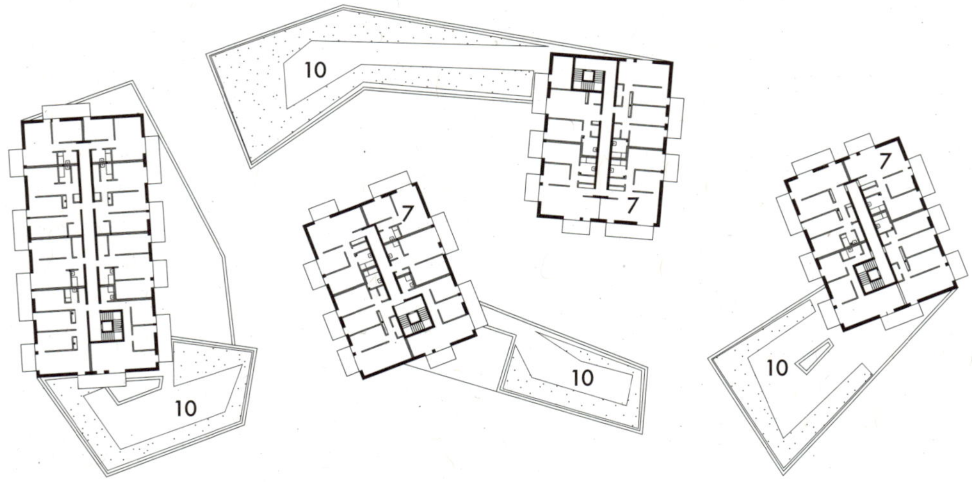

Ninth floor

Fourth floor

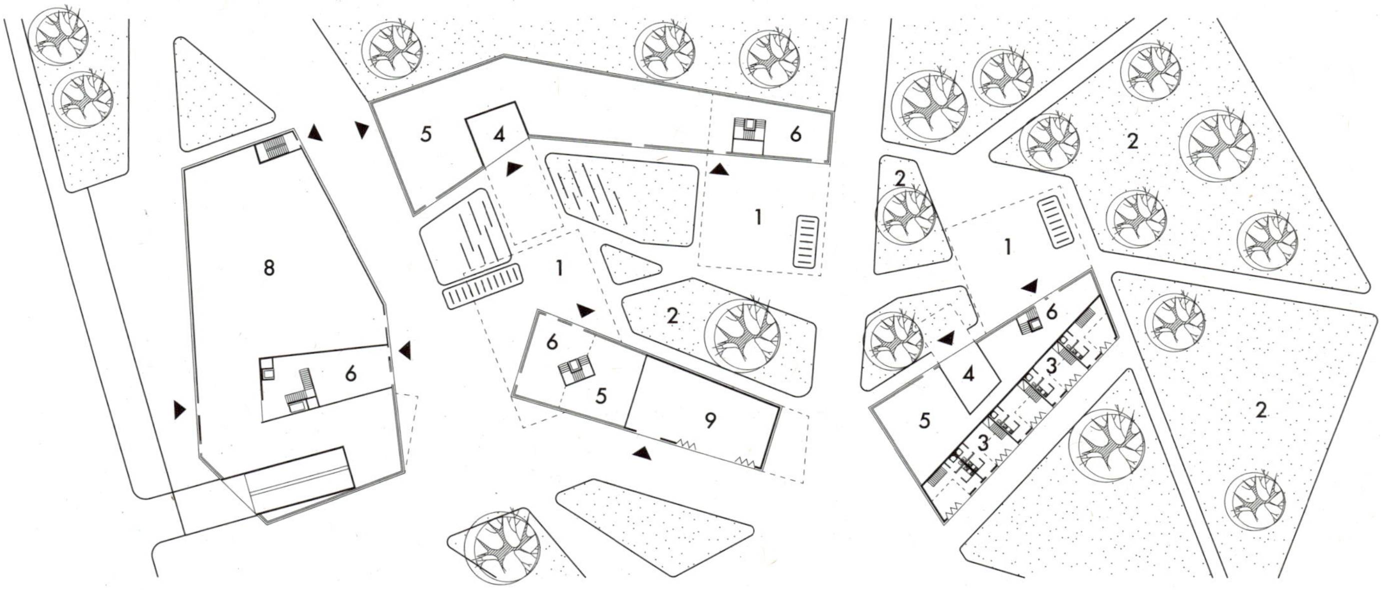

Ground floor
1:1,100

1	Entrance	6	Staircase
2	Green island	7	Apartments with balcony
3	Studio apartments	8	Grocery store
4	Common indoor spaces	9	Meeting point
5	Bike room	10	Communal terraces

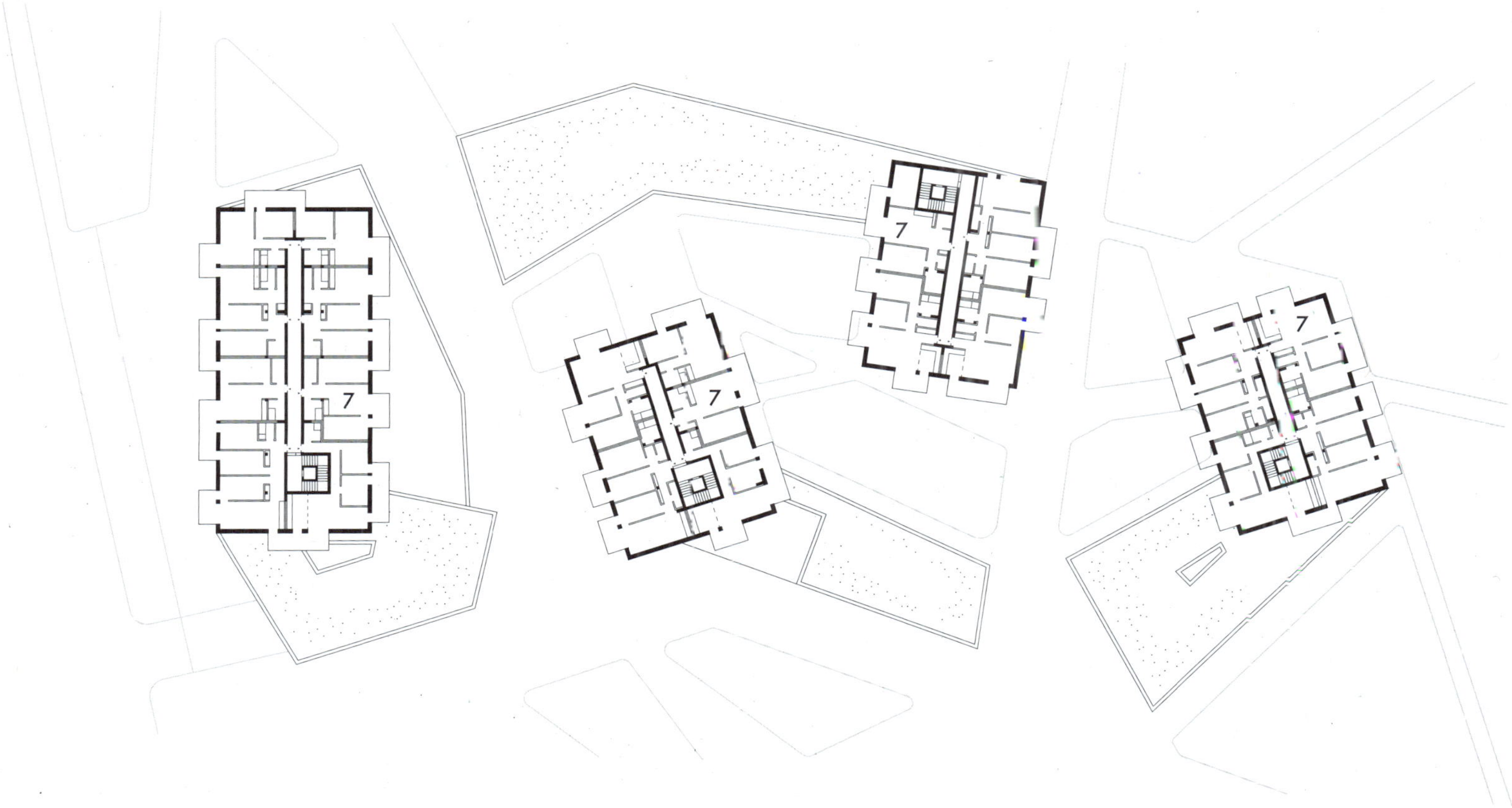

Typical floor plan

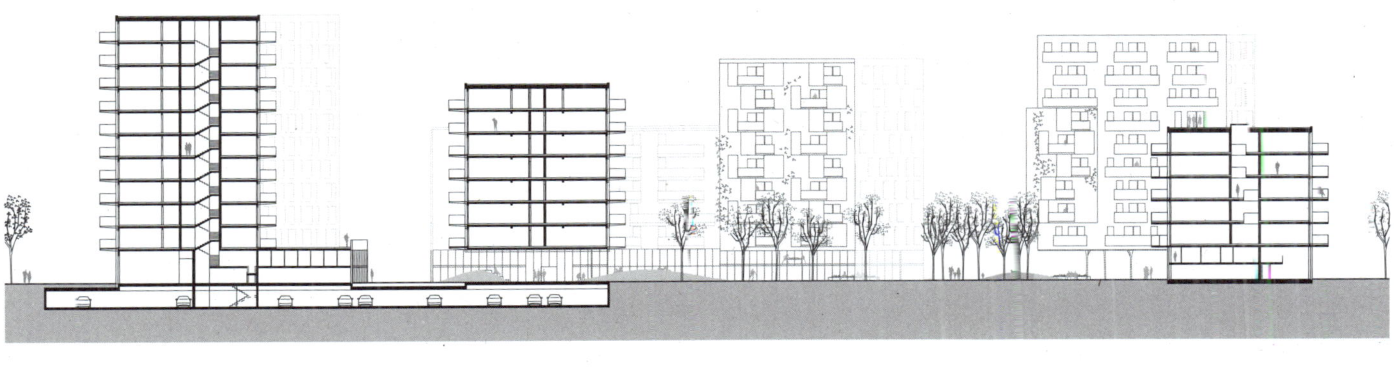

Section
1:850

low-rise courtyards
1220 Vienna, AT

PROGRAM
Residential settlement, carpet city, public and semipublic greens, private courtyards, communal spaces

DIMENSIONS
Plot area 26,727 m², GFA living area 11,627 m², green open space 7,618 m², private green area 2,448 m², private terraces 2,448 m², 136 housing units

CLIENT
Stadtplanung Wien

PROJECT TEAM
Marlies Breuss, Michael Ogertschnig, Adam Myczkowski

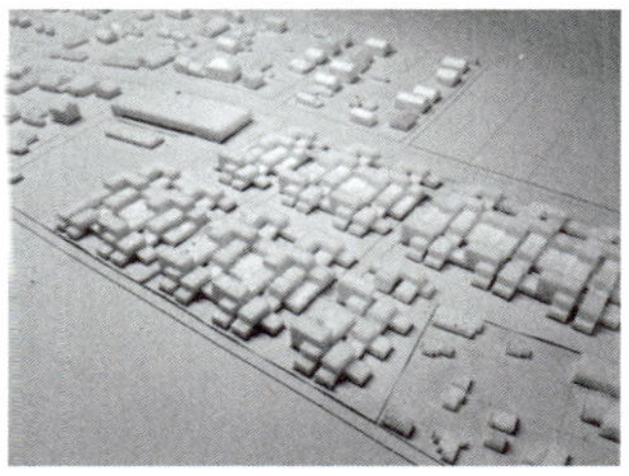

"Stacked atrium homes with open sun space for each unit. Densification with the living comfort of a single-family home."

—HOLODECK architects, project description, 2014 (trans. by the ed.)

Site plan
1:2,000

10 30 60 100 m

page 501

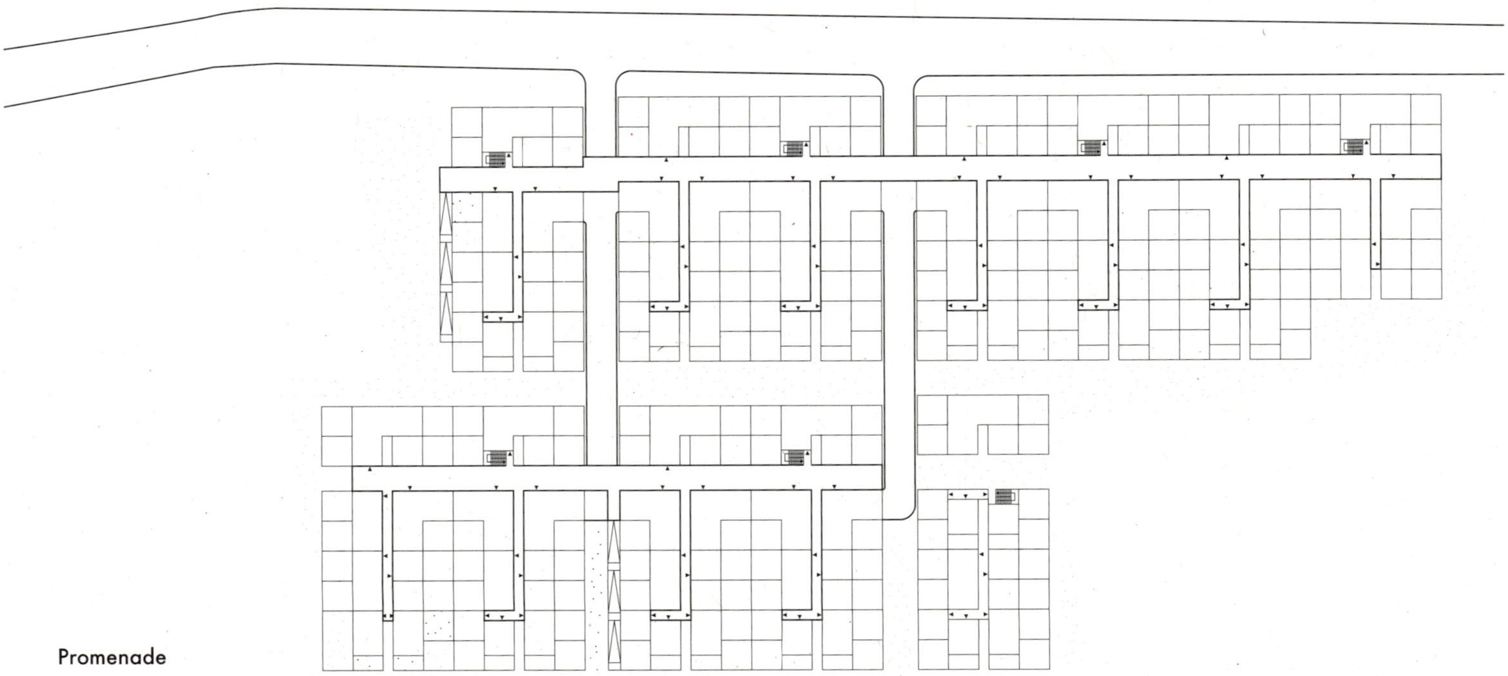

Promenade

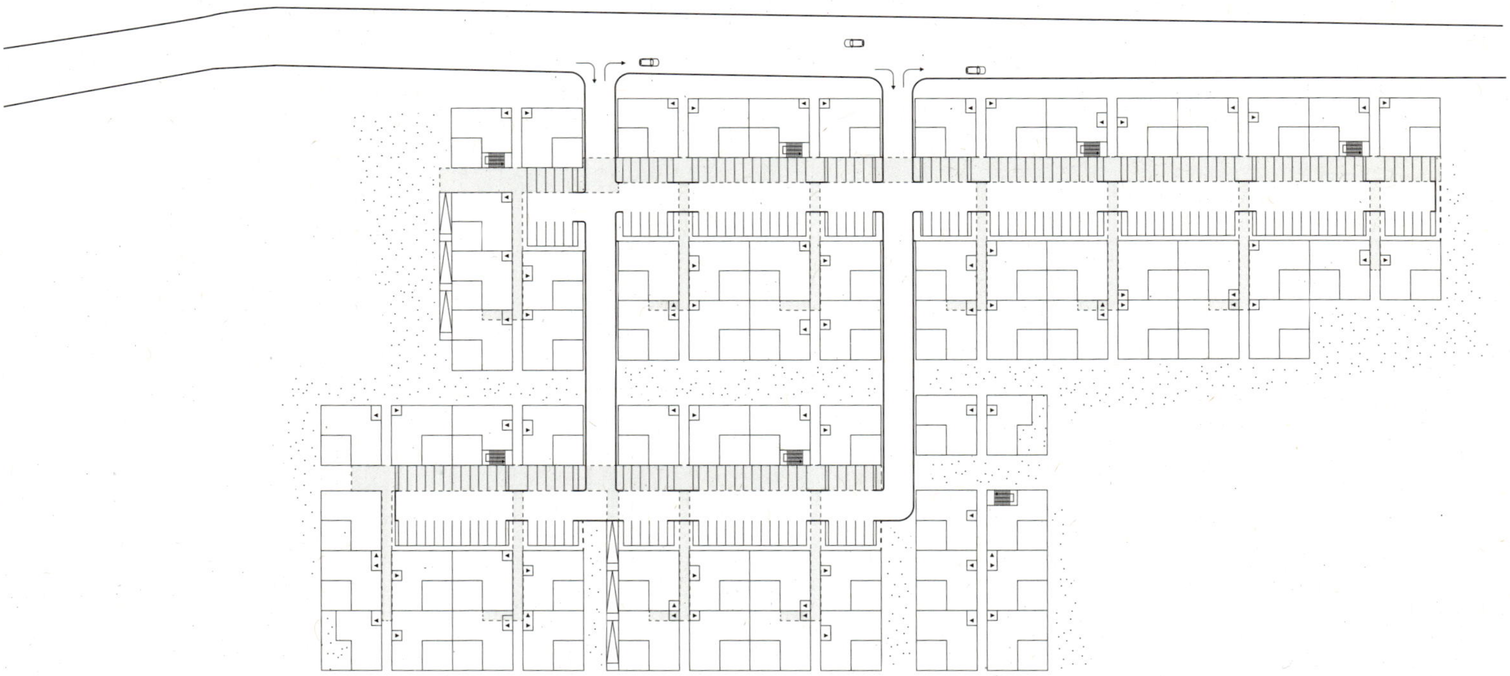

Ground floor
1:1,500

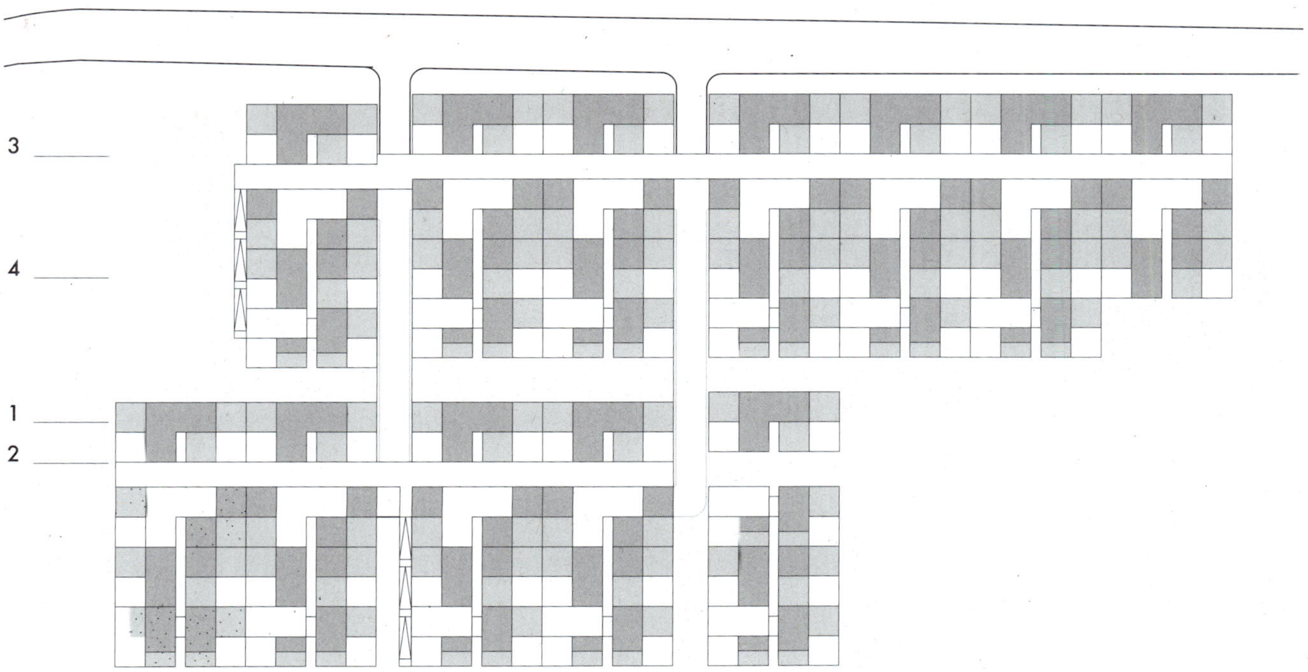

Top view

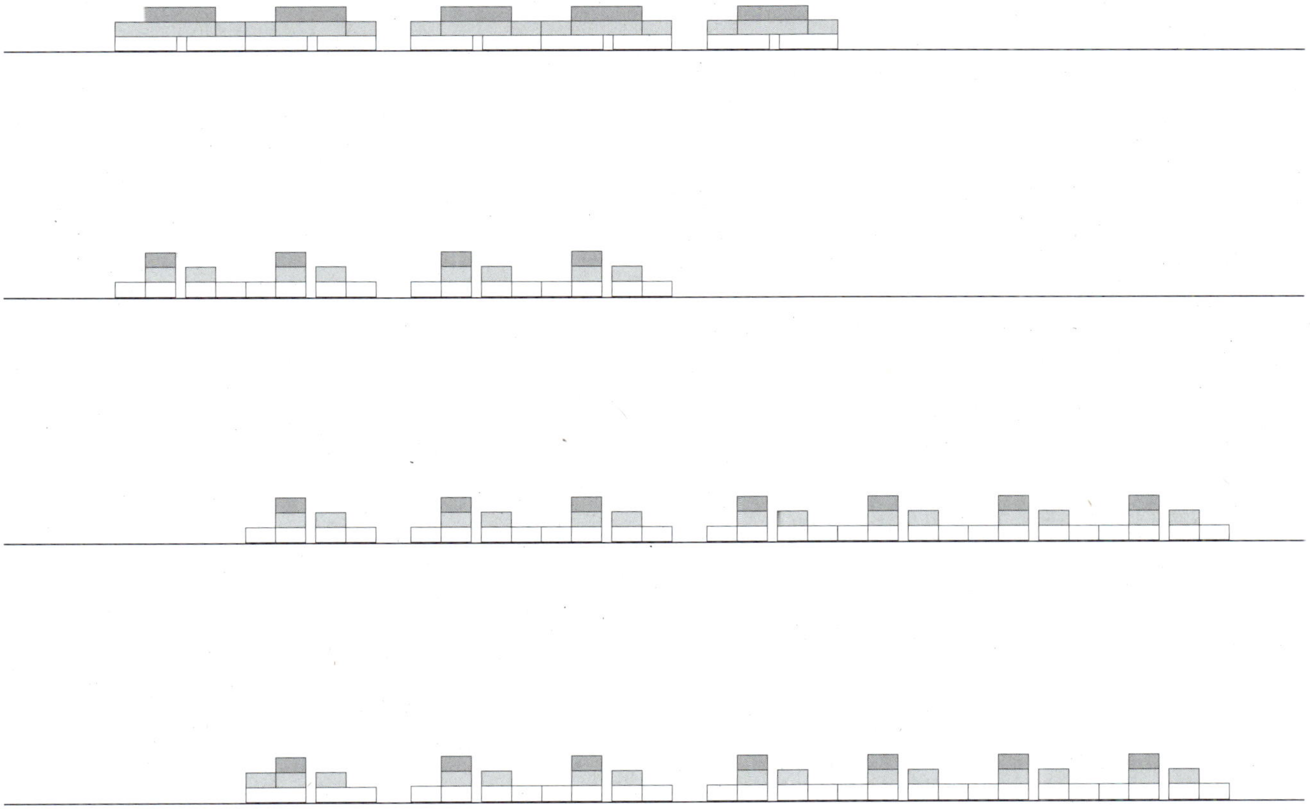

1-1

2-2

3-3

4-4

Sections
1:1,500

public square
7000 Eisenstadt, AT

PROGRAM
Urban development, public square, recreational areas, public services, undergraound parking, public greens

DIMENSIONS
Public square 2,272 m², terraces on three levels 1,584 m², entrance building and café 330 m²

CLIENT
LIB Landesimmobilien Burgenland

PROJECT TEAM
Marlies Breuss, Michael Ogertschnig, Arber Koni, Sarah Gold, Zois Alexandros Chionidis, Elisa Cesarini

CONSULTANTS
Karin Graf (landscape design)

AWARDS
First prize, international invited competition

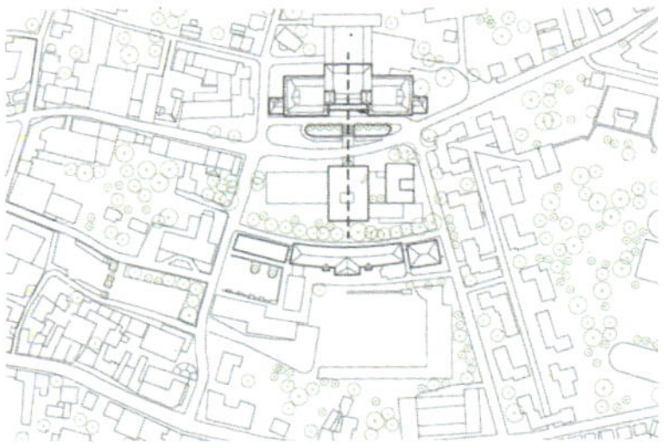

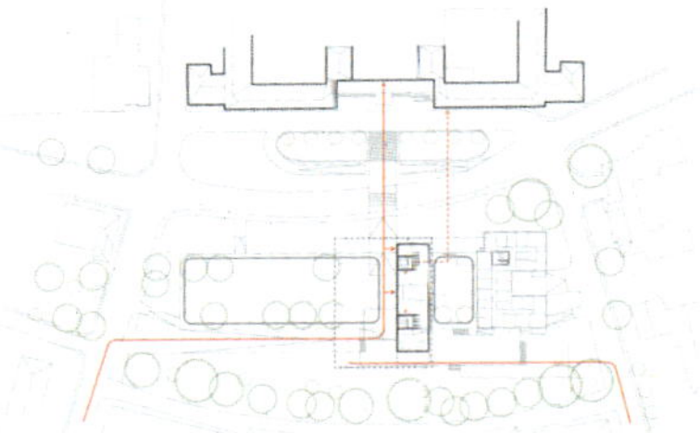

“In general, this approach pleases in the way the open space interacts with the planned and already existing buildings, using both the difficult topography and the existing green space to its best advantage.”

—Excerpt from the jury protocol 2021 (trans. by the ed.)

Site plan
1:1,000

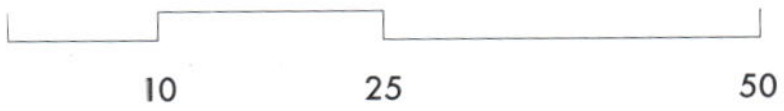

page 507

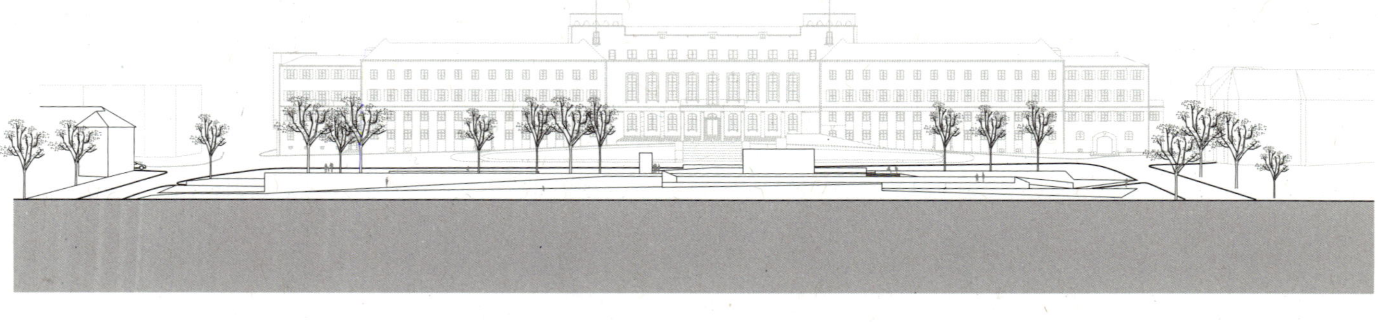

Elevation

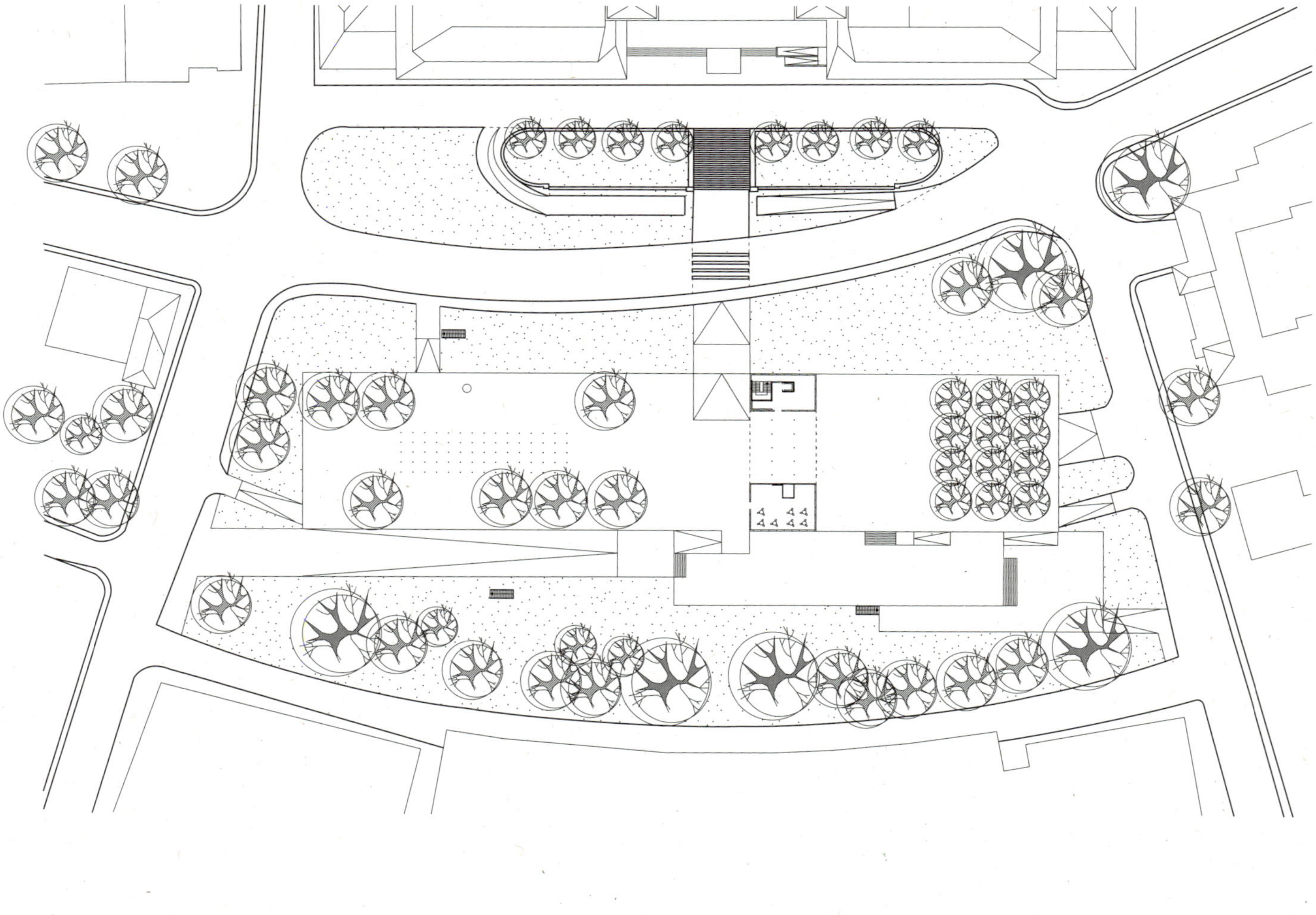

Design of the
public open space
1:1,125

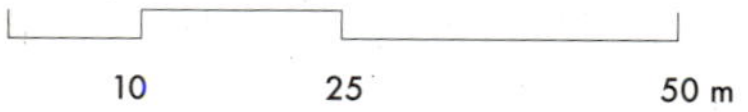

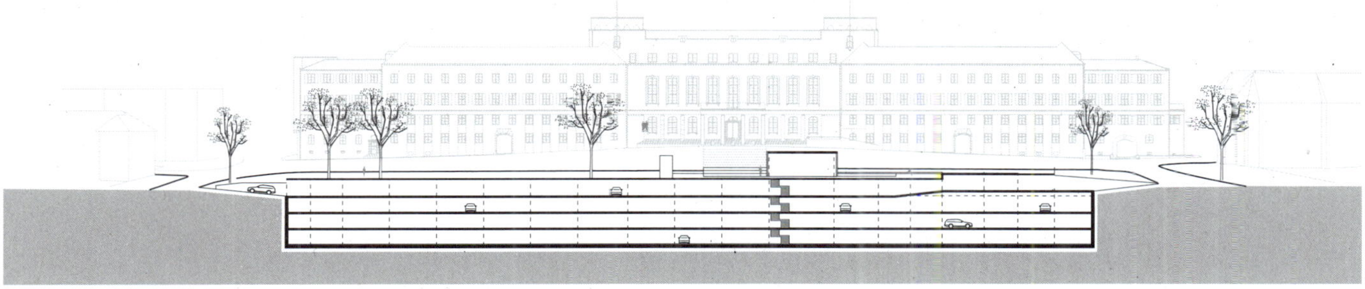

Section

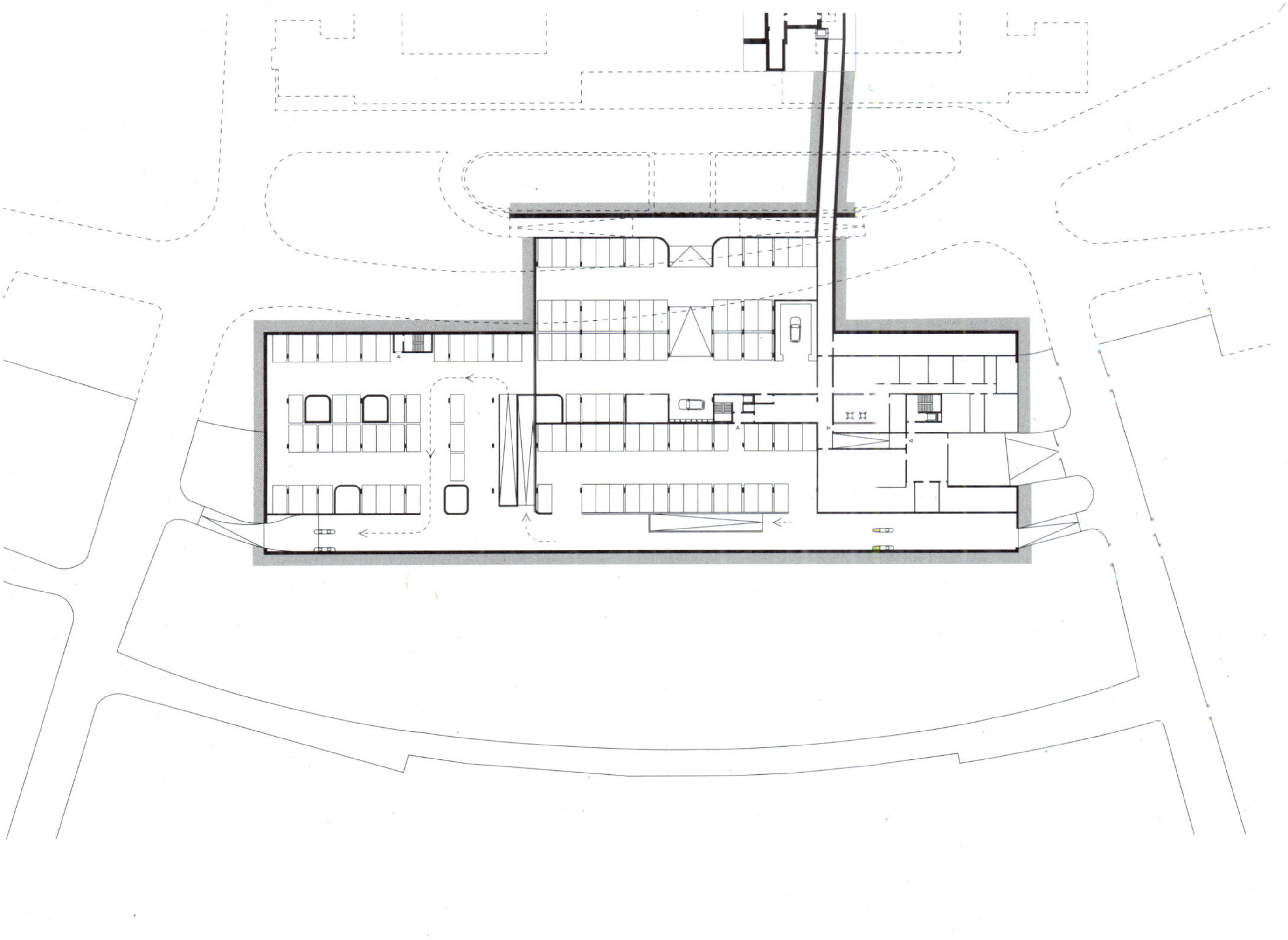

Basement floor
1:1,125

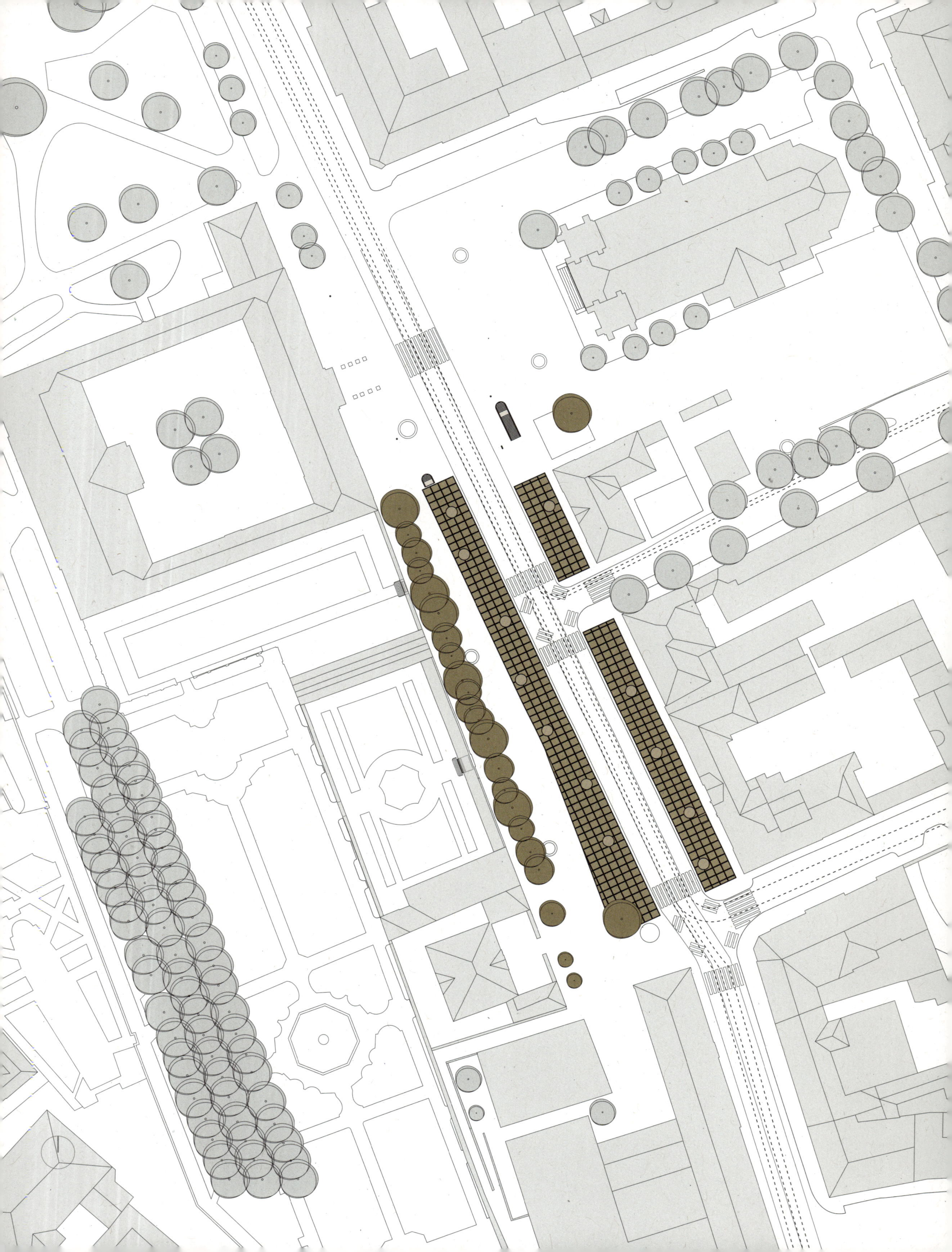

mirabellplatz s-link station
5020 Salzburg, AT

PROGRAM
Urban development, public square, mobility area, public transport, waiting areas, public greens

DIMENSIONS
Gross net area: mobility spaces underground 3,660 m², public amenities 460 m², shops 238 m²

CLIENT
Salzburger Regionalstadtbahn Projektgesellschaft

PROJECT TEAM
Marlies Breuss, Michael Ogertschnig, Sarah Gold, Arber Koni, Elisa Cesarini

CONSULTANTS
ghp gmeiner | haferl & partner zt gmbh (structural engineer)

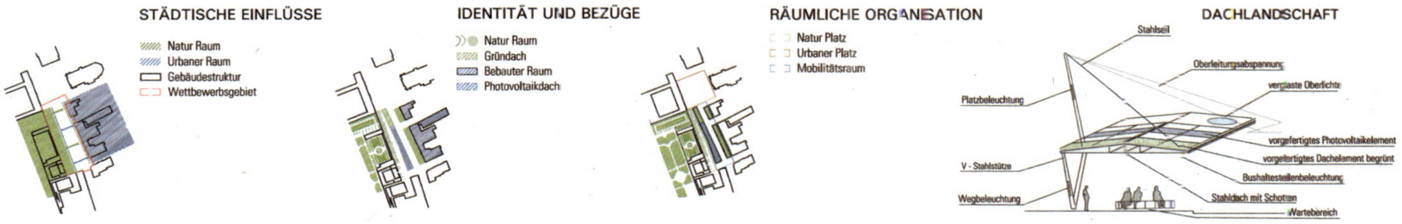

“This floating landscape of roof elements, which can be used in different ways, creates a pixelated, unmistakable image from above.”

—HOLODECK architects, project description for the competition, 2021 (trans. by the ed.)

Site plan
1:1,100

10 25 50 m

page 513

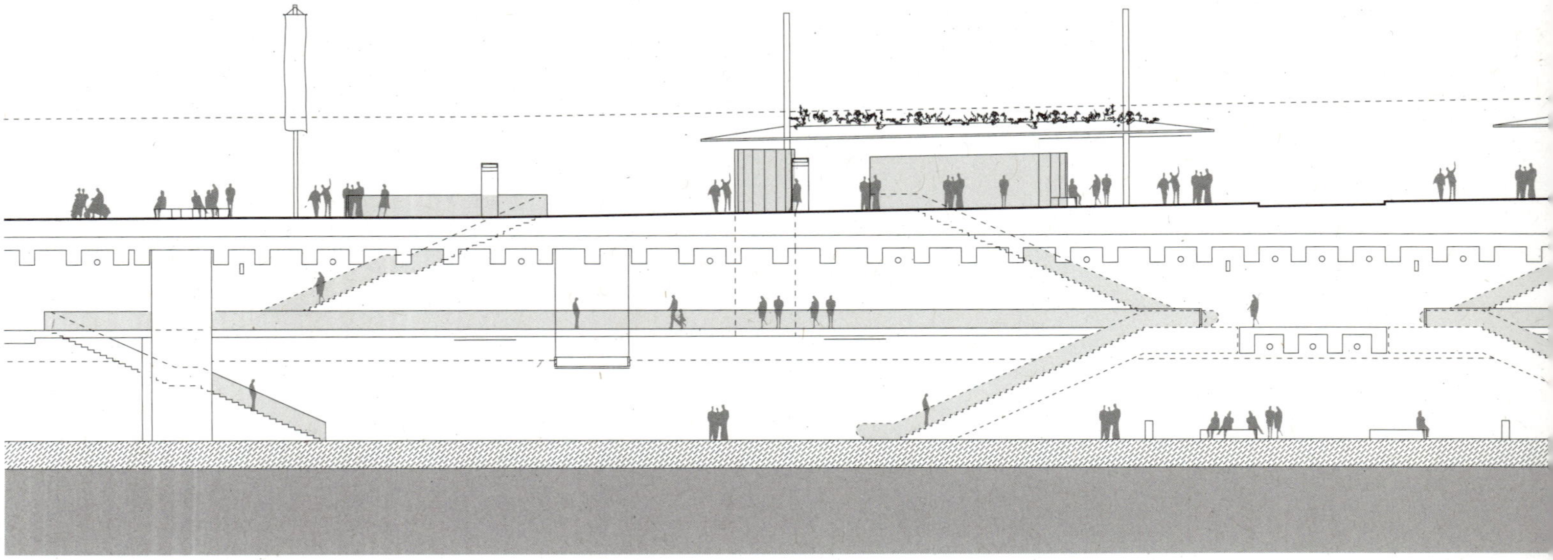

Longitudinal section

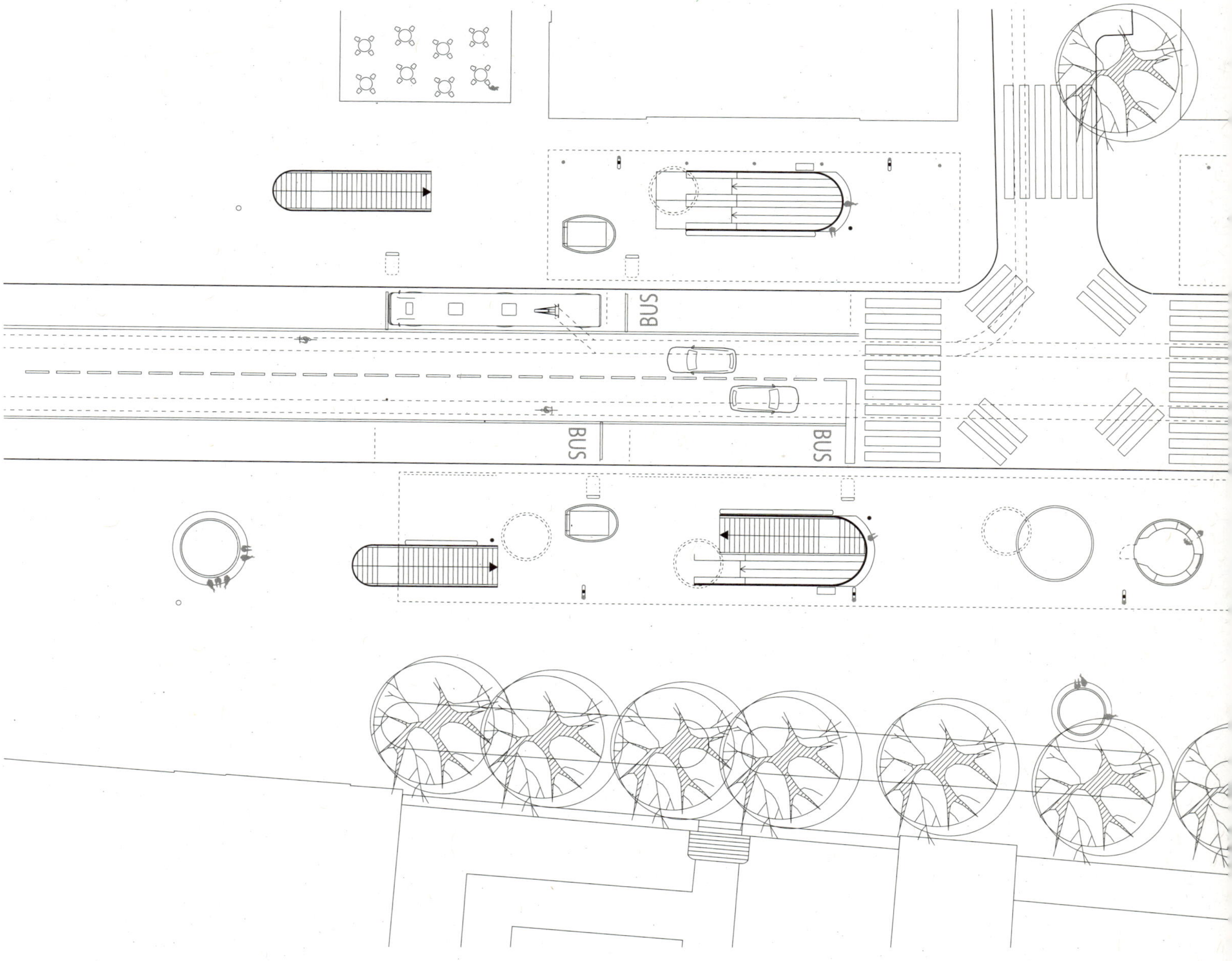

Ground floor
1:400

1 5 10 25 m

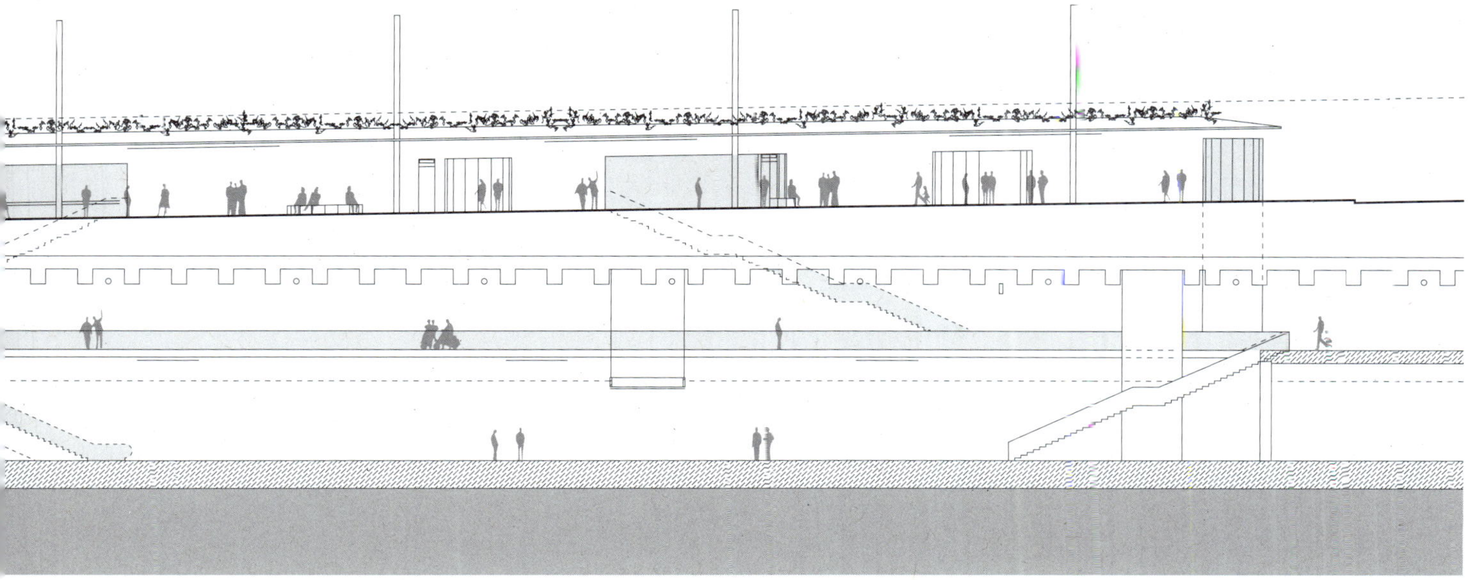

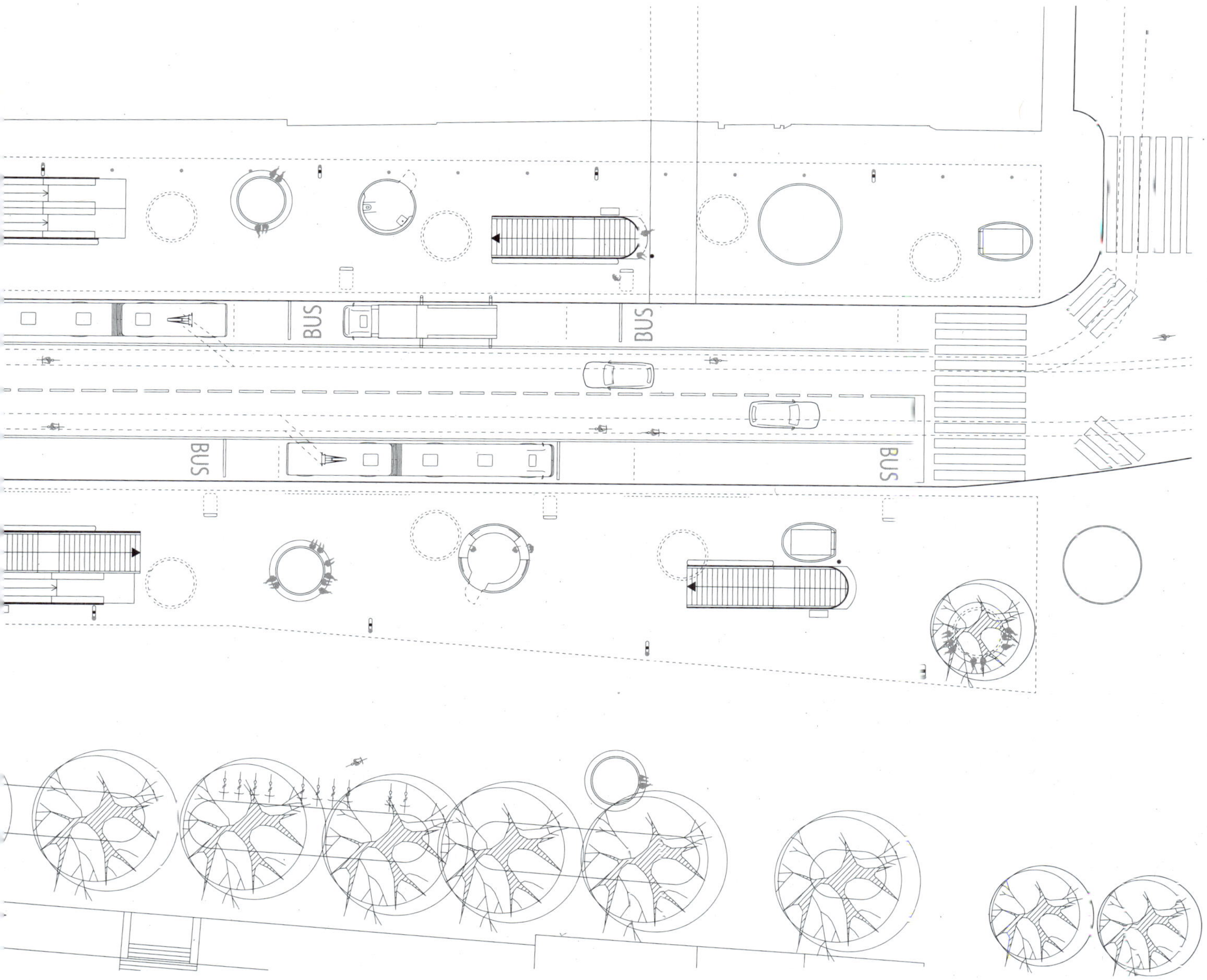
BUS
BUS
BUS
BUS

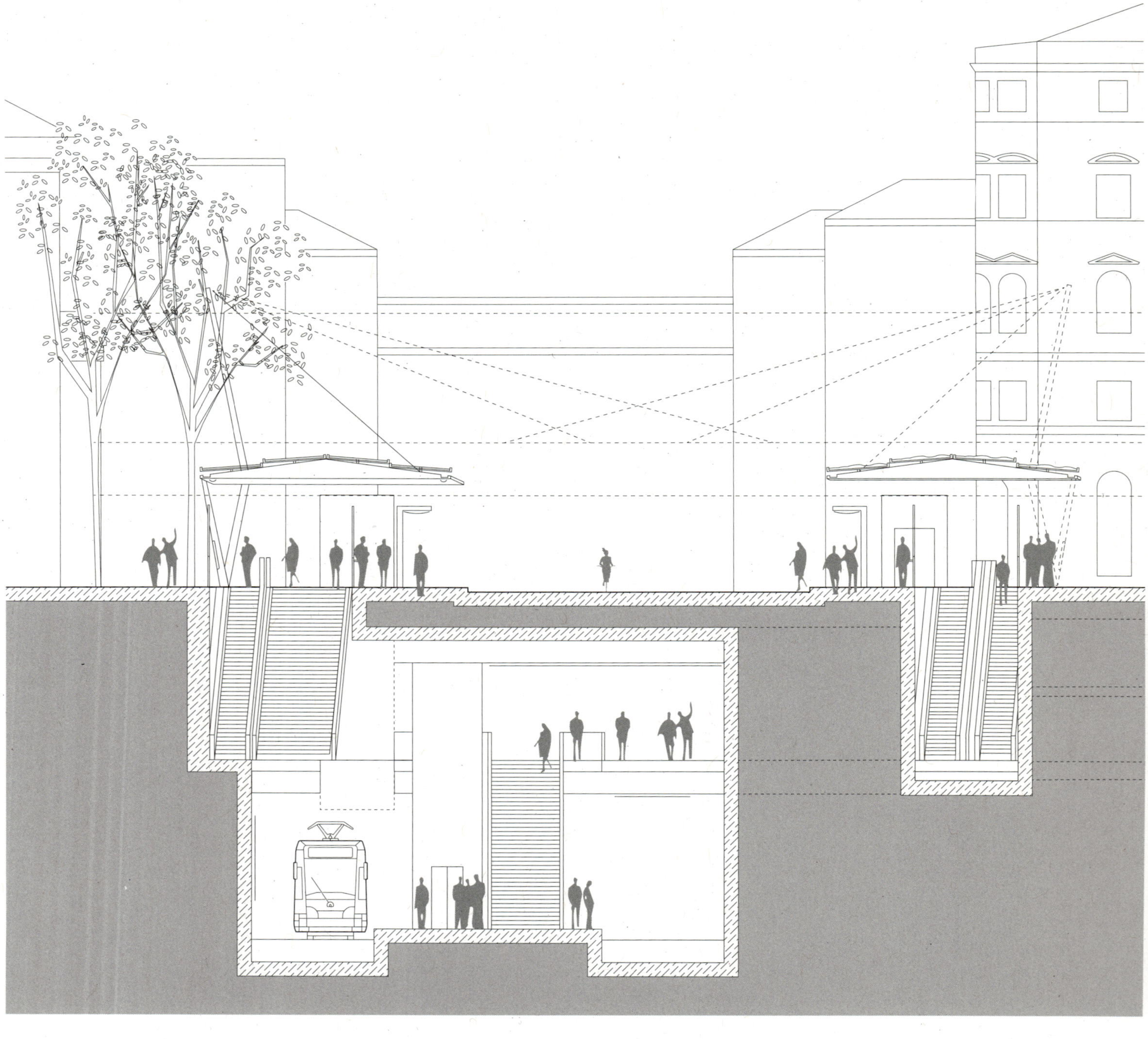

Section
1:200

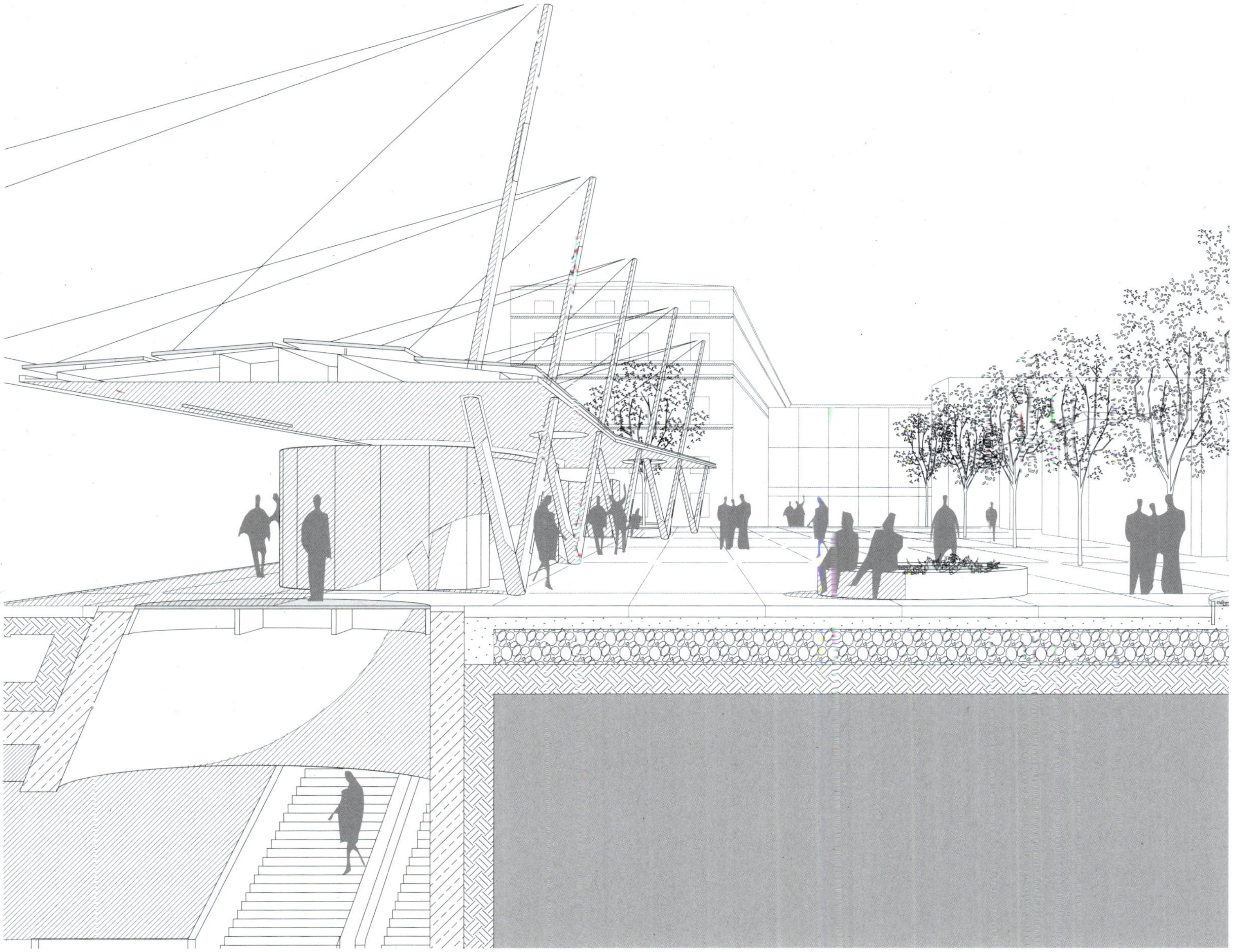

Sect on perspective
1:1C0

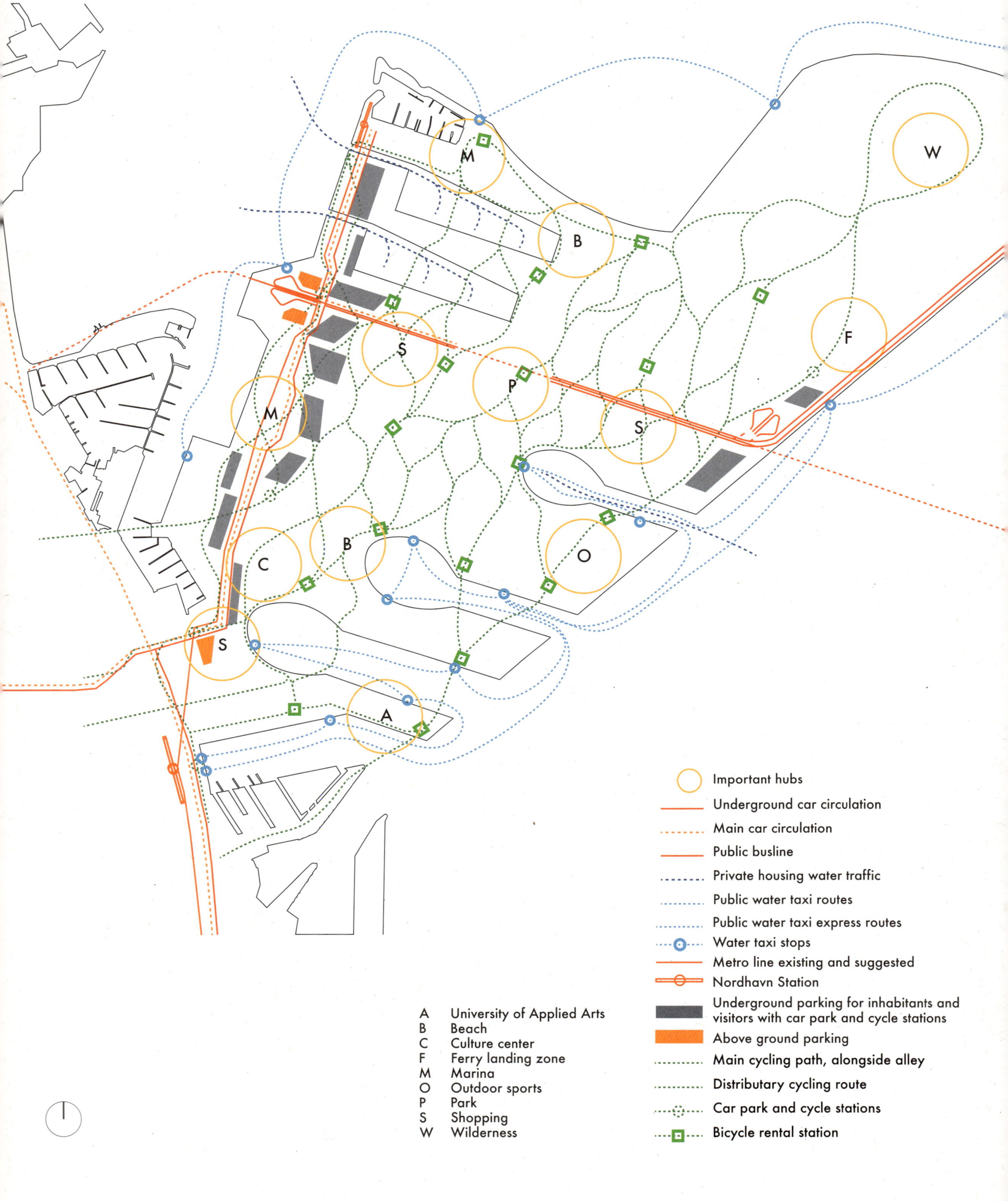

M
W
B
S
P
F
M
S
C
B
O
S
A
Important hubs
Underground car circulation
Main car circulation
Public busline
Private housing water traffic
Public water taxi routes
Public water taxi express routes
Water taxi stops
Metro line existing and suggested
Nordhavn Station
Underground parking for inhabitants and visitors with car park and cycle stations
Above ground parking
Main cycling path, alongside alley
Distributary cycling route
Car park and cycle stations
Bicycle rental station
A University of Applied Arts
B Beach
C Culture center
F Ferry landing zone
M Marina
O Outdoor sports
P Park
S Shopping
W Wilderness

2008
URBAN STRATEGIES

sustainable quarter
2150 Copenhagen, DK

PROGRAM
Infrastructural services, car-free zones, residential plots, balanced spatial arrangements, education, social and health, culture, sports, entertainment, commercial and offices, urban development

DIMENSIONS
GFA 670,000 m^2

CLIENT
City of Copenhagen, Denmark

PROJECT TEAM
Marlies Breuss, Michael Ogertschnig, Kristin Mueller, Simon Jakoby, Stefanie Gänger, Christin Kurze, Stefan Stähle, Mario Thaum

PUBLICATIONS (SELECTION)
Annett Zinsmeister and Tobias Wallisser, “Wie gehen wir warum wohin.” in *JOUR FIXE Zeitgenössische Positionen in Architektur, Design*, Berlin, DOM publishers, 2010 (ISBN 978-3-86922-034-5).

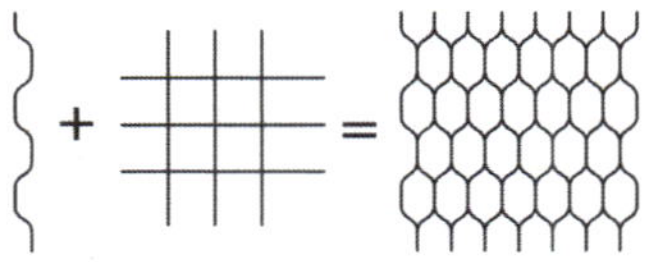

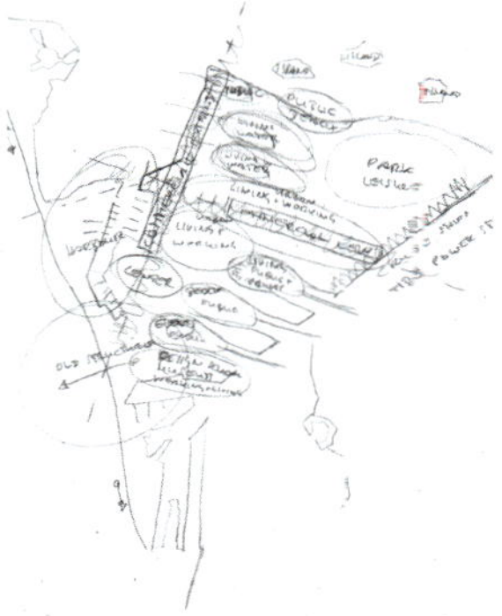

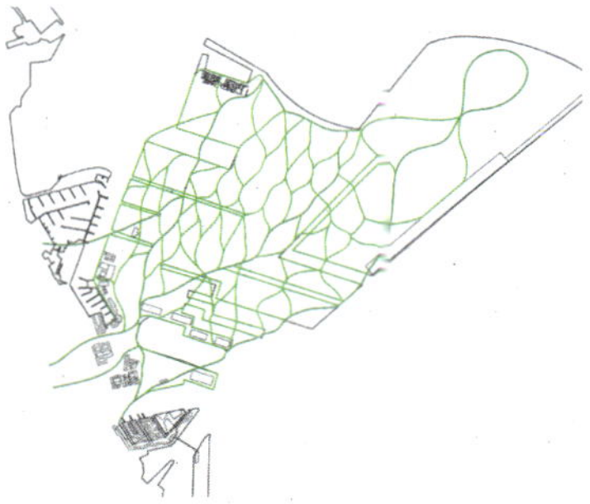

“In terms of sustainable development, we are creating a new cycling network. A kind of lattice structure, a flexible system that shapes the environment but also takes it into account.”

—HOLODECK architects, project description for the competition, 2008 (trans. by the ed.)

Bike network and distributional connections
1:14,000

100 500 1 km

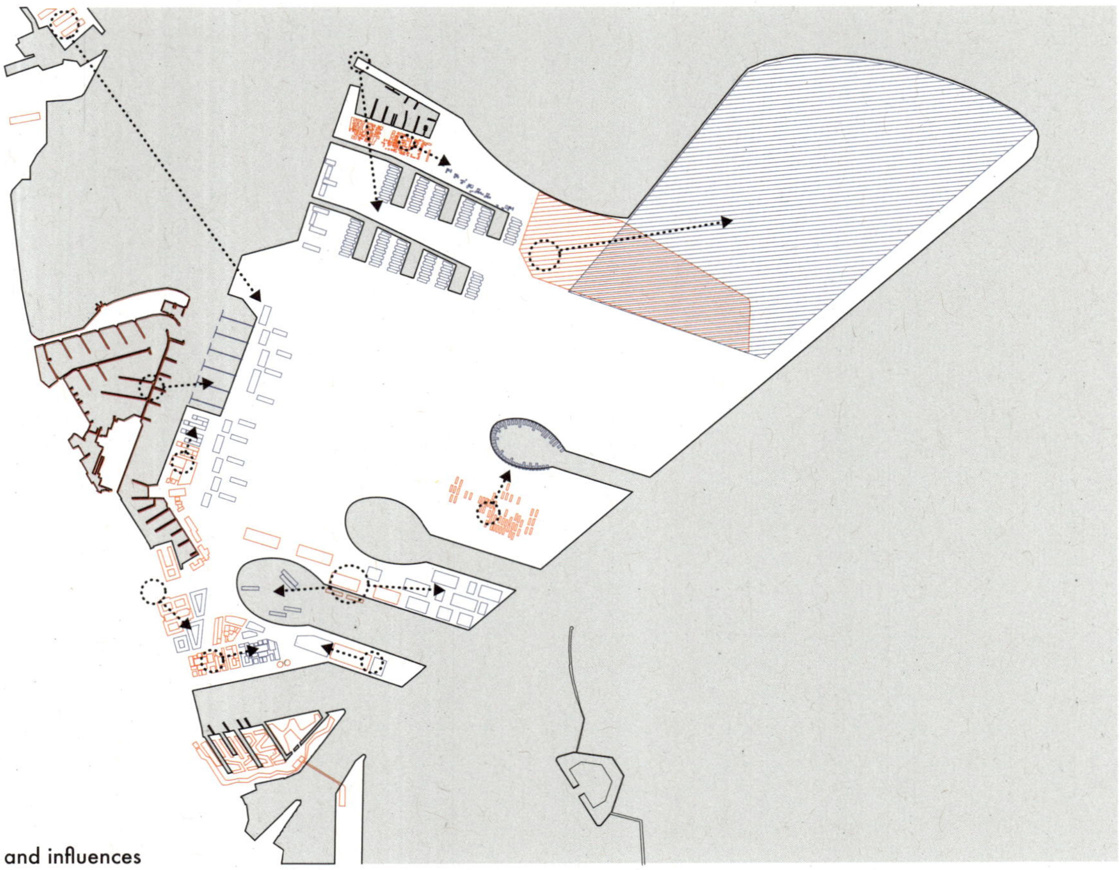

Existing conditions and influences

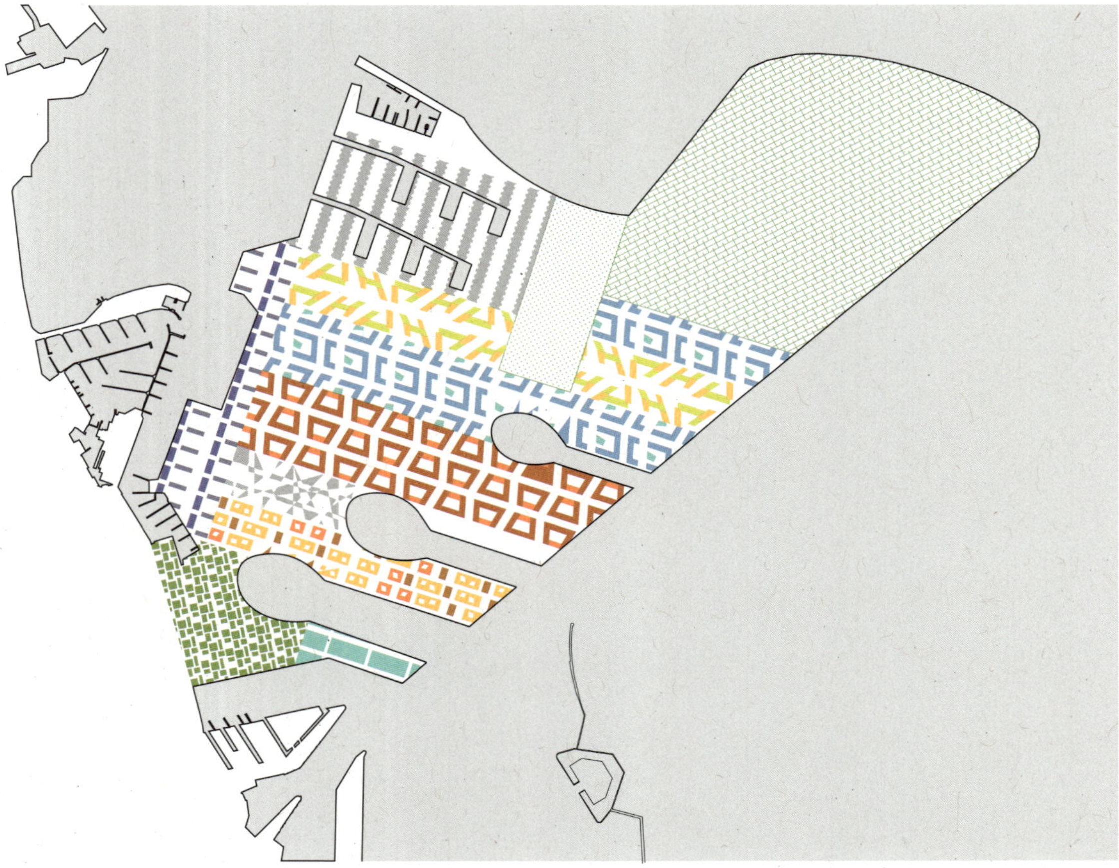

Typological diversity
1:26,000

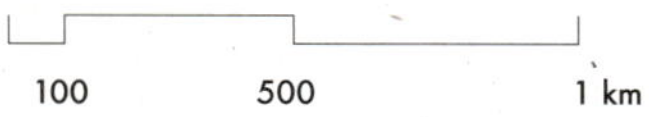

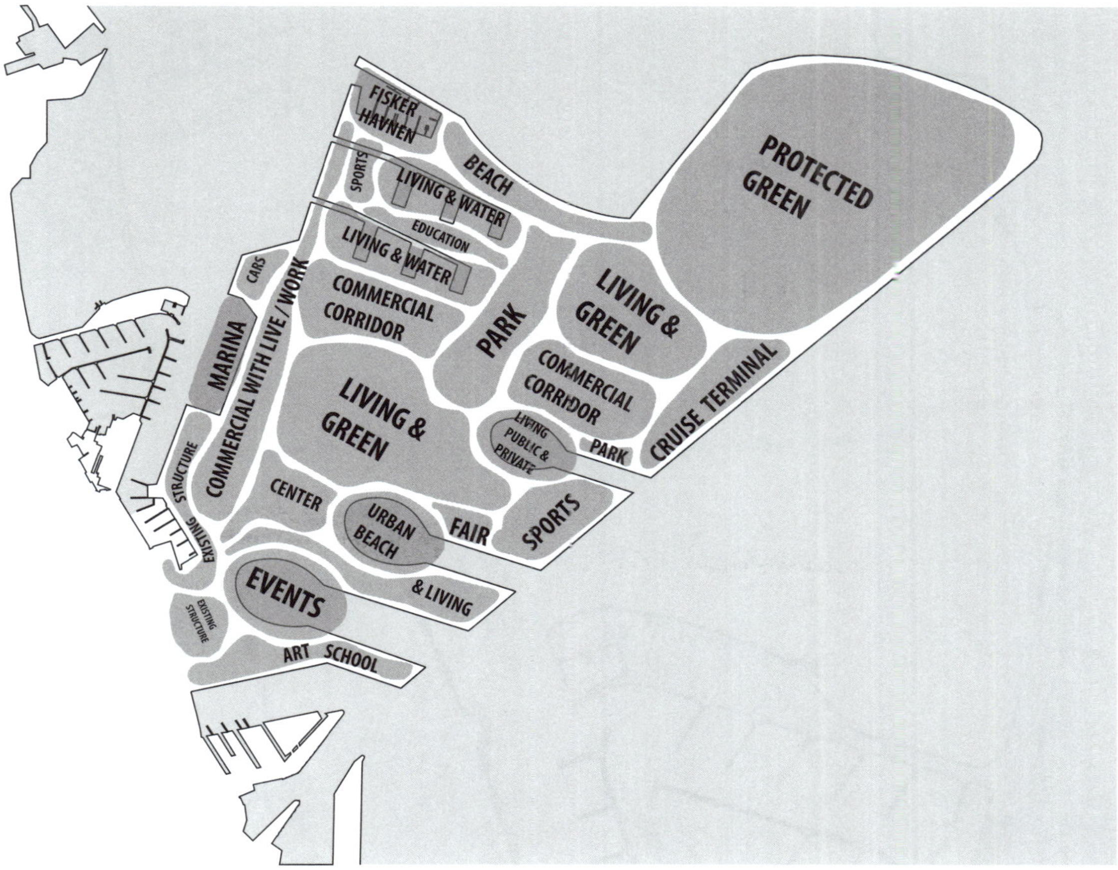

Functional program

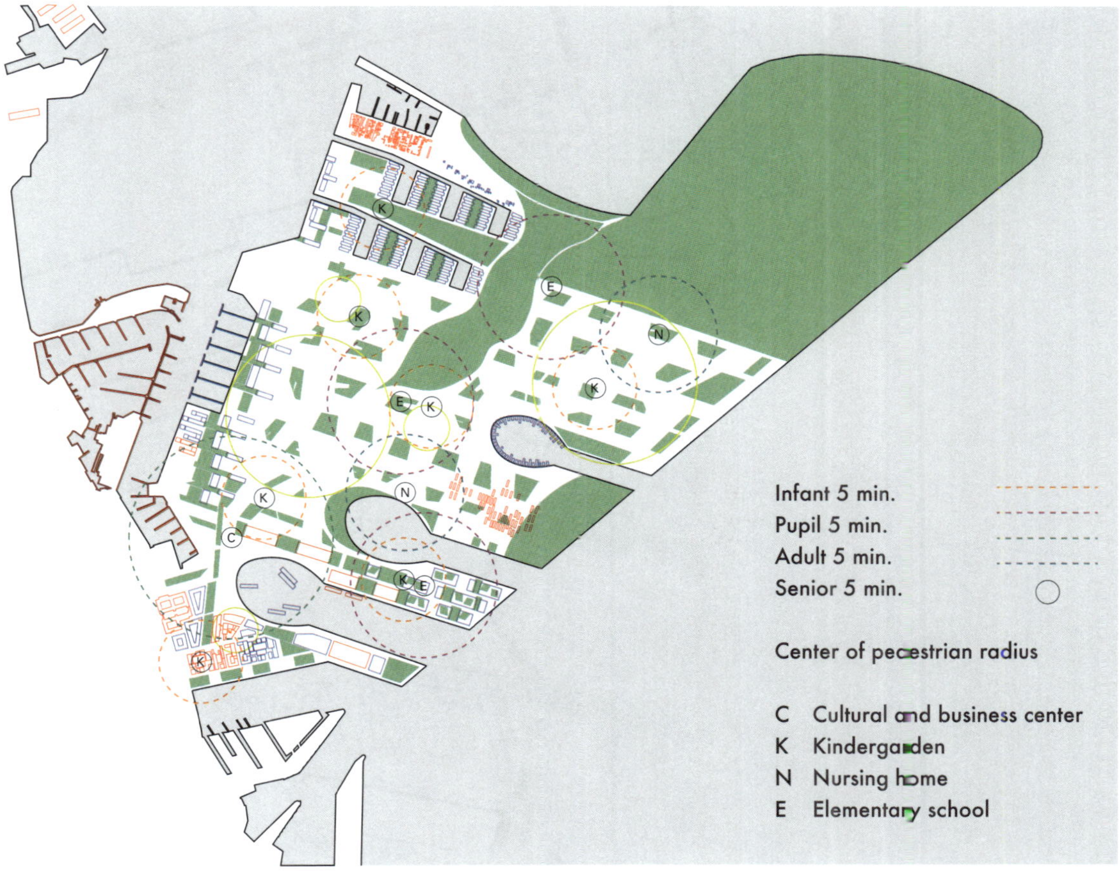

Walking inhabitants
and green areas
1:26,000

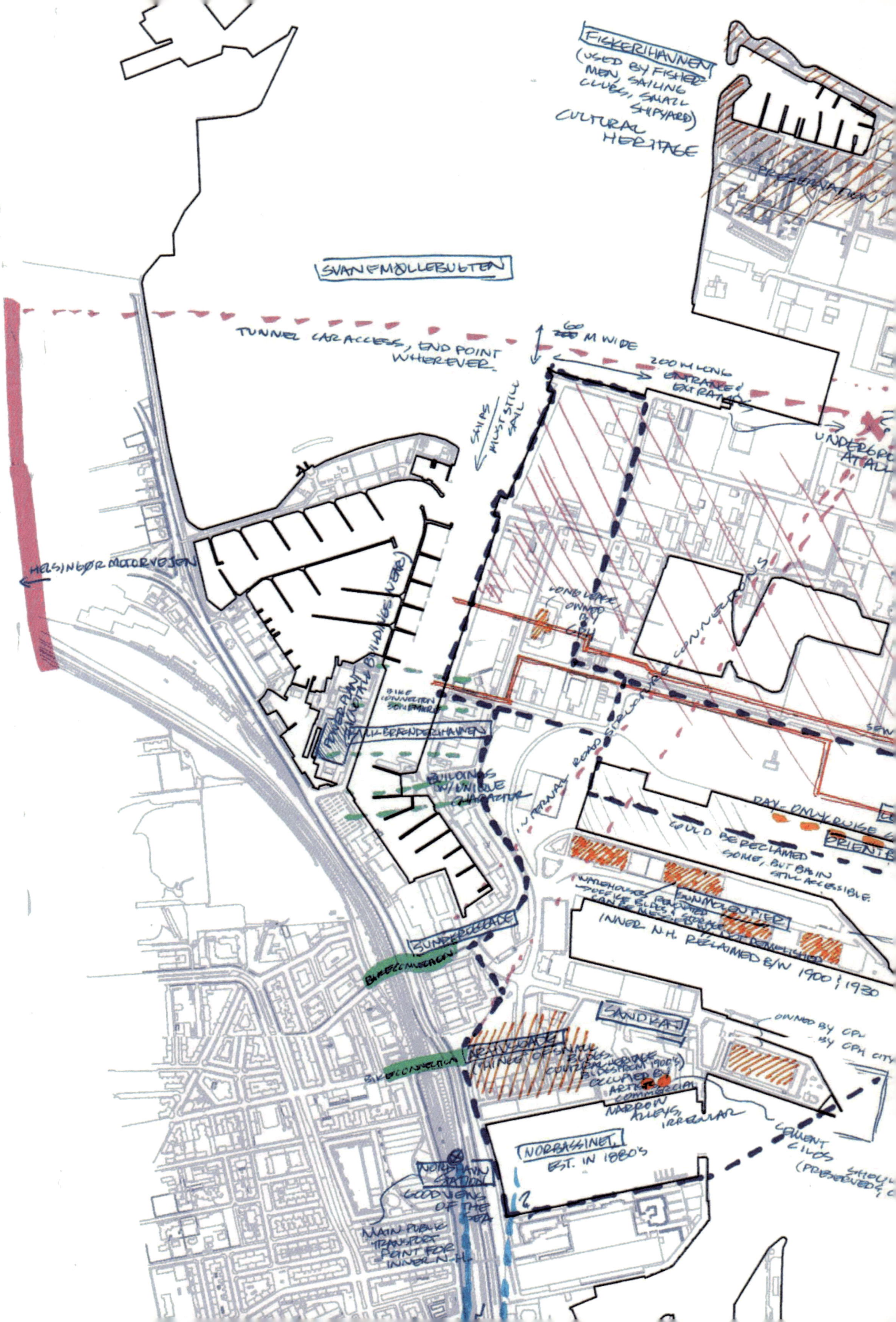

FISKERIHAVNEN
(USED BY FISHERMEN, SAILING CLUBS, SMALL SHIPYARD)
CULTURAL HERITAGE
PRESERVATION
SVANEMØLLEBUGTEN
TUNNEL CAR ACCESS, END POINT WHEREVER.
60 M WIDE
200 M LONG
SHIPS MUST STILL SAIL
HELSINGØR MOTORVEJEN
LONG LEASE, OWNED BY CPH
BIKE CONNECTION SOMEWHERE
KALKBRÆNDERIHAVNEN
BUILDINGS W/ UNIQUE CHARACTER
INTERNAL ROAD
COULD BE RECLAIMED SOME, BUT BASIN STILL ACCESSIBLE.
SUNDKROGSGADE
BIKE CONNECTION
INNER N.H. RECLAIMED B/W 1900 & 1930
SANDKAJ
OWNED BY CPH
ÅRHUSGADE
BIKE CONNECTION
NARROW ALLEYS, IRREGULAR
CEMENT SILOS
NORDBASSINET
EST. IN 1880's
NORDHAVN STATION
GOOD VIEWS OF THE SEA
MAIN PUBLIC TRANSPORT POINT FOR INNER N.H.

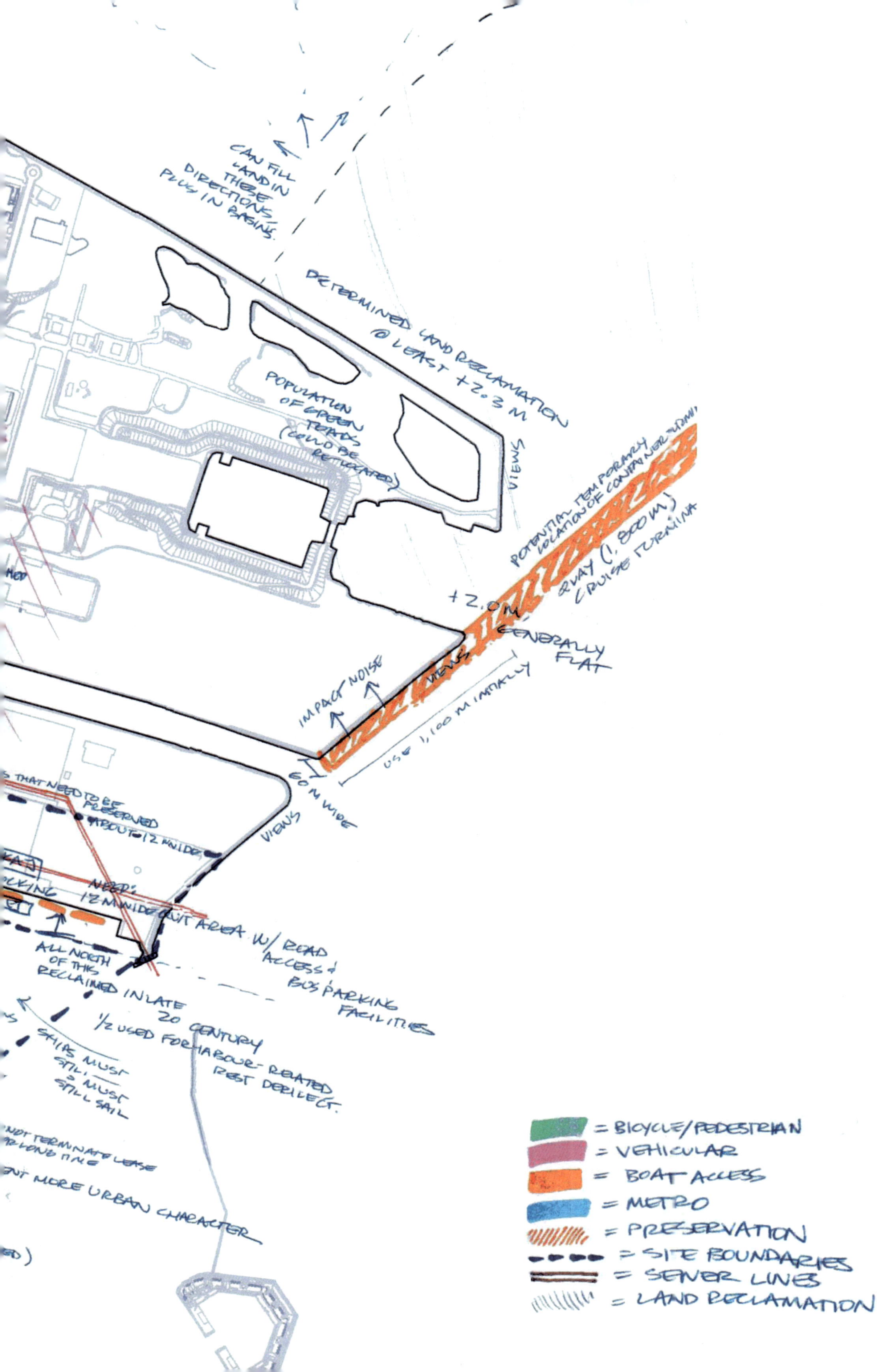
CAN FILL LAND IN THESE DIRECTIONS PLUS IN BASINS
DETERMINED LAND RECLAMATION @ LEAST +2.3 M
POPULATION OF GREEN TREADS (COULD BE RELOCATED)
VIEWS
POTENTIAL TEMPORARY LOCATION OF CONTAINER
QUAY (1,800 M) CRUISE
+2.0 M
GENERALLY FLAT
IMPACT NOISE
VIEWS
USE 1,100 M INITIALLY
60 M WIDE
VIEWS
THAT NEED TO BE PRESERVED ABOUT 12 M WIDE
NEED: 12 M WIDE
AREA W/ ROAD ACCESS & BUS PARKING FACILITIES
ALL NORTH OF THIS RECLAIMED IN LATE 20 CENTURY
1/2 USED FOR HARBOUR-RELATED REST DERELICT.
SHIPS MUST STILL, MUST STILL SAIL
NOT TERMINATE LEASE
MORE URBAN CHARACTER
= BICYCLE/PEDESTRIAN
= VEHICULAR
= BOAT ACCESS
= METRO
= PRESERVATION
= SITE BOUNDARIES
= SEWER LINES
= LAND RECLAMATION

Colophon

HOLODECK architects ZTGmbH
Friedrichstraße 6
1010 Vienna, Austria
Phone +43 1 524 81 33-0
vienna@holodeckarchitects.com
www.holodeckarchitects.com

Editors
Marlies Breuss
Michael Ogertschnig

Idea
Marlies Breuss

Concept
Marlies Breuss
Christine Schmauszer

Editorial Staff
Marlies Breuss
Alexandra Gamrot
Michael Ogertschnig

Editorial Assistance
Elena Perez y Schneider

Preparation of Plan Material
Julia Binder

Assistance in Plan Preparation
Angelika Krayer
Anika Lindwedel
Philipp Schulten

Project Descriptions
Marlies Breuss
Alexandra Gamrot

Layout, Imaging Editing, and Production
Christine Schmauszer
Michael Rieper

Translations from German into English
Ada St. Laurent
John Wheelwright

Copyediting
Dawn Michelle d'Atri
Ada St. Laurent
John Wheelwright

Text Credits
Rights to the text contributions are held by the respective authors and HOLODECK architects.

Photo Credits
austrian embassy bangkok: Ketsiree Wongwan (pp. 8–11, 14–20, 199), Pichak Thananchaibut (pp. 12–13)
making it: Christian Wachter (pp. 21, 185)
campus school: Kurt Hörbst (pp. 22–25, 223), Susanne Veit Aschenbrenner (pp. 26–27)
wirtschaftspark breitensee: Wolfgang Thaler (pp. 28–38, 243)
hall 01: AT.Neubau (pp. 39–43, 259)
gewerbehof missindorf: Wolfgang Thaler (pp. 44–49, 265)
urban topos: Hertha Hurnaus (pp. 50–55, 301)
stratified townscape: Hertha Hurnaus (pp. 56–61, 309)
roof transformations: Wolfgang Thaler (pp. 62–67, 317)
urban reflections: HOLODECK architects archive (pp. 68–69, 71, 325), Josef Herfert (p. 70)
spatial appropriation: Grazia Ike Branco (pp. 72–76, 339)
plus energy rooftop: HOLODECK architects archive (pp. 77–79), Thomas Jeschko (pp. 80–81)
rooftop 02: Veronika Hofinger (pp. 82, 84–87), Johannes Ifkovits (p. 83)
22 tops: Paul Ott (pp. 88–96, 351)
looped house: Veronika Hofinger (pp. 97–103, 365)
embedded house: Rita Laslberger/Günter Stöger (pp. 104–11, 371)
floating house: Hertha Hurnaus (pp. 112–19, 379)
benthouse: AT.Neubau (pp. 120–21)
shifthouse: Veronika Hofinger (pp. 122–29)
parkhouse: Veronika Hofinger (pp. 130–37)
kulturzentrum mattersburg/zentrum für kultur und forschung: Wolfgang Thaler (pp. 138–51, 397)
aktionsraum 1: Barbara Mair (pp. 152–54, 439)
marzona book collection: Veronika Hofinger (pp. 155–57, 449)
double vision dürer kentridge: Christian von Steffelin (pp. 158–63, 457)
space furniture: Pez Hejduk (pp. 164–65)
mobile 01: Peter Fattinger (pp. 190, 475)

Plan Credits
Aero Photovoltaic Solutions (p. 205)
Kapo Windows (p. 367)
David Keller, "Dramatic Growth of Neuronal Architecture from Birth to 2 years," in *The Pediatrician's Role in Addressing Childhood Poverty* (p. 407)
Exh. cat. AKTIONSRAUM 1, published August 1971 in Munich; copyright A 1 INFORMATIONEN VERLAGSGESELLSCHAFT mbH Munich, pp. 238–39; Calendar AKTIONSRAUM 1 from the collection Aktionsraum 1 Egidio Marzona (pp. 444–45)

In the status of competitions, drawings, plans, and realized projects differences may occur due to our will to show the progress of projects during the period of designing and building.

Printed on recycled paper Virus 89, 120 g/m² in white, and Allegro semimatte, 150 g/m²; book cover in gray paperboard, 2 mm, covered by SH Recycling paper in gray/gray, 140 g/m²; book blocks with open thread stitching glued into hardcover and fastened; closed dimensions 24 × 30.5 cm, unfolded dimensions 78 × 30.5 cm; English.

Printing Support
Ulli Arnold

Printing and Binding
Bösmüller Print Management GesmbH & Co. KG, Stockerau, Austria. Printed in Austria

For the publisher Birkhäuser Verlag, Vienna, Austria
Acquisitions Editor: David Marold
Content and Production Editor: Angelika Gaal

Library of Congress Control Number: 2022949536

Bibliographic information published by the German National Library
The German National Library lists this publication in the Deutsche Nationalbibliografie; detailed bibliographic data are available on the Internet at http://dnb.dnb.de.

ISBN 978-3-0356-2698-8
e-ISBN (PDF) 978-3-0356-2713-8

First published 2023

P.O. Box 44, 4009 Basel, Switzerland
Part of Walter de Gruyter GmbH, Berlin/Boston

9 8 7 6 5 4 3 2 1
www.birkhauser.com

We apologize for any unseen mistakes and to those whose names we may have failed to mention.

HOLODECK
ARCHITECTS

Marlies Breuss,
Michael Ogertschnig

It is our home already,
that starts shaping us.
It is the area that it is situated at,
the people that occupy it.
The environments that we work at,
the places that we visit,
the way the urban is
in a constant flux,
creating an imprint.

Philosophy and Method of Working

We understand architecture as the spatialization of different systems, based on multiple parameters that encompass social needs, local conditions, functional requirements, and visionary approaches. We take analytical steps to filter out the information that is relevant to the design, superimposing it with project-specific values that we have defined. We undertake this process not by simplifying the many components but by instead retaining their inherent complexity and thus creating the basis for our conceptual contextualism.

The concept developed through this approach provides the foundation for decision-making throughout all project phases and represents the logical structure intrinsic to the building. It is holistic and characteristic to each project, with the analyzed parameters resulting from the different connotations of each specific case. We consider architecture to be a mediator between landscapes and cities that respects ecological, social, economic, and structural fabrics—building, including, and evolving them to better meet the future. We are especially interested in researching unique features, historical references, and fractures, as well as in finding innovative, unexpected transformations by incorporating sociological trends, contemporary materials, and current uses. The projects we develop are low-tech buildings, carefully thought through from the first draft to the details of execution to utilize natural features such as passive solar energy, airflow patterns, cross-ventilation, and natural lighting. Technology supports the overarching architectural goal and individual user needs with minimal input, never becoming a determining element of the usage.

Over the last twenty-four years, we have worked in a substantial spectrum of architectural fields ranging from urban planning to exhibition architecture. For us, these various challenges and scales are essential to provoking other perspectives and reexamining tried-and-true approaches by posing new questions. Early participation in international competitions entails architectural possibilities that have given us a multitude of opportunities to explore our strategy, whether through competitions for the conception of a new urban fabric or for the creation of a temporary art institution in a business-dominated neighborhood. A particular concern of ours is togetherness, something that is subject to constant change in both private and public contexts and which we analyze, evolve, and shape to suit individual needs and overarching structures.

Typologies and Buildings

Even our first single-family homes, which—together with their occupants—we looked at as fields of experimentation in the landscape, are spatial representations of our ideas about living together as a family. The concepts are ultimately shaped by the local environment, which defines the architectural composition of the building and the usage of renewable energy. Our project *embedded house* is nestled into the hillside, inspired by the contours of the landscape and the orientation of the adjacent buildings. In contrast, *floating house* absorbs its surroundings to create a floating projection of the terrain around it. The buildings presented in this book show fluid spaces of togetherness, but also opportunities for retreat where individuals can meet their needs for privacy. However, due to the questionable way humans are consuming land, we critically approach the task of constructing free-standing, single-family homes and have not pursued it for almost ten years, while still recognizing that it enabled us to develop strategic solutions for other building typologies.

Parallel to the typology of the free-standing home, we have worked on attic conversions that have proven themselves well as an alternative way of creating living space within an already built infrastructure. This path means no further land consumption; water pipes, power supply, and sewer are all in place, and various upgrades for future uses can be installed together with the extension of the roof. The moderate densification of existing towns and cities is possible due to the good building fabric of the existing structures. Our various attic flat concepts—such as *roof transformations* and *urban reflections*—show strategies for opening up these existing spaces and making them livable, mostly as maisonettes. This layout of apartments with galleries enables an excellent spatial experience, yet it has almost disappeared from the residential building sector in recent years due to a number of new building regulations.

The nonprofit, publicly funded, and privately financed residential building sectors have shown an interest in experimenting together with us, putting a focus on public, semipublic, and private outdoor spaces as an extension of living areas as well as on flexible floor plans. The publicly funded housing complex *22 tops* is located on the edge of a single-family housing development and responds to it with large outdoor facilities in such a way that its volumes and siting are integrated into the single-family housing structure and well accepted despite its large scale. In contrast to this rural housing, the privately financed residential building *urban topos* is located in the midst of a dense urban area. Reacting to this situation, surrounding balconies and terraces create extensive exterior spaces reaching from one site boundary to another to enrich the interiors with additional outdoor areas that can be used as a garden and oasis of relaxation. Our investigations on communal interiors and exterior surfaces led us to the low-cost solution of the south-facing green structure used in *stratified townscape*. With no additional effort required, the green area turns the large living rooms into a conservatory filled with plants, while respecting the regulated site boundaries. In *spatial appropriation*, an in-depth analysis of functional flexibility brought us to the complete dissolution of wall divisions within a spacious loft, using floor-to-ceiling tarpaulins to create temporary spaces, a novel approach that gives the client complete freedom of living.

This highly flexible, temporary concept takes us on to exhibition architecture. When invited by the Architekturzentrum Wien in 2003 to create a spatial concept for the exhibition *Wie Bauen? Das Buch der Moderne* of the Egidio Marzona Collection, we immediately accepted—and our analytical and holistic approach was welcomed by the curator and collector. Invitations from the Prussian Cultural Heritage Foundation in Berlin and Dresden, the Kunsthalle Wien, and Vienna Museum of Modern Art followed, always with the byline "the budget is small," which we see as a challenge as long as it moves within the realm of what is possible.

Courageous clients have been with us since the very beginning, entrusting us with their developments and seeing us as a source of inspiration for their future projects. In fact, this is how the commercial project *hall 01* was designed alongside our first single-family home for a businessman in the metalworking field, including an old storage hall. In order to stay competitive, and despite the lack of a successor, the client decided to venture an annex and contracted us. Our idea to retain the filigree steel skeleton and to use the company's own materials, thus constructing a low-cost building with static improvements, was immediately well received by the client, and his building then became a showcase for his goods.

Working with existing structures and additions to old buildings has since become an essential field of our architectural work. *wirtschaftspark breitensee* and *remise amstetten* are both flexible, multifunctional buildings based on skeleton structures with prefabricated construction and facade elements that allow low-cost solutions and react to existing fabrics. The same strategy was used for our design restructuring the *WDR crossmedia house*, which sits at a prominent site in Cologne facing the cathedral. Despite its persuasive strategy and winning design, the second and third revision phases ultimately did not result in a contract.

In recent years, along with restructuring and expanding existing buildings, our interest in unique typologies has also grown, as standardization and construction norms have increasingly influenced residential buildings, not for reasons of affordability but rather for the liability and safety issues of real-estate developers.

Building culture is not a temporary phenomenon. It shapes our landscapes, cities, and therefore us humans, and we thus participate in fields of architecture that demand building culture. We feel committed to this holistic approach and choose projects and competitions that are based on a mandate of baukultur, as proven by the *austrian embassy bangkok* project for the Federal Ministry for European and International Affairs. A challenge for everyone involved, the building's winning architecture is documented by its substantial international awards and honors.

Book Conception

We have designed this book in two volumes that can be read in parallel, representing on the one hand the communication tools of the architectural language—sketches, drafts, studies, and models—and on the other photographs of our projects and essays on current topics written by personalities from different fields. This arrangement makes it possible to intensely study the architecturally concise depictions and the representational photographs at the same time, starting with our founding year of 1998 and ending with the printing of this book in 2022.

The book is organized into seven sections: Public Attitude, Flexible Reuse, Human Habitat, Allover Landscape, Social Culture, Art Positions, and Urban Strategies. In each, we explain several projects from concept to detail, showing the creative process and various methods of communicating architecture in all its diversity and complexity. The photo section of the book presents the completed buildings and surroundings, with their craftsmanship and mechanical precision captured in different formats by the photographers Ketsiree Wongwan, Pichak Thananchaibut, Wolfgang Thaler, Sigrun Appelt, Hertha Hurnaus, Veronika Hofinger, Paul Ott, Günter Stoeger, Rita Laslsberger, Christian von Steffelin, Barbara Maier, Kurt Hörbst, Grazia Ike Branco, and Pez Hejduk.

Statements on current issues by Anjalika Sagar, Gerhard Steixner, Quijxote Nuntanasirivikrom, Alexis Kalagas, Lisz Hirn, and Belinda Rukschcio are a particularly important part of the book. We invited these individuals to write about the state of our current time and the possible future implications based upon their beliefs and approaches in their own fields of activity.

PHOTOGRAPHS / POSITIONS OF INTERNATIONAL EXPERTS

CONCEPTS / SKETCHES / PLANS / MODELS / DESCRIPTIONS

making it
EINBAHN

HUBER
WERKZEUG
making it

ABUS

EINGANG
STIEGE 3
1. STOCK
W 29506 A

breitensee

barista

172
Goldschlagstraße
ZIEHEN

barista
restaurant
bar
cafe

barista
restaurant
bar
cafe

08
09

07

Einfahrt Freihalten

TURNERGASSE 24

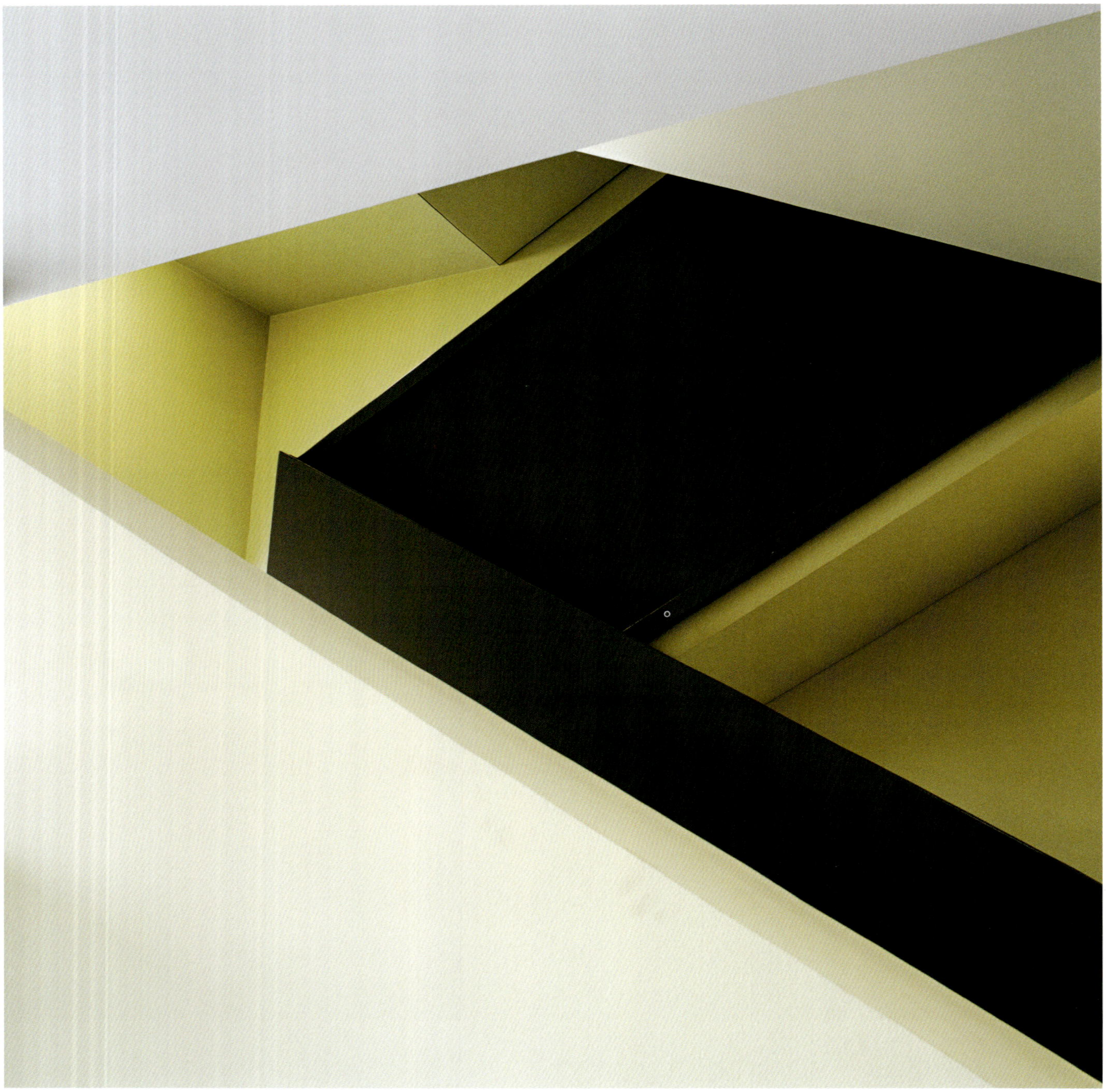

LÖWE

ATTENSAM

SPIELPLATZ

nr3 KAPLANWEG nr3

Is there life
on earth ?
FABBRO BEKLEIDUNG
AKTIONSRAUM

BRUS Zerreißprobe
Aktionsraum 1

DIBBETS
SECRETS

LE MODULOR

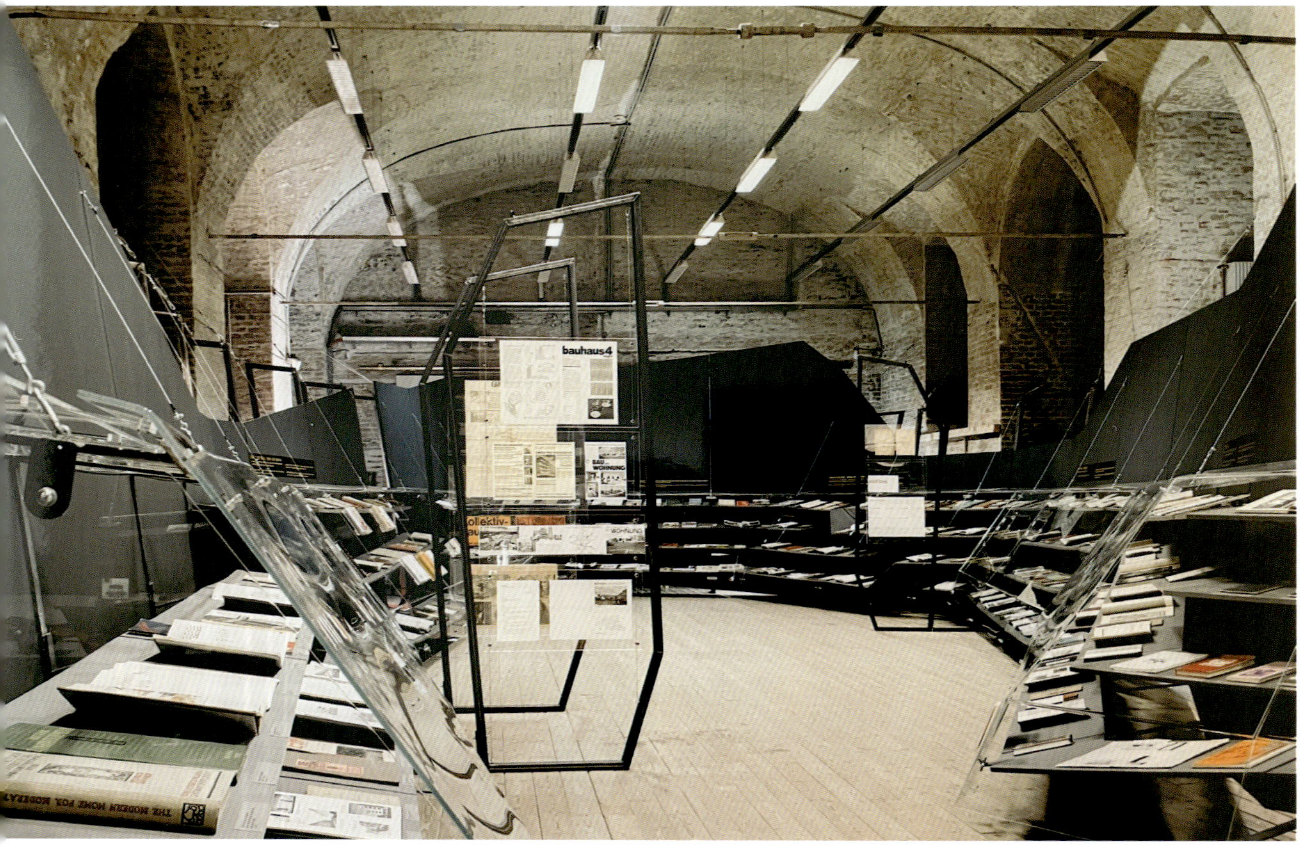
bauhaus4
BAU WOHNUNG
kollektiv-
THE MODERN HOME FOR MODERATE

ARARAT

ARARAT

LOOKING AT THE SUN
DOMESTICATING THE BICYCLE
LEAP BEFORE YOU LOOK
Greek Lexicon (Drawing Lesson 45) 2011
video, 0:37 min.
Intoxicating Liquor 2010
video, 1:31 min.
L'Exploration du Sahara 2010
video, 0:50 min.
Three Shadows

LOOKING AT THE SUN
AGAINST ARGUMENT (BUT NOT THIS ONE)
A SAFE SPACE FOR STUPIDITY
ANTI-ENTROPY
THE FULL STOP SWALLOWS THE SENTENCE
DOMESTICATING THE BICYCLE
THICK TIME
VERTICAL THINKING
TORSCHLUSS-PANIK
LEAP BEFORE YOU LOOK
THE PLEASURES OF SELF DECEPTION
POEMS I USED TO KNOW
THE INVENTION OF AFRICA

ht berühren / Please do not touch

DXG

The Dept. of Xenogenesis

2019–21 and onward

Anjalika Sagar

"What happens when we treat empirical objects as interscalar vehicles, as means of connecting stories and scales usually kept apart?"
— Gabriele Hecht

"I need to get closer to my public who understands these references. African cinema must teach; it must be a night school, which is something that Western cinema can afford to do without."
— Ousmane Sembène

Since 2002, together with many friends new and old and beyond, we have endeavored through the Otolith Group and Collective to create a context for thinking together. More importantly to create a speculative platform upon which the very question of what constitutes how we understand time, tempo, temporality, scale, politics, and political activity today can be reconsidered (the where, when, what, how, with whom). In fact, we found many of our fellow travelers and friends on this journey and in that process of thinking. We also have over the years taken great care to disactivate an ethos of enterprise, or one of competing expertise that condemns things that harvest a potentiating politics toward a transactional proviso of mastery, personal gain, or self-speculation.

The Dept. of Xenogenesis (DXG) formalizes this archive of a research-based artistic practice that has been developed through events, talks, screenings, and gatherings since 2002, whose name emerges from the projects that subtend the meanings and the methods entailed by *Xenogenesis*, the title of the international exhibition of the work of The Otolith Group curated by Annie Fletcher in 2019. *Xenogenesis* began at the Van Abbe Museum in Eindhoven in June to September 2019 and continued throughout 2020 to 2022, traveling from the Institute for Contemporary Art at Virginia Commonwealth University, Buxton Contemporary at University of Melbourne, Museum of Contemporary Art Metelkova, Ljubljana, and Southern Alberta Art Gallery, Lethbridge, Sharjah Art Foundation, Sharjah, and lastly to The Irish Museum of Modern Art, Dublin, in 2022.

Before, during, between, and after each of these institutional exhibitions, XG has operated as an ongoing experiment that subtends the ramifications and repercussions of the term Xenogenesis that was invented by the novelist Octavia Butler for her trilogy of science-fiction novels *Dawn* (1987), *Adulthood Rites* (1988), and *Imago* (1989). By adopting Octavia Butler's term for the exhibition, the artists aim to develop its potential as a vector that opens onto ongoing preoccupations with specific practices of study.

The Dept. of Xenogenesis offers a means for gathering around and staying with The Otolith Group's enduring preoccupations with questions of chronopolitics, matters of futurity, methods of science fiction, the desedimentation of Africanity, the interrogation of racial distinction, practices of Black feminist study, projects of Black study, the experiments of documentary engagement with alienation, the study of differing formulations of inhumanisms, and contending notions of posthumanisms.

These interscalar questions can be rendered more concrete and yet more abstract by a close study of the specific writings of Octavia Butler in relation to her importance for specific strands within twentieth- and twenty-first-century feminist thought. Thinkers such as Donna Haraway, Saidiya Hartman, Denise Ferreira da Silva, and Luciana Parisi have turned to moments within the novels of Octavia Butler in order to develop their own inquiries into the futures of biology, slavery, freedom and involuntary servitude, ontology and rationality, prediction, computability, and machine intelligence.

At its core, XG is a sustained engagement with Octavia Butler as a speculative thinker who used the generic conventions of science fiction as a narrative vehicle for a speculative inquiry into the denaturalization of human, Black female reproduction as the time machine for the afterlife of slavery, the extinction of the earth, the practice of the inexistent, the project of surrogacy as the revision of the human, the necropolitics of technofascism, and the becoming Black of the human.

Taking the writings of Octavia Butler seriously, devoting time and space to those writings, turning toward and subtending those writings, it becomes possible, in the words of Saidiya Hartman, to "tell an impossible story and to amplify the impossibility of its telling."

Let us start from the proposition that the world, however we define "world" and however we define "ourselves," changed when the SARS-CoV-2 virus appeared in Wuhan, Central China, in late December 2019. In what ways, then, has the world changed? What is the structure of feeling of this changed world? What is the social and political experience of this ongoing transformation? How can the dimensions of this transformation be comprehended, dramatized and metabolized, and expressed? What will happen to sociality as the fundamental fabric of life of education and learning?

Our exposure within accelerated scales of negative collapsing, interlocking infrastructures reveals historical imperialisms and ongoing categorical and escalating violence in its most totalizing sense. The fear of erasure and extinction is upon us. This is characterized by the seemingly uncontrollable clock of the earth's tectonic shifts or the increasing climate catastrophe as it takes the form of flooding or wildfires, to name the most obvious. To state the obvious is to state the imperial clocks of genocide, ecocide, the clocks of viruses, epidemics, syndemics, or pandemics. It is clear that we are confronted with an existence that is undergoing transformation at all levels of our reality and our relationship to time. A transformation whose interscalar dimensions require us to construct and assemble new structures of sensing, compose new ways of seeing, gather new ways of unlearning, and build new forms of thinking that can contribute to a counternarrative in the widest temporal frame.

We see The DXG as the occasion for thinking with our friends and friends to be, for contributing to the collective crystallization of the social, a propositional experience of transformation as an occasion for the collective precipitation of the social experience of global change. Of the lived collective reality and spectacle of the virus which demands nothing but an aesthetics of embodiment that moves from the center of the earth into the cosmos and all that lies between. If we approached the DXG as an interscalar vehicle in itself, then it could become the vehicle for exploring, investigating, mourning, dramatizing, socializing, processing, and metabolizing the harrowing social experience of the Racial Capitalocene.

Covid-19's exponential rate of infection amplifies all so-called preexisting inequalities. It heightens the local tendencies of the global neofascist, ethnonationalism, and anti-statist insurgency. Political regimes such as India, Brazil, and the United Kingdom have used their ever-increasing mortality rates to mobilize and financialize their eugenic policies. We can see how violence that takes underprivileged Black and Brown life in the Global West and in the Global South and works in tandem with corporate health systems in these states lets People of Color die. At the same time, the pandemic confuses political boundaries that political entrepreneurs exploit for their own ends. It engenders updated versions of Clara Zetkin's political asylum under which the politically homeless gather. It creates shelters for social media that nurture new semioviruses recombined from archaic conspiracy theories and tired vulnerable outdated forms of protest.

Covid-19, amongst other scales of apocalypse, confronts us with the threat, the promise, the danger, and the seduction of transformation. It forces us to ask ourselves how we will choose to live, even as we mourn those who have died from climate breakdown, infection, or who have been murdered by security forces, militarized police, or war. To live with the pandemic is to confront the virus as a fundamental test of solidarity that can bring us out of isolation and conjoin the hyperlocal with the nonlocal to comprehend the gravity of the issues that seem beyond our control.

It demonstrates the extent to which human and nonhuman protagonists are inextricably entangled in the age of the Capitalocene. It brings us face to face with conditions that are at the same time viral and social. It confronts us with conditions of living that carry the risks of dying. This vector of breathing in and breathing out indicates our fundamental dependency on air which climate activists have been warning us about and teaching for some time.

If we indeed think of The Dept. of Xenogenesis as a gathering that scales up this autodidactic impulse, then we can think of DXG as a pedagogical occasion to locate our complex local, situated knowledges of the deadly layers of the present within then onlocal scale of the planetary. Such an assembly aims to create pathways that direct attention toward the ways in which online and other screen-based, post-cinematic platforms operate as educational experiments for comprehending the dynamics at work in the present that open up the field of aesthetics to their widest syntax and to their material organization.

If we indeed turn the medium of our platform toward the question of interscalar travel in order to grasp the intrasectional dynamics of the pandemic, then the question becomes: How do we travel across these scales? And what kind of time traveler do we need to be? What if we see the pedagogic initiatives that have emerged in response to the Covid-19 pandemic as contemporary versions of the Senegalese film director, producer, and writer, Ousmane Sembène's idea of African cinema as a night school, *Ecole de soir*. What if we are witnessing the blowup of the screen and see the multiplicity of screens as a contemporary expression of Sembene's generous cinematic vision?

A yearning for discussion, dialogue, debate, and discourse induces an uncontrolled, uncoordinated, decentralized experiment in platform pedagogy. It is a proliferating experiment in collective study that is emerging as we speak. If we accept that we are living in the continuing aftermath of imperialism and its regressive enclosures, then one is aware that we are bearing witness to folded and related scenes of crimes. As Serge Daney writes in his essay "Cinemeteorology," on the film *Too Early Too Late* by the renowned French filmmakers Jean-Marie Straub and Danièle Huillet: "Starting off with sounds—all the sounds, from the most infinitesimal to the subtlest—they too identify a crime. Scene of the crime: the earth; victims: peasants; witnesses to the crime: landscapes. That is, clouds, roads, grass, wind."

When we think of the landscape as the Earthscape and Covid-19 as an embodiment of all that metabolizes our senses now in their folded complexity, perhaps we can ask metaphorically where, as filmmakers do, we situate the camera. Straub and Huillet search evidently for the right spot, where the camera can be unnoticed enough to see things unfold. Straub describes this situation almost as if to create a "structure of feeling"; when asked about the discrepant and distanced positionality deployed in the film, he says:

> I do not like the word distance much, because everyone thinks the word distance comes from Brecht. Distanciation (in French), Brecht never spoke of distanciation. He spoke of Verfremdung, which means strange, it is completely different.[1]

Deney describes the filmmakers as they shoot in Egypt as less meteorologists than acupuncturists who search for the spot, the only spot, the right spot where their camera can film without presence. In one long take, the camera is planted in front of a factory gate where Egyptian workers pass, enter, and leave; some of them glance directly into the direction of the camera, while the others react with indifference. The scene invites comparison with the Lumière Brothers' *Workers Leaving the Lumière Factory in Lyon 1895*, but in the present asks new questions of new labor, new subjects.

The structure of feeling, to quote Raymond Williams, is also that which has not yet crystallized into vocabulary or solidified into terminology. It requires moving through and attending to each other beyond the fear of death that is inflicted by precarity, the virus, or climate catastrophe. It requires gathering the autonomous movements and independent collectives that initiate practices of study which are inseparable from aesthetics of sociality and forming a curriculum that helps us bridge and move through these dark times out of a mire of necropolitical pedagogies that drive education today. It is through an awareness of these registers and these forces that we can create a curriculum of study, of Black, of Brown study, of resilient aesthetics, of a form of earthly study—of study of the unthought, of collective sensing where we can all dare to trespass.

1 Jean-Marie Straub in conversation with Celine Condorelli on October 20, 2010, published online in March 2011 as "Speaking of Revolutions: Too Early, Too Late," *LUX*, https://lux.org.uk/speaking-of-revolutions-too-early-too-late/ (accessed in October 2022)

Easy Living: Luxury for All

Gerhard Steixner

Housing is both urban planning and a political classification.

Almost a hundred years ago, in 1924, Vienna mayor Karl Seitz announced in the newspaper *Arbeiter-Zeitung* the beginning of a new era: "[F]rom the time of the 1870s and 1880s, we still remember the small houses with their large courtyards, which provided a place of recreation for the youth. Then came the building period of bleak rental barracks, where every last patch of land was made usable. That was a time in which the Viennese were struggling under capitalism, with anyone in a rental apartment dreading the terrible payment deadline.[1] … Now, we are entering a new building period, no longer building small, single houses with tiny courtyards, but instead large complexes with communal apartments in which people live together, but where everyone can also live separately according to their individuality. General needs for recreation and activity are fulfilled by beautiful shared parks for the benefit of everyone. We don't want to raise our youth to be individualists and loners; they should grow up to be sociable, brought up to be community members."[2]

At just a fraction of the building density of the *Gründerzeit* era, this political and humanitarian program was successfully implemented on a large scale within ten years and continues to be as internationally acclaimed as the buildings of Red Vienna.[3] Housing as a human right, not as a commodity. These buildings owe their worldwide reputation to the radical social program, its sheer size, and the innovative urban planning that went beyond the standard block grid. The architecture can be blunt and pompous at times, the appearance often defensive, with a tendency to obscure the profound quality of these large residential complexes: the apartments are designed for subsistence-level living, but they face quiet, park-like greenspaces filled with light, air, and sun, and are equipped with community facilities for education, culture and leisure, health, and everyday shopping needs. Autonomous islands. In a mere ten years, from 1923 to 1933, well over 60,000 apartments were built in this way, dwellings which remain exempt from the mechanisms of the market to this day.

In the aftermath of this Viennese model, starting in the mid-1960s, municipalities and cooperatives throughout Europe renewed their efforts to advance emancipation for the masses through residential and urban development. New urban forms of living combined the qualities of a single-family home with those of the dense city. Large experimental housing estates emerged in Paris, London, Berlin, Munich, and Vienna, to name only a few. "The greatest happiness for the greatest number" was the shared political leitmotif of the day. The aim was to allow everyone what previously only the rich could afford. It was the stepped terrace housing typology, invented as early as the 1920s, that promised to best meet this demand.

Stepped terrace housing is economical and offers a high level of living comfort, including a terrace and a garden, yet with minimal land consumption. People can plant whatever they wish on their own terrace, with the buildings' hanging gardens changing with the seasons and the residents' activities. The added value is not only aesthetic, but above all ecological, more important than ever in terms of the city's microclimate and in consideration of climate change.

During another mere decade, 1968 to 1978, numerous greened, high-quality, pedestrian residential complexes the size of neighborhoods were built this way, with buildings that not only looked good but that were user-friendly, well-maintained, and embraced by the community. For the most part, resource utilization in these buildings was minimal and very well controlled. When taken as a whole, the buildings were sustainable in the best sense of the word; a qualitative leap over the buildings of Red Vienna fifty years later. Although building density was once again much higher and room heights lower, apartments were now almost twice as large on average, often two-story, and equipped with bathrooms and closets. While earlier only balconies or loggias added to the living spaces, it was now achieved through terraces with gardens. While earlier buildings had paddling pools for children in the courtyard, there were now swimming pools on the roof, with saunas and sundecks for all to share—all embedded in spacious, traffic-free green spaces designed for relaxation, play, and sport. When everybody is doing well, then the entire community can prosper. This vision is realized through structures built with high functionality, efficiency, and economy. The architecture isn't trying to tell a story; it simply is what it is, and what the residents make of it. Prototypes for the green city to come.

But all that came to an end in the late 1970s, with conservative bourgeois forces declaring the large estates and stepped terrace housing a sin of construction. The incidence of light was then again reduced to the legally prescribed minimum, with value shifted back toward the facade. The idea of a society based on solidarity and a suitable portion of the increasing prosperity for everyone began to erode, right up to the "me" corporations of the first decade of the twenty-first century, and culminating in, among other things, the privatization of 60,000 high-quality apartments by the right-wing conservative government, something never before seen in Austria.[4]

The entanglement of the financial and real-estate markets created the starting point for the global financial crisis of 2008: banks faltered, the auto industry struggled with a slump in sales, and trade and services with a reluctance to consume. The state had to step in. A reduction in energy consumption and garbage, a decrease in automobile and air traffic, significantly fewer new car registrations, and cleaner air were positive yet short-lived consequences for the environment. The potential for optimization became apparent, and the fulfillment of lower CO_2-level targets appeared within reach.

But that didn't last long, maybe a year or two, and then almost everything returned to business as usual once again. The cities grew, land prices rose, and with them urban density. Living space was made to be "smart" and became the currency of escape; Airbnb emerged as the platform for bed-seekers. The Internet of Things and the great depth of residential construction regulations now seem to be preparing for the future total market penetration of household and nursing robots. The Boston Dynamics prototypes, for example, are quite promising.

What to do?

Keep cool, don't panic: cities can be planned, but cannot be bought. The selling of special rights through "urban development contracts" and the outsourcing of public responsibilities to private partners must (for the most part) be stopped. The republic itself must also set the goals of its companies—for example, readjusting *the long-term increase in values of high-quality real estate in Austria* and setting a future focus on social values in residential construction.[5]

Moving forward is not about wrapping buildings in foam and then greening them, but instead about constructing residential housing that fulfills

1 True again today: the discussion of affordability and high density.

2 This was a clear rejection of the Viennese settlement movement, which strove for autonomy and self-sufficiency, making it difficult to contain politically. Despite prominent protagonists such as Adolf Loos and Josef Frank, it was shut down in 1925, after about 3,000 settlement buildings had been built.

3 Floor space index and degree of development are each only a quarter of that of the *Gründerzeit* era.

4 For more information on the BUWOG scandal, see Wikipedia, s.v. "BUWOG-Affäre," last modified October 7, 2022, https://de.wikipedia.org/wiki/BUWOG-Aff%C3%A4re.

5 Concept from the Austrian Real Estate (ARE) website. Austrian Real Estate is a government company with a focus on residential construction in the luxury segment.

the wishes and needs of those who live there … about laying the ecological groundwork for a green city … about providing both private and shared open spaces, community facilities, and opportunities for appropriation.

Adequate housing is a human right. In this respect, the problem of affordability has been around for some time, and it is likely to be exacerbated by the impact of the pandemic. Housing costs are rising sharply, while household incomes have been stagnating for a long time now, and blue-collar incomes are even falling. Apartments will be affordable once their occupants return to earning decent wages for their work. Until then, urgent action on the part of the public sector, municipalities, and cooperatives is necessary to prevent the housing crisis from spreading, with measures that make the exploitation of living space unprofitable in the future, together with the communalization of land, as more of it cannot be made. To what extent such a containment succeeds will be revealed in the upcoming residential and urban development, as it is a strong indicator of the social and cultural state of a society.

A reset is necessary, a fresh attempt. It would be the third (following the 1920s and 1970s), heading toward democratization and the greening of architecture and urban development. The development that has radically called into question the past hundred years' social achievements seems to be nearing its lowest point. Now, in the 2020s, the next leap is imminent. A fifty-year leap. Realizations resulting from the pandemic have opened up a space for this. The goal must be luxury for all. More space, easy living, green cities. It is possible, and—in light of the climate crisis—it is the order of the day. In particular, youth will develop a feeling for it, will become involved, will not let themselves be lured down the wrong track by persistent, backward-looking forces that dream of the "European city," of "urban architecture," of showy facades along the edges of the block grids, the residents mere extras left behind in an architectural backdrop, using every opportunity to escape from their inhospitable homes, into nature.

It's the ecology, stupid! City and nature don't have to be a contradiction. The green city is a city of inhabitants, contributors to a living, constantly changing image. This is the transition to the fourth phase of modernity.

Ban Morh: Happiness Does Not Exist in This World, Only Tolerable Suffering Can Be Found Here

Quijxote Nuntanasirivikrom

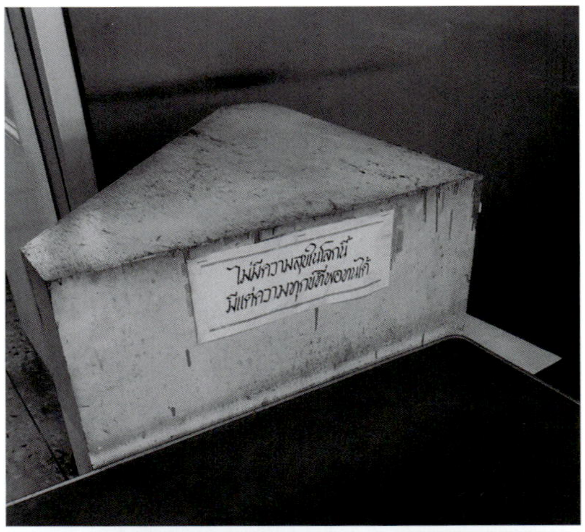

"Seeing comes before words. The child looks and recognizes before it can speak. But there is also another sense in which seeing comes before words. It is seeing which establishes our place in the surrounding world; we explain that world with words, but words can never undo the fact that we are surrounded by it. The relation between what we see and what we know is never settled."
— John Berger, *Ways of Seeing*

"Body" always bears a sense of containment. In order to experience how a body works within its environment, the relationships between what we see and what we know must be explored. In order to explore what a body is, the studio views the body through three lenses: captivating object (place), cultivated culture, capturing scenario.

Captivating Object (Place)

An object, a physical place, that is captivating always carries not only an aesthetic quality but also ones of performance and capability. These are based either on how it was built with a particular technique or how it works once in operation. To see what the body of an object is and how it works, this research-based analysis will explore this qualitative issue through the adaptation of basic knowledge.

"Happiness does not exist in this world, only tolerable suffering can be found here"

This Thai folk saying conveys the truth and provides comfort and could be regarded as a critical statement when applied to the urban context. It represents a common understanding of how people habitually evolve and sustain themselves to establish their effort and to respond to the dynamism of urban development. These implications comprise an in-depth understanding of architecture and its complexity. It is where qualitative issues crucially reciprocate with substantial quantitative issues. It is clear evidence of where deeper understanding and greater complexity play an important role in the analysis of the physical content of tangibles.

Here, we engage with the complex implications and reciprocal relationships of quantitative and qualitative issues of urban architecture using substantial empirical evidence: the simple physical factors that are the basic conditions of architecture. Moving forward to benefit stakeholders and improve regulations and sociopolitical economic factors, this could demonstrate a way for people to communally share and live together, to coexist in the architecture of the urban area. In order to do so, psychogeographic mechanisms for understanding the role of supporting factors are applied to create tools for observing the phenomena of the city.

The processes of negotiation between the various neighborhood agencies about the degree of sharing of architecture and urban spaces plays an important role in their claims of private and public. The shared rights held by each stakeholder at every level are physical and manifest visibly and tangibly as well as socially and economically. This driving mechanism determines the quantitative and qualitative value of an area, socially and economically generating public properties and shared living conditions between stakeholders. Public space and degree of publicness could, then, be generated, argued, and negotiated, thus dynamically evolving through time.

Cultivated Culture

Once an object (or place) is fitted into the context, the generative effects of the object begin taking place. This could be defined as the qualitative effect of the relationships between objects (or place) and their environment.

> "Geography, for example, deals with the determinant action of general natural forces, such as soil composition or climatic conditions, on the economic structures of a society, and thus on the corresponding conception that such a society can have of the world."
> — Guy Debord, *Introduction to a Critique of Urban Geography*, 1955

Although a city is a non-living organism, there is nonetheless a consensus that the city can be regarded as a living creature. Cities evolve through time in the context of specific conditions and factors. If we see the city as a living creature, its architecture could be considered an organ that sustains and ensures its functioning.

When the city and its architecture are treated organically, the driving forces within its built environment and organization become complex and delicate. Operative forces are generated by many factors, both individual and cumulative. Both physical and non-physical elements are active in and throughout the "place." Studying the common occurrences of any city and its architecture in light of the effects of the specific place and architectures is essential.

Here, we look at an area of the old town of Bangkok, called Ban Morh. We do not inquire what has been quantitatively realized but approach the city from a qualitative perspective instead. We show the dialogue and materials in an art piece of moving images as a space for thought and playful, inventive strategies for exploring the city, showing viewers habitats that are off the beaten path and jolting them into a new awareness of the urban landscape. In this video, quantitative content is examined and interrogated in a factual analysis. We explore the relationships and parameters of where and how factual content and actual extent are incorporated. Within the screenplay, there are categories of factors, criteria, and context. In the dialogue, actual synthesis is activated and qualitative extent is perceivable.

Capturing Scenario: Script and Narration

https://web.facebook.com/watch/?v=199180087871041

Ban Morh
Ban Morh Palace
Ban Morh Market
Ban Morh Plaza

<u>Ban Morh: What and how was it?</u>

In the past, clay pots were sold at market, brought in on the canal. There was a water gate, and boats came into the canal, not like today. The market was large but is now gone.

Groceries were moved to Pak Morh, as were the workers who lived there. The market has now been dissolved.

<u>Where did the jewelry businesses that used to be here go?</u>

Most moved and rented retail spaces in Silom (Bangkok Central Business District). Most of the jewelry stores have now moved into shopping malls, where there are proper parking lots. People were often frustrated when they couldn't park their cars here in the area.

<u>Where did the electronics stores come from?</u>

Cho-Chai Chana (an electronic appliance business) came first. They mainly provided appliance repair services and sold spare parts. The store is near here, at the crossroads. I (the interviewer) was interested in their skill, and I observed how they work. Once me and my friend were good enough, my pal started his own business. Nowadays, spare parts sales are dropping. Selling ready-made stereo systems has turned out to be a good business instead.

The Disappearance of the Night Market

About the storage, when nearby neighbors' ground floors are unoccupied or there is any extra space, they gladly welcome the hawkers renting their storage space. Most commercial stall space (1.5 × 1.5 m) is occupied and in high demand, $40–50 a month depending on location. They are not allowed to stay there the whole night long. They have to be packed up and stored, somewhere, somehow. Actually, stalls are not allowed in public space, but sometimes, someway, and somehow, they comply with regulations by negotiating with an officer. Temporary extensions are allowed for about 3 feet into public space. Back then, it was not possible for vehicles to pass through the alleyways.

"Happiness does not exist in this world, only tolerable suffering can be found here"

Good spot, trendy, ready for business.

Obsolete jewelry business, a new business comes (electronic appliances)

Leaseholders welcome the newcomers running their businesses. But rental space fees are quite high. (We street vendors have to do our best.) Other holders also see their chance. (OK, we [also leaseholders] will try, too.)

Boom! Electronics (a formulated identity of the place). The arrival of mass rapid transit, there are more visitors, new buildings go up (someway and somehow). The higher budget for operating the space is passed on to the leaseholder (renting the space from the landlord).

"Rental fees will be raised."—the Landlord

The landlord increases rents. "Affordable?" Depends. If it's not, you need to let go. The business owner is forced to increase cash flow. A new special deal with the street vendors is the solution. There is an agreement on arranging spaces without blocking the public flow. Hawkers get spaces to run their businesses; the leaseholders get their profit. Cashflow is smoother. "We thrive." We organize for our own ochlocracy, either against or beyond formal regulation and casual law.

"Place must be cleared and tidied up by six o'clock. You need to move out by six o'clock."—the municipal officer

There won't be any stalls at night. Where and how can we find storage? The other leaseholders provide storage space, all night long. Stalls now have storage, leaseholders have extra profits. There is less and less residential space. Residents move away, making room for more business. Dead by night, trading for higher cash flow and profits … "We thrive."

"……"—the Landlord

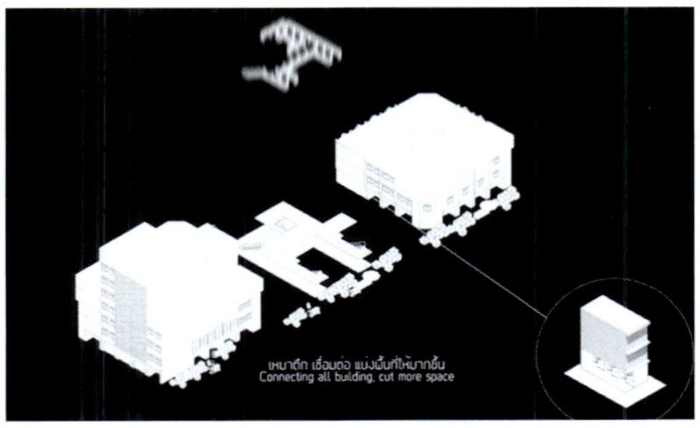

But the cash flow of the leaseholder is still stagnant. The solution is to get more leased properties, to combine and connect them for more rental space to welcome more businesses. Leaseholders gain more profits with the larger business area. With a higher degree of cash flow … "We thrive."

"Now what?"—the Landlord

But again, not for all, some leaseholders can't do this. An agent is brought in to negotiate.

The Agent: "Dear Landlord, we are here to negotiate lowering our rental fees."

"How dare you?"—the Landlord

The Agent: "If not, we can't survive. If not, we can't stay. All of us."

"Good. Find something that you can afford."—the Landlord

The Agent: "All of us."

"Well?"—the Landlord

Around here, it is tough for one person alone.

Afterword

Scene I

Leaseholder: I am interested in running my small business around here. I saw a sign about renting a space.

Landlord: Are you sure? Can you? Can you pay the monthly rental fee? It is unusually high.

Leaseholder: I can, it is not too much of a burden.

Landlord (thinking): Shall I run this business on my own? No way.

Leaseholder (thinking): The landlord is very demanding, I see it in his policy on quickly raising the rent.

Landlord: Do you know? There will be a policy on rapidly raising rents. Therefore, I must increase the price.

Leaseholder: Come on, if you do that, can I survive?

Landlord: If you can't, find something that suits you. Otherwise, just let it go.

Leaseholder (thinking): Come on, how far you gonna go?

Scene II

Street Vendor: Sir, this location is really good for running a business. Can I put my stall here in the public space in front of your property?

Leaseholder: How dare you? It will obstruct my storefront. Find somewhere else instead.

Street Vendor: Please, please. There are stalls everywhere around here. Most of the space is occupied.

Leaseholder: Well then, how do we share? Any ideas?

Street Vendor: Let's do it this way. I give you compensation for obstructing your shopfront. You gain more profit; I gain my space and profit. This is quite a fair trade, isn't it?

Leaseholder: OK, deal.

Later

Street Vendor: Hold on, please don't turn me down. I desperately need space to store my stuff. They won't allow anything in public space after 6 p.m.

Leaseholder: Yeah, let's do it this way: tuck everything in my building, there is lots of space left. By the way, you need to pay for it.

PS

Leaseholder: Sir, here is the monthly fee for the lease.

Landlord (thinking): Too bad, the rental fee doesn't reflect the property. In the end, what kind of business is this?

Psychogeography

"[T]he study of the precise laws and specific effects of the geographical environment, consciously organized or not, on the emotions and behavior of individuals."

— Guy Debord, *Introduction to a Critique of Urban Geography*, 1955

"Psychology is like the soul of Ban Morh. In terms of the place, it may be hard to recognize who has power over whom. The geographical conditions of the area generate the physical manifestation of Ban Morh. The conditions of Ban Morh focus solely on the static physicality of what still exists. In contrast, the physical characteristics of the area are expressed as the result of Ban Morh's desire: The desire to sustain oneself through mutual agreements within a uniform network of mutual trust. This can be seen as a mutual relationship."

— Kalayakorn Komvipak, screenplay author

"People form their habitual engagements with the place. People also realize the physical conditions of the area through their experiences, perceptions, conditions, and constraints. This was considered by using a research method that could address the intangible quality of the place."

— Chayapat Krainatsith,
screenplay author

"Psychogeography exists as the relationships of people in the 'place' and their ways of living. These relations can be conveyed in many ways, in many forms. In such a place, architecture is a crucial mechanism that can generate society and physical location."

— Chinnapatr Petchchad,
documentary narrator

"Psychogeography is a representation of describing the actions based on humanity. Psychogeography expresses the straightforward truth of needs and desires. It also expresses balance in society, especially regarding relationships of requiring and allowing, of what could or should be done. This phenomenon is applied on a place by its society, physically and relatively. Therefore, what emerges is an essential focusing on the inseparable relationships of people to their place."

— Nittipoom Nilketr,
voice (landlord)

"Psychogeography is the emergence of an agreement created and shared by certain groups of people based on their living conditions, their constraints, both physically or socially. Accordingly, this social occurrence generates an unassigned identity that is dynamic and transformable in itself. Architecture is a case in point of the exploitative power of this dynamic. Residential spaces can be turned into some kind of department store, small alleyways can be turned into a shop, the shop selling electrical appliances can be turned into a noodle shop that uses the household appliances at the site."

— Palin Sookatiwararattana,
moving image editing

"Psychogeography is the way of life, thoughts, and actions. The psychogeography of a place could be seen as a well-defined structure operatively differentiated through internal management. There are conditions and constraints, various types of interactions, both tangible through physical property and intangible through formless parameters. These can be seen in relationships, networks, ownership, trades, negotiations, stakeholdings."

— Pongsathorn Imsombbon,
scene and image arrangement and voice
(street vendor)

"As a place, Ban Morh represents the creation of arrangements by a local cast. In a place that is already dense yet still has a crucial need for growth, negotiation must be brought into play. All of these factors are crucial conditions that explicitly affect the physicality of the place."

— Pakawat Aroonangsuthorn,
moving image editing

"The psychogeography of Ban Morh is as simple as the infused savor of a papaya salad with extra crab and pickled fish mixed in a mortar. Even if the physical conditions inside of the mortar have been altered by the different ingredients, the original flavors still remain. The papaya salad is served on plates, just as the stores in the area have changed, yet the solutions to sustain themselves remain. These altered conditions are unrecognizable even to the local people. They still live their lives as usual, under their same old recognizable living conditions. From the first moment, only a few who have delicate tastes can sense the differences."

— Rattanachoke Saelee,
voice (leaseholder)

"Psychogeography is an architectural theory that aims to represent the effects and correlation between local habitat and physicality of place. In Ban Morh, the local habitat sustains itself someway and somehow. The emergence of quaint construction sites is clear evidence of this. They are working together for mass socialization, striving for sustainment. This can no longer be done individually."

— Apisama Larpmahanonta,
scene and image arrangement

De Conditio Urbana

Lisz Hirn

"People have lived in cities for just 1 percent of their 500,000 years of history. And this invention, the city, can disappear just as quickly as it began."[1]
— Alexander Kluge

"The concept of the city is becoming pointless. The utopias that once ushered the city into the modern era have run dry. The visions intended to help survive the twentieth century have entirely lost their sparkle and promise of happiness. The city's illusions and stories have become utterly banal. Both naïve and sentimental criticism fail when it comes to the city, just like the stupid, local economy focus of marketing, politics, and the administration."[2]
— Roger Behrens

People have always moved from the country to the city when convinced they will have a better life there. The city air will set you free after a year and a day. From its very beginnings, the city has served as a catalyst for civilization, culture, and innovation, as a social and political utopia in which the city dweller (*Homo Urbanus*) could be transformed into a beautiful spirit (*Urbanus Homo*). The term "urbanity" has been used to distinguish urban living from life in the country since the European Middle Ages. But how are people doing in their cities, which will be home to five billion people by 2030? How is this *Homo Urbanus* "dwelling," in the sense used by Heidegger?

If one understands dwelling not simply as one activity among many, but instead as the very way that humans exist on earth, then the concept of dwelling is no longer limited to the idea of merely "having a place to live," but instead becomes inextricably linked to the concept of "building." That is the goal of building: dwelling. "Where the word *bauen* still speaks in its original sense it also says how far the essence of dwelling reaches. … What then does *ich bin* mean? The old word *bauen*, to which the *bin* belongs, answers: *ich bin, du bist* mean: I dwell, you dwell. The way in which you are and I am, the manner in which we humans *are* on the earth, is *buan*, dwelling. To be a human being means to be on the earth as a mortal. It means to dwell."[3] Dwelling is the fundamental trait of being that defines all mortals. But how *are* these mortals in urban space? Which apartments produced by today's big cities are suspected of being places of "semiotic desolation?"[4] To what extent does urban morphology, particularly that of housing, alter our image of *Homo Urbanus*? If the essence of building is to let people dwell, as Heidegger writes, and if the process of building creates places by joining rooms, then the question arises as to which apartments and thus also norms of contemporary residential architecture are produced by the everyday life of the residents and translated into urban structures. "On all sides we hear talk about the housing shortage, and with good reason. Nor is there just talk; there is action too. We try to fill the need by providing houses, by promoting the building of houses, planning the whole architectural enterprise. However hard and bitter, however hampering and threatening the lack of houses remains, the *proper plight of dwelling* does not lie merely in a lack of houses. The proper plight of dwelling is indeed older than the world wars with their destruction, older also than the increase of the earth's population and the condition of the industrial workers. The proper dwelling plight lies in this, that mortals ever search anew for the essence of dwelling, that they must ever learn to dwell."[5] And this is true of both rural and urban living. Interpreting urbanity in terms of movements such as New Urbanism would mean evaluating less whether rural life is superior or preferable to urban life, but rather to what extent our human condition must be taken into account in urban environments in order to prevent the creation of urban dystopias such as urban sprawl (suburbanization), gentrification, high crime rates, and the excessive use of resources.

What can architects do to counter the dystopian elements of the city in order to save the utopian potential of urbanity? They would probably have to use their work to address the question of how humans want to live in the city, that is, the *conditio urbana* in the face of advancing suburbanization and post-urbanization. As early as 1953, Gilles Ivain wrote about architecture as the simplest means in his influential essay "Formulary for a New Urbanism": "Architecture is the simplest means of articulating time and space, of modulating reality and engendering dreams. It is a matter not only of plastic articulation and modulation expressing an ephemeral beauty, but of a modulation producing influences in accordance with the eternal spectrum of human desires and the progress in realizing them."[6] It would mean thinking about architects not only as economic or at best aesthetic accomplices of the respective city government, but also rediscovering them as utopian builders: that is, as builders of a city that has not yet come to be, but should exist.

The question of whether the *conditio humana* is constituted differently in the city than in rural areas does not change the fact that dwelling is still the essence of being. "Only if we are capable of dwelling, only then can we build. Our reference to the Black Forest farm in no way means that we should or could go back to building such houses; rather, it illustrates by a dwelling that has been how it was able to build."[7] In this sense, popular structural phenomena such as micro-apartments and loft extensions can possibly be examined in a more differentiated manner, perhaps even understood as being a harbinger of an approaching post-urbanism. As much as cities have fueled social and economic utopias and accelerated technological developments, they have also continuously produced dystopias of urban space, "tourist museums" (Jean-François Lyotard), and places of extreme material misery, a fact that, for example, the political scientist Benjamin Barber lays out in his book *If Mayors Ruled the World: Dysfunctional Nations, Rising Cities*.[8] To what extent architectural measures endanger the ontology of the urban or even promote a "new urban citizenship"[9] aimed at the legal, political, social, and cultural participation of all humans in urban space remains to be discussed.

1 Alexander Kluge, *Der Angriff der Gegenwart auf die übrige Zeit*, screenplay (Frankfurt am Main, 1985), p. 27 (trans. Ada St. Laurent).

2 Roger Behrens, "Die posturbane Gegen-Stadt," *Kunstforum International* 218 (2012), https://www.kunstforum.de/artikel/die-posturbane-gegen-stadt/ (all URLs accessed in June 2022; trans. Ada St. Laurent).

3 Martin Heidegger, "Building, Dwelling, Thinking," in *Basic Writings from Being and Time (1927) to The Task of Thinking (1964)* (New York: Harper & Row, 1977), p. 349.

4 Behrens, "Die posturbane Gegen-Stadt."

5 Heidegger, "Building, Dwelling, Thinking," p. 363.

6 Gilles Ivain, "Formulary for a New Urbanism," trans. Ken Knabb, October 1953, https://www.cddc.vt.edu/sionline/presitu/formulary.html.

7 Heidegger, "Building, Dwelling, Thinking," p. 362.

8 Benjamin Barber, *If Mayors Ruled the World: Dysfunctional Nations, Rising Cities* (New Haven, CT, and London: Yale University Press, 2013), pp. 177–78.

9 See Martin Krenn and Katharina Morawek, eds., *Urban Citizenship: Zur Demokratisierung der Demokratie* (Vienna: Verlag für moderne Kunst, 2017), p. 11.

Post-Pandemic Urbanism: Hustle and Flow

Alexis Kalagas

In 1997, a sixty-year-old Japanese electronic engineer and longtime executive at Hitachi, Tsugio Makimoto, quietly published a book called *Digital Nomad*. In it, he described a coming revolution, when ubiquitous new technologies would "unleash the ties of geography."[1] Smaller, cheaper, and more powerful personal devices, transmitting over high-capacity wireless communications networks, would deliver the ability to work and live on the move to millions of people. According to Tsugio Makimoto and his co-author David Manners, after ten thousand years of settled human existence, we would soon be faced with a simple question: Do we stay put, or do we roam? Yet twenty-three years later, we are still not living in a new age of migration. The proportion of the world's population residing in a country outside their place of birth (3 percent) has barely budged, despite six decades of unprecedented global integration through trade, investment, and information flows.[2]

What has spiked in the last two decades, however, is the number of highly skilled migrants, as well as the shorter-term and nonlinear mobility patterns that have come to define this professional class. Despite online boosters hyping "geoarbitrage" life hacks, and the "belong anywhere" mantra of technology startups targeting a new group of itinerant professionals mixing work and travel, digital nomadism is also yet to go mainstream. But migratory lifestyles have seeped into the wider global culture. From social-media-fueled romantic dreams of the open road (#vanlife), to the cold realities of twenty-first century labor markets (the growth of freelancing and "alternative work arrangements"), mobility is at once a perceived antidote to life in the rat race, and a non-negotiable demand imposed upon more and more workers hustling to stay afloat in the modern economy. "Roaming" may offer an escape route, but it is also the cost of staying put.

What does this have to do with architecture and urbanism? In comparison to biological processes of bodily decay, our cities are built to endure. Yet contemporary life—and especially contemporary urban life—is shaped by the collision of large-scale economic, social, and technological forces: corporate desires for nimble workforces drawn from a global talent pool, the gig economy explosion of independent contracting, and the more generalized shift to remote work, enabled by the widespread adoption of digital workflow practices in knowledge and service-based industries. Even before Covid-19 transformed overnight the way we think about formal divisions between work and home, along with the role of spatial proximity long understood to define what it means to be urban, our cities were already being remade by the migration of humans and capital, influencing everything from the financialization of housing to the reprogramming of the built environment through lean digital platforms like Airbnb.

Until the logistical feat of a worldwide coronavirus vaccine rollout enters an advanced stage, the open borders and free movement that furnished the invisible infrastructure of twenty-first century migration will remain frozen. But while the crisis conditions of 2020 can appear to have trapped us in an extended liminal state—we can no longer return to the world we left behind, and the exact contours of our "new normal" have yet to come into sharp focus—the pandemic is accelerating shifts that will have profound spatial implications, with the possibility for parallel new approaches to emerge in the way we design, program, and experience cities. Much commentary has been devoted to the potential for Covid-19 to foster a new localism, as the "biggest working from home experiment in history," together with the forced rediscovery of our immediate neighborhoods during lockdowns, is expected to lead to a revisiting of deadening commuter rituals and the received wisdom of centralized urban forms.

Yet once we are untethered completely from deep-rooted patterns of physical proximity, where do the new limits lie? Visions of a hyper-connected network of urban villages could be accommodated by everything from a garden city to a mega city.[3] But when corporations like Twitter and Microsoft announce that their employees need never work from an office again, we appear one step closer to the "permanent nomadism" of Superstudio's *Supersurface*, albeit absent that world's radical liberation from labor and consumerism.[4] Even as the shift to working from home has increased the agency of those with the capacity to benefit (while exposing the structural inequalities that have long constrained others), it has also revealed the extent to which countless jobs could be performed from anywhere with acoustic separation and high-speed Internet. Researchers had begun to speak of "virtual labor migration" in the form of digitally enabled outsourcing as early as 2006—it is not a leap to suggest that the growth of this kind of labor mobility will exacerbate existing trends toward insecure work and the precarious lifestyles that accompany it.[5]

Pre-Covid, market-led housing typologies like co-living sought to capitalize on the emerging plug-and-play lifestyles of an unsettled generation. In their most luxurious form, they represent an uneasy mash-up of decades-old Nordic co-housing ideas, traditional serviced apartments, and flexible short-stay accommodation. In their grimmer expressions, they can reflect a cynical zero-sum exercise in space versus yield. At the same time, projects like Andrés Jaque's *Rolling House for the Rolling Society* have explored how many of the same forces that gave rise to co-living were already transforming the way shared domestic space is informally occupied and adapted, through the melding of online and offline architectures. As Jaque wrote a decade ago about the reality experienced by more than 80 million people across the European Union alone, single-family residences occupied by aggregates of unfamiliar individuals had already come to demarcate a society shaped by transience.[6]

Speculating on the future of work, researchers tend to focus on the disruptive impact of artificial intelligence on processes of automation. The "defensible space" for humans is typically framed as jobs that require creativity or personal connection—from highly paid medical specialists to low-wage workers in the service economy. Again, the pandemic has exposed the fragility in entire sectors (like hospitality) that are intrinsically linked to how we experience cities. This is not a question of building back stronger after a societal *force majeure*. The rise of online meal delivery services predated mandatory shutdowns. In the United States, "off premise" restaurant spending had been expected to overtake "dine-in" revenue in 2020 for the first time on record.[7] The result has been the "logistification" of urban food systems, spawning phenomena like ghost kitchens and virtual food courts, while hospitality staff cast adrift by restaurant closures are left to become frontline components in this on-demand infrastructure of seamless movement.[8]

One could argue that the "great pause" of 2020 might ultimately be understood as triggering an even greater state of perpetual movement, defined by virtual and real labor migration in a despatialized economy, the precarious

1 Tsugio Makimoto and David Manners, *Digital Nomad* (Chichester: John Wiley & Sons, 1997).

2 World Bank, *Moving for Prosperity: Global Migration and Labor Markets* (Washington, DC: World Bank Publications, 2018), p. 1.

3 Dan Hill, "From Lockdown to Slowdown: Tokyo as Slowdown City," *The Slowdown Papers* 18 (April 2020).

4 Superstudio, *Supersurface*, first exhibited at *Italy: The New Domestic Landscape*, The Museum of Modern Art, New York, 1972.

5 A. Aneesh, *Virtual Migration: The Programming of Globalization* (Durham, NC, and London: Duke University Press, 2006).

6 Andrés Jaque, "Sheltering the Rolling Society: A Post-Typological Urbanism of Non-Familiar Shared Homes," *Volume* (December 2015), p. 86.

7 Derek Thompson, "The Booming, Ethically Dubious Business of Food Delivery," *The Atlantic* (August 2019).

8 Jesse LeCavalier, *The Rule of Logistics: Walmart and the Architecture of Fulfillment* (Minneapolis: University of Minnesota Press, 2016).

and contingent living arrangements that result, and the parallel hollowing out of ground-level urban spaces of sociality as our mediated retail and hospitality interactions are bookended by glowing touchscreens, real-time tracking, and contactless pickups. As evident in the earlier shift from the industrial to the postindustrial city though, the ruptures caused by wide-scale societal changes create opportunities—however fleeting—for new ideas, practices, and cultures to emerge. The task for architects in the post-pandemic environment is how best to contribute to holistic design responses which reassert the urban quality and collective values that continue to attract people to cities and which underpin our ability to address the deeper imperatives of escalating inequality and climate emergency.

Architecture alone is not the answer, especially when it elevates spatial conditions above all else. It is tempting to conclude that life on the move—whether literal or symbolic—demands mobile architecture, from fluidly modular or flexible interior spaces that optimize and economize, to updated countercultural nomadic living units, which unlock a technology-enabled migratory urbanism at scale. But in the same way that Covid-19 has demonstrated how curbing lifestyles shaped by paradigms of infinite growth produces immediately tangible environmental benefits, understanding the physical form of our cities as the visible expression of a more complex ecology suggests that an enduring design challenge is more likely to be found in the need to reimagine a new life for vacant office buildings left as the detritus of a transitioning economy and society. The added layer in this challenge will be to do so in a way that ties the fate of such structures into a low-waste, zero-carbon urban future.

The pandemic is increasingly being discussed as a smaller crisis within the larger crisis of climate collapse. Perhaps fittingly, the last time the global population worked from home en masse was just prior to the introduction of wage labor in the bleak early factories of the Industrial Revolution. The broad sweep of history that followed—from cottage industry to the "electronic cottage"—is what brought us to this moment.[9] The agglomeration effects of industrial capitalism (and subsequent modernist response to urban overcrowding and squalor) left an indelible mark on the design of cities that is still evident today. If we are to learn from this history, rather than respond myopically to the immediate problems of the present, we must harness our proven capacity to take collective action—the most heartening outcome of 2020—to support a form of strategic design that engages intelligently with the underlying drivers shaping our urban system.

9 Alvin Toffler, *The Third Wave* (New York: Bantam Books, 1980).

Craftsmanship in Architecture

Belinda Rukschcio

"Architects, sculptors, painters—we all must return to craftsmanship! For there is no such thing as 'art by profession.' There is no essential difference between the artist and the artisan," wrote Walter Gropius in his 1919 Bauhaus manifesto.[1] Mental and manual labor, the tools of creative work, were once inseparably linked in education. This changed, though—in Germany, for example—through the educational reforms of the 1960s and 1970s. Artisans without a high school diploma or university entrance exams were no longer able to access design or art courses. This curtailed one of the most important aspects of the trades: creative design competency and the communication and marketing thereof. With the goal of changing this, the German Confederation of Skilled Crafts (Zentralverband des Deutschen Handwerks, ZDH) established the Academies of Design in the mid-1980s.[2] Providing interdisciplinary advanced training created the state-recognized qualification as a "skilled craft designer."[3]

Design competency in the trades is important for architecture, too.

On the one hand, this is because having the earliest possible interaction between planning and execution is a relevant aspect of finding tailored solutions. Construction regulations are becoming increasingly complex; in Germany, for instance, there are almost 3,800 construction-related regulations. These must be taken into account, all without losing sight of the design approach, the powerful idea. At the same time, each and every construction process is accompanied by a great number of protagonists with different interests. And at the same time, construction activity has also been steadily increasing in recent years. Construction processes now make up half of all processes in Germany.[4]

On the other hand, because the construction sector is responsible for a significant share of our CO_2 emissions, it also holds tremendous potential for reduction. Innovation is called for, which must be designed. Craftsmanship is an important component of this, as can be seen, for example, in the development of technical building equipment. More than 120 years ago, architect Adolf Loos called plumbers the "top tradesmen of our nation," and even the "neighborhood makers of culture." Craftsmanship and its technical achievements have been a decisive aspect of modern architecture, and in the area of design as well. In the meantime, building systems equipment, including water and heating pipes, comprises a large portion of overall construction costs. In general, building systems are becoming more digital, smarter, and more system-based. Their average technical life span is thirty to forty years. This means that, within the life cycle of a building, the building systems will be entirely replaced one to two times. The materials that result from this demolition represent an important resource for circular economies. As early as 2016, there were 75 kilograms of building systems materials installed per inhabitant in Germany.[5]

Smart minds and experimentation are needed when it comes to addressing the energy revolution, which is one of the (but not the only) great challenges facing us in the years to come. However, technology is not the only answer to the questions that are arising. Holistic viewpoints that break up sectoral thinking and working can serve as a motor for innovation. Going beyond the immediate context, the view is broadened to include local resources and techniques as well as society overall. There is a great deal of potential for active participation by the skilled trades, because local ties and a strong knowledge of materials are essential features of many craft businesses.

A good example of the impressive symbiosis of planning and building can be found in Studio Mumbai, founded by architect Bijoy Jain in the early years of the twenty-first century. The studio's *Work-Place* contribution to the 2010 international architecture exhibition in Venice was a magnet for visitors. A workshop with models, building materials, and all the tools used with them was set up the Arsenale, a historic shipyard with impressive spaces. What made the contribution so special was the way that manual work processes and the people doing them were made visible. The working structures of an office are very different from those of the classic architecture firm, which is organized as a working group, with projects being developed and implemented in constant dialogue with skilled craftspeople right from the start. The personal experience and knowledge of the individual are used collectively as tools. For Bijoy Jain, the dialogue between thinking and doing that emerges from this approach is a crucial aspect of the studio's built results.[6] However, having such a close connection of skilled craft knowledge and architectural-spatial thinking in the collective, further development of a design idea is generally not a matter of course in everyday planning. Which is surprising, because the two disciplines are united by something very fundamental: according to sociologist Richard Sennett, craftspeople and architects are united by a will to achieve quality; they are motivated to do good work.[7] This is indeed the best prerequisite for successful collaboration.

How can this be successful? Increasingly, educational and training programs emphasize interdisciplinary communication between the planning and implementing professions in order to bolster mutual understanding. Numerous architectural firms are demonstrating how much sense it makes to include professional exchange in the very early project phases of day-to-day work, not just when tendering contracts to the various trades. This allows solutions to be jointly developed that go beyond the usual standard quality to deliver new approaches and make space for experimentation. Even though Walter Gropius later increasingly turned to industrial production methods with the Bauhaus, his manifesto remains relevant: We all must return to craftsmanship!

1 English translation from www.bauhausmanifesto.com.

2 Wikipedia, s.v. "Akademien für Gestaltung," online in German only at: https://de.wikipedia.org/wiki/Akademien_f%C3%BCr_Gestaltung (all URLs accessed in June 2022).

3 Arbeitsgemeinschaft der Akademien für Gestaltung im Handwerk, Gestaltung im Handwerk, https://www.gestaltung-im-handwerk.info/bildung/.

4 According to Werner Sobek at the online event "urbainable – stadthaltig: Sustainability in Construction – Greenwashing or Progress?" on November 17, 2020, organized by the Berlin Academy of Arts.

5 Bundesstiftung Baukultur (2018), *Baukulturbericht 2018/19: "Erbe – Bestand – Zukunft,"* https://www.bundesstiftung-baukultur.de/publikationen/baukulturbericht/2018–19.

6 Klaus-Peter Guest, "Auch in philosophischen Diskursen geht es um die Frage, wie man eine Idee Praxis werden lassen kann," interview with Bijoy Jain (Studio Mumbai), published in Bauwelt 31/2014, Berlin, https://www.bauwelt.de/dl/796408/bw_2014_31_0018-0031.2290735.pdf.

7 Richard Sennett, *The Craftsman* (London: Penguin Books, 2009).

Author Biographies

Marlies Breuss, architect
Marlies Breuss studied piano and composition at the music conservatory in Vorarlberg, and architecture at the Vienna University of Technology. She earned her postgraduate master's degree at the Southern California Institute of Architecture in Los Angeles. In 2019, she held a visiting professorship at the Vienna University of Technology in cooperation with Kasetsart University, Bangkok. Breuss has given lectures in Budapest, Banská Bystrica, Coburg, Hittisau, Paris, Prague, Milan, Salvador/BR, Stuttgart, and Zagreb.

Lisz Hirn, Dr.
Lisz Hirn studied philosophy and singing in Graz, Paris, Vienna, and Kathmandu. She works as a publicist, activist, and philosopher in youth and adult education, holding for instance the university course "Philosophical Practice" at the University of Vienna.

HOLODECK architects
HOLODECK architects was formed in 1998 by Marlies Breuss and Michael Ogertschnig and has been working with multicultural companions over the last twenty-four years. Susanne Schmall was a founding member and Hannes Zergoi was a partner on our team for about two years, while Marc Werner and Iva Olujic have now been team members for several years. HOLODECK architects has participated in exhibitions throughout the world, such as in Buenos Aires, Rome, Helsinki, Shanghai, Bratislava, Ljubljana, Saint Petersburg, Pärnu, Crete, Tel Aviv, Mumbai, and New York.

Alexis Kalagas
Originally a foreign policy advisor, Alexis Kalagas worked on projects across Europe, Latin America, and Africa with the Zurich-based design practice Urban-Think Tank. More recently, he has pursued his interest in the complex economic, social, and technological forces reshaping our experience of both urban space and the home as a Richard Rogers Fellow at Harvard Graduate School of Design, a Future Architecture Fellow, and through design research exhibited at the Seoul Biennale of Architecture and Urbanism and the Oslo Architecture Triennale. Kalagas is currently head of public programs at Molonglo.

Quijxote Nuntanasirivikrom, B.Arch, M.Arch, PhD candidate
Quijxote Nuntanasirivikrom obtained his bachelor's degree from the Faculty of Architecture, Silpakorn University, Thailand, under the "formal, common and conventional" training of modern pedagogy in architectural education, obtaining the Thai license of professional practice in 1993. He passed the related examination to be an instructor in the newly established school of architecture in Thailand in 1995. Nuntanasirivikrom was supported by the Royal Thai Government in continuing his studies in the United Kingdom (pursuing master's and doctoral degrees). Having spent over six years abroad, he returned to Thailand in 2002 after his scholarship expired, without completing his PhD thesis. Nuntanasirivikrom was appointed as associate professor in 2019.

Michael Ogertschnig, architect
Michael Ogertschnig studied architecture at the Vienna University of Technology and pursued his postgraduate studies at the Institute for Advanced Architectural Studies / Museu d'Art Contemporani de Barcelona. He is a university lecturer at the Vienna University of Technology and has given talks in Budapest, Prague, Milan, and Zagreb.

Belinda Rukschcio
Belinda Rukschcio studied architecture at the Vienna University of Technology and has worked in architectural education, including as project manager at the House of Architecture in Graz and for the Architecture Biennale in Venice. She has also taught at the Vienna University of Technology, Bauhaus University in Weimar, and Brandenburg University of Technology Cottbus. In 2014, she released her documentary film *Precise Poetry* about the Italian/Brazilian architect Lina Bo Bardi. From 2016 to 2020, Rukschcio was responsible for the Baukultur reports as project manager at the Bundesstiftung Baukultur, based in Potsdam. In 2021, she took over the management of Werkraum Bregenzerwald, an association of regional craft businesses that is committed both to contemporary quality craftsmanship and its communication and to craft training.

Anjalika Sagar, filmmaker and member of The Otolith Group
Anjalika Sagar studied social anthropology at the University of London School of Oriental and African Studies. She is interested in the film essay and in the relationship between image, text, and sound. Sagar works as a curator, moderator, essayist, film director, video-maker, and photographer. Her extensive work has been shown at exhibitions all over the world. Anjalika Sagar, together with Kodwo Eshun, founded The Otolith Group in 2002. The Otolith Group received acclaim for their project *A Long Time Between Suns* in 2010. In 2011, they exhibited at Bétonsalon in Paris, and in 2011 – 12, at MAXXI in Rome. Latest works include *INFINITY minus Infinity*, a 52-minute film that was performed at the *Forum Expanded* exhibition of the Berlinale in 2020.

Gerhard Steixner, Univ.-Prof. i. R., Mag.arch.
Gerhard Steixner studied architecture at the Academy of Fine Arts Vienna, in the master class of Roland Rainer. In 1983, he established his architectural firm, based in Vienna, with a focus on eco-solar building, prefabrication, and prototypes. From 2009 to 2019, Steixner was a university professor for building construction and head of the research unit "Building Construction and Design 2" at the Vienna University of Technology. His research on European and non-European modernism between 1958 and 1978 has focused on housing construction, among other topics.

Acknowledgments

Thanks to all team members who supported us during these intense twenty-four years and made it possible to maintain high quality in the complex world of architecture.

To the courageous clients that supported us in following the architectonic concept throughout the whole process until the commissioning of the buildings.

To the professors and adjunct professors giving their visions and experiences to us as interested students, supporting our curiosity, and guiding us through difficult periods of designing, without being too much focused on moving forward in their own careers. The years as students were important times for our personal development and we combined studying, working, and traveling to understand different cultures.

Special thanks to all family members and friends encouraging us on our architectonic path.

ALPHA
MOBILE
www.ljr.at